S0-ASM-563

FLORIDA

MACMILLAN • USA

Copyright © 1995 by Simon & Schuster Inc.
All rights reserved
including the right of reproduction
in whole or in part in any form.

Macmillan Travel
A Simon & Schuster Macmillan Company
15 Columbus Circle
New York, NY 10023

MACMILLAN is a registered trademark of Macmillan, Inc.

Manufactured in the United States of America

10 9 8 7 6 5 4 3 2 1

ISSN: 1079-3593
ISBN: 0-02-860145-9

SPECIAL SALES
Bulk purchases (10+ copies) of Frommer's travel guides are available to corporations at special discounts. The Special Sales Department can produce custom editions to be used as premiums and/or for sales promotion to suit individual needs. Existing editions can be produced with custom cover imprints such as corporate logos. For more information write to Special Sales, Simon & Schuster, 1230 Avenue of the Americas, New York, NY 10020

CONTENTS

INTRODUCTION

America on Wheels introduces a brand-new lodgings rating system—one that factors in the latest trends in travel preferences, technologies, and amenities and is based on thorough inspections by experienced travel professionals. We rate establishments from 1 to 5 flags, plus a unique rating we call Ultra, a special award reserved for only a handful of outstanding properties in each category. Our restaurant selections represent the ethnic diversity of today's dining scene and are categorized with symbols according to their special features, ambience, and services available. In addition, the series provides in-depth sightseeing information, including driving tours and best-of-the-state highlights.

STATE INTRODUCTIONS

Our coverage of each state in the *America on Wheels* series begins with background information that will help familiarize you with your destination. Included is a summary of the state's history and an overview of its geography, followed by practical tips that we hope you will find useful in planning your trip—what kind of weather to expect, what to pack, sources of information within the state, driving rules and regulations, and other essentials.

The "Best of the State" section provides you with a rundown of the top sights and attractions and the most popular festivals and special events around the state. It also includes information on spectator sports and an "A to Z" list of recreational activities available to you.

DRIVING TOURS

The scenic driving tours guide you along some of the most popular sightseeing routes. Every tour is keyed to a map and includes mileage information and precise directions, refreshment stops, and, for longer tours, recommended places to stay.

THE LISTINGS

The cities are organized alphabetically within each state. Below each city name, you'll find a map page number and map location. These refer to the color maps at the back of the book.

Types of Lodgings

Here's how we define the lodging categories used in *America on Wheels*.

Motel

A motel usually has 1 to 3 floors, and many of the guest rooms have doors facing the parking lot or outdoor corridors. A motel may only have a small, serviceable lobby and usually offers only limited services; the nearest restaurant may be down the street. A motel is most likely to be located alongside a highway or in a resort area.

Hotel

A hotel usually has 3 or more floors with elevators. It may or may not have parking, but if it does, entry to the guest rooms is likely to be through the lobby rather than directly from the parking lot. A range of lodgings is available (such as standard rooms, deluxe rooms, and suites), and a range of services is available (such as bellhops, room service, and a concierge). Many hotels have a restaurant or coffee shop open for breakfast, lunch, and dinner; they may have a cocktail lounge/bar. Recreational facilities may be available (such as a swimming pool, fitness center, and tennis courts).

Resort

A resort usually has more extensive facilities and recreational activities than a hotel, and offers 3 meals a day. The atmosphere is generally more informal than at comparable hotels.

Lodge

A lodge is essentially a small hotel in a rural, remote, or mountainous location. The atmosphere, service, and furniture may be more casual than you'd find in a regular hotel, and there may not be televisions or telephones in every guest room. The facilities usually include a coffee shop or restaurant, bar or cocktail lounge, game room, and indoor or outdoor swimming pool or hot tub. In ski areas, the lounge usually has a fireplace and facilities for storing ski gear.

Inn

An inn is a small-scale hotel or lodge, usually in an older building that may or may not have been designed for lodgings, and it is often located in interesting surroundings. An inn should have a warm, welcoming atmosphere, with a more homelike quality to its furnishings and facilities. The guest rooms may be individually decorated in a style appropriate to the inn's age and location, and the rooms may or may not have telephones, televisions, or private bathrooms. An inn usually has a lounge or sitting room for guests (with parlor games and perhaps a television) and a small dining room that may or may not be open to the public. Breakfast, however, is almost always served.

How the Lodgings Are Rated

Every hotel, motel, resort, inn, and lodge rated in this series has been subjected to a thorough hands-on inspection by our team of accomplished travel professionals. We ask the kinds of questions that readers would ask if they could inspect the rooms in advance for themselves (How good is the soundproofing? How firm is the bed? What condition are the room furnishings in?). Then all of the inspection reports are reviewed by regional editors who are experts on their territories. The top-rated properties are then rechecked by a special consultant who has been reviewing and critiquing luxury hotels around the world for almost 25 years. *Establishments are not charged to be included in our series.*

Our ratings are based on *average* guest rooms—not lavish suites or concierge floors—so they're not artificially high. Therefore, in some cases a hotel rated 4 flags may indeed have individual rooms or suites that might fall into the 5-flag category; conversely, a 4-flag hotel may have a few rooms in its lowest price range that might otherwise warrant 3 flags.

The detailed ratings vary by category of lodgings—for example, the criteria imposed on a hotel are more rigorous than those for a motel—and some features that are considered essential in, for example, a 4-flag city hotel are relaxed for a resort that offers alternative attractions, sporting facilities, and/or beautiful and spacious grounds. Likewise, amenities such as telephones and televisions—essential in hotels and motels—are not required in inns, often the destination for lovers of peace and quiet. Instead, the criteria take into account such features as individually decorated rooms and complimentary afternoon tea.

There are, of course, several basic attributes that apply to all lodgings across the board: the cleanliness and maintenance of the building as a whole; the housekeeping in individual rooms; safety, both indoors and out; the quality and practicality of the furnishings; the quality and availability of the amenities; the caliber of the facilities; the extent and/or condition of the grounds; the ambience and cleanliness in the dining rooms; and the caliber and professionalism of the service in relation to the rates and types of lodging. Since the *America on Wheels* rating system is highly rigorous, just because a property has garnered only 1 flag does not mean it is inadequate or substandard.

WHAT THE INDIVIDUAL RATINGS MEAN

≣ 1 Flag

These properties have surpassed the minimum requirements of cleanliness, safety, convenience, and amenities; the staff may be limited, but guests can generally expect a friendly, hospitable greeting. They will have basic amenities, such as air conditioning or heating where appropriate, telephones, and televisions. The bathrooms may have only showers rather than tubs, and just 1 towel for each guest, but showers and towels must be clean. The 1-flag properties are by no means places to avoid, since they can represent exceptional value.

≣ ≣ 2 Flags

In addition to having all of the basic attributes of 1-flag lodgings, these properties will have some extra amenities, such as bellhops to help with the luggage, ice buckets in each room, and better quality furnishings. Some extra services may include availability of cribs and irons, and wake-up service.

≣≣≣ 3 Flags

These properties have all the basics noted above but also offer a more generous complement of amenities, such as firmer beds, larger desks, more drawer space, extra blankets and pillows, cable or satellite TV, alarm clock/radios, room service (although hours may be limited), and dry cleaning and/or laundry services.

≣≣≣≣ 4 Flags

This is the realm of luxury, with refinements in amenities, furnishings, and service—such as larger rooms, more dependable soundproofing, 2 telephones per room, in-room movies, in-room safes, thick towels, hair dryers, twice-daily maid service, turndown service, concierge service, and 24-hour room service.

≣≣≣≣≣ 5 Flags

These properties have everything the 4-flag properties have, plus a more personal level of service and more sumptuous amenities, among them bathrobes, superior linens, and blackout drapes for lightproofing. Facilities normally include a business center and fitness center. Generally speaking, guests pay handsomely to stay in these properties.

✿ Ultra

This crème-de-la-crème rating is reserved for those rare hotels and resorts, possibly also motels and inns, that are truly outstanding in every or almost every department—places with a "Grand Hotel" presence, an almost flawless level of service, and a standard of dining equal to that of the finest restaurants.

Unrated

In the few cases where an inspector was not able to make a detailed inspection, the property is listed as "Unrated." Also, in some cases where a property was in the process of changing owners or managers, or if the property was undergoing the kind of major renovations that made formal evaluation impossible, then, again, the inspectors have listed it as "Unrated."

Types of Dining

Restaurant

A restaurant serves complete meals.

Refreshment Stop

A refreshment stop serves drinks and/or snacks only (such as an ice cream parlor, bakery, or coffee bar).

How the Restaurants Were Evaluated

All of the restaurants reviewed in this series have been through the kind of thorough inspection described for accommodations, above. Our inspectors have evaluated everything from freshness of ingredients to noise level and spacing of tables.

Unique to the *America on Wheels* series are the easy-to-read symbols that identify for you a restaurant's special features, ambience, and services. With them you can determine at a glance whether a place is a local favorite, offers exceptional value, or is "worth a splurge."

How to Read the Listings

LODGINGS

Introductory Information

The rating is followed by the establishment's name, address, neighborhood (if located in a major city), telephone numbers, and fax number (if there is one). When appropriate, you'll also find the location of the establishment, highway information with exit number, and/or more specific directions. In the resort listings, the number of acres is indicated. Also included are our inspectors' comments, which provide some description and discuss any outstanding features or special information about the establishment. If the lodging is not rated, it will be noted at the end of this section.

Rooms

The number and type of accommodations available is followed by the information on check-in/check-out times. If there is anything worth noting about rooms, whether the size or decor or furnishings, inspectors' comments will follow.

Amenities

The amenities available in the majority of the guest rooms are indicated by symbols and then a list. Because travelers usually expect air conditioning, telephones, and televisions in their guest rooms, we specifically note when those amenities are not available. If the accommodations have minibars, terraces, fireplaces, or Jacuzzis, we indicate that here.

Services

The services available are indicated by symbols and then a list. There may be a fee for some of the services. "Babysitting available" means the establishment can put you in touch with local babysitters and/or agencies. An establishment that accepts pets may nevertheless place restrictions on the types or size of pets allowed.

Facilities

The facilities available are indicated by symbols followed by a list; all are on the premises, except for cross-country and downhill skiing, which are within 10 miles. The lifeguard listed refers to a beach lifeguard, not a pool lifeguard. Our "Accessible for People With Disabilities" symbol appears where establishments claim to have guest rooms with such accessibility.

Rates

If the establishment's rates vary throughout the year, then the rates given are for the high season. The rates listed are EP (no meals included), unless otherwise noted. We'll tell you if there is a charge for an extra person to stay in a room; if children stay free, and if so, up to what age; if there are minimum stay requirements; if the rates are ever higher for special events or holidays; if AP (3 meals) or MAP (breakfast and dinner) rates are also available; and/or if special packages are available. The parking rates (if the establishment has parking) are followed by the credit card information.

Always confirm the rates when you are making your reservations, and ask about taxes and other charges, which are not included in our rates.

RESTAURANTS

Introductory Information

If a restaurant is a local favorite, an exceptional value, or "worth a splurge," this will be noted by a special symbol at the beginning of the listing. Then the establishment's name, address, neighborhood (if located in a major city), and telephone number are listed. Next comes the location of the establishment, highway information with exit number, and/or more specific directions, as appropriate. The types of cuisine are followed by our inspectors' comments on everything from decor to menu highlights.

The "FYI" Heading

After the reservations policy, we tell you if there is live entertainment, a children's menu, a dress code, and a no-smoking policy for the entire restaurant. If the restaurant does not offer a full bar, we tell you what the liquor policy is.

Hours of Operation

Under the "Open" heading, "HS" indicates that the hours listed are for the high season only; otherwise, the hours listed are year-round. It's a good idea to call ahead to confirm the hours of operation, especially in the off-season.

Prices

Prices given are for the dinner main courses (unless otherwise noted). If a prix-fixe dinner is offered during all of the dinner hours, that price is listed here, too. This section ends with credit card information, followed by any appropriate symbol(s).

Accessibility for People With Disabilities

The accessibility symbol appears in listings where the restaurant has a level entrance or an access ramp, a doorway at least 36 inches wide, and restrooms that are on the same floor as the dining room, with doorways at least 32 inches wide and properly outfitted stalls.

ATTRACTIONS

Introductory Information

The name, street address, neighborhood (if located in a major city), and telephone number are followed by a brief rundown of the attraction's high points and key attributes—so you can quickly determine if it's worth a full day of exploration or just a brief detour.

Hours of Operation & Admission

Service information includes hours of operation and the cost of admission. The cost is indicated by 1 to 4 dollar signs ($, $$, $$$, or $$$$) or by "Free," if no fee is charged. It's a good idea to call ahead to confirm the hours.

DISABLED TRAVELER INFORMATION

The Americans with Disabilities Act (ADA) of 1990 required that all public facilities and commercial establishments be made accessible to disabled persons by January 26, 1992. Any property opened after January 26, 1993, must be built in accordance with the ADA Accessible Guidelines. Note, however, that not all establishments have completed their renovations to conform with the law; be sure to call ahead to determine if your specific needs can be met.

TAXES

State and city taxes vary widely and are not included in the prices in this book. Always ask about the taxes when you are making your reservations. State sales tax is given under "Essentials" in the introduction to each state.

A DISCLAIMER

Readers are advised that prices fluctuate in the course of time and travel information changes under the impact of the varied and volatile factors that affect the travel industry. The publisher cannot be held responsible for the experiences of readers while traveling. Readers are invited to send ideas, comments, and suggestions for future editions to: *America on Wheels*, Macmillan Travel, 15 Columbus Circle, New York, NY 10023.

ABBREVIATIONS

A/C	air conditioning
AP	American Plan (rates include breakfast, lunch, and dinner)
avail	available
BB	Bed-and-Breakfast Plan (rates include full breakfast)
bldg	building
CC	credit cards
CI	check-in time
CO	check-out time
CP	Continental Plan (rates include continental breakfast)
ctges	cottages
ctr	center
D	double
effic	efficiencies
evnts	events
HS	high season
info	information
int'l	international
ltd	limited
maj	major
MAP	Modified American Plan (rates include breakfast and dinner)
Mem Day	Memorial Day
mi	miles
min	minimum
MM	mile marker
PF	prix fixe (a fixed-price meal)
pking	parking
refrig	refrigerator
rms	rooms
rsts	restaurants
S	single
satel	satellite
spec	special
stes	suites
svce	service
tel	telephone
univ	university
w/	with
wknds	weekends

TOLL-FREE NUMBERS

The following toll-free telephone numbers were accurate at press time; *America on Wheels* cannot be held responsible for any number that has changed. The "TDD" numbers are answered by a telecommunications service for the deaf and hard-of-hearing. Be sure to dial "1" before each number.

Lodgings

Best Western International, Inc
(800) 528-1234 Continental USA and Canada
(800) 528-2222 TDD

Budgetel Inns
(800) 4-BUDGET Continental USA and Canada

Budget Host
(800) BUD-HOST Continental USA

Clarion Hotels
(800) CLARION Continental USA and Canada
(800) 228-3323 TDD

Comfort Inns
(800) 228-5150 Continental USA and Canada
(800) 228-3323 TDD

Courtyard by Marriott
(800) 321-2211 Continental USA and Canada
(800) 228-7014 TDD

Days Inn
(800) 325-2525 Continental USA and Canada
(800) 325-3297 TDD

Doubletree Hotels
(800) 222-TREE Continental USA

Drury Inn
(800) 325-8300 Continental USA and Canada
(800) 325-0583 TDD

Econo Lodges
(800) 446-6900 Continental USA and Canada
(800) 228-3323 TDD

Embassy Suites
(800) 362-2779 Continental USA and Canada

Exel Inns of America
(800) 356-8013 Continental USA and Canada

Fairfield Inn by Marriott
(800) 228-2800 Continental USA and Canada
(800) 228-7014 TDD

Fairmont Hotels
(800) 527-4727 Continental USA

Forte Hotels
(800) 225-5843 Continental USA and Canada

Four Seasons Hotels
(800) 332-3442 Continental USA
(800) 268-6282 Canada

Friendship Inns
(800) 453-4511 Continental USA
(800) 228-3323 TDD

Guest Quarters Suites
(800) 424-2900 Continental USA

Hampton Inn
(800) HAMPTON Continental USA and Canada

Hilton Hotels Corporation
(800) HILTONS Continental USA and Canada
(800) 368-1133 TDD

Holiday Inn
(800) HOLIDAY Continental USA and Canada
(800) 238-5544 TDD

Howard Johnson
(800) 654-2000 Continental USA and Canada
(800) 654-8442 TDD

Hyatt Hotels and Resorts
(800) 228-9000 Continental USA and Canada
(800) 228-9548 TDD

Inns of America
(800) 826-0778 Continental USA and Canada

Intercontinental Hotels
(800) 327-0200 Continental USA and Canada

ITT Sheraton
(800) 325-3535 Continental USA and Canada
(800) 325-1717 TDD

La Quinta Motor Inns, Inc
(800) 531-5900 Continental USA and Canada
(800) 426-3101 TDD

Loews Hotels
(800) 223-0888 Continental USA and Canada

Marriott Hotels
(800) 228-9290 Continental USA and Canada
(800) 228-7014 TDD

Master Hosts Inns
(800) 251-1962 Continental USA and Canada

Meridien
(800) 543-4300 Continental USA and Canada

Omni Hotels
(800) 843-6664 Continental USA and Canada

Park Inns International
(800) 437-PARK Continental USA and Canada

Quality Inns
(800) 228-5151 Continental USA and Canada
(800) 228-3323 TDD

Radisson Hotels International
(800) 333-3333 Continental USA and Canada

Ramada
(800) 2-RAMADA Continental USA and Canada
(800) 228-3232 TDD

Red Carpet Inns
(800) 251-1962 Continental USA and Canada

Red Lion Hotels and Inns
(800) 547-8010 Continental USA and Canada

Red Roof Inns
(800) 843-7663 Continental USA and Canada
(800) 843-9999

Residence Inn by Marriott
(800) 331-3131 Continental USA and Canada
(800) 228-7014 TDD

Resinter
(800) 221-4542 Continental USA and Canada

Ritz-Carlton
(800) 241-3333 Continental USA and Canada

Rodeway Inns
(800) 228-2000 Continental USA and Canada
(800) 228-3323 TDD

Scottish Inns
(800) 251-1962 Continental USA and Canada

Shilo Inns
(800) 222-2244 Continental USA and Canada

Signature Inns
(800) 822-5252 Continental USA and Canada

Stouffer Renaissance Hotels International
(800) HOTELS-1 Continental USA and Canada
(800) 833-4747 TDD

Super 8 Motels
(800) 800-8000 Continental USA and Canada
(800) 533-6634 TDD

Susse Chalet Motor Lodges & Inns
(800) 258-1980 Continental USA and Canada

Travelodge
(800) 255-3050 Continental USA and Canada

Vagabond Hotels Inc.
(800) 522-1555 Continental USA and Canada

Westin Hotels and Resorts
(800) 228-3000 Continental USA and Canada
(800) 254-5440 TDD

Wyndham Hotels and Resorts
(800) 822-4200 Continental USA and Canada

Car Rental Agencies

Advantage Rent-A-Car
(800) 777-5500 Continental USA and Canada

Airways Rent A Car
(800) 952-9200 Continental USA

Alamo Rent A Car
(800) 327-9633 Continental USA and Canada

Allstate Car Rental
(800) 634-6186 Continental USA and Canada

Avis
(800) 331-1212 Continental USA and Canada

Budget Rent A Car
(800) 527-0700 Continental USA and Canada

Dollar Rent A Car
(800) 800-4000 Continental USA and Canada

Enterprise Rent-A-Car
(800) 325-8007 Continental USA and Canada

Hertz
(800) 654-3131 Continental USA

National Car Rental
(800) CAR-RENT Continental USA and Canada

Payless Car Rental
(800) PAYLESS Continental USA and Canada

Rent-A-Wreck
(800) 535-1391 Continental USA

Sears Rent A Car
(800) 527-0770 Continental USA and Canada

Thrifty Rent-A-Car
(800) 367-2277 Continental USA

U-Save Auto Rental of America
(800) 272-USAV Continental USA and Canada

Value Rent-A-Car
(800) 327-2501 Continental USA and Canada

Airlines

American Airlines
(800) 433-7300 Continental USA and Canada

Canadian Airlines International
(800) 426-7000 Continental USA
(800) 665-1177 Canada

Continental Airlines
(800) 525-0280 Continental USA
(800) 421-2456 Canada

Delta Air Lines
(800) 221-1212 Continental USA

Northwest Airlines
(800) 225-2525 Continental USA and Canada

Southwest Airlines
(800) 435-9792 Continental USA and Canada

Trans World Airlines
(800) 221-2000 Continental USA

United Airlines
(800) 241-6522 Continental USA and Canada

USAir
(800) 428-4322 Continental USA and Canada

Train

Amtrak
(800) USA-RAIL Continental USA

Bus

Greyhound
(800) 231-2222 Continental USA

THE TOP-RATED LODGINGS

5 Flags

Four Seasons Ocean Grand, Palm Beach
The Ritz-Carlton Palm Beach, Manalapan

4 Flags

The Alexander All-Suite Luxury Hotel, Miami
Amelia Island Plantation, Amelia Island
Bellevue Mido Resort Hotel, Clearwater
The Breakers, Palm Beach
Boca Raton Resort & Club, Boca Raton
Buena Vista Palace—Walt Disney World Village, Lake Buena Vista
Disney's Grand Floridian Beach Resort, Lake Buena Vista
Disney's Wilderness Lodge, Lake Buena Vista
The Fisher Island Club, Fisher Island
Four Seasons Ocean Grand, Palm Beach
Grand Bay Hotel, Miami
Grenelefe Golf and Tennis Resort, Haines City
Hyatt Regency Grand Cypress, Orlando
Hyatt Regency Miami
Hyatt Regency Westshore, Tampa
Innisbrook Hilton Resort, Palm Harbor
The Lodge and Bath Club at Ponte Vedra Beach
The Marquesa Hotel, Key West
Marriott at Sawgrass Resort, Ponte Vedra Beach
Marriott's Bay Point Resort, Panama City Beach
Marriott's Harbor Beach Resort, Fort Lauderdale
Ocean Reef Club, Key Largo
The Peabody Orlando
Pier 66 Crowne Plaza Resort & Marina, Fort Lauderdale
Ponte Vedra Inn & Club, Ponte Vedra Beach
The Registry Resort, Naples
The Ritz-Carlton Naples
Saddlebrook, Wesley Chapel
Sheraton Bal Harbour Resort, Bal Harbour
Stouffer Orlando Resort, Orlando
Stouffer Renaissance Vinoy Resort, St Petersburg
Turnberry Isle Resort & Club, North Miami
Walt Disney World Dolphin, Lake Buena Vista
Wyndham Harbour Island Hotel, Tampa

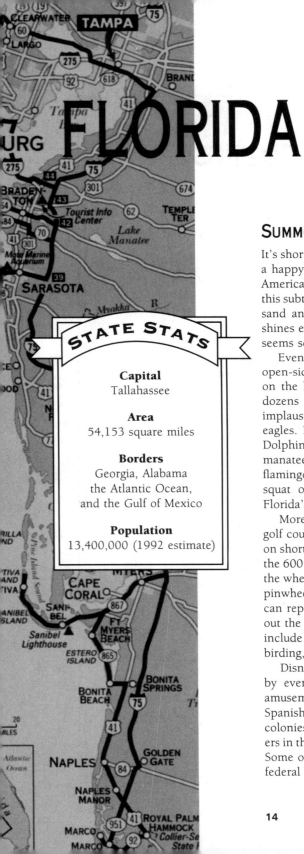

FLORIDA

STATE STATS

Capital
Tallahassee

Area
54,153 square miles

Borders
Georgia, Alabama
the Atlantic Ocean,
and the Gulf of Mexico

Population
13,400,000 (1992 estimate)

SUMMONS TO PARADISE

It's short on ski runs, but Florida revels in most of the other ingredients of a happy vacation, and in all seasons. Every year, millions of frostbitten Americans and Europeans from northerly climes funnel themselves into this subtropical state. Tens of thousands of them dig their heels into sugary sand and refuse to leave, having discovered a place in which the sun shines every day, flowered vines flutter in warm sea breezes, and no task seems so urgent it can't be put off until tomorrow.

Even sloth has its rewards, however, in afternoons lazed away in open-sided tiki bars or watching sportfishing boats return from their days on the high sea. Boredom is rare. Lovers of wildlife catch glimpses of dozens of native birds and mammals, which turn up in the most implausible places. Atop telephone poles are nests of osprey, as big as eagles. In the Keys are deer that stand no higher than a man's knees. Dolphins perform cartwheels out in the bays, and lovably homely manatees lumber in channels. Roseate spoonbills, great blue herons, pink flamingoes, and snowy egrets stalk mud flats and marshlands. Pelicans squat on dock pilings. Alligators and armadillos are reminders that Florida's genealogy dates back to the days of the dinosaurs.

More active visitors can exhaust themselves on any of more than 1,000 golf courses and on the tennis courts that adjoin every other hotel. Even on short excursions, novice snorkelers and scuba divers can spot scores of the 600 species of marine creatures that inhabit these waters. Anglers with the wherewithal can troll the edges of the Gulf Stream for such prey as the pinwheeling sailfish and the awesome marlin. Those with thinner wallets can replicate those big-time thrills from dinghies or from shore, seeking out the "Big Three" of tarpon, snook, and permit. More passive pursuits include shelling on the islands off the southwest edge of the peninsula and birding, especially in the vast Everglades basin.

Disney's sprawling kingdom dominates central Florida, but it is ringed by ever-increasing concentric circles of competing theme parks and amusement centers. Attractions include 16th-century forts built by Spanish conquistadores and a space center that may eventually establish colonies among the stars. Mansions built by fabulously wealthy northerners in the last century and in the early years of this one dot both coastlines. Some of them can be visited, for a look at life before the dire fact of the federal income tax.

Those who crave a brisk urban beat find it in abundance beside the hip southern strand of Miami Beach and along Calle Ocho, the effervescent Latino enclave of its sister city across the bay. Visitors seeking nonstop nightly parties bump into kindred spirits just about everywhere, but especially in the earthy resorts of the Panhandle, on the lively downtown streets of Key West, beside the busy canals of Fort Lauderdale, and, during the famed spring break for college students, at Daytona Beach. Florida is invitingly sensual, and delightfully diverse, and it beckons even the most satiated of travelers. Knowing where to look helps.

A Brief History

THE FLOWERY LAND   Middle-aged Ponce de León, conqueror of Puerto Rico, sailed north in 1513 in quest of an alleged fountain of youth, and in April, he sighted the glistening sands of an unknown land. Given the time of year, he dubbed it "Pascua Florida"—Easter—and claimed it for the Spanish crown. As it happens, "florida" also means "flowery," a happy coincidence given the profusion of blossoms he surely found. His continued search proved fruitless and the native peoples he encountered were not friendly. On a return visit in 1521, he was felled in battle and died soon after.

Subsequent expeditions ran afoul of hurricanes and assorted other hardships and barely left a trace, their leaders more interested in booty than in permanence. The first determined Spanish settlers didn't arrive until 1565, when Pedro Menéndez de Avilés put ashore with a force of 1,500 soldiers and settlers. They swept aside a French trading post called Fort Caroline and established their own St Augustine, 25 miles south of the present Jacksonville. It was to become the oldest continually occupied European settlement in the future United States, established 42 years before the English first put down roots in Virginia. The moated castle they built still stands.

THE BRITISH ARE COMING   The people of St Augustine endured yellow fever, malaria, vicious tropical storms, and brigands. (Sir Francis Drake, for one, sacked the town in 1586.) No matter the calamity, they always rebuilt. But mere survival wasn't enough to attract other colonists and no gold was discovered in Florida.

There had been an earlier Spanish outpost at Pensacola, on the Gulf Coast, but it was abandoned after only 2 years, and the Spanish didn't return there until 1698. Pensacola took on a measure of strategic importance 4 years later, when France and Spain were allied against England and Austria in what was called Queen Anne's War. Such coalitions were short-lived. Six years after the treaty ending the war was signed, France launched repeated attacks against Pensacola from Louisiana, taking the colony in 1719 only to hand it back to Spain in 1723.

Imperial maneuvering between Spain, France, and Britain, their New World battles an extension of Old World struggles, continued through mid-century. By 1763, the end of the Seven Years War (known on this side of the Atlantic as the French and Indian War), England had taken charge of the territory. All this churning and bloodshed was curious, however, since, except for St Augustine, Pensacola, and a few small outlying ports, most of Florida was a backwater, and not many people other than the native Creeks and

---

✆ *Fun Facts* ✆

• *The oldest city of European origin in the United States is St Augustine. It was founded as a Spanish colony on September 8, 1565.*

• *Florida is home to more golf courses than any other state. More than 55 million rounds of golf are played annually on the state's 1,032 courses.*

• *No location in Florida is more than 60 miles from saltwater.*

• *The first integrated professional baseball game was played on March 17, 1946, at City Island Ball Park in Daytona Beach. Future Hall-of-Famer Jackie Robinson represented the minor league Montreal Royals in the game.*

• *Three-quarters of the oranges consumed in the United States are grown in Florida.*

• *Walt Disney World covers 43 square miles, making the theme park approximately the same size as San Francisco!*

Seminoles wished to live there. A 1771 census tallied only 1,200 whites and slaves east of the Apalachicola River.

THE AMERICANS TAKE OVER   The British didn't stay long. At the end of the American Revolution, the Treaty of Paris ceded Florida back to Spain. When the expansionist young republic to the north purchased the Louisiana Territory from the French in 1803, it insisted that west Florida was part of the package. Various groups nibbled at the region, and Andrew Jackson marched on Pensacola in 1813, returning in 1818 to make war against the Seminoles. Three years later, Spain gave Florida to the United States in return for clear title to Texas. That bargain wasn't to hold for long, but Jackson was on hand again to preside at the Spanish concession.

A site midway between St Augustine and Pensacola —Tallahassee—was declared the capital of the new territory. (Three log cabins served as legislative buildings.) Another bitter war with the Seminoles erupted in 1835. In a hardly unique act of perfidy, the army arrested Chief Osceola when he came to them under a flag of truce. In 1842, nearly 4,000 Seminoles and runaway slaves who lived among them were deported to Arkansas.

STATEHOOD & CONFLICT   A new brick capital was completed in Tallahassee in 1845, just in time for statehood. Florida signed on with the Confederacy during the Civil War, although it wasn't destined to play a major role, because of its small population. Its troops held forts in the northeastern and northwestern parts of the state, while Union forces dominated in strategically more important Key West and the Dry Tortugas. The war over, a new state constitution in 1868 granted suffrage to all male citizens, regardless of race. Suddenly, enfranchised blacks actually outnumbered whites, some of whom flocked to the Ku Klux Klan. In 1871 alone, the KKK lynched 163 black people in a single Florida county.

RAILWAYS TO THE SUN   After the withdrawal of Federal troops in 1877, investors finally began to see the enormous agricultural and touristic potential of the undeveloped peninsula. Industrialist Henry B Plant financed a new rail line running diagonally across the state between Jacksonville and Tampa on the Gulf

Coast (1884), and oil magnate Henry M Flagler commenced construction of his East Coast Railway from St Augustine south to Miami. Linking the luxury hotels he built along the way, his "Railroad That Went to Sea" eventually reached Key West.

A post–World War I land boom poured millions of speculative dollars into the economy. Immigration and tourism grew apace. Criminals flourished, too, for this was the Prohibition era and Florida, with its 1,800 miles of coastline, was a magnet for rumrunners. The bubble burst in 1926, when investors began to discover that much of the acreage they had purchased unseen didn't exist or was underwater. The final blow was a devastating hurricane the same year that all but leveled Miami, leaving almost 200 dead.

BUST TO BATTLESHIPS   Seven years later, yet another hurricane destroyed much of Flagler's railroad between Miami and Key West. The state acquired the right-of-way and constructed a road, which opened for traffic in 1938, aiding in the economic revival of the Keys. The Great Depression was beginning to ease by then, due to New Deal social programs and the industrial and military buildup prior to World War II. Florida was deemed crucial to the defense of Gulf shipping and the Panama Canal.

BLAST-OFF   With the recovery following Japan's surrender, Americans sought sun and frolic as never before. Resorts, hotels, and condominium complexes sprang up along the two coasts. Rapacious developers and municipalities sucked so much water from interior lakes and aquifers that the great Everglades began to shrink, an alarming process and one that has yet to be resolved.

When NASA set up shop on Cape Canaveral in 1958, launching the Apollo missions that landed the first men on the moon, the state received a shot of scientific prestige as well as a further boost to tourism. Theme parks contributed to the increasing tides of visitors. Cypress Gardens and Busch Gardens led the way and they still thrive, but it took the phenomenon named Disney to transform central Florida into the world's most popular tourist destination. Disney's Magic Kingdom opened in 1971.

MICKEY, MINNIE, MARGARITA   Monumental demographic and economic change was prompted by the

Cuban Revolution, which caused waves of refugees to flee to south Florida. Many of them were prosperous and educated, with the drive and vision to invigorate the society they found waiting for them. Miami soon became the de facto capital of the Caribbean.

Another revolution took place with the arrival of contemporary versions of Prohibition's rumrunners. America's escalating taste for illicit drugs was—and is—a bonanza for drug traffickers and the pilots and boat captains they hired to dump tons of cocaine and marijuana on these shores every week.

That challenge, and those of rapid growth and the depleted environment, will dog the state for decades. Now the 4th largest state in population—it was only tenth in 1960—it is destined to move up to 3rd place, after California and Texas and ahead of New York, by the end of this century. Even then, the worst thing about Florida will be having to leave.

A CLOSER LOOK
Geography

The elongated thumb of land pointing at the tropics is the youngest part of the United States, geologically speaking. For the most part, it is as flat as a billiard table, with any elevation higher than a 3-story building qualifying as a hill. Its highest "peak" is 345 feet, 2 miles from the Georgia border. Otherwise, the state offers a remarkably diverse landscape, with dense forests of live oak and cypress, hundred of rivers and streams, barrier reefs and islands protecting long stretches of both coasts, the primordial wilderness known as the Everglades, and over 10,000 lakes, including Okeechobee, second-largest in the United States. And yes, beaches—over 1,000 miles of them.

The **Florida Keys** trail off the south tip of the peninsula like a broken necklace drifting in the current. These hundreds of coral and mangrove islands are largely uninhabited, apart from those linked by US 1, the "Overseas Highway." Off Key Largo, at the northern end, is John Pennekamp Coral Reef State Park. From there down, only Islamorada and Marathon have significant populations until the southernmost terminus of US 1, Key West. That island city is closer to Cuba than to Miami.

Moving north to the mainland, Homestead is a modest introduction to the glittery **Miami** region,

DRIVING DISTANCES:

Jacksonville
90 miles NW of Daytona Beach
202 miles NE of Tampa
358 miles E of Pensacola
463 miles SE of Birmingham, AL
503 miles N of Key West

Miami
164 miles NE of Key West
229 miles SE of Orlando
268 miles SE of Daytona Beach
348 miles SE of Jacksonville
663 miles SE of Atlanta, GA

Orlando
84 miles NE of Tampa
166 miles NW of West Palm Beach
232 miles NW of Miami
258 miles SE of Tallahassee
648 miles SE of New Orleans, LA

Tampa
78 miles SW of Orlando
201 miles SW of Jacksonville
238 miles SE of Tallahassee
269 miles NW of Miami
440 miles SW of Charleston, SC

which includes cosmopolitan Miami itself, an ethnic and racial mosaic that reflects its magnetism for peoples throughout the Western Hemisphere, and its adjacent sister city of Miami Beach, with a rejuvenated art deco district. Snuggled against them are Hialeah, famed for its racetrack, and the lush residential community of Coral Gables. Continuing north, Fort Lauderdale signals the beginning of the **Gold Coast,** whose busy canals prompt chamber of commerce comparisons to Venice. Strung along the shore, with resort hotels and luxurious homes at every turn, are the wealthy communities of Boca Raton, Delray Beach, Boynton Beach, and Palm Beach, the last established by Henry Flagler for his monied chums. West of Miami and the Gold Coast, the Everglades stretch all the way to the Gulf Coast, nearly empty of human habitation apart from the Miccosukee Seminoles who were there thousands of years before Europeans arrived. The expanse is crossed by I-75, known as Alligator Alley.

On this side of the state, the less urban and more sedate Lee County coast incorporates upscale **Naples** and engagingly frowsy **Fort Myers,** winter home to Thomas Edison. Offshore are Sanibel, Captiva, Estero, and Marco resort islands, bearing a relatively tranquil family identity and incorporating notable wildlife refuges.

Farther north, the **Central Gulf Coast** centers on the cities and resorts that ring **Tampa Bay** and constitute the largest concentration of population on the Florida Gulf Coast. Sarasota, slightly south of the entrance to the bay, enjoyed the beneficence of circus mogul John Ringling, who left 3 important museums. Tampa is the hub, with its fine airport, hotels, nightlife, and the popular Busch Gardens theme park. St Petersburg, nearly as large, has the beaches and marinas Tampa lacks.

Orlando and **Central Florida** spell one thing to most people anticipating a visit with a carful of youngsters: Disney. That's understandable, given the way the Disney empire keeps expanding, with the Magic Kingdom begetting EPCOT Center begetting MGM Studios. New attractions, restaurants, and hotels are added by the month, but that picture is incomplete. There are many quiet corners, as in the gracious municipality of Winter Park and in peaceful Bok Tower Gardens.

The **Central Atlantic Coast,** often called the Space or Treasure Coast, is a short drive east of Orlando. Its shore is protected by a rarely broken string of barrier islands from Fort Pierce to Daytona Beach. Cape Canaveral and the Kennedy Space Center contrast space-age technology with the surrounding nature refuge and with the rural character of nearby Indian River, famed for its citrus groves.

In the **Northeast,** sometimes referred to as the Crown of Florida, is historic St Augustine, the oldest continuously occupied town in the United States and a prize that has thrived under 5 flags—Spanish, French, English, Old Glory, and the Stars and Bars of the Confederacy. Jacksonville is a thriving metropolis straddling the broad St John's River. Beyond the city, in the last corner of the state before Georgia, is Amelia Island, with a trove of several hundred Victorian dwellings behind its impressive sand dunes.

The northwest arm of the state, which reaches under Alabama toward Mississippi, is commonly known as the **Panhandle.** At its eastern edge is the capital, Tallahassee, its antebellum plantation houses and venerable trees lending a distinctive Old South flavor. Pensacola, at the western border, is older, with a village of restored houses harking back to the 18th century. Nearby is the Pensacola Naval Air Station, with an impressive aircraft museum. From there, the "Emerald Coast" curves southeast through the bustling Gulfside resorts of Fort Walton Beach, Destin, and Panama City. This strip has its honky-tonk aspects, but it also has segments protected by state and national recreation areas. Soon, both give way to secluded cottage colonies and drowsy old-time fishing villages. Apalachicola, on the bay of the same name, has a good-size shrimp fleet and is famous for its oysters.

Climate

Warm breezes and blue skies rule throughout the state. There is ample room for variations, however, since it is over 500 miles from the Georgia border to the tip of Key West.

While January in Jacksonville won't remind anyone of New Year's Day in Minneapolis, it is usually cool during the day and chilly at night. Freezing temperatures, albeit short in duration, are an almost yearly threat to citrus crops as far down the coast as Palm Beach. From Miami on south, though, frosts are virtually unknown, even in deepest winter. Residents of South Florida and the Keys, who fear the onset of chilbains if the temperature falls below 65°F, even at Christmas, pay a price in heavier rainfall during the off-season (May through October), when thunderstorms and lightning are frequent. That period is also hot and can be stiflingly humid, but not much worse than in northern cities in summer. Interior sections of the state, notably around Orlando, tend to be less comfortable in summer than the coastal cities.

June through October is also hurricane season, which usually peaks in July and August. While past storms have brought great tragedy and even altered the course of the state's history, the National Hurricane Center in Miami gives ample warning of possible danger, and routes of escape.

The Florida sun is extremely powerful, especially on or near water, beaches, and other reflective surfaces.

AVERAGE MONTHLY TEMPERATURES (°F) & INCHES OF RAINFALL		
	Miami	Jacksonville	Tampa
Jan	67/2.1	53/3.1	60/2.2
Feb	68/2.1	55/3.5	61/3.0
Mar	72/1.9	61/3.7	66/3.5
Apr	75/3.1	68/3.3	72/1.8
May	79/6.5	74/4.9	77/3.4
June	81/9.2	79/5.4	81/5.3
July	83/6.0	81/6.5	82/7.4
Aug	83/7.0	81/7.2	82/7.6
Sept	82/8.1	78/7.3	81/6.2
Oct	78/7.1	70/3.4	74/2.3
Nov	73/2.7	61/1.9	67/1.9
Dec	69/1.9	55/2.6	61/2.1

Visitors of all complexions are cautioned to wear hats and use protective sunscreen lotions *whenever* spending time outside, and to reapply it liberally and often. Failure to do so can result in discomfort at the least and a severe health risk at the worst. Parents should pay particular attention to protection for their children. If possible, avoid outdoor activities between 10am and 3pm.

What to Pack

In winter months, a sweater is necessary even in South Florida, where there can be unexpected cold snaps with temperatures occasionally dropping into the 50s. A light, water-repellent windbreaker is useful, especially from June to October, when short showers are an almost daily occurrence. Take it along, too, when spending time on a boat.

Comfortable walking shoes are a must for tramping through theme parks. Rubber soles are essential for boats. With the exception of a handful of restaurants, most of them in Miami or Palm Beach, men won't need ties unless on a business trip. A blazer and trousers will do for almost all social situations, with a cocktail dress or two for women. Leave splashy jewelry at home, especially when traveling in the larger cities. The rest of the time, shorts or jeans or light cotton dresses should do. And no one needs to be told to take a swimsuit or two to Florida.

A camera is all but essential, and birders will need their binoculars. Tuck in a bottle of sunscreen lotion with an SPF of 15 or higher, or buy some immediately upon arrival, as well as insect repellent for comfort in forested areas, marshes, swamps, and even on beaches. Other necessities are a sunhat, and sandals or flip-flops to protect feet on hot sand.

Tourist Information

Contact the Florida Division of Tourism at 126 West Van Buren St, Tallahassee, FL 32399 or call 904/487-1462 to obtain the free *Florida Vacation Guide* and road maps, as well as answers to general questions. Those wishing more specific information about towns and regions throughout the state will find the addresses and telephone numbers of local visitors bureaus or chambers of commerce in the same publication.

For information about Walt Disney World, contact the Walt Disney World Company, PO Box 10000, Lake Buena Vista, FL 32830-1000 (tel 407/824-4321). General information about accommodations can be obtained from the Florida Hotel and Motel Association, Box 1529, Tallahassee, FL 32302-1529 (tel 904/488-1133). Welcome centers at highway entry points along the state border have a wealth of brochures and maps available for the taking, and many cities have centrally located kiosks serving the same purpose.

Driving Rules & Regulations

Seat belts are mandatory for all front-seat passengers, and for children 4 or 5 years old anywhere in the vehicle. Every child under 3 must use an approved safety seat. Speed limits are 55 mph on state roads unless otherwise posted, and 55 or 65 mph on interstate highways. Liability insurance is required.

Persons caught driving while under the influence of alcohol or drugs are punished severely, but that doesn't stop many from doing it. Alert defensive driving is always in order.

Renting a Car

Visitors wanting to rent a car on arrival in Florida are faced with a bewildering profusion of offers. To save time, it is preferable to ask a travel agent to sort through the possibilities and make advance reservations. An agent can also suggest packages that include not only airfare and rental car but lodging, sightseeing tours, and other features.

If you prefer to make your own arrangements, call several rental companies to compare prices, since fee structures are complicated and promotional deals appear and disappear frequently. Members of some national organizations, such as AARP, are eligible for discounts, so be sure to ask. Keep in mind that some car rental companies have minimum age requirements.

All major rental companies are represented, including:

* **Alamo** (tel toll free 800/327-9633)
* **Avis** (tel toll free 800/331-1212)
* **Budget** (tel toll free 800/527-0700)
* **Dollar** (tel toll free 800/365-5276)
* **Hertz** (tel toll free 800/654-3131)
* **National** (tel toll free 800/227-7368)
* **Thrifty** (tel toll free 800/367-2277)

Essentials

Area Codes: The area code for northern Florida, including Jacksonville and Tallahassee, is 904; for the west coast from Tampa south, it's 813; for the central part of the state east to the Atlantic Coast, it's 407; for the southeast, from West Palm Beach through Miami to Key West, it's 305.

Emergencies: To summon the police, the fire department, or an ambulance from anywhere in the state, call 911.

Liquor Laws: The minimum legal age to buy or consume alcoholic beverages in Florida is 21, although the law is observed with varying degrees of rigor. Bars are open at least until midnight, and often as late (or early) as 4 or even 6am. They are closed Sunday mornings.

Smoking: While there are no statewide and few municipal anti-smoking regulations, most restaurants have nonsmoking areas, many hotels have smoke-free rooms, and the major airports forbid smoking except in designated areas.

Taxes: Florida's sales tax is 6%. Many municipalities and counties impose additional taxes, especially on hotel and restaurant bills.

Time Zone: Most of the state observes Eastern Standard Time, but the section of the Panhandle west of the Apalachicola River, including Pensacola and Panama City, is on Central Standard Time, an hour behind the rest of Florida. Daylight Savings Time is observed.

Best of the State

Florida's cultural institutions may lag behind those of some northern cities, and overdevelopment and unfettered commercialism may have blighted long stretches of the coast and interior. But the state has sun, almost all the time; inviting bodies of water, fresh and salt, for swimming, fishing, and boating; over 1,000 miles of beaches; and exotic wildlife. It also has world-famous resorts and theme parks, ancient forts and historic homes, luxuriant gardens, and vivacious cities.

What to See & Do

FAMILY FAVORITES

An abundance of family-oriented attractions ensures that parents and children can enjoy every minute of a vacation together, no matter how long the stay.

THEME PARKS Almost everyone who crosses the border journeys into the heart of the state, where the Disney organization has spawned its own clutch of theme parks and inspired a dozen or so commendable competitors. **Walt Disney World** is really 3 theme parks in one, beginning with **the Magic Kingdom,** a repository of nostalgia, Americana, and fantasy, with electrifying rides through a faux mountain, a sanitized jungle, and over water. Next came **EPCOT Center,** a semi-educational paean to technology and the future. Most popular of its entertainments is Spaceship Earth, a 15-minute sojurn through the entire history of the planet. Youngest of the 3 complexes is **Disney–MGM Studios,** where rides and multimedia theaters revel in Hollywood lore, and visitors plunge into replications of famous film scenes as well as a couple of imaginative water parks.

Also in Orlando is **Sea World,** with its performing dolphins, killer whales, and flock of penguins. One of the most popular exhibits is an underwater glass tunnel that allows spectators to look out at sharks and barracudas on the prowl. Shamu the killer whale is the headliner, with his own stadium. **Universal Studios Florida,** easily the equal of the Disney-MGM collaboration, is also in the neighborhood, making the most of its associations with hit films and Hollywood lore. Besides movie sets, stunt shows, and state-of-the-art films, it includes impressive sound stages actually used in film production. Out of the Orlando orbit, but deserving of consideration, is **Busch Gardens,** near Tampa Bay. A full day is barely enough to take in its extensive animal exhibits, which include apes, lions, zebras, and giraffes.

BEACHES   They are never far away, but some are better known than others, for a variety of reasons. **Daytona Beach,** famed for its automobile races and as the destination of choice for college students on spring break, is a wide avenue of sand so hard-packed that sun-worshipers can drive right up to the spot they choose to pitch their blankets. Odds-on favorite for the "most glamorous" are the miles of reconstructed sands alongside fashionable south **Miami Beach.** Manmade **Smathers Beach** in Key West draws crowds as diverse as the residents of the island itself. In the Tampa Bay area, avoid swimming in bays, which may look fine but are subject to pollution. Instead, head south to the barrier islands off Sarasota—**South Lido Beach** is long and well equipped—or Bradenton, where the top choice for families is **Manatee County Beach.** Farther south, the gulf beaches of **Captiva** and **Sanibel Islands** are famous for shelling. In the Panhandle, superb strands are among the several accessible portions of

Gulf Island National Seashore, opposite Pensacola, and they have none of the commercial clutter associated with beaches farther east along the Panhandle.

FORTS   Most kids get a kick out of clambering over the walls and battlements of fortresses the Spanish left behind in northern Florida, especially those with costumed docents and displays of musketry. One of the largest and best restored is the **Castillo de San Marcos** in St Augustine. Over on the Gulf Coast, Pensacola has the 1844 **Fort Barrancas,** built over older Spanish fortifications contained within the sprawling Pensacola Naval Air Station. On the island of Santa Rosa, which enclosed Pensacola Bay, is **Fort Pickens.** Now part of a national seashore park, it once served as a prison for the Apache warrior Geronimo.

HISTORICAL BUILDINGS

The wealthy men and women responsible for developing Florida around the turn of the century left eye-popping hotels and mansions all along the east coast, especially in St Augustine, Palm Beach, and Miami.

James Deering's Italianate seaside villa **Vizcaya** and its extensive gardens are fabulously theatrical. Despite its Spanish name, the 70-room mansion and its outbuildings are Venetian in style; interiors are lavishly appointed with imported tiles, coffered ceilings, and collections of European decorative and fine arts. The estate, a decided must-see, is on the outskirts of Miami.

Also make time for the 1902 **Whitehall** mansion, built in Palm Beach by the oil and railroad tycoon who was responsible in great measure for Florida's development. Now officially named the Henry M Flagler Museum, it has scores of rooms replete with paintings, carpets, sculptures, and furnishings of the period, many of them original to Flagler. His private railroad car is also on display.

Many of the distinctive designs of the flamboyant architect **Addison Mizner** survive as restaurants, hotels, and private homes in the Boca Raton–Fort Lauderdale area. Noted for his use of Mediterranean styles and materials in combinations entirely his own, he created structures that are enjoyed more for their exuberance than for their contributions to the art of architecture. Two Mizner creations accessible to the public are La Vieille Maison restaurant and portions of the Boca Raton Hotel and Club.

In Pensacola's **Seville District,** preserved blocks of dozens of houses dating from the colonial period cluster around Seville Square and along streets named after Spanish cities—Tarragona, Zaragoza, Alcañiz. Eleven of the buildings constitute **Historic Pensacola Village,** and function as museums illustrating the heritage, commerce, and industries of the city or as examples of colonial and antebellum architecture. Earnest guides in period garb conduct tours.

The Spanish founded **St Augustine** and occupied it for over 250 years, apart from a 20-year interim of British control. While little remains from the 16th and 17th centuries, the **Spanish Quarter** does contain a large number of buildings surviving from the early 1700s and 1800s and most are intriguing. The majority are Spanish in origin, with British and French overlays, and have been much restored. Many are used as shops and cafes, while some serve as mini-museums.

The youngest preservation district in the state is the **Miami Beach Art Deco District** of south Miami Beach (also known as SoBe). Its buildings, dating from the 1930s and early 1940s, are reminiscent of old radios and between-the-wars passenger liners. Neon, bands of pastel colors, eyebrow windows, mock portholes, and stylized representations of palm trees and sunsets inform block after block of restored structures. Many are now boutique hotels, clubs, and restaurants, a scene that has attracted the attention of model agencies and big-time Hollywood stars and investors.

STATE & NATIONAL PARKS

Quite apart from the artificial naturalism of commercial safari parks and aviaries, wildlife and a profusion of luxuriant subtropical vegetation can be viewed up close and personal in the waters and fields outside every town, as well as in parks that are never far away from any urban center.

In **Everglades National Park,** easily the best environment for viewing native fauna, the ecosystem's birds of prey, lizards, giant turtles, wading birds, and alligators can be seen in abundance from escorted trams and elevated walkways. The profoundly endangered Florida panther also makes the swamp its home, but not even the resident park rangers are likely to spot one. Hurricane Andrew caused considerable damage to visitor facilities and the grasslands, and both are still recovering.

John Pennekamp Coral Reef State Park, the first underwater state park in the continental United States, embraces almost 80 square miles of ocean floor east of Key Largo, northernmost of the hundreds of Florida Keys. Snorkeling party boats make the short trip to the park's central feature, a long coral reef, almost every day. The reef provides shelter and sustenance to fish so brilliantly hued they look like fragments spilled from a broken kaleidoscope. Farther north, just outside the Miami city limits, another section of the same reef system was the motivation for the creation of **Biscayne National Park.**

North of the bustling Orlando area lies **Ocala National Forest,** a large preserve virtually surrounded by lakes and rivers inviting to campers, hikers, canoeists, and anglers. With 13 major campgrounds, there are ample bases from which to engage in these activities as well as exploration of the large springs that dot the region. Surrounding farms and estates are known for horse breeding, with wranglers tending to their charges under trees draped in Spanish moss.

Canaveral National Seashore, a protected marine environment adjoining the grounds of the Kennedy Space Center, has opportunities for sightings that are legend among bird-watchers. Over 300 types of waterfowl and other species have been identified. Pristine beaches attract swimmers and sunbathers, and the preserve also contains Mosquito Lagoon, where alligators and egg-laying sea turtles are often observed.

Take binoculars for the circuit of the small but engaging **J N "Ding" Darling National Wildlife Refuge.** Along the park's 5-mile Wildlife Drive visitors can spot roseate spoonbills, egrets, herons, pelicans, and alligators, among others, most of them accommodating enough to roost and wade beside signs that announce their presence.

CUISINE

Once characterized as a gastronomic wasteland of chicken shacks and barbecue joints, Florida now boasts a burgeoning cadre of 3-star chefs, many of them immigrants from New York and Europe. They are fashioning a distinctive "sunshine cuisine," giving inventive twists to the produce and ideas of Caribbean and Latin American kitchens. The best of this innovative breed are in Palm Beach, Fort Lauderdale, Miami, and Key West, but other areas are catching up. Whether in evolving forms of cookery that are yet to be given labels or in more traditional domestic or imported cuisines, the growing American taste for spicy, even fiery, dishes is abundantly served.

Creole/Cajun cooking has successfully made the short journey from its birthplace, Louisiana, especially in the northwestern part of the state. The lowly crawfish and vegetable greens have been raised to epicurean status, and the vogue for blackened redfish threatened the very existence of that species until the technique was applied to other types of fish.

The **Cuban** culinary repertoire, by contrast, is more limited in scope but well worth seeking out, if only for the tasty toasted sandwiches of layered ham, pork, Swiss cheese, pickles, and tangy sauce. Many Cuban recipes have their origins in Spain, naturally, as with paella and arroz con pollo. Others take advantage of Caribbean fruits and produce, as in *lechon al trozo*—roast pork with rice, black beans, and yucca, often with fried plantains on the side. **Jamaican** food is increasingly popular, using similar ingredients, but usually with a hotter kick. Jerked pork is typical. Look for these and related Caribbean cuisines in South Florida, especially in Miami.

Seafood figures prominently on all restaurant menus. Some of it rarely travels north, so visitors inevitably encounter fish and crustaceans with which they are unfamiliar. Mahimahi is a Hawaiian name often applied to the delectable *fish* properly called dolphin. This is not—repeat, *not*—the lovable mammal we know as Flipper. Ground or diced conch (pronounced "conk") is a rubbery shellfish served in chowder and fritters, each of which merits a taste. Stone crabs are a happily renewable resource. Properly harvested, they are made to surrender only one claw and are then returned to the sea, where they obligingly grow another. A restaurant in Miami Beach is so devoted to the stone crab that it closes its doors when the delectable creature is out of season.

Events/Festivals

The Keys

- **Old Island Days,** Key West. Various events and celebrations, including house and garden tours, parades, boat races, arts and craft shows. Mid-January to April. Call 305/294-9501 for information.
- **Seven-Mile Bridge Run,** Marathon. Foot race across the namesake bridge, with international participants. April. Call 305/743-8513.
- **Hemingway Days,** Key West. Story competition, Hemingway look-alike contest, arm wrestling. Mid-July. Call 305/294-4440.
- **Fantasy Fest,** Key West. Bizarre, often ribald costume parties and Halloween parades. October. Call 305/296-1817.

Miami & the Gold Coast

- **Orange Bowl,** Miami. One of the 5 major postseason college football games, preceded by the King Orange parade. New Year's Day. Call 305/642-1515 for information.
- **Taste of the Grove,** Coconut Grove, Miami. Two days of food and music. Mid-January. Call 305/624-3714.
- **Art Deco Festival,** Miami Beach. Street fair, dances, music in South Beach's restored Deco district. Mid-January. Call 305/672-2014.
- **Arts Festival,** Coconut Grove, Miami. Hundreds of local artists display their work; food and music. Mid-February. Call 305/447-0401.
- **Sistrunk Historical Festival,** Fort Lauderdale. Street fair celebrates the African-American experience with food, music, and crafts displays. February. Call 305/357-7514.
- **International Boat and Sailboat Show,** Miami. Mid- to late February. Call 305/531-8410.
- **Seminole Tribal Fair,** Hollywood. Traditional Native American music, dance, crafts. Late February. Call 305/321-1000.
- **Grand Prix,** Miami. Formula One cars race on Biscayne Boulevard. Late February to early March. Call 305/379-7223.
- **Calle Ocho/Carnavale,** Miami. Festivities include parades and dancing in Little Havana. Early March. Call 305/324-7349.
- **Broward County Fair,** Hallandale. A week of rides, games, concerts, and food. November. Call 305/923-3247.
- **Winterfest Boat Parade,** Fort Lauderdale. Scores of gaily decorated craft sail and chug along the Intracoastal Waterway. Many other events fill the month. December. Call 305/767-0686.

The Gulf Coast

- **Hall of Fame Bowl,** Tampa. New Year's Day college football extravaganza, with road race and concerts. Call 800/448-2672 for information.
- **Gasparilla Festival,** Tampa. Buccaneers sail into the bay and "invade" the city. Torchlight parade, road races, golf tournaments, and parties fill out the month-long celebration. Late January to early February. Call 800/448-2672.
- **Florida State Fair,** Tampa. A classic. Dozens of rides and a midway packed with games and food booths. Country music stars, agricultural exhibits, and prize-winning livestock. February. Call 800/345-3247.
- **Edison Festival of Light,** Fort Myers. The inventor of the electric light is honored by 2 weeks of festivities, including foot races, regatta, dancing, shell show, and parade. February. Call 813/334-2550.
- **Medieval Fair,** Sarasota. Knights and ladies besport themselves at jousts and games at the Ringling Museum of Art. Theatrical performances. Early March. Call 813/355-5101.
- **Jazz Festival,** Sarasota. Blues shouters, combos, and big bands rejoice. Week in early April. Call 813/366-1552.
- **Tropicool Fest,** Naples. Canoe races, concerts, and art shows stretch the winter season by 2 weeks. Mid-May. Call 813/262-6141.
- **Music Festival,** Sarasota. Concerts by chamber and symphony orchestras with prominent guest artists. June. Call 813/953-4252.
- **Jazz on the Green,** Sanibel. Annual jazz festival with food prepared by noted area chefs. October. Call 813/481-2011.

Orlando & Central Florida

- **Citrus Bowl,** Orlando. One of Florida's several post-season college football matchups. New Year's Day. Call 407/423-2476 for information.
- **Scottish Highland Games,** Orlando. Highland games, dancing, and athletic events, all to the skirl of bagpipes. Last weekend in January. Call 407/672-1682.
- **Silver Spurs Rodeo,** Kissimmee. One of the most important rodeos in the country, featuring many top-rated cowboys. February and July. Call 407/677-6336.

- **Bluegrass Festival,** Kissimmee. Gospel and bluegrass singers, with crafts shows and down-home cookery. March. Call 800/472-7773.
- **Sun 'n' Fun Fly-In,** Lakeland. Week-long meeting of the Experimental Aircraft Association, featuring unusual planes and aerobatics. 2nd week of April. Call 813/644-2431.
- **Florida State Air Fair,** Kissimmee. Nostalgic throwback to barnstorming air shows of the past. Vintage planes. Late October or early November. Call 407/933-7998.
- **Light Up Orlando.** Parade and street festival with food and live entertainment kicking off the winter season. November. Call 407/648-4010.

Central Atlantic Coast

- **Speed Weeks,** Daytona Beach. Three weeks of NASCAR races at the Daytona Speedway. February. Call 904/253-7223 (RACE) for information.
- **Bike Week,** Daytona Beach. Championship motorcycle races. February. Call 904/255-0981.
- **Daytona 500,** Daytona Beach. The number one stock car race in the United States. At Daytona Speedway. February. Call 904/253-7223 (RACE).
- **Air Show,** Titusville. Mock dogfights and precision flying by World War II fighter planes and antique aircraft. March. Call 407/268-1944.
- **Space Week,** Brevard County. Commemoration of the Apollo 11 moon landing. Concerts, hot-air balloons, other events. July. Call 407/452-2121.

The Northeast

- **Gator Bowl,** Jacksonville. Fireworks and other entertainments spark the hours leading to a post-season college football game. New Year's Day. Call 904/353-1188 for information.
- **Blessing of the Fleet,** Jacksonville. An excuse for lavish food festival, live music, and boat show. Palm Sunday. Call 904/396-4900.
- **Easter Parade,** St Augustine. Floats, bands, and horse-drawn carriages circle through downtown. Late March or early April. Call 904/692-1032.
- **Flagler County Bluegrass Jamboree,** Bunnell. Accomplished bluegrass musicians play throughout the day; games and pony rides for kids, and a Civil War reenactment. May. Call 904/437-0106.

- **Heritage Days,** Jacksonville. Actors in period costumes stage vignettes from Florida's past. May. Call 904/356-6307.
- **Mug Race,** Palatka. Sailboats race 40 miles downriver to Jacksonville. Entertainment. First Friday in May (usually). Call 904/264-4094.
- **Cross and Sword,** St Augustine. Popular musical drama depicts establishment of the colony by the Spanish. Mid-June to late August. Call 904/471-1965 or 829-6476.
- **Jazz Festival,** Jacksonville. Major event with many stars and up-and-comers of the jazz world. 2nd weekend in October. Call 904/353-7770.
- **Grand Illumination,** St Augustine. Torchlight parade winds through the historic district. Mid-December. Call 904/824-9550 or 829-6476.

The Panhandle

- **Natural Bridge Battlefield Reenactment,** Tallahassee. Staged Civil War battle. Early March. Call 800/628-2866 or 904/681-9200 for information.
- **Springtime Tallahassee.** Arts and crafts exhibits, processions, house and garden tours, and a hot-air balloon race, among many events. Mid-March to early April. Call 800/628-2866 or 904/681-9200.
- **Eglin Air Show,** Fort Walton Beach. Mock dogfights and breathtaking aerobatics by the illustrious Navy Thunderbirds. April. Call 800/322-3319 or 904/651-7131.
- **Hog's Breath Hobie Regatta,** Fort Walton Beach. Some 200 boats dance all day across the Gulf past party boats loaded with spectators. All-night pig roast. May. Call 800/322-3319 or 904/651-7131.
- **Fiesta of Five Flags,** Pensacola. Parades on water and land, waterskiing competitions, and other events commemorate the 1st Spanish explorers. Mid-June. Call 800/874-1234.
- **Volleyball Tournament,** Destin/Fort Walton Beach. One of the country's premier beach volleyball tourneys. September. Call 800/322-3319 or 904/651-7131.
- **Fishing Rodeo,** Destin/Fort Walton Beach. A month-long fishing tournament, open to all. Prizes. October. Call 904/837-6241.
- **Florida Seafood Festival,** Apalachicola. The drowsy fishing port comes alive in celebration of its meal ticket—the succulent Apalachicola oyster.

Parades, eating contests. First Saturday in November. Call 904/653-8051.
- **Blue Angels Homecoming Airshow,** Pensacola. The renowned Navy aerobatics team performs free of charge from its home base. November. Call 800/874-1234.

Spectator Sports

AUTO RACING Daytona Beach is one of the country's prime venues for stock car and hot rod racing. Events are held throughout the year at **Daytona International Speedway,** site of the famous Daytona 500. Call 904/254-2700 for schedule information. Miami attracts cars and drivers from around the world for its annual Formula One **Toyota Grand Prix,** held on a course plotted along downtown streets, usually in February or March. Call 305/379-5660 for dates, 305/379-7223 for tickets.

Hot rodders and drag racing enthusiasts flock to the **Gatornationals,** held in Gainesville in March (tel 904/377-0046), and there are weekly events during the winter at **Hialeah Speedway** (tel 305/821-6644). The thrilling **Twelve Hours of Sebring** thunders around Sebring International Raceway in March (tel 813/655-1442).

BASEBALL Until 1991, Floridians hungering for big-league baseball had to settle for its short spring "Grapefruit League," when professional teams from other states arrived for a few weeks of training. Now, they have a home team to root for, the **Florida Marlins.** The National Leaguers play at Joe Robbie Stadium (tel 305/779-7070), a short drive north of Miami.

Twenty rival clubs spend the late winter and early spring in Florida conducting their training camps, including the **Philadelphia Phillies** (tel 813/442-8496) in Clearwater, the **Pittsburgh Pirates** (tel 813/747-3031) in Bradenton, the **Toronto Blue Jays** (tel 813/733-9302) in Dunedin, the **Cincinnati Reds** (tel 813/752-7337) at Plant City, the **Chicago White Sox** (tel 813/954-7699) in Sarasota, the **New York Yankees** (tel 305/776-1921) in Fort Lauderdale, the **Texas Rangers** (tel 813/625-9500) at Port Charlotte, the **New York Mets** (tel 407/871-2115) at Port St Lucie, the **St Louis Cardinals** (tel 813/822-3384) in St Petersburg, the **Minnesota Twins** (tel 813/768-4278) and **Boston Red Sox** (tel 813/334-4700) in Fort

Myers, the **Atlanta Braves** (tel 407/683-6100) and the **Montreal Expos** (tel 407/689-9121) at West Palm Beach, and the **Los Angeles Dodgers** (tel 407/569-4900) at Vero Beach. Almost all exhibition games sell out weeks in advance, so it's wise to plan ahead.

BASKETBALL   Florida has joined the National Basketball Association with a vengeance, with 2 basketball teams that have recently begun to make an impact on the standings. The **Miami Heat** play at the downtown Miami Arena (305/577-4328). Central Florida has its own **Orlando Magic,** with star center Shaquille O'Neal, playing in the gleaming new Orlando Arena (407/896-2442).

FOOTBALL   Teams from 3 universities in the state are routinely ranked among the top 20 in national polls. Hailed as a cradle of superstar quarterbacks, the **Hurricanes** of the **University of Miami** harass their opponents at the Orange Bowl (305/643-7100). At Gainesville, 34,000 students and uncounted supporters cheer on the **Gators** of the **University of Florida,** who appear at Doak Campbell Stadium (904/644-1830). And the **Seminoles** of **Florida State University,** who play their tough home schedule in Tallahassee, do their work at Ben Griffin Stadium (904/375-4683).

Florida's first professional club was the **Miami Dolphins,** the only NFL team ever to post an unbeaten season. They perform at Joe Robbie Stadium (305/620-5000), named for the Dolphins owner who built it when he grew dissatisfied with the creaky Orange Bowl, their former home. The **Tampa Bay Buccaneers** were the 2nd expansion team. While they haven't enjoyed the same level of success as their cross-state rivals, their followers are no less loyal. Buccaneer games are played at Tampa Stadium (813/879-2827). In 1995, the new **Jacksonville Jaguars** join the roster, clawing their way to contention at the Gator Bowl (904/633-2000).

GREYHOUND RACING   Controversial though it may be, the dog racing industry thrives, with many venues throughout the state. Pari-mutuel betting is the lure, and tracks are open on a staggered basis throughout the year.

In the Northeast, Jacksonville has **Orange Park Kennel Club, St John's Greyhound Park,** and the **Jacksonville Kennel Club.** They have alternating schedules, so at least one is open at almost any time of

the year. Call 904/646-0001 for information about all 3. Over in the Panhandle is the **Pensacola Greyhound Track** (904/455-8598), with an air-conditioned grandstand.

In the Tampa Bay area, the active tracks are **Derby Lane** in St Petersburg (813/576-1361), **Sarasota Kennel Club** (813/355-7744), and **Tampa Greyhound Track** (813/932-4313). To the south of Tampa, races are held all year at the **Naples–Fort Myers Greyhound Track** (813/992-2411).

Central Florida has **Seminole Greyhound Park** (407/699-4510) in Casselberry and **Sanford Orlando Kennel Club** (407/831-1600) in Longwood. Gold Coast venues are the venerable **Palm Beach Kennel Club** (407/683-2222), the **Hollywood Greyhound Track** (305/454-9400) and, in the Miami area, the **Biscayne Kennel Club** (305/754-3484) and the **Flagler Dog Track** (305/649-3000).

HOCKEY   As unlikely a locale as it might seem, Florida now has 2 major league professional hockey teams. The **Tampa Bay Lightning** of the NHL can be followed at the Exposition Hall (813/229-8800). Miami has its own **Florida Panthers,** sharing Miami Arena (305/577-4328) with the Miami Heat basketballers. Minor-league clubs represent Jacksonville, Daytona Beach, West Palm Beach, and Lakeland.

HORSE RACING   **Hialeah Park** (305/885-8000), with its extravagant clubhouse and resident flock of hundreds of flamingoes, is a virtual synonym for the sport of kings. In Miami, **Calder Race Course** (305/625-1311) has an air-conditioned grandstand, which makes it possible to hold races throughout the year. The periods of activity vary annually, however, so call ahead. For harness racing, the only possibility is **Pompano Track** (305/972-2000) in Pompano Beach. Its future is uncertain, so, again, call ahead. In nearby Fort Lauderdale, thoroughbreds run at **Gulfstream Park** (305/454-7000), site of the famous Breeders Cup. It observes a winter season. On the Gulf Coast, **Tampa Bay Downs** (813/855-4401) hosts thoroughbreds from late December to early May.

JAI ALAI   The ancient Basque sport provokes furious and complicated betting. Players catch the ball (*pelota*) in a long curved wicker basket (*cesta*) strapped to the arm, then fling it against a wall of the 3-sided court (*fronton*) in the same fluid action. Ball speeds have been recorded at nearly 190 mph. Jai alai was introduced to the United States here, where the betting is legal and the game is played all year at various venues.

Frontons are found in Dania (tel 305/428-7766), Fort Pierce (tel 407/464-7500), Miami (tel 305/633-6400), Ocala (tel 904/591-2345), Orlando (tel 407/699-4510), Palm Beach (tel 407/844-2444), and Tampa (tel 813/831-1411).

Activities A to Z

BICYCLING   Hills are low and the flatlands vast, so pleasant excursions of an hour or two or demanding tours covering 100 miles and more are equally possible and easy to plot. All cities and most of the larger towns have shops with bicycles for rent and advice about local trails and precautions. Many resort hotels make bikes available to guests, as well. For a free guide to cycling trails write the Florida Department of Transportation, Mail Station 82, 605 Suwanee St, Tallahassee, FL 32399 or call 904/487-1200.

CAMPING   There are private campgrounds throughout the state, but the most desirable facilities and settings are usually found in state-owned recreation areas. About half of the 3 dozen preserves have campsites. Usage fees are rarely more than $20 a night. Stays are limited and there are restrictions on pets. Additional fees are charged for features and services such as waterfront locations, use of boat ramps, nature tours, and electrical hookups.

For a copy of the *Florida State Parks Guide,* write the Bureau of Parks Planning, Department of Natural Resources, Mail Station 535, 3900 Commonwealth Blvd, Tallahassee, FL 32399 or call 904/488-9872. For information about private campgrounds, write the Florida Campground Association, 1638 North Plaza Dr, Tallahassee, FL 32308, or call 904/656-8878.

CANOEING   Enthusiasts find stretches of inviting water throughout the state, often with marked trails, as between Everglades City and Flamingo, along the Santa Fe River in the northeast, and on Little Manatee River, north of Tampa Bay. For information, write the Florida Association of Canoe Liveries and Outfitters, PO Box 1764, Arcadia, FL 33821 or call 813/494-1215.

DIVING/SNORKELING   It is estimated that Florida's offshore waters hold over 4,000 shipwrecks, from Spanish galleons to German U-Boats. High underwater visibility and ideal temperatures contribute mightily to the diving and snorkeling experience, especially on expeditions to the only living coral reef in the continental United States, which lies a short distance east of the Keys, part of it contained by John Pennekamp State Park. Snorkelers can visit by party boat, and only average swimming ability is required.

Special certification is required for scuba diving. Most coastal localities have dive shops that provide lessons, and some resort hotels have intensive programs that can qualify students in a matter of days.

For a brochure about diving in the state, write the Florida Sports Foundation, 107 West Gaines St, Tallahassee, FL 32399 or call 904/488-8347.

FISHING   With thousands of miles of coastline, hundreds of miles of rivers and streams, and over 7,700 lakes of 10 acres or more, Florida can be likened to a 500-mile pier down the middle of a giant tank packed with fish. Anglers can wet their lines from a chartered sportfishing yacht, a thronged party boat, a dinghy, or a bridge or beach; every inclination and wallet can be accommodated. **Licenses** are required for both saltwater and freshwater fishing. Nonresidents can obtain licenses good for as few as 7 days. They are sold in the bait-and-tackle shops found near every promising body of water. Rods, reels, and bait are provided by guides and chartered boats, with the client expected to provide food and drink, as a rule. Tackle can usually be rented at waterside hotels and tackle shops.

For a brochure, write the Florida Sports Foundation, 107 West Gaines St, Tallahassee, FL 32399 or call 904/488-8347. Questions about **freshwater fishing** can be addressed to the Florida Game and Fresh Water Fish Commission, Ferris Bryant Building, 620 South Meridian St, Tallahassee, FL 32399 or call 904/488-1960. Send questions about **saltwater fishing** to the Florida Department of Natural Resources, Mail Station 30, 3900 Commonwealth Blvd, Tallahassee, FL 32399 or call 904/488-7326.

GOLF   Apart from the short but sudden downpours often experienced during the hottest months, Florida is a nearly ideal place to challenge the world's most prominent designers of golf courses. The presence of 20 PGA and LPGA tournaments every year is testimony to that happy fact, as are the more than 1,000 courses— more than in any other state. The PGA itself is head- quartered in Palm Beach. While knowing a member or being the guest of a participating hotel is necessary for entrance to some courses, many others are open to all, and many of the best courses are owned by resort hotels rather than country clubs. Consult a travel agent about current golf packages.

To obtain a guide listing important details about all the state's courses, write the Florida Sports Foundation, 107 West Gaines St, Tallahassee, FL 32399 or call 904/488-8347.

GUIDED TOURS   There is no end to the opportuni- ties for informative and entertaining escorted tours, from the Conch Train that circulates through colorful Key West to the walks led by costumed lecturers through the historic district of Pensacola. The Ever- glades inspire many companies to offer a variety of excursions: riveting airboat rides from bases along the Tamiami Trail to Miccosukee ''villages'' deep in the swamp; 2-hour and daylong cruises from Fort Lauder- dale, Flamingo, and Everglades; tram tours from Shark Valley and Flamingo; even customized ecology-minded tours out of Miami of several days' duration.

Sightseeing boats steam around the Port of Miami and along the New River from Fort Lauderdale, while trolley tours take in the major sights on land in the same cities. Orientation tours of theme parks in the Orlando region are a virtual necessity and most of the major attractions provide them.

For information about the organizations affording these services, contact the chamber of commerce in the appropriate locality.

TENNIS   Resort hotels with their own golf courses typically have tennis courts, too—something to keep in mind when making travel arrangements. Visitors stay- ing in less expensive lodgings have access to over 7,700 courts throughout the state, many of them run by municipalities and open to all. Year-round playing conditions make Florida highly attractive; grass, clay, and hard courts are all available and many of them are lighted for night play.

For a brochure, write the Florida Tennis Association, 801 NE 167th St, Suite 301, North Miami Beach, FL 33162 or call 305/652-2866.

WINDSURFING   Also known as sailboarding, this increasingly popular aquatic sport is pursued both on the ocean and on thousands of inland lakes. Most waterside resorts have sailboards for rent and provide instruction.

SCENIC DRIVING TOUR #1

ST AUGUSTINE, DAYTONA BEACH & CAPE CANAVERAL

Start: Jacksonville
Finish: Kennedy Space Center
Distance: About 325 miles round-trip
Time: 3 days
Highlights: Historic sites, a marine life park, sugar mill ruins, pristine beaches, NASA facilities and exhibits

This trip along the coast south of Jacksonville takes you to a number of historic places: St Augustine, with restored 18th-century buildings and homes; Fort Matanzas, an 18th-century Spanish defense outpost; and Bulow Plantation Ruins, with the remains of a sugar mill. You also stop at several small seaside towns and the world-renowned Daytona Beach, where the Daytona 500 auto race is held each year. After driving through an undeveloped natural seashore area, you will end your trip on a high note at the John F Kennedy Space Center at Cape Canaveral.

For additional information on accommodations, restaurants, and attractions in the region covered by the tour, look under specific cities in the listings portion of this book.

From downtown Jacksonville, take I-95 southbound to exit 98 and pick up US 1 south. Continue about 30 miles to:

1. **St Augustine.** Although this charming city has palm-fringed beaches, St Augustine is primarily known for its sense of history, with a 17th-century fort, horse-drawn carriages, cobblestone streets, old city gates, and the restored 18th-century Spanish Quarter. On Easter in 1513, Spanish explorer Juan Ponce de León claimed the land that was to become St Augustine for Spain, but the city wasn't founded until 1565 by Pedro Menéndez de Avilés, a Spanish admiral who arrived that year with some thousand settlers and a priest. St Augustine became America's 1st city, established 55 years before the Pilgrims landed at Plymouth Rock.

The city was owned by both the Spanish and the British over the years until Spain sold it to the

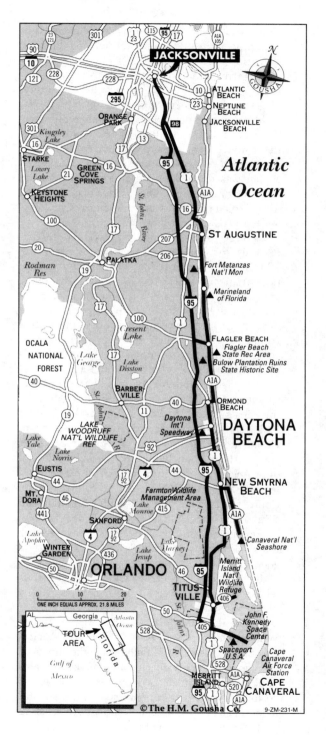

United States in 1821. Union forces occupied St Augustine from 1862 until the end of the Civil War. In 1883, Standard Oil magnate Henry Flagler arrived to develop the area as a fashionable resort for the wealthy. By the turn of the century, Flagler had expanded tourism throughout Florida, building posh hotels and developing rail lines along the eastern coastline. In 1887 and again in the early 1900s, fires destroyed several of St Augustine's original buildings. Then in the 1950s, a plan was devised to preserve and restore the remaining historic buildings, which may be visited today. You'll probably want to spend a day exploring Florida's past on foot.

Centrally located at St George St and Cathedral Place is the **Visitor Information Center** (tel 904/825-1064) situated at the beginning of a pedestrian walkway lined with shops, restaurants, and historic buildings. On sale at the center is a walking tour brochure (95¢) covering 2 main areas of the city. One tour begins and ends at the **Oldest House,** at 14 St Francis St. From here, the tour covers 33 stops; it turns up Marine St and wanders through the neighborhood, passing a number of 18th- and 19th-century homes and Marin House, Countess de Montjoye House, St Francis Barracks, the King's Bakery, St Francis Inn, and St Francis Park. The 2nd tour begins at the **Plaza de la Constitucion,** south of the information center. It covers 31 stops, including the Basilica Cathedral of St Augustine, Government House, Flagler College, St Augustine City Hall, St John's County Court House, Palm Row, St Joseph's Convent, and Trinity Episcopal Church, as well as Victorian homes and bed-and-breakfast inns. These walking tours take about 3–4 hours total and provide a good overview of the city.

If you would like to visit a few sights rather than take a prescribed walking tour, here are a few highlights:

Authentic Old Jail, 167 San Marco Ave, at Williams St (tel 904/829-3800). This 1890 Victorian brick prison was built with the financial assistance of Henry Flagler and served the area until 1953. During the day, tours are conducted by costumed guides; visitors are shown the sheriff's living quarters, the kitchen, and prison cells, as well as exhibits relating to the jail's history.

Castillo de San Marcos National Monument, 1 Castillo Dr, between Orange and Charlotte Sts (tel 904/829-6506). This fort, designed to protect the city against British attacks, took the Spanish 23 years (1672–1695) to complete; it was made of massive coquina (shell rock) walls, with a double drawbridge entrance over a 40-foot moat. The Castillo was so well built that it was never captured in battle, nor did its walls ever crumble. Today you can tour the vaulted powder-magazine room, a dank prison cell, a chapel, and guard rooms. Old storerooms now house exhibits on the fort's history. You can also walk the upper-level gundeck; many of the copper and cast-iron cannons still present are at least 200 years old.

Lightner Museum, 75 King St, at Granada St (tel 904/824-2874). Henry Flagler's lavish Spanish Renaissance–style Alcazar Hotel, constructed during 1889, was bought in 1948 by publishing magnate Otto Lightner to house his collection of Victoriana. The 1st floor is devoted to a Victorian village with shopfront windows filled with period wares. Among the various displays are Victorian furnishings, porcelain and glass, automated musical instruments, artifacts, stuffed birds, train models, toys, and even an Egyptian mummy from 500 BC.

The Oldest House, 14 St Francis St, at Charlotte St (tel 904/824-2972). The Gonzales-Alvarez House, named after 2 of its past prominent owners, evolved from a 2-room coquina dwelling built between 1702 and 1727. Rooms are furnished to simulate various historical times. Abandoned wells are on the site, and Native American, Spanish, and British artifacts (some of them found in the wells) are displayed.

St Augustine Alligator Farm, 999 Anastasia Blvd (Fla A1A), at Old Quarry Rd (tel 904/824-3337). First opened in 1893, this attraction houses the world's largest collection of crocodilians, including alligators, crocodiles, caymans, and gavials.

St Augustine's Restored Spanish Quarter, entrance on St George St, between Cuna and Orange Sts (tel 904/825-6830). This 2-block area south of the City Gate is St Augustine's most comprehensive historical neighborhood, re-creating Spanish colonial period architecture and landscape. Although about 90% of the area's buildings are reconstructions, several structures date back to the mid-18th century, including a few homes, such as the **Triay, Gómez, Gallegos, Gonzáles,** and **José Peso de Burgo and Francisco Pellicer houses.** Guides and craftspeople dressed in 18th-century attire are on site to provide information, and at the blacksmith shop hardware is manufactured using 18th-century methods.

☕
REFRESHMENT STOP

Finding a place to eat won't be hard in the restored Spanish Quarter. One pleasant, casual establishment in the area is the **Florida Cracker Cafe,** 81 St. George St (tel 904/829-0397), a lively eatery with hearty food and seating indoors and out.

If you got a late start from Jacksonville, you may want to spend a night in St Augustine, which has a variety of lodging choices. Some bed-and-breakfasts are housed in historic inns, such as the **Kenwood Inn,** 38 Marine St (tel 904/824-2116). Also consider **Ponce de León Golf & Conference Resort,** 4000 US 1 N (tel 904/824-2821), a 350-acre complex with all the facilities of a traditional hotel. Many of the chain hotels have properties in town; look along Fla A1A for family-oriented motels.

Next, from St Augustine, cross the Intracoastal Waterway to Fla A1A and head south 14 miles until you reach:

2. **Fort Matanzas.** At this 298-acre national park, you can take a ferry (operating daily 9am–4:30pm except Tuesday) from the visitors center on the Anastasia River across the Matanzas River to an 18th-century fort on Rattlesnake Island. Completed in 1742, Fort Matanzas prevented enemy vessels from passing through the inlet south of the fort, thus protecting St Augustine.

As you enter the building's main stairway, imagine the approach by wooden ladder 200 years ago. The 2 original cast-iron cannons, left behind by the Spanish when they departed in 1821, can still be seen guarding the fortress. The lower level once housed 7 to 10 enlisted men who brought supplies in longboats. A low wall kept the powder magazine away from open flames used for heat and light in the officers' quarters. Up a narrow ladder, the observation deck provides a good view of the inlet to the south. The fort is open Wednesday–Monday 8:30am–5:30pm. Admission free.

While the island doesn't offer picnicking areas, you may wish to take a dip in the ocean across Fla A1A, opposite the visitors center entrance, and enjoy your picnic there. A $4 parking fee is charged for the beach.

From Fort Matanzas, continue on Fla A1A a little over 3½ miles south to:

3. **Marineland,** 9507 Ocean Shore Blvd (Fla A1A) (tel 904/471-1111). First opened in 1938 as an underwater motion picture studio and tourist attraction, this marine park on the Atlantic Ocean and the Intracoastal Waterway has long been known for its dolphin shows held in the Dolphin Stadium tank. The performing dolphins leap as high as 16 feet in the air to take food from a jumpmaster's hand. The 20-minute shows are held 5 times a day.

You can also observe the circular **Oceanarium,** home of a permanent colony of Atlantic bottlenose dolphins. This underwater setting is created with 400,000 gallons of filtered sea water. In another, rectangular Oceanarium are 1,000 specimens representing 124 different species of game and predator fish and other marine life. Fish are hand-fed 4 times a day by scuba divers.

Other attractions include colorful fish of the Pacific in the new **"Secrets of the Reef"** exhibit, and the **"Wonders of the Spring"** aquarium, the world's largest freshwater fish display, with native Florida species of gar, largemouth bass, sunfish, and crappie. At the **Aquarius Theatre,** a 22-minute, 3-D film is shown throughout the day. More than 6,000 rare shells may be admired at the **Margaret Herrick Shell Museum.**

Marineland is open daily 9am–5:30pm. Admission is $14.95 for adults, $9.95 for teens 13–18, and $7.95 for children 3–12; children under 3 are admitted free, and visitors 65 and older receive 20% off the adult price.

Turn right out of Marineland and go 14 miles south on Fla A1A to Fla 100 and the Bulow loop. Take FL 100 a little more than 3 miles west until you see the turnoff, left or south, to:

4. **Bulow Plantation Ruins State Historic Site** (tel 904/439-2219). Continue 3 miles, past the Bulow Campground, to the entrance of the historic site. The plantation site has a dirt road on the left leading into a wooded area. About 1 mile ahead is a walking path known as the Bulow Woods Hiking Trail, a 4-mile loop for those interested in communing with nature. A bit further onward, visitors are required to pay a $2 entrance fee per vehicle. Beyond the entrance are picnic tables and parking.

Established in 1821 by Major Charles William Bulow, the plantation once contained 2,200 acres of sugar cane, cotton, rice, and indigo. Under the management of Bulow's son, John, it thrived until the outbreak of the Second Seminole War when John abandoned it and moved northward. Around 1836, the Seminoles burned "Bulowville," and all that is left are the ruins of the sugar mill and the crumbling mansion foundation. Visitors can walk the grounds or drive along a 2.7-mile scenic loop.

Stop at the interpretive center near the ruins for an informative history of the plantation, and have lunch at the picnic area overlooking Bulow Creek. Open 9am–5pm.

Just south of the cutoff to Bulow Plantation is:

5. **Flagler Beach.** This stretch of sand's most visible landmark is the 898-foot pier extending out into the Atlantic. To walk onto the pier costs 75¢. If

---

REFRESHMENT STOP

Pier Restaurant on Flagler Beach, 215 S Fla A1A, Flagler Beach (tel 904/439-3891), serving mostly seafood, offers a great view of the ocean and the pier. Another good local spot for the freshest fish is **High Tides at Shack Jack's,** 2805 S Fla A1A (904/439-3344).

---

you bring your own rod and reel, you can fish for $2.75. There's also a shack at the pier entrance that rents fishing equipment.

Continue 3 miles south on Fla A1A from the pier area to:

6. **Gamble Rogers Memorial State Recreation Area,** at Flagler Beach, 3100 S Fla A1A (tel 904/439-2474). This fine family camping area is a 145-acre park bordering the Atlantic Ocean on the east and the Intracoastal Waterway on the west. From the campgrounds, cross the dune walkovers for swimming and surf fishing along the beach; pompano, whiting, and bluefish are frequently caught here. Stroll the shell-strewn beaches and observe pelicans and sandpipers.

From May to September sea turtles return to the beach here to lay their eggs. You can also catch sight of various songbirds as they migrate along the Atlantic Flyway in the spring and fall.

The park has a boat ramp on the Intracoastal Waterway, a picnic area with shelters, and hiking trails.

As you continue the drive south on Fla A1A, you'll notice the sea oats and scrub oak that protect the dunes. Leaving Flagler Beach city limits, you will enter the North Peninsula State Recreation Area. After driving 14 miles, you'll pass Ormond Beach, where hotels, condominiums, and shopping centers vie for tourists' attention. Then, 3 miles south of Ormond Beach, is:

7. **Daytona Beach.** This world-renowned beach is 23 miles long and 500 feet wide at low tide, and you can still drive and park on the sand (maximum speed is 10 mph). Opportunities for boating, tennis, golf, and watersports abound. The area, however, becomes much less relaxed when the Daytona 500 comes to town; the event is the culmination of Speedweeks, held from late January to mid-February at the Daytona International Speedway (see below). Also in February, during Bike Week, thousands of leather-clad motorcyclists congregate here. Finally, the area plays host to thousands of college students from around the country during their spring break. (You'll especially want to avoid Daytona Beach at this time if you're looking for a peaceful holiday.)

Daytona is filled with hotels, though few can be considered standouts. One of the nicer large hotels is the **Daytona Beach Marriott,** 100 N Atlantic Ave (tel 904/254-8200). If you're seeking something cozier, you might want to try **Captain's Quarters Inn,** 3711 S Atlantic Ave (tel 904/767-3199). For the budget-minded, there's the **Days Inn Daytona Central,** 1909 S Atlantic Ave (tel 904/255-4492).

If the beach doesn't have enough to keep you busy, you can visit the **Birthplace of Speed Museum,** 160 E Granada Blvd (tel 904/672-5657), a small showcase of exhibits on racing history; the **Daytona International Speedway,** 1801 W International Speedway Blvd (US 92) (tel 253-RACE), with a visitors center that has tours of the racing facility; the **Museum of Arts and Sciences,** 1040 Museum Blvd (tel 904/255-0285), with a notable collection of Cuban art; and **Ponce de Leon Inlet Lighthouse,** 4931 S Peninsula Dr (tel 904/761-1821), the 2nd-tallest US lighthouse, with 203 steel steps for you to climb to the top.

From Daytona Beach, continue south along the US 1 about 12 miles into New Smyrna Beach. Turn left, or east, at Fla 44 and follow that road, which becomes Fla A1A and leads to:

8. **Canaveral National Seashore.** Continue on Fla A1A for about 9 miles, when you'll see a sign welcoming visitors to this undeveloped, gorgeous natural seashore; about a mile further is the visitors center (tel 904/428-3384), open daily 8am–4:30pm. You're now in the north district of the seashore.

Retrace your steps to US 1 and drive south 29 miles into **Titusville** and turn left on Fla 406. Follow this road 7 miles to **Merritt Island** and the south district of Canaveral National Seashore. Merritt Island, which has its own visitors center (tel 904/861-0667), encompasses a refuge for endangered waterfowl, birds, alligators, and other wildlife. The pristine beaches here are lovely to stroll along. Both the north and south districts of the Seashore are administered by the National Park Service. Continue to the ocean for a view of the uninhabited, pristine beach.

Follow signs from Merritt Island to:

9. **Cape Canaveral** and the **John F Kennedy Space Center.** Cape Canaveral, practically synonymous with NASA, is where all US manned space missions are launched. From the early 1960s and America's first manned space flight to today's manned and unmanned shuttle launches, the events at Cape Canaveral have captured the world's attention. The Kennedy Space Center comprises the Air Force Museum, the main space center, the Astronauts Memorial, US Space Camp, and Spaceport USA.

Spaceport USA (tel 407/452-2121), the center's main exhibition hall, features two 5½-story screens in the IMAX Theater, which shows 3 space-exploration films: *Destiny in Space, Blue Planet,* and *The Dream Is Alive,* which features footage filmed by NASA astronauts. Admission to the theater is $4 for adults and $2 for children 3–11. Other parts of Spaceport USA are free, including a full-size replica of a space shuttle dubbed *Explorer.* Here you can see a cockpit, a payload bay cargo area, and flight crew living quarters. The best time to visit Spaceport USA is before 11am, when lines are shortest.

Guided tours originate at Spaceport USA. Don't miss the tour that includes the *Apollo 11* and space shuttle launch sites, the Flight Crew Training Building, and the Vehicle Assembly Building. Another tour takes you to the Air Force Museum, which has military rockets that have been modified for NASA use. Other points of interest include the mission control station for the *Gemini* and *Mercury* projects and a memorial to the original 7 astronauts.

Exit Spaceport USA on Fla 405 and drive west to US 1, or cross US 1 and continue on Fla 405 to I-95 N, which is the faster route back to Jacksonville, a distance of about 165 miles.

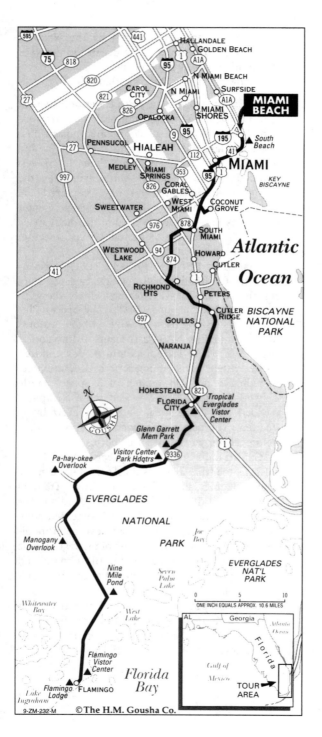

© The H.M. Gousha Co.

9-ZM-232-M

SCENIC DRIVING TOUR #2

MIAMI TO THE EVERGLADES

Start: Miami
Finish: Everglades National Park
Distance: About 160 miles round-trip
Time: 1 day
Highlights: Art deco district, scenic drive, nature trails, cruises, outdoor recreation

For those seeking to escape the hectic pace of Miami and the neon glitter of Miami Beach, this fairly short tour takes you to Everglades National Park, a majestically beautiful subtropical wildlife sanctuary that allows you to observe delicate plant and animal life up close in their natural state. First, however, you may opt for a quick refreshment stop in either the art deco district of South Miami Beach or the trend-setting community of Coconut Grove before setting off on the longer drive to the wildlife refuge. At the park, you can drive a scenic 38-mile road, walk on nature trails, take a sightseeing cruise, have a picnic lunch, or, if you're feeling more adventurous, rent a canoe for an afternoon. If you're looking to escape crowds, you may wish to drive to the park either during midweek or on an overcast day.

You should also keep in mind that mosquitoes and other biting insects can make your visit particularly unpleasant from May through the summer months. However, if you do visit the park during this time, *be sure to bring insect repellent.* Otherwise, winter is a better time to explore the park, when the mosquitoes are on vacation as well. All park activities are in full operation during the winter months, and the best viewing of wildlife is from December through March.

For additional information on accommodations, restaurants, and attractions in the region covered by the tour, look under specific cities in the listings portion of this book.

1. **Miami and Miami Beach.** Any first-time visitor to South Florida usually spends at least 2 nights in Miami, Florida's largest city, known around the world for its white sand beaches, glistening waters, sun-filled days, and vibrant multicultural population. Miami Beach is clearly the main draw for visitors. Although tourism declined here in the 1960s and 1970s, the area has witnessed a resur-

gence in visitors since the late 1980s. Its huge self-contained resort hotels, with restaurants, activities, and entertainment, appeal to international tourists and large convention crowds.

2. **South Beach.** Located at the southern end of Miami Beach, this neighborhood contains the largest concentration of **art deco architecture** in the world. The district culminates in the chic 15-block beachfront stretch known as **Ocean Drive;** most of the glamorous old and not-so-old hotels with flowing designs and pastel exteriors on this strip were built in the late 1930s and early 1940s. South Beach, or SoBe, as it is also called, is a thrilling renaissance community populated by poor artists, up-and-coming young investors, pensioners, and the usual mixture of Miami's ethnic groups. The trendy clubs and cafes along Ocean Drive attract working models and photographers, celebrities, musicians, writers, artists, and vacationers.

From Miami Beach, take Washington St or Collins Ave south to reach 5th St W, which becomes the MacArthur Causeway (US 41) and turns into I-395. First you'll pass Star Island on your right. Stay in the left lanes so you don't end up taking a wrong exit, but take a quick look at the cruise ships docked in the Port of Miami. You'll likely see a dozen or so of these vessels on weekends.

From I-395 enter I-95, heading south while the downtown area whizzes by on your left. Stay in the middle lanes and shortly you'll see the Key Biscayne exit. That's your cue that I-95 will end in half a mile to become US 1, a 3-lane highway hemmed in on one side by concrete overpasses and strip shopping centers.

From here you can choose to continue immediately on to the Everglades or to make the next stop on this tour. Off US 1, also known as Dixie Hwy at this point, go left on Lejeune Rd and left again on Poinciana Ave into the center of:

3. **Coconut Grove,** a colorful upscale community of pedestrian walkways, boutiques, nightspots, restaurants, and cafes, which lend themselves to great people-watching, especially at night. Sidewalks are often packed with business types, col-

lege students, and a multitude of foreign tourists. The heart of Coconut Grove lies at the intersection of Grand Ave, Main Hwy, and McFarlane Rd. At the turn of the century, workers came here from the Bahamas for employment at a new hotel called the Peacock Inn; today Bahamian-style wooden homes, built by these early transplants, still stand on Charles St.

☕ REFRESHMENT STOP

If you are leaving Miami early in the day, make a stop at one of Coconut Grove's many sidewalk cafes. **Joffrey's Coffee & Tea Co,** 3434 Main Hwy (tel 305/448-0848), will provide you with a caffeine fix to keep you perky until noon. If you stop in the area later in the day, **Green Street Cafe,** 3468 Commodore Plaza (tel 444-0244), will serve you more substantial fare like rack of lamb and various pastas, as well as satisfying coffee and dessert. **Qui du Crepes,** 3115 Commodore Plaza (tel 446-7964), offers light sandwiches and crepes any time of day.

Take US 1 south from Coconut Grove. About 9 miles south of downtown is Fla 878, also known as the Snapper Creek Expressway. Take the right here under the overpass and head west: You'll avoid several miles of stop-and-go traffic. Continue on Fla 878 until it enters the Don Shula Expressway and a tollgate (25¢).

After you exit the tollgate, you're now driving on what is known as Florida's Turnpike. Continue for 8 miles to the next toll (50¢). Along this route is mostly flat farmland. In another 10 miles, the turnpike ends at US 1 in Florida City.

At US 1, you'll see a sign for **Everglades National Park.** About 1,000 feet past the turnoff, on the right next to the Burger King, is the:

4. **Tropical Everglades Visitor Association,** 160 US 1, in Florida City (tel 305/245-9180 or toll free 800/388-9669), operated by the Greater Miami

Convention and Visitors Bureau. The office provides brochures and information about the area and is open daily 8am–5pm.

From the turnoff to the Everglades National Park Main Visitors Center, proceed 14 miles on Fla 9336. At the 4-way stop sign near the Robert Is Here farm stand, make a left onto 192nd Ave SW; after driving 1½ miles you'll come to another stop sign, where you turn right onto 376th St SW. The area around here is mostly farmland, and from fall to early spring several trucks are parked at this intersection selling fresh vegetables and fruits.

Just before the entrance to Everglades National Park is a small picnic area called **Glenn Garrett Memorial Park,** with a handful of picnic tables and palm trees on hand but little more. You may prefer to wait until you get into the park to choose a picnic site.

At the tollgate to the park, visitors pay $5 per carload; hikers and cyclists pay $3 per person. The gatehouse is open 24 hours. On the right is the:

5. **Main Visitors Center** (tel 305/242-7700), which is open daily 8am–5pm. The center has orientation brochures and maps of the park, as well as rest rooms and refreshments in vending machines.

Everglades National Park covers the entire southern tip of the Florida peninsula and encompasses more than 2,000 square miles and 1.5 million acres. The term "everglades" came into use more than a century ago as a corruption of "river glades," which was used on an 18th-century map. The term refers to the sheets of slow-moving water clogged with tall sawgrass that characterize the Everglades. This unique, marshy tropical area, dotted by hammocks of hardwood trees and clumps of coastal mangroves, contains a treasure trove of plant and animal life.

Originally, water flowed unimpeded from **Lake Okeechobee,** the main source of water nourishing the land. But beginning in the late 1800s, large tracts were drained through a system of canals in the hopes of using the swampland for agriculture. In the late 1920s, 2 hurricanes caused extensive flooding and loss of life in South Florida, and the southern end of Lake Okeechobee was diked. The retaining walls built in the 1960s at this end of the

lake, together with land development in Big Cypress Swamp (another major source of water) have partially choked off the natural flow of water to the Everglades, threatening its many fragile ecosystems. Today, nesting and wading birds are only a small fraction of their former number. The federal government is currently working with the state as part of a water- and land-management agreement to preserve the Everglades and reverse its decline.

Meanwhile, visitors come here to experience what the Everglades still has to offer: beautiful and unusual vegetation; tens of thousands of birds, including beautiful white egrets, blue herons, and eagles; and otters, tiny tree frogs, alligators, racoons, bobcats, deer, and many other creatures, all trying to survive in a shrinking homeland.

For your 1 day in the park, take the single road that winds its way for about 38 miles from the Main Visitors Center to the **Flamingo Visitors Center** (open daily 7:30am–5pm) in the southwest corner of the state. This scenic drive provides a lovely introduction to the area; along the road, you'll drive through a half-dozen distinct ecosystems, including a dwarf cypress forest, endless saw grass, and thick mangroves. You'll also discover well-marked walking trails, elevated boardwalks, and informative signs.

Just beyond the main entrance, at the Royal Palm Visitors Center, are 2 of the park's most well-trodden paths. All year, you can usually be assured of seeing wildlife on the **Anhingo Trail,** a ½-mile loop on a boardwalk popular for photographing birds and alligators. The **Gumbo Limbo Trail** took a beating from Hurricane Andrew in 1992, but it's still open for a walk through tropical hardwood hammock. Experienced hikers can get advice at the Main Visitors Center for more challenging hikes around the park. The staff can direct you to pineland, marsh, and hammock trails. Those looking for less demanding routes will appreciate the boardwalk trails, ranging from ¼- to ½-mile in length, along the main park road; these trails include Pa-hay-okee Overlook, West Lake Trail, Pinelands Trail, and Mahogany Hammock.

At the end of the 38 miles on the park's main road lies the tiny "town" of Flamingo, and the:

6. **Flamingo Lodge Marina and Outpost Resort,** 1 Flamingo Lodge Hwy (tel 305/253-2241 or 813/695-3101). The starting point for several sightseeing excursions, it is the only lodging inside the park. The clean, simple rooms overlook Florida Bay, and the hotel has a swimming pool and gift shop. It is most busy in February.

> 🍵
>
> ### REFRESHMENT STOP
>
> The Flamingo Lodge complex includes the 2nd-floor **Flamingo Lodge Restaurant,** which serves a mostly traditional American menu and a few regional dishes at moderate prices. You have a fine view here of Florida Bay.

The day-tripper might plan his or her day by arriving in the park before noon and lunching at the Flamingo Restaurant or taking a picnic lunch in a canoe. This could be followed by an afternoon tour or hike to complete your introduction to the park.

Just steps away from the Flamingo Lodge is the:

7. **Flamingo Visitor Center,** which provides information on park activities such as canoe rentals. For advance information on sightseeing tours and times, contact the Flamingo Lodge Marina (see above).

The marina is the starting point for 2 cruises which travel around nearby estuaries and sandbars for a look at local plant and animal life. The 90-minute **Florida Bay Cruise,** held daily, gives you a chance to observe egrets, herons, ibis, ospreys, bald eagles, and pelicans (cost: $8.50 adults, $4.50 children 6–12; children under 6 free). On the 2-hour **White Water Bay Cruise,** you see the same wildlife species as on the other tour, but you'll also sight alligators and crocodiles; this trip also runs daily (cost: $12 adults, $6 children 6–12, children under 6 free).

A 2-hour tour on the **Wilderness Tram** takes visitors through tropical hardwood hammock and mangrove forests, where you're likely to encounter turtles, alligators, snakes, and other wildlife and plant species. A naturalist guide narrates each tour. The tram departs from Flamingo Lodge from November to April only (cost: $7.50 adults, $4 children 6–12, children under 6 free).

To do sightseeing on your own, you may elect to rent a skiff with a 15-horsepower motor for $65 for an entire day or $47 for a half day. Canoes rent for $7 an hour, $20 for a half day, $25 for a full day. A full-day rental begins at 7am and runs to 5pm. Half-day rentals are good for up 5 hours. Bicycles rent for $2.50 per hour, $7 for half days, or $12 for full days. A small office at the marina provides rental equipment.

Hardcore nature lovers may come to the Everglades to do some backcountry exploring by canoe to remote campsites dotting the shoreline, from the Flamingo Visitor Center in the south to the Gulf Coast Visitor Center in Everglades City in the north. Everglades City is accessed from Miami via US 41 and Fla 29, which should not be confused with the Florida City route into the Everglades.

The **Wilderness Waterway,** between the 2 visitor centers, is open to both canoes and powerboats and meanders for 99 miles through the largest mangrove forest in the United States. A considerably more modest canoe route goes from Flamingo around Cape Sable, providing a good opportunity to see majestic sunsets on an overnight round trip of 10 miles. In addition, the 9-mile **Canoe Trail** offers viewing of wading birds and other wildlife such as alligators, as well as a freshwater marsh. Canoeists can do some hiking on this trip to a ground site or backcountry chickee (a wooden platform with partial roof) for staying overnight.

Visitors who would rather camp out than stay overnight at the Flamingo Lodge Marina & Outpost Resort can use park **campsites** when they bring their own equipment. The Flamingo camping area on the Florida Bay has 300 sites and provides free (cold) outdoor showers. At Long Pine Key, a pine forest that wraps partly around a lake, 100 sites for camping and RVs are available, with a dumping station but no hookups. Campers can arrange for space on a first-come, first-served basis by calling the Main Visitor Center (tel 813/695-3941) for reservations. The busiest time for camping is February.

Exiting the park at about 5pm allows you to return to Miami in daylight. Retrace your steps, following the road to the park entrance and continuing to the 4-way intersection, where you turn right on Fla 9336, which leads to Florida City and US 1 N. A nonstop drive to downtown Miami takes about 75 minutes in normal traffic. And if you haven't yet made it to Coconut Grove, now is a good time on your way back.

SCENIC DRIVING TOUR #3

ORLANDO & CENTRAL FLORIDA

Start: Orlando
Finish: Lakeland
Distance: About 130 miles round-trip
Time: 1 day
Highlights: Rural countryside, baseball stadiums, lavish gardens, the lake district, horticultural amusement park, Frank Lloyd Wright–designed college buildings

Everything is at your fingertips when you vacation in central Florida. Orlando is less than 1 hour from Cape Canaveral and the John F Kennedy Space Center, 90 minutes from Tampa and exciting Busch Gardens, 1 hour from the famous Daytona Beach, and of course, in the middle of a magical kingdom called Walt Disney World. On this tour, the varied route takes you to amusement parks, historic sights, and quiet countryside. Realistically, you can't do all these activities in 1 day, especially with children in tow, so plan your itinerary selectively.

For additional information on accommodations, restaurants, and attractions in the region covered by the tour, look under specific cities in the listings portion of this book.

From almost anywhere in the Orlando area, you can hop on I-10 to begin this trip. Heading west on I-10 through Kissimmee, you'll cross under the overpass of US 192, also known as Irlo Bronson Memorial Hwy, which runs north-south. Following this road south would bring you to Florida's Turnpike, but instead keep heading west on I-10 for 9 miles to exit 23 and US 27, and:

1. **Baseball City.** It's mainly an area of chain restaurants and hotels, but if you look left or east from the highway you'll immediately spot **Baseball City Stadium,** a sports complex that is the spring training camp site for the Kansas City Royals.

   Five miles south from the exit, on US 27 past citrus groves, is **Webb's Candy Factory.** If it's not too early, you may wish to sample the candy factory's goat-milk fudge or ice cream.

   Continue south an additional 2 miles on US 27 and you'll reach the:

2. **Haines City Tourist Information Center** (tel 813/422-3751), located on the southwest corner of US 27 and Commerce Ave. Operated by the Chamber of Commerce, the center, which is open Monday–Friday 8:30am–4:30pm, can provide helpful information on golf and freshwater fishing in Haines City. For the more adventurous, the center will provide names of companies who offer airboat rides and hang-gliding instruction.

   If you're in the Haines City area in the evening, you can take the whole family to:

3. **Southern Country Danceland,** 117 N 7th St, just north of US 92 and east of US 27 (tel 813/422-1642). This dance hall sponsors evening line dancing Monday–Thursday 7:30–10pm for beginners, and children are welcome. Friday and Saturday is open dance night (8pm–midnight) with a DJ and band. Smoking and alcohol are not permitted so that the place may retain a family atmosphere. Admission is $5.30 for adults, $2.65 for children 6–12.

   Next continue 1 mile from the tourist information center along US 27 to US 17 and US 92 west to Winter Haven (see below). Cypress Gardens is a 13-mile drive from here, and Lake Wales is a 16-mile drive. If you wish to spend the day playing golf, you can take Fla 544 east from Winter Haven through Dundee to the **Grenelefe Golf and Tennis Resort,** 3200 Fla 546, Haines City (tel 813/422-7511), about 7 miles away.

   Nine miles south of Haines City on US 27 is the Cypress Gardens turnoff, also known as Fla 540. You can take this road west to the gardens if you want a nonstop route. But to get to the next stop on this tour continue on US 27 another 6 miles into Lake Wales. Turn left on County Rd 17A and go 1½ miles to Alternate US 27. (It may seem as though you're going south on 17A, but the sign says north.) Take a right on Alternate US 27 and continue to the entrance of:

4. **Bok Tower Gardens** (tel 813/676-9412). This sanctuary was envisioned by the editor and publisher Edward William Bok (1863–1930). The 128-acre estate comprises the lovely Pinewood House and Gardens, a cafe and gift shop, picnic areas, and a visitor center where lecture films are

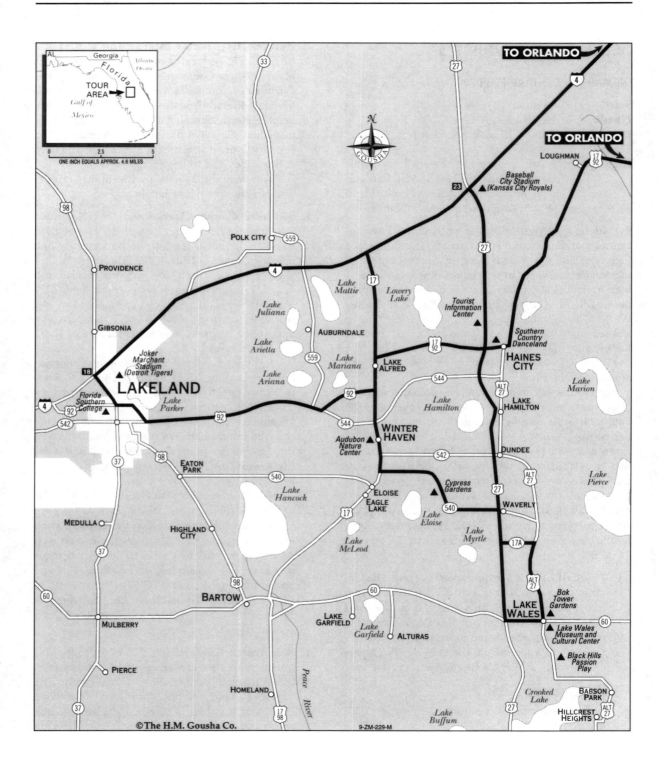

Georgia

Florida

TOUR AREA

Gulf of Mexico

AL

Atlantic Ocean

ONE INCH EQUALS APPROX. 4.6 MILES

0   2.5   5

TO ORLANDO

TO ORLANDO

LOUGHMAN

Baseball City Stadium (Kansas City Royals)

Tourist Information Center

Southern Country Danceland

HAINES CITY

Lake Marion

POLK CITY

PROVIDENCE

GIBSONIA

Lake Mattie

Lowery Lake

Lake Juliana

Lake Arietta

AUBURNDALE

Lake Mariana

LAKE ALFRED

Lake Hamilton

LAKE HAMILTON

Lake Ariana

Joker Marchant Stadium (Detroit Tigers)

LAKELAND

Florida Southern College

Lake Parker

Lake Hamilton

DUNDEE

Lake Pierce

EATON PARK

Lake Hancock

WINTER HAVEN

Audubon Nature Center

Cypress Gardens

WAVERLY

MEDULLA

HIGHLAND CITY

ELOISE

EAGLE LAKE

Lake Eloise

Lake Myrtle

Lake McLeod

BARTOW

MULBERRY

LAKE GARFIELD

Lake Garfield

ALTURAS

LAKE WALES

Bok Tower Gardens

Lake Wales Museum and Cultural Center

Black Hills Passion Play

PIERCE

HOMELAND

Peace River

Crooked Lake

BABSON PARK

HILLCREST HEIGHTS

Lake Buffum

©The H.M. Gousha Co.

9-ZM-229-M

presented. The grounds include walking paths and landscaped grounds bursting with azalea and camellia. More than 125 species of birds live within the gardens.

A central attraction is a 205-foot pink marble and coquina stone structure known as the **Bok Singing Tower,** dedicated by President Calvin Coolidge in 1929. Atop the tower is a carillon where recitals are held each day at 3pm; clock music is heard every half hour beginning at 10am. The 57-bell carillon houses bronze bells that weigh from 17 pounds to nearly 12 tons. Bok Tower Gardens is open daily all year from 8am to 6pm.

☕

REFRESHMENT STOP

Shaded by lovely trees, the **Garden Cafe and Gift Shop** inside Bok Tower Gardens makes an excellent stop for a late morning bite or a full lunch, with hot and cold entrees and a daily special. The cafe operates daily from 9am–5pm, although the menu is on the lighter side from 3pm till closing.

As you exit the gardens, continue on Tower Blvd, which leads to:

5. **Lake Wales.** Here you can relax by the small, serene lake or stroll through the charming downtown **historic district,** listed on the National Register of Historic Places and featuring an arcade of shops and restaurants.

If you exit the gardens and turn right on Burns Ave, you'll head back toward Alternate US 27. Tower Blvd ends at the water, where the road comes to a T; turn right here on N Lakeshore Blvd and then right again at Central Ave and follow signs to US 27. Stop by the:

6. **Lake Wales Museum and Cultural Center,** 325 S Scenic Hwy (Alternate US 27) (tel 813/676-5443), housed in a restored 1928 railroad station that was once a stop on the Atlantic Coast Line. You can see a 1916 Pullman train car, a locomo-

tive from 1944, a 1926 caboose, and more railroad memorabilia.

Lake Wales is also the winter home of the **Black Hills Passion Play** (tel 813/676-1495), whose season runs from mid-February through mid-April and Easter Sunday. The very popular 2-hour matinee and evening performances illustrate the last days of Christ. Reserve tickets well in advance.

Follow US 27 north, then Fla 540 west, and 4 miles later you'll reach:

7. **Cypress Gardens,** Cypress Gardens Blvd, Winter Haven (tel 813/324-2111, or toll free 800/237-4826, 800/282-2123 in FL). Opened in 1936 as Florida's 1st theme park with 16 acres of public gardens, Cypress Gardens now extends over 200 lush acres and features more than 8,000 varieties of flowers and plants from more than 75 countries. The gardens are combined with park rides and shows for the young and young-at-heart. Among the many offerings here are a lake cruise on a pontoon boat; a revolving platform rising 153 feet above the gardens for a bird's-eye view; an entertaining bird show starring macaws, cockatoos, and Amazon parrots; boat rides on inner canals; and exhibits ranging from hundreds of antique radios to a fine sculpture garden.

Each season has its own floral splendor. In late winter and early spring, you can see more than 40 varieties of bougainvillea, 60 kinds of azalea, and 500 types of roses in bloom. Late spring brings the scent of crape myrtles, magnolias, and gardenias. During the summer, visitors are dazzled by jasmine, hibiscus, and birds of paradise. Autumn is notable for the floss silk trees, camellias, and golden rain trees, while winter brings displays of thousands of red, white, and pink poinsettias, as well as chrysanthemums, and trees decorated for the holiday season.

You can easily spend several hours here viewing the gardens and watching the shows, which include the famous year-round **waterskiing show.** There are a variety of indoor and outdoor dining spots in the park for both snacks and full meals, at reasonable prices.

Cypress Gardens is open daily 9:30am–5:30pm, except on Christmas Eve (shorter hours), and November 25 through January 8 (when the park closes at 10pm). Admission (excluding tax) is $24.95 for adults, $21.20 for senior citizens over 55, and $16.45 for children 3–9; children under 3 are admitted free.

From Cypress Gardens, bird-watchers and other nature enthusiasts will want to turn right onto Fla 540 E, and go 2 miles to visit the:

8. **Audubon Nature Center,** 115 Lameraux Rd, Winter Haven (tel 813/324-7304), a 40-acre refuge partly embracing Lake Ned. Here you can stroll along 2 nature trails or stop for a picnic. Bring binoculars for up-close views of eagles, blue herons, and ospreys.

If instead you turn *left* on Fla 540 from Cypress Gardens and drive 5 miles west, you will come to:

9. **Winter Haven.** This area, with 14 lakes, is a mecca for freshwater fishing, particularly for largemouth bass, bream, black crappie, and sunshine bass.

Meanwhile, baseball's **Cleveland Indians** call Winter Haven their home in winter. The **Holiday Inn Winter Haven/Cypress Gardens,** 1150 3rd St SW (tel 813/294-4451), becomes headquarters for the American League team during spring training.

If at this point you wish to head on to Orlando, you have a choice of taking US 17 north about 12 miles to I-4 and heading east to Orlando proper, 53 miles away; or staying on US 17 as it joins US 92 northward, and proceeding east to Orlando via the backroads of Orange and Osceola counties. The backroads are a bit more adventuresome as you drive through Haines City, Davenport, Loughman, and Kissimmee back to the familiar territory of the Beeline Expressway, International Dr, and everything else at Walt Disney World's doorstep.

From Winter Haven, head north on US 17, then west on US 92 for about 20 miles, at which point you will reach:

10. **Lakeland.** From US 92, turn left on Florida Ave and proceed 1 mile to Pine St, and turn left again for some antique shopping in this small city's **antiques district,** which begins a block from Florida Ave.

Lakeland is the winter home of the **Detroit Tigers** baseball team, who play about 30 "Grapefruit League" exhibition games from early March to early April, half of them at Joker Marchant Stadium, 2305 Lakeland Hills Blvd (tel 813/682-1401).

An exciting spectacle takes place here each April, when as many as 300,000 visitors gather to watch and participate in Lakeland's weeklong **Sun 'n' Fun EAA Fly-In and Annual Aviation Convention,** held in back of Linder Regional Airport, 4175 Medulla Rd. See air shows, lectures, and aircraft displays. Adjacent to the airport is a 40-acre campus housing the **Sun 'n' Fun Air Museum and Aviation Center** (tel 813/644-0741), with its many informative displays on the history of flight. The museum hours are Monday–Friday 9am–5pm, Saturday 10am–4pm, Sunday noon–4pm.

From the Pine St turnoff that took you into the antiques district, continue 3 miles to McDonald St and turn left. Proceed 6 blocks to Johnson St (which dead-ends at Lake Hollingsworth) and take a right. You are now on the west side of the campus of:

11. **Florida Southern College,** Johnson and McDonald Sts (tel 813/680-4110), a liberal arts institution affiliated with the United Methodist Church. Concentrated on the west side of the campus are 12 buildings designed by Frank Lloyd Wright, which are usually open to the public throughout the day, except during holiday recess and weekends.

The **Thad Buckner Building,** completed in 1945, was originally a library but today houses the **Frank Lloyd Wright Visitors Center.** Among the classic Wright touches here are the use of geometric shapes and design, fireplaces, and clerestory windows. There are exhibits of furniture pieces as well as drawings and photographs. The center is open Tuesday–Friday 11am–4pm, Saturday 10am–2pm, and Sunday 2pm–4pm. For a monthly calendar of events, call 813/860-4597 or 813/680-4110.

The **Annie Pheiffer Chapel,** also designed by Wright, was constructed with student labor between 1939 and 1941. Its tower is fondly referred to as a "bicycle rack in the sky." Wright used leaded glass to complete the **William Danforth Chapel,** with a frame constructed of native Florida tidewater red cypress wood. He also designed the pews and cushions that were constructed by industrial arts and home economics students. The last Wright building erected on campus was the 1958 **Polk County Science Building,** which contains the only planetarium Wright designed that was actually built. Among the other Wright buildings on campus are the **Industrial Arts Center,** featuring a series of 30°, 60°, and 90° triangles, each lying on its hypotenuse; the **Water Dome,** completed in 1948; the skylighted **Hawkins Seminar Building;** and the **Benjamin Fine Administrative Building,** with a copper-lined ceiling.

From the campus, return to Florida Ave and turn right for about 6 miles, crossing US 92. Florida Ave becomes US 98 N and runs into I-4. The Disney World exits off I-4 begin about 35 miles from Lakeland; downtown Orlando is 55 miles away.

SCENIC DRIVING TOUR #4

THE SUNCOAST & THE SEASHELL COAST

Start: Tampa
Finish: Don Cesar Beach Resort
Distance: About 400 miles round-trip
Time: 3 days
Highlights: Gulf Coast beaches, Florida's cultural center, quaint beach towns, beautiful islands, shopping, and glamorous resorts

This tour concentrates on the heart of Florida's central west coast as you explore the Tampa Bay area, often known as the Suncoast, and the Seashell Coast, which encompasses Fort Myers and Naples. You'll stop at pleasant beach villages, serene islands, and lively resort cities with plenty of opportunities for shopping, watersports, and fine dining. Culture fans will especially enjoy Sarasota, with its arts and music festivals and the Ringling Museum Complex. The trip allows you to be comfortable in sandals and shorts, but you can also dress up, if you wish, for a night on the town.

For additional information on accommodations, restaurants, and attractions in the region covered by the tour, look under specific cities in the listings portion of this book.

1. **Tampa.** Sitting on the Hillsborough River and rimmed by Hillsborough Bay and Tampa Bay, the city of Tampa has numerous waterfront views and activities that attract vacationers year-round. This metropolis of nearly 300,000 inhabitants is a major business hub on Florida's west coast and the 7th largest US port. From Tampa's city center, get on the South Crosstown Expressway (Fla 618) heading east and continue 12 miles to I-75. Take I-75 southbound toward Naples.

After continuing 28 miles to where I-75 meets I-275 (exit 44), you're given the opportunity to make your way toward St Petersburg and St Petersburg Beach. Continue another 3 miles to exit 43 and the:

2. **Tourist Information Office,** where you can pick up information on the area and Anna Maria Island, the next stop. The office (tel 813/729-7040) is open daily 7:30am–5:30pm and has vending machines and rest rooms. Return to I-75 south

and go to exit 42. At this point, you've driven about 38 miles from where you first got on I-75.

At exit 42, take Fla 64 west about 17 miles, crossing part of Sarasota Bay to:

3. **Anna Maria Island.** Spanish explorers made their way to Anna Maria Island in the early 1500s. Legend has it that early settlers were so taken with the island's beauty that they named it "Ana-Maria Cay," in honor of Mary, the mother of Jesus, and her mother, Anne. Except for the presence of low-rise buildings, much of the 7½-mile island, with its long stretches of white sand beaches studded with sea oats, remains the same as in the past. The island's narrow streets are a favorite of cyclists and walkers who come to the town of Anna Maria to explore its old buildings and quaint boutiques and crafts shops. The town shares the island with 2 other communities, Holmes Beach and Bradenton Beach.

You'll enter Anna Maria Island via Fla 64 and the Manatee Avenue Bridge at about mid-island. The **Chamber of Commerce,** located south of Manatee Ave on East Bay Dr (tel 813/778-1541), has a tourist information center open Monday–Friday 9am–5pm. Here you're just south of Holmes Beach.

REFRESHMENT STOP

Beachside Restaurant, 200 N Gulf Dr, Bradenton Beach (tel 813/778-5608), south of the tourist office, serves a fresh catch of the day along with some tempting desserts. A deck provides outdoor dining. The **Sandbar,** 100 Spring Ave, Anna Maria Island (tel 813/778-0444), overlooking the Gulf of Mexico, has a menu of seafood combo plates, steaks, pastas, and chicken. Another local choice, **Rotten Ralph's,** 902 S Bay Blvd, Anna Maria Island (tel 813/778-3953), offers crab cakes, deep-fried oysters, and other fish platters, as well as British favorites like fish-and-chips and steak-and-kidney pie.

For the next part of the tour, follow Gulf of Mexico Dr (also known just as Gulf Dr) on Anna Maria Island, via Fla 789 south, through Longboat Key up to St Armands Key and Lido Beach. The drive is about 21 miles from Anna Maria to St Armands Key, depending upon the nooks and crannies you explore. First, take Fla 789 south from Anna Maria Island for about 8 miles to:

4. **Longboat Key.** One of Florida's wealthiest areas, this island contains private homes and condominiums in gated communities between the Gulf of Mexico and Sarasota Bay. A number of hotels lined along the Gulf shore provide fine accommodations in a variety of settings, though this is not an area for economy lodging.

The area has a number of moderately priced and expensive hotels to consider, starting on the north end with the **Holiday Inn Longboat Key,** 4949 Gulf of Mexico Dr (tel 813/383-3771), and followed by **Longboat Key Hilton Beach Resort,** 4711 Gulf of Mexico Dr (tel 813/383-2451), the **Colony Beach and Tennis Resort,** 1620 Gulf of Mexico Dr (tel 813/383-6464), and the **Resort at Longboat Key Club,** 301 Gulf of Mexico Dr (tel 813/383-8821).

REFRESHMENT STOP

Chart House, 210 Gulf of Mexico Dr, Longboat Key (tel 813/383-5593), cooks steaks and prime rib to order and also has an extensive seafood menu, with lobster, swordfish, mahimahi, shrimp, and scallops. It features panoramic views of the water and a large bar, if you're simply looking for a cool drink.

On the southern side of Longboat Key, about a mile from the resorts on Gulf Dr, is:

5. **St Armands Key,** a delightful enclave named after Charles St Amand (early spelling), a 19th-century French homesteader. The community has a traffic rotary, known as **St Armands Circle,** lined with

flower beds and filled with trendy shops, boutiques, sidewalk cafes, and restaurants. The circle
is a must-see attraction. Plan to spend a couple of
hours here looking at shops and relaxing at a
sidewalk cafe as you people-watch.

Little more than 100 yards south of St Armands
Circle is:

6. **Lido Beach.** This fine stretch of public beach on a
lively, well-developed island has ample parking,
concession stands, changing rooms, and rest rooms.
You can bring lunch in a cooler here and sit at one
of the picnic tables.

From Lido Beach, take the John Ringling Causeway (Fla 789) south to downtown:

7. **Sarasota.** This tourist mecca is known as the
cultural center of Florida and serves as the home
of the Florida West Coast Symphony, which performs at **Van Wezel Performing Hall,** 777 N
Tamiami Trail (tel 813/953-3366); and the Asolo
Performing Arts Center (see below). Annual
events include the Sarasota French Film Festival,
which screens premieres that often draw French
celebrities; the Sarasota Jazz Festival; the Sarasota
Music Festival; and the Sarasota Festival of New
Plays.

Although the early European settlers of Florida's west coast never achieved their dream of
finding gold and silver treasure, today's visitors
will find Sarasota one of the richest and most
beautiful parts of the state. With about 50,000
people, this vibrant city has 361 days of sunshine
per year and encompasses 150 miles of waterfront, 11 beaches, 6 barrier islands, and a number
of distinct communities, including Longboat Key,
Lido Beach, and St Armands Key (see above);
Siesta Key, an island resort and arts center; and
Venice, Englewood, and Northport, all quiet
beach havens.

The area was originally established by the region's early Native American inhabitants, the
Calusas, whose ancient mounds and middens can
be seen along the coastline and the keys. As in
much of Florida, Hernando de Soto is noted as
being the first European to explore the area in the
16th century. According to legend, the city was
named after de Soto's daughter, Sara. Later arrivals

included adventurous Scots, who, after hewing out
a bustling city from the palmetto and pine forests,
introduced the game of golf to the region in their
spare time.

By the early 1900s, northern socialites arrived
to begin building palatial winter retreats on Sarasota Bay. The region soon attracted a large following among the wealthy and influential, who continue to come to Sarasota today. Among the early
magnates was circus entrepreneur **John Ringling,**
who arrived in Sarasota in the 1920s and left his
imprint (see below).

US 41 is the major north-south traffic artery in
Sarasota. For a look at the city's most renowned
attraction, take US 41 north from downtown to
DeSoto Rd and turn left onto Ringling Plaza and
soon you'll approach the:

8. **Ringling Museum Complex,** 5401 Bayshore Rd
(tel 813/359-5700). This impressive, larger-than-
life 60-acre site, the former estate of John Ringling, has 4 primary attractions. Ringling, a real
estate mogul, was a partner in the world-famous
Ringling Bros and Barnum & Bailey Circus. He
spent his winters in Sarasota and eventually
moved the circus here for its winter home. Ringling also spent much time in Europe searching for
fine works of art and became enamored of Italian
and Spanish art and architecture.

Eventually he needed a museum to house the
world-class paintings and other priceless art works
he had acquired. The result was the **John and
Mable Ringling Museum of Art,** which was
constructed in the 1920s in the style of a fabulous
pink Italian Renaissance villa. Today the building
is Florida's official state art museum, with 22
galleries featuring exquisite works by Rubens, Van
Dyck, Velázquez, Hals, Poussin, and others. It also
displays decorative arts and antiques as well as
traveling exhibits.

Outside the museum are elaborate grounds
with beautiful rose gardens, the Dwarf Garden,
and fountained courtyards, including one with 91
columns and a 17-foot bronze of Michelangelo's
David, 1 of only 3 replicas and the only one in
the Western Hemisphere. Also on the complex
grounds is the 30-room **Ca'd'Zan** (House of
John), the Ringling winter residence modeled after

a Venetian palace, and the **Circus Museum,** with a vast collection of circus memorabilia that encompasses parade wagons, calliopes, costumes, posters, and the Barlow Animated Miniature Circus, a scale replica of a famous circus from the 1930s.

Finally, the grounds include the **Asolo Center for the Performing Arts,** 5555 N Tamiami Trail (tel 813/351-8000), which has a year-round program of plays, concerts, lectures, and art films. The center incorporates an Italian-style court playhouse with interior friezes, carved box fronts, and cornice work from the Dunfermline Opera House in Scotland.

The complex is open daily 10am–5:30pm, except Thanksgiving, Christmas, and New Year's Day. Admission is $8.50 adults, $7.50 seniors; free for children under 12. Admission to the art galleries only is free on Saturdays.

To reach another Sarasota attraction take the causeway to St Armands Circle, and head north on Fla 789 toward the bridge at Longboat Key. Just to the right, at the foot of the bridge, is:

9. **Mote Marine Aquarium,** 1600 Ken Thompson Pkwy, City Island Park (tel 800/691-MOTE). Part of the Mote Marine Laboratory complex, a world-renowned research center, the aquarium concentrates on marine life in the Sarasota area. You can see more than 200 varieties of sea life, and even touch some of them in the 30-foot touch tank. Displays include a living mangrove swamp and seagrass environment, a shark tank, loggerhead turtles, dolphins, manatees, and an extensive shell collection. Well-informed guides are on hand to tell you about the creatures and the work of the laboratory. Open daily 10am–5pm; closed Easter, Thanksgiving, and Christmas.

On your 2nd day, plan to get an early start. St Armands Circle is a good place to stop for a coffee and danish to go. Leaving the circle, take the John Ringling Causeway to the traffic light at the intersection of US 41 and pick up Fla 780; take Fla 780 west to exit 39 and head south on I-75 for a speedy 75-minute trip to:

10. **Fort Myers.** Fort Myers is home to a great many "snowbirds," who come south to escape the cold

northern winters. This dignified city, with palm-tree-covered boulevards, began as a humble US Army outpost named Fort Harvie in 1844. Today Fort Myers is an easy-going place where you can stroll or ride a bike, stay in a comfortable hotel, dine in good restaurants, play golf, and participate in watersports. Prices here are reasonable.

Fort Myers is also home base to baseball's Minnesota Twins and Boston Red Sox, who both play in Florida's Grapefruit League during spring training. Both teams play at the Lee County Sports Complex. For schedules, call 813/768-4210. Tickets must be purchased well in advance.

To visit the former residence of one of Fort Myers's most famous citizens, take US 41 north to Colonial Blvd and go west to McGregor Blvd (Fla 867), where you'll find the:

11. **Thomas Alva Edison Winter Home,** 2350 McGregor Blvd (tel 813/334-3614). Situated on the riverfront, this lovely 14-acre estate contains inventor Thomas Alva Edison's former winter retreat, Seminole Lodge, as well as his laboratory and botanical gardens (with the world's largest banyan tree). Edison created thousands of inventions at his laboratory here. Inside the museum on the grounds are some of his inventions, such as early motion picture equipment and talking machines. Open Monday–Saturday 9am–5:30pm, Sunday noon–5:30pm.

Right next door is the **Henry Ford Winter Home** (same address and telephone number as the Edison home). This restored former winter dwelling of billionaire industrialist Henry Ford is modestly decorated and furnished in 1920s style, and features tropical landscaping.

From the Edison Winter Home, go east past US 41 to:

12. **Fort Myers Historical Museum,** 2300 Peck St (tel 813/332-5955). Contained in a former Spanish Mediterranean–style Atlantic Coast line railroad depot, this museum devoted to Fort Myers's and southwest Florida's history has rare artifacts, photographs, and exhibits dealing with the area's past settlers. You can see a replica fort, the exceptional Cooper Glass Collection of carnival and depression glass, and "Esperanza," the long-

est and last of the fancy Pullman private railroad cars. Open Monday–Friday 9am–4:30pm, Sunday 1–5pm.

Make your way back to McGregor Blvd and head west for about 17 miles, following the well-marked signs to:

13. **Sanibel and Captiva islands.** These 2 islands are accessed via Sanibel Bridge with a $3 round-trip toll. As soon as you enter Sanibel Island, stop at the Visitors Information Center at Causeway Rd (tel 813/472-1080), on your right, to pick up brochures on the island, local restaurants, and island accommodations. From the center, you can make reservations at local hotels. Sanibel and Captiva islands make for a wonderful weekend. Pirates treasured these islands 200 years ago, and they are still held in high regard.

Sanibel is the larger island, about 12 miles long and 3 miles wide. Connected to Sanibel by a bridge, Captiva is about 6 miles long and even narrower than Sanibel. The islands have wide, white sand beaches touched by clear, iridescent gulf waters, colorful tropical flora, and wooded areas of pine and banyan trees. Much of the land area of the islands consists of wildlife sanctuaries. It's easy to get around Sanibel and Captiva, as there are only a couple of major roads.

One of the main attractions here is the 1842 **lighthouse** on the eastern end of Sanibel, which is surrounded by refuge lands that attract as many as 50 species of birds each winter. This is one of Florida's few operational lighthouses, marking the entrance from the Gulf of Mexico into San Carlos Bay. The peaceful nature of both islands encourages shelling, bird-watching, and cycling. The more adventurous might try a canoe trip, an organized walking tour, or a visit to the small **Island Historical Museum,** 850 Dunlop Rd (tel 813/472-4648), housed in a Florida pine home. Its displays cover the islands' early history, and you can see old photographs and clothing and other fascinating memorabilia. Open Wednesday–Saturday 10am–4pm.

Those with an interest in environment and ecology will want to visit **CROW** (Care and Rehabilitation of Wildlife), Sanibel-Captiva Rd (tel 813/472-3644), a sanctuary for recuperating local hawks, owls, pelicans, otters, and other wildlife; **Ding Darling National Wildlife Refuge** (tel 813/472-1100), encompassing approximately 5,000 acres and serving as a home to hundreds of species of birds and migrating waterfowl, as well as alligators, raccoons, and otters; and the **Sanibel/Captiva Conservation Foundation,** 333 Sanibel-Captiva Rd (tel 813/472-2329), which offers information about the islands' ecosystem. Call ahead for hours or consult the Visitors Information Center (see above).

You can reach Captiva from Sanibel on the appropriately named Sanibel-Captiva Rd. The road from the causeway to the northern end of Captiva is only about 10 miles long. Along this stretch, you'll find many beaches fronting the hotels and resorts.

☕

REFRESHMENT STOP

Captiva has a number of good restaurants. Try **Sunshine Cafe,** Captiva Village Sq (tel 813/472-6200), offering continental cuisine in a friendly cafe atmosphere, and **Bellini's of Captiva,** Andy Rosse Lane (tel 813/472-6866), serving northern Italian entrees in a romantic setting.

When you depart Sanibel Island and cross the causeway back to McGregor Blvd, stay to the right and continue on Summerlin Rd until you reach San Carlos Blvd, where you'll take a right. Continue south and drive through:

14. **Fort Myers Beach.** Located on Estero Island off the coast at the city of Fort Myers, Fort Myers Beach is a casual, laid-back community, with quaint cottages, garden apartments, and high-rise hotels available for tourists. Estero Island has all the amenities of a city, yet with small-town friendliness. The area's least endearing aspect is the traffic which continuously clogs the bridge to the island and Estero Blvd. Usually the traffic is

northbound in the afternoon as beachgoers head back to Fort Myers.

World-class fishing is the attraction for many who visit this beach locale. More than 30 species of fish inhabit the waters, and professional charters are available to take you deep-sea fishing (no individual license is required). Rental boats are also available from the marina for exploring the back bays on your own. Other options include fishing from the beach and from the 500-foot pier.

Fort Myers Beach has additional opportunities for windsurfing, waterskiing, sailing, and jet skiing. If you're interested in shelling, the beach has plenty of pretty shells to spare, especially at low tide during the winter. Bird-watchers will find many species of wading birds, shorebirds, and waterfowl native to the area. For more information, contact the **Fort Myers Beach Chamber of Commerce,** 394 Estero Blvd (tel 813/454-7500), open Monday–Friday 9am–5pm.

From Fort Myers Beach, continue 19 miles south on Estero Blvd (Fla 865) toward:

15. **Bonita Springs.** A former fishing village, this area has white sand beaches and acres of wildlife habitats and parks. The gulf and back bays are popular spots for saltwater and freshwater fishing.

From Bonita Springs, cross east to the mainland on Bonita Beach Rd until you reach US 41 (about 4 miles); head south on US 41 for 8 miles to:

16. **Naples.** One of Florida's most glamorous communities, Naples exudes charm, elegance, and sophistication without being snobbish. This highly regarded beach resort has its fair share of cultural diversions, art galleries, high-fashion shops, and fine dining spots, as well as golf courses and tennis courts. Although Naples has a strong appeal for the affluent who live and holiday here, the city also caters to families and travelers on more modest budgets.

It isn't surprising that Naples is home to some of Florida's finest lodging establishments, including the **Ritz-Carlton Naples,** 280 Vanderbilt Beach Rd (tel 813/598-3300 or toll free 800/241-3333). Some good moderately priced lodgings

include **Cove Inn Resort and Marina,** 1191 8th St S (tel 813/262-7161 or toll free 800/255-4365) or **La Playa Beach and Racquet Inn,** 9891 Gulf Shore Dr (tel 813/597-3123 or toll free 800/237-6883). For those looking to spend even less, try **Days Inn,** 1925 Davis Blvd (tel 813/774-3117 or toll free 800/272-0106), or **Hampton Inn,** 3210 Tamiami Trail N (tel 813/261-8000 or toll free 800/732-4667).

Naples has several impressive nature reserves, such as **Big Cypress National Preserve,** accessible by I-75 and US 41 (tel 813/695-4111), a 2,000-square-mile sanctuary for alligators, deer, and numerous birds; the **Conservancy Nature Center,** Goodlette Rd on 14th Ave N (tel 813/262-0304), with a science museum, nature trails, butterfly atrium, and aviary; and **Corkscrew Swamp Sanctuary,** Sanctuary Rd (tel 813/657-3771), an 11,000-acre wilderness, maintained by the National Audubon Society, that features alligators as well as migratory and wading birds.

To come to Naples and not visit the fine boutiques and galleries is like missing a mouse named Mickey in the Magic Kingdom. The **Fifth Avenue South** district has more than 100 shops, galleries, and restaurants, and for many it is Naples's finest shopping area. **Old Naples,** along 3rd St S and the avenues, is a 9-square-block historic area in the southern part of the city between the Gulf and Naples Bay. It has handsomely restored old balconied buildings, trendsetting shops, art galleries, and top restaurants. Additional shopping centers include **Coastland Center,** 1900 Tamiami Trail N; **Coral Isle Factory Shops,** on Fla 951; **Tin City,** at US 41 and Goodlette Rd; the **Village on Venetian Bay,** 4200 Gulf Shore Blvd N; and the **Waterside Shops at Pelican Bay,** Seagate Dr and Tamiami Trail N.

From Naples, drive 8 miles south on US 41 to Isle of Capri Rd (Fla 951); proceed another 7 miles and go over the bridge to:

17. **Marco Island,** about a half-hour drive from Naples. Ordinarily, Marco Island requires its own overnight stay, at least if you're a beachgoer. The pace here is slow and you can easily slip from your

bed to a hammock without skipping a page from your best-seller.

Like Sanibel Island but a bit more commercialized, Marco Island has a number of boutiques, art galleries, and casual restaurants. **Tiger Tail Beach State Park** has a nice beach that offers opportunities for swimming and watersports, as well as changing rooms and showers.

At Isle of Capri Rd turn right, away from Marco Island, and continue 7 miles to I-75 N. From here,

---

REFRESHMENT STOP

Stan's Idle Hour Seafood Restaurant (tel 813/394-3041) is located in Goodland, less than a 10-minute drive east from Marco Island's center, just off to the right before the bridge on Fla 92. Stan Gober owns this rustic seafood eatery on the dock, where locals like to gather for good food, drinks, and sometimes live entertainment. Besides the fresh fish and seafood entrees, try the frogs' legs (seasonal), the large fried onion rings, and the buffalo chicken wings. The outdoor patio with thatched huts is fun for lunch or dinner.

---

the drive is approximately 125 miles north to the interchange of I-75 and I-275. To proceed to St Petersburg Beach, take exit 44 from I-75 and drive toward St Petersburg until you see signs for the beach. Follow these signs to Gulf Blvd, where you'll see the:

18. **Don Cesar Beach Resort,** 3400 Gulf Blvd (tel 813/360-1881), a big pink National Landmark hotel sitting magnificently on 7½ miles of beachfront. This 1928 palace, combining Moorish and Mediterranean architecture, was renovated in the 1980s. You'll enjoy looking at its elegant interior, with classic high windows and archways, crystal chandeliers, marble floors, and artworks on display. Enjoy drinks on the terrace, a romantic dinner in the fine dining room, or stroll the grounds and slip off your shoes for a walk on the beach.

Turn right out of the Don Cesar and drive north on Gulf Blvd from St Petersburg Beach. Take this drive at a leisurely pace as you continue past a handful of little beach towns, including Treasure Island, Madeira Beach, Redington Beach, Indian Rocks Beach, Belleair, and Clearwater. At Clearwater Beach, proceed east on Fla 60 to the Courtney Campbell Causeway (Fla 60). It's about 30 minutes from Clearwater back to downtown Tampa.

SCENIC DRIVING TOUR #5

JACKSONVILLE TO THE GOLDEN ISLES & SAVANNAH

Start: Jacksonville
Finish: Savannah, GA
Distance: About 300 miles round-trip
Time: 3 days
Highlights: Luxurious resorts, semitropical barrier islands, historic homes and inns, romantic neighborhoods

This 3-day tour from Jacksonville to Georgia should especially please history buffs and those interested in diverse architectural styles. Along the way, you'll stop at historic landmarks dating from the 18th century (when English settlers first arrived in the area) and the Civil War. You'll visit homes built in a range of styles, among them Victorian, federal, and regency. And if you're traveling with someone special, you'll find it easy to discover places to share intimate dinners, relax with a cup of coffee in front of a fireplace, and walk arm in arm along cobblestone streets.

Those concerned with watching their budget should be forewarned before starting this trip. While a commercial center such as Jacksonville has less expensive hotel rooms available on weekends when business is lighter, rooms in Savannah actually become more costly. Savannah's best lodging choices—its lovely historic inns—charge higher rates on the weekend, when couples like to take a romantic vacation. If your schedule allows, you may wish to consider traveling to Savannah during midweek when prices are usually lower.

1. **Jacksonville.** From the downtown part of the city, take I-95 north 21 miles to exit 129; near the exit, you'll find a fruit and vegetable stand displaying the season's freshest produce. Here you can get on Fla 200 and continue toward Fernandina Beach, which lies another 14 miles from the exit. After about 10 miles, you'll cross the Amelia River and see the sign for Amelia Island Plantation shortly beyond the bridge. If you turn right at the sign and drive 3½ miles, you will reach:

2. **Ritz-Carlton Amelia Island,** 4750 Amelia Island Plantation (tel 904/277-1100), a posh hotel over-

looking the beach and the Atlantic and set on lushly landscaped grounds. The interior decor of this impressive building is much like that of other Ritz hotels: fine antiques and other museum-quality furnishings, rich carpets and upholstery, and soft lighting. If you plan a Sunday departure from Jacksonville, the Ritz-Carlton makes an ideal stop for a Sunday buffet (served 7–11am). (See also the listing in this book under "Amelia Island.")

The Ritz-Carlton is located on the **Amelia Island Plantation,** which is an extensive enclave of private homes, villas, and other accommodations. The plantation is a gated community that has golf and tennis opportunities, in a lovely wooded setting with its own stretch of private beach.

Exit the Ritz-Carlton and retrace your steps to I-95: 3½ miles back to Fla 200, left or west just over 10 miles to exit 129, and then up the ramp to I-95 northbound. The Georgia state line is 9 miles north on I-95. Cross the bridge when you reach the state line and pull into the:

3. **Visitors Welcome Center** (tel 912/729-3253), a half-mile ahead. The center provides helpful information on Georgia, including maps and brochures on hotels and inns on St Simons Island, Sea Island, and Jekyll Island, and in Savannah. If you didn't have time for breakfast on Amelia Island, the center has vending machines and rest rooms. It's open 9am–5pm.

Continue north on I-95, passing the serene landscape of wildflowers, trees, and flowering bushes along the way. Located 28 miles north of the visitors center is exit 6; from here, US 17 will take you to the Jekyll Island and St Simons Causeways and the **Golden Isles.** The Golden Isles comprise 4 lush, semitropical barrier islands: Jekyll Island, St Simons Island, Sea Island, and Little St Simons Island.

Shortly after taking exit 6 and following US 17, you'll come across the turnoff on the right to the Jekyll Island Causeway. As soon as you cross the causeway prepare to pay a $2 toll, referred to as a parking fee, to get onto:

4. **Jekyll Island,** which is known for its wonderful golf courses: three 18-hole beauties called Ole-

ander, Indian Mound, and Pine Lakes. There's also the Oceanside Nine, which is designed like the course in St Andrews, Scotland. America's millionaires once came to play at Oceanside Nine during the winter.

The island first became the leisure home of several wealthy Yankee industrialists who bought the island for a mere $125,000 in the late 1800s. They built beautiful homes, some of them with as many as 25 rooms, and called these estates "cottages." Their mansions were known collectively as Millionaires Village, until a group of 2nd-generation millionaires sold the island to the state of Georgia in 1947.

The **Jekyll Island Historic District** maintains several of the original homes. One of these Victorian residences has been restored as the:

5. **Jekyll Island Club Hotel,** 371 Riverview Dr (tel 912/635-2600). While the Rockefellers, Morgans, and Vanderbilts aren't guests any longer, this Radisson Hotel property still retains much of its original charm. The rambling, turreted, clapboard structure features elaborately detailed woodwork and fine hardwood floors. There is a lovely dining room where you can enjoy an evening meal after a day at the nearby beach club, and the casual, atmospheric little cafe-delicatessen is ideal for a sandwich or ice cream cone.

In all, the Historic District has 33 structures, although some of them are still being restored. If you have time, visit a few of the former cottages now open to the public, among them the Villa Ospo, Crane, Goodyear, and DuBignon cottages. The Faith Chapel is worth a stop to look at the stained-glass windows by Louis Tiffany and D Maitland Armstrong.

Jekyll Island also has more modest accommodations—run by Holiday Inn, Clarion, and Comfort—that line the beach area near the Radisson property. The island **beaches,** all of which are open to the public, are excellent and measure almost 10 miles. The main beach has plenty of free parking, rest rooms, and changing facilities. Much of the pace on Jekyll Island is as slow as it was 2 generations ago.

Return to the causeway and make your way to US 17, turn right and proceed to the St Simons

Causeway, which takes you to **St Simons** and **Sea Island.** A good introduction to St Simons comes from the area known as:

6. **The Village,** with a pier that once took visitors by ferry to the mainland. The little village thrives thanks to a few shops and restaurants and its focal point, the St Simons Lighthouse, which is part of the Museum of Coastal History.

To reach the lighthouse and the museum, turn right from the St Simons Causeway (also known as the Torras Causeway) onto Kings Way; take a right on Mallory St, a left on Beachview Dr, and finally a right onto 12th St.

7. **The St Simons Lighthouse,** 1 of only 5 such remaining structures in Georgia, is now an automated light that shines 18 miles out over the ocean, directing marine traffic along the coast and into St Simons Sound. You can climb the 129 steps to the top of the lighthouse for a view of the island.

The structure was built in 1872 after Confederate forces blew up the original lighthouse in 1862 so that it would not be used by Union troops. That original building was constructed in what was known as Fort Brown. The fort's history traces back even further—to the early 1700s, when English General James Oglethorpe commissioned the land as Fort St Simons to protect the island.

8. **The Museum of Coastal History,** 101 12th St (tel 912/638-4666), includes exhibits contained in the former lighthouse keeper's quarters, constructed in an 1890 brick house that is now operated by the Coastal Georgia Historical Society. The museum and lighthouse are open Tuesday–Saturday 10am–5pm, Sunday 1:30–5pm.

Between the lighthouse and pier is a casino building and an old bandstand. If you want more information on the island, you can stop at the **Chamber of Commerce** (tel 912/729-3253 or toll free 800/525-8678), located in the casino. Open Monday–Friday 9am–5pm, Saturday 10am–2pm.

Turn left from 12th St onto Demere Rd and proceed to:

9. **Bloody Marsh Battle Site,** administered by the National Park Service, and the location of a brief but important battle between the Spanish and British in 1742. A large contingency of British troops surprised the Spanish forces and overwhelmed them to prevent an attack at Fort Frederica (see below).

Depart the historic site on Demere Rd and turn right onto Frederica Rd, following signs across Sea Island Rd to:

10. **Fort Frederica National Monument** (tel 912/638-3639). Only 3 years after British General James Oglethorpe founded Savannah, he came to St Simons in the 1730s and built Fort Frederica to protect the area from Spanish invasion. A park ranger leads tours of the fort, or you can take your own self-guided tour. A film, presented every half hour, covers the fort's history. Open daily May through Labor Day 8am–6pm; closes at 5pm the rest of the year.

From the fort, you may choose to turn left onto Lawrence Rd toward the dock where a ferry will take you to:

11. **Little St Simons Island.** This unspoiled 10,000-acre privately owned island has 6 miles of beaches good for swimming, fishing, horseback riding, and birdwatching. Some of the expensive lodges on the island date back to the 1920s.

If you decide to skip the ferry ride, head back on Frederica Rd to Sea Island Rd and turn left. Then proceed to Sea Island Dr and:

12. **Sea Island.** Industrialist Howard Coffin purchased this northernmost of the Golden Isles in 1927 and built a small causeway to the 5-mile island, connecting it to St Simons Island. Coffin developed a resort that is today one of the South's most famous, the Cloister.

Leaving the Cloister, follow Sea Island Dr back to the causeway and go right (north) on US 17 for 12 miles to I-95. From I-95, exit 9 continues north over the Altamaha River, but do not take this exit. About 50 miles further, I-95 crosses I-16 at exit 17; take this exit onto I-16 east and drive 8 miles into downtown:

13. **Savannah.** In this tour, Savannah is the ultimate destination, where the first-time visitor will probably want to invest most of his time. Although most

---

> ☕
> ## REFRESHMENT STOP
> The **Cloister,** Sea Island (tel 912/638-3611), is a spectacular resort in Moorish style with a red-tiled roof and elaborate public rooms that encourage you to linger. The exquisite dining rooms are perfect for a romantic evening. The hotel is also a fine place to stop for lunch. You may wish to stay here overnight instead of staying in Savannah for more than 1 night.

of its major sights can be covered in 2 days, this seductive city easily lends itself to a longer stay. Savannah has landmark historic buildings, delightfully restored squares, and charming cobblestone streets.

The city usually has something to offer during every month of the year. One of the most popular events here is the **St Patrick's Day Parade** (March 17), a festival second in size only to New York City's. Later in the month, there's an annual **4-day tour** of homes, museums, churches, and gardens, followed closely in April by the **Savannah Seafood Festival** and the **Night in Old Savannah,** which involves the participation of the city's ethnic communities.

Other annual highlights include the 5-day **Savannah Jazz Festival** in September and the **Oktoberfest** held on River Street. At Christmastime, the Downtown Neighborhood Association sponsors tours of **historic homes,** and 7 homes are shown on each day during Christmas weekend. The celebration includes candlelight tours, hand-bell ringers, carolers, and horse-drawn carriage rides. You can also conduct your own self-guided tour of the city's historic inns that dress up for the holidays and welcome visitors with refreshments and tales of old Savannah.

Plan to stay in one of the city's **historic inns** if you can find a room and if the price fits your budget. These inns feature individually decorated rooms full of style and charm and are served by caring, warm staffs. Savannah has more than a dozen such inns; 4 are highlighted below.

Perhaps the best historic inn in town is **Kehoe House,** 123 Habersham St, Columbia Sq (tel 912/231-0208). This grand Victorian mansion is filled with exquisitely displayed antiques. The music room, the dining room, and parlors are all decorated to create an ambience of refined elegance. The guest rooms—with fabulous 4-poster beds, puddled drapes, and rich upholstered furniture—will make you want to retire early to luxuriate in the romantic atmosphere.

Another top lodging choice is **The Gastonian,** 220 E Gaston St (tel 912/232-2869 or toll free 800/322-6603). The exquisitely decorated rooms, some with fireplaces and whirlpool tubs, are just what Cupid ordered. You can expect a gourmet breakfast when you come down to the dining room, and if you'd like a cup of tea or another beverage, the staff will be pleased to oblige. The 2 Italianate brick buildings here are joined by a walkway where a hot tub is tucked away for everyone to enjoy.

Two other inns are worth a look. The **Ballastone Inn,** 14 E Oglethorpe Ave (tel 912/236-1484 or toll free 800/822-4553), a 19th-century townhouse that sits next to the Juliette Gordon Low Girl Scout shrine, features a tasteful array of rooms from the original servants' quarters and elegant formal rooms with 14-foot ceilings. There's a lively bar as well. The owners of the **Foley House Inn,** 14 W Hull St (tel 912/232-6622 or toll free 800/647-3708), are so sure you'll like what you see, they guarantee your stay with a money-back offer. The rooms are comfortable and charming, most with 4-poster beds and a few with whirlpools; 16 rooms have fireplaces.

Of course, Savannah also has a handful of traditional hotels, including the **Hyatt Regency Savannah,** 2 W Bay St (tel 912/238-1234 or toll free 800/228-9000); the **Radisson Plaza Hotel Savannah,** 100 General McIntosh Blvd (tel 912/233-7722 or toll free 800/333-3333; and the **Days Inn Historic District,** 201 W Bay St (tel 912/236-4440 or toll free 800/325-2525). The Hyatt, situated on the riverfront, is one of the more expensive chain hotels, while the Days Inn, convenient to historic buildings, will appeal to those on a budget.

In 1733, General James Oglethorpe came to

the area that is now Savannah with just over 100 English settlers who yearned to start their lives over in the New World. Oglethorpe set out to create a town that would provide houses for each resident along with a garden plot to be arranged

---

☕

REFRESHMENT STOP

Savannah and the Historic District have a number of small pubs and cafes for a morning coffee break, a bagel sandwich, a cold lemonade, or a cold beer. Some inns provide afternoon tea. The Ballastone Inn (see above) has a nice little bar. In the waterfront area, you'll find a variety of dining spots, but your best bet is to amble about with no particular agenda and enter a place that strikes your fancy.

---

around a series of 24 town squares. The natural deep harbor brought in commerce and a lively sea trade, which in turn attracted immigrants from Spain, Portugal, Germany, Ireland, and Scotland. During the Revolutionary War, the British took Savannah on December 29, 1778, and held it until July 1782; an attempt by French and American forces to retake the city in 1779 failed miserably. Just following the Declaration of Independence in 1776, Savannah was named the state capital, which it remained until 1807, when it was moved to Milledgeville.

Savannah prospered between the end of the colonial era and the Civil War, as construction continued in the classic revival, Georgia colonial, and regency styles. The port sustained the town's growth and economy. Cotton and tobacco became important crops in Savannah. With the invention of the cotton gin in 1793, cotton farming and production boomed, and a railroad was soon built that linked the port town with the cotton fields.

Savannah remains special today because so much of its early architecture has been preserved. Of the original 1,100 buildings, 800 remain, along with 20 squares in what is today known as the

Historic District. (This is the largest National Historic District; it measures 2½ square miles.) South of the Historic District lies the Victorian neighborhood, with fine examples of post–Civil War architecture.

The best way to see the Historic District is on foot. Begin with:

14. **Davenport House,** 324 E State St (tel 912/236-8097), on Columbia Sq, is a distinguished federal-style (circa 1815) house that 7 determined women preserved from destruction in the 1950s. Today on a tour of the home, you can observe the elliptical stairway and lovely ironwork. Open Monday–Wednesday, Friday–Saturday 10am–4pm, Sunday 1:30–4:30pm.

    Turn right out of the Davenport House and walk 2 blocks to the:

15. **Owens-Thomas House and Museum,** 124 Abercorn St (tel 912/233-9743). Considered one of the finest surviving examples of regency architecture, this abode was designed in 1816 by English architect William Jay for a cotton merchant and was later inherited by the Telfair Academy (now the Telfair Museum of Art). Inside is a collection of decorative arts. Open Tuesday–Saturday 10am–5pm, Sunday–Monday 2–5pm.

    Continue walking west on State St until you reach Bull St. Turn left and walk past Wright Sq, with its impressive landscaping, en route to Oglethorpe Ave, where you'll find the:

16. **Juliette Gordon Low Girl Scout National Center,** 142 Bull St at Oglethorpe Ave (tel 912/233-4501). This regency-style house was home to the founder of the Girl Scouts, originally formed in Savannah in 1912. Today the building is maintained as a memorial to her and operates as the National Program Center. The 1818 house had additions built in the Victorian style in 1886. Open Monday–Tuesday, Thursday–Saturday 10am–4pm, Sunday 12:30–4:30pm.

    Turn left out the front door and proceed 5 blocks via Chippewa Sq to Madison Sq and W Macon St, where you'll discover the:

17. **Green-Meldrim Home,** 14 W Macon St (tel 912/233-3845). When Union General William T

Sherman occupied Savannah in 1864, this Gothic-style house was his headquarters. Reportedly, Sherman sent a telegram to President Lincoln offering him Savannah as a Christmas present. Part of the home is used by St John's Church as a rectory but other sections are open to the public. Visitors can view the former slave quarters, kitchen, and stables. Open Tuesday, Thursday–Saturday 10am–4pm.

Leave via Madison Sq and head south 1 block to Charlton St. Turn left and go 2 blocks to:

18. **Andrew Low House,** 329 Abercorn St (tel 912/233-6854). Facing Lafayette Sq, this classic 19th-century home served as the home of Andrew Low and his wife Juliette Gordon Low, the founder of the Girl Scouts. In 1870, the Lows hosted a gala in the double parlor, and Robert E Lee was on the guest list. William Makepeace Thackeray also visited here; you can see the desk where the English novelist worked in one of the bedrooms. Be sure to take note of the detail work in the construction, the chandeliers, the ironwork, and the lovely carved woodwork. Open Monday–Wednesday, Friday–Saturday 10:30am–4pm, Sunday 12–4pm.

From the Low house, keep walking east until you arrive at the:

19. **Flannery O'Connor Childhood Home,** 207 E Charlton St (tel 912/233-6014). Flannery O'Connor is best remembered for her short stories, which etched highly original portraits of southern characters. Between October and May, the home sponsors lectures, readings, and seminars about O'Connor and other southern writers. Open Friday–Sunday 1–4pm.

From here you can proceed toward the Savannah River via Abercorn St, past the Colonial Park Cemetery, through Oglethorpe Sq and Reynolds Sq to E Bay St and:

20. **Factor's Walk.** Here along the riverfront, you'll find a host of charming boutiques, restaurants, and taverns in what used to be brokers' offices and warehouses. The brick buildings, dating from the early 1800s, are strung along a high bluff at the river's edge and rise 3 or more stories above River St. Each level has its own street—River Street, Lower Factors' Walk, Upper Factors' Walk—and

there are bridgeways connecting each level to streets along the bluff. The entrance ramps are paved with cobblestones that crossed the Atlantic as ballast in sailing ships.

Your last morning can be spent exploring places that you didn't have time to investigate before. In fact, this morning gives you a chance to

---

⛾

REFRESHMENT STOP

The River St area provides plenty of opportunities to sample a taste of Low Country cuisine. Some recommended choices are: **Huey's,** 115 River St (tel 912/234-7385), an Italian cafe with sidewalk dining; **Kevin Barry's Irish Pub,** W River St (tel 912/233-9626), whose name says it all; and **River House,** 125 W River St (tel 912/234-1900), offering seafood and a wonderful bakery.

---

drop into a few shops to collect some souvenirs. A good buy is a collection of southern recipes gathered from various local women's clubs. And for your last dining experience in Savannah, plan on a visit to the following local institution:

21. **Mrs. Wilkes's Dining Room,** 107 W Jones St (tel 912/232-5997). This restaurant is only open for breakfast and lunch, and since breakfast is included in your rate if you're staying at a historic inn, you probably will have lunch here. Since the 1940s, Mrs Wilkes has been serving generous portions of barbecued chicken, black-eyed peas, fresh corn, and other Savannah cuisine. Breakfast offers eggs, grits, sausage, bacon, and ham. Everything is served family-style with big dishes piled high. There's no sign outside to direct you here: The owner says that would make her place too commercial and not at all like home.

To leave Savannah, you can take any of the streets running parallel to the river for the first dozen blocks or so south of River St to get to Martin Luther King, Jr Blvd. This latter road will take you to I-16 for the 10-mile drive west to I-95. In about 2 hours, you'll be back in Jacksonville.

SCENIC DRIVING TOUR #6

THE GULF COAST

Start: Pensacola
Finish: Bellingrath Gardens, Theodore, Alabama
Distance: 125 miles round-trip
Time: 1–2 days
Highlights: Miles of bleached-white beaches, a ferry ride, an arts community, historic forts, southern gardens

This tour introduces you to the splendors of the Gulf Coast area, beginning in Pensacola and proceeding to historic and scenic sights in Alabama, where you end your trip at serene, beautifully landscaped southern gardens. If you plan to drive only for 1 day, you'll need to plan ahead and pick which stops you wish to cover. A typical day may include a drive along the beaches (get out for a picture-taking moment and have coffee); a stop in charming Foley, with flower baskets hanging from utility poles; a look at the USS *Alabama,* a battleship in the Mobile area; and a stroll through Bellingrath Gardens.

Some sights may not appeal to the whole family, but if you get an early start, the Mobile Bay Ferry ride should prove entertaining to everyone. Younger children who may not appreciate the USS *Alabama,* Foley, or Bellingrath Gardens will likely warm up to Zooland Animal Park and Fort Morgan in Gulf Shores. It may be

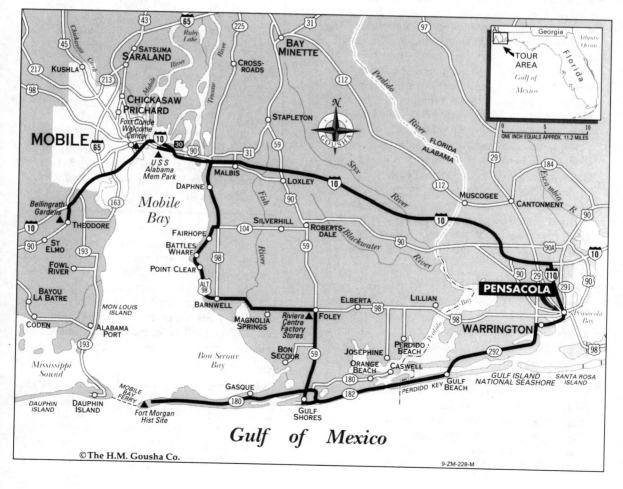

© The H.M. Gousha Co.

9-ZM-228-M

too ambitious to try to see everything on this tour in 1 day; consider staying overnight in Point Clear, AL.

1. **Pensacola, FL.** This city on Florida's westernmost tip combines urban sophistication with the pleasures of sun, sand, and sea just across a causeway, where miles of platinum white beaches are splashed by the Gulf of Mexico. Besides serving as the home to the US Naval Air Station with one of the world's largest aerospace museums, the city has historic forts and architecture that recall the Spanish, French, and British settlers who once claimed the area as their own. Begin your trip from downtown Pensacola at the intersection of Main and Jefferson Sts. From here, drive west 1½ miles to Barrancas Ave. Turn left and continue to S Pace Blvd, where you once again turn left and drive over a drawbridge. Perry's Seafood Restaurant—a bright red landmark building in the city—is on the right.

Continue west, going through the Navy Blvd intersection onto Gulf Beach Hwy (Navy Blvd becomes Gulf Beach Hwy). While continuing this westward route for about 5 miles, you'll have a view of the northwest Florida woods of stately pines, scrub oaks, and live oaks. This road leads to Blue Angel Pkwy, past Perdido Bay Resort and Country Club, and to Innerarity Point.

At Sorrento Rd and Innerarity Point Rd, continue through the intersection and drive onto **Innerarity Point Bridge,** which takes you over the **Gulf Intracoastal Waterway.** The bridge also provides a spectacular view of the Gulf of Mexico and Perdido Bay.

2. **Perdido Key.** A "Welcome to Perdido Key" sign greets visitors as they descend the bridge. Veer to the right as the road curves past Johnson Beach and continue west on Perdido Key Dr, also known as Fla 292, which runs parallel with the Gulf of Mexico and becomes Ala 182 in Alabama.

Perdido Key is a stretch of quaint, family-owned beach shops, restaurants, condominiums, and beach houses. Families can also enjoy the quiet of **Perdido Key State Recreation Area.** The bright, ultra-wide white sand beaches, with undulating sand dunes and golden sea oats, are spotted with natural foliage that provide a haven to

birds and wildlife. Come here to swim, picnic, or just relax.

🍺

REFRESHMENT STOP

The **Flora-Bama Lounge,** 17401 Perdido Key Dr (tel 904/492-0611), is just minutes away from the Perdido Key beaches. This saloon located on the Florida and Alabama state line is famous for its colorful, eclectic crowd from the blue-haired set to Harley Davidson bikers to yuppies and beach bunnies. The establishment has a raw oyster bar and a menu that emphasizes seafood. During the day, the place is family-oriented, but it's not suitable for children after 9pm. Flora-Bama is known for its country music entertainment and sponsors the Frank Brown International Songwriters Festival each November. Past festivals have featured some top names in country songwriting. Open 8am–2:30am.

Besides the Flora-Bama Lounge, songwriters perform at various venues in the Greater Perdido area, including **Zeke's Landing,** 26619 Perdido Beach Blvd, Orange Beach (tel 205/981-4001).

From the beach, head west on Perdido Key Dr through Orange Beach and travel over the Alabama Point Bridge into Alabama.

Keep driving west on what has now become Ala 182 for about 12 miles, taking in the scenery as you pass **Gulf State Park** and its white sand beaches, the **Gulf State Park Resort and Campground,** and restaurants and beach boutiques, until you reach:

3. **Gulf Shores, AL,** situated at the southernmost tip of the state. This 30,000-acre island is 50 miles southeast of Mobile and 35 miles west of Pensacola on Ala 59 and Ala 182, and it is easily accessible from I-65 and I-10. The island encompasses 32 miles of bleach-white beaches on the Gulf of

Mexico. The beaches at Gulf Shores are typical of others on the Gulf Coast, with dazzling sand, tall sand dunes, golden sea oats, and brilliant, blue-green waters. The inland is wooded with live oaks and pines, and freshwater lakes, rivers, bayous, and coves add thousands of acres of protected waterfront to the area.

For the spring break college crowd, most of the action is found at the intersection of Ala 182 and Ala 59 N, with its barrage of "souvenir cities," gift shops, and sportswear and fashion boutiques. Gulf Shores provides plenty of options for the activity-minded. Rental companies all along the beach offer jet skis, Wave Runners, catamarans, boogie bodyboards, mopeds, bicycles, and more. Thrill-seekers can get their adrenaline pumping with parasail rides and bungee jumping.

The island also offers deep-sea fishing and party boat charters, or you can simply cast your line from the Gulf State Park Fishing Pier, which extends 824 feet into the Gulf of Mexico. Freshwater fishing is also popular. The Bob Secour River, the 700-acre freshwater Lake Shelby, and the other protected areas provide anglers with a variety of fishing holes.

A popular recreation spot, located about a mile from the beaches, is **Zooland Animal Park and Mini Golf,** 1204 Gulf Shores Pkwy (Ala 59) (tel 205/968-4910), which features 250 exotic and endangered animals, some in their natural habitat. Less exotic deer can be seen wandering the park. There's also a petting zoo and rides for small children; during summer, 2 shows each day introduce kids to various animals. Next door is **Waterville,** 906 Gulf Shores Pkwy (tel 205/948-2106), a water theme park with 7 major slides, a wave pool, and a lazy river, and, on dry land, two 18-hole mini-golf courses, a roller coaster, and a video arcade.

For a shopping diversion, head south from Zooland a half-mile on Ala 59 to **Bayou Village Shopping and Dining Plaza,** where you'll find various arts and crafts boutiques, gift shops, and several restaurants, including an oyster house.

After sampling Gulf Shores, turn left on Fort Morgan Rd (Ala 180 W) from Ala 59 and venture to the western end of the island to:

4. **Fort Morgan.** One of the last southern forts to fall to Union forces, the 450-acre Fort Morgan (tel 205/540-7125) is actually the site of 2 forts: Fort Bowyer, built in 1813, and Fort Morgan, built between 1819 and 1834 to replace the earlier structure and to guard the entrance to Mobile Bay. Here Union Admiral David Farragut issued his now-famous command, "Damn the torpedoes! Full speed ahead!" The park, which includes a museum displaying military artifacts from the War of 1812 through World War II, is open daily from 8am until sunset for self-guided walking tours; during June to mid-August, a guided walking tour is available. The park has picnic tables and concessions, as well as a 250-foot pier that provides a good fishing opportunity. Admission is $2 adults, $1 students and senior citizens.

If you have the time, take a scenic 30-minute ride on:

5. **The Mobile Bay Ferry,** the car-passenger ferry that connects Fort Morgan to Dauphin Island. The ferry departs several times daily from both sides of the bay, providing an alternate route to the beaches of Gulf Shores and Orange Beach. Fare is $12 for cars and $1 for walk-on passengers.

If you bypass the fort, continue out of Gulf Shores northward. After driving 9 miles, you'll reach:

6. **The Riviera Centre Factory Stores,** in Foley, AL, an undeniable lure for shoppers with 85 manufacturers' outlets. The Riviera Centre features designer names such as Liz Claiborne, J Crew, Ralph Lauren, and more. The stores in this sprawling shopping mecca carry everything from housewares to lingerie to home electronics. (If you're taking this tour in 1 day, you may want to save shopping for another time.)

Leaving Riviera Centre, turn right and head west again. If you departed Pensacola early, Foley makes a good stop for lunch.

Upon leaving Foley, go west on US 98. This oak-lined stretch will take you through rural farm fields, pecan groves, and corn fields; antique shops sprinkle the landscape. Pass through **Magnolia Springs,** home to the 500-year-old Inspiration Oak.

Take Alternate US 98 for the scenic entrance to nearby:

7. **Point Clear, AL,** about 23 miles northwest of Foley via Barnwell. The road, which curves to the right and parallels Mobile Bay, is dotted with state-

---

☕

REFRESHMENT STOP

From the Riviera Centre, drive 2 miles to the intersection of Ala 59 and US 98. The **Gift Horse Restaurant and Bakery,** 209 W Laurel Ave (US 98), Foley (tel 205/943-3663), serves home-style southern dishes and other specialties in a former 1912 social hall decorated with antique chandeliers, stained-glass panels, and a lovely indoor fountain. The 28-foot Duncan Phyfe buffet table, which today displays about 20 salads, meat dishes, and vegetables, once stood in the White House.

---

ly magnolias and Spanish moss–draped oaks. The bay is lined with winter getaway homes and year-round residences, complete with front porches and rocking chairs and built in Florida Cracker-style and Gulf Coast Vernacular; each home greets visitors with welcome signs such as "Happy Ours," "Extra Point," "Point of It All," "McLeod Crowd," or "Panoramic Point."

The **Wash House Restaurant,** 17111 Scenic Hwy 98 (Alt US 98), near County Hwy 32 (tel 205/928-1500), in an 1897 southern mansion, is a family-run candy and confection business that offers demonstrations of candy and fudge making. The family uses locally grown pecans in their famous pralines. The mansion also contains a museum showcasing the original furniture. The main restaurant is contained in the former wash house and kitchen of what was once known throughout the South as the "big house."

Press onward on US 98 W, driving past **Marriott's Grand Hotel,** 1 Grand Blvd (tel 205/928-9201 or toll free 800/228-9290) in Point Clear. If you decide to take this tour in 2 days, you can stay

overnight at this commendable hotel, with lovely grounds and good restaurants. A central fireplace is the focal point of a grand octagonal pine-paneled public room furnished with fine antiques. The guest rooms provide views of Mobile Bay.

About 2 miles west of the hotel on US 98 is:

8. **Fairhope.** This enchanting town and artists' colony has art galleries, espresso cafes, old-fashioned ice cream parlors, bookstores, specialty food and gift shops, and antique dealers. Flower baskets hang from poles in the streets, and the entrance of each shop is adorned with overflowing flower boxes filled with geraniums, impatiens, periwinkles, and asparagus ferns. The town also has manicured parks skirting Mobile Bay, an English-style rose garden, and a magnificent fountain at the Fairhope Pier, a popular site for weddings and picnics. You can take a bicycle ride on one of the town's many paths.

From Fairhope, return to US 98 and drive north about 20 miles through Daphne and Malbis. Take I-10 west to exit 30, at US 90 and Battleship Pkwy. Here, at **Battleship USS *Alabama* Memorial Park,** you can board the:

9. **USS *Alabama*** and the **USS *Drum*,** a submarine (tel 205/433-2703). A total of 21 battle stars were bestowed upon these vessels during World War II. The *Alabama* allows visitors to see 12 decks of living quarters, the command center, and the bridge; a video program features old war veterans recalling the ship's past. Also on view in the park are 20 aircraft, including the B-52 bomber *Calamity Jane* and an A-12 Blackbird secret spy plane. Unfortunately, you cannot board the planes, although various displays do provide background on their history and use. The park also has a lovely rose garden as well as a gift shop.

If time permits, take a moment to experience pure southern charm by driving about 5 miles west on Battleship Pkwy from Battleship Memorial Park to the **Oakleigh Plantation,** 350 Oakleigh Place, at Savannah St (tel 205/432-1281), in Mobile. The **Oakleigh Period House Museum,** part of the plantation, is a 2-story T-shaped Greek revival home dating from 1833. Union soldiers spared the house, which was a social center after the Civil

War. House tours operate Mon–Sat 10am–4pm and Sun 2–4pm.

Return to I-10 W at exit 30 and continue through the tunnel (free) to the downtown exit, staying in the right-hand lane, then follow the "?" sign for tourist information at:

10. **Mobile's welcome center,** 150 S Royal St (tel 205/434-7304), located in reconstructed Fort Condé, which is still furnished as it was in the 1740s under French rule. Costumed guides chronicle the French, British, Spanish, and American occupations of Mobile.

Next door to the tourist welcome center, on Theater St, is the city's first official jail, now known as the **Condé-Charlotte Museum House** (tel 205/432-4722); it is located in the Church Street East Historic District, Mobile's largest and second-oldest neighborhood. The museum houses 19th-century antiques and artifacts, as well as a period kitchen and Spanish garden.

Return to I-10 and go west and south 20 miles to exit 15A and:

11. **Bellingrath Gardens,** 12401 Bellingrath Garden Rd, Theodore, AL (tel 205/973-2217, or 205/973-

2365 for recorded information). This landscaped 65-acre floral wonderland has great views of the Isle-aux-Oies River amid the scent of dogwoods, roses, wisteria, and azaleas, the crowning glory of the South. The gardens are situated on a 906-acre estate including the Bellingrath home, a chapel, and the Delchamps Gallery, which has the world's largest public display of Boehm porcelain. The home, listed on the National Register of Historic Places, is furnished with antiques, fine china, and rare porcelain and is open to a small number of visitors at a time.

The gardens bloom all year, with each season offering its own splendor. In spring, azaleas in white, pink, lavender, purple, and rose adorn the grounds; summer serves a lush spread of hibiscus, allamandas, and mandevillas; autumn plays host to 60,000 cascading chrysanthemums; and in winter, a Christmas presentation is equally colorful with a spread of poinsettias, camellias, and winter annuals.

At dusk, when Bellingrath Gardens closes, you can retrace your steps to I-10 and head east 75 miles for a speedy return back to downtown Pensacola.

ALTAMONTE SPRINGS

Map page M-7, C2

Hotels 🏨

Altamonte Springs Hilton and Towers, 350 S North Lake Blvd, Altamonte Springs, FL 32715; tel 407/830-1985 or toll free 800/HILTONS; fax 407/830-9378. Exit 48 off I-4 E. More a corporate address than one for tourists. Sleek and appealing, and well maintained. **Rooms:** 325 rms and stes; 2 ctges/villas. CI 3pm/CO noon. Nonsmoking rms avail. Rooms have been recently renovated. **Amenities:** 🛎 🐾 A/C, cable TV w/movies, refrig. All units w/minibars. **Services:** ✗ ⊨ 🚐 ⌂ 🔑 Car-rental desk. **Facilities:** 🛗 🚗 & 1 rst, 1 bar, whirlpool. Guests receive free membership in Bally's Fitness Center across the highway. **Rates:** HS Jan–Mar $99–$129 D; from $250 ste; from $150 ctge/villa. Children under 18 stay free. Lower rates off-season. Higher rates for spec evnts/hols. AP and MAP rates avail. Spec packages avail. Pking: Outdoor, free. Maj CC.

Days Inn & Lodge, 450 Douglas Ave, Altamonte Springs, FL 32714; tel 407/862-7111 or toll free 800/327-2221. Exit 48 off I-4. A lowrise complex with a tree-filled courtyard. **Rooms:** 331 rms and stes. CI 3pm/CO 11:30am. Nonsmoking rms avail. **Amenities:** 🛎 A/C, cable TV, refrig, in-rm safe. Some units w/terraces. **Services:** ✗ ⊨ 🚐 ⌂ 🔑 Car-rental desk. **Facilities:** 🛗 🚗 1 rst, 1 bar, playground, washer/dryer. **Rates:** HS Dec/June–Sept $29–$59 S or D; from $39 ste. Children under 18 stay free. Lower rates off-season. Higher rates for spec evnts/hols. Spec packages avail. Pking: Outdoor, free. Maj CC. Weekly and monthly rates avail.

Embassy Suites Orlando North, 225 E Altamonte Dr, Altamonte Springs, FL 32701; tel 407/834-2400 or toll free 800/EMBASSY; fax 407/834-2117. Exit 48 off I-4. A modern all-suites hotel within walking distance of the local mall. **Rooms:** 210 stes. CI 3pm/CO noon. Nonsmoking rms avail. **Amenities:** 🛎 🐾 🖥 A/C, cable TV w/movies, refrig. All units w/terraces. Wet bars, microwaves. **Services:** ✗ 🚐 ⌂ 🔑 ⑊ Evening social hour. **Facilities:** 🛗 🏋 🚗 & 1 rst, 1 bar, games rm, sauna, steam rm, whirlpool, washer/dryer. **Rates (BB):** HS Jan–May from $134 ste. Extra person $15. Children under 17 stay free. Lower rates off-season. Higher rates for spec evnts/hols. Spec packages avail. Pking: Outdoor, free. Maj CC.

Hampton Inn Altamonte Springs, 151 N Douglas Ave, Altamonte Springs, FL 32714; tel 407/869-9000 or toll free 800/HAMPTON; fax 407/788-6746. Exit 48 off I-4. Offers pleasant surroundings and good value. Has been undergoing remodeling. **Rooms:** 210 rms. CI 4pm/CO noon. Nonsmoking rms avail.

Amenities: 🛎 🐾 A/C, cable TV, refrig. **Services:** ⊨ ⌂ 🔑 Car-rental desk. **Facilities:** 🛗 🏋 🚗 🖥 & 1 rst, whirlpool, washer/dryer. **Rates (CP):** $55–$62 S or D. Children under 18 stay free. Higher rates for spec evnts/hols. Pking: Outdoor, free. Maj CC.

Holiday Inn, 230 W Fla 436, Altamonte Springs, FL 32714; tel 407/862-4455 or toll free 800/242-6862; fax 407/682-5982. Exit 48 off I-4. A 4-story building with a pretty driveway leading to a well-maintained lobby and public area. The building wraps around the courtyard, which contains the pool and deck. **Rooms:** 197 rms and stes. CI 2pm/CO noon. Nonsmoking rms avail. **Amenities:** 🛎 🐾 A/C, cable TV w/movies. **Services:** ✗ 🆅🅿 🚐 ⌂ 🔑 Car-rental desk. **Facilities:** 🛗 🏋 🚗 & 1 rst, 1 bar (w/entertainment), games rm, playground, washer/dryer. **Rates:** HS Jan–May $69–$99 D; from $129 ste. Lower rates off-season. Higher rates for spec evnts/hols. Spec packages avail. Pking: Outdoor, free. Maj CC.

La Quinta Motor Inn, 150 S Westmonte Dr, Altamonte Springs, FL 32741; tel 407/788-1411 or toll free 800/531-5900; fax 407/788-6472. Exit 48 off I-4. Standardized, basic motel. **Rooms:** 115 rms and stes. CI noon/CO noon. Nonsmoking rms avail. **Amenities:** 🛎 🐾 A/C, cable TV w/movies. Some units w/terraces. **Services:** 🚐 ⌂ 🔑 ⑊ **Facilities:** 🛗 🚗 & Washer/dryer. **Rates (CP):** $59–$86 S or D; from $82 ste. Extra person $7. Children under 18 stay free. Higher rates for spec evnts/hols. Pking: Outdoor, free. Maj CC.

Residence Inn by Marriott, 270 Douglas Ave, Altamonte Springs, FL 32714; tel 407/788-7991 or toll free 800/331-3131; fax 407/869-5468. Exit 48 off I-4. A condo-like community featuring units ranging from studios with full kitchens to large units with separate bedrooms and living rooms with fireplaces. **Rooms:** 128 stes. CI 3pm/CO noon. Nonsmoking rms avail. **Amenities:** 🛎 🐾 🖥 A/C, cable TV w/movies, refrig, stereo/tape player. All units w/terraces, all w/fireplaces. Units outfitted with microwaves, icemakers, dishwashers, utensils, and ample cupboard space. **Services:** 🚐 ⌂ 🔑 ⑊ Guests have free use of Bally's Fitness Center. **Facilities:** 🛗 🚗 & Whirlpool, washer/dryer. **Rates (CP):** HS Mar–June from $89 ste. Lower rates off-season. Higher rates for spec evnts/hols. Spec packages avail. Pking: Outdoor, free. Maj CC.

Motel

Sundance Inn, 205 W Fla 436, Altamonte Springs, FL 32714; tel 407/862-8200; fax 407/862-8200. Exit 48 off I-4. Basic accommodations, with limited facilities and services. **Rooms:** 150 rms. CI 4pm/CO noon. Nonsmoking rms avail. **Amenities:** 🛎 A/C, cable TV. **Services:** ⌂ Continental breakfast. **Facilities:** 🛗 🚗 1 bar. **Rates (CP):** HS Mar–June $42–

$64 D. Children under 18 stay free. Lower rates off-season. Higher rates for spec evnts/hols. Spec packages avail. Pking: Outdoor, free. Maj CC.

AMELIA ISLAND
Map page M-5, B4

Resorts 🛏

🏳🏳🏳🏳 **Amelia Island Plantation**, Fla A1A S, Amelia Island, FL 32034; tel 904/261-6161 or toll free 800/874-6878; fax 904/277-5159. 6 mi S of Fla 200. 1,250 acres. One of Florida's most extensive resorts, sprawled along pristine ocean shoreline and encompassing a vast array of accommodations and dining and recreational facilities. Sure to please the tennis and golf enthusiast, as well as those seeking simple relaxation. **Rooms:** 525 rms and effic. CI 4pm/CO noon. Express checkout avail. Nonsmoking rms avail. **Amenities:** 🕾🔆📺 A/C, cable TV w/movies, refrig, voice mail, in-rm safe. Some units w/minibars, all w/terraces, some w/fireplaces, some w/Jacuzzis. **Services:** ✕ 🔑 🚐 ⛵ 🔧 Twice-daily maid svce, car-rental desk, social director, masseur, children's program, babysitting. Hard-working, highly competent management and staff ensure guests' needs are met. **Facilities:** 🏕 🚲 ⛰ 🎣 ▶45 ▲ 🏀 🏊15 🏊 🛩 600 🖥 ⅙ 6 rsts, 6 bars (1 w/entertainment), 1 beach (ocean), lifeguard, games rm, lawn games, racquetball, spa, sauna, steam rm, whirlpool, beauty salon, day-care ctr, playground, washer/dryer. **Rates:** HS Mar–Apr $175–$207 S; $180–$212 D; from $225 effic. Extra person $3.50. Children under 12 stay free. Lower rates off-season. Spec packages avail. Pking: Outdoor, free. Maj CC.

🏳🏳🏳🏳 **Ritz-Carlton Amelia Island**, 4750 Amelia Island Pkwy, Amelia Island, FL 32034; tel 904/277-1100 or toll free 800/241-3333; fax 904/261-9063. 26 mi N of Jacksonville, exit 129 off I-95. 26 acres. A fine deluxe establishment, constructed with the care and attention to detail familiar in other Florida Ritz-Carlton properties. Plush interior styling. Superior recreational facilities. **Rooms:** 449 rms and stes. CI 3pm/CO noon. Nonsmoking rms avail. All rooms have rich appointments and ocean views. **Amenities:** 🕾🔆🎽 A/C, cable TV w/movies, refrig, in-rm safe, bathrobes. All units w/minibars, all w/terraces, some w/fireplaces, some w/Jacuzzis. **Services:** 🍽 🔑 🅥🅟 ⛵ 🔧 Twice-daily maid svce, car-rental desk, social director, masseur, children's program, babysitting. **Facilities:** 🏕 🚲 ▶18 🏀 🏊6 🏊 🛩 🎱 🖥 ⅙ 2 rsts, 3 bars (1 w/entertainment), 1 beach (ocean), lawn games, spa, sauna, steam rm, whirlpool, beauty salon, playground. One of the pools is indoor. **Rates:** HS Oct 2–Nov 5 $205–$285 S or D; from $495 ste. Extra person $15.

Children under 18 stay free. Lower rates off-season. Higher rates for spec evnts/hols. Spec packages avail. Pking: Indoor/outdoor, free. Maj CC.

Attractions 🏛

Centre Street Historic District; tel 904/261-3248. This 50-block historic area of downtown Fernandina Beach boasts many restored 19th-century buildings housing shops, restaurants, and many homes in a carefully preserved Victorian setting that recalls the city's "golden age."

Amelia Island Museum of History, 233 S Third St; tel 904/261-7378. On display are artifacts from an excavation of a nearby 17th-century Spanish mission, many documents, and several greatly enlarged photographs of 19th-century Fernandina. A research library is here as well. A walking tour of the 50-block Centre Street Historic District includes interiors of a church and a Victorian home, and complimentary tea at a 19th-century inn. Tour begins at the Depot, Thurs and Fri at 3pm. Museum tours given Mon–Sat 11am and 2pm. **Open:** Mon–Fri 10am–5pm. $$

Fort Clinch State Park, 2601 Atlantic Ave; tel 904/277-7274. Two-thirds of this 1,100-acre park consist of hardwood hammock, the remainder of sandy dunes. The masonry fort built here in 1867 could garrison more than 500 men and had 74 gun emplacements. Rangers in period uniform stage a reenactment of life at the fort at the beginning of each month. Swimming, fishing, boating, hiking, camping, nature trail. **Open:** Daily 8am–sunset. $$

ANNA MARIA ISLAND
Map page M-8, B1

Restaurants 🍴

The Anchorage, 101 S Bay Blvd, Anna Maria, Anna Maria Island; tel 813/778-9611. **Seafood/Steak.** A relaxed, comfortable eatery with lovely beach and ocean views. The daily fresh fish offerings might include grouper, tuna, or mahimahi, and can be prepared grilled or blackened Cajun-style. **FYI:** Reservations accepted. Band/dancing. Children's menu. **Open:** Daily 11:30am–10pm. Closed Dec 25. **Prices:** Main courses $6.95–$19.95. Maj CC. 🏞 💟 ⅙

Rotten Ralph's, 902 S Bay Blvd, Anna Maria, Anna Maria Island; tel 813/778-3953. **American/British/Seafood.** Relax in a casual setting overlooking the bay as you dine on the fisherman's platter, crab cakes, deep-fried oysters, or chicken pot pie.

A good value. **FYI:** Reservations not accepted. **Open:** Daily 11am–9pm. Closed some hols. **Prices:** Main courses $9.95–$19.95. Ltd CC. ♿

Sandbar, 100 Spring Ave, Anna Maria, Anna Maria Island; tel 813/778-0444. Take Gulf Dr to Spring Ave. **Seafood.** Dine overlooking the Intracoastal Waterway. Menu highlights include crab dishes, shrimp sautéed with mushrooms and white wine, scallops in a light garlic butter, and various seafood combinations. Dinner discounts are offered in conjunction with an affiliated boat cruise. **FYI:** Reservations recommended. Guitar. Children's menu. **Open:** Lunch daily 11:30am–3pm; dinner daily 4–10pm. **Prices:** Main courses $9.95–$16.95. Maj CC. ♥ ♿

Shells in the Island Centre, 3200 E Bay Blvd, Holmes Beach, Anna Maria Island; tel 813/778-5997. **Seafood/Steak.** This brightly colored seafood restaurant, with mounted fish on the walls, is known for its large portions. A good value. **FYI:** Reservations not accepted. Children's menu. **Open:** Sun–Thurs 4–10pm, Fri–Sat 4–11pm. Closed Dec 25. **Prices:** Main courses $4.95–$14.95. Maj CC. ♿

APALACHICOLA

Map page M-3, D3

Attractions 💼

John Gorrie State Museum, 6th St at D Street; tel 904/653-9347. Seeking a way to cool the hospital rooms of malaria and yellow fever patients, Dr John Gorrie developed the first artificial cooling device, a forerunner of modern ice-makers and air conditioners. A model of the machine is on display, with a diagram of how it worked; there is also a diorama of the sick room first cooled by the machine. This small museum also houses exhibits on early Apalachicola history. **Open:** Thurs–Mon 9am–5pm; usually closed noon–1pm. Closed some hols. $

St George Island State Park; tel 904/927-2111. On St George Island, just south of Apalachicola via the toll bridge, this park offers miles of undeveloped, near-primitive beaches, plus dunes, forests, and marshes. Gulf swimming, fishing, boating, hiking, nature trails, camping. **Open:** Daily 8am–sunset. $$

St Vincent National Wildlife Refuge; tel 904/653-8808. Most of the refuge's 12,000 acres are on St Vincent Island, an undeveloped barrier island in Apalachicola Bay. Originally established as a waterfowl preserve, the refuge has broadened its scope to include such endangered species as bald eagles and loggerhead sea turtles. The visitor center houses exhibits on the wetlands and wildlife of the refuge and on Apalachicola Bay. Swimming in gulf, fishing, boating, hiking along old logging roads. **Open:** Refuge, daily dawn–dusk; visitor center Mon–Fri 8am–4:30pm. Closed some hols. Free.

APOPKA

Map page M-7, C1

Attraction 💼

Wekiwa Springs State Park, Wekiwa Circle; tel 407/884-2009. The varied topography of this 7,000-acre park includes everything from pine flatwoods and sand hills to hammock and swampland; 13 miles of trails survey much of it. Swimming, fishing, boating, canoe rentals, camping, hiking, nature trails. **Open:** Daily 8am–sunset. $$

ATLANTIC BEACH

Map page M-5, C4

Hotel 🛏

Sea Turtle Inn, 1 Ocean Blvd, Atlantic Beach, FL 32233; or toll free 800/874-6000; fax 904/241-7439. Just minutes from I-95 and I-10 via the 9A interchange. This 8-story oceanfront hotel offers ocean views from all rooms. Unrated. **Rooms:** 194 rms. CI 3pm/CO noon. Nonsmoking rms avail. Guest rooms have matching drapes, spreads, and valances. **Amenities:** 🛁 ♨ A/C, cable TV w/movies. Some units w/terraces. **Services:** ✗ 🚗 🖼 ♫ Babysitting. Complimentary coffee and newspaper daily. Happy hour held afternoons in lounge. **Facilities:** 🏋 600 ♿ 1 rst, 1 bar (w/entertainment), 1 beach (ocean), washer/dryer. **Rates:** HS Mar–Oct $89–$115 S or D. Children under 18 stay free. Min stay spec evnts. Lower rates off-season. Spec packages avail. Pking: Outdoor, free. Maj CC.

Restaurant 🍴

★ **Ragtime Tavern Seafood & Grill**, 207 Atlantic Blvd, Atlantic Beach; tel 904/241-7877. **Seafood/Vegetarian.** A home-style eatery with exposed brick and a country atmosphere. The bar, known as the Tap Room Brewery, serves beer made on the premises. The owner's mother makes award-winning key lime cheese cake. Live jazz at Sunday brunch. **FYI:** Reservations not accepted. Band/blues/jazz. Children's menu. **Open:** Sun–Thurs 11am–10:30pm, Fri–Sat 11am–11pm. Closed some hols. **Prices:** Main courses $4.95–$17.95. Maj CC. ♥ ♿

BAL HARBOUR

Map page M-11, B2

Hotel 🏨

▰▰▰▰ **Sheraton Bal Harbour Resort**, 9701 Collins Ave, Bal Harbour, FL 33154; tel 305/865-7511 or toll free 800/999-9898; fax 305/864-2601. 11 acres. A major force in the hotel market north of Miami Beach, featuring a fancy lobby and comfortable rooms. **Rooms:** 663 rms and stes; 26 ctges/villas. CI 3pm/CO noon. Express checkout avail. Nonsmoking rms avail. **Amenities:** 🎍 🏧 📺 🍷 A/C, cable TV w/movies, refrig, voice mail, bathrobes. Some units w/minibars, some w/terraces, some w/Jacuzzis. **Services:** ✗ ☎ 🆅🅿 📷 🍴 🛎 Car-rental desk, social director, children's program, babysitting. Security guards patrol beach and outdoor shower areas. **Facilities:** 🎣 ⛱ 🏊 🍹2 🍸 🎱 2.5K 💻 🚹 4 rsts, 2 bars, 1 beach (ocean), lifeguard, board surfing, games rm, snorkeling, playground. **Rates:** HS Oct–Dec $240–$300 S or D; from $500 ste; from $400 ctge/villa. Extra person $25. Children under 17 stay free. Lower rates off-season. Spec packages avail. Pking: Indoor, $9. Maj CC.

BELLEAIR BEACH

Map page M-6, E2

Motel 🏨

▰▰ **Belleair Beach Resort Motel**, 2040 Gulf Blvd, Belleair Beach, FL 34635; tel 813/595-1696 or toll free 800/780-1696; fax 813/593-5433. 3 mi S of Clearwater Beach. Directly on the beach and handy to shopping and restaurants. **Rooms:** 43 rms and effic. CI 2pm/CO 11am. **Amenities:** 🎍 🏧 A/C, cable TV, refrig. Some units w/terraces. **Services:** 🍴 **Facilities:** 🎣 1 beach (ocean), washer/dryer. Sailing and boating available nearby. **Rates:** HS Jan–Apr $68–$72 S or D; from $77 effic. Extra person $5. Children under 5 stay free. Min stay spec evnts. Lower rates off-season. Pking: Outdoor, free. Maj CC.

BIG PINE KEY

Map page M-10, E3

Motel 🏨

▰ **Parmer's Place Cottages**, Barry Ave near MM 28.5, PO Box 28.5, Big Pine Key, FL 33043; tel 305/872-2157; fax 305/872-2014. Modest but comfortable cottages available in a variety of configurations. Every unit is different: Some face the water while others are just a short walk away. Most contain 2 separate units that can be combined into one for large families. **Rooms:** 44 rms and effic. CI 3pm/CO 11am. Nonsmoking rms avail. Sparsely decorated but very clean. Some cottages have small kitchenettes, while others hold just a bedroom. **Amenities:** 🏧 A/C, cable TV. No phone. All units w/terraces. **Services:** 🍴 🛎 **Facilities:** 🎣 25 🚹 Washer/dryer. **Rates (CP):** HS Jan–Apr/July–Aug $66–$85 S or D; from $85 effic. Extra person $6.25–12.50. Min stay spec evnts. Lower rates off-season. Pking: Outdoor, free. Maj CC.

Restaurants 🍴

Baltimore Oyster House, Overseas Hwy, MM 30, Big Pine Key; tel 305/872-2314. **New American/Seafood.** Sea shells and fish netting adorn this casual restaurant. Sautéed reef snapper, deep-sea scallops, shrimp dishes. **FYI:** Reservations not accepted. Children's menu. Beer and wine only. **Open:** Mon–Sat 11:30am–10pm. Closed some hols. **Prices:** Main courses $8.95–$14.50. Maj CC. 🚹

Island Reef, Overseas Hwy, MM 31.3, Big Pine Key; tel 305/872-2170. **Regional American.** Overhead fans keep the breeze swirling in this nautically inspired cafe. Seafood dishes prepared a variety of ways. **FYI:** Reservations not accepted. Children's menu. Beer and wine only. **Open:** HS Dec–Apr breakfast Mon–Sat 6:30am–2:30pm, Sun 7am–1:30pm; dinner daily 5–9:30pm. Reduced hours off-season. Closed Dec 25. **Prices:** Main courses $8.95–$17.95. Ltd CC. 🚹

Attractions 🖼

Leda–Bruce Galleries, Overseas Hwy, MM 30.2; tel 305/372-0212. In short, this is the finest gallery between Miami and Key West. Some of the best works from the Keys' most important artists are exhibited. Also for sale are vintage clothes and antiques. **Open:** Mon–Sat 9am–5pm. Free.

National Key Deer Refuge, Overseas Hwy, MM 30; tel 305/872-2239 or toll free 800/872-2239. A preservation area for about two-thirds of the population of Key deer, which can most likely be observed in early morning or early evening. There is a nature walk 1.5 miles north of Watson Blvd on Key Deer Blvd. Nearby is Blue Hole, a depleted rock quarry inhabited by alligators. Refuge headquarters are located north of US 1 between Key Deer Blvd and Wilder Ave. **Open:** Daily; headquarters Mon–Fri. Free.

Bahia Honda State Park, Overseas Hwy, MM 37; tel 305/872-2353. The best park in the Lower Keys is spread out across

635 acres and offers large stretches of white sandy beach, the only natural sand beach in the Keys (most are coral). Deep waters close to shore are perfect for snorkeling and diving, and there are miles of trails packed with unusual plants and animals. Docking and camping facilities; beachside picnic areas with tables and grills. **Open:** Daily 8am–sunset. $$

Boca Grande

Map page M-8, D2

Motel ▣

≣ **Waterfront Motel**, Railroad and 11th Sts, Boca Grande, FL 33921; tel 813/964-2294; fax 813/964-0382. As its name implies, this motel is right on the water—in this case the Intracoastal Waterway. The 2-story coral-colored structure has a gravel driveway dotted with a handful of palms. **Rooms:** 32 rms and effic. CI 2pm/CO 11am. **Amenities:** ▣ ▣ A/C, cable TV, refrig. All units w/terraces. **Services:** ⊸ ⊸ **Facilities:** ▣ Restaurants are within walking distance. The old railroad bed out front is now used as a bicycle path and walking trail that extends the length of the island. **Rates:** HS Feb–July $100 S or D; from $125 effic. Extra person $10. Children under 10 stay free. Min stay HS and wknds. Lower rates off-season. Pking: Outdoor, free. Ltd CC.

Inn

≣ ≣ **Gasparilla Inn**, 5th Ave at Palm, Boca Grande, FL 33921; tel 813/964-2201; fax 813/964-2733. Built just after the turn of the century, this is a fine example of traditional innkeeping. The 3-story, bleached yellow-and-white structure is fronted by a porch. Inside is a look at a bygone era. **Rooms:** 145 rms and stes; 15 ctges/villas. CI 2pm/CO 11am. **Amenities:** ▣ A/C. Some units w/terraces, some w/fireplaces, all w/Jacuzzis. TVs are rented for $5. **Services:** ✕ ▣ ▣ ⊸ ⊸ Car-rental desk, social director, masseur, babysitting, afternoon tea served. **Facilities:** ▣ ⬤ ▶₁₈ ▣ ▣ ⬤ 2 rsts, 2 bars (1 w/entertainment), 1 beach (ocean), lifeguard, games rm, sauna, beauty salon, playground, guest lounge w/TV. **Rates (AP):** HS Dec–Apr $197–$400 S or D; from $392 ste; from $322 ctge/villa w/shared bath. Extra person $82. Children under 2 stay free. Lower rates off-season. Pking: Outdoor, free. Ltd CC. Closed: Mid June–Nov.

Restaurant ▮▮▮

Theater Restaurant, in Old Theatre Mall, 4th and Park Aves, Boca Grande; tel 813/964-0806. **Seafood/Steak/Pasta.** This 2-story restaurant with an outdoor dining room uses unpainted

wood and candlelight to create a natural, intimate atmosphere. Daily specials regularly include 5 kinds of fresh fish. The key lime chicken is a specialty. **FYI:** Reservations recommended. Guitar. Children's menu. **Open:** Lunch Mon–Sat 11:30am–2:30pm; dinner Mon–Sat 5:30–10pm. Closed Dec 25; Aug–Sept. **Prices:** Main courses $12–$22. Ltd CC. ▣ ⬤

Attractions ▣

Cayo Costa Island State Park; tel 813/964-0375. The park encompasses most of the Cayo Costa, an unspoiled island paradise of deserted white sand beaches, pine forest, mangrove swamp, and oak palm hammocks. Shelling is especially good on the northern portion of the island, and the swimming is excellent. Fishing, boating, picnicking, and primitive camping are allowed. Access by boat only. For cabin rentals and information contact Barrier Islands GEO Park, PO Box 1150, Boca Grande, FL 33921. **Open:** Daily 8am–sunset. $

Gasparilla Island State Recreation Area; tel 813/964-0375. Located on the southern end of Gasparilla Island, the park features year-round swimming and excellent saltwater fishing in the Gulf of Mexico. The historic Boca Grande Lighthouse (circa 1890) is located at the southern tip of the park. It has been completely restored and current plans include the addition of an interpretive center. Picnic areas. **Open:** Daily 8am–sunset. $

Boca Raton

Map page M-9, E4

Hotels ▣

≣ ≣ ≣ **Boca Raton Marriott Crocker Center**, 5150 Town Center Circle, Boca Raton, FL 33486; tel 407/392-4600 or toll free 800/962-9786; fax 407/369-9223. Exit 39 off I-95. This business hotel leader features a handsome marble lobby that makes a nice first impression. Near a shopping mall. **Rooms:** 256 rms and stes. CI 3pm/CO noon. Nonsmoking rms avail. **Amenities:** ▣ ⬤ A/C, cable TV w/movies. All units w/minibars, all w/terraces. **Services:** ✕ ▣ ▣ ⊸ Car-rental desk, babysitting. **Facilities:** ▣ ▣ ▣ ⬤ 1 rst, 1 bar, steam rm, whirlpool. **Rates:** HS Dec–Apr $159 S or D; from $209 ste. Extra person $15. Children under 18 stay free. Lower rates off-season. Higher rates for spec evnts/hols. Spec packages avail. Pking: Outdoor, $6.50. Maj CC.

≣ ≣ ≣ **The Bridge Hotel**, 999 E Camino Real, Boca Raton, FL 33432; tel 407/368-9500 or toll free 800/327-0130; fax 407/362-0492. Located on a waterway next to a small bridge, from which the hotel takes its name. This commendable hotel has a cozy lobby and attractive guest rooms. **Rooms:** 121 rms and stes. CI 3pm/CO noon. Nonsmoking rms avail. **Amenities:** 🎁 ⚗ 🍷 A/C, cable TV. All units w/terraces. **Services:** ✗ 🆅🅿 🛆 ⌇ Babysitting. **Facilities:** 🖼 ⚙ ⚠ 🏌 🔲 ⅙ 2 rsts, 2 bars (1 w/entertainment), sauna. Rooftop restaurant. **Rates:** HS Dec–Apr $140–$175 S; $150–$185 D; from $280 ste. Extra person $10. Children under 18 stay free. Min stay HS. Lower rates off-season. Spec packages avail. Pking: Indoor/outdoor, free. Maj CC.

🏢🏢 **Courtyard by Marriott**, 2000 NW Executive Court, Boca Raton, FL 33431; tel 407/998-7621 or toll free 800/321-2211; fax 407/241-7080. Exit 39 off I-95. A pretty and well-kept facility offering pleasing accommodations and better-than-average decor. **Rooms:** 152 rms and stes. CI 3pm/CO noon. Express checkout avail. Nonsmoking rms avail. **Amenities:** 🎁 ⚗ 🔲 A/C, cable TV w/movies, voice mail. Some units w/terraces. **Services:** 🛆 ⌇ **Facilities:** 🖼 🏌 🔲 ⅙ 1 rst, 1 bar (w/entertainment), whirlpool, washer/dryer. Restaurant open for breakfast only. **Rates:** HS Dec–Apr $110 S; $120 D; from $130 ste. Children under 18 stay free. Lower rates off-season. Pking: Outdoor, free. Maj CC.

🏢🏢🏢 **Crown Sterling Suites Hotel**, 701 NW 53rd St, Boca Raton, FL 33487; tel 407/997-9500 or toll free 800/433-460; fax 407/994-3565. Exit 40 off I-95. A Southwest-accented hotel marked by a handsome courtyard. **Rooms:** 182 stes. CI 3pm/CO 1pm. Express checkout avail. Nonsmoking rms avail. **Amenities:** 🎁 ⚗ 🔲 A/C, cable TV w/movies, refrig, voice mail. All units have microwaves. **Services:** ✗ 🛆 ⌇ 🍴 Babysitting. **Facilities:** 🖼 ⚙ 🔲 ⅙ 1 rst, whirlpool, washer/dryer. **Rates (BB):** HS Dec–Apr $149 S; $159 D. Extra person $10. Children under 12 stay free. Lower rates off-season. Spec packages avail. Pking: Outdoor, free. Maj CC.

🏢🏢🏢 **Embassy Suites Boca Raton**, 661 NW 53rd St, Boca Raton, FL 33487; tel 407/994-8200 or toll free 800/521-9183; fax 407/994-9518. Exit 40 off I-95. An appealing, midrise, all-suites hotel. Atrium. **Rooms:** 263 stes. CI 3pm/CO noon. Nonsmoking rms avail. **Amenities:** 🎁 ⚗ 🔲 🍷 A/C, cable TV w/movies, refrig, voice mail, in-rm safe. All units w/terraces. **Services:** ✗ 🔜 🆅🅿 🛆 ⌇ Car-rental desk, masseur, babysitting. **Facilities:** 🖼 ⚙ 🏌 🔲 ⅙ 1 rst, 1 bar, games rm, sauna, whirlpool, washer/dryer. **Rates (BB):** HS Dec–Apr from $159 ste. Extra person $10. Children under 12 stay free. Lower rates off-season. Higher rates for spec evnts/hols. Spec packages avail. Pking: Indoor/outdoor, free. Maj CC.

🏢🏢🏢 **Holiday Inn Glades Road**, 1950 W Glades Rd, Boca Raton, FL 33431; tel 407/368-5200 or toll free 800/HOLIDAY; fax 407/395-4783. Exit 39 off I-95. Featuring a lobby set in Mexican tile adjoining a sunny courtyard. **Rooms:** 185 rms and

stes. CI 2pm/CO noon. Nonsmoking rms avail. Upholstered reading chairs in each room. **Amenities:** 🎁 ⚗ A/C, cable TV w/movies. All units w/terraces, some w/Jacuzzis. **Services:** ✗ 🛆 ⌇ Car-rental desk. **Facilities:** 🖼 🏌 🔲 ⅙ 1 rst, 3 bars (1 w/entertainment), games rm, whirlpool, beauty salon. **Rates:** HS Dec–Apr $125–$150 S; $135–$160 D; from $199 ste. Extra person $5. Children under 16 stay free. Lower rates off-season. Pking: Indoor/outdoor, free. Maj CC.

🏢🏢 **Holiday Inn West**, 8144 Glades Rd, Boca Raton, FL 33434; tel 407/482-7070 or toll free 800/HOLIDAY; fax 407/482-6076. Glades Rd exit off Fla Tpk. Satisfactory lodging with a bar that's probably more popular than the hotel. **Rooms:** 100 rms. CI 2pm/CO noon. Nonsmoking rms avail. A few units open to the pool area. **Amenities:** 🎁 ⚗ A/C, cable TV w/movies. Some units w/terraces. **Services:** ✗ 🛆 ⌇ Babysitting. **Facilities:** 🖼 ⅙ 1 rst, 2 bars (1 w/entertainment), games rm. Extremely busy restaurant and sports bar has memorabilia of baseball great Pete Rose, who is a part-owner. **Rates:** HS Dec–Apr $99 S; $105 D. Extra person $6. Children under 18 stay free. Lower rates off-season. Higher rates for spec evnts/hols. Spec packages avail. Pking: Outdoor, free. Maj CC.

🏢🏢🏢 **Radisson Suites Hotel**, 7920 Glades Rd, Boca Raton, FL 33434; tel 407/483-3600 or toll free 800/333-3333; fax 407/479-2280. Very appealing hotel earns high marks for its good blend of business and leisure facilities. Public areas are noteworthy for their eye-catching look. Hardworking housekeeping staff keeps everything spotless. **Rooms:** 200 stes. CI 3pm/CO noon. Nonsmoking rms avail. **Amenities:** 🎁 ⚗ 🔲 🍷 A/C, cable TV w/movies, VCR, stereo/tape player, voice mail, bathrobes. All units w/minibars, some w/terraces. **Services:** 🛆 ⌇ 🍴 Babysitting. **Facilities:** 🖼 🏌 🔲 ⅙ 1 rst, 1 bar, whirlpool, washer/dryer. **Rates (BB):** HS Feb–Apr from $175 ste. Extra person $10. Children under 18 stay free. Lower rates off-season. Pking: Outdoor, free. Maj CC.

🏢🏢 **Ramada Hotel of Boca Raton**, 2901 N Federal Hwy, Boca Raton, FL 33431; tel 407/395-6850 or toll free 800/228-2828; fax 407/368-7964. Between Glades Rd and Spanish River Rd on US 1. A tropical-themed, 4-story hotel with a rather glitzy lobby with a fountain and lots of jungle foliage. **Rooms:** 93 rms and stes. CI 3pm/CO noon. Nonsmoking rms avail. **Amenities:** 🎁 A/C, cable TV. Some units w/terraces. **Services:** ✗ 🛆 ⌇ Twice-daily maid svce. **Facilities:** 🖼 🔲 ⅙ 1 rst, 1 bar, spa, whirlpool. **Rates:** HS Dec–Apr $85–$95 S or D; from $105 ste. Children under 18 stay free. Lower rates off-season. Pking: Outdoor, free. Maj CC.

🏢🏢🏢 **Residence Inn by Marriott**, 525 NW 77th St, Boca Raton, FL 33487; tel 407/994-3222 or toll free 800/331-3131; fax 407/994-3339. Congress Ave exit off I-95. Located on a manmade lake, this all-suites hotel in a pastoral setting features a sports court with tennis, volleyball, and basketball. **Rooms:** 120 stes. CI 3pm/CO noon. Nonsmoking rms avail. **Amenities:** 🛍 ⚕️ 🖭 A/C, cable TV w/movies, refrig. Some units w/terraces, all w/fireplaces. VCRs available on request. **Services:** 🛆 ⌁ 🐾 Babysitting. Social hour held Mon–Thurs 5–7pm. **Facilities:** 🚣 🍴 🎾 & Whirlpool, washer/dryer. Breakfast served in club-house with fireplace. Gold's Gym is free to guests. **Rates (CP):** HS Dec–Apr from $169 ste. Children under 18 stay free. Lower rates off-season. Pking: Outdoor, free. Maj CC.

≣≣≣ **Sheraton Boca Raton Hotel & Towers**, 2000 NW 19th St, Boca Raton, FL 33431; tel 407/368-5252 or toll free 800/394-7829; fax 407/750-5437. 2.5 mi E of Fla Tpk. Glades Rd W exit off I-95. Close to a mall. **Rooms:** 192 rms and stes. CI 3pm/CO noon. Nonsmoking rms avail. **Amenities:** 🛍 ⚕️ A/C, cable TV w/movies. Some units w/terraces. **Services:** ✗ 🛆 ⌁ Twice-daily maid svce, car-rental desk, babysitting. **Facilities:** 🚣 🍴 🎾 600 & 1 rst, 1 bar (w/entertainment), games rm, washer/dryer. **Rates (CP):** HS Dec–Apr $125 S or D; from $195 ste. Extra person $10. Children under 12 stay free. Lower rates off-season. Higher rates for spec evnts/hols. Spec packages avail. Pking: Outdoor, free. Maj CC.

Motel

≣ **Shore Edge Motel**, 425 N Ocean Blvd, Boca Raton, FL 33432; tel 407/395-4491 or toll free 800/BOCA SUN. 1 block N of Palmetto Park Rd. A mom-and-pop motel. **Rooms:** 16 rms and effic. CI 1pm/CO 11am. Efficiencies with full baths, standard rooms with showers only. **Amenities:** 🛍 A/C, cable TV, refrig. **Services:** ⌁ **Facilities:** 🚣 Washer/dryer. **Rates:** HS Dec–Apr $55–$75 S or D; from $75 effic. Extra person $10. Lower rates off-season. Pking: Outdoor, free. Ltd CC.

Resort

≣≣≣≣ **Boca Raton Resort & Club**, 501 E Camino Real, PO Box 5025, Boca Raton, FL 33431; tel 407/395-3000 or toll free 800/327-0101; fax 407/391-3183. Exit 38 or 37 off I-95. 356 acres. Back in the 1920s, the Cloisters, as it was then known, was one of the pace-setting pamperers to winter-weary northerners, and a pioneer of the Spanish-Moorish style of Florida's grand hotels. The original Cloister wing still retains its placid courtyards and tiled fountains, but the Boca Raton now incorporates a 27-story tower and a midrise beach resort across the Intracoastal Waterway. And the nabobs have been replaced by conventioneers (3 guests in every 4 are there for a business meeting); some vacationers may think twice about checking into a resort with signs saying "Shhhh! You're friends are sleeping. . ." However, if resorts were judged solely on their sports

facilities, the Boca Raton would rate 6 out of 5—everything here is offered in duplicate or better. **Rooms:** 963 rms, stes, and effic; 120 ctges/villas. Exec-level rms avail. CI 3pm/CO noon. Express checkout avail. Nonsmoking rms avail. Lodgings vary from cramped and makeshift to spacious and sunny, with the most stylish in the Beach Club, although many guests prefer the traditional styling of the Cloister, especially those rooms facing the inner courtyard. **Amenities:** 🛍 ⚕️ 🖭 A/C, cable TV w/movies, refrig, voice mail, in-rm safe, bathrobes. All units w/minibars, some w/terraces, 1 w/Jacuzzi. **Services:** 🍴 🖭 🖭 🔴 🛆 ⌁ Twice-daily maid svce, car-rental desk, social director, masseur, children's program, babysitting. Concierge International Program; Shuttle service 7am–3am to Beach Club and Country Club. **Facilities:** 🚣 🎿 🔺 🚤 🛥36 🎣 🏊23 🎾 ➤ 🍴 🎱 & 8 rsts, 8 bars (2 w/entertainment), 1 beach (ocean), lifeguard, games rm, lawn games, racquetball, snorkeling, squash, sauna, steam rm, whirlpool, beauty salon, day-care ctr, playground. 2 croquet courts, 4 indoor racquetball courts, 3 fitness centers, 111 beach cabanas, 24-slip marina (offering sailing, fishing, power craft, even Wave Runners and boogie boards). The original El Patio Restaurant in imposing Spanish grandee style has now been relegated to a breakfast room. **Rates:** HS Dec 20–Apr 30 $220–$390 S or D; from $375 ste. Extra person $30. Children under 16 stay free. Lower rates off-season. AP and MAP rates avail. Spec packages avail. Pking: Outdoor, $8. Maj CC. Rates determined by location rather than size or amenities, the least expensive being in the original wing, the most expensive by the beach.

Restaurants 🍽️

Baci, in Mizner Park, 344 Plaza Real, Boca Raton; tel 407/362-8500. **Italian.** A casual, upscale Italian eatery with a festive atmosphere. You can sit indoors in wrought-iron chairs at black-topped tables and watch your meal being prepared in the spotless open kitchen. Or, if you prefer, dine on the outdoor patio as you watch the crowds go by. Poached pear and pecan risotto, and angel hair pasta with shrimp, scallops, and mussels are specialties. **FYI:** Reservations accepted. **Open:** Lunch Mon–Sat 11:30am–2:30pm; brunch Sun 11am–3pm. Closed Dec 25. **Prices:** Main courses $9.95–$16.95. Maj CC. 🍷 🖭 &

Bistro l'Europe, in Mizner Park, 346 Plaza Real, Boca Raton; tel 407/368-4488. **Continental/French.** Rich walnut furnishings and flooring, French artwork, and an attractively displayed selection of wines set the scene at this relaxed, civilized bistro. The menu, featuring continental cuisine with a French flair, includes rack of lamb, couscous-stuffed cornish game hen, veal medallions, and black angus steak au poivre. **FYI:** Reservations recommended. **Open:** Lunch Mon–Sat 11:30am–5pm; dinner daily 6–11pm. **Prices:** Main courses $16–$24; PF dinner $55. Maj CC. ♙ VP &

Cafe Ole, in Arvida Parkway Center, 7860 Glades Rd, Boca Raton; tel 407/852-8063. Exit 75 off Fla Tp. **Mexican.** Spanish tile and nuevo Mexican decor help to create a comfortable, festive atmosphere here. The cantina's covered patio overlooks a manmade lake. The chili relleno is a house specialty. Three fresh fish entrees are offered daily. **FYI:** Reservations accepted. Children's menu. Beer and wine only. **Open:** Mon–Thurs 5:30–10pm, Fri–Sat 5–10:30pm, Sun 5–9:30pm. Closed Thanksgiving. **Prices:** Main courses $7–$14. Maj CC. ♙ VP &

Coppola's, in Crocker Center, 5250 Town Center Circle, Boca Raton; tel 407/368-7400. **Italian/Seafood.** Sophisticated, with an elaborate wine selection. The menu includes lobster from South Africa as well as Maine, veal, chicken, and pasta dishes. **FYI:** Reservations recommended. **Open:** Lunch Mon–Sat 11:30am–2:30pm; dinner Sun–Thurs 5:30–10pm, Fri–Sat 5:30–11pm. Closed Thanksgiving. **Prices:** Main courses $10–$22; PF dinner $50. Maj CC. ♙ VP &

♥ **The Gazebo Cafe**, 4199 N Federal Hwy, Boca Raton; tel 407/395-6033. **French.** An excellent dining experience on all counts. Decorated in antiques, crisp linen, and French art, with a marble-topped bar overlooking the spotless open kitchen. A grand chandelier dominates the room. The French menu regularly includes rack of lamb, chateaubriand for two, fresh salmon and scallops, and veal medallion. **FYI:** Reservations accepted. Piano/singer. **Open:** Lunch Mon–Fri 11:30am–3pm; dinner daily 5:30–10pm. Closed some hols. **Prices:** Main courses $16–$29. Maj CC. ♥ &

Joe Muer Seafood, 6450 N Federal Hwy, Boca Raton; tel 407/997-6688. **Seafood.** A favorite South Florida spot for fresh seafood at good prices. Scallops, mussels, stone crabs, and many other kinds of ocean treats are served in a relaxing atmosphere. **FYI:** Reservations accepted. Piano. Children's menu. **Open:** Mon–Fri 11:30am–10pm, Sun 3:30–10pm. **Prices:** Main courses $14–$27. Maj CC. ♥ VP &

La Finestra, 171 E Palmetto Park Rd, Boca Raton; tel 407/392-1838. **Italian.** A petite, romantic Italian cafe adorned with pink linen and fresh roses. Fare includes antipasti as well as pasta, chicken, fish, and beef tenderloin dishes. The pasta with crabmeat, clams, and shrimp in a light tomato sauce is a house specialty. **FYI:** Reservations accepted. Beer and wine only. **Open:** Daily 6–10pm. **Prices:** Main courses $12.95–$28.95. Maj CC. &

L'Auberge le Grillon, 6900 N Federal Hwy, Boca Raton; tel 407/997-6888. **French.** A tiny, antique-filled, vine-covered cottage with an intimate atmosphere. The traditional French menu typically includes veal and beef tenderloin medallions, the chef's fresh seafood specialty, and a particularly good vegetable platter. There is a fine selection of wines. Banquet facilities are available for small or large parties. **FYI:** Reservations recommended. Dress code. Beer and wine only. No smoking. **Open:** Daily 6–9:30pm. **Prices:** Main courses $19.95–$31.95; PF dinner $19.94. Maj CC. VP &

♥ ❋ **La Vieille Maison**, 770 E Palmetto Park Rd, Boca Raton; tel 407/391-6701. 1½ blocks W of Fla A1A. **French.** An old, rustic Mediterranean-style manor house filled with antiques, handsome dark carpets, and loads of country-French charm. Dine in one of several intimate rooms, each of which holds only 2 or 3 cozy linen-covered tables. This restaurant is celebrated for both its service and its classic cuisine. Appetizers include bell pepper soup and open-faced ravioli with duck confit and sage butter. For dinner, options include roast rack of lamb with thyme and goat cheese, and salmon wrapped in rice paper. **FYI:** Reservations recommended. Dress code. **Open:** Daily 6–9:30pm. **Prices:** Main courses $17–$35; PF dinner $35–$49. Maj CC. ▪ VP &

Le Truc, 299 E Palmetto Park Rd, Boca Raton; tel 407/392-4568. **Vietnamese.** Authentic Vietnamese dishes served in simple but attractive surroundings. Popular among locals. French pastries for dessert. **FYI:** Reservations accepted. Beer and wine only. **Open:** Lunch Mon–Sat 11am–2:30pm; dinner Mon–Sat 5–10pm, Sun 5–9pm. **Prices:** Main courses $11–$16. Maj CC.

Maxaluna Tuscan Grill, in the Crocker Center, 5050 Town Center Circle No 245, Boca Raton; tel 407/391-7177. **Italian.** Trendy, stylish restaurant serving innovative contemporary northern Italian cuisine, with many dishes prepared on the Tuscan oak-fired grill. Wide selection of wines by the glass. **FYI:** Reservations accepted. **Open:** Lunch Mon–Fri 11:30am–2:30pm; dinner Sun–Fri 6–10pm, Sat 6pm–10:30. Closed Thanksgiving. **Prices:** Main courses $16–$33. Maj CC. ♙ &

Max's Grille, in Mizner Park, 404 Plaza Real, Boca Raton; tel 407/368-0080. **New American.** A casually elegant art-deco bistro and bar with an innovative menu that includes New York strip steak or yellowfin tuna prepared on the oak wood grill, as well as a variety of creative salads. **FYI:** Reservations accepted. **Open:** Dinner Mon–Thurs 5:30–10:30pm, Fri–Sat 5–11pm, Sun 5–10pm; brunch Sat 11:30am–2:30pm, Sun 11:30am–3pm. Closed Dec 25. **Prices:** Main courses $9.95–$19.95. Maj CC. VP &

Morada Bar & Grill, in Crocker Center, 5100 Town Center Circle, Boca Raton; tel 407/395-0805. **Regional American.** An architecturally impressive dining room downstairs and a plum-toned bar upstairs. Consider the homemade pasta such as the black linguine or half-moon ravioli, or one of the more tradition-al dishes, like baby-back ribs or rack of lamb. **FYI:** Reservations recommended. **Open:** Lunch Mon–Fri 11:30am–2:30pm; dinner daily 5:30–10:30pm. **Prices:** Main courses $13–$30. Maj CC. 🚢 ☑ VP ⅙

Nick's Italian Fishery, in One Boca Place, 2255 Glades Rd, Boca Raton; tel 407/994-2201. **Seafood/Pasta.** Enjoy seafood dishes prepared Italian-style in an attractive, upbeat dining room with a wall of windows and a thousand-gallon aquarium. The popular eatery is known for its huge portions. **FYI:** Reservations recommended. Band/piano. Children's menu. Dress code. **Open:** Lunch daily 11:30am–2:30pm; dinner daily 5–11pm. **Prices:** Main courses $14–$25. Maj CC. ♥ 🚢 ☑ VP ⅙

Outback Steakhouse, in the Shoppes at Village Pointe, 6030 18th St SW, Boca Raton; tel 407/338-6283. **Seafood/Steak.** This rustic steakhouse, housed in a vibrant pink edifice, keeps its patrons happy with enormous portions and a rollicking atmo-sphere. **FYI:** Reservations not accepted. Children's menu. **Open:** Mon–Thurs 4:30–10:30pm, Fri–Sat 4–11:30pm, Sun 4–10:30pm. Closed Dec 25. **Prices:** Main courses $9–$18. Maj CC. ⅙

Peking, 2300 N Federal Hwy, Boca Raton; tel 407/392-0666. **Chinese.** Standard Chinese menu offered in a casual setting. **FYI:** Reservations accepted. Dress code. **Open:** Daily 11:45am–10pm. Closed Thanksgiving. **Prices:** Main courses $6.95–$14.95. Maj CC. ⅙

Prezzo, in Arvida Parkway Center, 7820 Glades Rd, Boca Raton; tel 407/451-2800. Glades Rd exit off Fla Tpk. **Italian/Pizza.** A stylish, upbeat restaurant with a contemporary northern Italian menu designed to make the most of the kitchen's wood-fired brick oven. A young and friendly staff serves brick-oven pizzas and other house specialties. If you have to wait for a table at this popular place, you can enjoy a drink at one of the attractive bar area's granite-topped tables. **FYI:** Reservations not accepted. Children's menu. **Open:** Lunch Mon–Fri 11:30am–2:30pm; dinner Mon–Thurs 5:30–11pm, Fri–Sat 5pm–midnight, Sun 5–10pm. Closed Thanksgiving. **Prices:** Main courses $8–$16. Maj CC. ⅙

Tom's Place, 7251 N Federal Hwy, Boca Raton; tel 407/997-0920. **Soul/Southern.** A casual eatery with vinyl table-cloths and customers' pictures on the walls. Known for its food, not its decor. The specialties here are Tom's meaty baby-back ribs, his St Louis–style barbecue, and chicken prepared to order,

either barbecued or fried. **FYI:** Reservations not accepted. Children's menu. Beer and wine only. **Open:** Mon 4–10pm, Tues–Fri 11:30am–10pm, Sat noon–10pm. Closed some hols. **Prices:** Main courses $5.95–$16.50. Ltd CC. ⅙

Uncle Tai's, in Crocker Center, 5250 Town Center Circle, Boca Raton; tel 407/368-8806. **Chinese.** The menu is as sophisticat-ed as the decor in this handsome, refined Chinese restaurant, done in linen and polished woods. Specialties include Hunan-style sliced lamb. **FYI:** Reservations accepted. **Open:** Lunch Mon–Sat 11:30am–2:30pm; dinner Sun–Thurs 5–10pm, Fri–Sat 5–10:30pm. Closed Thanksgiving. **Prices:** Main courses $8–$17. Maj CC. 🚢 ☑ VP ⅙

Wilt Chamberlain's, in Somerset Shoppes, 8903 W Glades Rd, Boca Raton; tel 407/488-8881. **American.** Sports memorabilia, TV monitors, and video games fill this gala sports bar and restaurant. Both the food and the atmosphere make this a great family eatery. However, the same features that make this place festive and fun can also make it a madhouse at times. **FYI:** Reservations not accepted. Children's menu. **Open:** Daily 11:30am–1:30am. Closed Thanksgiving. **Prices:** Main courses $5.45–$14. Maj CC. 🎮 ⅙

Woolley's Cafe, in Royal Palm Plaza, 25 Royal Palm Plaza, Boca Raton; tel 407/392-2977. **Cafe.** A cheerful, casual cafe where you can enjoy a variety of salads and sandwiches, as well as frozen yogurt. **FYI:** Reservations not accepted. Children's menu. No liquor license. No smoking. **Open:** Mon–Sat 9am–5:30pm, Sun 11am–4pm. Closed some hols. **Prices:** Main courses $3.25–$10. No CC. ⅙

Attractions 💼

Boca Raton Museum of Art, 801 W Palmetto Park Rd; tel 407/392-2500. In addition to a small permanent collection that is strongest in 19th-century European oils, the museum holds temporary exhibitions by local and international artists. **Open:** Mon–Fri 10am–4pm, Sun noon–4pm. Closed some hols. $

Children's Science Exploratorium, 131 SE Mizner Blvd, Suite 15; tel 407/395-8401. Located in the Royal Palm Plaza shopping center. Interactive exhibits teach children how things work. Displays on magnetic fields, bridge construction, gravitational forces, and computer technology. **Open:** Tues–Sat 10am–5pm, Sun noon–5pm. Closed some hols. $

BOKEELIA
Map page M-8, D3

Restaurant 🍴

Bokeelia Crab Shack, Main St, Bokeelia; tel 813/283-2466. **Seafood.** Enjoy the water view while dining at this seafood palace. Among the tasty selections are a variety of shrimp dishes and oysters served on the half-shell. Follow your meal with a piece of key lime pie. **FYI:** Reservations not accepted. **Open:** Daily 11am–9pm. **Prices:** Main courses $5–$17. No CC. ♿

BONITA SPRINGS
Map page M-8, E4

Motel 🛏

≣≣ Comfort Inn Motel, 9800 Bonita Beach Rd, Bonita Springs, FL 33923; tel 813/992-5001 or toll free 800/892-3605; fax 813/992-9283. Exit 18 off I-75. A 3-story motel featuring a handsome courtyard with oversized pool. **Rooms:** 69 rms. CI 3pm/CO 11am. Nonsmoking rms avail. **Amenities:** 🛎 🅐 A/C, cable TV w/movies, refrig, in-rm safe. All units w/terraces. All units with wet bars. **Services:** 🖼 🍴 **Facilities:** 🔒 ♿ 1 rst, 1 bar, whirlpool, washer/dryer. **Rates:** HS Dec–Apr $90 S; $95 D. Extra person $5. Children under 10 stay free. Lower rates off-season. Pking: Outdoor, free. Maj CC.

Restaurants 🍴

McCully's Rooftop, in Rooftop Plaza, 25999 Hickory Blvd, Bonita Springs; tel 813/992-0033. **Continental.** The bar, shaped like a ship's bow, and the views of Back Bay give this spot nautical atmosphere. Watch the sun set on the gulf as you dine. Consider the roast beef, the seafood strudel, the prime rib, or the catch of the day for dinner. **FYI:** Reservations accepted. Dancing/piano/singer. Children's menu. Dress code. **Open:** HS Dec–Apr daily 11:30am–midnight. Reduced hours off-season. Closed Dec 25. **Prices:** Main courses $8–$22. Maj CC. 🏔 🆅🅿 ♿

Springs Garden Restaurant & Lounge, 24080 N Tamiami Trail, Bonita Springs; tel 813/947-3333. 5 mi N of Bonita Beach Rd. **Continental/French.** Decorated with artificial flowers to create the atmosphere of a spring garden. A fake tree is the bar's centerpiece. The veal and the prime rib are the most popular entrees. **FYI:** Reservations accepted. Band/jazz. Children's menu. **Open:** Mon–Fri 11:30am–2am, Sat–Sun 4pm–2am. **Prices:** Main courses $10–$17. Maj CC. 🖤 ♿

BOYNTON BEACH
Map page M-9, D4

Hotel 🛏

≣≣ Holiday Inn–Catalina, 1601 N Congress Ave, Boynton Beach, FL 33436; tel 407/737-4600 or toll free 800/23-HOTEL; fax 407/734-6523. 1 mi N of Boynton Beach Blvd. A fine choice off the beach, good for families and business clientele alike. Spanish-style courtyard with pool and palms is popular among guests. Boynton Beach Mall is next door. **Rooms:** 152 rms and effic. CI 2pm/CO noon. Nonsmoking rms avail. **Amenities:** 🛎 🅐 A/C, cable TV w/movies. All units w/terraces. **Services:** ✕ 🖼 🍴 Car-rental desk. Housekeeping can be a little slow. **Facilities:** 🔒 🏊 ♿ 1 rst, 1 bar, whirlpool. Popular dance club. **Rates:** HS Dec–Apr $105–$120 S or D; from $120 effic. Children under 18 stay free. Lower rates off-season. Pking: Outdoor, free. Maj CC.

Hotels 🛏

≣≣ Holiday Inn Express, 480 W Boynton Beach Blvd, Boynton Beach, FL 33435; tel 407/734-9100 or toll free 800/HOLIDAY; fax 407/734-9100 ext 252. Exit 44 off I-95. No surprises here, just the basic amenities. A slimmed-down version of the bigger Holiday Inns. Only 1 mile from the beach. **Rooms:** 102 rms. CI 2pm/CO noon. Nonsmoking rms avail. **Amenities:** 🛎 🅐 A/C, cable TV. **Services:** 🍴 Cocktail party offered Mon–Sat 5–7pm. **Facilities:** 🔒 🏊 ♿ **Rates (CP):** HS Dec–Apr $59 S; $69 D. Children under 19 stay free. Lower rates off-season. Pking: Outdoor, free. Maj CC. AARP discounts available.

Restaurants 🍴

✶ **Banana Boat Restaurant**, 739 E Ocean Ave, Boynton Beach; tel 407/732-9400. **American/Seafood.** This popular waterside eatery features 2 indoor bars and 1 outdoors. A great place to mingle with beautiful people enjoying après-sun delights. The menu features a catch of the day; the oreo cheesecake is the special dessert. **FYI:** Reservations not accepted. Band. **Open:** Mon–Sat 11am–12:30am, Sun 9am–12:30am. **Prices:** Main courses $8–$20. Maj CC. ⛴ 🏔 ♿

✶ **Benvenuto**, 1730 N Federal Hwy, Boynton Beach; tel 407/364-0600. 1 mi N of Boynton Beach Blvd. **Continental/Italian.** Housed in a restored 1929 abode designed by Addison Mizner, this restaurant consists of 3 upbeat, stylized rooms, all with lovely appointments. The cuisine is well-known for both its quality and presentation. Menu highlights include lamb chops, snapper, and salmon dishes. **FYI:** Reservations recommended.

No smoking. **Open:** HS Nov–May daily 5–9:30pm. Reduced hours off-season. Closed Dec 25. **Prices:** Main courses $12–$18; PF dinner $22. Maj CC. ♥ 🖼 VP &

Attraction 💼

Arthur R Marshall Loxahatchee National Wildlife Refuge; tel 407/734-8303. This 145,000-acre refuge protects such endangered species as the snail kite and wood stork, and threatened species like the American alligator. Migrating waterfowl flock here in the winter. Observation tower, visitor center with exhibits and introductory slide show; also nature trails and a 5.5-mile canoe trail. The refuge also offers fishing, boating, and birdwatching opportunities at its 3 recreation areas. **Open:** Daily 6am–sunset. Closed Dec 25. $$

BRADENTON

Map page M-8, B2

Hotels 🏨

≣≣ **Bradenton Inn**, 2303 1st St E, Bradenton, FL 34208; tel 813/747-6465 or toll free 800/447-6465. Nicely kept property convenient to local attractions and close to town. **Rooms:** 150 rms and effic. CI 1pm/CO 11am. Nonsmoking rms avail. Recently renovated rooms are quite clean and comfortable. **Amenities:** 🛁 A/C, cable TV w/movies. **Services:** 🕹 **Facilities:** 🔦 🏊 & Playground, washer/dryer. **Rates (CP):** HS Jan–Apr $50–$55 S or D; from $75 effic. Extra person $6. Children under 12 stay free. Lower rates off-season. Pking: Outdoor, free. Maj CC.

≣≣ **Days Inn**, 3506 1st St W, Bradenton, FL 34208; tel 813/746-1141 or toll free 800/325-2525; fax 813/745-2382. Within 7 miles of gulf coast beaches and centrally located to area attractions. The friendly staff caters to families. **Rooms:** 134 rms. CI 3pm/CO noon. Nonsmoking rms avail. **Amenities:** 🛁 A/C, cable TV w/movies, in-rm safe. **Services:** 🕹 🔌 Local weather forecast is posted in the lobby. **Facilities:** 🔦 🏊 & Playground. **Rates (CP):** HS Jan–Mar $75–$80 S; $80–$85 D. Extra person $5. Children under 12 stay free. Lower rates off-season. Spec packages avail. Pking: Outdoor, free. Maj CC.

≣≣ **Holiday Inn Riverfront**, 100 Riverfront Dr, Bradenton, FL 34205; tel 813/747-3727 or toll free 800/HOLIDAY; fax 813/746-4289. A quiet hotel with mission-style architecture. Attractive river view from a courtyard pool nestled among gardens and waterfalls. **Rooms:** 153 rms and stes. CI 2pm/CO noon. Nonsmoking rms avail. **Amenities:** 🛁 🔌 🍴 A/C, cable TV w/movies. All units w/terraces. **Services:** ✕ 🖼 🕹 Babysitting. **Facilities:**

🔦 🛁 🏊 & 1 rst, 1 bar. Poolside bar has a covered outside terrace overlooking the courtyard. **Rates:** HS Jan–Apr $99–$109 S or D; from $129 ste. Extra person $10. Children under 18 stay free. Lower rates off-season. MAP rates avail. Spec packages avail. Pking: Outdoor, free. Maj CC.

≣≣ **Park Inn Club**, 4450 47th St W, Bradenton, FL 34210; tel 813/795-4633 or toll free 800/437-PARK; fax 813/795-0808. Spacious motel with relaxing, comfortable atmosphere. **Rooms:** 128 rms and stes. CI 3pm/CO noon. Nonsmoking rms avail. **Amenities:** 🛁 🔌 🍴 A/C, cable TV. **Services:** ✕ 🖼 🕹 🔌 Continental breakfast, coffee, and evening cocktails are all complimentary. **Facilities:** 🔦 🛁 🏊 & 1 rst, 1 bar, whirlpool. **Rates (CP):** HS Nov–Apr 15 $57 S; $63 D; from $83 ste. Extra person $6. Children under 18 stay free. Lower rates off-season. Spec packages avail. Pking: Outdoor, free. Maj CC.

Motel

≣ **Knights Inn**, 668 67th St Circle E, Bradenton, FL 34208; tel 813/745-1876 or toll free 800/843-5644; fax 813/745-1876 ext 615. Exit 42 off I-75. Situated off the highway, it's fine for a night's rest. Fast food restaurants are few yards away. **Rooms:** 105 rms and effic. CI 3pm/CO 11am. Nonsmoking rms avail. **Amenities:** 🛁 A/C, cable TV. **Services:** 🕹 🔌 **Facilities:** 🔦 Washer/dryer. **Rates:** HS Jan–May $50 S; $55 D; from $60 effic. Extra person $5. Children under 18 stay free. Lower rates off-season. Pking: Outdoor, free. Maj CC.

Restaurants 🍴

Leverock's Seafood House, 12320 Manatee Ave W, Bradenton; tel 813/794-8900. Exit 42 off I-75. **Seafood.** A spectacular waterfront dining room with a great bar. Dine on sundry fruits of the sea as you watch a bevy of boats enter and leave the nearby marina. **FYI:** Reservations not accepted. Children's menu. **Open:** Mon–Fri 11:30am–3pm, Sat–Sun 11:30am–10pm. Closed some hols. **Prices:** Main courses $6.95–$19.95. Maj CC. 🔲 💟 &

Miller's Dutch Kitchen, 3401 14th St W, Bradenton; tel 813/746-8253. 1.5 mi S of Bradenton; exit 42 off I-75. **American.** This family-style eatery, popular with seniors, has a proud, friendly owner. Daily dinner specials. **FYI:** Reservations not accepted. Children's menu. No liquor license. No smoking. **Open:** Mon–Sat 11am–8pm. Closed some hols. **Prices:** Main courses $5.40–$7.25. No CC. 🔳 &

The Pier, 1200 1st Ave W, Bradenton; tel 813/748-8087. **Seafood/Steak.** Located at the end of the wharf for which it was named, this restaurant has panoramic harbor views and a nautical theme; the decor includes a saltwater aquarium and mounted sports fish. **FYI:** Reservations recommended. Band/ guitar. Children's menu. **Open:** Mon–Thurs 11:30am–9pm, Fri– Sat 11:30am–10pm, Sun 11am–9pm. **Prices:** Main courses $7.95–$16.95. Maj CC. 🍴 🏞 🍴 VP ♿

Attractions 🖼

South Florida Museum and Bishop Planetarium, 201 10th St W; tel 813/746-4131. Florida's history, from prehistory to the modern age, is told in exhibits that include a Native American collection with life-size dioramas; a replica of a 16th-century Spanish courtyard; and an indoor aquarium. The adjacent Bishop Planetarium features a 50-foot hemispherical dome for laser light shows and star-gazing activities. Star show is offered at 1:30pm and 3pm. **Open:** Tues–Sat 10am–5pm, Sun noon–6pm. Closed some hols. $$$

Manatee Village Historical Park, 6th Ave E and 15th St E; tel 813/749-7165. This national historic site, located in a tree-shaded park, showcases restored buildings from Bradenton and the surrounding county. Among the structures are the Manatee County Courthouse, dating to 1860; a Methodist church built in 1887; and the Wiggins General Store, dating to 1912 and full of local memorabilia and antique furnishings. **Open:** Mon–Fri 9am–4:30pm, Sun 1:30–4:30pm. Closed Sun July–Aug. Free.

De Soto National Memorial Park, 75th St NW; tel 813/ 792-0458. Commemorates Spanish explorer Hernando de Soto's 1539 landing in Florida. The park features a restoration of de Soto's original camp site, as well as a scenic nature trail through a mangrove swamp that leads to the ruins of one of the first settlements in the area. From December through March, park employees dress in 16th-century costumes and portray the lifestyle of the early settlers, including demonstrations of musket-firing and cooking. The visitor center displays weapons and armor from the era. **Open:** Daily 9am–5pm. Free.

Anna Maria Island; tel 813/778-1541. A 7½-mile stretch of quiet, tree-shaded beaches that rim the Gulf of Mexico. West of downtown Bradenton, the island is accessible by 2 causeways (Fla 64 and Fla 684). On the northern end is Anna Maria Bayfront Park, a favorite for finding seashells and sand dollars. At the southern tip of the island is Coquina Beach, a secluded area of sand dunes, pines, and extensive picnic facilities. Manatee County maintains a walk-in visitor center at 5030 US 301, Ellenton (tel 813/729-7040), open daily 8:30am–5:30pm.

BRADENTON BEACH
Map page M-8, B1

Motels 🏨

🏨 🏨 **Catalina Beach Resort**, 1325 Gulf Dr N, Bradenton Beach, FL 34217; tel 813/778-6611; fax 813/778-6748. Take Cortez Road over the bridge to Bradenton Beach. Small family-owned hostelry directly across from the beach. A good value for family vacations. **Rooms:** 35 rms, stes, and effic. CI 2pm/CO 11am. **Amenities:** 🛁 🐾 🍴 A/C, cable TV, refrig. Some units w/terraces. **Services:** ✗ 🛎 Babysitting. **Facilities:** 🛗 ♿ 1 rst, 1 beach (ocean), washer/dryer. Gas grills available. **Rates:** HS Feb–Apr $77 S or D; from $107 ste; from $92 effic. Extra person $6. Children under 3 stay free. Lower rates off-season. Higher rates for spec evnts/hols. Spec packages avail. Pking: Outdoor, free. Maj CC.

🏨 **Sand & Sea Motel**, 2412 Gulf Dr, Bradenton Beach, FL 34217; tel 813/778-2231. Between Cortez Rd and Manatee Ave (Fla 64). Simple but pleasant 3-story elongated building on the gulf. **Rooms:** 28 rms and effic. CI 2pm/CO 11am. **Amenities:** 🛁 🍴 A/C, cable TV, refrig. Some units w/terraces. Units equipped with dishes, utensils, and other items for multiple-night stays. **Services:** 🛎 **Facilities:** 🛗 ♿ 1 beach (ocean), washer/dryer. Gas grill on premises. **Rates:** HS Feb–Apr 15 $85 S or D; from $90 effic. Extra person $5. Children under 5 stay free. Min stay spec evnts. Lower rates off-season. Higher rates for spec evnts/ hols. Pking: Outdoor, free. Ltd CC.

Restaurant 🍴

Beachhouse Restaurant, 200 Gulf Dr N, Bradenton Beach; tel 813/779-2222. **Seafood/Steak.** A casual eatery with an outdoor deck overlooking the gulf. Sample one of the nightly specials or the fresh catch of the day and follow your choice with the pound cake and vanilla ice cream topped with a raspberry. **FYI:** Reservations not accepted. Band. Children's menu. **Open:** Daily 11:30am–10pm. **Prices:** Main courses $9.95–$15.95. Maj CC. 🍴 🏞 ♿

BRISTOL
Map page M-3, B3

Attraction 🖼

Torreya State Park; tel 904/643-2674. Located on Fla 12 north of Bristol, this park along the Apalachicola River was named for the Torreya tree, an endangered species that grows naturally only in this area. There is a 7-mile loop trail that is unusually hilly for Florida; wildflowers bloom profusely along the trailside in the spring. A small primitive campsite is accessible only by a 1¼-mile hike. The Gregory House, an 1840s plantation home furnished in period style, is open for 1-hour guided tours. Swimming, fishing, hiking, camping. **Open:** Daily 8am–sunset. $$

CAPE CORAL

Map page M-8, D3

Hotel 🏨

≣≣ **Quality Inn–Fort Myers/Cape Coral**, 1538 Cape Coral Pkwy, Cape Coral, FL 33904; tel 813/542-2121 or toll free 800/221-2222; fax 813/542-6319. Exit 21 off I-75. A good value. Roomy lobby done in a casual Florida style. **Rooms:** 142 rms. CI 1pm/CO 11am. Nonsmoking rms avail. **Amenities:** 🛁 👤 A/C, cable TV. Some units w/terraces. **Services:** 🚗 🖼 🍴 🐾 Babysitting. **Facilities:** 🔥 🏊 👤 1 bar (w/entertainment), washer/dryer. **Rates (CP):** HS Jan–Apr $70–$75 S; $75–$80 D. Extra person $10. Children under 18 stay free. Lower rates off-season. Pking: Outdoor, free. Maj CC.

Resort

≣≣≣ **Cape Coral Golf and Tennis Resort**, 4003 Palm Tree Blvd, Cape Coral, FL 33904; tel 813/542-3191 or toll free 800/648-1475; fax 813/542-4694. Exit 21 off I-75. 205 acres. A heavenly holiday for the racquet and club enthusiast. **Rooms:** 99 rms. CI 3pm/CO noon. **Amenities:** 🛁 A/C, cable TV, refrig. **Services:** ✗ 🖼 🍴 Car-rental desk. **Facilities:** 🔥 ▶18 🏌 🏊 👤 2 rsts, 1 bar, lifeguard. Restaurants range from the upscale Tee Cafe to the casual poolside bar and grill. **Rates:** HS Jan–Apr $87–$98 S or D. Extra person $15. Children under 17 stay free. Lower rates off-season. Spec packages avail. Pking: Outdoor, free. Maj CC.

Restaurants 🍴

Dario's Restaurant and Lounge, in Coral Pointe Shopping Center, 1805 De Prado Blvd, Cape Coral; tel 813/574-7798. **Continental/Northern Italian.** The menu includes veal prepared several ways. **FYI:** Reservations accepted. **Open:** Lunch Mon–Fri 11:30am–2pm; dinner Mon–Sat 4–10pm, Sun 5–9pm. Closed some hols. **Prices:** Main courses $7.95–$17.95. Maj CC. 📺 👤

Iguana Mia, 1027 Cape Coral Pkwy, Cape Coral; tel 813/945-7755. 2 mi W of the Cape Coral toll bridge. **Mexican.** All the familiar choices are offered, including fajitas, burritos, and taco salads. A good value. **FYI:** Reservations not accepted. Children's menu. **Open:** Sun–Thurs 11am–10pm, Fri–Sat 11am–11pm. Closed some hols. **Prices:** Main courses $4–$9. Ltd CC. 👤

CAPE HAZE

Map page M-8, D2

Resort 🏨

Palm Island Resort, 7002 Placida Rd, Cape Haze, FL 33946; tel 813/697-4800 or toll free 800/824-5412, 800/282-6142 in FL; fax 813/697-0696. Exit 35 off I-75. 200 acres. Between the mainland and an island lies this complex of privately owned condominiums, most of which are 3-story clusters on stilts located on the island. Mainland suites are at a marina (where registration is). Two miles of beaches circle the island. This is a private retreat for those who want to drop anchor and stay put. Unrated. **Rooms:** 160 stes and effic. CI 2:30pm/CO 11:30am. **Amenities:** 🛁 👤 📺 A/C, cable TV, refrig. All units w/terraces. **Services:** 🍴 Social director, children's program, babysitting. Daily maid service on request. **Facilities:** 🔥 🚲 🔺 🏊 🍷11 🐾 🎾80 1 rst, 1 bar, 1 beach (ocean), snorkeling, whirlpool, playground, washer/dryer. **Rates:** From $85 ste; from $210 effic. Extra person $15. Children under 6 stay free. Min stay HS. Higher rates for spec evnts/hols. Spec packages avail. Pking: Outdoor, free. Maj CC. Summer packages are available. Rates do not include a one-time boat fee of $15–$20 per person.

CAPTIVA ISLAND

Map page M-8, D3

Hotel 🏨

≣≣ **'Tween Waters Inn**, 15951 Captiva Dr, Captiva Island, FL 33924; tel 813/472-5161 or toll free 800/223-5865, 800/282-7560 in FL; fax 813/472-0249. 1.5 miles N of Captiva Bridge. Separated from its own beach by a road, this low-key lodging on the northern end of the island attracts both couples and families. The friendly staff partakes in the weekly activities, which include the long-standing tradition of crab races. **Rooms:** 74 rms and effic; 51 ctges/villas. CI 4pm/CO noon. Nonsmoking rms avail. **Amenities:** 🛁 👤 📺 📞 A/C, cable TV, refrig, in-rm safe. Some units w/terraces, some w/fireplaces. **Services:** ✗ 🍴 🐾 Babysitting. **Facilities:** 🔥 🚲 🔺 🏊 🐾 🎾100 👤 3 rsts (see also

"Restaurants" below), 3 bars (1 w/entertainment), 1 beach (ocean), board surfing, games rm, washer/dryer. **Rates:** HS Dec–Apr $190 S or D; from $210 effic; from $240 ctge/villa. Extra person $15. Children under 18 stay free. Lower rates off-season. Higher rates for spec evnts/hols. Spec packages avail. Pking: Indoor/outdoor, free. Ltd CC.

Resort

South Seas Plantation Resort and Yacht Harbour, 5400 Captiva Road, Captiva Island, FL 33924; tel 813/472-5111 or toll free 800/237-3102; fax 813/472-7541. Exit 21 off I-75. W to Fla 869; S to Sanibel Causeway to tip of Captiva Island. 330 acres. One of the largest resorts in this region, occupying the southern end of Captiva Island. It could take days to explore the entire complex. The entirely self-sufficient facility provides all the resort amenities as well as maximum privacy. Security gate ensures safety. **Rooms:** 160 rms, stes, and effic. CI 4pm/CO noon. Nonsmoking rms avail. Many units offer Gulf or other water vistas. **Amenities:** A/C, cable TV w/movies, refrig, in-rm safe. Some units w/minibars, all w/terraces, some w/Jacuzzis. **Services:** Car-rental desk, social director, masseur, children's program, babysitting. **Facilities:** 14 3 rsts, 3 bars (w/entertainment), 1 beach (ocean), board surfing, games rm, snorkeling, whirlpool, beauty salon, playground, washer/dryer. **Rates:** HS Feb–Apr $260 S or D; from $275 ste; from $265 effic. Extra person $25. Children under 12 stay free. Lower rates off-season. Higher rates for spec evnts/hols. Spec packages avail. Pking: Outdoor, free. Ltd CC.

Restaurants

Bellini's of Captiva, Andy Rosse Lane, Captiva Island; tel 813/472-6866. **Northern Italian.** An attractive enclosed patio and wood furnishings create an informal atmosphere at this bistro. The northern Italian cuisine includes filet of salmon Capriccio, fettuccine Alfredo, and a variety of veal and chicken entrees. **FYI:** Reservations recommended. Piano. Children's menu. **Open:** Dinner daily 5:30–10pm. **Prices:** Main courses $10.50–$24. Maj CC.

★ **Bubble Room**, 15001 Captiva Dr, Captiva Island; tel 813/472-5558. **New American.** A small cottage restaurant with bubbles painted on the facade, white wrought-iron furniture, and memorabilia from the 1930s and '40s. A popular spot with locals, who are attracted by the great lunch deals. A unique Florida dining experience. **FYI:** Reservations not accepted. Children's menu. **Open:** HS Dec–Apr lunch daily 11:30am–2:30pm; dinner daily 5–10pm. Reduced hours off-season. Closed Dec 25. **Prices:** Main courses $13.50–$27. Maj CC.

Captiva Inn, 11509 Andy Rosse Lane, Captiva Island; tel 813/472-9129. **New American/Continental.** An intimate and romantic dining room adorned with crystal, china, linen, and lace. Despite these extravagances, the atmosphere is relaxed and informal. Yellowfin tuna steak, filet of salmon, filet mignon, and nightly dinner specials. **FYI:** Reservations recommended. Beer and wine only. No smoking. **Open:** Dinner daily 5:30–9:30pm. Closed Dec 25. **Prices:** Main courses $13.95–$23.95; PF dinner $37.50. Maj CC.

The Moonlight, in Captiva Village Square, 14970 Captiva Dr, Captiva Island; tel 813/472-1956. **Southwestern.** An immaculate, southwestern-inspired eatery with an upbeat atmosphere. The menu includes wood-grilled fillet of beef, herb-crusted rack of lamb, and a nightly selection of fish entrees. **FYI:** Reservations recommended. Beer and wine only. **Open:** Dinner daily 5–9:30pm. Closed Dec 25. **Prices:** Main courses $6–$24. No CC.

Old Captiva House, in 'Tween Waters Inn, Captiva Rd, Captiva Island; tel 813/472-5161. **Seafood/Steak.** An elegant inn, with a beautiful dining room and an informal piano bar, located next to the beach. A variety of seafood, chicken, and pork dishes are available. The menu includes a great selection of desserts fresh from the bakery. **FYI:** Reservations accepted. Piano. Children's menu. Dress code. No smoking. **Open:** Breakfast daily 7:30–10:30am; lunch daily noon–3pm; dinner daily 5:30–10pm. **Prices:** PF dinner $14.95. Ltd CC.

Sunshine Cafe, in Captiva Village Square, 14900 Captiva Dr, Captiva Island; tel 813/472-6200. **New American.** An upbeat, casual little cafe with crisp white linen and an open kitchen. Fresh fish selections are served nightly; sandwiches and salads are available for lunch. **FYI:** Reservations recommended. Beer and wine only. **Open:** Daily 11:30am–9:30pm. Closed some hols. **Prices:** Main courses $5.95–$21.95. No CC.

CHIEFLAND

Map page M-4, E4

Attraction

Manatee Springs State Park; tel 904/493-6072. A 2,000-acre park centered around a natural spring. Swimming, fishing, hiking, camping, nature trails. **Open:** Daily 8am–sunset. $$

CHIPLEY

Map page M-3, A2

Attractions 🏛

Ponce de León Springs State Recreation Area, US 90; tel 904/836-4281. The centerpiece of this 440-acre park is its natural spring, which produces 16 million gallons of clear water each day. Swimming, fishing, nature trails. **Open:** Daily 8am–sunset. $

Falling Waters State Recreation Area; tel 904/638-6130. Located just south of Chipley off Fla 77A, this is certainly one of Florida's most distinctive geological attractions. A 67-foot waterfall drops into a 100-foot-deep, 20-foot-wide sinkhole with moss-and-fern-covered walls; an overlook platform provides an excellent vantage point. The park offers swimming, hiking, picnicking, and overnight camping. For information write to the park at Rte 5, Box 660, Chipley, FL 32428. **Open:** Daily 8am–sunset. $$

CLEARWATER

Map page M-6, E2

Hotels 🏨

Best Western Clearwater Central, 21338 US 19 N, Clearwater, FL 34625; tel 813/799-1565 or toll free 800/528-1234; fax 813/797-6801. Modest low-rise hotel recommended for short stays and its convenient highway location. **Rooms:** 149 rms and stes. CI 1pm/CO noon. Nonsmoking rms avail. **Amenities:** A/C, cable TV. Some units w/minibars, some w/terraces. **Services:** **Facilities:** Washer/dryer. **Rates:** HS Feb–Apr $60–$70 S or D; from $70 ste. Extra person $5. Children under 12 stay free. Lower rates off-season. Pking: Outdoor, free. Maj CC.

Comfort Inn, 3580 Ulmerton Rd, Clearwater, FL 34622; tel 813/573-1171 or toll free 800/221-2222; fax 813/572-8736. Exit 18 off I-275. Comfortable lodgings located across from popular dinner theater and 9 miles from gulf beaches. **Rooms:** 120 rms and stes. CI 3pm/CO noon. Nonsmoking rms avail. **Amenities:** A/C, cable TV w/movies. Some units w/terraces. **Services:** X **Facilities:** Whirlpool. **Rates (CP):** HS Jan–Apr $65–$75 S or D. Extra person $6. Children under 18 stay free. Lower rates off-season. Pking: Outdoor, free. Maj CC.

Courtyard by Marriott, 3131 Executive Dr, Clearwater, FL 34622; tel 813/572-8484 or toll free 800/321-2211; fax 813/572-6991. Exit 16 off I-275. Conveniently located yet in a tranquil, pastoral setting. **Rooms:** 149 rms and stes. CI 3pm/CO noon. Express checkout avail. Nonsmoking rms avail. **Amenities:** A/C, cable TV w/movies. All units w/terraces. **Services:** Babysitting. **Facilities:** 1 rst, 1 bar, whirlpool, washer/dryer. **Rates:** HS Jan–Apr $89 S; $99 D; from $102 ste. Extra person $10. Children under 12 stay free. Lower rates off-season. Spec packages avail. Pking: Outdoor, free. Maj CC.

Days Inn, 3910 Ulmerton Rd, Clearwater, FL 34622; tel 813/572-8540 or toll free 800/638-2343; fax 813/373-3334. Exit 18 off I-275. Adequate accommodations, for business or leisure. **Rooms:** 118 rms. CI 3pm/CO noon. Nonsmoking rms avail. **Amenities:** A/C, cable TV w/movies, in-rm safe. **Services:** Car-rental desk. **Facilities:** Washer/dryer. Complimentary admission to nearby Bally's Health Spa. **Rates (CP):** HS Jan–Apr $64 S; $74 D. Extra person $6. Children under 16 stay free. Lower rates off-season. Higher rates for spec evnts/hols. Pking: Outdoor, free. Maj CC.

Hampton Inn, 3655 Hospitality Lane, Clearwater, FL 34622; tel 813/577-9200 or toll free 800/HAMPTON; fax 813/572-8931. Exit 18 off I-275. Designed for the value-conscious traveler. **Rooms:** 118 rms and effic. CI 3pm/CO noon. Nonsmoking rms avail. **Amenities:** A/C, cable TV w/movies. Free continental breakfast and happy hour. **Services:** **Facilities:** Sauna, whirlpool, washer/dryer. Golf and tennis courts are within walking distance. **Rates (CP):** HS Jan–Apr $66–$76 S or D; from $86 effic. Extra person $5. Children under 18 stay free. Lower rates off-season. Pking: Outdoor, free. Maj CC.

Holiday Inn, 3535 Ulmerton Rd, Clearwater, FL 34622; tel 813/577-9100 or toll free 800/HOLIDAY; fax 813/573-5022. Exit 18 off I-275. This 5-story property, outfitted with all the essentials, attracts a largely business clientele. **Rooms:** 174 rms and stes. CI 3pm/CO noon. Nonsmoking rms avail. **Amenities:** A/C, cable TV w/movies. **Services:** X **Facilities:** 1 rst, 1 bar, whirlpool, washer/dryer. **Rates:** HS Jan–Apr $90–$108 S or D; from $108 ste. Extra person $10. Lower rates off-season. MAP rates avail. Spec packages avail. Pking: Outdoor, free. Maj CC.

Holiday Inn Clearwater Central, 21030 US 19 N, Clearwater, FL 34642; tel 813/797-8173 or toll free 800/HOLIDAY; fax 813/791-7759. Well-liked by the shop-till-you-drop crowd for its location opposite the Clearwater Mall. Families that don't require an on-beach hotel will find this a suitable locale as well. **Rooms:** 193 rms and stes. CI 3pm/CO

11am. Nonsmoking rms avail. **Amenities:** 📺 A/C, cable TV w/movies. **Services:** ✗ 🖾 ↵ **Facilities:** 🔂 🔟 ⅙ 1 rst, 1 bar, games rm, washer/dryer. **Rates:** HS Dec–Apr $58–$62 S; $85–$105 D; from $150 ste. Extra person $10. Children under 18 stay free. Lower rates off-season. Higher rates for spec evnts/hols. Spec packages avail. Pking: Indoor, free. Maj CC.

📰📰 **Holiday Inn Express**, 13625 Icot Blvd, Clearwater, FL 34620; tel 813/536-7275 or toll free 800/HOLIDAY; fax 813/530-3053. Exit 18 off I-275. A mid-range hotel with many conveniences for families or corporate guests. **Rooms:** 128 rms and stes. CI 2pm/CO noon. Nonsmoking rms avail. **Amenities:** 🔂 🕪 🕾 A/C, cable TV w/movies. Some units w/Jacuzzis. Television speaker and phone extension in bathroom. **Services:** 🖾 ↵ ↩ Babysitting. **Facilities:** 🔂 🖳 🔟 ⅙ Whirlpool. **Rates (CP):** HS Feb–Apr $56 S; $61 D; from $71 ste. Extra person $5. Children under 18 stay free. Lower rates off-season. Pking: Outdoor, free. Maj CC.

📰📰 **Howard Johnson Hotel**, 20967 US 19 N, Clearwater, FL 34625; tel 813/799-1181 or toll free 800/741-1181; fax 813/797-8504. This otherwise standard facility sets itself apart from nearby properties with its newly renovated rooms and on-site comedy club. **Rooms:** 115 rms and stes. CI 3pm/CO noon. Nonsmoking rms avail. **Amenities:** 🔂 A/C, cable TV w/movies. **Services:** ✗ 🖾 ↵ ↩ **Facilities:** 🔂 🔟 ⅙ 1 rst, 1 bar (w/entertainment), washer/dryer. **Rates:** HS Feb–Apr $62–$75 S or D; from $75 ste. Extra person $6. Children under 12 stay free. Lower rates off-season. Higher rates for spec evnts/hols. Spec packages avail. Pking: Outdoor, free. Maj CC.

📰📰 **La Quinta Inn**, 3301 Ulmerton Rd, Clearwater, FL 34622; tel 813/572-7222 or toll free 800/531-5900; fax 813/572-0076. Exit 18 off I-275. This modern hotel is set back from the highway in a quiet area. **Rooms:** 115 rms. CI 2pm/CO noon. Nonsmoking rms avail. **Amenities:** 🔂 🕪 A/C, cable TV w/movies. **Services:** 🚐 🖾 ↵ ↩ **Facilities:** 🔂 🖳 🔟 ⅙ Whirlpool, washer/dryer. **Rates (CP):** HS Jan–Apr $73–$80 S or D. Extra person $6. Children under 18 stay free. Lower rates off-season. Pking: Outdoor, free. Maj CC.

📰📰 **Ramada Inn–Countryside**, 26508 US 19 N, Clearwater, FL 34621; tel 813/796-1234 or toll free 800/2-RAMADA; fax 813/796-0452. At the intersection of US 19 N and Countryside Blvd. Tries to impart a rural setting. Noteworthy for its pool and lighted tennis courts. **Rooms:** 128 rms and stes. CI 3pm/CO noon. Nonsmoking rms avail. **Amenities:** 🔂🗖 A/C. Some units w/terraces, some w/Jacuzzis. **Services:** ✗ 🖾 ↵ **Facilities:** 🔂 🖳 🔟 1 rst, 1 bar (w/entertainment), washer/dryer. **Rates:** HS Feb–Apr $69–$99 S; $79–$109 D; from $99 ste. Extra person $10. Children under 18 stay free. Lower rates off-season. Pking: Outdoor, free. Maj CC.

📰📰 **Residence Inn by Marriott**, 5050 Ulmerton Rd, Clearwater, FL 34620; tel 813/573-4444 or toll free 800/331-3131; fax 813/572-4446. Exit 18 off I-275. Condominium-style living in a professional environment; popular with repeat business and leisure travelers. **Rooms:** 88 rms. CI 3pm/CO noon. Nonsmoking rms avail. Each unit is self-contained with kitchen facilities. **Amenities:** 🔂🕪🗖 A/C, cable TV w/movies, refrig. Some units w/terraces, all w/fireplaces. **Services:** 🖾 ↵ ↩ Happy hour in the lobby Monday–Thursday, when beer and wine is complimentary. **Facilities:** 🔂 🕪 🔟 ⅙ 1 rst, whirlpool, washer/dryer. **Rates (CP):** HS Jan–Apr $90–$140 S or D. Lower rates off-season. Spec packages avail. Pking: Outdoor, free. Maj CC.

Resorts

📰📰📰📰 **Bellevue Mido Resort Hotel**, 25 Belleview Blvd, PO Box 2317, Clearwater, FL 34617; tel 813/442-6171 or toll free 800/237-8947; fax 813/441-4173. 20 acres. A turn-of-the-century architectural tour de force that is sure to appeal to couples and other romantics. This is to Clearwater what the Don Cesar is to St Petersburg. **Rooms:** 260 rms and stes. CI 3pm/CO noon. Nonsmoking rms avail. Delightfully decorated in period style. **Amenities:** 🔂 🕪 A/C, cable TV. All units w/minibars, some w/terraces. **Services:** ✗ 🆅🅿 🖾 ↵ Masseur, babysitting. **Facilities:** 🔂 ▶18 🔟 🕪4 🖳 🔟 ⅙ 2 rsts, 3 bars (1 w/entertainment), lawn games, spa, sauna, steam rm, whirlpool. Cabana beach club requires a ride from the hotel but food service is provided there. **Rates:** HS Jan–Apr $190–$210 S or D; from $260 ste. Extra person $20. Children under 18 stay free. Lower rates off-season. Spec packages avail. Pking: Outdoor, free. Maj CC.

📰📰📰 **Sheraton Sand Key Resort**, 1160 Gulf Blvd, Clearwater, FL 33515; tel 813/595-1611 or toll free 800/325-3535; fax 813/596-8488. Fla 60 to Gulf Blvd S across bridge. 20 acres. A major resort in the area. Set on spacious grounds with views all around. **Rooms:** 390 rms and stes. CI 3pm/CO 11am. Nonsmoking rms avail. Some rooms need more attention and a renovation, but they are in generally decent repair. **Amenities:** 🔂🕪🗖 A/C, cable TV w/movies. All units w/terraces. **Services:** ✗ 🗝 🖾 ↵ Social director, masseur, children's program, babysitting. **Facilities:** 🔂 🚲 ⚠🕪🖳 🔟🖳 ⅙ 2 rsts, 2 bars, 1 beach (ocean), games rm, snorkeling, sauna, steam rm, whirlpool, playground, washer/dryer. **Rates:** HS Feb–Apr $110–$160 S; $120–$170 D; from $240 ste. Extra person $10. Children under 18 stay free. Lower rates off-season. Spec packages avail. Pking: Outdoor, free. Maj CC.

Restaurants 🍴

Leverock's Seafood House, 551 Gulf Blvd, Clearwater; tel 813/446-5884. Just before the Sand Key Bridge. **Seafood/Steak.** Enjoy the great view from either indoors or out at this cheerful waterside restaurant. Seafood specials, early bird bargains, and affordable prices make this a popular stop. **FYI:** Reservations not accepted. Children's menu. **Open:** Daily 11:30am–10pm. Closed some hols. **Prices:** Main courses $6.95–$19.95. Maj CC. 🏔️✅♿

♥★ 9th Aero Squadron, 84 Fairchild Dr, Clearwater; tel 813/563-0409. Exit 18 off I-275. **Eclectic.** Award-winning cuisine is presented in authentic country-French surroundings. The romantic setting is enhanced by candlelight and crackling fires. Sup on prime New York strip steak and other continental fare. **FYI:** Reservations recommended. Children's menu. **Open:** HS Nov–Apr lunch Mon–Fri 11:30am–3pm; dinner Mon–Thurs 5–10pm, Fri–Sat 5–10:30pm, Sun 4:30–10pm; brunch Sun 10:30am–2:30pm. Reduced hours off-season. Closed some hols. **Prices:** Main courses $11.95–$28.95. Maj CC. 💟🖼️🏔️✅♿

Tio Pepe's, 2930 Gulf-to-Bay Blvd, Clearwater; tel 813/799-3082. **Spanish.** An Old Spanish restaurant with rustic decor, a festive atmosphere, a celebrated menu, and an award-winning wine list. **FYI:** Reservations recommended. Children's menu. Dress code. **Open:** Tues–Thurs 5–11pm, Fri–Sat 5–11:30pm, Sun 4–10pm. Closed some hols. **Prices:** Main courses $10.95–$54.45. Maj CC. 💟🖼️♿

Attractions 📷

Florida Military Aviation Museum, 16055 Fairchild Dr; tel 813/535-9007. This outdoor museum is devoted to aircraft from all branches of military aviation, from Word War II patrol bombers to supersonic jet fighters. **Open:** Tues, Thurs, Sat 10am–4pm, Sun 1–5pm. $

Clearwater Marine Science Center, 249 Windward Passage; tel 813/447-0980. Located on an island in Clearwater Harbor, this facility is dedicated to the rescue and rehabilitation of marine mammals and sea turtles. A turtle hatchery releases more than 3,000 hatchlings each year in local waters. Visitors can view a 400-pound sea turtle and baby turtles, a bottle-nosed dolphin, and a coral reef tank. **Open:** Mon–Fri 9am–5pm, Sat 9am–4pm, Sun 11am–4pm. $$

Moccasin Lake Nature Park, 2750 Park Trail Lane; tel 813/462-6024. A 51-acre wildlife preserve with a 5-acre lake, nature trails, and an aviary, plus exhibits on animals, birds of prey, reptiles, plants, and energy sources. **Open:** Tues–Fri 9am–5pm, Sat–Sun 10am–6pm. Closed some hols. $

Jack Russell Stadium, 800 Phillies Dr; tel 813/442-8496. The Philadelphia Phillies conduct their spring training activities at this stadium. Exhibition season mid-Feb–Mar. $$$

CLEARWATER BEACH
Map page M-6, E2 (W of Clearwater)

Hotels 🏨

🏖️🏖️🏖️ **Adam's Mark Caribbean Gulf Resort**, 430 South Gulfview Blvd, Clearwater Beach, FL 33515; tel 813/443-5714 or toll free 800/444-2326; fax 813/442-8389. Fla 60 to Gulfview Blvd. Right on the beach, it's a local favorite and popular with younger folks for its many bars. **Rooms:** 216 rms and stes. CI 4pm/CO 11am. Nonsmoking rms avail. Generally good-quality accommodations are a bit dated in places. Balconies afford ocean views. **Amenities:** 🔌 A/C, cable TV w/movies. All units w/terraces. **Services:** ✖️ VP 🛗 Car-rental desk, children's program, babysitting. **Facilities:** 🏊 500 ♿ 2 rsts, 2 bars (w/entertainment), 1 beach (ocean), games rm, whirlpool, washer/dryer. Guests have use of nearby health club for a fee. **Rates:** HS Feb–Apr $124–$169 S or D; from $195 ste. Extra person $10. Children under 18 stay free. Lower rates off-season. Spec packages avail. Pking: Indoor, free. Maj CC.

🏖️🏖️ **Best Western Sea Stone Resort**, 445 Hamden Dr, Clearwater Beach, FL 34630; tel 813/441-1722 or toll free 800/444-1919; fax 813/461-1680. At Gulfview Blvd. Although not on the beach, this better-than-average establishment is right near a public one, and it has its own marina. **Rooms:** 109 rms and stes. CI 4pm/CO noon. Nonsmoking rms avail. Guests staying in suites section will be pleased with the new upbeat decor and the extra space for relaxing. **Amenities:** 🔌 A/C, cable TV, refrig, in-rm safe. All units w/terraces. **Services:** ✖️ Car-rental desk, children's program, babysitting. **Facilities:** 🏊 100 ♿ 1 rst, 1 bar (w/entertainment), whirlpool, beauty salon, washer/dryer. **Rates:** HS Feb–Apr $99–$119 S or D; from $166 ste. Extra person $10. Children under 18 stay free. Min stay spec evnts. Lower rates off-season. Spec packages avail. Pking: Indoor/outdoor, free. Maj CC.

🏖️🏖️ **Best Western Sea Wake Inn**, 691 S Gulfview Blvd, Clearwater Beach, FL 34630; tel 813/443-7652 or toll free 800/444-1919; fax 813/461-2836. Families make up a large part of the guests at this sun-drenched lodging. **Rooms:** 110 rms and effic. CI 4pm/CO noon. Nonsmoking rms avail. Rooms are tastefully decorated with updated furnishings. Beachfront rooms are usually well-booked because of their balconies and sunset views. **Amenities:** 🔌 A/C, TV, in-rm safe. Some units w/terraces. **Services:** ✖️ Babysitting. Free pass provided for

Clearwater Beach Trolley. **Facilities:** 🔥 📶 1 rst, 1 bar (w/entertainment), 1 beach (ocean), playground. Children's program is available during summer months (no fee). Beachside pool and bar. **Rates:** HS Feb–Apr $115–$140 S or D; from $150 effic. Extra person $10. Children under 17 stay free. Lower rates off-season. Spec packages avail. Pking: Outdoor, free. Maj CC.

≣≣≣ **Clearwater Beach Hilton**, 715 S Gulfview Blvd, Clearwater Beach, FL 34630; tel 813/447-9566 or toll free 800/445-8677, 800/282-3566 in FL; fax 813/447-9566 ext 2168. This sprawling complex on the Gulf offers a variety of rooms from highrise to beachside lowrise units for both couples and families. **Rooms:** 210 rms and stes. CI 4pm/CO 11am. Nonsmoking rms avail. **Amenities:** 🛅 🅰 A/C, cable TV w/movies, in-rm safe. All units w/minibars, all w/terraces. Some rooms have coffeemakers. **Services:** ✕ 🖼 🐾 Masseur, babysitting. Scarce front-desk staff sometimes leaves guests stranded. **Facilities:** 🔥 ⚓ 🏊 📶 📶 2 rsts, 2 bars (w/entertainment), 1 beach (ocean), games rm, playground, washer/dryer. **Rates:** HS Feb–Apr $119–$139 S or D; from $239 ste. Extra person $10. Children under 18 stay free. Lower rates off-season. Spec packages avail. Pking: Outdoor, free. Maj CC.

≣≣≣ **Clearwater Beach Hotel**, 500 Mandalay Ave, Clearwater Beach, FL 34630; tel 813/441-2425 or toll free 800/292-2295; fax 813/449-2083. This holdover from a bygone era still retains much of its splendor. The well-appointed lobby features high-backed chairs and artwork. **Rooms:** 156 rms, stes, and effic. Exec-level rms avail. CI 3pm/CO noon. **Amenities:** 🛅 A/C, cable TV. Some units w/terraces. **Services:** ✕ 🖼 🖼 🐾 🥂 Babysitting. **Facilities:** 🔥 📶 🅱 1 rst (see also "Restaurants" below), 1 bar (w/entertainment), 1 beach (ocean). Library with fireplace. Beachside bar adjacent to the pool. **Rates:** HS Feb–Apr $135–$155 S or D; from $200 ste; from $160 effic. Extra person $8. Lower rates off-season. Higher rates for spec evnts/hols. Pking: Indoor/outdoor, free. Maj CC.

≣≣ **Holiday Inn Gulfview**, 521 S Gulfview Blvd, Clearwater Beach, FL 34630; tel 813/447-6461 or toll free 800/HOLIDAY; fax 813/443-5888. Located in the midst of the beach district, though its own frontage is not ideal for swimming. Public beach is close by. **Rooms:** 288 rms. CI 4pm/CO 11am. Nonsmoking rms avail. **Amenities:** 🛅 🅰 🅱 A/C, cable TV w/movies. All units w/minibars, all w/terraces. **Services:** 🍽 🖼 🥂 Car-rental desk, babysitting. **Facilities:** 🔥 📶 🅱 2 rsts, 2 bars (1 w/entertainment), games rm, beauty salon. **Rates:** HS Feb $100–$125 S; $110–$135 D. Extra person $10. Children under 19 stay free. Lower rates off-season. Higher rates for spec evnts/hols. Spec packages avail. Pking: Outdoor, free. Maj CC.

≣≣≣ **Holiday Inn Surfside**, 400 Mandalay Ave, Clearwater Beach, FL 34630; tel 813/461-3222 or toll free 800/753-3954;

fax 813/461-0610. At Gulfview Blvd on Fla 60. This large beachfront staple has long been favored by families. It garners awards from within the Holiday Inn chain for service and quality. The lively public areas always seem to have something going on. **Rooms:** 428 rms and stes. CI 4pm/CO 11am. Nonsmoking rms avail. Rooms throughout offer gulf views. Appointments are of high quality. **Amenities:** 🛅 🅰 A/C, cable TV w/movies. Some units w/terraces. **Services:** ✕ 🖼 🖼 🐾 Children's program, babysitting. **Facilities:** 🔥 📶 📶 🅱 2 rsts, 3 bars (1 w/entertainment), 1 beach (ocean), games rm, washer/dryer. **Rates:** HS Feb–Apr $120–$215 S or D; from $225 ste. Extra person $10. Children under 18 stay free. Lower rates off-season. Spec packages avail. Pking: Indoor/outdoor, free. Maj CC.

≣≣ **Palm Pavilion Inn**, 18 Bay Esplanade, Clearwater Beach, FL 34630; tel 813/446-6777 or toll free 800/433-PALM; fax 813/446-4255. Three-story art deco-style hotel with beach access. **Rooms:** 29 rms and effic. CI 2pm/CO noon. Furnishings are sparse but acceptable. **Amenities:** 🛅 🅰 A/C, cable TV w/movies. **Services:** 🥂 **Facilities:** 🔥 🅱 1 beach (ocean). Rooftop sundeck. Gift shop and burger stand next door. **Rates:** HS Feb–Apr $75–$110 S or D; from $95 effic. Extra person $8. Children under 16 stay free. Lower rates off-season. Higher rates for spec evnts/hols. Pking: Outdoor, free. Maj CC.

≣≣ **Quality Inn Beach Resort**, 655 S Gulfview Blvd, Clearwater Beach, FL 34630; tel 813/442-7171 or toll free 800/228-5151; fax 813/446-7177. A recently renovated, mid-rise beachfront property that commands great sunset views. **Rooms:** 90 rms, stes, and effic. CI 3pm/CO noon. Nonsmoking rms avail. Bright colors with many private balconies and floral print spreads. Rooms are attractively decorated in bright colors and well-insulated from neighbors. **Amenities:** 🛅 🅰 A/C, TV, in-rm safe. Some units w/terraces. **Services:** ✕ 🖼 🥂 Babysitting. **Facilities:** 🔥 🅱 1 rst, 1 bar, 1 beach (ocean), playground, washer/dryer. Marina nearby. The restaurant is a chain pancake house with inexpensive fare. **Rates:** HS Feb–Apr $105–$115 S or D; from $145 ste; from $125 effic. Extra person $20. Children under 18 stay free. Lower rates off-season. Spec packages avail. Pking: Outdoor, free. Maj CC.

≣≣≣ **Radisson Suite Resort**, 1201 Gulf Blvd, Clearwater Beach, FL 34630; tel 813/596-1100 or toll free 800/333-3333; fax 813/595-4292. On Sand Key. Fresh and appealing, this operation the waterfront is one of the top hotels on the beach. The spacious lobby is only an introduction to the other smart-looking public areas. The adjacent string of shops and restaurants makes for a good non-beach diversion. **Rooms:** 220 stes. CI 4pm/CO noon. Nonsmoking rms avail. **Amenities:** 🛅 🅰 🅱 A/C, cable TV w/movies, refrig, stereo/tape player. All units w/minibars, all w/terraces, some w/Jacuzzis. All w/microwaves.

Services: ✗ 🔑 VP 🖼 🛎 Car-rental desk, social director, masseur, children's program, babysitting. Shuttle to beach operates every half hour; also takes guests to town for nightlife until very late. **Facilities:** 🏊 ⛳ 🎾 ⛵ ⛳ 🍴 🍺 ⚓ ♿ 2 rsts, 2 bars (w/entertainment), 1 beach (bay), games rm, lawn games, spa, sauna, whirlpool, beauty salon, day-care ctr, playground, washer/dryer. **Rates:** HS Dec–Apr from $150 ste. Extra person $10. Children under 18 stay free. Min stay spec evnts. Lower rates off-season. Spec packages avail. Pking: Outdoor, free. Maj CC.

Motels

🏨 **Aegean Sands Resort Motel**, 421 Gulfview Blvd S, Clearwater Beach, FL 34630; tel 813/447-3464 or toll free 800/942-3432; fax 813/446-7169. Opposite a public beach, this hotel prides itself on its family comforts and ambience. Popular among European vacationers. **Rooms:** 65 rms and stes. CI 3pm/CO noon. Rooms vary from motel-style units to efficiencies and 2-bedroom apartments. **Amenities:** 🛏 🖥 A/C, TV. Some units w/terraces. **Services:** 🛎 🍷 Babysitting. **Facilities:** 🏖 1 beach (ocean), washer/dryer. **Rates:** HS Feb–Apr $80–$105 S or D; from $100 ste. Extra person $5. Children under 18 stay free. Lower rates off-season. Pking: Outdoor, free. Maj CC.

🏨 **Flamingo Motel Apartments and Suites**, 450 N Gulfview Blvd, Clearwater Beach, FL 34630; tel 813/441-8019 or toll free 800/821-8019; fax 813/446-6599. Take Fla 60 to Mandalay Ave then turn left onto N Gulfview Blvd. A mom-and-pop-style motel that's a mainstay for families on a budget. **Rooms:** 35 rms, stes, and effic. CI 2pm/CO 10am. Lodgings vary in size from apartments with separate bedrooms to studios w/sofabeds. Some beachfront rooms. **Amenities:** 🛏 🖥 A/C, cable TV, refrig, bathrobes. All units w/terraces. **Services:** 🛎 **Facilities:** 🏊 🎾 1 beach (ocean), sauna, washer/dryer. A quiet street separates units from the large pool. **Rates:** HS Feb–Apr $60–$80 S or D; from $95 ste; from $70 effic. Extra person $6. Children under 16 stay free. Lower rates off-season. Higher rates for spec evnts/hols. Pking: Outdoor, free. Ltd CC.

🏨 **Sun West Beach Motel**, 409 Hamden Dr S, Clearwater Beach, FL 34630; tel 813/442-5008. A small family-run harborside motel with a private dock; only a short walk from the beach. **Rooms:** 14 rms and effic. CI 1pm/CO 10am. Poolside rooms are the favorites, although they may be a little more noisy. **Amenities:** 🛏 🍷 🖥 A/C, cable TV, refrig. **Facilities:** 🏊 ♿ Washer/dryer. The pool deck leads directly to the dock, where guests can fish or just relax. **Rates:** HS Feb–Apr $59–$61 S or D; from $67 effic. Extra person $5. Lower rates off-season. Spec packages avail. Pking: Outdoor, free. Ltd CC.

Restaurants 🍴

Bob Heilman's Beachcomber, 447 Mandalay Ave, Clearwater Beach; tel 813/442-4144. 1 block N of Fla 60. **New American/Continental.** A simple, casual restaurant with a jumbo bar area. Menu highlights include seafood, steaks, and prime rib. **FYI:** Reservations accepted. Piano. **Open:** Mon–Sat 11am–midnight, Sun noon–midnight. **Prices:** Main courses $8.95–$23.95. Maj CC. 💟 VP ♿

Cha Cha Coconuts, in the Shops of Sand Key, 1241 Gulf Blvd, Clearwater Beach; tel 813/596-6040. **Burgers.** Neon lights and tropical colors illuminate this festive bar, which caters to the younger set. The menu offers burgers, salads, Jamaican jerk chicken, sandwiches, and other munchies. **FYI:** Reservations not accepted. Band. Children's menu. **Open:** Mon–Thurs 11am–midnight, Fri–Sat 11am–1am, Sun 11am–10pm. **Prices:** Main courses $3.95–$6.25. Maj CC. 🍴 ♿

Chateau Madrid, 415 Cleveland St, Clearwater Beach; tel 813/447-2211. **Continental/Spanish.** Spanish touches accent the simple decor. Filet mignon, veal marsala, and fresh seafood entrees are offered. **FYI:** Reservations accepted. Children's menu. **Open:** Lunch Tues–Fri 11am–2pm; dinner Tues–Thurs 5–10pm, Fri–Sat 5–11pm, Sun 4–10pm. Closed Thanksgiving. **Prices:** Main courses $8–$18. Maj CC. 💟 ♿

Clearwater Beach Hotel Dining Room, in Clearwater Beach Hotel, 500 Mandalay Ave, Clearwater Beach; tel 813/441-2425. **New American/Continental.** This attractive, men's club-style room is casual for lunch and upscale for dinner. Traditional menu. **FYI:** Reservations recommended. Piano. Children's menu. **Open:** Breakfast daily 7–11am; lunch daily 11:30am–2:30pm; dinner daily 5–10pm. **Prices:** Main courses $9.95–$23.95. Maj CC. ♥ 💟 VP ♿

The Columbia, in the Sand Key Shopping Center, 1241 Gulf Blvd, Clearwater Beach; tel 813/596-8400. Just across Sand Key Bridge. **New American/Cuban/Spanish.** Beautiful, colorful Mediterranean tile sets the mood in this relaxed waterside restaurant. Menu items such as filet mignon, bean soup, and the catch of the day are served Spanish style. **FYI:** Reservations accepted. Children's menu. Dress code. **Open:** Sun–Thurs 11am–10pm, Fri–Sat 11am–11pm. **Prices:** Main courses $8.95–$16.95. Maj CC. 💟 ♿

Frenchy's Cafe, 41 Baymount St, Clearwater Beach; tel 813/446-3607. **Cafe.** The cafe and its adjacent bar share a relaxed, casual atmosphere. Specialties include grouper burger, buffalo shrimp, and Greek salad. **FYI:** Reservations not accepted. **Open:** Mon–Thurs 11:30am–11pm, Fri–Sat 11:30am–midnight, Sun 1–11pm. **Prices:** Main courses $2.75–$5.75. Ltd CC.

Frenchy's Rockaway Grill and Beach Club, 7 Rockaway St, Clearwater Beach; tel 813/446-4844. **Seafood/Grill.** A tavern-style establishment very popular with the college crowd. Walk in right off the beach for a beer and a burger. **FYI:** Reservations not accepted. Band. **Open:** Sun–Thurs 11am–midnight, Fri–Sat 11am–1am. **Prices:** Main courses $2.75–$9.95. Ltd CC. 🍴 ♿

Island House, 452 Mandalay Ave, Clearwater Beach; tel 813/442-2373. 1 block N of Holiday Inn Surfside. **New American/Greek.** Kids have their very own menu at this very casual eatery. Specialties for the grown-ups include seafood, beef, pork, and Greek salads. **FYI:** Reservations accepted. Children's menu. **Open:** Daily noon–10:30pm. **Prices:** Main courses $6.95–$16.95. Maj CC. 🅿 💳 ♿

Jesse's Flagship, 20 Island Way, Clearwater Beach; tel 813/443-6210. **Seafood.** This casual restaurant with several rooms is a fun spot for both families and the older generation. Early dinner specials are a good value. **FYI:** Reservations not accepted. Children's menu. **Open:** Daily 11:30am–10pm. **Prices:** Main courses $4.99–$22. Maj CC. 💳 ♿

Seafood and Sunsets at Julie's, 351 S Gulfview Blvd, Clearwater Beach; tel 813/441-2548. **Cafe.** The great beach location attracts a young crowd. Menu includes sandwiches, seafood, burgers, and fresh salads. Don't miss the fun bar upstairs. **FYI:** Reservations not accepted. Children's menu. Beer and wine only. **Open:** Daily 11am–10pm. Closed Thanksgiving. **Prices:** Main courses $4.95–$14.95. Maj CC. 🅿 💳 ♿

Ⓢ **Waterfront Pizza Restaurant**, 490 Mandalay Ave, Clearwater Beach; tel 813/442-3684. **Greek/Italian.** A busy, neon-lit eatery that offers good food at low prices. The diverse menu includes Italian and Greek dishes and gourmet pizzas. **FYI:** Reservations not accepted. Beer and wine only. **Open:** Daily 7am–11pm. **Prices:** Main courses $4.75–$14.95. Maj CC. ♿

Attraction 💼

The Admiral Tour Boat, 25 Causeway Blvd, Clearwater Beach Marina; tel 813/462-2628 or toll free 800/444-4814. This air-conditioned, 400-passenger, triple-decker craft tours Clearwater Bay in both the afternoon and evening. Afternoon sightseeing cruises, offered with an optional luncheon, depart at 12:30pm and last 2 hours. Evening dinner/dance cruises with live band and sit-down dinner depart at 7pm and run 3 hours (3½ hours on Sat). Cruises operate Tues–Sun. Boarding is half-hour before departure time; reservations required for meal cruises. $$$

CLERMONT
Map page M-7, C1

Motel 🏨

▤▤ **Orlando Vacation Resort**, 1403 US 27 N, Clermont, FL 34711; tel 904/394-6171 or toll free 800/874-9064; fax 904/394-1069. Convenient to Magic Kingdom, this informal compound offers welcome hospitality. But renovation, being planned at time of inspection, is needed. **Rooms:** 463 rms. CI 3pm/CO noon. **Amenities:** 🛁 A/C, cable TV. **Services:** 🚐 🛏 **Facilities:** 🏊 2 rsts, 1 bar (w/entertainment), playground, washer/dryer. **Rates:** $30–$45 S or D. Children under 18 stay free. Higher rates for spec evnts/hols. Pking: Outdoor, free. Maj CC.

COCOA
Map page M-7, D3

See also Kennedy Space Center

Hotel 🏨

▤▤ **Best Western Cocoa Inn**, 4225 W King St, Cocoa, FL 32926; tel 407/632-1065 or toll free 800/528-1234; fax 407/631-3302. 12 mi W of Cocoa Beach, exit 75 off I-95. An economical 2-story property embracing a pool and courtyard area. **Rooms:** 120 rms. CI noon/CO 11:30am. Nonsmoking rms avail. **Amenities:** 🛁 🔔 A/C, cable TV. **Services:** 🚐 ▤ 🛏 🛎 Car-rental desk, babysitting. **Facilities:** 🏊 🟦 ♿ 1 rst, 1 bar, games rm, washer/dryer. Barbecue grills and picnic area. Covered wooden deck. **Rates:** HS Jan–Apr $49–$59 S or D. Children under 18 stay free. Lower rates off-season. Spec packages avail. Pking: Outdoor, free. Maj CC.

Motels

▤▤ **Econolodge Space Center**, 3220 N Cocoa Blvd, Cocoa, FL 32926; tel 407/632-4561 or toll free 800/446-6900; fax 407/632-3756. A 3-story budget motel near several highways. **Rooms:** 150 rms. CI 3pm/CO 11am. Nonsmoking rms avail. **Amenities:** 🛁 A/C, cable TV w/movies. **Services:** 🚐 🛏 🛎 Car-rental desk. **Facilities:** 🏊 🟦 1 rst, 1 bar, lawn games, washer/dryer. **Rates:** HS Jan–Apr $40 S; $45–$65 D. Children under 18 stay free. Lower rates off-season. Higher rates for spec evnts/hols. Spec packages avail. Pking: Outdoor, free. Maj CC.

▤▤ **Ramada Inn Kennedy Space Center**, 900 Friday Rd, Cocoa, FL 32926; tel 407/631-1210 or toll free 800/2-RAMA-

DA; fax 407/636-8661. Exit 76 off I-95. A pleasant place for families to stay. Guests can feed the ducks in the pond nearby. **Rooms:** 150 rms. CI 2pm/CO noon. Nonsmoking rms avail. **Amenities:** 🔒 🐾 A/C, cable TV. **Services:** ✕ 🚐 🛒 🛎 Car-rental desk. **Facilities:** 🎣 🏊 🏌 ⚓ 1 rst, 1 bar (w/entertainment), games rm, lawn games, washer/dryer. **Rates:** HS Jan–Apr $55–$69 S or D. Children under 18 stay free. Lower rates off-season. Spec packages avail. Pking: Outdoor, free. Maj CC.

Attraction 🖼

Brevard Museum, 2201 Michigan Ave; tel 407/632-1830. This history and science museum chronicles Florida's history from the Ice Age to the Space Age. The Discovery Room has games, computers, and toys for children and features an aquarium and active beehive. Traveling exhibits. **Open:** Tues–Sat 10am–4pm, Sun 1–4pm. Closed some hols. $

COCOA BEACH

Map page M-7, D4

See also Kennedy Space Center

Hotels 🏨

🏨🏨 **Cape Colony Resort**, 1275 N Atlantic Ave, Cocoa Beach, FL 32931; tel 407/783-2252 or toll free 800/795-2252; fax 407/783-4485. Exit 77 off I-95. A commendable tourist-class hotel situated away from beach but near local attractions like the JFK Space Center. **Rooms:** 128 rms and effic. CI 3pm/CO 11am. Nonsmoking rms avail. Plain rooms. **Amenities:** 🔒 A/C, cable TV, in-rm safe. **Services:** 🚐 🖼 🛎 🛒 Car-rental desk. **Facilities:** 🎣 🏊 ⚓ 1 rst, 2 bars, games rm, lawn games, beauty salon, washer/dryer. **Rates:** HS Mar–Apr/July–Aug $76–$96 S or D; from $81 effic. Children under 18 stay free. Lower rates off-season. Higher rates for spec evnts/hols. Pking: Outdoor, free. Maj CC.

🏨🏨🏨 **Cocoa Beach Hilton**, 1550 N Atlantic Ave, Cocoa Beach, FL 32931; tel 407/799-0003 or toll free 800/526-2609; fax 407/799-0344. Exit 77 off I-95. The clear leader among hotels in this area, with a fine reputation. The tropical motif creates a fun yet still professional look. Guests can stroll across the boardwalk over the dunes to the beach. **Rooms:** 297 rms and stes. CI 3pm/CO 11am. Nonsmoking rms avail. Most rooms have ocean views. **Amenities:** 🔒 🐾 A/C, cable TV. **Services:** ✕ 🖙 🚐 🖼 🛒 Car-rental desk, babysitting. **Facilities:** 🎣 ⛱ 🏊 ⚓ 1 rst, 2 bars, 1 beach (ocean), board surfing, games rm, whirlpool, washer/dryer. **Rates:** HS Feb–Apr/July–Aug $70–

$145 S or D; from $100 ste. Extra person $15. Children under 18 stay free. Lower rates off-season. Spec packages avail. Pking: Outdoor, free. Maj CC.

🏨🏨 **Comfort Inn & Suite Resort**, 3901 N Atlantic Ave, Cocoa Beach, FL 32931; tel 407/783-2221 or toll free 800/247-2221; fax 407/783-0461. Exit 77 off I-95. Mid-rise hotel featuring a courtyard with a waterfall and fish pond. **Rooms:** 144 rms, stes, and effic. CI 2pm/CO 11am. Express checkout avail. Nonsmoking rms avail. **Amenities:** 🔒 🐾 🖨 🍷 A/C, cable TV w/movies, refrig, in-rm safe. Some units w/terraces. **Services:** 🚐 🖼 🛒 Car-rental desk. Complimentary cocktail hour. **Facilities:** 🎣 🏊 ⚓ 2 bars, games rm, lawn games, whirlpool, playground, washer/dryer. Poolside snackbar. **Rates:** HS Feb–Apr/June–Aug $71–$119 S or D; from $95 ste; from $67 effic. Extra person $8. Children under 12 stay free. Lower rates off-season. Spec packages avail. Pking: Outdoor, free. Maj CC.

🏨🏨 **Holiday Inn Cocoa Beach**, 1300 N Atlantic Ave, Cocoa Beach, FL 32931; tel 407/783-2271 or toll free 800/226-6587; fax 407/784-8878. A sprawling complex with a beach from where guests (if lucky enough) can watch space shuttle launches. **Rooms:** 500 rms, stes, and effic. CI 4pm/CO 11am. Express checkout avail. Nonsmoking rms avail. Two-floor lofts available. **Amenities:** 🔒 🐾 A/C, cable TV. Some units w/terraces. **Services:** ✕ 🖙 🚐 🖼 🛒 Car-rental desk, social director, children's program, babysitting. **Facilities:** 🎣 🚲 🏊 🎾 🍴 🏊 ⚓ 3 rsts, 3 bars (1 w/entertainment), 1 beach (ocean), board surfing, games rm, lawn games, whirlpool, beauty salon, day-care ctr, playground, washer/dryer. Reggae band plays weekends at the luau. **Rates:** $105–$250 S or D; from $235 ste; from $175 effic. Extra person $15. Children under 18 stay free. Higher rates for spec evnts/hols. Spec packages avail. Pking: Outdoor, free. Maj CC.

🏨🏨 **Howard Johnson Plaza Hotel**, 2080 N Atlantic Ave, Cocoa Beach, FL 32931; tel 407/783-9222 or toll free 800/55-BEACH; fax 407/799-3234. Exit 77 off I-95. A 6-story, oceanfront facility that draws a leisure-business mix. **Rooms:** 210 rms, stes, and effic. CI 3pm/CO 11am. Nonsmoking rms avail. Some rooms are arranged for families. **Amenities:** 🔒 🐾 A/C, cable TV. Some units w/terraces. **Services:** ✕ 🖙 🚐 🖼 🛒 Car-rental desk, babysitting. **Facilities:** 🎣 🍴 🏊 ⚓ 2 rsts, 3 bars (1 w/entertainment), 1 beach (ocean), games rm, lawn games, playground, washer/dryer. Special observation deck allows guests to watch space shuttle launches. **Rates:** HS Feb–Apr/July–Aug $55–$115 S; $65–$125 D; from $85 ste; from $95 effic. Extra person $10. Children under 18 stay free. Lower rates off-season. Spec packages avail. Pking: Outdoor, free. Maj CC.

🏨🏨🏨 **Ocean Landings Resort & Racquet Club**, 900 N Atlantic Ave, Cocoa Beach, FL 32931; tel 407/783-9430 or toll free 800/323-8413; fax 407/783-1339. This oceanfront property offers many activities to keep vacationing guests busy. **Rooms:** 226 rms, stes, and effic. CI 5pm/CO 11am. Express checkout avail. Florida-inspired furnishings in homestyle guest rooms. **Amenities:** 🛁 🗔 🍷 A/C, cable TV, refrig. Some units w/terraces, some w/Jacuzzis. **Services:** 🚙 🍴 Car-rental desk, social director, babysitting. **Facilities:** 🛗 🗔 📺 🔥 160 🏊 1 rst, 1 bar (w/entertainment), 1 beach (ocean), board surfing, lawn games, racquetball, squash, sauna, steam rm, whirlpool, playground, washer/dryer. **Rates:** HS Feb–Sept $52–$136 S or D; from $76 ste; from $106 effic. Children under 18 stay free. Lower rates off-season. Spec packages avail. Pking: Outdoor, free. Maj CC.

Restaurants 🍴

Alma's, 306 N Orlando Ave, Cocoa Beach; tel 407/783-1981. **Italian.** A comfortable, old-fashioned restaurant of several rooms, all ornamented with artwork, tile flooring, and potted plants. The menu offers a variety of seafood and beef entrees, as well as traditional Italian dishes. **FYI:** Reservations accepted. Children's menu. **Open:** Daily 5–10pm. Closed some hols. **Prices:** Main courses $15–$19. Maj CC. 🌑 🏃

Bernard's Surf, 2 S Atlantic Ave, Cocoa Beach; tel 407/783-2401. At Fla A1A and Minute Man Causeway. **Seafood.** A dimly lit, casual restaurant with an extensive menu offering sandwiches and burgers as well as pasta, seafood, and beef entrees. **FYI:** Reservations recommended. **Open:** Daily 11am–11pm. Closed Dec 25. **Prices:** Main courses $12–$25. Maj CC. 🌑 🏃

Mango Tree, 118 N Atlantic Ave, Cocoa Beach; tel 407/799-0513. Corner of 1st St N and N Atlantic Ave. **American/Continental.** Probably the best restaurant in the area, with a romantic ambience, an elaborate continental menu, and an attentive staff. The conscientious owner oversees all aspects of the daily operation. The dining room sports a saltwater fish tank, and the beautifully landscaped garden features a lovely gazebo. **FYI:** Reservations recommended. Piano. Dress code. **Open:** Tues–Sun 6–10pm. Closed some hols. **Prices:** Main courses $18.95–$39. Maj CC. 💗 🏃

Attraction 🖼

Cocoa Beach Pier, 401 Meade Ave; tel 407/783-7549. This pier, extending 800 feet into the Atlantic Ocean, has restaurants, nightclubs, shops, and a bait and tackle store that rents fishing equipment. **Open:** Daily 11am–11pm (closing hours vary at each establishment). Closed Dec 25. Free.

COCONUT GROVE

See Miami

CORAL GABLES

Map page M-11, B2

Hotels 🛏

≣≣ **Holiday Inn**, 2051 LeJeune Rd, Coral Gables, FL 33134; tel 305/443-2301 or toll free 800/HOLIDAY; fax 305/446-6827. An excellent business hotel; each floor houses a business room equipped with a modem, fax machine, and laptop print cables. **Rooms:** 168 rms and stes. CI 2pm/CO noon. Nonsmoking rms avail. Pastel decor, with wicker headboards and dark furnishings. **Amenities:** 🛁 🗔 A/C, cable TV. **Services:** ✕ VP 🚙 🛅 🍴 Babysitting. **Facilities:** 🛗 🔥 250 1 rst, 1 bar (w/entertainment), washer/dryer. Exercise room is planned in the former sauna. **Rates:** HS Dec 15–Apr 30 $80–$85 S or D; from $140 ste. Extra person $10. Lower rates off-season. Higher rates for spec evnts/hols. Spec packages avail. Pking: Outdoor, free. Maj CC.

≣≣ **Hotel Place St Michel**, 162 Alcazar, Coral Gables, FL 33134; tel 305/444-1666; fax 305/529-0074. At Ponce de Leon Blvd. This romantic hotel in a 3-story corner building is something of a charmer, a look back to a time when elevators were manned and guest rooms were individually decorated. Has an elegant old-world atmosphere. **Rooms:** 27 rms and stes. CI 2pm/CO noon. Rooms may have an antique or two; some have original marble floors and original fixtures. **Amenities:** 🛁 🗔 🍷 A/C, TV. 1 unit w/terrace. **Services:** ✕ 🛅 🍴 Babysitting. **Facilities:** 125 🏃 1 rst (*see also* "Restaurants" below), 1 bar (w/entertainment). **Rates (CP):** HS Nov–Apr $125 S or D; from $150 ste. Extra person $10. Children under 12 stay free. Lower rates off-season. Spec packages avail. Pking: Outdoor, Maj CC.

≣≣≣≣ **Omni Colonnade Hotel**, 180 Aragon Ave, Coral Gables, FL 33134; tel 305/441-2600 or toll free 800/533-1337; fax 305/445-3929. A wonderful hotel housed in a historic building containing many striking architectural features. Grand rotunda entrance, luxurious public areas, lovely appointments. Hotel is supported by a dedicated staff. **Rooms:** 157 rms and stes. CI 3pm/CO noon. Nonsmoking rms avail. **Amenities:** 🛁 🗔 🍷 A/C, cable TV w/movies, bathrobes. All units w/minibars. **Services:** 🍽 🛎 🛅 Car-rental desk, masseur, babysitting. **Facilities:** 🛗 🔥 700 💻 2 rsts (*see also* "Restaurants" below), 1 bar (w/entertainment), sauna, whirlpool, beauty salon. Sophisticated, very popular bar. **Rates:** HS Oct–Apr 15 $215–$255 S or D; from $295 ste. Extra person $30. Lower rates off-season. Spec packages avail. Pking: Indoor, $8.50. Maj CC.

Restaurants 🍴

Aragon Cafe, in the Omni Colonnade Hotel, 180 Aragon Ave, Coral Gables; tel 305/448-9966. **New American/French.** A formal restaurant with quiet elegance and an international flair. The menu is as appealing as the ambience. Seafood is the house specialty, and salmon is the fish of choice. The menu also features duck sausage and various veal selections. **FYI:** Reservations accepted. Piano. **Open:** Tues–Sat 6–11pm. **Prices:** Main courses $17–$25. Maj CC. ♥ &

Bistro, 2611 Ponce de Leon Blvd, Coral Gables; tel 305/442-9671. **Continental/French.** A cozy Italian eatery, particularly popular with families. House specialties include veal scaloppine marsala and a variety of pastas. **FYI:** Reservations accepted. Beer and wine only. **Open:** Lunch Mon–Fri 11:30am–2pm; dinner Mon–Thurs 6–10:30pm, Fri–Sat 6–11pm. **Prices:** Main courses $18–$29. Maj CC. 🎦

★ **Caffe Abbracci**, 318 Aragon Ave, Coral Gables; tel 305/441-0700. **Italian.** An appealing, upscale northern Italian eatery. The dark, finely furnished bar and stylish dining rooms create an aura of affluence. The menu features such specialties as risotto al Porcini, grilled Norwegian salmon, and a swordfish, shrimp, and salmon combination. **FYI:** Reservations recommended. Dress code. **Open:** Lunch Mon–Fri 11:30am–3pm; dinner Sun–Thurs 6–11:30pm, Fri–Sat 6pm–12am. **Prices:** Main courses $16–$23. Maj CC. ♥ &

Caffe Baci, 2522 Ponce de Leon Blvd, Coral Gables; tel 305/442-0600. **Italian/Mediterranean.** A bright, cozy cafe. Romantic pink pastel interior is adorned with Roman prints and fresh floral displays. **FYI:** Reservations accepted. Beer and wine only. **Open:** Lunch Mon–Fri 12:00–3:00pm; dinner Mon–Thurs 6:30–11:00pm, Fri–Sat 6:30–11:30pm, Sun 6:00–10:30pm. **Prices:** Main courses $13.50–$23.50. Maj CC. ♥ VP

Casa Rolandi, 1930 Ponce de Leon Blvd, Coral Gables; tel 305/444-2187. At Navarre St. **Italian.** An attractive eatery renowned for its creative northern Italian cooking. **FYI:** Reservations accepted. Beer and wine only. **Open:** Lunch Mon–Fri noon–3pm; dinner daily 6–11pm. Closed some hols. **Prices:** Main courses $13–$25. Maj CC. ♥

Charade, 2900 Ponce de Leon Blvd, Coral Gables; tel 305/448-6077. **French.** You'll feel like Cary Grant or Audrey Hepburn as you dine in splendor. The beautiful, classically styled restaurant is adorned with fresh flowers and a glittering chande-

lier. Piano music. **FYI:** Reservations recommended. Jacket required. **Open:** Lunch Mon–Sun 11:30–3:30pm; dinner Sun–Thurs 5:30–11pm, Fri–Sat 5:30pm–midnight. **Prices:** Main courses $19.95–$29.95. Maj CC. ♥

Christy's, 3101 Ponce de Leon Blvd, Coral Gables; tel 305/446-1400. **Continental/Steak.** A landmark steakhouse, styled like a gentleman's club, where you can rub elbows with longtime area residents. Cozy atmosphere. **FYI:** Reservations recommended. Dress code. **Open:** Mon–Thurs 11:30am–11pm, Fri 11:30am–midnight, Sat 5pm–midnight, Sun 5–11pm. **Prices:** Main courses $16–$32. Maj CC. ♥ &

Domenico's, 2271 Ponce de Leon Blvd, Coral Gables; tel 305/442-2033. **Italian.** A smart, casual restaurant. Popular dishes include half a lobster served in zesty sauce with an assortment of other seafood, center-cut swordfish, and pasta stuffed with spinach and ricotta. **FYI:** Reservations recommended. Beer and wine only. **Open:** Lunch daily 11am–2:30pm; dinner daily 6–11pm. Closed some hols. **Prices:** Main courses $11.95–$26.95. Maj CC. ♥ &

House of India, 22 Merrick Way, Coral Gables; tel 305/444-2348. 1 block N of Miracle Mile. **Indian.** This dark restaurant, with its soft Indian music, is a real treat. The very reasonably priced lunch and dinner buffets include chicken, lamb, shrimp, fish, and bread prepared authentically in a tandoor, the clay oven of India. **FYI:** Reservations accepted. **Open:** Lunch daily 11:30am–3pm; dinner Sun–Thurs 5–10pm, Fri–Sat 5–11pm. Closed some hols. **Prices:** Main courses $7–$10. Maj CC. &

Le Festival, 2120 Salzedo St, Coral Gables; tel 305/442-8545. 5 blocks N of Miracle Mile. **French.** Elegant French dining in a refined, flower-filled setting. Seafood, steak, chicken, and wild game dishes are served, followed by splendid desserts. **FYI:** Reservations recommended. **Open:** Lunch Mon–Fri 11:45am–2:30pm; dinner Mon–Thurs 6–10:30pm, Fri–Sat 6–11pm. Closed July 4. **Prices:** Main courses $15.75–$24.95. Maj CC. &

Peppy's in the Gables, 216 Palermo Ave, Coral Gables; tel 305/448-1240. **Northern Italian.** Northern Italian cuisine served by a friendly staff in a cozy, Euro-style dining room. **FYI:** Reservations accepted. Beer and wine only. **Open:** Lunch Mon–Fri 11:30am–2pm; dinner Tues–Thurs 5–11pm, Fri–Sat 5pm–midnight. **Prices:** Main courses $12–$21. Maj CC. ♥ &

♣ **Restaurant St Michel**, in Hotel Place St Michel, 162 Alcazar Ave, Coral Gables; tel 305/446-6572. **New American/French.** A very elegant, rather formal dinner spot (slightly more casual for lunch) with chandeliers, antiques, hardwood floors, and beautiful flowers. A wide variety of entrees is available, including grilled veal with pink peppercorn and mustard cream sauce, roast Long Island duckling, yellowtail snapper, and fresh Maine lobster. The changing wine list is extensive. **FYI:** Reservations accepted. Piano. **Open:** Breakfast Mon–Fri 7–9:30am; lunch Mon–Sat 11am–3pm; dinner Sun–Thurs 6–10:30pm, Fri–Sat 5–11:30pm; brunch Sun 11am–3pm. **Prices:** Main courses $13.95–$26.95. Maj CC. ♥ ✉ ♿

Ristorante Tanino, 2312 Ponce de Leon Blvd, Coral Gables; tel 305/446-1666. **Italian.** A quiet, charming, unpretentious French eatery favored by couples. The menu includes a selection of fine seafood dishes as well as rack of lamb and veal steak in lemon sauce. **FYI:** Reservations recommended. Beer and wine only. **Open:** Lunch Mon–Fri 11:30am–2:30pm; dinner Mon–Fri 5:30–11pm, Sat 6–11pm. Closed some hols. **Prices:** Main courses $9–$20. Maj CC. ♥ ✉ ♿

Two Sisters, in the Hyatt Hotel, 50 Alhambra Plaza, Coral Gables; tel 305/445-1234. **Caribbean/Health/Spa.** A spacious, stylish, and romantic setting for the Spanish-influenced dishes. The tapas are popular. **FYI:** Reservations accepted. Children's menu. **Open:** Breakfast daily 7–11am; lunch Mon–Sat 11am–3pm; dinner daily 6–11pm; brunch Sun 11am–3pm. **Prices:** Main courses $12–$24. Maj CC. ♥ VP ♿

Yuca, 177 Giralda, Coral Gables; tel 305/444-4448. **Cuban/Latin.** An immaculate, upscale new Cuban restaurant where smartly dressed chefs prepare inspired gourmet entrees. Inventive specialties include grilled veal chops with black beans, rice, and chayote slaw seasoned with onion essence, as well as citrus-planked salmon with mango-mustard glaze. **FYI:** Reservations recommended. Band. **Open:** Lunch Mon–Sat noon–4pm; dinner Mon–Thurs 4–11pm, Fri–Sat 4pm–midnight; brunch Sun 11:30am–3:30pm. **Prices:** Main courses $18–$28. Maj CC. VP ♿

Attractions

Fairchild Tropical Gardens, 10901 Old Cutler Rd; tel 305/667-1651. These large botanical gardens feature a veritable rain forest of both rare and exotic plants. Narrated tram tours are available; phone ahead for the schedule. **Open:** Daily 9:30am–4:30pm. Closed Dec 25. $$$

Venetian Pool, 2701 De Soto Blvd; tel 305/460-5356. Miami's most unusual swimming pool, dating from 1924, is hidden behind pastel stucco walls and is honored with a listing in the National Register of Historic Places. The pool is ornamented with palm-studded paths, Venetian-style bridges, and coral rock caves. Visitors are free to swim and sunbathe here year-round. **Open:** Call for hours. Closed some hols. $$

CORTEZ
Map page M-8, B1

Restaurant 🍴

Seafood Shack, 4110 127th St W, Cortez; tel 813/794-1235. At Cortez Rd. **Seafood/Steak.** Overlooking the Intracoastal Waterway. You can take the showboat over to the restaurant and receive $7 off dinner. Pay a visit to the Marina Grill lounge, located downstairs. **FYI:** Reservations not accepted. Children's menu. **Open:** Sun–Thurs 11:30am–9pm, Fri–Sat 11:30am–10pm. Closed some hols. **Prices:** Main courses $6.95–$22.95. Maj CC. ♿

CRYSTAL RIVER
Map page M-6, B3

Hotel 🛏

≡≡ Days Inn Resort, 2380 US 19 N, PO Box 785, Crystal River, FL 32629; tel 904/795-2111 or toll free 800/343-4230; fax 904/795-4126. Exit 40 off I-75. ½ mile N of Crystal River Mall. Family-oriented, with manicured grounds and a landscaped courtyard. **Rooms:** 106 rms, stes, and effic. CI 3pm/CO noon. Nonsmoking rms avail. **Amenities:** 🛏 A/C, cable TV. 1 unit w/terrace. **Services:** ✕ 🚐 ↺ ↺ Free shuttle to mall. **Facilities:** 🛎 200 1 rst, 1 bar (w/entertainment), lawn games, washer/dryer. **Rates:** HS Feb–Mar $50–$55 S or D; from $90 ste; from $55 effic. Extra person $6. Children under 18 stay free. Lower rates off-season. Pking: Outdoor, free. Maj CC.

Resort

≡≡≡ Plantation Inn & Golf Resort, 9301 W Fort Island Trail, PO Box 1116, Crystal River, FL 34423; tel 904/795-4211 or toll free 800/632-6262; fax 904/795-1368. 420 acres. Columned, white-brick "estate" with a classic interior and some antiques. **Rooms:** 155 rms, stes, and effic. CI 2pm/CO noon. Nonsmoking rms avail. **Amenities:** 🛏 ♨ 🖥 A/C, cable TV w/movies. Some units w/terraces. **Services:** ✕ 🚐 ↺ ↺ **Facilities:** 🛎 ⛳ ▸27 🏊 🚤 500 ♿ 2 rsts, 3 bars (1 w/entertainment), games rm, lawn games, snorkeling, sauna, washer/dryer. Marina. **Rates:** HS Jan–Mar $88–$107 S or D; from $118 ste; from $310 effic. Extra person $15. Children under 12 stay free. Lower rates off-season. AP rates avail. Spec packages avail. Pking: Outdoor, free. Maj CC.

Attraction 🖼

Crystal River State Archeological Site, 3400 N Museum Pointe; tel 904/795-3817. Archeologists have recovered numerous artifacts from this site, mainly from about 200 BC to AD 1400, when a community of pre-Columbian mound-builders resided here. Six mounds, used for various purposes, remain in the park, and there are two large limestone boulders thought to have been used as part of a solar calendar system. An on-site museum focuses on the mound-builders, but also has pieces recovered from even earlier settlements. A half-mile loop trail is marked with plaques explaining many features of the mounds. Gift shop, picnic area. **Open:** Park, daily 8am–dusk; museum, daily 9am–5pm. $

CYPRESS GARDENS

Map page M-7, E1

See Winter Haven

DANIA

Map page M-11, A2

Hotels 🛏

≣≣≣ **Fort Lauderdale Airport Hilton**, 1870 Griffin Rd, Dania, FL 33004; tel 305/920-3300 or toll free 800/445-8667, 800/426-8578, 800/654-8266 in FL; fax 305/920-0517. 11 acres. A spiffy hotel with good security. Tropical motif, airy 3-story lobby. **Rooms:** 388 rms and stes. Exec-level rms avail. CI 3pm/CO noon. Nonsmoking rms avail. Rooms are appointed with quality furnishings. **Amenities:** 🔒 🏠 A/C, cable TV w/movies. Some units w/minibars, some w/terraces, 1 w/Jacuzzi. **Services:** ⏾ ➤ 🆅🅿 🚗 🖾 ⏾ Twice-daily maid svce, car-rental desk, masseur, babysitting. **Facilities:** 🔥 🏊 ⛳ 💇 🕿 [IK] 🖥 2 rsts, 3 bars (1 w/entertainment), sauna, steam rm, whirlpool. Rooftop terrace on 8th floor. **Rates:** HS Dec–Apr $119 S; $129 D; from $195 ste. Extra person $15. Children under 18 stay free. Lower rates off-season. Higher rates for spec evnts/hols. Spec packages avail. Pking: Indoor/outdoor, free. Maj CC.

≣≣≣ **Sheraton Design Center**, 1825 Griffin Rd, Dania, FL 33004; tel 305/920-3500 or toll free 800/325-3535; fax 305/920-3571. 5 minutes from Ft Lauderdale Int'l Airport. A stylish, first-rate commercial hotel. **Rooms:** 251 rms and stes. Exec-level rms avail. CI 3pm/CO noon. Nonsmoking rms avail. **Amenities:** 🔒 🏠 🖭 A/C, cable TV w/movies, voice mail,

bathrobes. **Services:** ⏾ ➤ 🚗 🖾 ⏾ 🕊 Twice-daily maid svce, babysitting. **Facilities:** 🔥 🚲 🕿 💇 [400] 🖥 🔥 4 rsts, 2 bars (1 w/entertainment), lawn games, racquetball, sauna, steam rm, whirlpool. **Rates:** HS Jan–Apr $150–$170 S; $160–$180 D; from $275 ste. Extra person $10. Children under 18 stay free. Lower rates off-season. Pking: Outdoor, free. Maj CC.

DAVIE

Map page M-11, A2

Restaurant 🍴

Tarks, in Pine Island Plaza, 8970 Fla 84, Davie; tel 305/475-8275. **New American.** Casual tavern, with pooltables and neon beer signs. Chicken sandwiches, chicken caesar salads, burgers, fried clams. Daily lunch specials are $3.95. **FYI:** Reservations accepted. Children's menu. **Open:** Mon–Thurs 11am–11pm, Fri–Sat 11am–midnight, Sun noon–10pm. Closed Dec 25. **Prices:** Main courses $3.95–$9.95. Ltd CC. 🔥

DAYTONA BEACH

Map page M-7, A3

See also Daytona Beach Shores, New Smyrna Beach, Ormond Beach, Ponce Inlet

Hotels 🛏

≣≣ **Acapulco Inn**, 2505 S Atlantic Ave, Daytona Beach, FL 32110; tel 904/761-2210 or toll free 800/874-7420; fax 904/761-2216. Exit 87 off I-95. This 8-story property is popular with students during spring break and with couples and others off-peak. **Rooms:** 133 rms and effic. CI 3pm/CO 11am. Nonsmoking rms avail. Sturdy rooms in tropical colors, furnished with adequate appointments for this grade of hotel. Units are categorized oceanview or oceanfront. **Amenities:** 🔒 🏠 🖭 A/C, cable TV w/movies, refrig, in-rm safe. All units w/terraces. Some have microwaves. **Services:** 🚗 🖾 ⏾ Car-rental desk, children's program. **Facilities:** 🔥 🏊 🔥 1 rst, 1 bar, 1 beach (ocean), games rm, lawn games, whirlpool, washer/dryer. Restaurant provides ocean vistas. **Rates:** HS Feb–Aug $159–$173 S or D; from $167 effic. Extra person $10. Children under 18 stay free. Lower rates off-season. Pking: Outdoor, free. Maj CC.

≣≣ **The Aladdin Inn**, 2323 S Atlantic Ave, Daytona Beach, FL 32110; tel 904/255-0476 or toll free 800/874-7517; fax 904/255-3376. Exit 87 off I-95. A 6-story oceanfront hotel flanked on one side by a pool and furnished with a routine mix of accommodations. **Rooms:** 120 rms, stes, and effic. CI 3pm/CO 11am. **Amenities:** 🔒 A/C, cable TV, refrig, in-rm safe. All units w/terraces. **Services:** 🍴 📠 🛎 Car-rental desk, children's program, babysitting. **Facilities:** 🏊 1 beach (ocean), games rm, lawn games, washer/dryer. **Rates:** HS June–Aug $72–$139 S or D; from $139 ste; from $82 effic. Children under 18 stay free. Lower rates off-season. Higher rates for spec evnts/hols. Spec packages avail. Pking: Outdoor, free. Maj CC.

🏕🏕 **The American Beach Lodge Resort**, 1260 N Atlantic Ave, Daytona Beach, FL 32118; tel 904/255-7431 or toll free 800/874-1824; fax 904/253-9513. Exit 88 off I-95. An aging, balconied highrise hotel on beach. Continues to prosper with a steady flow of beachgoers and other tourists. **Rooms:** 182 rms, stes, and effic. CI 4pm/CO 11am. **Amenities:** 🔒 A/C, cable TV, refrig. Some units w/terraces. **Services:** 🔑 🍴 📠 🛎 Car-rental desk, social director, masseur, children's program, babysitting. **Facilities:** 🏊 🏋 ♿ 2 rsts, 3 bars (1 w/entertainment), 1 beach (ocean), games rm, lawn games, sauna, whirlpool, washer/dryer. Kung Fu offered twice weekly in the fitness center, a facility more ambitious than usually found in a hotel of this grade. **Rates:** HS Apr–Aug $58–$95 S or D; from $85 ste; from $68 effic. Extra person $8. Children under 12 stay free. Lower rates off-season. Higher rates for spec evnts/hols. Spec packages avail. Pking: Outdoor, free. Maj CC.

🏕🏕 **Beachcomber Oceanfront Inn**, 2000 N Atlantic Ave, Daytona Beach, FL 32118; tel 904/252-8513 or toll free 800/874-7420; fax 904/252-7400. Exit 87A off I-95. Away from the fray of beach action, this modest but attractive 7-story hotel has accommodations facing the ocean or street. Couples and others hoping to avoid boom boxes and corridor parties will be happy here. **Rooms:** 174 rms and effic. CI 3pm/CO 11am. Nonsmoking rms avail. **Amenities:** 🔒 🍴 A/C, cable TV w/movies, in-rm safe. All units w/terraces. Some have coffeemakers and small refrigerators. **Services:** 🍴 📠 🛎 **Facilities:** 🏊 ♿ 1 rst, 1 bar, 1 beach (ocean), games rm, lawn games, whirlpool, washer/dryer. **Rates:** HS June–Aug $48–$174 S or D; from $76 effic. Extra person $8. Children under 18 stay free. Min stay spec evnts. Lower rates off-season. Higher rates for spec evnts/hols. Spec packages avail. Pking: Outdoor, free. Maj CC.

🏕🏕 **Boardwalk Beach Resort**, 400 N Atlantic Ave, Daytona Beach, FL 32118; tel 904/255-0251 or toll free 800/535-2036; fax 904/238-0907. Exit 87 off I-95. Busy motel in the center of spring break activity. An alert staff and maintenance crew manages to keep most problems in check. **Rooms:** 196 rms and effic. CI 4pm/CO 11am. Nonsmoking rms avail. More than a half-dozen categories of room grades. **Amenities:** 🔒 A/C, cable TV w/movies. All units w/terraces. **Services:** 📠 🛎 **Facilities:** 🏊 🏊 ♿ 1 rst, 3 bars (1 w/entertainment), 1 beach (ocean),

lifeguard, games rm, washer/dryer. Country-western theme to top-floor restaurant. **Rates:** HS Mar–mid-Apr $55–$79 S or D; from $79 effic. Children under 18 stay free. Min stay spec evnts. Lower rates off-season. Higher rates for spec evnts/hols. Spec packages avail. Pking: Outdoor, free. Maj CC.

🏕🏕 **Captain's Quarters Inn**, 3711 S Atlantic Ave, Daytona Beach, FL 32127; tel 904/767-3119 or toll free 800/332-3119; fax 904/767-0883. Exit 8S off I-95. This all-suites hotel has fine accommodations with hardwood floors and quality appointments. Limited public areas. **Rooms:** 26 stes. CI 3pm/CO 11am. **Amenities:** 🔒 🍴 📺 A/C, cable TV, refrig, VCR. All units w/terraces, 1 w/fireplace, 1 w/Jacuzzi. **Services:** ✕ 📠 🛎 **Facilities:** 🏊 ♿ 1 rst, 1 beach (ocean), washer/dryer. **Rates:** HS June–Aug from $75 ste. Extra person $5. Children under 18 stay free. Lower rates off-season. Higher rates for spec evnts/hols. Pking: Outdoor, free. Maj CC.

🏕🏕 **Days Inn Daytona Central**, 1909 S Atlantic Ave, Daytona Beach, FL 32118; tel 904/255-4492 or toll free 800/224-5056; fax 904/238-0632. Exit 87 off I-95. A 9-story, beachfront tourist hotel. **Rooms:** 191 rms and effic. CI 4pm/CO noon. Nonsmoking rms avail. Rooms with partial or full ocean views. Oceanfront efficiencies. **Amenities:** 🔒 🍴 A/C, cable TV w/movies, in-rm safe. All units w/terraces. **Services:** 🍴 📠 🛎 🛎 **Facilities:** 🏊 🏊 1 bar, 1 beach (ocean), games rm, washer/dryer. **Rates:** HS Feb–Apr $75–$95 S or D; from $85 effic. Extra person $6. Children under 18 stay free. Lower rates off-season. Higher rates for spec evnts/hols. Spec packages avail. Pking: Outdoor, free. Maj CC.

🏕🏕🏕 **Daytona Beach Hotel**, 2637 S Atlantic Ave, Daytona Beach, FL 32110; tel 904/767-7350 or toll free 800/525-7350; fax 904/760-3651. Volusia Ave exit off I-95. An attractive highrise hotel located on the beach. Spacious lobby. **Rooms:** 214 rms, stes, and effic. CI 3pm/CO 11am. Express checkout avail. Nonsmoking rms avail. First-class accommodations are neat and stylish, with excellent ocean and beach views. **Amenities:** 🔒 🍴 📺 A/C, cable TV w/movies, refrig, in-rm safe. Some units w/minibars, some w/terraces. Some rooms have coffeemakers. **Services:** ✕ 🔑 VP 🍴 📠 🛎 Car-rental desk, babysitting. **Facilities:** 🏊 🎾 🏋 🏊 🎱 ♿ 2 rsts, 2 bars (1 w/entertainment), 1 beach (ocean), games rm, lawn games, whirlpool, beauty salon, washer/dryer. Large motorist entrance is joined by a skywalk to additional parking across the street. **Rates:** HS Feb–Apr/July $89–$170 S or D; from $145 ste; from $145 effic. Extra person $15. Children under 18 stay free. Lower rates off-season. Spec packages avail. Pking: Indoor/outdoor, free. Maj CC.

🏕🏕🏕 **Daytona Beach Marriott**, 100 N Atlantic Ave, Daytona Beach, FL 32118; tel 904/254-8200 or toll free 800/228-9290; fax 904/253-8841. Exit 89 off US 92E. This is

Daytona's most luxurious—and most central—beachfront hotel, located right at the clock tower and bandshell. It makes a striking architectural statement in a resort city where blasé is the norm. The 3-story marble lobby is shiny and impressive. The style and craftsmanship in this hotel really shows. **Rooms:** 402 rms and stes. CI 4pm/CO 11am. Express checkout avail. Nonsmoking rms avail. Every room offers a beautiful ocean view. **Amenities:** 🔒 🗚 A/C, cable TV w/movies. **Services:** ✗ 🗁 VP 🚗 🗻 🗂 Car-rental desk, babysitting. **Facilities:** 🗲 🐠 ⚠ 🗋 🖳 🗀 🗲 2 rsts, 3 bars (1 w/entertainment), 1 beach (ocean), board surfing, lawn games, sauna, steam rm, whirlpool, beauty salon, washer/dryer. **Rates:** HS Feb–Apr $149 S or D; from $265 ste. Extra person $20. Children under 18 stay free. Lower rates off-season. Spec packages avail. Pking: Indoor/outdoor, free. Maj CC.

≣≣ Hawaiian Inn, 2301 S Atlantic Ave, Daytona Beach, FL 32118; tel 904/255-5411 or toll free 800/922-3023, 800/922-3023 in the US, 800/635-3502 in Canada; fax 904/253-1209. Exit 87 off I-95. A popular stop for college students on spring break who don't require anything but the most basic facilities and certainly don't expect much service. **Rooms:** 200 rms and effic. CI 3pm/CO 11am. Nonsmoking rms avail. Accommodations take a battering each year, but management tries to smooth the edges as best it can. **Amenities:** 🔒 A/C, cable TV, refrig, in-rm safe. All units w/terraces. **Services:** ✗ 🚗 🗻 🗂 Car-rental desk, babysitting. **Facilities:** 🗲 🗀 🗲 2 rsts, 2 bars (1 w/entertainment), 1 beach (ocean), games rm, lawn games, whirlpool, playground, washer/dryer. **Rates:** HS Mar–Sept $95–$105 S or D; from $100 effic. Children under 18 stay free. Lower rates off-season. Higher rates for spec evnts/hols. Spec packages avail. Pking: Outdoor, free. Maj CC.

≣≣ Holiday Inn Daytona Beach Oceanfront, 2560 N Atlantic Ave, Daytona Beach, FL 32118; tel 904/673-6793 or toll free 800/238-8000; fax 904/677-8811. Exit 87 off I-95. Renovations are taking place in both the public areas and rooms of this beachfront hotel. **Rooms:** 144 rms and effic. CI 3pm/CO 11am. Nonsmoking rms avail. All rooms have mini- or full kitchens. **Amenities:** 🔒 🗚 🗐 A/C, cable TV w/movies, refrig, in-rm safe. All units w/terraces. **Services:** 🍽 🗻 🗂 **Facilities:** 🗲 🗀 🗲 1 rst, 1 bar, 1 beach (ocean), lawn games, whirlpool, washer/dryer. Sunny pool is partly embraced by building. **Rates:** HS June–Aug $92–$102 S or D; from $83 effic. Children under 18 stay free. Min stay spec evnts. Lower rates off-season. Higher rates for spec evnts/hols. Pking: Outdoor, free. Maj CC.

≣≣ Holiday Inn Oceanside, 905 S Atlantic Ave, Daytona Beach, FL 32118; tel 904/255-5432 or toll free 800/334-4484; fax 904/254-0885. Exit 87 off I-95. A clean, stable, and attractive choice, it does a commendable job under the pressure of the annual spring break influx and an even better one off-season. Alert staff. **Rooms:** 107 rms and effic. CI 3pm/CO 11am. Express checkout avail. Nonsmoking rms avail. **Amenities:** 🔒 🗚 A/C, cable TV w/movies, in-rm safe. Some units w/minibars, all w/terraces. **Services:** ✗ 🚗 🗻 🗂 Car-rental desk, babysitting. **Facilities:** 🗲 🗀 1 rst, 1 bar, 1 beach (ocean), lawn games, washer/dryer. Reserved and intimate restaurant is a surprise for a beach city. Fireplace in lounge. **Rates:** HS Feb–Mar/June–July $85–$125 S or D; from $85 effic. Extra person $10. Children under 18 stay free. Lower rates off-season. Higher rates for spec evnts/hols. Spec packages avail. Pking: Outdoor, free. Maj CC.

≣≣≣ Howard Johnson Hotel and Conference Center, 600 N Atlantic Ave, Daytona Beach, FL 32118; tel 904/255-4471 or toll free 800/767-4471; fax 904/253-7543. Exit 87 off I-95. Comprising 2 highrise towers, this lively hotel is an attractive, solid choice. **Rooms:** 323 rms, stes, and effic. CI 4pm/CO noon. Nonsmoking rms avail. Modern rooms are nicely decorated and maintained. **Amenities:** 🔒 A/C, cable TV, in-rm safe. Some units w/terraces, some w/Jacuzzis. Guests may request a refrigerator if room is not equipped with one. **Services:** ✗ 🚗 🗻 🗂 Car-rental desk. **Facilities:** 🗲 🗀 🗲 1 rst, 4 bars (2 w/entertainment), 1 beach (ocean), games rm, lawn games, washer/dryer. Popular nightclub. **Rates:** HS Feb–Apr/June–July $79–$119 S or D; from $165 ste; from $135 effic. Children under 18 stay free. Lower rates off-season. Higher rates for spec evnts/hols. Spec packages avail. Pking: Indoor/outdoor, free. Maj CC.

≣≣ La Playa Inn, 2500 N Atlantic Inn, Daytona Beach, FL 32118; tel 904/672-0990 or toll free 800/874-6996; fax 904/677-0982. Exit 88 off I-95. Highrise hotel on the north end of the beach, opposite a shopping plaza. **Rooms:** 239 rms, stes, and effic. CI 3pm/CO 11am. Nonsmoking rms avail. Rooms are more than adequately furnished and outfitted. Each offers an ocean-view; some have oceanfront balconies. **Amenities:** 🔒 🗚 A/C, cable TV w/movies, refrig, in-rm safe. All units w/terraces. Coffeemakers in some rooms. **Services:** ✗ 🚗 🗻 🗂 Car-rental desk, babysitting. **Facilities:** 🗲 🗀 🗀 🗲 1 rst, 2 bars (1 w/entertainment), 1 beach (ocean), games rm, lawn games, sauna, steam rm, whirlpool, washer/dryer. Chain restaurant next door also owned by hotel. **Rates:** HS June–Aug $91–$107 S or D; from $140 ste; from $97 effic. Extra person $6. Children under 17 stay free. Lower rates off-season. Higher rates for spec evnts/hols. Spec packages avail. Pking: Indoor/outdoor, free. Maj CC.

≣≣ Ocean Sands Hotel, 1024 N Atlantic Ave, Daytona Beach, FL 32118; tel 904/255-1131 or toll free 800/543-2923; fax 904/255-5670. This 8-story lodging set on very limited grounds has a sunny pool and ocean-facing accommodations that help to compensate for the drabness of the street side of the building.

Rooms: 94 rms and effic. CI 3pm/CO 11am. Nonsmoking rms avail. **Amenities:** 🕾 A/C, cable TV w/movies, refrig, in-rm safe. All units w/terraces, 1 w/Jacuzzi. **Services:** ✗ 🚐 🔼 🥤 Car-rental desk. **Facilities:** 🔼 ᕁ 1 beach (ocean), games rm, washer/dryer. **Rates:** HS Feb–Apr/June–Aug $69–$92 S or D; from $82 effic. Children under 18 stay free. Lower rates off-season. Higher rates for spec evnts/hols. Spec packages avail. Pking: Outdoor, free. Maj CC.

Palm Plaza, 3301 S Atlantic Ave, Daytona Beach, FL 32118; tel 904/767-1711 or toll free 800/DAYTONA; fax 904/756-8394. Exit 85 off I-95. A cheerful highrise on the south side of town, it presents a fresh, tropical face. Its pleasant, well-kept lobby provides an ocean view. **Rooms:** 98 effic. CI 3pm/CO 11am. Nonsmoking rms avail. **Amenities:** 🕾 🗐 A/C, cable TV w/movies, refrig, in-rm safe. All units w/terraces. **Services:** 🚐 🔼 🥤 Car-rental desk, social director, children's program, babysitting. **Facilities:** 🔼 ᕁ 1 beach (ocean), games rm, whirlpool, washer/dryer. **Rates:** HS June–Sept from $75 effic. Children under 18 stay free. Lower rates off-season. Higher rates for spec evnts/hols. Pking: Outdoor, free. Maj CC.

Perry's Ocean Edge Resort, 2209 S Atlantic Ave, Daytona Beach, FL 32118; tel 904/255-0581 or toll free 800/447-0002; fax 904/258-7315. A modest family operation offering quite extensive facilities. **Rooms:** 204 rms, stes, and effic. CI 4pm/CO 11am. Standard motel appointments. **Amenities:** 🕾 🗐 A/C, cable TV. Some units w/terraces. **Services:** 🚐 🔼 🥤 Car-rental desk, social director, children's program, babysitting. **Facilities:** 🔼 ⑤₀ ᕁ 1 rst, 1 beach (ocean), games rm, lawn games, whirlpool, washer/dryer. **Rates (CP):** HS June–Aug $60–$120 S or D; from $85 ste; from $85 effic. Children under 12 stay free. Lower rates off-season. Higher rates for spec evnts/hols. AP and MAP rates avail. Spec packages avail. Pking: Outdoor, free. Maj CC.

South Beach Resort, 701 S Atlantic Ave, Daytona Beach, FL 32118; tel 904/255-8431 or toll free 800/633-7010; fax 904/253-7425. This 8-story structure has long been a stomping ground for seemingly every fraternity brother and sorority sister this side of South Padre Island. Its nightclub is a prime draw and is immensely popular. The hotel also does a steady business after spring break. **Rooms:** 149 rms and stes. CI 4pm/CO 11am. Some units have kitchenettes. Inexpensively appointed rooms follow a minimalist philosophy in decor. **Amenities:** 🕾 A/C, cable TV. All units w/terraces. **Services:** 🚐 🔼 🥤 Car-rental desk, babysitting. **Facilities:** 🔼 1 rst, 1 bar (w/entertainment), 1 beach (ocean), games rm, lawn games, washer/dryer. **Rates:** HS Feb–Apr/June–Aug $39–$109 S or D; from $59 ste. Extra person

$10. Children under 16 stay free. Lower rates off-season. Higher rates for spec evnts/hols. Spec packages avail. Pking: Outdoor, free. Maj CC.

Motel

La Quinta Motor Inn, 2725 Volusia Ave, Daytona Beach, FL 32114; tel 904/255-7412 or toll free 800/531-5900; fax 904/255-5350. Exit 87 off I-95. Located immediately off the exit ramp. Handy to the Speedway and the dog track, this superior budget hotel focuses on good housekeeping and routine maintenance. **Rooms:** 143 rms and stes. CI 1pm/CO noon. Nonsmoking rms avail. **Amenities:** 🕾 🗐 A/C, cable TV. All units w/terraces. **Services:** 🔼 🥤 ⑨ **Facilities:** 🔼 ⑤₀ ᕁ Washer/dryer. **Rates:** HS Jan–Apr $60 S; $68 D; from $95 ste. Extra person $8. Children under 18 stay free. Lower rates off-season. Higher rates for spec evnts/hols. Pking: Outdoor, free. Maj CC.

Resort

Indigo Lakes Resort Limited, 2620 W International Speedway Blvd, Daytona Beach, FL 32120; tel 904/258-6333 or toll free 800/874-9918, 800/223-4161 in FL; fax 904/254-3615. Exit 87 off I-95. 7 acres. Large-scale resort close to the Speedway and a 5-minute drive to the beach. The handsome accommodations are housed in 2-story tan stucco buildings set on beautifully landscaped grounds that contain duck-filled lakes and lagoons spanned by arched bridges. **Rooms:** 211 rms, stes, and effic. CI 3pm/CO 11am. Nonsmoking rms avail. Rooms attractively decorated in earth tones, with dark oak furnishings. **Amenities:** 🕾 🗐 🗐 🍽 A/C, cable TV w/movies, refrig. All units w/terraces. **Services:** ✗ 🚐 🔼 🥤 Masseur, babysitting. **Facilities:** 🔼 ▶₁₈ ⛳₁₀ 🎾 ⑤₀₀ 🖥 ᕁ 2 rsts, 2 bars, lawn games, washer/dryer. Championship golf course with putting green and pro shop. **Rates:** HS Feb–Apr/June–July $85–$109 S or D; from $105 ste; from $85 effic. Extra person $10. Children under 18 stay free. Min stay spec evnts. Lower rates off-season. Higher rates for spec evnts/hols. Spec packages avail. Pking: Outdoor, free. Maj CC.

Restaurants 🍴

Anna's Italian Trattoria, 304 Seabreeze Blvd, Daytona Beach; tel 904/239-9624. At Peninsula Dr. **Italian.** An attractive pasta house with a romantic atmosphere. You can choose from a wide selection of appetizing pasta dishes. Veal and chicken entrees are also served. **FYI:** Reservations accepted. **Open:** Daily 5–10pm. **Prices:** Main courses $8.50–$16.50. Maj CC. ᕁ

Live Oak Inn, 448 S Beach St, Daytona Beach; tel 904/252-4667. **New American/Continental.** A Victorian-styled restaurant with a romantic ambience. Its 2 dining rooms have dark pine walls and lace-curtained windows; french doors open onto an enclosed porch. The menu changes frequently, and might include grilled filet mignon with mushrooms as well as fresh fish dishes. **FYI:** Reservations recommended. **Open:** Lunch Mon–Fri 11:30am–1:30pm; dinner daily 5–9:30pm. **Prices:** Main courses $14–$18. Maj CC. ♥ ⅋

Riccardo's, 610 Glenview Blvd, Daytona Beach; tel 904/253-3035. **Italian.** A romantic restaurant with a candlelit interior and stained-glass panels. The menu offers a selection of pasta entrees, including the house specialty, shrimp Riccardo (shrimp sautéed in garlic butter and served over fettuccine). **FYI:** Reservations not accepted. Children's menu. **Open:** Daily 5–10pm. Closed Dec 25. **Prices:** Main courses $7.50–$14.50. Maj CC. ♥ ⅋

St Regis Restaurant, 509 Seabreeze Blvd, Daytona Beach; tel 904/252-8743. Between Wild Olive and Grandview Aves. **Continental.** This old Victorian home with hardwood floors provides a nice backdrop for a dinner that might include the St Regis lasagna, caesar salad with shrimp, or one of the daily specials. **FYI:** Reservations accepted. Guitar. **Open:** Lunch Mon–Fri 11:30–2; dinner Mon–Thurs 5:30–10, Fri–Sat 5:30–11. Closed some hols. **Prices:** Main courses $6.95–$21.95. Maj CC. ⅋

Sophie Kay's Top of Daytona, 2625 S Atlantic Ave, Daytona Beach; tel 904/767-5791. **Seafood/Steak.** Enjoy the views from the 29th floor as you dine. Menu highlights include the queen-cut roast prime rib, shrimp scampi, and chicken parmigiana. **FYI:** Reservations accepted. Piano/singer. Children's menu. **Open:** Daily 3–10pm. **Prices:** Main courses $8.95–$23.95. Maj CC. 🖼️ 💟 ⅋

Attractions 📷

Daytona International Speedway, 1801 W International Speedway Blvd (US 92); tel 904/253-RACE (tickets) or 254-2700 (info). Opened in 1959 with the inaugural Daytona 500, the "World Center of Racing" presents about 8 weekends of major racing events annually, featuring stock cars, sports cars, motorcycles, and go-karts, and is also used for automobile testing. Its grandstand seats nearly 98,000 and is a mile long. Major annual races include the Daytona 500 by STP, the world's most prestigious stock car racing event; the Rolex 24, a major event for sports cars; and the Daytona 200 by Arai, which features motorcycles.

The **Visitors' Center** at the west end of the Speedway is the departure point for 30-minute guided van tours of the facility, given every half-hour from 9am to 4:30pm, except during races, special events, or car testing. Also here are a gift shop; the

Gallery of Legends, with photographs and memorabilia documenting the history of motor racing in the Daytona Beach area; and the Budweiser Video Wall. **Open:** Daily. Closed some hols. $$

Museum of Arts and Sciences, 1040 Museum Blvd; tel 904/255-0285. An eclectic museum featuring both art and natural science exhibits. Displayed are fine and folk art from Cuba; American fine and decorative art; African art and objects; graphic art; and the Pre-History of Florida collection, which features Pleistocene-era fossils and a 130,000-year-old, 13-foot-tall skeleton of a giant ground sloth. Contemporary sculpture garden and planetarium. **Open:** Tues–Fri 9am–4pm, Sat–Sun noon–5pm. Closed some hols. $

Halifax Historical Museum, 252 S Beach St; tel 904/255-6976. This small museum contains pieces of local history that date from early Native American settlements. Also items from Spanish colonial period, antiques, and memorabilia from the War of 1812 through World War II. Library and gift shop. **Open:** Tues–Sat 10am–4pm. Closed some hols. $

Daytona Beach Kennel Club, 2201 W International Speedway Blvd (US 92); tel 904/252-6484. Greyhound racing and pari-mutuel betting. Pavilion Clubhouse Restaurant overlooks race-track. Night races Mon–Sat at 7:45pm; matinees Mon, Wed, and Sat at 1pm. $

DAYTONA BEACH SHORES

Map page M-7, A6

Hotels 🛏️

■■ **Days Inn Oceanfront South**, 3209 S Atlantic Ave, Daytona Beach Shores, FL 32118; tel 904/761-2050 or toll free 800/722-DAYS; fax 904/761-3922. Exit 85 off I-95. **Rooms:** 196 rms, stes, and effic. CI 3pm/CO 11am. Nonsmoking rms avail. **Amenities:** 🛢️ 🗊 A/C, cable TV, refrig, in-rm safe. All units w/terraces. **Services:** 🚐 🖼️ 🖐 Car-rental desk, children's program, babysitting. **Facilities:** 🔄 🚲 ⚠ 🗊 ⛱ ⅋ 1 rst, 1 bar, 1 beach (ocean), board surfing, games rm, washer/dryer. **Rates:** $95–$150 S or D; from $150 ste; from $125 effic. Extra person $6. Children under 18 stay free. Spec packages avail. Pking: Outdoor, free. Maj CC.

■■ **Seagarden Inn**, 3161 S Atlantic Ave, Daytona Beach Shores, FL 32118; tel 904/761-2335 or toll free 800/245-0575;

fax 904/756-6676. A neat, friendly hotel with smart appointments. **Rooms:** 144 rms and effic. CI 3pm/CO 11am. Nonsmoking rms avail. **Amenities:** ☎ A/C, cable TV w/movies, in-rm safe. All units w/terraces. **Services:** 🚗 🖼 🛎 Car-rental desk, children's program, babysitting. **Facilities:** 🎣 🔲 ⅋ 1 rst, 2 bars (1 w/entertainment), 1 beach (ocean), whirlpool, washer/dryer. Restaurant offers pool views. **Rates:** HS Feb–Mar $60–$85 S or D; from $75 effic. Extra person $6. Children under 18 stay free. Lower rates off-season. Higher rates for spec evnts/hols. Spec packages avail. Pking: Outdoor, free. Maj CC.

≣≣ Turtle Inn Beach Club, 3233 S Atlantic Ave, Daytona Beach Shores, FL 32118; tel 904/761-0426; fax 904/761-5396. Exit 85 off I-95. Pleasant 4-story oceanfront complex offers studios and 1- and 2-bedroom units. The small room count ensures that guests won't get lost in the shuffle. **Rooms:** 39 effic. CI 3pm/CO 10am. **Amenities:** ☎ 🔯 🖃 A/C, cable TV, refrig. Some units w/terraces, some w/Jacuzzis. **Services:** 🚗 ⅋ **Facilities:** 🎣 🔲 1 beach (ocean), whirlpool, washer/dryer. **Rates:** HS June–Sept from $70 effic. Children under 18 stay free. Lower rates off-season. Spec packages avail. Pking: Outdoor, free. Maj CC.

DEERFIELD BEACH

Map page M-11, A2

Hotels 🛏

≣≣ Comfort Suites, 1040 E Newport Center Dr, Deerfield Beach, FL 33442; tel 305/570-8887 or toll free 800/228-5150; fax 305/570-5346. Exit 36C off I-95. Set amid pleasant surroundings, this hotel shares its dining facilities with the Quality Suites next door. The young staff is chipper and outgoing. **Rooms:** 100 stes. CI 3pm/CO noon. Nonsmoking rms avail. Suites are small by industry standards. **Amenities:** ☎ 🔯 A/C, cable TV w/movies, refrig, voice mail. **Services:** 🖼 ⅋ **Facilities:** 🎣 🔲 ⅋ 1 rst, 1 bar, games rm, whirlpool, washer/dryer. **Rates (CP):** HS Dec–Apr from $94 ste. Extra person $10. Children under 7 stay free. Lower rates off-season. Pking: Outdoor, free. Maj CC.

≣≣≣ Deerfield Beach/Boca Raton Hilton, 100 Fairway Dr, Deerfield Beach, FL 33441; tel 305/427-7700 or toll free 800/624-3606; fax 305/427-2308. Exit 37 off I-95. The area's leading hotel, a sophisticated operation that incorporates an interesting array of architectural styles. It will likely enthrall guests with its fine public areas, more stylish than those usually found in a beach town. **Rooms:** 220 rms and stes. CI 3pm/CO noon. Nonsmoking rms avail. **Amenities:** ☎ 🔯 A/C, cable TV w/movies. Some units w/terraces. **Services:** ✗ 🖼 ⅋ Babysit-

ting. **Facilities:** 🎣 ⛳ 🔲 ⅋ 2 rsts, 1 bar (w/entertainment), whirlpool. **Rates:** HS Dec–Apr $135–$149 S; $145–$159 D; from $225 ste. Extra person $10. Children under 18 stay free. Lower rates off-season. Higher rates for spec evnts/hols. Spec packages avail. Pking: Outdoor, free. Maj CC.

≣≣≣ Deerfield Beach Resort, 950 SE 20th Ave, Deerfield Beach, FL 33441; tel 305/426-0478 or toll free 800/433-4600; fax 305/360-0539. Exit 37 off I-95. Breezy decor and style at this beachfront location. Attentive staff bolts to assist arriving guests. **Rooms:** 244 stes. CI 3pm/CO noon. Nonsmoking rms avail. Few suite hotels offer 2 bathrooms per unit like this one does. **Amenities:** ☎ 🔯 🖃 A/C, cable TV w/movies, refrig, VCR. All units w/terraces. Also equipped with 2 TVs, wet bar, microwave. **Services:** ✗ 🖙 VP 🖼 ⅋ Car-rental desk, children's program, babysitting. **Facilities:** 🎣 🔲 ⅋ 1 rst, 1 bar (w/entertainment), games rm, washer/dryer. **Rates (BB):** HS Dec–Apr from $195 ste. Extra person $10. Children under 12 stay free. Lower rates off-season. Higher rates for spec evnts/hols. Pking: Indoor, $5–$7. Maj CC.

≣≣ Howard Johnson Ocean Resort Hotel & Conference Center, 2096 NE 2nd St, Deerfield Beach, FL 33441; tel 305/428-2850 or toll free 800/426-0084; fax 305/480-9639. Exit 37 off I-95. A great location for an otherwise ordinary offering. Opposite the beachfront and pier. **Rooms:** 177 rms and stes. CI 3pm/CO noon. Nonsmoking rms avail. **Amenities:** ☎ 🔯 A/C, cable TV w/movies, in-rm safe, bathrobes. Some units w/terraces. **Services:** ✗ 🖼 ⅋ **Facilities:** 🔲 ⅋ 1 rst, 1 bar, games rm. **Rates:** HS Dec–Apr $145–$185 S; $165–$185 D; from $285 ste. Extra person $10. Children under 18 stay free. Min stay spec evnts. Lower rates off-season. Pking: Outdoor, free. Maj CC.

≣≣ Oceanside Inn, 50 SE 20th Ave, Deerfield Beach, FL 33441; tel 305/428-0650 or toll free 800/827-4735; fax 305/427-2666. At Hillsboro Blvd and Fla A1A. Superior budget property. **Rooms:** 69 rms and effic. CI 2pm/CO 11am. Nonsmoking rms avail. **Amenities:** ☎ A/C, cable TV w/movies. **Services:** ✗ ⅋ Babysitting. **Facilities:** 🎣 🔲 ⅋ 1 rst, 1 bar, games rm, washer/dryer. **Rates:** HS Dec–Apr $99–$129 S or D; from $109 effic. Children under 18 stay free. Min stay HS. Lower rates off-season. Pking: Outdoor, free. Maj CC.

≣≣≣ Quality Suites, 1050 E Newport Center Dr, Deerfield Beach, FL 33442; tel 305/570-8888 or toll free 800/221-2222; fax 305/570-5346. Exit 36C off I-95. Rooms have a bit more flair than most in this price category. **Rooms:** 107 stes. CI 3pm/CO noon. Nonsmoking rms avail. **Amenities:** ☎ 🔯 A/C, cable TV w/movies, refrig, VCR, voice mail. Some units w/terraces. **Services:** ✗ 🖼 ⅋ Babysitting. **Facilities:** 🎣 🔲 ⅋ 1 rst, 1 bar, games rm, whirlpool, washer/dryer. **Rates (CP):** HS Dec–Apr from $129 ste. Extra person $10. Children under 18 stay free. Lower rates off-season. Pking: Outdoor, free. Maj CC.

≣≣ **Ramada Inn**, 1401 S Federal Hwy, Deerfield Beach, FL 33431; tel 305/421-5000 or toll free 800/283-9946; fax 305/426-2811. 1 mi S of Hillsboro Blvd. Lowrise, pink-toned highway hotel. Peaceful courtyard. **Rooms:** 107 rms, stes, and effic. CI noon/CO noon. Nonsmoking rms avail. **Amenities:** ☎ A/C, cable TV w/movies. Some units w/terraces. **Services:** ✗ ⌂ ⌐ **Facilities:** ⌂ ⌐ 1 rst, 1 bar, beauty salon, washer/dryer. **Rates:** HS Dec–Apr $55–$68 S; $65–$78 D; from $85 ste; from $75 effic. Extra person $10. Children under 18 stay free. Lower rates off-season. Higher rates for spec evnts/hols. Pking: Outdoor, free. Maj CC.

≣≣ **Wellesley Inn**, 100 SW 12th Ave, Deerfield Beach, FL 33442; tel 305/428-0661 or toll free 800/444-8888; fax 305/427-6701. Exit 37 off I-95. With newly renovated guest rooms. Well-liked for its affordability. **Rooms:** 79 rms and stes. CI 2pm/CO 11am. Nonsmoking rms avail. **Amenities:** ☎ ⌂ A/C, cable TV. **Services:** ⌂ ⌐ ⌐ **Facilities:** ⌂ & Washer/dryer. **Rates (CP):** HS Dec–Apr $80 S or D; from $99 ste. Children under 18 stay free. Lower rates off-season. Pking: Outdoor, free. Maj CC.

Motel

≣≣ **La Quinta Motor Inn**, 351 W Hillsboro Blvd, Deerfield Beach, FL 33441; tel 305/421-1004 or toll free 800/531-5900; fax 305/427-8069. Exit 37 off I-95. Popular, basic, budget motel. **Rooms:** 130 rms. CI 2pm/CO noon. Nonsmoking rms avail. **Amenities:** ☎ ⌂ A/C, cable TV. **Services:** ⌂ ⌐ ⌐ Babysitting. **Facilities:** ⌂ ⌐ & 1 rst, washer/dryer. **Rates (CP):** HS Dec–Apr $70–$77 S; $80–$87 D. Extra person $7. Children under 17 stay free. Lower rates off-season. Pking: Outdoor, free. Maj CC.

Restaurant ⍾

★ **Riverview**, 1714 Riverview Rd, Deerfield Beach; tel 305/428-3463. At Hillsboro Blvd and Intracoastal Waterway. **Regional American/Seafood.** A quietly elegant hideaway in a historic building where whirling fans overhead and warm colors and woods set the tone. Dine as you gaze at passing watercraft. Specialties include yellowtail snapper, and cinnamon ice cream for dessert. **FYI:** Reservations accepted. **Open:** Lunch Mon–Fri 12–2:30pm; dinner Mon–Sat 5–10pm. **Prices:** Main courses $10–$22; PF dinner $21. Maj CC. ⊡ ⌂ ⌂ ⌂ &

DE FUNIAK SPRINGS
Map page M-2, A4

Attractions ⌂

Circle Drive. Along Circle Drive, a 1-mile road encircling the perfectly round natural lake that lies in the center of town, are magnificent Victorian homes with ornate turrets and fancy "gingerbread" trimmings. All are as elegantly furnished as when these prestigious residences were built in the 1880s. At certain times of the year, the historic homes are open for touring.

Chautauqua Vineyards, 1330 Freeport Rd; tel 904/892-5887. Located at the intersection of I-10 and US 331, this is Florida's largest winery. Tastings are offered during the free daily tours. A wine festival is held usually in early September. **Open:** Tour schedule varies; phone ahead. Free.

DELAND
Map page M-7, B2

Attractions ⌂

DeLand Museum of Art, 600 N Woodland Blvd; tel 904/734-4371. The small permanent collection consists mostly of works by Florida artists in various media, and a collection of Native American craftwork. Traveling exhibitions are presented each year; guided tours are available upon request. Every other year the Florida Watercolor Exhibition, a juried show open to artists from the southeastern states, is held here. **Open:** Tues–Sat 10am–4pm, Sun 1–4pm. $

Hontoon Island State Park, 2039 River Ridge Rd; tel 904/736-5309. Located on an island in the St Johns River, this 1,600-acre park is accessible only by ferry. The island was once home to a population of Timucuan Indians, who left behind a mound 300 feet long and 20 feet high. A reflection of their diet, it is composed mainly of shells, including those of snails, various shellfish, and turtles. The park also has an 80-foot observation tower. Fishing, boating, hiking, camping, nature trails. $$

DELRAY BEACH
Map page M-9, E4

Hotels 🧳

≣≣ The Colony, 525 E Atlantic Ave, PO Box 970, Delray Beach, FL 33447; tel 407/276-4123 or toll free 800/552-2363; fax 407/274-0035. 1½ mi E of I-95. This west-of-the-shore oldie offers very basic accommodations considered dowdy by some but adored by others, who keep coming back for the bygone look year after year. And the New England hospitality is genuine—these folks work half the year in Kennebunkport, Maine. All that's missing from the working 1920s switchboard is Ernestine. **Rooms:** 80 rms and stes. CI 2pm/CO noon. Nonsmoking rms avail. **Amenities:** 🏧 Cable TV, bathrobes. No A/C. **Services:** ✕ 🛄 🍴 🛎 Social director, babysitting. **Facilities:** 🏧 🟦 1 rst, 1 bar (w/entertainment), 1 beach (ocean), beauty salon. The dining room is a real look back in time. **Rates (MAP):** HS Dec–Apr $150–$190 D; from $190 ste. Lower rates off-season. Spec packages avail. Pking: Outdoor, free. Maj CC.

≣≣ Holiday Inn Camino Real, 1229 E Atlantic Ave, Delray Beach, FL 33483; tel 407/278-0882 or toll free 800/23-HOTEL; fax 407/278-1845. Atlantic Ave E exit off I-95. Adorned with Spanish and Mediterranean touches, this standard-bearer opposite the beach does a brisk winter business. **Rooms:** 150 rms and stes. CI 3pm/CO noon. Nonsmoking rms avail. **Amenities:** 🏧 🟦 🟦 🍴 A/C, cable TV w/movies. All units w/terraces. **Services:** ✕ 🅥🅟 🛄 🍴 Babysitting. **Facilities:** 🏧 🚲 🟦 🛄 1 rst, 2 bars (1 w/entertainment), whirlpool. Roof restaurant provides ocean views. **Rates:** $169–$209 S or D; from $179 ste. Children under 15 stay free. Min stay spec evnts. Higher rates for spec evnts/hols. Spec packages avail. Pking: Indoor/outdoor, free. Maj CC.

≣≣≣ Seagate Hotel & Beach Club, 400 S Ocean Blvd, Delray Beach, FL 33483; tel 407/276-2421 or toll free 800/233-3581; fax 407/243-4714. A pleasant facility located across the road from the beach, with its own beach property. **Rooms:** 70 stes and effic. CI 3pm/CO noon. **Amenities:** 🏧 🟦 🟦 A/C, cable TV, refrig, in-rm safe. All units w/terraces, 1 w/Jacuzzi. **Services:** ✕ 🅥🅟 🛄 🍴 Car-rental desk, social director, children's program, babysitting. Coffee and muffins are set out every morning in the lobby. **Facilities:** 🏧 🚲 🔺 🟦 1 rst, 1 bar (w/entertainment), 1 beach (ocean), board surfing, washer/dryer. Lending library in lobby. Freshwater and saltwater pools. Vendor operates watersports. **Rates:** HS Jan–Mar from $223 ste; from $96 effic. Extra person $15. Children under 18 stay free. Min stay spec evnts. Lower rates off-season. Pking: Outdoor, free. Maj CC.

Motel

≣ Riviera Palms Motel, 3960 N Ocean Blvd, Delray Beach, FL 33438; tel 407/276-3032. This family-owned outfit is fine for the budget-minded traveler who doesn't require many amenities. Just a short walk to the beach. **Rooms:** 17 rms, stes, and effic. CI 2pm/CO 11am. Decor is 1960s and '70s, with baths out of the '50s. **Amenities:** 🏧 A/C, cable TV, refrig. Phone supplied on request. **Services:** 🍴 **Facilities:** 🏧 **Rates:** HS Dec–Apr $50–$60 S or D; from $60 ste; from $55 effic. Extra person $6. Min stay. Lower rates off-season. Pking: Outdoor, free. No CC.

Restaurants 🍽

★ **Boston's on the Beach**, 40 S Fla A1A, Delray Beach; tel 407/278-3364. **American.** This oceanfront restaurant, popular with beachgoers, is a great spot for people-watching. The menu includes a selection of seafood entrees as well as sandwiches and burgers. **FYI:** Reservations not accepted. Band/island music/jazz. **Open:** Mon 11am–2am, Tues 11am–1am, Wed–Fri 11am–2am, Sat 6:30pm–2am, Sun 6:30pm–1am. **Prices:** Main courses $6–$18. Maj CC. 🛥 ✦

Busch's Seafood, 840 E Atlantic Blvd, Delray Beach; tel 407/278-7600. **Seafood.** A rather sophisticated fish house with a sizeable bar area and great water views. The menu includes sautéed grouper and a clambake special. **FYI:** Reservations accepted. Piano. Children's menu. Dress code. **Open:** Sun–Thurs 11:30am–10pm, Fri–Sat 11:30am–11pm. Closed some hols. **Prices:** Main courses $14–$24. Maj CC. 💙 🖼 💟 🅥🅟 ✦

Scoundrel's, in Royal Palm Mortgage Bldg, 100 E Linton Blvd, Delray Beach; tel 407/265-1313. **Continental.** A casual American eatery with a nondescript brick and wood interior and a standard menu. Lunch and dinner specials are offered, as is Sunday brunch. **FYI:** Reservations accepted. Band. **Open:** Sun 11am–8pm, Mon–Sat 11am–2am. Closed some hols. **Prices:** Main courses $7–$18. Maj CC. ✦

Tom Jr's Rib Shack, 1211 S Dixie Hwy, Delray Beach; tel 407/278-0505. **Barbecue.** This little shack is known for its ribs. Great for takeout. **FYI:** Reservations not accepted. No liquor license. No smoking. **Open:** Wed–Sun 11:30am–9pm. Closed some hols. **Prices:** Main courses $5.50–$11. No CC.

Refreshment Stop 🥤

Doc's All-American Diner, 10 N Swinton Ave, Delray Beach; tel 407/278-DOCS. **Diner.** The simplest of diners, offering up American fast food favorites, including hamburgers, hot dogs, hot and cold sandwiches, and omelettes, as well as ice cream, milk shakes, and pies. **Open:** Daily 11am–8pm. Closed some hols. No CC. ♨

Attraction 🏛

Morikami Museum and Japanese Garden, 4000 Morikami Park Rd; tel 407/495-0233. This museum in Morikami Park showcases traveling exhibitions of Japanese arts, crafts, history, and culture. The main building houses expansive galleries, a teahouse with a viewing gallery, a 225-seat theater, and an electronic multimedia resource center.

Located a short distance away, the original museum building (called the Yamato-kan), modeled after a Japanese residence, contains a permanent exhibit chronicling the history of the Yamato Colony. The colony was founded by a group of Japanese farmers who settled in this area around the turn of the century. Although the colonists eventually dispersed, the park and museum were created as a memorial to these settlers, on property bequeathed to the state by one of the members who remained. The 200-acre park also has nature trails, lakes and ponds, Japanese-style gardens, picnic areas, and a rare bonsai tree collection. **Open:** Museum, Tues–Sun 10am–5pm; garden, daily dawn–dusk. Closed some hols. $$

DESTIN

Map page M-2, B3

Hotel 🛏

≣≣≣ **Holiday Inn of Destin**, 1020 US 98 E, Destin, FL 32541; tel 904/837-6181 or toll free 800/HOLIDAY; fax 904/837-1537. 4 mi W of Mid-Bay Bridge. A 9-story property featuring the trademark Holidome indoor recreation and lounging area. **Rooms:** 233 rms. CI 3pm/CO 11am. Nonsmoking rms avail. Rooms have undergone recent renovation. **Amenities:** 🛖 ♨ 🍷 A/C, cable TV, in-rm safe. All units w/terraces, 1 w/Jacuzzi. **Services:** ✗ 🔔 Children's program, babysitting. **Facilities:** 🛠 ⛳ 🎱 ♿ 3 rsts, 3 bars, 1 beach (ocean), lifeguard, games rm, spa, sauna, whirlpool. **Rates:** HS Mar–Sept $100–$135 S or D. Extra person $10. Children under 18 stay free. Lower rates off-season. Higher rates for spec evnts/hols. Spec packages avail. Pking: Outdoor, free. Maj CC.

Motel 🏩

≣ **The Village Inn**, 215 US 98 E, Destin, FL 32541; tel 904/837-7413 or toll free 800/821-9342; fax 904/654-3394. This is an exceptional value at a great location for the sport-fishing

enthusiast. It's immediately across from a charter fishing fleet. **Rooms:** 100 rms. CI 3pm/CO 11am. Nonsmoking rms avail. Rooms are basic, but offer ample space. **Amenities:** 🛖 A/C, cable TV. **Facilities:** 🛠 ♿ **Rates:** HS Jan–Sept $30–$50 S or D. Extra person $6. Children under 18 stay free. Min stay spec evnts. Lower rates off-season. Higher rates for spec evnts/hols. Pking: Outdoor, free. Maj CC.

Inns

≣≣ **Frangista Beach Inn Destin**, 4150 Old US 98 E, Destin, FL 32541; tel 904/654-5501 or toll free 800/382-2612; fax 904/654-5876. 5 mi E of Destin. A charming beachfront inn accented with Adirondack chairs and other homey features. **Rooms:** 23 stes and effic. CI 3pm/CO 11am. The whitewashed rooms have wicker furnishings and hardwood floors. **Amenities:** 🛖 ♨ 🍷 🍷 A/C, cable TV w/movies, refrig. All units w/terraces. Ceiling fans. **Services:** 🔔 **Facilities:** ♿ 1 beach (ocean), lifeguard, washer/dryer. **Rates:** HS June–Aug from $115 ste; from $109 effic. Extra person $10. Children under 18 stay free. Min stay spec evnts. Lower rates off-season. Higher rates for spec evnts/hols. Pking: Outdoor, free. Ltd CC.

≣≣≣ **Henderson Park Inn**, 2700 Scenic Beach Hwy 98 E, Destin, FL 32541; tel 904/654-0400 or toll free 800/336-4853; fax 904/654-0405. Couples flock to this romantic beachfront inn for a quiet retreat in a cozy atmosphere. Unsuitable for children under 18. **Rooms:** 38 rms and stes; 18 ctges/villas. CI 3pm/CO 11am. Rooms are eclectic in decor and layout. **Amenities:** 🛖 🍷 A/C, cable TV, refrig, in-rm safe. Some units w/terraces, some w/fireplaces, some w/Jacuzzis. **Services:** ✗ 🔺 🔔 Twice-daily maid svce, babysitting, wine/sherry served. Free beach lounges and umbrellas. **Facilities:** 🛠 ⛳ 🎱 ♿ 1 rst, 1 beach (ocean), lifeguard. Casual restaurant with sparkling views. **Rates (CP):** HS May–Aug $175 S or D w/shared bath; from $195 ste. Extra person $10. Lower rates off-season. Higher rates for spec evnts/hols. Spec packages avail. Pking: Outdoor, free. Ltd CC.

Resorts

Sandestin Beach Resort, 5500 US 98E, Destin, FL 32541; tel 904/267-8150 or toll free 800/277-0800; fax 904/267-8222. 4 mi E of Mid-Bay Bridge. 2,400 acres. Expansive resort consisting of 2 towers, with ample facilities and direct access to the beach. Very popular with families. Unrated. **Rooms:** 550 stes and effic; 667 ctges/villas. CI 4pm/CO 11am. Express checkout avail. Nonsmoking rms avail. **Amenities:** 🛖 ♨ A/C, cable TV, refrig, voice mail. Some units w/terraces, some w/fireplaces, some w/Jacuzzis. **Services:** ✗ ➡ 🅥🅟 🚗 🔺 🔔 Car-rental desk, social director, masseur, children's program, babysitting. **Facilities:** 🛠 🚲 ⛳ 🎣 ▶45 🏊 🏖 🎱 🎾 ♿ 3 rsts, 2 bars (1 w/entertainment), 1 beach (ocean), board surfing, spa, sauna, steam rm, whirlpool, beauty salon, washer/dryer. **Rates:** HS June–Aug from $173 ste; from $173 effic; from $170 ctge/villa. Children under 18 stay free. Min stay wknds. Lower rates off-season. Spec packages avail. Pking: Indoor/outdoor, free. Ltd CC.

Tops'l Beach & Racquet Club, 5550 US 98 E, Destin, FL 32541; tel 904/267-9222 or toll free 800/476-9222; fax 904/267-2955. 6 mi E of Mid-Bay Bridge. Combination highrise and condo partially located on the beach and the strip. Nothing special, but fine for couples and families without any great expectations. Unrated. **Rooms:** 180 effic. CI 3pm/CO 11am. Nonsmoking rms avail. **Amenities:** 🛋 🐾 📺 A/C, cable TV w/movies, refrig, VCR, stereo/tape player. All units w/terraces, some w/fireplaces, some w/Jacuzzis. **Services:** ✗ 🖐 🔔 Babysitting. **Facilities:** 🗗 ⚠ 🏊 🏌 🍴 [250] ⅃ 2 rsts, 2 bars, 1 beach (ocean), games rm, racquetball, sauna, steam rm, whirlpool, beauty salon, washer/dryer. **Rates:** HS May–Aug from $215 effic. Children under 18 stay free. Lower rates off-season. Higher rates for spec evnts/hols. Spec packages avail. Pking: Indoor/outdoor, free. Maj CC.

Restaurants 🍽

AJ's Seafood and Oyster Bar, 116 US 98 E, Destin; tel 904/837-1913. ½ mi E of the Destin Bridge. **Seafood.** A seafood restaurant overlooking the nearby marina and the ocean beyond it. Enjoy lunch or dinner in the maritime-styled dining room, or merely relax with a beverage in the open-air upstairs bar. **FYI:** Reservations not accepted. Band/island music/jazz. Children's menu. **Open:** HS June–Sept daily 11am–11pm. Reduced hours off-season. Closed some hols. **Prices:** Main courses $9–$18. Maj CC. 🍽 🖼 📺 ⅃

Buster's Oyster Bar and Seafood Restaurant, in Delchamps Plaza, Delchamps Plaza, Destin; tel 904/837-4399. **New American.** A family-oriented seafood palace with a maritime theme. It not only welcomes kids, but is dedicated to making them happy. **FYI:** Reservations not accepted. Children's menu. **Open:** Daily 11am–11pm. **Prices:** Main courses $4–$16.95. Maj CC. 📺

★ Destin Diner, 1038 E US 98, Destin; tel 904/654-5843. **Diner.** A fun, diner-style eatery with the popular hits of yesterday and today continually playing in the background. **FYI:** Reservations not accepted. Children's menu. No liquor license. **Open:** Daily 24 hrs. **Prices:** Main courses $3.50–$6.25. No CC. 📺 ⅃

Harbor Docks, 538 US 98 E, Destin; tel 904/837-2506. **Seafood/Steak.** A fun, casual, rustic eatery overlooking Destin Harbor. The menu offers a variety of steaks and seafood dishes.

FYI: Reservations not accepted. Band. Children's menu. **Open:** Daily 11am–11pm. Closed Dec 25. **Prices:** Main courses $9–$20. Maj CC. 🍽 🖼 📱 ⅃

♣ Marina Cafe, 320 US 98E, Destin; tel 904/837-7960. US 98 E next to Yacht Club. **Continental.** An art deco restaurant and bar with a comfortable atmosphere and fabulous water views. The extensive menu offers pizzas and pastas as well as seafood and steaks. **FYI:** Reservations accepted. **Open:** Daily 5–11pm. Closed some hols; Jan. **Prices:** Main courses $17–$27. Maj CC. 🖼 📺 ⅃

Scampi's, US 98 E, Destin; tel 904/837-7686. **Seafood/Steak.** Surf-and-turf lovers should enjoy this nautically themed restaurant. Enjoy steaks and seafood stuffed, baked, or cajun-style. **FYI:** Reservations not accepted. Children's menu. **Open:** Daily 4:30–9:30pm. Closed Dec 25. **Prices:** Main courses $10–$15. Maj CC. 📱 ⅃

Attractions 💼

Museum of the Sea and Indian, 4801 Beach Hwy; tel 904/837-6625. Many marine and Native American artifacts on display; cassette-guided tour describes each exhibit. Two ponds with ducks and alligators, also peacocks and pheasants. **Open:** Daily 9am–5pm. Closed some hols. $$

Destin Fishing Museum, Moreno Plaza, 35 US 98E; tel 904/654-1011. World- and state-record catches, from blue marlin to red snapper, are displayed along with thousands of photos and various maritime memorabilia. Hands-on tidal pool and dry walk-through aquarium. **Open:** Tues–Sat noon–4pm, Sun 1–4pm. Closed some hols. $

Henderson Beach State Recreation Area, 1700 Emerald Coast Pkwy; tel 904/837-7550. Located just east of Destin, this is one of the 18 beaches of South Walton. A natural environment for magnolias, scrub oaks, sand pines, and a variety of wildflowers, the park has miles of white sand, towering dunes, and clear emerald waters. For information, contact the park at 1700 Emerald Coast Pkwy, Destin, FL 32541. **Open:** 8am–dusk. $

DUNDEE

Map page M-7, E1

Hotel 🛏

≣≣ Holiday Inn–Cypress Gardens/Dundee, 339 US 27 N, Dundee, FL 33838; tel 813/439-1591 or toll free 800/HOLI-DAY; fax 813/439-5297. 15 mi S of Cypress Gardens. Convenient for visiting some area attractions and a popular stopping-off point for truckers and other motorists. **Rooms:** 100 rms. CI 2pm/CO 11am. Nonsmoking rms avail. **Amenities:** 🔒 ☕ A/C, cable TV w/movies. **Services:** ✕ 🛍 ↺ ↻ **Facilities:** 🏊 🈐 ⅙ 1 rst, 1 bar, washer/dryer. **Rates (CP):** HS Jan–Apr $60–$70 S or D. Extra person $5. Children under 18 stay free. Lower rates off-season. Spec packages avail. Pking: Outdoor, free. Maj CC.

DUNEDIN

Map page M-6, E2

Hotel 🛏

🏳🏳 **Best Western Jamaica Inn**, 150 Marina Plaza, Dunedin, FL 34698; tel 813/733-4121 or toll free 800/447-4728; fax 813/736-4365. Perched at the water's edge—so close, in fact, that you can hear water lapping outside your door. **Rooms:** 55 rms and effic. CI 3pm/CO 11am. Nonsmoking rms avail. Second-floor units have cathedral ceilings. **Amenities:** 🔒 🈂 A/C, cable TV. All units w/terraces. Large chairs on balconies. **Services:** ↺ **Facilities:** 🏊 🈐 1 rst (see also "Restaurants" below), 1 bar, lawn games. **Rates:** HS Dec–Apr $59–$87 S or D; from $69 effic. Extra person $7. Children under 12 stay free. Lower rates off-season. Pking: Outdoor, free. Maj CC.

Restaurants 🍴

★ **Bon Appetit**, in Best Western Jamaica Inn, 148 Marina Plaza, Dunedin; tel 813/733-2151. **American/German.** A bistro popular with elderly area residents for its quiet, relaxing atmosphere and pretty locale on the water. Serves rack of lamb, crabcakes, fresh local fish, and French bistro classics like onion soup, steak frites, and pot au feu. **FYI:** Reservations recommended. Children's menu. Dress code. **Open:** Daily 7am–10pm. **Prices:** Main courses $9–$19. Maj CC. 🍴 🖼 💟 🆅🅿

Sabal's, 315 Main St, Dunedin; tel 813/734-3463. **New American.** This moderately priced, informal, contemporary American cafe is noted for its inventive dishes, such as linguine primavera, filet mignon served in a Roquefort sauce, and garlic shrimp. Lamb chops and chicken dishes are also offered. **FYI:** Reservations recommended. Dress code. Beer and wine only. **Open:** Tues–Thurs 6–9pm, Fri–Sat 6–10pm, Sun 6–9pm. **Prices:** Main courses $12–$22. Ltd CC. ⅙

Attractions 🛄

Grant Field, 311 Douglas Ave; tel 813/733-0429. The spring training site for the Toronto Blue Jays. Exhibition games are played here throughout March. $$$

Caladesi Island State Park, Causeway Blvd; tel 813/469-5918. Three miles long and a half-mile wide, this is one of Florida's few remaining undisturbed barrier islands. No cars are allowed, and access is only by private boat or by ferry boat from Honeymoon Island (tel 813/734-5263). Ideal for swimming, shelling, and scuba diving, the island's beaches front the Gulf of Mexico. Facilities include palm-shaded picnic pavilions, snack bar, boardwalks, and shower houses. **Open:** Daily 8am–sunset. $

ELLENTON

Map page M-8, B2

Attraction 🛄

Gamble Plantation, 3708 Patten Ave; tel 813/723-4536. The oldest structure on the southwest coast of Florida, and a fine example of an antebellum plantation home. Built in the late 1840s by Maj Robert Gamble, it is maintained as a state historic site and includes an excellent collection of 19th-century furnishings. The only opportunity to view the interior is through guided tours given Thurs–Mon at 9:30 and 10:30am, and at 1, 2, 3, and 4pm. Visitor center open 8am–sunset. Closed some hols. $

ESTERO

Map page M-8, E4

Attraction 🛄

Koreshan State Historic Park; tel 813/992-0311. Located off US 41 along the Estero River, this historic landmark was the site inhabited by a now-extinct religious sect, the Koreshan Unity Movement, which believed that man lived inside the Earth. Several buildings and gardens have been restored, and a museum explains the sect's story. Nature trails and canoe trails run through the settlement. Boating, canoe rentals, hiking, camping. **Open:** Daily 8am–sunset. $$

EVERGLADES CITY
Map page M-10, B3

Restaurant 🍴

Captain's Table Restaurant, 125 Collier Blvd, Everglades City; tel 813/695-2727. **American/Seafood.** This is one of only a handful of full-service restaurants in the area. The interior is cool and pleasant. The menu includes alligator piccata, snapper, catfish, and fisherman's plate. **FYI:** Reservations accepted. Children's menu. **Open:** Daily 11am–9:30pm. **Prices:** Main courses $12–$20. Maj CC. 🍽 🏞 ♿

EVERGLADES NATIONAL PARK
Map pages M-10 to M-11

For lodging and dining, see Everglades City, Flamingo

Encompassing over 2,000 square miles and 1.5 million acres, Everglades National Park covers the entire southern tip of Florida. Established as a national park in 1947, it comprises one of America's most unique regions. Unlike Yosemite or Grand Canyon National Parks, the Everglades' awesome beauty is more subtle. The park is a wildlife sanctuary, set aside for the protection of its delicate plant and animal life. Species making their home here include deer, otters, great white egrets, hawks, herons, and—of course—alligators.

The **Main Visitor Center** (tel 305-247-7700) is located on the east side of the park, just outside of Homestead. Fla 9336 runs to the park entrance (follow signs). This is the park's official headquarters, housing audiovisual exhibits on the park's fragile ecosystems. A single road winds its way for 38 miles from the Main Visitor Center to the **Flamingo Visitor Center,** in the southwest corner of the park. The scenic drive provides a beautiful introduction as it passes through several distinct ecosystems, including a dwarf cypress forest, endless saw grass, and dense mangroves. Well-marked trails and elevated boardwalks are plentiful along the entire stretch; all contain informative signs.

In addition to a small visitor center and bookstore, **Shark Valley** (tel 505/221-8455) offers an elevated boardwalk, hiking trails, bike rentals, and an excellent tram tour that delves 7.5 miles into the wilderness to a 50-foot observation tower. Built on the site of an old oil well, the tower gives sweeping views of the park. Tours run regularly, year-round (phone for details).

At the **Miccosukee Indian Village,** (tel 305/223-8380), visitors can take a half-hour, high-speed airboat "safari" through the rushes. Birds scatter as the boats approach, and when they slow down, alligators and other animals appear. Rides offered daily (phone for details).

FISHER ISLAND
Map page M-11, B2 (S of Miami Beach)

Resort 🏨

▆▆▆▆ **The Fisher Island Club**, 1 Fisher Island Dr, Fisher Island, FL 33109; tel 305/535-6029 or toll free 800/537-3708; fax 305/535-6003. Star Island exit off MacArthur Causeway then by car ferry (every 15 minutes) from the island's private dock. 216 acres. If you're looking for security, resorts and hideaways don't come more secure than this one. On a private island only a few miles from downtown Miami, it is accessible only by private launch and private car ferry (or, rather, limo ferry). The swank, full-service apartments are augmented by a restored, antique-filled Vanderbilt mansion and its attendant cottages. **Rooms:** 60 rms, stes, and effic; 4 ctges/villas. CI 3pm/CO noon. Rooms and suites echo the style and decor of a New England inn; apartments date from the 1980s and sport California contemporary decor, some with views of the sea and cruise ships. Some self-contained cottages have private patios and spas. **Amenities:** 🛁 🧺 📺 🍴 A/C, cable TV, refrig, bathrobes. All units w/minibars, some w/terraces, 1 w/fireplace, some w/Jacuzzis. Ceiling fans in rooms and suites. Every guest room comes with golf cart for getting around the island. Bedside carafe of sherry. Toothbrushes and mini loofahs in inn rooms. **Services:** ✗ 🅅🅿 🚗 🛎 Twice-daily maid svce, masseur, children's program, babysitting. Attendant hoses down windshield of your rental car when you drive off the ferry. **Facilities:** 🏌 🚴 🎣 📺 🏖 🏊 🎳 🍴 ♿ 7 rsts, 4 bars (2 w/entertainment), 1 beach (ocean), lifeguard, lawn games, snorkeling, spa, sauna, steam rm, whirlpool, beauty salon, day-care ctr, playground, washer/dryer. The island's exclusive golf course has hosted President Clinton. Marina can handle luxury yachts up to 200 feet. Acclaimed full-service Spa Internazionale includes private rooms for VIP pampering. Posh restaurant in library of mansion; 4 other moderately priced dining spots throughout the island. **Rates:** HS Nov–Apr $325 S or D; from $475 ste; from $575 effic; from $525 ctge/villa. Children under 12 stay free. Min stay spec evnts. Lower rates off-season. Spec packages avail. Pking: Outdoor, free. Maj CC. Quoted rates do not include daily membership fee of $20 per room.

FLAGLER BEACH
Map page M-7, A2

Restaurants 🍴

★ **High Tides at Shack Jack's**, 2805 S Ocean Shore Blvd, Flagler Beach; tel 904/439-3344. 2 miles S of the pier. **American/Seafood.** A casual, screened-in eatery with picnic tables, peachy, rustic decor, and great ocean views. House specialties include steak sandwiches and New England clam chowder. **FYI:** Reservations not accepted. Band. Beer and wine only. **Open:** Daily 11am–11pm. Closed some hols. **Prices:** Main courses $7–$11. No CC. 🍴 ⛰

Pier Restaurant on Flagler Beach, 215 S Fla A1A, Flagler Beach; tel 904/439-3891. **American/Seafood.** A seafood eatery with maritime decor and large windows offering lovely ocean and pier views. The daily menu usually includes lemon flounder, salmon, and homemade crabcakes. **FYI:** Reservations not accepted. Children's menu. **Open:** Daily 7am–9pm. Closed Dec 25. **Prices:** Main courses $7–$13. Maj CC. ⛰ ♥

FLAMINGO
Map page M-10, D4

Motel 🛏

═ ═ **Flamingo Lodge Marina & Outpost Resort**, 1 Flamingo Lodge Hwy, Flamingo, FL 33034; tel 305/253-2241 or toll free 800/600-3813; fax 813/695-3921. 38 mi S of Everglades National Park Visitors Center. The only game in town, this motel has clean cottages with fully equipped kitchens. Nothing fancy, but popular in season. **Rooms:** 103 rms and stes; 24 ctges/villas. CI 3pm/CO 11am. Nonsmoking rms avail. **Amenities:** 🔒 A/C, TV. **Services:** 🛎 Breakfast is not offered during summer at restaurant, so continental breakfast is served in registration area. **Facilities:** 🚤 ⚓ ⛵ 🏊 ⛴ 1 rst (see also "Restaurants" below), 1 bar, washer/dryer. **Rates:** HS Dec–Apr $74–$87 S or D; from $110 ste; from $87 ctge/villa. Extra person $10. Children under 12 stay free. Lower rates off-season. Pking: Outdoor, free. Maj CC.

Restaurant 🍴

Flamingo Lodge Restaurant, in the Flamingo Lodge, 1 Flamingo Lodge Hwy, Flamingo; tel 813/695-3101. 38 miles S of Everglades National Park Visitors Center. **American/Caribbean.** This well-regarded multilevel restaurant in the Everglades

provides a stunning view of Florida Bay. Fresh fish prepared a variety of ways is offered along with several meat and poultry selections. **FYI:** Reservations accepted. Children's menu. No smoking. **Open:** HS Dec–Apr breakfast daily 7–10am; lunch daily 11:30am–3pm; dinner daily 5–9pm. Reduced hours off-season. **Prices:** Main courses $6–$16. Maj CC. ⛰ ♥

FORT LAUDERDALE
Map page M-11, A2

See also Dania, Hollywood, Hollywood Beach, Lauderdale-by-the-Sea, North Lauderdale, Pompano Beach, Port Everglades, Wilton Manors

Hotels 🛏

═ ═ ═ **Best Western Oceanside Inn**, 1180 Seabreeze Blvd, Fort Lauderdale, FL 33316; tel 305/525-8115 or toll free 800/367-1007; fax 305/527-0957. A small hotel nestled among the highrises. **Rooms:** 100 rms. CI 3pm/CO 11:30am. Express checkout avail. Nonsmoking rms avail. **Amenities:** 🔒 🍴 A/C, cable TV w/movies, refrig, in-rm safe. All units w/minibars, some w/terraces. **Services:** ✕ 🛎 Car-rental desk. Complete buffet breakfast provided. **Facilities:** 🚤 ⛵ ⛱ 🏊 ⛴ 75 🖥 ⛴ 1 rst, 1 bar, 1 beach (ocean), snorkeling, washer/dryer. Access to public beach's widest section, with its picnic tables, volleyball nets, barbecues, and showers. **Rates (BB):** HS Dec–Apr $94–$104 S; $104–$114 D. Extra person $10. Children under 12 stay free. Lower rates off-season. Spec packages avail. Pking: Indoor, free. Maj CC.

═ ═ ═ **Crown Sterling Suites**, 1100 SE 17th St, Fort Lauderdale, FL 33316; tel 305/527-2700 or toll free 800/433-4600; fax 305/760-7202. A Mediterranean-accented hotel that stands comfortably away from the beach. Convenient for those heading to Port Everglades. **Rooms:** 358 stes. CI 3pm/CO noon. Express checkout avail. Nonsmoking rms avail. Suites have a pleasing mix of Florida style and Mediterranean flair. All have microwaves. **Amenities:** 🔒 🍴 A/C, cable TV, refrig, voice mail. All units w/terraces. **Services:** ✕ 🛎 🚗 ⛱ 🛎 Car-rental desk, babysitting. **Facilities:** 🚤 500 ⛴ 1 rst, 1 bar (w/entertainment), sauna, steam rm, whirlpool, washer/dryer. **Rates (BB):** HS Oct–Apr 15 from $209 ste. Extra person $10. Children under 12 stay free. Lower rates off-season. Spec packages avail. Pking: Outdoor, free. Maj CC.

═ ═ **Fort Lauderdale Beach Resort**, 909 Breakers Ave, Fort Lauderdale, FL 33304; tel 305/566-8800 or toll free 800/741-7869; fax 305/566-8802. At NW 19th Ave. A commendable offering located in the fray of beach activity but set off from the strip. **Rooms:** 210 rms, stes, and effic. CI 4pm/CO 11am. Pastel interiors. Some Murphy beds or sofa beds in larger units. **Amenities:** 📺 🛗 🗄 🍴 A/C, cable TV, refrig. **Services:** 🔑 VP 🖨 🍷 Car-rental desk, social director, masseur, babysitting. **Facilities:** 🎣 🚲 🏓 🎳 ⚓ 1 bar, games rm, snorkeling, sauna, whirlpool, washer/dryer. **Rates:** HS Dec–Apr $130–$190 S or D; from $200 ste; from $99 effic. Extra person $10. Children under 16 stay free. Lower rates off-season. Spec packages avail. Pking: Indoor/outdoor, free. Maj CC.

≣≣≣ **Fort Lauderdale Marriott North**, 6650 N Andrews Ave, Fort Lauderdale, FL 33309; tel 305/771-0440 or toll free 800/343-2459; fax 305/772-9834. A smart address appropriately tuned to the needs of business travelers. **Rooms:** 321 rms. CI 3pm/CO noon. Express checkout avail. Nonsmoking rms avail. Stylish look is presented in rooms with dark woods and light fabrics. Executive floor offers a few more perks. **Amenities:** 📺 🛗 A/C, cable TV w/movies. Some units w/minibars, some w/terraces. **Services:** ✕ VP 🖨 🍷 🛎 Car-rental desk. **Facilities:** 🎣 🏓 🍴 💻 ⚓ 1 rst, 1 bar, sauna, whirlpool, washer/dryer. Free admission to nearby Gold's Gym. **Rates:** HS Jan–Mar $109–$124 S; $119–$134 D. Extra person $10. Children under 17

stay free. Lower rates off-season. Higher rates for spec evnts/hols. AP rates avail. Spec packages avail. Pking: Indoor/outdoor, free. Maj CC.

≣≣ **Holiday Inn Fort Lauderdale Beach Galleria**, 999 N Atlantic Blvd, Fort Lauderdale, FL 33304; tel 305/563-5961 or toll free 800/HOLIDAY; fax 305/564-5261. At Jct 838 (East Sunrise Blvd). A highrise facility close to shopping and beach action. A popular rendezvous for the beach crowd. Renovations to accommodations are underway. **Rooms:** 240 rms and stes. CI 3pm/CO 11am. Nonsmoking rms avail. **Amenities:** 📺 🛗 A/C, cable TV w/movies, refrig. **Services:** 🍽 VP 🖨 🍷 Twice-daily maid svce, babysitting. **Facilities:** 🎣 🏖 ⚓ 2 rsts, 1 bar, 1 beach (ocean), lifeguard, games rm. Waffle house restaurant. **Rates:** HS Dec–Apr $89–$145 S or D; from $150 ste. Extra person $14. Children under 18 stay free. Lower rates off-season. Higher rates for spec evnts/hols. Spec packages avail. Pking: Outdoor, free. Maj CC.

≣≣ **Mark 2100 Resort Hotel**, 2100 N Atlantic Blvd, Fort Lauderdale, FL 33305; tel 305/566-8383 or toll free 800/334-6275; fax 305/566-4325. A complex of almost a dozen

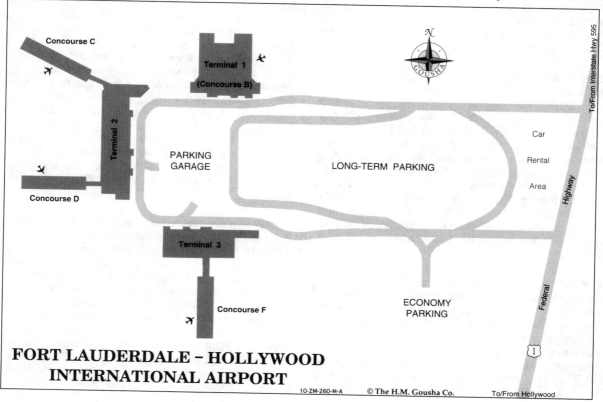

FORT LAUDERDALE – HOLLYWOOD
INTERNATIONAL AIRPORT

10-ZM-260-M-A   © The H.M. Gousha Co.

buildings, set on a quiet section of beach. Appeals to a more mature crowd. The property, reportedly up for sale, needs some renovation. **Rooms:** 123 rms, stes, and effic. CI 1pm/CO 11am. Nonsmoking rms avail. **Amenities:** ⛶ A/C, cable TV, voice mail. **Services:** ✗ ⬛ ⌇ Babysitting. **Facilities:** ⛶ ⬛ ⛴ 2 rsts, 4 bars (2 w/entertainment), 1 beach (ocean), games rm. Pool needs better landscaping; but the boardwalk area along the beach is inviting. **Rates:** HS Dec–Apr $69–$129 S or D; from $129 ste; from $89 effic. Extra person $10–15. Children under 12 stay free. Lower rates off-season. Spec packages avail. Pking: Outdoor, free. Maj CC.

≡≡ Ocean Manor Resort, 4040 Galt Ocean Dr, Fort Lauderdale, FL 33308; tel 305/566-7500 or toll free 800/955-0444; fax 305/564-3075. Lobby replete with a chandelier and marble coffee tables makes a smart impression. **Rooms:** 84 rms, stes, and effic. CI 3pm/CO noon. Rooms are clean and cool with pastel decor. **Amenities:** ⛶ A/C, cable TV, refrig. Some units w/terraces. **Services:** ✗ ▬ 🅥🅟 ⌇ Car-rental desk, social director, children's program, babysitting. **Facilities:** ⛶ ⬛ ⛴ 2 rsts, 2 bars (1 w/entertainment), 1 beach (ocean), lifeguard, games rm, beauty salon, washer/dryer. **Rates:** HS Dec–Apr $129–$179 S or D; from $219 ste; from $149 effic. Extra person $15. Children under 17 stay free. Min stay spec evnts. Lower rates off-season. AP rates avail. Spec packages avail. Pking: Outdoor, free. Maj CC.

≡≡ Pelican Beach Resort, 2000 N Atlantic Blvd, Fort Lauderdale, FL 33305; tel 305/568-9431 or toll free 800/525-6232; fax 305/565-2622. A comfortable place, where the owners are on hand to keep everything running smoothly. **Rooms:** 62 rms, stes, and effic. CI 3pm/CO 11am. Express checkout avail. Handsome sunlit rooms in pastel tones with white appointments. Some have ocean views. **Amenities:** ⛶ 🄳 A/C, cable TV, refrig. All units w/terraces, 1 w/Jacuzzi. **Services:** ⌇ Babysitting. Bagels, muffins, juice, and coffee served mornings. **Facilities:** ⛶ 1 beach (ocean), washer/dryer. **Rates (CP):** HS Jan–Apr 15 $95–$115 S or D; from $145 ste; from $115 effic. Extra person $10. Children under 12 stay free. Min stay spec evnts. Lower rates off-season. Spec packages avail. Pking: Outdoor, free. Maj CC.

≡≡≡ Ramada Beach Resort, 4060 Galt Ocean Dr, Fort Lauderdale, FL 33308; tel 305/565-6611 or toll free 800/678-9022; fax 305/564-7730. Tropically flavored throughout; fresh flowers and fine appointments in public areas. **Rooms:** 223 rms and stes. CI 3pm/CO noon. Nonsmoking rms avail. **Amenities:** ⛶ A/C, cable TV, refrig, in-rm safe. All units w/minibars, some w/terraces, some w/Jacuzzis. **Services:** ✗ ▬ 🅥🅟 ⬛ ⌇ Car-rental desk, babysitting. **Facilities:** ⛶ ⚠ ⛴ ▶ ⬛ ⬛ ⛴ 2 rsts, 2 bars (1 w/entertainment), 1 beach (ocean),

board surfing, games rm. Watersports rentals available from vendor on beach. **Rates:** HS Dec–Apr $110–$165 S or D; from $295 ste. Extra person $10. Children under 17 stay free. Min stay HS. Lower rates off-season. MAP rates avail. Spec packages avail. Pking: Outdoor, $3. Maj CC.

≡≡ Riverside Hotel, 620 E Las Olas Blvd, Fort Lauderdale, FL 33301; tel 305/467-0671 or toll free 800/325-3280; fax 305/462-2145. Enchanting 1936 building with muraled facade. Lobby with Mexican tile, and a coral-rock fireplace creates a romantic atmosphere. **Rooms:** 110 rms and stes. CI 3pm/CO 11am. Nonsmoking rms avail. Oak furnishings and original tile floor in bath. **Amenities:** ⛶ 🄳 A/C, cable TV, refrig. Some units w/terraces. **Services:** ✗ 🚐 ⬛ ⌇ Twice-daily maid svce, babysitting. **Facilities:** ⛶ ⬛ ⛴ 2 rsts, 1 bar, lawn games. Lighted walkways. 560 feet of dockage on New River. **Rates:** HS Dec–Apr $99–$149 S or D; from $179 ste. Extra person $15. Children under 16 stay free. Lower rates off-season. Higher rates for spec evnts/hols. Spec packages avail. Pking: Outdoor, free. Maj CC.

≡≡≡ Sheraton Yankee Clipper Beach Resort, 1140 Seabreeze Blvd, Fort Lauderdale, FL 33316; tel 305/524-5551 or toll free 800/325-3535; fax 305/523-5376. A longtime favorite stop on the beach scene, this multi-building complex caters to beachgoers and some spring-breakers. Hotel can be a hectic place in mid-winter. **Rooms:** 504 rms and stes. CI 3pm/CO noon. Express checkout avail. Nonsmoking rms avail. **Amenities:** ⛶ 🄳 🍴 A/C, cable TV w/movies, in-rm safe. Some units w/terraces. **Services:** ✗ 🅥🅟 ⬛ ⌇ Car-rental desk, babysitting. **Facilities:** ⛶ ⚓ ⬛ ⛴ 1 rst, 1 bar (w/entertainment), 1 beach (ocean), games rm, snorkeling, washer/dryer. Guests also have use of facilities at the nearby sibling hotel, the Sheraton Yankee Trader (see below). **Rates:** HS Dec–Apr $110–$180 S or D; from $250 ste. Extra person $20. Children under 15 stay free. Lower rates off-season. Spec packages avail. Pking: Outdoor, $5. Maj CC.

≡≡≡ Sheraton Yankee Trader Resort, 321 N Atlantic Blvd, Fort Lauderdale, FL 33304; tel 305/467-1111 or toll free 800/325-3535; fax 305/462-2342. Between Sunrise Blvd and Las Olas Blvd. Two highrise towers opposite the beach. It's a favorite stomping ground for beachgoers and has exchange privileges with its sister hotel, the Sheraton Yankee Clipper. **Rooms:** 465 rms and stes. CI 3pm/CO noon. Express checkout avail. Nonsmoking rms avail. Standardized rooms are outfitted in tropical motif. **Amenities:** ⛶ 🄳 🍴 A/C, cable TV w/movies, in-rm safe. **Services:** ✗ 🚐 ⬛ ⌇ Car-rental desk, social director, babysitting. **Facilities:** ⛶ ⚓ ⚓ ⬛ ⛴ 2 rsts, 4 bars (2 w/entertainment), 1 beach (ocean), lifeguard, games rm, washer/dryer. Restaurants and lounges are often social meccas for the bikini and Speedo set. **Rates:** HS Dec–Apr $70–$90 S or D; from $175 ste. Extra person $15. Children under 18 stay free. Lower rates off-season. Spec packages avail. Pking: Outdoor, $5. Maj CC.

≡≡≡ The Westin Hotel Cypress Creek, 400 Corporate Dr, Fort Lauderdale, FL 33334; tel 305/772-1331 or toll free 800/228-3000; fax 305/481-9087. 1 block east of I-95 and Cypress Creek Rd. A deluxe business-class hotel that is set on a lake and easily accessible from the interstate. Receives high marks from many business guests who come to use its smart and attractive facilities. **Rooms:** 293 rms and stes. CI 3pm/CO 1pm. Express checkout avail. Nonsmoking rms avail. **Amenities:** 🛁 🐾 📺 🖥 A/C, cable TV w/movies, refrig, voice mail, bathrobes. All units w/minibars, some w/terraces. Fax machines being installed in all executive rooms. **Services:** 🍽 🅥🅟 🚐 🛄 🛎 🐕 Twice-daily maid svce, car-rental desk, masseur, babysitting. **Facilities:** 🔧 🚴 ⚠ 📷 🎿 🌐 💻 & 2 rsts, 2 bars (1 w/entertainment), sauna, whirlpool. **Rates:** HS Jan–mid-Apr $169–$199 S or D; from $199 ste. Extra person $10. Children under 18 stay free. Lower rates off-season. Higher rates for spec evnts/hols. Spec packages avail. Pking: Outdoor, free. Maj CC.

Motels

≡≡ Banyan Marina Apartments, 111 Isle of Venice, Fort Lauderdale, FL 33301; tel 305/524-4430; fax 305/764-5629. A charming apartment complex situated on one of the intracoastal islands. **Rooms:** 10 rms, stes, and effic. CI 3pm/CO 11am. Black and white leather pieces and light-colored decor. **Amenities:** 🛁 🐾 📺 A/C, cable TV, refrig. Limited groceries supplied upon check-in. **Services:** 🐕 Private phone numbers may be arranged for long-term guests. **Facilities:** 🔧 Washer/dryer. Dock for boats. **Rates:** HS Dec–Apr $75 S or D; from $120 ste; from $110 effic. Extra person $15. Children under 6 stay free. Lower rates off-season. Pking: Outdoor, free. Ltd CC.

≡≡ Lauderdale Colonial, 3049 Harbor Dr, Fort Lauderdale, FL 33316; tel 305/525-3676; fax 305/463-3787. A sophisticated residence, more for couples and retirees who prefer the quiet life. Most guests are repeat ones. **Rooms:** 14 rms and effic. CI 2pm/CO 11am. Nonsmoking rms avail. Rattan furniture and lots of details make rooms comfortable and first-rate. Some units may be combined to make larger ones. **Amenities:** 🛁 🐾 📺 A/C, cable TV, refrig. Some units w/terraces. **Services:** 🐕 **Facilities:** 🔧 Washer/dryer. Tiki area for barbecues or private parties. **Rates:** HS Dec–Apr $90–$100 S or D; from $105 effic. Extra person $15. Lower rates off-season. Spec packages avail. Pking: Outdoor, free. Ltd CC.

≡ Oakland East Motor Lodge, 3001 N Federal Hwy, Fort Lauderdale, FL 33306; tel 305/565-4601 or toll free 800/

633-6279; fax 305/565-0384. **Rooms:** 110 rms, stes, and effic. CI 2pm/CO 11am. Nonsmoking rms avail. **Amenities:** 🛁 🐾 A/C, cable TV, VCR, stereo/tape player, voice mail, in-rm safe. Some units w/Jacuzzis. **Services:** 🐕 **Facilities:** 🔧 & 1 bar (w/entertainment), washer/dryer. **Rates (CP):** HS Dec 31–Easter $60–$80 S or D; from $85 ste; from $70 effic. Extra person $10. Children under 12 stay free. Lower rates off-season. Pking: Outdoor, free. Maj CC.

≡ Surf and Sun Hotel and Apartments, 521 N Atlantic Blvd, Fort Lauderdale, FL 33304; tel 305/564-4341 or toll free 800/248-0463; fax 305/522-5174. This well-situated budget property promises additional room renovations. **Rooms:** 22 rms and effic. CI noon/CO 11am. Basic rooms offered without frills. **Amenities:** 🛁 A/C, cable TV, refrig. 1 unit w/terrace. Coffeemakers, microwaves, and utensils available free from office. Beach chairs provided for guests. **Services:** 🐕 **Facilities:** 🏊 Washer/dryer. Barbecue area. **Rates:** HS Dec–Apr $59 S or D; from $74 effic. Extra person $4. Children under 16 stay free. Lower rates off-season. Pking: Outdoor, free. Maj CC.

Resorts

≡≡≡ Bahia Mar Resort & Yachting Center, 801 Seabreeze Blvd, Fort Lauderdale, FL 33316; tel 305/764-2233 or toll free 800/327-8154; fax 305/523-5424. 40 acres. Located on a marina in a complex of buildings connected by a skywalk to the oceanside. **Rooms:** 295 rms. CI 3pm/CO noon. Express checkout avail. Nonsmoking rms avail. Cheerful rooms, some with ocean views. **Amenities:** 🛁 🐾 📺 A/C, cable TV w/movies. Some units w/terraces. **Services:** ✕ 🅥🅟 🚐 🛄 🐕 Twice-daily maid svce, masseur, babysitting. **Facilities:** 🔧 🚴 ⚠ 🏊 🔱 🌐 💻 2 rsts, 1 bar, 1 beach (ocean), lifeguard, games rm, snorkeling, beauty salon, washer/dryer. Children under 7 eat free in restaurants. **Rates:** HS Dec–Apr $149–$159 S; $159–$169 D. Extra person $20. Lower rates off-season. MAP rates avail. Spec packages avail. Pking: Outdoor, $5. Maj CC.

≡≡≡ Bonaventure Resort & Spa, 250 Racquet Club Rd, Fort Lauderdale, FL 33326; tel 305/389-3300 or toll free 800/327-8090; fax 305/384-0563. Exit 1 off I-595. 1,250 acres. A glamourous resort operation with beautiful grounds, catering to affluent golfers and spa-goers. **Rooms:** 504 rms and stes. CI 3pm/CO noon. Express checkout avail. Nonsmoking rms avail. Rich appointments and attention to detail in rooms. **Amenities:** 🛁 📺 A/C, cable TV w/movies, refrig. Some units w/minibars, some w/terraces. **Services:** ✕ 🍴 🅥🅟 🚐 🛄 🐕 Twice-daily maid svce, car-rental desk, social director, masseur, children's program. **Facilities:** 🔧 🚴 🏌 ⛳ 📷 🎾 🔱 🎿 💻 & 4 rsts, 2 bars (w/entertainment), lifeguard, racquetball, squash, spa, sauna, steam rm, whirlpool, beauty salon, playground. Extensive conference facilities. **Rates:** HS Jan–May $195–$225 S or D; from $275 ste. Extra person $15. Children under 17 stay free. Lower rates off-season. Spec packages avail. Pking: Outdoor, free. Maj CC.

≣≣≣ **Lago Mar**, 1700 S Ocean Lane, Fort Lauderdale, FL 33316; tel 305/523-6511; fax 305/524-6627. 10 acres. Architecturally impressive Mediterranean-styled hotel set amid lush tropical plantings, with beautiful fountains surrounded by wrought-iron benches and flower beds. **Rooms:** 176 rms and stes. CI 3pm/CO noon. Great attention to detail in rooms and suites. Tailored spreads, bed ruffles, bleached tropical colors, and fine furniture. **Amenities:** 🛎 📺 A/C, cable TV, refrig, voice mail. Some units w/terraces. **Services:** ✕ ☛ 🆅🅿 🛄 🛏 Car-rental desk, children's program, babysitting. **Facilities:** 🏋 🏊 🛶 🎱 💻 🚪 4 rsts, 2 bars (w/entertainment), 1 beach (ocean), board surfing, games rm, snorkeling, playground, washer/dryer. Outdoor pool table, volleyball, hammocks under palms. Super-clean beach. **Rates:** HS Dec 15–May 1 $155–$180 S or D; from $245 ste. Lower rates off-season. Pking: Indoor/outdoor, free. Maj CC.

≣≣≣≣ **Marriott's Harbor Beach Resort**, 3030 Holiday Dr, Fort Lauderdale, FL 33316; tel 305/525-4000 or toll free 800/ 222-6543; fax 305/766-6152. 16 acres. Directly on the beach, it is likely the best of the local Marriotts, at least for overall beach atmosphere. Breezy tropical style throughout. **Rooms:** 659 rms and stes. CI 4pm/CO 11am. Express checkout avail. Nonsmoking rms avail. Rattan-furnished rooms with pastel colors. **Amenities:** 🛎 📺 A/C, cable TV w/movies, refrig, voice mail, in-rm safe. All units w/minibars, all w/terraces. **Services:** 🍴 ☛ 🆅🅿 🛄 🛏 Car-rental desk, social director, masseur, children's program, babysitting. Shuttle operates to Bonaventure Country Club for golf. **Facilities:** 🏋 🚲 🏊 🏌 🛶 🍴 🚪 💻 🛄 5 rsts, 3 bars (1 w/entertainment), 1 beach (ocean), lifeguard, board surfing, games rm, spa, whirlpool, beauty salon, washer/dryer. **Rates:** HS Jan–Apr $249–$330 S or D; from $500 ste. Children under 18 stay free. Min stay spec evnts. Lower rates off-season. Spec packages avail. Pking: Indoor, $6. Maj CC.

≣≣≣≣ **Pier 66 Crowne Plaza Resort & Marina**, 2301 SE 17th St Causeway, Fort Lauderdale, FL 33316; tel 305/525-6666 or toll free 800/334-5774; fax 305/728-3541. 22 acres. Arguably the top dog in town, this deluxe choice caters to the yachting crowd (who dock their boats in the marina) and those who appreciate the civilized service and surroundings but can survive without a beachfront position. Its lovely grounds all but compensate for the lack of beach. **Rooms:** 388 rms and stes. CI 4pm/CO noon. Express checkout avail. Nonsmoking rms avail. Major renovations have left units in top shape, with pastel tones, bed ruffles, and fancy window dressings. **Amenities:** 🛎 📺 📞 A/C,

cable TV w/movies, refrig, voice mail, in-rm safe, bathrobes. All units w/minibars, all w/terraces, some w/Jacuzzis. **Services:** 🍴 ☛ 🆅🅿 🛄 🛏 🔔 Social director, masseur, children's program, babysitting. **Facilities:** 🏋 🏊 🏌 🛶 🎱 🛶 📞 800 💻 🛄 4 rsts, 1 bar (w/entertainment), lifeguard, spa, sauna, steam rm, whirlpool, beauty salon, washer/dryer. Whirlpool will accommodate up to 40 people. Tower is topped by a revolving lounge. **Rates:** HS Jan–Apr 15 $219–$259 S or D; from $500 ste. Extra person $15. Children under 18 stay free. Lower rates off-season. Higher rates for spec evnts/hols. Spec packages avail. Pking: Outdoor, $5. Maj CC.

≣≣ **Rolling Hills Hotel & Golf Resort**, 3501 W Rolling Hills Circle, Fort Lauderdale, FL 33328; tel 305/475-0400 or toll free 800/327-7735; fax 305/474-9967. At 30th St SW and University Dr. Set away from the beach area in its own enclave, the training camp headquarters for the Miami Dolphins has its own following for its golf courses. While its facilities are of resort status, the accommodations, maintenance, and service do not measure up, and resort ambience is lacking. **Rooms:** 290 rms and stes. Exec-level rms avail. CI 3pm/CO noon. Nonsmoking rms avail. Standard motel-like rooms. **Amenities:** 🛎 A/C, cable TV w/movies. Some units w/terraces. **Services:** ✕ 🆅🅿 🛄 🛏 Twice-daily maid svce, car-rental desk, babysitting. **Facilities:** 🏋 ⛳27 🏊 1K 💻 🛄 2 rsts, 1 bar, whirlpool. **Rates:** $80–$90 S or D; from $150 ste. Extra person $10. Children under 12 stay free. Min stay spec evnts. Higher rates for spec evnts/hols. AP and MAP rates avail. Spec packages avail. Pking: Outdoor, free. Maj CC.

Restaurants 🍴

Bimini Boat Yard, in Quay Shopping Center, 1555 SE 17th St Causeway, Fort Lauderdale; tel 305/525-7400. **New American.** An upscale eatery with water views, a yuppie crowd, and a rollicking Friday night happy hour. The menu includes fresh blackened mahimahi served with couscous and Jamaican jerk ribs. **FYI:** Reservations not accepted. Dancing/guitar/piano. **Open:** Mon–Thurs 11:30am–11pm, Fri 11:30am–11:30pm, Sat noon–11:30pm, Sun 10:30am–11pm. Closed Dec 25. **Prices:** Main courses $12.95–$17.95. Maj CC. 📷 🆅🅿 ♿

★ **By Word of Mouth**, 3200 NE 12th Ave, Fort Lauderdale; tel 305/564-3663. **Continental.** A stylish, appealing bistro-style cafe that began as a catering company. The interior is attractively accented with fresh gladiolas. Regularly changing gourmet menu. Known for its brownie desserts. **FYI:** Reservations recommended. Beer and wine only. **Open:** Lunch Mon–Fri 11am–3pm; dinner Wed–Thurs 5–9pm, Fri–Sat 5–10pm. Closed some hols; early Aug. **Prices:** Main courses $17–$25. Maj CC. ♿

Cafe de Paris, 715 E Las Olas Blvd, Fort Lauderdale; tel 305/467-2900. **French.** Bedecked in wrought iron and green marble. Live piano music wafts through the air as you dine. The outdoor patio is reminiscent of a true Parisian cafe. The menu includes scampi and baby rack of lamb. Fine wine list. **FYI:** Reservations recommended. Piano. Dress code. **Open:** Lunch Mon–Sat 11:30am–2:30pm; dinner Sun–Thurs 5:30–10pm, Fri–Sat 5:30–10:30pm. **Prices:** Main courses $15–$25; PF dinner $15–$20. Maj CC. ♥ ⬢ ⬤

The Chart House, 301 SW 3rd Ave, Fort Lauderdale; tel 305/523-0177. **Seafood/Steak.** Located in two of Fort Lauderdale's oldest homes, the Bryant Homes, located on the New River. Off-season, early-bird specials are available. Local seafood, prime rib, caesar salad, mud pie. **FYI:** Reservations recommended. Children's menu. **Open:** Daily 5–10pm. **Prices:** Main courses $16–$28. Maj CC. ⬛ ⬜ ⬤ VP &

Down Under, 3000 E Oakland Park Blvd, Fort Lauderdale; tel 305/563-4123. **New American.** Copious floral arrangements, Victorian antiques, and garden rooms filled with lush, colorful foliage make this an inviting dining spot. The patio overlooks flower gardens and the Intracoastal Waterway. The menu includes Idaho trout and steak au poivre. **FYI:** Reservations accepted. **Open:** HS Sept–May lunch Tues–Fri 11am–2pm; dinner Sun–Sat 5–11pm. Reduced hours off-season. **Prices:** Main courses $15–$30. Maj CC. VP &

15th St Fisheries, 1900 SE 15th St, Fort Lauderdale; tel 305/763-2777. **Seafood.** A Florida-casual waterside seafood eatery with dining both upstairs and down. The menu includes sautéed snapper, tuna filet mignon, blackened redfish, and Lake Superior whitefish. **FYI:** Reservations recommended. Children's menu. **Open:** Daily 11:30am–10pm. Closed Dec 25. **Prices:** Main courses $11–$30. Maj CC. ⬢ ⬜ ⬤ VP &

French Quarter, 215 SE 8th Ave, Fort Lauderdale; tel 305/463-8000. **Cajun/Creole.** A lovely, romantic hideaway with stained glass and gardens. The country French interior with lush foliage has a garden-like atmosphere. Red snapper, beef Wellington, Dover sole. **FYI:** Reservations recommended. Jacket required. **Open:** Lunch Mon–Fri 11:30am–3pm; dinner Mon–Sat 5:30–11:30pm. Closed some hols. **Prices:** Main courses $14.50–$26; PF dinner $25. Maj CC. ♥ ⬤ VP &

Gibby's, 2900 NE 12th Terrace, Fort Lauderdale; tel 305/565-2929. **Seafood/Steak.** A very busy yet low-key old-fashioned steakhouse with a brick interior. Specialties like baked stuffed salmon served in addition to steaks. **FYI:** Reservations recommended. **Open:** Dinner Mon–Fri 5–10pm, Sat–Sun 4:30–10pm. **Prices:** Main courses $14–$28; PF dinner $22–$25. Maj CC. ⬤ VP &

Houston's, in Del Mar Shopping Center, 1451 N Federal Hwy, Fort Lauderdale; tel 305/563-2226. 3 blocks N of Sunrise Blvd. **New American.** A dimly lit, romantic restaurant with an open kitchen and cheerful staff. The menu offers a good selection of quality beef, fresh fish, and chicken. **FYI:** Reservations not accepted. **Open:** Sun–Thurs 11:30am–11pm, Fri–Sat 11:30am–midnight. Closed some hols. **Prices:** Main courses $7.25–$15.75. Maj CC. ♥ &

Il Tartuffo, 2980 N Federal Hwy, Fort Lauderdale; tel 305/564-0607. **Italian.** Northern Italian favorites are served in a cozy, casual setting. Some dishes prepared in the woodburning oven. **FYI:** Reservations recommended. Beer and wine only. **Open:** Tues–Sat 5–11pm, Sun 5–10pm. Closed some hols. **Prices:** Main courses $12.95–$22.50. Maj CC. ♥ VP &

La Coquille, 1619 E Sunrise Blvd, Fort Lauderdale; tel 305/467-3030. Between 15th Ave and 16th Terrace. **French.** Traditional French cuisine is served in a charming, casual French-accented setting. **FYI:** Reservations recommended. Beer and wine only. **Open:** HS Oct–May lunch Fri 11:30am–2pm; dinner daily 5:30–10pm. Reduced hours off-season. Closed Aug. **Prices:** Main courses $12.50–$21.50. Maj CC. &

La Ferme, 1601 E Sunrise Blvd, Fort Lauderdale; tel 305/764-0987. **French.** A warm and inviting restaurant made up of a series of separate cozy rooms. Tables are covered with pink linen and lace. Lump crab meat and avocado salad is a notable starter. Entrees include roasted duck served with apricot sauce, and filet mignon in a pepper and orange sauce. The dessert specialty is Grand Marnier soufflé. **FYI:** Reservations recommended. **Open:** HS Nov–May daily 5:30–10pm. Reduced hours off-season. Closed Aug. **Prices:** Main courses $15.75–$22.50. Maj CC. ♥ ⬤ &

Le Dome, 333 Sunset Dr, Fort Lauderdale; tel 305/463-3303. **American/Continental.** A Provençal-style restaurant reminiscent of an old-world château. The interior is done in soft tones and is graced with fluted columns and lovely water views. The menu includes rack of lamb, 3-pound Maine lobster, and swordfish. There's a separate bar area and a full-time wine steward. **FYI:** Reservations recommended. Guitar/piano. Dress code. **Open:** Daily 5:30–10pm. **Prices:** Main courses $15.50–$28. Maj CC. ♥ ⬜ VP &

Left Bank, 214 SE 6th Ave, Fort Lauderdale; tel 305/462-5376. 1 block N of Las Olas Blvd. **New American/French.** A romantic hideaway with soft floral wallpaper and a country French ambience. The chef, host of a nationally televised PBS cooking show, calls the Florida-French fare here "sunshine cuisine." The menu includes sesame-seared tuna and rack of lamb. The caesar salad is prepared tableside. **FYI:** Reservations recommended. Dress code. Beer and wine only. **Open:** Daily 6–11pm. **Prices:** Main courses $18–$26; PF dinner $27. Maj CC. ♥ &

Mai Kai, 3599 N Federal Hwy, Fort Lauderdale; tel 305/563-3272. Between Oakland Park and Commercial Blvds. **Polynesian.** Traditional Polynesian entrees are served in a lavish South Seas setting with a casual atmosphere. Relax and enjoy a tropical drink amid thatch, torches, waterfalls, lagoons, and lush gardens. **FYI:** Reservations recommended. Guitar. Children's menu. **Open:** Sun–Thurs 5–10pm, Fri–Sat 5–11pm. **Prices:** Main courses $16–$30. Maj CC. ♥ VP &

Newman's La Bonne Auberge, in 4300 Plaza, 4300 N Federal Hwy, Fort Lauderdale; tel 305/491-5522. **Continental/French.** A romantic, elegant bistro with a country French decor. Calf's liver, sautéed veal chops, fresh trout, large shrimps in saffron sauce. **FYI:** Reservations recommended. **Open:** Lunch Mon–Fri 11:30–2:30; dinner Mon–Sat 5:30–10pm. Closed Aug. **Prices:** Main courses $13.50–$24.50. Maj CC. ♥ ♥ &

Paesano, 1301 E Las Olas Blvd, Fort Lauderdale; tel 305/467-3266. **Italian.** A rather formal trattoria serving northern Italian fare. Soft music plays in the background. The menu features veal dishes, baked stuffed shrimp, and pasta Venetian. The adjacent bar area is less formal. **FYI:** Reservations recommended. Dress code. **Open:** Mon–Sat 5:30–10:30pm. **Prices:** Main courses $15–$26. Maj CC. ♥ VP

The Plum Room, 3001 E Oakland Park Blvd, Fort Lauderdale; tel 305/561-4400. At SW corner of Intracoastal Waterway. **New American/Continental.** This polished art deco restaurant with a wonderful collection of artwork is the perfect setting in which to enjoy the elegant continental cuisine. Specialties include tricolor ravioli filled with lobster, wild mushrooms, and fresh herbs; and Maine lobster poached in white wine and whiskey and served with mushrooms. **FYI:** Reservations not accepted. Jacket required. **Open:** Mon–Thurs 5–10pm, Fri–Sat 5–10:30pm, Sun 5–9:30pm. **Prices:** Main courses $17–$30. Maj CC. VP &

Primavera, 830 E Oakland Park Blvd, Fort Lauderdale; tel 305/564-6363. Between NE 6th Ave and Dixie Hwy. **Italian.** Casually elegant restaurant serving original Italian cuisine. Specialties include veal chops with wild mushrooms, lobster with a light brandy and ginger sauce, and beef tenderloin sautéed in rosemary and balsamic vinaigrette. **FYI:** Reservations recommended. **Open:** Tues–Thurs 5–10, Fri–Sun 5–11. **Prices:** Main courses $15–$25. Maj CC. &

★ **Ruth's Chris Steak House**, 2525 N Federal Hwy, Fort Lauderdale; tel 305/565-2338. **Steak.** A basic, casual steakhouse

with romantic lighting and a cozy lounge. Veal, chicken, and fish also served. **FYI:** Reservations recommended. **Open:** Mon–Sat 5–11pm, Sun 5–10pm. **Prices:** Main courses $17.50–$29.50. Maj CC. ▣ VP &

★ **Seawatch**, 6002 N Ocean Blvd, Fort Lauderdale; tel 305/781-2200. 1 mi N of Commercial Blvd on Fla A1A. **Seafood/Steak.** This favorite beach area hideaway is situated in a 2-story space complete with an upbeat nautical decor, great ocean views, and outdoor dining. The staff, dressed in striped sailor tops, serves a variety of seafood dishes and grilled specialties. **FYI:** Reservations accepted. Children's menu. **Open:** Lunch daily 11:30am–3:30pm; dinner daily 5–10pm. Closed Dec 25. **Prices:** Main courses $12–$31. Maj CC. ▣ ▣ ▣ VP

Sheffield's, in Marriott's Harbor Beach Resort, 3030 Holiday Dr, Fort Lauderdale; tel 305/525-4000. **Continental.** Classy, formal setting. Continental dishes include beef Wellington and chateaubriand. Attentive service. **FYI:** Reservations recommended. Jacket required. **Open:** HS Sept–May daily 6–10:30pm. Reduced hours off-season. **Prices:** Main courses $20.75–$31.25. Maj CC. ♥ VP &

Yesterday's, 3001 E Oakland Park Blvd, Fort Lauderdale; tel 305/561-4400. **New American/Continental.** Every table at this stunning 3-tiered restaurant enjoys sweeping views of the Intracoastal Waterway. Both the dining room and the high-energy nightclub are popular with Palm Beach's jet set. Specialties include pistachio-encrusted dolphin sautéed with ginger and key lime–butter sauce. **FYI:** Reservations recommended. **Open:** Mon–Thurs 5–10:30pm, Fri–Sat 5–11pm–Sun 4:30–10:30pm. **Prices:** Main courses $12–$25. Maj CC. ▣ VP &

Attractions ▣

Museum of Discovery & Science, 401 SW 2nd St; tel 305/467-6637. This interactive science museum features 7 permanent exhibits, including Florida EcoScapes, KidScience, Space Base, and Choose Health. The Blockbuster IMAX Theater shows large-format films on a 5-story screen. **Open:** Mon–Fri 10am–5pm, Sat 10am–8:30pm, Sun noon–5pm. $$$

International Swimming Hall of Fame, 1 Hall of Fame Dr; tel 305/462-6536. The world's largest repository of swimming memorabilia, with Olympic gold medals won by some of the sport's greats, as well as films, books, interactive video displays, and more. The complex also houses 2 Olympic-size swimming pools. **Open:** Daily 9am–7pm. $

Bonnet House, 900 N Birch Rd; tel 305/563-5393. A historic 35-acre sub-tropical plantation-style home and estate designed by Chicago muralist Frank Clay Bartlett and completed in 1921. Tours are given May–Nov, Tues–Fri at 10am and 1pm, Sun at 1 and 2pm. $$$

Ocean World, 1701 SE 17th St; tel 305/525-6611 (recorded info). Six animal shows run continuously throughought the day. Performers range from dolphins and sea lions to river otters and exotic birds; also on view are tortoises, alligators, and tropical fish. A 1-hour narrated sightseeing cruise along the Intracoastal Waterway departs 3 times each day (additional fee required). Snack bars, gift shop. **Open:** Daily 10am–6pm. $$$$

Hugh Taylor Birch State Recreation Area, 3109 E Sunrise Blvd; tel 305/564-4521. Almost 200 acres with access to the ocean. Swimming, fishing, canoe rentals, hiking/nature trails. **Open:** Daily 8am–sunset. $$

FORT MYERS

Map page M-8, D3

Hotels 📇

Courtyard by Marriott, 4455 Metro Pkwy, Fort Myers, FL 33901; tel 813/275-8600 or toll free 800/321-2211; fax 813/275-7087. Exit 22 off I-75. After you exit, go west for 3 miles; the hotel is located at the intersection of Colonial Blvd and Metro Pkwy. Standing in the busy commercial district, the lowrise structure presents a familiar look, including the trademark courtyard. **Rooms:** 149 rms and stes. CI 4pm/CO noon. Express checkout avail. Nonsmoking rms avail. Handsome rooms are carefully maintained and outfitted with tasteful appointments. **Amenities:** 📦 🅰 🖥 A/C, cable TV w/movies. Some units w/terraces. **Services:** 🚗 🖎 🍽 🛎 Babysitting. **Facilities:** 🔥 🍴 [50] 🔥 1 rst, 1 bar, whirlpool, washer/dryer. **Rates:** HS Jan–Apr $110–$128 S or D; from $139 ste. Children under 18 stay free. Lower rates off-season. Higher rates for spec evnts/hols. Spec packages avail. Pking: Outdoor, free. Maj CC.

Holiday Inn Airport, 13051 Bell Tower Dr, Fort Myers, FL 33907 (Southwest Florida Regional Airport); tel 813/482-2900 or toll free 800/HOLIDAY. Exit 21 off I-75. Right in the thick of a shopping center area and 5 minutes from a major mall, it's geared more toward business travelers than leisure guests. **Rooms:** 231 rms and stes. CI 3pm/CO noon. Nonsmoking rms avail. **Amenities:** 📦 🅰 A/C, cable TV w/movies, refrig. Some units w/minibars. **Services:** ✕ 🚗 🖎 🍽 Car-rental desk, babysitting. **Facilities:** 🔥 🍴 [450] 🔥 1 rst, 1 bar (w/entertainment), washer/dryer. **Rates:** HS Feb–Apr $149–$189 S or D; from $209 ste. Extra person $10. Lower rates off-season. Spec packages avail. Pking: Outdoor, free. Maj CC.

Holiday Inn Central, 2431 Cleveland Ave, Fort Myers, FL 33901; tel 813/332-3232 or toll free 800/998-0466; fax 813/332-0590. 1 mi S of downtown Fort Myers. A midrise hotel with southwestern styling that is handy to downtown and the nearby mall. If you can live without a beach location, this is a good find. **Rooms:** 126 rms and stes. CI 3pm/CO noon. Nonsmoking rms avail. Spiffy rooms are colorful and upbeat. **Amenities:** 📦 🅰 🗣 A/C, cable TV w/movies, refrig. **Services:** ✕ 🚗 🖎 🍽 🛎 Twice-daily maid svce, babysitting. **Facilities:** 🔥 🍴 [75] 🔥 1 rst, 1 bar (w/entertainment), sauna, steam rm, whirlpool. **Rates:** HS Feb–Mar $129 S or D; from $260 ste. Extra person $10. Children under 18 stay free. Lower rates off-season. Higher rates for spec evnts/hols. Spec packages avail. Pking: Outdoor, free. Maj CC.

Radisson Inn Sanibel Gateway, 20091 Summerlin Rd, Fort Myers, FL 33908; tel 813/466-1200 or toll free 800/333-3333; fax 813/466-3797. A smartly decorated establishment that manages to make the most of its off-beach location, with an inviting courtyard that provides a nice alternative for tired beachgoers. Fountain in registration area is a fun touch. **Rooms:** 157 rms. CI 3pm/CO noon. Nonsmoking rms avail. **Amenities:** 📦 🅰 A/C, cable TV w/movies, refrig, in-rm safe. 1 unit w/Jacuzzi. **Services:** ✕ 🖎 🍽 🛎 Babysitting. **Facilities:** 🔥 ⚽ 🍴 [40] 1 rst, 1 bar, games rm, whirlpool, washer/dryer. **Rates:** HS Feb–Apr $115–$125 S or D. Children under 18 stay free. Lower rates off-season. Higher rates for spec evnts/hols. Spec packages avail. Pking: Outdoor, free. Maj CC.

Ramada Airport Hotel, 12635 Cleveland Ave, Fort Myers, FL 33907; tel 813/936-4300 or toll free 800/368-3027; fax 813/936-2058. At College Pkwy. Satisfactory facility housed in a 5-story brick building. **Rooms:** 224 rms and stes. CI 4pm/CO 11am. Nonsmoking rms avail. Bathrooms scheduled for renovation. **Amenities:** 📦 🅰 A/C, cable TV w/movies. **Services:** ✕ 🚗 🖎 🍽 **Facilities:** 🔥 🎱 [350] 1 rst, 2 bars (w/entertainment), lawn games, washer/dryer. Nearby health club offers free access to guests. Volleyball court on premises. **Rates:** HS Dec–Apr $79–$99 S or D; from $149 ste. Extra person $8. Children under 18 stay free. Lower rates off-season. Spec packages avail. Pking: Outdoor, free. Maj CC.

Shell Point Village Guest House, 15000 Shell Point Blvd, Fort Myers, FL 33908; tel 813/466-1111. 1 mi E of the Sanibel tollgate. This hostelry in a Christian retirement village set on 75 acres is certainly not for everyone, but it may appeal to those who desire a quiet retreat or vacation in a wholesome environment. No drinking or smoking is allowed, and there is no dancing in public. A security gate controlls access to the village. **Rooms:** 39 rms. CI 3pm/CO 11am. Nonsmoking rms avail. **Amenities:** 📦 A/C, cable TV. Some units w/terraces. **Services:**

↵ **Facilities:** 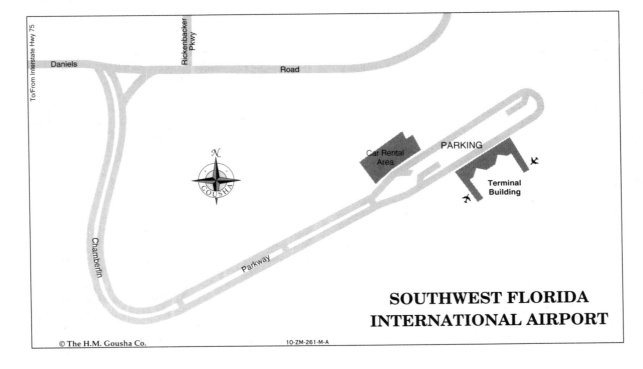 1 rst, washer/dryer. There's a bank within the village. **Rates:** HS Dec–Apr $70 S; $80 D. Extra person $6. Children under 18 stay free. Lower rates off-season. Pking: Outdoor, free. Ltd CC.

Sheraton Harbor Place, 2500 Edwards Dr, Fort Myers, FL 33901; tel 813/337-0300 or toll free 800/833-1620; fax 813/337-1530. Exit 25W off I-75. This downtown highrise offers a variety of accommodations and facilities capable of satisfying the needs of both business and leisure clients. **Rooms:** 417 rms and stes. CI 3pm/CO noon. Nonsmoking rms avail. **Amenities:** A/C, cable TV w/movies. **Services:** ✗ Babysitting. **Facilities:** 1 rst, 2 bars (1 w/entertainment), games rm, whirlpool, washer/dryer. **Rates:** HS Feb–Apr $119–$151 S; $129–$161 D; from $139 ste. Extra person $10. Children under 17 stay free. Lower rates off-season. Higher rates for spec evnts/hols. Spec packages avail. Pking: Indoor/outdoor, free. Maj CC.

Victoria Pier House Inn, 2220 W 1st St, Fort Myers, FL 33901; tel 813/334-3434; fax 334-3844. 1 mi W of US41. Enjoying somewhat of a resurgence in popularity now that some of its renovations have been completed, it nonetheless has a "vacant" feeling. **Rooms:** 170 rms, stes. CI 3pm/CO 11am. **Amenities:** A/C, cable TV. **Services:** ↵ **Facilities:**

1 rst, 2 bars (1 w/entertainment). The restaurant is quite popular with outsiders. **Rates:** HS Jan–Apr $99–$119 S or D; from $89 ste. Extra person $10. Children under 18 stay free. Lower rates off-season. Pking: Outdoor, free. Maj CC.

Motels

La Quinta Motor Inn, 4850 S Cleveland Ave, Fort Myers, FL 33907; tel 813/275-3300 or toll free 800/531-5900; fax 813/275-6661. Simple accommodations for the motorist on a budget. Not far from area attractions. **Rooms:** 130 rms and stes. CI 3pm/CO noon. Nonsmoking rms avail. **Amenities:** A/C, cable TV. **Services:** ↵ **Facilities:** Washer/dryer. **Rates (CP):** HS Jan–Mar $69 S; $79 D; from $87 ste. Extra person $10. Children under 18 stay free. Lower rates off-season. Pking: Outdoor, free. Maj CC.

Travelodge, 2038 W 1st St, Fort Myers, FL 33901; tel 813/334-2284 or toll free 800/578-7878; fax 813/334-2366. ¼ mi W of US 41. **Rooms:** 48 rms. CI 2pm/CO 11am. Nonsmoking rms avail. **Amenities:** A/C, cable TV. Some units w/terraces. **Services:** ↵ **Facilities:** **Rates:** HS Jan–Apr $49–$69 S or D. Extra person $3. Children under 12 stay free. Lower rates off-season. Higher rates for spec evnts/hols. Pking: Outdoor, free. Maj CC.

SOUTHWEST FLORIDA INTERNATIONAL AIRPORT

© The H.M. Gousha Co.   10-ZM-261-M-A

≣≣ **Wellesley Inn**, 4400 Ford St, Fort Myers, FL 33916; tel 813/278-3949 or toll free 800/444-8888; fax 813/278-3670. Exit 22 off I-75. Basic lodgings, featuring an attractive lobby with marble floor and potted palms. **Rooms:** 106 rms and stes. CI 2pm/CO 11am. Nonsmoking rms avail. **Amenities:** 📺 🗗 A/C, cable TV. **Services:** ✕ 🖼 🗗 🕾 **Facilities:** 🗗 🚹 🕭 Washer/dryer. **Rates (CP):** HS Dec 15–Apr 15 $70 S or D; from $100 ste. Extra person $5. Children under 17 stay free. Lower rates off-season. Pking: Outdoor, free. Maj CC.

Resort

≣≣≣ **Sanibel Harbour Resort & Spa**, 17260 Harbour Point Rd, Fort Myers, FL 33908; tel 813/466-4000 or toll free 800/767-7777; fax 813/466-2150. 80 acres. This local favorite offers the most complete package in Ft Myers or Sanibel, except possibly for the South Seas Plantation. Situated on dozens of landscaped acres, the resort exudes good taste without being too formal. It's well respected for its dining and recreational diversions and spa facilities. The tall windows in the lobby look out to the harbor. **Rooms:** 364 rms, stes, and effic. CI 3pm/CO noon. Nonsmoking rms avail. **Amenities:** 📺 🗗 A/C, cable TV w/movies. Some units w/minibars, all w/terraces. **Services:** ✕ 🖛 📞 🖼 🗗 Car-rental desk, social director, masseur, children's program, babysitting. Numerous young staffers are friendly and efficient. **Facilities:** 🗗 🔺 🏊 🞼 🐟12 🞼12 🍴 600 🖳 🕭 3 rsts, 3 bars (2 w/entertainment), 1 beach (bay), games rm, racquetball, spa, sauna, steam rm, whirlpool, beauty salon. **Rates:** HS Dec–Apr $230–$270 S or D; from $325 ste; from $285 effic. Extra person $20. Children under 18 stay free. Lower rates off-season. Higher rates for spec evnts/hols. AP and MAP rates avail. Spec packages avail. Pking: Indoor/outdoor, free. Maj CC.

Restaurants 🍴

The Chart House, 2024 W 1st St, Fort Myers; tel 813/332-1881. **Seafood/Steak.** An excellent chain restaurant featuring map-topped tables, a central bar, and lovely water views. This location features fine seafood, as well as a few beef and chicken dishes to satisfy landlubbers. **FYI:** Reservations recommended. Children's menu. **Open:** Sun–Thurs 5–10pm, Fri–Sat 5–11pm. **Prices:** Main courses $16.95–$21.95. Maj CC. 🖼 🗹 🕭

Outback Steakhouse, in Bell Tower Shops, 12995 S Cleveland Ave, Fort Myers; tel 813/936-1021. **Steak.** A casual eatery popular with families for the good value it offers. The varied menu features entrees like grilled baby-back ribs and 12-ounce center-cut sirloin. There is a bar area as well, with dark wood tables, booths, and a TV. **FYI:** Reservations accepted. Children's

menu. **Open:** Mon–Thurs 3:30–10:30pm, Fri–Sat 3–11:30pm, Sun noon–10:30pm. Closed some hols. **Prices:** Main courses $4.95–$17.95. Maj CC. 🕭

Peter's La Cuisine, 2224 Bay St, Fort Myers (Downtown); tel 813/332-2228. Adjacent to the Harborside Convention Center. **French.** This upscale dining room has a noteworthy lounge area and jazz bar upstairs. Specialties include seafood, veal, beef, and pasta dishes. Lunch is a more casual affair than dinner. **FYI:** Reservations recommended. Blues. Dress code. **Open:** Lunch Mon–Fri 11:30am–2:30pm; dinner daily 5:30–9:30pm. **Prices:** Main courses $16.95–$23. Maj CC. 🕭

The Prawnbroker Restaurant and Fish Market, in Cypress Square, 13451 McGregor Blvd, Fort Myers; tel 813/489-2226. **Seafood/Steak.** This seafood restaurant and shop with basic decor is a good choice for families and the older crowd. A great value for fresh fish. **FYI:** Reservations recommended. Reservations accepted. Children's menu. **Open:** Daily 4–9:45pm. Closed some hols. **Prices:** Main courses $10.95–$24.95. Maj CC. 🕭

Smitty's, 2240 W 1st St, Fort Myers (Downtown); tel 813/334-4415. ½ mi W of the Caloosahatchee River Bridge. **Seafood/Steak.** Elegant and dark, this is the spot for romance. Hand-selected and custom-aged beef, home-baked breads and rolls, and sinfully delicious desserts are the house specialties. For the health-conscious, a lighter menu is available. **FYI:** Reservations accepted. Children's menu. **Open:** Lunch Mon–Fri 11am–4pm, Sun 11:30–4; dinner Mon–Thurs 4:30–9:30pm, Fri–Sat 4–10pm, Sun 4–9pm. Closed Dec 25. **Prices:** Main courses $8.95–$18.95. Maj CC. ❤ 🗹 🕭

Tootie McGregor's Gulfshore Grille, in Fort Myers Country Club, 3583 McGregor Blvd, Fort Myers; tel 813/939-7300. 1 mi S of the Edison Winter Home and Museum. **Seafood.** This place serves the best Sunday brunch in southwest Florida. The great menu features seafood strudel, stone crab cakes, grilled jumbo shrimp, and grilled Caribbean-jerk pork chops. Live entertainment and valet parking are some of the amenities available. Don't miss happy hour. **FYI:** Reservations accepted. Singer. Children's menu. **Open:** Lunch Mon–Sat 11am–2:30pm; dinner Sun–Thurs 4:30–9pm, Fri–Sat 4:30–10pm; brunch Sun 10am–2pm. Closed Dec 25. **Prices:** Main courses $4.95–$18.95. Maj CC. 🗹 🕭

Veranda, 2122 2nd St, Fort Myers; tel 813/332-2228. Across from City Hall. **Continental.** Experience southern comfort and elegance in an antique-filled Victorian house steeped in character, a fine place for special occasions. Entrees include a rack of New Zealand lamb, marinated grilled prawns, and vegetable ravioli. Among dessert choices are southern praline tart and peanut butter fudge pie. **FYI:** Reservations recommended. Piano. Children's menu. Dress code. No smoking. **Open:** Lunch Mon–Fri 11am–2:30pm; dinner Mon–Sat 5:30–10:30pm. Closed Dec 25. **Prices:** Main courses $13.95–$22.95. Maj CC. VP &

Attractions 📷

Edison Winter Home, 2350 McGregor Blvd; tel 813/334-3614. Regularly scheduled tours are conducted of inventor Thomas Alva Edison's winter retreat, in which he lived with his wife and their family until his death in 1931. Tour includes a visit to the gardens of the estate, with wild orchids and an enormous banyan tree that Edison grew from a seedling; the laboratory, which contains the original equipment used for his rubber research from 1928 to 1931; and the museum, with vintage light bulbs, phonographs, early movie projectors, and other interesting gadgets and memorabilia. **Open:** Mon–Sat 9am–4pm, Sun 12:30–4pm. Closed some hols. $$$

Ford Winter Home, 2350 McGregor Blvd; tel 813/334-3614. "Mangoes," industrialist Henry Ford's winter home, is next door to the Edison home and was purchased so the two friends could be neighbors. Tours are given of the interior of the house, which contains 1920s-style furnishings, and of the grounds. **Open:** Mon–Sat 9am–4pm, Sun 12:30–4pm. Closed some hols. $$$

Fort Myers Historical Museum, 2300 Peck St; tel 813/332-5955. Artifacts, graphic depictions, and photos present the history of Fort Myers, from the Calusa and Seminole civilizations to the first European settlers and beyond. There are scale models, a collection of Ethel Cooper glass, and the "Esperanza," the last (and longest) of the plush Pullman railroad cars, which is parked outside the museum. **Open:** Mon–Sat 9am–4:30pm, Sun 12:30–4:30pm. Closed some hols. $

Burroughs Home, 2505 1st St; tel 813/332-1229. A 1901 Georgian revival mansion. "Living history" tours are conducted by the 2 Burroughs sisters, local historians who dress up in period fashion and talk to visitors about life in the mansion. The garden overlooks the Caloosahatchee River. **Open:** Tours, Mon–Fri 10am–4pm, Sun noon–4pm. $

Lee County Nature Center, 3450 Ortiz Ave; tel 813/275-3435. Nature trails wind through over 100 acres of pinewood flatland and cypress swamp. Visitors can also visit the aviary, live reptile exhibit, saltwater aquarium, and museum store. Planetarium features star and laser shows. **Open:** Mon–Sat 9am–5pm, Sun 11am–5pm. $

Six Mile Cypress Slough Preserve, Penzance Crossing and Six Mile Cypress Pkwy; tel 813/338-3300. Visitors can walk along a mile-long boardwalk through this 2,000-acre wetland ecosys-

tem, exploring southwest Florida's diverse flora and fauna. Subtropical ferns, wild orchids, and such birds as herons, egrets, spoonbills, and storks. **Open:** Daily 8am–5pm. $

FORT MYERS BEACH
Map page M-8, E3

Hotels 🏨

■■ **Days Inn at Lover's Key**, 8701 Estero Blvd, Fort Myers Beach, FL 33931; tel 813/765-4422 or toll free 800/325-2525; fax 813/765-4422. 7 mi S of Sky Bridge. This architecturally unremarkable highrise offers a private beach with a view of the bridge at Big Bonita Pass, and water activities. The sunsets make up somewhat for the dull decor. **Rooms:** 110 effic. CI 3pm/CO 11am. Nonsmoking rms avail. **Amenities:** 🛁 A/C, cable TV w/movies, refrig, in-rm safe. All units w/terraces. Continental breakfast and cocktails at sunset are complimentary. **Services:** ✗ 🍷 🍽 Babysitting. **Facilities:** 🛗 ⚖ 👣 1 rst, 1 beach (cove/inlet), lawn games, washer/dryer. Picnic tables in the shade. Cheerful, casual cafe has outdoor seating. **Rates:** HS Feb–Apr from $139 effic. Extra person $10. Children under 12 stay free. Lower rates off-season. Higher rates for spec evnts/hols. Pking: Outdoor, free. Maj CC.

■■■ **Holiday Inn**, 6890 Estero Blvd, Fort Myers Beach, FL 33931; tel 813/463-5711 or toll free 800/HOLIDAY; fax 813/463-7038. 4½ mi S of Sky Bridge. Appealing for its sunny, landscaped pool area wrapped by a 1- and 2-story section, with some rooms opening directly to the pool. **Rooms:** 103 rms, stes, and effic. CI 3pm/CO noon. Express checkout avail. Nonsmoking rms avail. **Amenities:** 🛁 👣 A/C, cable TV w/movies, refrig. Some units w/terraces. **Services:** ✗ 🍷 🍽 Babysitting. **Facilities:** 🛗 🎱 [40] 👣 1 rst, 2 bars (1 w/entertainment), 1 beach (ocean), games rm, lawn games, washer/dryer. Thatched umbrellas and lounge chairs beside pool. **Rates:** HS Feb–Apr $141–$186 S or D; from $325 ste; from $186 effic. Extra person $6. Children under 18 stay free. Lower rates off-season. Pking: Outdoor, free. Maj CC.

■■■ **Lani Kai Island Resort**, 1400 Estero Blvd, Fort Myers Beach, FL 33931; tel 813/463-3111 or toll free 800/237-6133; fax 813/463-2986. A midrise structure located on a fine stretch of beach; may appeal to families who don't require much in the way of facilities. **Rooms:** 100 rms, stes, and effic. CI 3pm/CO 11am. Maintenance is not quite up to par, and a committee must have decorated—too many patterns and colors are used in the units. Rooms have great views, however, and good-sized decks, from which you can hear the waves crashing below. **Amenities:** 🛁 A/C, TV, refrig. All units w/terraces. **Services:** 🍽 Babysitting.

Facilities: 🔥 🚲 ⛱ ▶ 🏊 ♿ 1 rst, 3 bars (2 w/entertainment), 1 beach (ocean), games rm, beauty salon, playground, washer/dryer. **Rates:** HS Dec–Mar $150 S or D; from $195 ste; from $170 effic. Extra person $5. Children under 12 stay free. Lower rates off-season. Pking: Outdoor, free. Ltd CC.

≣≣≣ Mariner's Pink Shell Beach and Bay Resort, 275 Estero Blvd, Fort Myers Beach, FL 33931; tel 813/463-6181 or toll free 800/237-5786; fax 813/463-1229. This sprawling complex on both sides of the road at the north end of island offers a good stretch of beach and various recreational opportunities. **Rooms:** 135 rms and effic; 40 ctges/villas. CI 4pm/CO 11am. Standard rooms are to be transformed into efficiencies for 1995. **Amenities:** 🛏 🕓 📺 A/C, cable TV, refrig, VCR, in-rm safe. All units w/terraces. **Services:** 🍴 Children's program, babysitting. **Facilities:** 🔥 🚲 ⛱ 🎾 ▶ 🏊 ♿ 1 rst, 2 bars, 1 beach (ocean), games rm, playground, washer/dryer. Outdoor dining room features lovely bay views. **Rates:** HS Dec–Apr $105–$164 S or D; from $99 effic; from $129 ctge/villa. Extra person $5. Children under 18 stay free. Min stay HS. Lower rates off-season. Higher rates for spec evnts/hols. Spec packages avail. Pking: Outdoor, free. Maj CC.

≣≣ Pointe Estero, 6640 Estero Blvd, Fort Myers Beach, FL 33931; tel 813/765-1155 or toll free 800/237-5141; fax 813/765-0657. An attractive, upscale, slender condominium highrise on the beach. Boasts a sunny freeform pool and deck enhanced by foliage. **Rooms:** 60 effic. CI 3pm/CO 10am. Express checkout avail. Full-sized units are decorated with luxury appointments, including such details as silk flower arrangements. **Amenities:** 🛏 🕓 📺 A/C, cable TV w/movies, refrig, VCR, voice mail. All units w/terraces, some w/fireplaces, all w/Jacuzzis. **Services:** ⛱ 🍴 Social director, children's program, babysitting. **Facilities:** 🔥 ♿ 1 beach (ocean), whirlpool. Independent vendor operates watersports on beach. Barbecue grills available. **Rates:** HS Dec–Apr from $140 effic. Children under 18 stay free. Min stay HS. Lower rates off-season. Higher rates for spec evnts/hols. Pking: Outdoor, free. Maj CC.

≣≣ Santa Maria All-Suite Resort, 7317 Estero Blvd, Fort Myers Beach, FL 33931; tel 813/765-6700 or toll free 800/765-6701; fax 813/765-6909. 5 mi S of Sky Bridge. Condominium resort on a canal is minutes away from gulf beaches and boasts a full-service marina. **Rooms:** 53 stes. CI 3pm/CO 10am. Tastefully appointed 1-, 2-, and 3-bedroom units have tropical decor. **Amenities:** 🛏 🕓 📺 A/C, cable TV, refrig. All units w/terraces. **Services:** 🍴 Children's program, babysitting. **Facilities:** 🔥 ♿ Sauna, whirlpool, washer/dryer. Volleyball court. **Rates:** HS Feb–Apr from $135 ste. Children under 18 stay free. Min stay. Lower rates off-season. Higher rates for spec evnts/hols. Pking: Outdoor, free. Maj CC.

≣≣ Seawatch-on-the-Beach, 6550 Estero Blvd, Fort Myers Beach, FL 33931; tel 813/463-4469 or toll free 800/448-2736; fax 813/463-3926. 5 mi S of Sky Bridge. Considered a frontrunner in the condo market, a hotel away from the center of beach activity but still convenient to it. **Rooms:** 42 effic. CI 3pm/CO 10am. **Amenities:** 🛏 🕓 📺 A/C, cable TV, refrig, VCR. All units w/terraces, all w/Jacuzzis. **Services:** 🍴 Social director. **Facilities:** 🔥 ♿ 1 beach (ocean), games rm, whirlpool. Nearby health club offers free access to guests. No restaurant on premises. **Rates:** HS Feb–Apr from $189 effic. Children under 18 stay free. Min stay HS. Lower rates off-season. Higher rates for spec evnts/hols. Pking: Outdoor, free. Ltd CC.

Restaurants 🍴

Anthony's on the Gulf, 3040 Estero Blvd, Fort Myers Beach; tel 813/463-2600. **New American/Italian.** Excellent informal dining overlooking the water. The bar area is comfortable and inviting. The food is basic but good Italian, with veal, chicken, and seafood dishes populating the menu. **FYI:** Reservations not accepted. Band. Children's menu. **Open:** Lunch daily 11:30am–3pm; dinner daily 4:30–11pm. **Prices:** Main courses $7.95–$13.95. Maj CC. 🖼 📺 VP ♿

The Bridge, 708 Fisherman's Wharf, Fort Myers Beach; tel 813/765-0050. **Seafood/Steak.** This waterside restaurant, a comfortable, open room furnished in oak, is popular with locals and tourists alike. The dinner menu abounds with beef and seafood dishes, including Maine lobster. Sandwiches and salads are available at lunch. **FYI:** Reservations accepted. Children's menu. **Open:** Mon–Thurs 11am–10pm, Fri–Sun 11am–midnight. Closed Dec 25. **Prices:** Main courses $10.95–$15.95. Maj CC. ♿

Channel Mark, 19001 San Carlos Blvd, Fort Myers Beach; tel 813/463-9127. 1¼ mi N of the Skybridge. **Italian/Seafood/Steak.** An altogether pleasant dining experience. Sit at a table inside the light, airy dining room or outdoors overlooking the water. The menu includes sandwiches, fresh local seafood, and pasta-seafood combinations. **FYI:** Reservations not accepted. Jazz. Children's menu. **Open:** Daily 11am–11pm. Closed Dec 25. **Prices:** Main courses $13–$18. Maj CC. 🖼 📺 VP ♿

Crab Louie's Seafood Restaurant and Lounge, 1661 Esero Blvd, Fort Myers Beach; tel 813/463-2722. **New American/Seafood.** A relaxed spot to enjoy a meal after a day at the beach. Outdoor dining tables overlook Estero Blvd. Choose from a variety of steaks, seafood, pasta, and special dishes. Good values on the breakfast menu. **FYI:** Reservations accepted. Dancing. Children's menu. **Open:** Daily 8am–2am. **Prices:** Main courses $7.95–$18.95. Maj CC. ♿

Gulf Shore Restaurant, 1270 Estero Blvd, Fort Myers Beach; tel 813/463-9551. **Seafood/Steak.** A basic waterside eatery with a simple menu featuring seafood and steaks. An adjacent bar, the Cottage, caters to a college crowd. **FYI:** Reservations accepted. Children's menu. **Open:** Daily 7am–10pm. **Prices:** Main courses $9.95–$15. Maj CC. 🖤 🆅🅿

Skipper's Galley Restaurant, 3040 Estero Blvd, Fort Myers Beach; tel 813/463-6139. 2 mi SE of beach on Fla 865. **Seafood/Steak.** A nicely furnished eatery with a relaxed atmosphere and a great view of the beach. The menu offers fresh seafood, prime beef, veal Oscar, and the special dish, chicken Skipper. **FYI:** Reservations not accepted. Children's menu. **Open:** HS Dec–Apr daily 4–10pm. Reduced hours off-season. **Prices:** Main courses $13.95–$19.95. Maj CC. 🖼 🖤 ♿

FORT PIERCE

Map page M-9, B3

See also Indian River Shores, Jensen Beach, Port St Lucie, Stuart, Vero Beach

Hotels 🏨

Econo Lodge, 7050 Okeechobee Rd, PO Box 1, Fort Pierce, FL 34945; tel 407/465-8600 or toll free 800/424-4777. Exit 65 off I-95. A bare-bones pit stop for motorists, adequate for an overnight stay but otherwise charmless. Restaurants are close by. **Rooms:** 60 rms. CI 2pm/CO 11am. Nonsmoking rms avail. **Amenities:** 🛏 A/C, cable TV w/movies. **Services:** ⟲ ⟳ **Rates:** HS Dec–Apr $39 S; $44 D. Extra person $5. Children under 18 stay free. Lower rates off-season. Pking: Outdoor, free. Maj CC.

Holiday Inn Surfside North Hutchinson Island, 2600 N Fla A1A, Fort Pierce, FL 34949; tel 407/465-6000 or toll free 800/253-8673; fax 407/489-2354. Modest lodging directly on the beach. Home to a boxing training camp. **Rooms:** 153 rms. CI 3pm/CO noon. Nonsmoking rms avail. **Amenities:** 🛏 ♨ A/C, cable TV w/movies. All units w/terraces. **Services:** ✕ 🛎 ⟲ Car-rental desk. **Facilities:** 🔗 ♻ 🛆 🔲 ⚓ 🎱 ♿ 1 rst, 2 bars (1 w/entertainment), 1 beach (ocean), board surfing, games rm, snorkeling, washer/dryer. Children's pool. Sports cafe and poolside dining. **Rates:** HS Jan–Apr $65–$135 S or D. Extra person $10. Children under 19 stay free. Lower rates off-season. Higher rates for spec evnts/hols. Spec packages avail. Pking: Outdoor, free. Maj CC.

Motels

Days Inn–South Hutchinson Island, 1920 Seaway Dr, Fort Pierce, FL 34949; tel 407/461-8737 or toll free 800/447-4732; fax 407/460-2218. 2½ mi E of US 1. Set on the Intracoastal Waterway, 350 feet from the beach. Offers economy-class rooms and suites, facing pool, grounds, or Intracoastal. **Rooms:** 31 rms and stes. CI 2pm/CO 11am. Nonsmoking rms avail. **Amenities:** 🛏 A/C, cable TV w/movies. Some units w/terraces. **Services:** ⟲ Babysitting. **Facilities:** 🔗 ♿ Washer/dryer. **Rates:** HS Dec–Apr $95–$135 S or D; from $107 ste. Extra person $6. Children under 13 stay free. Lower rates off-season. Higher rates for spec evnts/hols. Pking: Outdoor, free. Maj CC.

Edgewater Motel and Apartments, 1156 Seaway Dr, Fort Pierce, FL 34949; tel 407/468-3555 or toll free 800/433-0004. At Seaway Dr and Alhambra St. A plain mom-and-pop operation located on the inlet, with standard motel rooms and a few efficiencies or units with a separate bedroom and dining and living areas. Affiliated with the pricier Harbor Light Inn next door (see below). **Rooms:** 14 rms and effic. CI 1pm/CO 11am. **Amenities:** 🛏 A/C, cable TV, refrig. **Services:** ⟲ **Facilities:** 🔗 Whirlpool, washer/dryer. Boat dock available by reservation. **Rates:** HS Dec 20–Apr $46 S or D; from $59 effic. Extra person $10. Children under 14 stay free. Min stay spec evnts. Lower rates off-season. Pking: Outdoor, free. Maj CC.

Harbor Light Inn, 1160 Seaway Dr, Fort Pierce, FL 34949; tel 407/468-3555. Located on Fort Pierce Inlet, this low-key hotel with an appealing nautical theme is a good choice for boating and fishing enthusiasts, as it offers boat slips and a pier for fishing. **Rooms:** 21 rms and effic. CI 1pm/CO 11am. Nonsmoking rms avail. Simply decorated, adequate rooms. **Amenities:** 🛏 A/C, cable TV, refrig. Some units w/terraces. **Services:** ⟲ **Facilities:** 🔗 ♿ Whirlpool, washer/dryer. **Rates:** HS Dec 20–Apr $78–$90 S or D; from $95 effic. Extra person $10. Children under 14 stay free. Min stay spec evnts. Lower rates off-season. Pking: Outdoor, free. Maj CC.

Restaurants 🍴

Captain's Galley, 827 N Indian River Dr, Fort Pierce; tel 407/466-8495. **New American/Seafood.** Cheerful, colorful eatery offering such selections as blackened grouper and New York strip steak prepared to order. All entrees include soup or salad, potato or rice, and vegetables. **FYI:** Reservations not accepted. Children's menu. Beer and wine only. **Open:** HS Jan–Apr Mon–Sat 7am–9pm, Sun 7am–noon. Reduced hours off-season. Closed some hols. **Prices:** Main courses $8.95–$12.95. Ltd CC. 🖤 ♿

Mangrove Mattie's, 1640 Seaway Dr, Fort Pierce; tel 407/466-1044. **American/Seafood.** An open, airy eatery with Casablanca-style ceiling fans and a jungle of plants. Menu specialties include baked mahimahi and prime rib. **FYI:** Reservations recommended. Guitar/jazz. Children's menu. **Open:** Daily 11:30am–10pm. Closed Dec 25. **Prices:** Main courses $9–$19. Maj CC. 🖼 💟 ♿

PV Martin's, 5150 N Fla A1A, Fort Pierce; tel 407/465-7300. **New American.** Most customers recommend reserving a window table at this lovely oceanfront restaurant. Menu highlights include leg of lamb, roast beef, and a selection of seafood dishes. The Friday night seafood buffet is a good value. **FYI:** Reservations recommended. Guitar. Children's menu. **Open:** Lunch Mon–Sat 11am–3:30pm; dinner Mon–Sat 5–10pm, Sun 3–10pm; brunch Sun 10:30am–2:30pm. **Prices:** Main courses $12.95–$16.95. Maj CC. 🖼 💟 ♿

Sevenseas Restaurant, 2041 Seaway Dr, Fort Pierce; tel 407/466-0311. **Seafood/Steak.** A lively, casual seafood restaurant that's a popular hangout for locals. Outdoor diners are entertained by a live band. **FYI:** Reservations accepted. Band. Beer and wine only. **Open:** Mon–Sat 11am–11pm, Sun 8am–11pm. **Prices:** Main courses $6–$17. Maj CC. 🍴

Theo Thudpucker's Raw Bar & Seafood Restaurant, 2025 Seaway Dr, Fort Pierce; tel 407/465-1078. **Seafood/Steak.** A casual spot with interesting decor—the ceiling is covered with autographed money and a hanging alligator. Menu offerings include stuffed grouper, captain's platters, and a selection of daily specials. **FYI:** Reservations not accepted. Beer and wine only. **Open:** Mon–Thurs 11:30am–9:30pm, Fri–Sat 11:30am–11pm, Sun 1–9:30pm. Closed Dec 25. **Prices:** Main courses $9–$23. No CC.

Attractions 📷

Underwater Demolition Team–SEAL Museum, 3300 N Fla A1A; tel 407/489-3597 or 595-1570. This tribute to the US Navy Underwater Demolition Team and their successors, the SEAL (sea, air and land) teams, is located in Pepper Park on Hutchinson Island, where the first "frogmen" began their training. Dioramas trace the history of these naval commandos; exhibits show diving gear, weapons, and other equipment used. **Open:** Tues–Sat 10am–4pm, Sun noon–4pm. Closed some hols. $

Fort Pierce Inlet State Recreation Area, 905 Shorewinds Dr; tel 407/468-4007. This park located off Fla A1A consists of 343 ocean-fronted acres, offering swimming, fishing, and nature trails. $$

FORT WALTON BEACH

Map page M-2, B3

Hotels 🏨

🏳🏳 **Carousel Beach Resort**, 571 Santa Rosa Blvd, Fort Walton Beach, FL 32548; tel 904/243-7658 or toll free 800/523-0208; fax 904/244-4330. 1 mi S of US 98. Noteworthy for its beachfront ground-level rooms that offer great views of the ocean and dunes. Strict management policy contains several caveats; ask about them before reserving. **Rooms:** 108 rms, stes, and effic. CI 2pm/CO 11am. **Amenities:** 🛏 A/C, cable TV, refrig, in-rm safe. Some units w/terraces. **Services:** 🖐 Babysitting. **Facilities:** 🛋 1 bar (w/entertainment), 1 beach (ocean), lifeguard, lawn games, washer/dryer. **Rates:** HS Mar–Aug $64–$78 S or D; from $84 ste; from $80 effic. Extra person $10. Children under 12 stay free. Min stay spec evnts. Lower rates off-season. Higher rates for spec evnts/hols. Pking: Outdoor, free. Maj CC. Accommodations are priced in 13 categories.

🏳🏳 **Islander Beach Resort**, 790 Santa Rosa Blvd, Fort Walton Beach, FL 32548; tel 904/244-4137 or toll free 800/523-0209; fax 904/664-6264. **Rooms:** 106 rms and effic. CI 4pm/CO 11am. **Amenities:** 🛏 A/C, cable TV. Some units w/terraces. **Services:** 🍴 🖐 Babysitting. **Facilities:** 🛋 🏊 ♿ 1 rst, 2 bars (1 w/entertainment), 1 beach (ocean), washer/dryer. **Rates:** HS Mar–Sept $69 S; $119 D; from $100 effic. Children under 12 stay free. Lower rates off-season. Higher rates for spec evnts/hols. Spec packages avail. Pking: Outdoor, free. Maj CC.

Marina Bay Resort, 80 Miracle Strip Pkwy, Fort Walton Beach, FL 32548; tel 904/244-5132; fax 904/244-0491. An all-condo waterside resort with plenty of the at-home conveniences desirable for longer stays. Unrated. **Rooms:** 121 rms, stes, and effic. CI 3pm/CO 10am. Well-maintained rooms, some with water views. **Amenities:** 🛏 🍴 🖥 A/C, cable TV, refrig. Some units w/terraces. **Services:** 🖐 🖐 Babysitting. **Facilities:** 🛋 🚲 🏊 🏋 🏊 ♿ Games rm, lawn games, spa, sauna, whirlpool, washer/dryer. Fishing pier, putting green. **Rates:** HS May–Sept $59–$79 D; from $119 ste; from $50 effic. Lower rates off-season. Higher rates for spec evnts/hols. Pking: Outdoor, free. Maj CC.

🏳🏳🏳 **Ramada Beach Resort**, 1500 Miracle Strip Pkwy US 98, Fort Walton Beach, FL 32548; tel 904/243-9161 or toll free 800/874-8962; fax 904/243-2391. 1 mi E of Brooks Bridge. A resort-style hotel that seems more Las Vegas than Florida Panhandle. Central pool and waterfall. **Rooms:** 454 rms and stes. CI 3pm/CO 11am. Express checkout avail. Nonsmoking rms avail. **Amenities:** 🛏 🍴 🖥 A/C, cable TV, in-rm safe. All units w/terraces. **Services:** 🍴 🖐 🖐 🖐 Masseur, babysitting.

Facilities: [icons] 4 rsts, 5 bars (2 w/entertainment), 1 beach (ocean), sauna, steam rm, whirlpool. Swim-up bar stationed under the pool waterfall. **Rates:** HS Apr–Sept $95–$135 S or D; from $230 ste. Extra person $10. Children under 18 stay free. Min stay spec evnts. Lower rates off-season. Spec packages avail. Pking: Outdoor, free. Maj CC.

Motel

≣**Conquistador Inn**, 847 Venus Court, Fort Walton Beach, FL 32548; tel 904/244-6155 or toll free 800/824-7112. A favorite among spring-breakers, it offers an array of units ranging from motel rooms to 3-bedroom oceanfront penthouses. **Rooms:** 87 rms and stes. CI 2pm/CO 11am. All oceanfront units have kitchens. **Amenities:** [icon] A/C, cable TV. Some units w/terraces. All oceanfront units have dishwashers but utensils are not provided. **Services:** [icons] Babysitting. **Facilities:** [icon] 1 beach (ocean), lifeguard, lawn games, washer/dryer. **Rates:** HS Mar–Aug $55 S or D; from $80 ste. Extra person $10. Children under 12 stay free. Min stay spec evnts. Lower rates off-season. Spec packages avail. Pking: Outdoor, free. Maj CC.

Restaurant [icon]

The Lighthouse Restaurant, 132 Miracle Strip Pkwy, Fort Walton Beach; tel 904/664-2828. 1½ mi E of Brooks Bridge. **Seafood/Steak.** A great spot for families and budget-seekers— 4:30–8pm, much of the menu is half price. **FYI:** Reservations not accepted. Children's menu. **Open:** Mon–Sat 4:30–9pm. Closed some hols. **Prices:** Main courses $14–$27. Maj CC. [icons]

Attractions [icon]

Eglin Air Force Base; tel 904/882-3933. The world's largest air force base, at more than 700 square miles. Free tours include demonstrations at McKinley Climatic Laboratory, an environmental test chamber; a look into the 33rd Tactical Fighter Wing; and more. The **US Air Force Armament Museum** (tel 904/882-4189), has reconnaisance, fighter, and bomber planes, and a fighter-cockpit simulator. Also displayed are war films, photographs, rockets, bombs, and missiles. **Open:** Museum, daily 9:30am–4:30pm. Closed some hols. Free.

Indian Temple Mound and Museum, 139 SE Miracle Strip Pkwy; tel 904/243-6521. One of the largest ceremonial mounds ever discovered, dating back to around 1400. The small adjacent museum houses artifacts testifying to 12,000 years of Native American settlement of the Choctawhatchee Bay region. **Open:** Sept–May, Mon–Fri 11am–4pm, Sat 9am–4pm; June–Aug, Mon–Sat 9am–4pm. $

Focus Center, 139 Brooks St; tel 904/664-1261. Exhibits in this children's science museum include the Hall of Life, about the human body, and "What If You Couldn't...," which deals with disabilities. **Open:** Sat–Sun during school year, 1–5pm; rest of year, daily 1–5pm. Closed some hols. $

Gulfarium, 1010 Miracle Strip Pkwy SE (US 98E); tel 904/244-5169. One of the nation's original marine parks, featuring dolphin and sea lion shows. Other exhibits showcase gray seals, otters, alligators, Ridley turtles, penguins, tropical birds, and numerous fish. **Open:** Daily 9am–dusk. $$$$

FRUITLAND PARK

Map page M-6, B1

Attraction [icon]

Lake Griffin State Recreation Area, 3089 US 441/27; tel 904/787-7402. This 427-acre park encompasses mostly floating marsh and islands. Fishing, boating, canoe rentals, camping, nature trails. $$

GAINESVILLE

Map page M-5, D2

Hotels [icon]

≣≣**Holiday Inn University Center**, 1250 W University Ave, Gainesville, FL 32601; tel 904/376-1661 or toll free 800/HOLIDAY; fax 904/336-8717. Exit 76 off I-75. At NW 13th St. This well-kept hotel is centrally located and within walking distance to the University of Florida. **Rooms:** 167 rms and stes. Exec-level rms avail. CI 2pm/CO noon. Express checkout avail. Nonsmoking rms avail. **Amenities:** [icons] A/C, cable TV w/movies. **Services:** X [icons] Car-rental desk. **Facilities:** [icons] 1 rst, 1 bar. **Rates:** HS Aug–Dec $83 S; $93 D; from $175 ste. Extra person $7. Children under 18 stay free. Min stay spec evnts. Lower rates off-season. Higher rates for spec evnts/hols. Pking: Indoor/outdoor, free. Maj CC.

≣≣≣**Radisson Hotel**, 2900 SW 13th St, Gainesville, FL 32608; tel 904/377-4000 or toll free 800/344-5866; fax 904/371-1159. This hotel, located on a scenic wildlife preserve, caters to the business traveler. **Rooms:** 195 rms and stes. CI 3pm/CO noon. Express checkout avail. Nonsmoking rms avail. **Amenities:** [icons] A/C, cable TV w/movies. All units w/terraces. **Services:** X [icons] **Facilities:** [icons] 1 rst, 1 bar, washer/

dryer. **Rates:** HS Feb–Mar $79–$99 S; $89–$109 D; from $150 ste. Children under 17 stay free. Min stay spec evnts. Lower rates off-season. Spec packages avail. Pking: Outdoor, free. Maj CC.

Residence Inn by Marriott, 4001 SW 13th St, Gainesville, FL 32608; tel 904/371-2101 or toll free 800/331-3131; fax 904/371-2101 ext 66. Exit 74 off I-75. 2 mi NE on US 331. For the more independent traveler who desires a complete home-like atmosphere in overnight lodging. **Rooms:** 80 effic. CI 3pm/CO noon. Nonsmoking rms avail. Self-contained units vary in size from studios with a full kitchen to large suites with separate bedrooms, living areas, full kitchens, and fireplaces. **Amenities:** A/C, cable TV, refrig. Some units w/terraces, all w/fireplaces. **Services:** Facilities: Whirlpool, washer/dryer. **Rates (CP):** From $91 effic. Children under 12 stay free. Higher rates for spec evnts/hols. Spec packages avail. Pking: Outdoor, free. Maj CC.

Motels

Cabot Lodge, 3726 SW 40th Blvd, Gainesville, FL 32608; tel 904/375-2400 or toll free 800/843-8735; fax 904/335-2321. Exit 75 off I-75. A relaxing, home-like atmosphere. The comfortable atrium with central fireplace, antler chandeliers, and unique wooden end tables is the perfect place to unwind. **Rooms:** 208 rms. Exec-level rms avail. CI 3pm/CO 11am. Express checkout avail. Nonsmoking rms avail. **Amenities:** A/C, cable TV w/movies. Some units w/terraces. **Services:** Babysitting. Evening activities include a 2-hour cocktail reception with popcorn. **Facilities:** 1 bar. **Rates (CP):** $49–$66 S; $56–$63 D. Extra person $7. Min stay spec evnts. Higher rates for spec evnts/hols. Spec packages avail. Pking: Outdoor, free. Maj CC.

Fairfield Inn, 6901 NW 4th Blvd, Gainesville, FL 32607; tel 904/332-8292 or toll free 800/228-2800. Modest accommodations; friendly atmosphere. **Rooms:** 135 rms. CI 3pm/CO noon. Nonsmoking rms avail. **Amenities:** A/C, cable TV w/movies. **Services:** Facilities: **Rates (CP):** HS Jan–Apr $45 S; $52 D. Children under 18 stay free. Lower rates off-season. Higher rates for spec evnts/hols. Pking: Outdoor, free. Maj CC.

Holiday Inn West, 7417 NW 8th Ave, Gainesville, FL 32605; tel 904/332-7500 or toll free 800/551-8206; fax 904/332-0487. Exit 76 off I-75. Modern hotel with southwestern-style architecture. It boasts ample meeting facilities for its business clientele as well as 2 enticing courtyard pools. **Rooms:** 280 rms and stes. Exec-level rms avail. CI 3pm/CO noon. Nonsmoking rms avail. **Amenities:** A/C, cable TV w/movies, in-rm safe. **Services:** Facilities:

1 rst, 1 bar (w/entertainment), washer/dryer. **Rates:** HS Sept–Nov/Feb–Apr $69 S or D; from $69 ste. Children under 18 stay free. Min stay spec evnts. Lower rates off-season. Higher rates for spec evnts/hols. Pking: Outdoor, free. Maj CC.

Howard Johnson Lodge, 7400 NW 8th Ave, Gainesville, FL 32605; tel 904/332-3200 or toll free 800/IGO-HOJO; fax 904/332-5500. Exit 76 off I-75. With its convenient location, this is an acceptable choice for long or short stays, business or pleasure. **Rooms:** 64 rms. CI 2pm/CO noon. Nonsmoking rms avail. **Amenities:** A/C, cable TV w/movies. Some units w/terraces. **Services:** **Facilities:** Playground, washer/dryer. **Rates:** HS Sept–Dec $33–$39 S; $33–$49 D. Children under 18 stay free. Min stay spec evnts. Lower rates off-season. Higher rates for spec evnts/hols. Pking: Outdoor, free. Maj CC.

La Quinta Inn, 920 NW 69th Terrace, Gainesville, FL 32605; tel 904/332-6466 or toll free 800/591-5900; fax 904/332-7074. Exit 76 off I-75. Economical lodging without frills or fanfare. **Rooms:** 134 rms and stes. CI 3pm/CO noon. Nonsmoking rms avail. **Amenities:** A/C, cable TV w/movies. Some units w/terraces. **Services:** **Facilities:** **Rates (CP):** HS Aug–Nov $48 S; $58 D; from $62 ste. Extra person $10. Children under 18 stay free. Min stay spec evnts. Lower rates off-season. Pking: Outdoor, free. Maj CC.

Restaurant

Sovereign, 12 SE 2nd Ave, Gainesville; tel 904/378-6307. Exit 76 off I-75. **Continental.** An attractive, romantic restaurant housed in a converted carriage barn. Menu options range from fresh flounder to beef Wellington; choose the chocolate mousse cake as a postscript. **FYI:** Reservations recommended. Piano. **Open:** Mon–Thurs 5:30–10:30pm, Fri–Sat 5:30–11pm. Closed Dec 25; Aug 7–21. **Prices:** Main courses $16.50–$24.95. Maj CC. ♥

Attractions

Samuel P Harn Museum of Art, SW 34th St at Hull Rd; tel 904/392-9826. Located on the University of Florida campus, this is one of the largest of Florida's art museums. Exhibits range from pre-Columbian to contemporary art; American, Latin American, and African collections are featured. **Open:** Tues–Fri 11am–5pm, Sat 10am–5pm, Sun 1–5pm. Closed some hols. Free.

Fred Bear Museum, 4600 SW 41st Blvd (Fred Bear Dr); tel 904/376-2411. This natural history museum exhibits ancient archery and bowhunting artifacts, including a broadhead arrow tip dating from 2700 BC. On display are more than 100 mounted animals, as well as Native American artwork. **Open:** Wed–Sun 10am–6pm. Closed Dec 25. $$

Marjorie Kinnan Rawlings State Historic Site, County Rd 325 (in Cross Creek); tel 904/466-3672. This typical 1930s Florida farmstead located 11 miles south of Gainesville was the home of the Pulitzer Prize–winning author of *The Yearling* and *Cross Creek*. Tours include the house and the surrounding citrus grove and are limited to 10 persons per tour. Thurs–Sun, tours at 10 and 11 am, and on the hour 1–4pm. Closed Aug–Sept and some hols. $

GREEN ACRES

Map page M-9, D4

Restaurant ▦

Bohemian Garden, 5450 Lake Worth Rd, Green Acres; tel 407/968-4111. 3 mi E of Fla Tpk. **Continental.** A popular, rather elegant, old-world-style restaurant with burgundy and pink linens adorning glass-topped tables. Menu offerings range from duck and frogs' legs to veal and Bohemian specialties. The early-bird specials are a great value. **FYI:** Reservations accepted. Children's menu. **Open:** Tues–Sat 5–10pm, Sun 4–9pm. Closed Mid-Aug–mid-Sept. **Prices:** Main courses $7–$18. Maj CC. ▨ &

GULF BREEZE

Map page M-2, B2

Hotel ▦

▤▤ **Holiday Inn–Bay Beach**, 51 Gulf Breeze Pkwy, Gulf Breeze, FL 32561; tel 904/932-2214 or toll free 800/HOLIDAY; fax 904/932-2214 ext 299. Chase St exit off I-10. A short drive north of Pensacola Beach. Pleasant hotel with beautiful scenic bay views from many guest rooms. **Rooms:** 168 rms. CI 3pm/CO 11am. Nonsmoking rms avail. **Amenities:** ▦ ⌂ A/C, cable TV. Some units w/terraces. **Services:** ✕ ▦ ▦ ⌂ Car-rental desk. Complimentary drinks served Monday–Thursday in cocktail suite. **Facilities:** ⌂ ▦ & 1 rst, 1 beach (bay), washer/dryer. **Rates:** HS Mem Day–Labor Day $58–$100 S or D. Extra person $8. Children under 18 stay free. Lower rates off-season. Higher rates for spec evnts/hols. Spec packages avail. Pking: Outdoor, free. Maj CC.

Attractions ▦

The ZOO, 5701 Gulf Breeze Pkwy; tel 904/932-2229. More than 700 animals make their home within this 50-acre zoo and botanical garden, not the least of which is Colossus, one of the largest gorillas in captivity. The Safari Line, a 20-minute miniature train tour through a wildlife preserve, allows visitors a look at free-roaming animals. The giraffe feeding tower allows guests a rare face-to-face meeting. Elephant shows and elephant rides; petting zoo. Restaurant and snack shop. **Open:** Daily 9am–5pm. Closed some hols. $$$

GULF ISLANDS NATIONAL SEASHORE

Gulf Islands National Seashore, 1801 Gulf Breeze Pkwy; tel 904/934-2600. Established in 1971, the protected beach area actually stretches from Gulfport, Mississippi to Destin, Florida, providing a natural environment for at least 280 different species of birds. Pristine white sand beaches and rolling sand dunes await visitors, who can enjoy swimming, boating, fishing, picnicking, camping, and ranger-led walks. The seashore area also contains Fort Pickens and Fort Barrancas (see below) as well as other historic fortifications on the grounds of the **Naval Air Station**. For information write to Gulf Islands National Seashore, 1801 Gulf Breeze Pkwy, Gulf Breeze, FL 32561. Free.

Fort Barrancas; tel 904/455-5167. Located on the grounds of the Naval Air Station. Originally built by the Spanish in the 16th century and later fortified by the British in the 19th century, the fort has been authentically restored and preserved. Visitors can stroll nature trails and picnic in the surrounding area. Guided tours available. **Open:** Nov–Mar, daily 10:30am–4pm, Apr–Oct, daily 9:30am–5pm. Free.

Fort Pickens; tel 904/934-2600. Located across the bay from Fort Barrancas at the western tip of Santa Rosa Island are the substantial remains of this slave-built fort. Dating from the 1830s, it was meant to protect Pensacola from seaborne attack. Chief Geronimo was imprisoned here during the 1880s along with a group of fellow Apaches. A small museum details the history of the structure, as well as the flora and fauna of the national seashore area. Free guided tours are regularly scheduled. Free.

HAINES CITY

Map page M-7, D1

Hotel 🏨

▤▤ **Holiday Inn–South of Disney World Area**, US 27 at I-4, PO Box 1536, Haines City, FL 33845; tel 813/424-2211 or toll free 800/422-2414; fax 813/424-3312. 13 mi S of Walt Disney World. A fine starting point for covering the central Florida attractions. **Rooms:** 250 rms. CI 3pm/CO noon. Nonsmoking rms avail. **Amenities:** 🛏 👜 🍴 A/C, cable TV w/movies. **Services:** ✕ 🛎 🐾 Complimentary shuttle to Walt Disney World. Staff can suggest day trips to local attractions. **Facilities:** 🏊₁ 🏊 🖵 ♿ Games rm, whirlpool, playground, washer/dryer. **Rates (CP):** HS Jan–Apr $69–$79 S or D. Lower rates off-season. Spec packages avail. Pking: Outdoor, free. Maj CC.

Resort 🏨

▤▤▤▤ **Grenelefe Golf and Tennis Resort**, 3200 State Rd 546, Haines City, FL 33844; tel 813/422-7511 or toll free 800/237-9549; fax 813/421-5000. 6 mi E of Haines City. 1,000 acres. A villa resort that's a golfer's paradise. The modern facilities sparkle and the extensive grounds are expertly manicured. **Rooms:** 900 rms, stes, and effic. CI 3pm/CO 11am. Express checkout avail. Nonsmoking rms avail. Each villa is fully equipped with kitchen and views of the fairways. **Amenities:** 🛏 👜 A/C, cable TV w/movies, refrig. All units w/terraces. **Services:** ✕ 🛎 🐾 Car-rental desk, social director, masseur, children's program, babysitting. **Facilities:** 🏊 🚲 🎣 ▶18 ⛳ ♦9 🏊 1.6K 🖵 ♿ 3 rsts, 1 bar (w/entertainment), games rm, sauna, whirlpool, playground, washer/dryer. Lake, nature trails. Miniature golf. **Rates:** HS Feb–Apr $180–$385 S or D; from $220 ste; from $385 effic. Extra person $20. Children under 18 stay free. Lower rates off-season. AP rates avail. Spec packages avail. Pking: Outdoor, free. Ltd CC.

HIGHLAND BEACH

Map page M-9, E4

Hotel 🏨

▤▤▤ **Holiday Inn Oceanside**, 2809 S Ocean Blvd, Highland Beach, FL 33487; tel 407/278-6241 or toll free 800/234-6835; fax 407/278-6241. 1 mi S of Linton Blvd. Housed in 3-story and 6-story buildings on the water. **Rooms:** 119 rms. CI 3pm/CO noon. Nonsmoking rms avail. **Amenities:** 🛏 👜 🍴 A/C, cable TV w/movies. Some units w/terraces. **Services:** ✕ 🛎 🐾

Babysitting. **Facilities:** 🏊 🍽 ♿ 1 rst, 2 bars (1 w/entertainment), 1 beach (ocean), games rm, washer/dryer. Cabanas operate on beach Dec–Sept. **Rates:** HS Dec–Apr $119–$159 S; $129–$169 D. Extra person $10. Children under 18 stay free. Lower rates off-season. MAP rates avail. Pking: Outdoor, free. Maj CC.

HOLLYWOOD

Map page M-11, A2

Hotels 🏨

Hollywood Beach Intracoastal Resort and Hotel, 4000 S Ocean Dr, Hollywood, FL 33019; tel 305/458-1900 or toll free 800/338-7800; fax 305/458-7222. On Fla A1A at Hallandale Beach Blvd. A midrise hotel across the street from the beach; a good business choice. Unrated. **Rooms:** 306 rms and stes. Exec-level rms avail. CI 3pm/CO noon. Express checkout avail. Nonsmoking rms avail. Balconies offer views of Intracoastal Waterway and pool. **Amenities:** 🛏 👜 A/C, cable TV w/movies, refrig, in-rm safe. All units w/minibars, all w/terraces. **Services:** ✕ VP 🛎 🐾 Car-rental desk, masseur, children's program, babysitting. **Facilities:** 🏊 🏊₂ 🍽 🖵 ♿ 3 rsts, 2 bars (1 w/entertainment), games rm, sauna, whirlpool, beauty salon. **Rates:** HS Dec–Apr $145–$215 S or D; from $385 ste. Extra person $10. Children under 18 stay free. Lower rates off-season. Higher rates for spec evnts/hols. Spec packages avail. Pking: Indoor, $4.50. Maj CC.

▤▤ **Hollywood Beach Resort Hotel**, 101 N Ocean Dr, Hollywood, FL 33019; tel 305/921-0990 or toll free 800/331-6103; fax 305/920-9480. Dating to 1925, it's housed in a landmark building that still needs much work. Privately owned accommodations prevent any consistency in room decoration. **Rooms:** 355 rms, stes, and effic. CI 4pm/CO 11am. **Amenities:** 🛏 📺 A/C, cable TV, refrig, voice mail, in-rm safe. Some units w/terraces. **Services:** 🍽 VP 🚐 🛎 🐾 Car-rental desk, masseur. **Facilities:** 🏊 🚲 ⛳ 🍽 🍽 ♿ 1 rst, 1 bar, 1 beach (ocean), lifeguard, games rm, spa, beauty salon, washer/dryer. **Rates:** HS Dec–Apr $95–$128 S or D; from $135 ste; from $175 effic. Extra person $10. Lower rates off-season. Spec packages avail. Pking: Outdoor, $6. Maj CC.

Restaurants 🍴

Martha's, 6024 N Ocean Dr, Hollywood; tel 305/923-5444. At the foot of the Dania Beach Blvd bridge. **Seafood/Steak.** A comfortable eatery with views of the Intracoastal Waterway through floor-to-ceiling windows. The menu includes pan-cooked Florida snapper and grilled tuna, as well as salad plates. **FYI:** Reservations recommended. Band/dancing/piano. Children's menu. **Open:** Lunch Mon–Sat 11:30am–4pm; dinner daily 4pm–midnight; brunch Sun 11am–3pm. **Prices:** Main courses $13–$35. Maj CC. ♥ VP &

Wan's Mandarin House, in Sheridan Park Plaza, 3331 Sheridan St, Hollywood; tel 305/963-6777. 1 mile W of I-95. **Chinese.** Basic Chinese eatery serving traditional Szechuan cuisine. The lunch combination specials, which include selections like honey-garlic chicken and chicken curry, are both delightful and a good value. Food can be ordered spicy hot or mild. **FYI:** Reservations accepted. **Open:** Mon–Thurs 11:30am–10pm, Fri–Sat 11:30am–10:30pm, Sun 1–10pm. Closed Thanksgiving. **Prices:** Main courses $7.50–$10.50. Maj CC. &

Attractions 💼

Graves Museum of Archeology and Natural History, 481 S Federal Highway; tel 305/925-7770. Features artifacts of the Maya, the Inca, and the Aztec such as pottery, metals, and textiles. Egyptian temple replica; tribal masks, wood carvings, and textiles from Africa; tools and fossils from prehistoric Florida. **Open:** Tues–Sat 10am–4pm, Sun 1–4pm. $$

Hollywood Beach Boardwalk. This paved beach path runs from Sheridan St to Georgia St. It is 3 miles long and 27 feet wide, and is packed with retirement-age residents and French Canadian tourists who take their daily strolls past the path's gift shops, cafes, and restaurants. The boardwalk also has a bicycling lane and in-line skate rentals.

HOLLYWOOD BEACH

Map page M-11, A2

Hotel 🛏

≣≣ **Holiday Inn SunSpree Resort**, 2711 S Ocean Dr, Hollywood Beach, FL 33019; tel 305/923-8700 or toll free 800/237-4667; fax 305/923-7059. On Fla A1A ½ mi N of Hallandale Beach Blvd. On a clean stretch of beach, it has remade itself since changing owners and sports a new look. **Rooms:** 195 rms, stes, and effic. CI 4pm/CO 11am. Nonsmoking rms avail. Rooms overlook the pool and ocean. **Amenities:** 🛁 🔥 🖭 A/C, cable TV w/movies, refrig. Some units w/terraces. **Services:** ✕ VP 🗺 🛗 Car-rental desk, social director, children's program, babysitting. **Facilities:** 🔥 🐴 🛁 & 1 rst, 1 bar (w/entertainment), 1 beach (ocean), lifeguard, games rm, playground, washer/dryer. Children under 12 eat free in restaurant. **Rates:** HS Dec–Apr $115–

$135 S or D; from $165 ste; from $155 effic. Extra person $10. Lower rates off-season. Spec packages avail. Pking: Outdoor, free. Maj CC.

HOMESTEAD

Map page M-11, C1

Refreshment Stop ☕

Robert Is Here Fruit Stand & Farm, 19200 SW 344th St, Homestead; tel 305/246-1592. **Fruit Stand.** Wide selection of fresh fruits and vegetables as well as freshly canned goods. Fresh fruit milkshakes come in a variety of flavors, from key lime to strawberry. **Open:** HS Dec–Apr daily 8am–7pm. Reduced hours off-season. No CC.

Attractions 💼

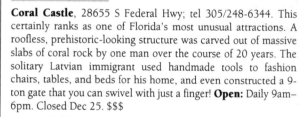

Coral Castle, 28655 S Federal Hwy; tel 305/248-6344. This certainly ranks as one of Florida's most unusual attractions. A roofless, prehistoric-looking structure was carved out of massive slabs of coral rock by one man over the course of 20 years. The solitary Latvian immigrant used handmade tools to fashion chairs, tables, and beds for his home, and even constructed a 9-ton gate that you can swivel with just a finger! **Open:** Daily 9am–6pm. Closed Dec 25. $$$

Orchid Jungle, 26715 SW 157th Ave; tel 305/247-1990. One of the world's largest outdoor orchid gardens, showcasing a wide variety of rare tropical flora, including rare palms. Many varieties are offered for sale, and there is a gift shop. Although severely damaged by Hurricane Andrew in 1992, the garden has been restored to its former beauty. **Open:** Daily 10am–5pm. Closed some hols. $$

Preston B Bird and Mary Heinlein Fruit and Spice Park, 24801 SW 187th Ave; tel 305/247-5727. This 20-acre living plant museum shows off more than 200 species of tropical plants and 500 varieties of fruits, nuts, and spices from around the world. A shop sells dried and canned fruits and spices, horticultural supplies, and books. Tours Sat–Sun at 1 and 3pm. **Open:** Daily 10am–5pm. $

Biscayne National Underwater Park, 9700 SW 328th St; tel 305/247-7275. This is America's largest underwater park; only 10 percent of its 181,500 acres are above the surface. On dry land is a visitor center, which has exhibits, videos, and a slide presentation. A boardwalk connects the mainland with 2 rock jetties, from which fishing is permitted. A 3-hour glass-bottom boat tour departs at 10am for a trip out to the coral reef and its colorful variety of marine life, and a snorkeling and scuba diving expedition departs at 1:30pm (fees required). Reservations are recommended for all tours; phone 247-2400 for further details. **Open:** Park, 8am–sunset; visitor center, Mon–Fri 8:30am–4:30pm, Sat–Sun 8am–5pm. Free.

HOMOSASSA

Map page M-6, C3

Hotel 🏨

≣≣ **Riverside Inn–Downtown**, 4076 S Suncoast Blvd, Homosassa, FL 34448; tel 904/628-4311; fax 904/628-4311. A restful spot on a busy commercial strip. The lobby has 2 antique automobiles. Good for children. **Rooms:** 105 rms and stes. CI 3pm/CO 11am. Nonsmoking rms avail. **Amenities:** 🛋 A/C, cable TV. Some units w/terraces. **Services:** ✕ 🔄 🔄 **Facilities:** 🔂 🔄 🔄 🔄 & 1 rst, 1 bar, games rm, playground. **Rates:** HS Dec–Mar $69 S or D; from $95 ste. Extra person $10. Children under 12 stay free. Lower rates off-season. Pking: Outdoor, free. Maj CC.

Motel

≣≣ **Riverside Inn Resort**, Fla 490, PO Box 258, Homosassa, FL 34487; tel 904/628-2474 or toll free 800/442-2040; fax 904/628-5208. Family-operated local staple. **Rooms:** 79 rms and effic. CI 4pm/CO 11am. Nonsmoking rms avail. Deluxe riverside rooms. **Amenities:** 🛋 A/C, cable TV. **Services:** 🔄 🔄 **Facilities:** 🔂 🔄 🔄 🔄 🔄 & 1 rst, 1 bar (w/entertainment), games rm, snorkeling, washer/dryer. **Rates:** $59–$69 S or D; from $79 effic. Extra person $7. Children under 12 stay free. Min stay wknds. Spec packages avail. Pking: Outdoor, free. Maj CC.

HUTCHINSON ISLAND

See Jensen Beach, Stuart

INDIALANTIC

Map page M-7, D4

Hotels 🏨

≣≣ **Holiday Inn–Melbourne Oceanfront**, 2605 N Fla A1A, Indialantic, FL 32903; tel 407/777-4100 or toll free 800/

HOLIDAY; fax 407/773-6132. Double-tower oceanfront property, perfectly suitable for beachgoers. **Rooms:** 299 rms and stes. CI 4pm/CO noon. Nonsmoking rms avail. **Amenities:** 🛋 🔄 🔄 A/C, cable TV w/movies. Some units w/terraces. **Services:** ✕ 🔄 🔄 🔄 🔄 🔄 Children's program, babysitting. **Facilities:** 🔂 🔄 6 🔄 & 1 rst, 2 bars (w/entertainment), 1 beach (ocean), lawn games, whirlpool, washer/dryer. Pool receives some shade from the hotel's towers. **Rates:** HS Feb–Apr/June–Aug $99–$119 S or D; from $159 ste. Children under 18 stay free. Lower rates off-season. Spec packages avail. Pking: Outdoor, free. Maj CC.

≣≣≣ **Melbourne Beach Hilton Oceanfront**, 3003 N Fla A1A, Indialantic, FL 32903; tel 407/777-5000 or toll free 800/624-0073; fax 407/777-3713. This highrise set on pretty landscaped grounds stands head and shoulders above other hotels on the beach, both literally and figuratively. The snazzy architecture is a welcome change from most humdrum beach offerings. **Rooms:** 118 rms and stes. Exec-level rms avail. CI 3pm/CO noon. Express checkout avail. Nonsmoking rms avail. **Amenities:** 🛋 🔄 🔄 A/C, cable TV w/movies, in-rm safe. All units w/terraces. **Services:** ✕ 🔄 🔄 Children's program, babysitting. Water sports rentals available on beach through independent vendor. **Facilities:** 🔂 🔄 🔄 🔄 🔄 & 1 rst, 3 bars (1 w/entertainment), 1 beach (ocean), lawn games. **Rates:** HS Jan–Apr $135–$145 S or D; from $160 ste. Children under 18 stay free. Lower rates off-season. Higher rates for spec evnts/hols. MAP rates avail. Spec packages avail. Pking: Outdoor, free. Maj CC.

≣≣ **Quality Suites Oceanside**, 1665 Fla A1A N, Indialantic, FL 32903; or toll free 800/876-4222; fax 407/768-2438. Twin-tower facility is joined by lowrise public area. **Rooms:** 208 stes. CI 3pm/CO noon. Express checkout avail. Nonsmoking rms avail. **Amenities:** 🛋 🔄 A/C, cable TV w/movies, refrig, VCR, stereo/tape player, in-rm safe. All units w/minibars, all w/terraces. **Services:** 🔄 🔄 🔄 Masseur, babysitting. Breakfast buffet served daily. **Facilities:** 🔂 🔄 🔄 🔄 & 1 rst, 2 bars, 1 beach (ocean), games rm, lawn games, sauna, whirlpool, washer/dryer. The restaurant offers pool and ocean views. **Rates (CP):** HS Feb–Apr/May–Aug from $89 ste. Extra person $10. Children under 18 stay free. Lower rates off-season. Spec packages avail. Pking: Outdoor, free. Maj CC.

Restaurant 🍴

Villa Palma, 111 5th Ave, Indialantic; tel 407/951-0051. At corner of Fla A1A. **Northern Italian.** A cozy, romantic, Euro-style eatery. The restaurant, housed in a former private home filled with works of art, maintains a comfortable, homestyle atmosphere. The diverse menu includes stuffed breast of chicken, pan-fried veal, baked fish with ricotta, and a variety of pasta dishes. **FYI:** Reservations accepted. Beer and wine only. **Open:** Sun–Thurs 5–10pm, Fri–Sat 5–10:30pm. **Prices:** Main courses $13.95–$28. Maj CC. ◉ ⟨

INDIAN ROCKS BEACH

Map page M-6, E2

Motel ⬛

≋≋ **Pelican East & West**, 108 21st Ave, Indian Rocks Beach, FL 34635; tel 813/595-9741. At 1st St, ½ block E of Gulf Blvd. Very attractive facility with private beach. **Rooms:** 13 rms and effic. CI 2pm/CO 10:30am. Most units have kitchens. **Amenities:** ⟨ ▣ A/C, cable TV, refrig. No phone. **Services:** ⟨♌ **Facilities:** 1 beach (ocean). **Rates:** HS Jan 15–Apr $50 S or D; from $70 effic. Extra person $3. Lower rates off-season. Higher rates for spec evnts/hols. Spec packages avail. Pking: Outdoor, free. Ltd CC.

Restaurant ⏐⏐⏐

Crabby Bill's, 401 Gulf Blvd, Indian Rocks Beach; tel 813/595-4825. **Seafood.** An informal eatery offering a variety of seafood platters. Stone crab claws are a specialty. **FYI:** Reservations accepted. Children's menu. **Open:** Mon–Thurs 11:30am–10pm, Fri–Sat 5:30–9:30pm, Sun noon–10pm. Closed Dec 25. **Prices:** Main courses $4.50–$12.95. Ltd CC. ☑ ⟨

Attraction ▥

Starlite Princess, Hamilin's Landing, 401 2nd St E; tel 813/595-1212. Four types of cruises are offered aboard this authentic, 300-passenger paddlewheeler: sightseeing only (with optional lunch), a luncheon/dance cruise (lunch also optional), a dinner/dance cruise, and 6-hour excursion to the Pier of St Petersburg. Boarding is half-hour before scheduled departure time. Snack bar and optional cocktail service available. Lunch cruise, Tues and Fri–Sat noon–2pm; luncheon/dance cruise, Wed noon–3pm; dinner/dance cruise, Tues–Wed and Fri–Sun 7:30–10:30pm; cruise to St Petersburg, Thurs 10am–4pm. $$$

INDIAN SHORES

Map page M-9, A3

Restaurant ⏐⏐⏐

Scandia, 19829 Gulf Blvd, Indian Shores; tel 813/595-5525. Between Park Blvd and Fla 688. **Scandinavian.** If a Viking came for dinner, he would be right at home in this Scandinavian-inspired restaurant. Specialties include stuffed filet of sole with a delightful seafood dressing, and roasted leg of lamb served with mint jelly. **FYI:** Reservations accepted. Children's menu. **Open:** Tues–Sat 11:30am–9pm, Sun noon–8pm. Closed July 4; Sept. **Prices:** Main courses $6.95–$14.95. Ltd CC. ☑ ⟨

Attraction ▥

Suncoast Seabird Sanctuary, 18328 Gulf Blvd; tel 813/391-6211. The largest wild-bird hospital in the United States, the sanctuary is dedicated to the rescue, treatment, recuperation, and release of sick and injured wild birds. Visitors are free to wander around this tree-lined open-air sanctuary and photograph the wide variety of birds, as well as the bird hospital and various other facilities. Tours Wed and Sun at 2pm. **Open:** Daily 9am–dusk. Free.

INVERNESS

Map page M-6, C3

Attraction ▥

Fort Cooper State Park, 3100 S Old Floral City Rd; tel 904/726-0315. This 700-acre day-use park sits on the site of Fort Cooper, which was built during the Second Seminole War; one wall of the fort has been reconstructed. Canoe and paddleboat rentals are available. Swimming, fishing, camping, nature trails. **Open:** Summer, daily 8am–sunset; winter, daily 8am–5pm. $

ISLAMORADA

Map page M-11, D1

Hotels ⬛

≋≋≋ **Chesapeake Resort**, 83409 Overseas Hwy, PO Box 909, Islamorada, FL 33036; tel 305/664-4662 or toll free 800/338-3395; fax 305/664-8595. At MM 83.5 on US 1. This family-run facility attracts seclusion-seekers desiring attractive accommodations set on tropical grounds. Guests may prefer units with cooking facilities, as there is no restaurant on premises. **Rooms:** 14 ctges/villas. CI 3pm/CO 11am. **Amenities:** 🔐 💧 A/C, cable TV w/movies, refrig, in-rm safe. All units w/terraces, some w/Jacuzzis. **Services:** 🛎 Babysitting. **Facilities:** 🎣 ⚠ 🏊¹ 🚤 🚣 1 beach (ocean), lawn games, spa, whirlpool, playground, washer/dryer. **Rates:** HS Dec–Apr $130–$210 S or D; from $290 ste; from $140 effic; from $175 ctge/villa. Extra person $15. Children under 12 stay free. Min stay spec evnts. Lower rates off-season. Pking: Indoor/outdoor, free. Maj CC.

🏖🏖 Holiday Isle Resort, Overseas Hwy MM 84, Islamorada, FL 33036; tel 305/664-2711 or toll free 800/327-7070; fax 305/664-2703. A large hotel drawing watersports enthusiasts and sun-seekers. **Rooms:** 71 rms, stes, and effic. CI 3:30pm/CO 11am. Clean, brightly-colored units. **Amenities:** 🔐 A/C, cable TV w/movies, in-rm safe. Some units w/terraces, 1 w/Jacuzzi. **Services:** 🛎 **Facilities:** 🎣 ⚠ 🏊 🚤 🚣 🍴 & 5 rsts, 9 bars (4 w/entertainment), 1 beach (ocean), games rm, snorkeling, playground, washer/dryer. Beach area has thatched umbrella tables. Volleyball. Free weights in gym. Express photo lab. **Rates:** HS Dec–Apr $135–$165 S or D; from $225 ste; from $190 effic. Extra person $10–$15. Children under 12 stay free. Min stay wknds and spec evnts. Lower rates off-season. Higher rates for spec evnts/hols. Spec packages avail. Pking: Outdoor, free. Maj CC.

Motels

🏖🏖 Breezy Palms Resort, Overseas Hwy, MM 80, PO Box 767, Islamorada, FL 33036; tel 305/664-2361; fax 305/664-2572. Varied accommodations, many with excellent water views. Casual atmosphere throughout. **Rooms:** 39 rms and effic. CI 3pm/CO 11am. **Amenities:** 🔐 🎨 A/C, cable TV w/movies, refrig, VCR. Some units w/terraces. **Services:** 🛎 Babysitting. **Facilities:** 🎣 🚲 ⚠ 🏊 🚣 🛶 1 beach (ocean), lawn games, snorkeling, washer/dryer. **Rates:** HS Dec–Apr $75 S or D; from $80 effic. Extra person $10. Children under 12 stay free. Min stay wknds. Lower rates off-season. Higher rates for spec evnts/hols. Pking: Outdoor, free. Maj CC.

🏖🏖 Campolo's Sunset Resort, US 1 MM 82.2, PO Box 269, Islamorada, FL 33036; tel 305/664-4427 or toll free 800/666-4427; fax 305/664-3063. Basic rooms, friendly atmosphere. **Rooms:** 60 rms and effic. CI 2pm/CO 11am. **Amenities:** 🔐 A/C, cable TV. Some units w/terraces. **Services:** 🛎 🛥 **Facilities:** 🎣 🏊 1 rst, 3 bars (1 w/entertainment), games rm. **Rates:** HS Dec–Apr $115 D; from $145 effic. Extra person $10. Children under 12 stay free. Lower rates off-season. Spec packages avail. Pking: Outdoor, free. Maj CC.

🏖 Islander Motel, US 1 MM 82.1, PO Box 766, Islamorada, FL 33036; tel 305/664-2031; fax 305/664-5503. Solid offering with a family atmosphere. **Rooms:** 114 rms and effic. CI 3pm/CO 11am. **Amenities:** 🔐 A/C, cable TV, refrig. All units w/terraces. **Services:** 🛎 **Facilities:** 🎣 🏊 1 beach (ocean), washer/dryer. Saltwater and freshwater pools. Tennis nearby. **Rates:** HS Dec 15–Apr 14 $70–$95 S or D; from $80 effic. Extra person $7. Children under 13 stay free. Min stay spec evnts. Lower rates off-season. Pking: Outdoor, free. Maj CC.

🏖 Ocean 80 Resort, US 1 MM 80.5, PO Box 949, Islamorada, FL 33036; tel 305/664-4411; fax 305/664-4411 ext 217. Midrise motel set on attractive landscaped grounds. **Rooms:** 82 rms and effic. CI 4pm/CO 10am. Nice views from balconied rooms. **Amenities:** 🔐 📺 A/C, cable TV, refrig. All units w/terraces. **Services:** 🛎 **Facilities:** 🎣 🏊 1 bar (w/entertainment), 1 beach (ocean), games rm, sauna, whirlpool, washer/dryer. Pier. **Rates:** HS Aug–Sept $105–$200 S or D; from $128 effic. Children under 18 stay free. Lower rates off-season. Pking: Outdoor, free. Maj CC.

🏖🏖 Pelican Cove Resort, 84457 Old Overseas Hwy, MM 84.5, Islamorada, FL 33036; tel 305/664-4435 or toll free 800/445-4690; fax 305/664-5134. Set on the water, with a clean, sandy beach. Newly renovated accommodations. **Rooms:** 63 rms, stes, and effic. CI 4pm/CO 11am. **Amenities:** 🔐 A/C, cable TV, refrig. All units w/terraces, some w/Jacuzzis. **Services:** 🛎 **Facilities:** 🎣 ⚠ 🏊 🏊¹ & 1 rst, 1 bar, 1 beach (ocean), snorkeling, whirlpool, playground. **Rates:** HS Dec 17–Apr $165–$285 S or D; from $285 ste; from $185 effic. Extra person $15. Children under 16 stay free. Min stay spec evnts. Lower rates off-season. Higher rates for spec evnts/hols. Pking: Outdoor, free. Maj CC.

Resort

🏖🏖🏖 Cheeca Lodge, MM 82, Overseas Hwy, PO Box 527, Islamorada, FL 33036; tel 305/664-4651 or toll free 800/327-2888; fax 305/664-2893. 27 acres. An extensive resort complex that is one of the Keys' most enduring facilities. It comprises about two dozen buildings housing first-rate accommodations and handsome public areas. Served by dedicated young staff. **Rooms:** 203 rms and stes. CI 3pm/CO noon. Nonsmoking rms avail. **Amenities:** 🔐 💧 🍴 A/C, cable TV, VCR, bathrobes. All units w/minibars, some w/terraces, 1 w/Jacuzzi. **Services:** ✕ 🛎 VP 🚗 🖼 🛎 Car-rental desk, social director, masseur, children's program, babysitting. **Facilities:** 🎣 🚲 ⚠ 🏊 🏌⁹ 🎾 🏊 🛶 🚣 & 2 rsts (see also "Restaurants" below), 2 bars, 1 beach (ocean), board surfing, lawn games, snorkeling, spa, whirlpool, playground. **Rates:** HS Dec–Apr $225–$500 S or

D; from $300 ste. Extra person $25. Children under 16 stay free. Lower rates off-season. AP and MAP rates avail. Spec packages avail. Pking: Outdoor, free. Maj CC.

Restaurants 🍴

Atlantic's Edge, in Cheeca Lodge, Overseas Hwy MM 82, Islamorada; tel 305/664-4651. **New American.** Upscale eatery where wraparound windows provide great views of private beaches and the ocean beyond. Menu highlights include a selection of fresh fish prepared blackened, grilled, or braised, filet of beef, jumbo sea scallops, and cheese-filled saffron pasta spirals. **FYI:** Reservations recommended. Children's menu. Dress code. **Open:** HS Labor Day–Mem Day dinner daily 5:30–11pm; brunch Sun 11am–3pm. Reduced hours off-season. **Prices:** Main courses $18–$38; PF dinner $32. Maj CC. 🏞 VP 🛆

⭐ **Lazy Days Oceanfront Bar and Seafood Grill**, Overseas Hwy MM 79.5, Islamorada; tel 305/664-5256. **Seafood/Steak.** A relaxed restaurant with a maritime theme and great water views. Extensive seafood menu. **FYI:** Reservations accepted. **Open:** Tues–Sun 11:30am–10pm. Closed some hols. **Prices:** Main courses $11–$21. Maj CC. 🍴 🏞 🛆

Manny and Isa's Kitchen, Overseas Hwy MM 81.6, Islamorada; tel 305/664-5019. **New American/Cuban.** A simple, no-frills eatery known for its food rather than its decor. Traditional Cuban-American menu; key lime pie. A special Cuban dinner can be prepared with 1 day's advance notice. **FYI:** Reservations not accepted. Beer and wine only. **Open:** Sun–Mon 11am–9pm, Wed–Sat 11am–9pm. **Prices:** Main courses $2.50–$14.95. Maj CC.

Papa Joe's, Overseas Hwy MM 79.7, Islamorada; tel 305/664-8109. **Seafood/Steak.** Basic, dark restaurant and bar, with lovely water and marina views. Fish is prepared broiled, fried, or sautéed; stone crab claws are always available. **FYI:** Reservations accepted. Children's menu. **Open:** Wed–Mon 11am–10pm. Closed some hols. **Prices:** Main courses $9.95–$16.95. Maj CC. 🏞 🛆 🛆

Sid and Roxie's, in Green Turtle Inn, Overseas Hwy MM 81.5, Islamorada; tel 305/664-9031. **Seafood/Steak.** A dark, cool restaurant with nautical overtones and a menu featuring a variety of seafood, steaks, and chops. **FYI:** Reservations not accepted. Singer. Children's menu. **Open:** Tues–Sun noon–10pm. Closed Thanksgiving. **Prices:** Main courses $10–$27. Maj CC. 🛆 🛆

Attraction

Theater of the Sea, Overseas Hwy, MM 84.5; tel 305/664-2431. One of the world's oldest marine zoos, featuring dolphin and sea lion shows. **Open:** Daily 9:30am–4pm. $$$$

ISLE OF CAPRI

Map page M-10, A2

Restaurant 🍴

♣ **Blue Heron Inn**, 387 Capri Blvd, Isle of Capri; tel 813/394-6248. **Eclectic.** Watch the sun set over the marina and the rest of Johnson Bay as you dine. Many fresh fish specialties are offered on the rotating menu, which is changed every 2 weeks. **FYI:** Reservations recommended. Dress code. Beer and wine only. **Open:** HS Oct–Apr Mon–Sat 5:30–10pm. Reduced hours off-season. Closed some hols; Aug–Sept. **Prices:** PF dinner $28–$32. Maj CC. ♥ 🏞

JACKSONVILLE

Map page M-5, C3

See also Atlantic Beach, Jacksonville Beach, Ponte Vedra Beach

TOURIST INFORMATION

Jacksonville and the Beaches Convention and Visitors Bureau, 3 Independent Dr, north of Water St at Main St (tel 904/798-9148). Open Mon–Fri 8am–5pm.

PUBLIC TRANSPORTATION

Jacksonville Transit Authority Buses Operate 4am–2am; hours vary, depending on route. Local fare 60¢ adults, 45¢ teens under 17 with student ID, children and seniors free. Buses to beach $1.10. For information call 904/630-3100.

Hotels

🏨🏨 **Best Western Bradbury Suites Hotel**, 8277 Western Way Circle, Jacksonville, FL 32256; tel 904/737-4477 or toll free 800/528-1234; fax 904/739-1649. Baymeadows Rd exit off I-95. Contemporary-style tourist hotel. **Rooms:** 111 stes. CI 3pm/CO noon. Nonsmoking rms avail. **Amenities:** 🛆 🛆 A/C, cable TV w/movies, refrig. Some units have bathroom TVs. **Services:** 🛆 🛆 Complimentary breakfast buffet, evening cocktails. **Facilities:** 🛆 🛆 🛆 Washer/dryer. Free passes available to nearby fitness center. **Rates (BB):** From $45 ste. Extra person $6. Children under 18 stay free. Higher rates for spec evnts/hols. Spec packages avail. Pking: Outdoor, free. Maj CC.

Comfort Suites Hotel, 8333 Dix Ellis Trail, Jacksonville, FL 32256; tel 904/739-1135 or toll free 800/228-5150; fax 904/731-0752. Exit 100 off I-95. SW of Baymeadows Rd exit. The lobby, which features a tile floor, potted trees, and a wicker-furnished seating area, provides a comfortable introduction to the modest suites within. **Rooms:** 128 stes. Exec-level rms avail. CI 3pm/CO 11am. Nonsmoking rms avail. Units have sleeper sofas and large bathrooms. **Amenities:** A/C, cable TV, refrig. Some units w/terraces. **Services:** Car-rental desk, babysitting. Evening cocktail reception. **Facilities:** Lawn games, whirlpool, washer/dryer. **Rates (CP):** HS Feb–Apr/June–Aug from $49 ste. Children under 18 stay free. Lower rates off-season. Higher rates for spec evnts/hols. Spec packages avail. Pking: Outdoor, free. Maj CC.

Courtyard by Marriott, 4600 San Pablo Rd, Jacksonville, FL 32224; tel 904/223-1700 or toll free 800/321-2211; fax 904/223-1026. Butler Blvd exit off I-95. Guests are primarily those with business at the Mayo Clinic next door. **Rooms:** 146 rms and stes. CI 3pm/CO noon. Nonsmoking rms avail. **Amenities:** A/C, cable TV w/movies. All units w/terraces. **Services:** Babysitting. **Facilities:** Whirlpool, day-care ctr, washer/dryer. Trademark courtyard with pool. **Rates:** $94–$104

S; $104–$114 D; from $110 ste. Children under 18 stay free. Higher rates for spec evnts/hols. Spec packages avail. Pking: Outdoor, free. Maj CC.

Days Inn, 1057 Broward Rd, Jacksonville, FL 32218; tel 904/757-0990 or toll free 800/325-2525. Broward Rd exit off I-95. Typical of the chain. Attracts the budget-conscious for its low rates. **Rooms:** 185 rms. CI 3pm/CO 11am. Nonsmoking rms avail. **Amenities:** A/C, cable TV. All units w/terraces. **Services:** **Facilities:** 1 rst, games rm, washer/dryer. **Rates:** $39 S; $44 D. Extra person $5. Children under 18 stay free. Higher rates for spec evnts/hols. Spec packages avail. Pking: Outdoor, free. Maj CC.

Doubletree Hotel, 4700 Salisbury Rd, Jacksonville, FL 32256; tel 904/281-9700 or toll free 800/528-0444; fax 904/281-1957. Exit 101 off I-95. Popular with both business travelers and families, who like to take advantage of its attractive pool, whirlpool, and fitness facility. Near downtown. **Rooms:** 167 rms and stes. CI 3pm/CO 1pm. Express checkout avail. Nonsmoking rms avail. **Amenities:** A/C, cable TV w/movies. Some rooms have refrigerators. **Services:** **Facilities:** 1 rst, 1 bar, whirlpool. **Rates:** $99 S; $119 D; from $119 ste. Extra person $10. Children under 16 stay free. Spec packages avail. Pking: Outdoor, free. Maj CC.

Embassy Suites, 9300 Baymeadows Rd, Jacksonville, FL 32256; or toll free 800/851-4185; fax 904/731-4972. Exit 100 off I-95. Its richly decorated lobby leads out to a lush

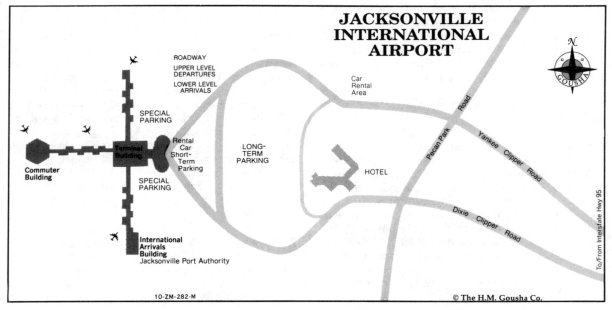

JACKSONVILLE INTERNATIONAL AIRPORT

10-ZM-282-M   © The H.M. Gousha Co.

courtyard traversed by terraced walkways and graced with waterfalls. **Rooms:** 210 stes. Exec-level rms avail. CI 3pm/CO noon. Express checkout avail. Nonsmoking rms avail. Kitchenette. **Amenities:** 🛅 🅰 🖭 A/C, cable TV w/movies, refrig, voice mail. Some units w/terraces. 2 TVs. **Services:** ✗ 🚗 🖼 🍴 Car-rental desk, babysitting. Full breakfast and evening cocktail reception are included in rates. **Facilities:** 🔥 ⛳ 🎾 ⛳ ⚓ 1 rst, 1 bar, games rm, whirlpool, washer/dryer. **Rates (BB):** From $110 ste. Extra person $10. Children under 18 stay free. Higher rates for spec evnts/hols. Spec packages avail. Pking: Outdoor, free. Maj CC.

🏨🏨🏨 Holiday Inn Airport, I-95 at Airport Rd, Jacksonville, FL 32218 (Jacksonville Int'l Airport); tel 904/741-4404 or toll free 800/HOLIDAY; fax 904/741-4907. Exit 27 off I-95. A snazzy airport choice that's convenient to the interstate and noteworthy for its Holidome recreation center attached to the 2- and 6-story structure. **Rooms:** 489 rms. CI 11am/CO noon. Nonsmoking rms avail. Modern accommodations are kept commendably neat and clean. **Amenities:** 🛅 🅰 A/C, cable TV, in-rm safe. **Services:** ✗ 🖥 🚗 🖼 🍴 Car-rental desk, babysitting. **Facilities:** 🔥 🎾 🏊 ⚓ 1 rst, 2 bars (1 w/entertainment), games rm, sauna, washer/dryer. **Rates:** $50–$76 S; $64 D. Extra person $4. Children under 18 stay free. Higher rates for spec evnts/hols. Spec packages avail. Pking: Outdoor, free. Maj CC.

🏨🏨 Holiday Inn Baymeadows, 9150 Baymeadows Rd, Jacksonville, FL 32256; tel 904/737-1700 or toll free 800/HOLIDAY; fax 904/737-0207. Exit 100 off I-95. With ample banquet facilities and an inexpensive family restaurant, this is a reliable spot for business travelers and families. **Rooms:** 249 rms. Exec-level rms avail. CI 3pm/CO noon. Express checkout avail. Nonsmoking rms avail. **Amenities:** 🛅 🅰 🖭 A/C, cable TV w/movies. Some units w/terraces. **Services:** ✗ 🖼 🍴 Babysitting. **Facilities:** 🔥 🎾 🏊 🖥 ⚓ 1 rst, 1 bar, washer/dryer. **Rates:** $69–$74 S or D. Extra person $5. Children under 18 stay free. Higher rates for spec evnts/hols. Spec packages avail. Pking: Outdoor, free. Maj CC.

🏨🏨 Holiday Inn Commonwealth Ave, I-295 and Commonwealth Ave, PO Box 37888, Jacksonville, FL 32236; tel 904/781-6000 or toll free 800/HOLIDAY; fax 904/781-2784. One of this chain's Holidome hotels, featuring an indoor courtyard housing a pool, whirlpool, and other recreational amenities. **Rooms:** 178 rms. CI 3pm/CO noon. Nonsmoking rms avail. Some rooms open to Holidome atrium. **Amenities:** 🛅 A/C, cable TV. All units w/terraces. **Services:** ✗ 🚗 🖼 🍴 **Facilities:** 🔥 🎾 🏊 ⚓ 1 rst, 1 bar, games rm, sauna, whirlpool. **Rates:** $59–$79 S or D. Children under 18 stay free. Higher rates for spec evnts/hols. Spec packages avail. Pking: Outdoor, free. Maj CC.

🏨🏨 Holiday Inn East, 5865 Arlington Expressway, Jacksonville, FL 32211; tel 904/724-3410 or toll free 800/874-3000; fax 904/727-7606. Caters largely to the business crowd and is well-liked for its large convention rooms and amphitheater. **Rooms:** 270 rms and stes. CI 3pm/CO noon. Express checkout avail. Nonsmoking rms avail. **Amenities:** 🛅 🅰 A/C, cable TV. Some units w/terraces. **Services:** ✗ 🚗 🖼 🍴 🍷 Babysitting. **Facilities:** 🔥 🎾 🏊 ⚓ 1 rst, 2 bars, whirlpool. Full-service conference facilities. 1950s-style soda shop. **Rates:** $45–$75 S or D; from $125 ste. Extra person $10. Children under 18 stay free. Higher rates for spec evnts/hols. Spec packages avail. Pking: Outdoor, free. Maj CC.

🏨🏨 Homewood Suites, 8737 Baymeadows Rd, Jacksonville, FL 32256; tel 904/733-9299 or toll free 800/CALL HOME; fax 904/448-5889. Baymeadows Rd exit off I-95. Take hard right off ramps. Comfortable, clean suites. **Rooms:** 116 stes. CI 3pm/CO noon. Nonsmoking rms avail. Rooms offer modern decor, full kitchens, and separate sleeping areas. **Amenities:** 🛅 🅰 🖭 🍷 A/C, cable TV w/movies, refrig, VCR, voice mail. Some units w/terraces, some w/fireplaces. **Services:** 🚗 🖼 🍴 🍷 Car-rental desk, babysitting. Complimentary breakfast and evening beverages; free daily newspaper. Staff will shop for groceries. **Facilities:** 🔥 🎾 🏊 🖥 ⚓ Lawn games, whirlpool, washer/dryer. **Rates (CP):** From $109 ste. Children under 18 stay free. Higher rates for spec evnts/hols. Spec packages avail. Pking: Outdoor, free. Maj CC.

🏨🏨🏨 Jacksonville Marriott at Southpoint, 4670 Salisbury Rd, Jacksonville, FL 32256; tel 904/296-2222 or toll free 800/228-9290; fax 904/296-7561. Butler Rd exit off I-95. This highrise hotel, just minutes from the beach and downtown attractions, is a top choice in the area. Plushly furnished marble-floored lobby lends a polished look. The fine staff has a knack for pleasing guests. **Rooms:** 256 rms and stes. CI 3pm/CO noon. Express checkout avail. Nonsmoking rms avail. Handsomely decorated rooms with mahogany furnishings. **Amenities:** 🛅 🅰 A/C, cable TV. Some units w/Jacuzzis. **Services:** ✗ 🖥 🆅🅿 🚗 🖼 🍴 Babysitting. **Facilities:** 🔥 🎾 🏊 🖥 ⚓ 1 rst (see also "Restaurants" below), 1 bar, sauna, steam rm, whirlpool. Health club has excellent facilities, better than you're likely to find at other hotels in this category. **Rates:** HS Aug–Dec/Jan–Apr $114 S; $124 D; from $175 ste. Extra person $10. Children under 18 stay free. Lower rates off-season. Spec packages avail. Pking: Outdoor, free. Maj CC.

🏨🏨 Marina Hotel & Conference Center, 1515 Prudential Drive, Jacksonville, FL 32207; tel 904/396-5100 or toll free 800/342-4605; fax 904/396-7154. On the south side of the St Johns River. This 5-story hotel sports a nautical look, evident in its huge, ship-like lobby with exposed pipes and corrugated tin ceiling. Major renovations to public areas and guest rooms were completed recently. **Rooms:** 322 rms and stes. CI 3pm/CO noon. Express checkout avail. Nonsmoking rms avail. Cheerful, tidy rooms, many with river views. New upholstery and carpeting in most rooms. **Amenities:** 🛏 🛆 A/C, cable TV. Some units w/minibars, some w/terraces, 1 w/Jacuzzi. **Services:** ✗ 🚗 🛆 🛎 Babysitting. **Facilities:** 🛗 4k 🛆 1 rst, 1 bar, games rm. **Rates:** $99 S; $109 D; from $165 ste. Extra person $10. Children under 18 stay free. Min stay spec evnts. Spec packages avail. Pking: Outdoor, free. Maj CC.

■■■ Omni Jacksonville Hotel, 245 Water St, Jacksonville, FL 32202; tel 904/355-6664 or toll free 800/THE OMNI; fax 354-2970. Located across from Jacksonville Landing and its dining, shopping, and entertainment options, this is one of the city's major downtown hotels, a spectacle of glass, polished wood, and marble. **Rooms:** 354 rms and stes. Exec-level rms avail. CI 3pm/CO noon. Express checkout avail. Nonsmoking rms avail. **Amenities:** 🛏 🛆 A/C, cable TV w/movies. All units w/minibars. **Services:** ✗ VP 🚗 🛆 🛎 Babysitting. Discounts offered to 2 area golf courses. Use of YMCA facilities for $5. **Facilities:** 🛗 🛳 900 🛆 1 rst, 1 bar. **Rates:** $109–$134 S or D; from $250 ste. Children under 18 stay free. Higher rates for spec evnts/hols. Spec packages avail. Pking: Outdoor, $6. Maj CC.

■■ Ramada Inn Mandarin Conference Center, 3130 Hartley Rd at Cagle Rd, Jacksonville, FL 32257; tel 904/268-8080 or toll free 800/2-RAMADA; fax 904/262-8718. Exit 102 off I-95 N. Known for the professional attention and service provided conference-goers. **Rooms:** 152 rms and stes. CI 3pm/CO noon. Nonsmoking rms avail. **Amenities:** 🛏 🛆 A/C, cable TV w/movies. Some units w/terraces. **Services:** ✗ 🛆 🛎 🛎 **Facilities:** 🛗 900 🛆 1 rst, 2 bars (w/entertainment), whirlpool, washer/dryer. Comedy club. Restaurant features all-you-can-eat buffets. **Rates (CP):** $53–$58 S; $48–$53 D; from $85 ste. Extra person $5. Children under 18 stay free. Min stay spec evnts. Higher rates for spec evnts/hols. Spec packages avail. Pking: Outdoor, free. Maj CC.

■■ Residence Inn by Marriott, 8365 Dix Ellis Trail, Jacksonville, FL 32256; tel 904/733-8088 or toll free 800/331-3131; fax 904/731-8354. Exit 100 off I-95. Comfortable, condominium-style accommodations. **Rooms:** 112 effic. CI noon/CO noon. Nonsmoking rms avail. Full kitchen, living area, sleeping area or separate bedrooms. **Amenities:** 🛏 🛆 🛗 A/C, cable TV, refrig, voice mail. Some units w/fireplaces. Microwaves; irons and ironing boards. **Services:** 🚗 🛆 🛎 🛎 Car-rental desk, babysitting. **Facilities:** 🛗 40 🛆 Lawn games, whirlpool, washer/dryer. **Rates (CP):** From $65 effic. Children under 18 stay free. Higher rates for spec evnts/hols. Spec packages avail. Pking: Outdoor, free. Maj CC.

■■ Skycenter Hotel, 2101 Dixie Clipper Rd, Jacksonville, FL 32218 (Jacksonville Int'l Airport); tel 904/741-4747 or toll free 800/453-5109; fax 904/741-0002. The closest hotel to the airport terminal. A one-time Radisson affiliate, now doing well even without a major brand name. **Rooms:** 160 rms and stes. CI 2pm/CO noon. Nonsmoking rms avail. **Amenities:** 🛏 A/C, cable TV w/movies. Some units w/terraces. **Services:** VP 🚗 🛆 🛎 🛎 Babysitting. **Facilities:** 🛗 🛳 300 🛆 Washer/dryer. **Rates (CP):** $65–$75 S or D; from $85 ste. Extra person $5. Children under 18 stay free. Higher rates for spec evnts/hols. Spec packages avail. Pking: Outdoor, free. Maj CC.

Motels

■ Econo Lodge, 5221 W University Blvd, Jacksonville, FL 32216; tel 904/737-1690 or toll free 800/553-2666; fax 904/448-5638. Exit 102 off I-95. Basic budget accommodations. **Rooms:** 180 rms. CI 3pm/CO noon. Nonsmoking rms avail. **Amenities:** 🛏 A/C, cable TV w/movies. **Services:** 🛎 **Facilities:** 🛗 250 1 rst, washer/dryer. **Rates:** HS Mar–Sept/Oct–Jan $36 S; $46 D. Lower rates off-season. Higher rates for spec evnts/hols. Pking: Outdoor, free. Maj CC.

■■ Fairfield Inn, 8050 Baymeadow Circle W, Jacksonville, FL 32256; tel 904/739-0739 or toll free 800/228-2800. Exit 100 off I-95. Economical lodging. A PGA golf course lies adjacent. **Rooms:** 102 rms, stes, and effic. CI 3pm/CO noon. Nonsmoking rms avail. Loft suites offer mini-kitchenettes. **Amenities:** 🛏 🛆 A/C, cable TV. Some units w/terraces, some w/Jacuzzis. **Services:** 🛆 🛎 **Facilities:** 🛗 75 🛆 Whirlpool. **Rates (CP):** $50 S; $56 D; from $63 ste; from $63 effic. Children under 12 stay free. Pking: Outdoor, free. Maj CC.

■ Motel 6, 8286 Dix Ellis Trail, Jacksonville, FL 32256;; fax 904/730-0781. Exit 100 off I-95. Clean, no-frills rooms. Within walking distance of many restaurants. **Rooms:** 109 rms. CI 2pm/CO noon. Nonsmoking rms avail. **Amenities:** 🛏 🛆 A/C, satel TV w/movies. **Services:** 🛎 🛎 **Facilities:** 🛗 🛆 **Rates:** $28 S; $32 D. Pking: Outdoor, free. Maj CC.

■■ Ramada Inn South, 5624 Cagle Rd, Jacksonville, FL 32211; tel 904/737-8000 or toll free 800/2-RAMADA; fax 904/448-8624. Exit 103 off I-95. In a convenient location off the interstate. A good value. **Rooms:** 110 rms. CI 1:30pm/CO noon. Nonsmoking rms avail. **Amenities:** 🛏 🛆 A/C, cable TV, in-rm safe. **Services:** 🛆 🛎 🛎 **Facilities:** 🛗 45 🛆 1 rst, 1 bar (w/entertainment), washer/dryer. **Rates:** $30 S; $36 D. Children under 18 stay free. Higher rates for spec evnts/hols. Pking: Outdoor, free. Maj CC.

Restaurants 🍴

Banyan's, in the Jacksonville Marriott at Southpoint, 4670 Salisbury Rd, Jacksonville; tel 904/296-2222. **New American.** A casual, family-style restaurant. The breakfast buffet offers a wide selection at a low price. Dinner entrees include Caribbean-grilled mahimahi. **FYI:** Reservations accepted. Harp. Children's menu. **Open:** Breakfast Mon–Fri 6:30–11am, Sat 7–11am, Sun 7–10:30am; lunch Mon–Fri 11am–2pm, Sat–Sun 10:30am–2pm; dinner Mon–Thurs 5–10pm, Fri–Sat 5–11pm, Sun 5–10pm. **Prices:** Main courses $8.95–$15.95. Maj CC. 💟 VP &

Cafe Carmon, 1986 San Marco Blvd, Jacksonville; tel 904/399-4488. Between Carlo St and Waldo Ave. **New American.** Casual restaurant located in the heart of the San Marco shopping district. Cajun stuffed grouper is a specialty. Enjoy cappuccino and dessert on the patio. **FYI:** Reservations not accepted. Beer and wine only. **Open:** Mon–Fri 7am–11pm, Fri 7am–midnight, Sat 8:30am–midnight, Sun 9am–3pm. Closed some hols. **Prices:** Main courses $7.50–$14.95. Maj CC. 💟 &

The Chart House, in St John's Place, 601 Hendricks Ave, Jacksonville; tel 904/398-3353. **Seafood/Steak.** A casual steakhouse located in the heart of the shopping district. The attractive black-and-white decor is accented by ceiling fans and exposed brick. Every table has river views. The salad bar has more than 60 items from which to choose. On weekend evenings this place is jammed with moviegoers who come in afterward for dessert and coffee. **FYI:** Reservations recommended. **Open:** Sun–Thurs 5–10pm, Fri–Sat 5–11pm. **Prices:** Main courses $12.95–$23.95. Maj CC. 🖼 💟 &

Chili's Grill & Bar, in Baymeadow Commons Shopping Center, 9500 Baymeadows Rd, Jacksonville; tel 904/739-2476. **Southwestern.** Locals love the lounge here, with its foliage and tiled table tops. Burger platters, chicken, and caesar salad are good values. **FYI:** Reservations not accepted. Children's menu. **Open:** Mon–Thurs 11am–11pm, Fri–Sat 11am–midnight, Sun 11am–10:30pm. Closed some hols. **Prices:** Main courses $5.65–$9.95. Maj CC. &

★ **Ciao Gianni Ristorante**, Jacksonville Landing, Jacksonville; tel 904/353-2626. At Water and Hogan Sts. **Italian.** An attractive Italian bistro with marble-topped tables and an open kitchen. The menu offers many pasta dishes. Popular with locals for candlelit dinners. **FYI:** Reservations accepted. **Open:** Sun–Thurs 11:30am–10:30pm, Fri–Sat 11:30am–10pm. Closed Dec 25. **Prices:** Main courses $9–$15. Maj CC. &

L & N Seafood Grill, in Jacksonville Landing, 2 Independent Dr, Jacksonville; tel 904/358-7737. **Seafood/Steak/Pasta.** This riverside seafood restaurant offers beautiful views from its wrap-around windows. The interior has a maritime theme. The menu includes grilled shrimp, top sirloin, and spicy shrimp linguine. **FYI:** Reservations not accepted. Children's menu. **Open:**. Lunch daily 11am–5pm; dinner Sun–Thurs 5–10pm, Fri–Sat 5–11:30pm. Closed some hols. **Prices:** Main courses $8.50–$15.95. Maj CC. &

Sand Dollar, 9716 Heckscher Dr, Jacksonville; tel 904/251-2449. ⅛ mi N of the Mayport Ferry. **Seafood/Steak.** You can view the activity at the nearby marina from your table. The menu offers swordfish, shrimp, oysters, and a steak and lobster combo. **FYI:** Reservations not accepted. Children's menu. **Open:** Sun–Thurs 11am–9:30pm, Fri–Sat 11am–10pm. **Prices:** Main courses $4.25–$14.95. Ltd CC. 💟

Silver Spoon, in Jacksonville Landing, 2 Independent Dr, Jacksonville; tel 904/353-4503. **Cafe/Continental.** Comfortable, with good views of the St John River. Menu highlights include gourmet pizzas as well as the southwestern grilled daily fish. **FYI:** Reservations recommended. Children's menu. **Open:** Mon–Thurs 11am–11pm, Fri–Sat 11am–midnight. Closed Dec 25. **Prices:** Main courses $5.99–$10.99. Maj CC.

Attractions 🏛

Jacksonville Museum of Science & History, 1025 Museum Circle (Gulf Life Dr); tel 904/396-7062. This hands-on interactive children's museum located on the Riverwalk focuses on science and northern Florida history. Exhibits include a small aviary of Florida songbirds and a 10,000-gallon aquarium. Planetarium shows for adults and children are scheduled daily. **Open:** Mon–Fri 10am–5pm, Sat 10am–6pm, Sun 1–6pm. Closed some hols. $$

Jacksonville Art Museum, 4160 Boulevard Center Dr; tel 904/398-8336. On permanent display is a notable pre-Columbian collection containing artifacts from northern Mexico to southern Peru, dating from 3000 BC through AD 1500. A separate collection of contemporary paintings includes works by Picasso, Lichtenstein, and Nevelson. Changing exhibits are held regularly. **Open:** Tues–Wed and Fri 10am–4pm, Thurs 10am–10pm, Sat–Sun 1–5pm. Closed some hols. Free.

Jacksonville Landing, 2 Independent Dr; tel 904/353-1188. A dining, shopping, and entertainment center on the north bank of the St Johns River, home to street performers, festivals, concerts, and other special events. The complex offers over 65 shops plus a market with open-air stalls displaying an array of meats, cheeses, fresh seafood, baked goods, flowers, and produce. **Open:** Mon–Thurs 10am–8pm, Fri–Sat 10am–9pm, Sun noon–5:30pm. Closed some hols. Free.

Riverwalk, 851 N Market St; tel 904/396-4900. This 1.2-mile wooden boardwalk on the south bank of the St Johns River is one of Jacksonville's most popular attractions, the scene of numerous festivals and special events throughout the year. Food vendors and restaurants line the route. At the west end is the massive Friendship Fountain, particularly pretty at night, when it is illuminated with colored lights. **Open:** Daily 24 hours. Free.

Cummer Gallery of Art, 829 Riverside Ave; tel 904/356-6857. Set amidst stunning formal gardens with fountains and reflecting pools, the museum boasts collections of 18th-century Meissen porcelain and 18th- and early 19th-century Japanese Netsuke ivory carvings. Also displayed are 18th- and 19th-century American landscapes and portraits by the likes of Thomas Eakins, Winslow Homer, John Singer Sargent, James Whistler, and Frederic Remington. **Open:** Tues–Fri 10am–4pm, Sat noon–5pm, Sun 2–5pm. Closed some hols. $

Jacksonville Zoological Garden, 8605 Zoo Rd; tel 904/757-4462 or 757-4463. Lushly landscaped zoo exhibiting over 700 mammals, birds, and reptiles, many of them in large, natural enclosures that simulate native habitats. Breeding programs involve such endangered species as the white rhino and the Florida panther. At the Educational Center (open weekends and holidays only, 10am–4pm) hands-on exhibits offer the opportunity to examine birds' eggs and nests, peer at insects through a microscope, or touch a giraffe vertebra or tiger skull. **Open:** Daily 9am–5pm. Closed some hols. $$

Anheuser-Busch Brewery, 111 Busch Dr; tel 904/751-8116. Visitors can tour the brewing and bottling facilities and learn about the company's history from its inception in 1852 to the present. Free samples of the final product in the Hospitality Room at the end of the tour. **Open:** Mon–Sat 9am–4pm. $

Fort Caroline National Memorial, 12713 Fort Caroline Rd; tel 904/641-7155. A triangular fort of earth and wood on the St Johns River, this was a French outpost during the European struggle for dominance in the New World. Arriving in 1562, the French colonists, mostly Huguenots, suffered great privation due to famine and Indian hostility. By 1565, 7 ships loaded with food and more settlers narrowly prevented the abandonment of the colony. But soon thereafter the colony was attacked and overrun by Spanish forces, who held the fort almost continuously for the next 250 years.

Today a replica of Fort Caroline near the original site is under the auspices of the National Park Service, as is the nearby 600-acre **Theodore Roosevelt Area,** beautiful woodland undisturbed since the Civil War. On a 2-mile hike along a centuries-old park trail, you'll see a wide variety of birds (including bald eagles, wood storks, and pelicans), wildflowers, and maritime hammock forest. There are picnic areas at the visitor center and at the trailhead.

Ranger-guided tours of Fort Caroline are given Sat–Sun at 1pm, followed by guided nature walks through Theodore Roosevelt Area at 2:30pm. **Open:** Daily 9am–5pm. Closed Dec 25. Free.

Zephaniah Kingsley Plantation, 11676 Palmetto Ave; tel 904/251-3537. Over 200 slaves tended the 30,000 acres of Sea Island cotton, sugarcane, and other crops grown on this 19th-century plantation, located just off Fla A1A. Visitors can tour the 2-story residence, kitchen house, barn/carriage house, and the remains of 23 slave cabins made of tabby, a kind of primitive concrete composed of sand, water, and crushed oyster shells. The National Parks Service schedules tours throughout the day; call ahead for times. **Open:** Daily 9am–5pm. Closed Dec 25. Free.

JACKSONVILLE BEACH

Map page M-5, C4

Hotels 🏨

🏨 **Comfort Inn Oceanfront**, 1515 N 1st St, Jacksonville Beach, FL 32250; tel 904/241-2311 or toll free 800/654-8776; fax 904/349-3830. Fronted by 3,000 feet of pristine white sand, this economical choice is very popular with families. Miles of sand beaches provide some wonderful views. **Rooms:** 180 rms and stes. CI 3pm/CO 11am. Nonsmoking rms avail. Many rooms with beach views. **Amenities:** 🛁 🐾 A/C, cable TV. Some units w/terraces. **Services:** 🛎 🍴 **Facilities:** 🛗 ⛳ 🏊 🐾 1 rst, 1 bar (w/entertainment), 1 beach (ocean), lawn games, whirlpool. Large pool has rock waterfalls and sun deck. Restaurant and lounge have both beach and pool views. **Rates (CP):** HS Feb–Aug $59–$89 S or D; from $135 ste. Children under 18 stay free. Lower rates off-season. Higher rates for spec evnts/hols. Spec packages avail. Pking: Outdoor, free. Maj CC.

🏨 **Days Inn Oceanfront Resort**, 1031 S 1st St, Jacksonville Beach, FL 32250; tel 904/249-7231 or toll free 800/321-2037; fax 904/249-7924. Butler Blvd exit off I-95. Located directly on the beach, at dunes' edge, this facility boasts panoramic ocean views from all its rooms. **Rooms:** 155 rms and stes. CI 3pm/CO noon. Nonsmoking rms avail. **Amenities:** 🛁 A/C, cable TV. All units w/terraces. **Services:** ✕ 🛎 🍴 🐾 Babysitting. **Facilities:** 🛗 🏊 🐾 1 bar (w/entertainment), 1 beach (ocean), lifeguard, lawn games, washer/dryer. Beach volleyball. Poolside patio bar. Restaurant and lounge have ocean views. **Rates:** HS Feb–Apr

$64–$69 S or D; from $125 ste. Children under 18 stay free. Lower rates off-season. Higher rates for spec evnts/hols. Spec packages avail. Pking: Outdoor, free. Maj CC.

Jacksonville Beach Oceanfront Hotel, 1617 N 1st St, Jacksonville Beach, FL 32250; tel 904/249-9071 or toll free 800/590-4767; fax 904/241-4321. From I-95 take Fla 10 east to Fla A1A then south to hotel. Former Holiday Inn. The 7th floor, dedicated as meeting space, features floor-to-ceiling windows affording a panoramic ocean view. Unrated. **Rooms:** 160 rms and effic. CI 3pm/CO 11am. Nonsmoking rms avail. **Amenities:** 📺 ♨ A/C, cable TV w/movies. All units w/terraces. **Services:** 🖾 🖘 Babysitting. **Facilities:** 🔗 🕹 🚘 ᕙ 1 bar (w/entertainment), 1 beach (ocean), lawn games, washer/dryer. **Rates (CP):** HS June–Aug $50–$60 S or D; from $65 effic. Children under 18 stay free. Lower rates off-season. Higher rates for spec evnts/hols. Spec packages avail. Pking: Outdoor, free. Maj CC.

Attraction 🖼

American Lighthouse Historical Society, 1011 N Third St (Fla A1A); tel 904/241-8845. Extensive collection of photographs, artifacts, and historical and technical data on more than 1,000 lighthouses in the United States. Artifacts, oil paintings, scale models, navigational aids, and blueprints help preserve the place of the lighthouse in American history. **Open:** Tues–Sat 10am–4pm. Closed some hols. Free.

JENSEN BEACH

Map page M-9, B4

Hotels 🏨

🔳🔳 **Courtyard by Marriott**, 10978 S Ocean Dr, Jensen Beach, FL 34957; tel 407/229-1000 or toll free 800/321-2211; fax 407/229-0253. 1 mi N of Jensen Beach Causeway. Popular with families for location near beach-going and island activities. **Rooms:** 110 rms and stes. CI 3pm/CO noon. Express checkout avail. Nonsmoking rms avail. Contemporary appointments. Some rooms with ocean views. **Amenities:** 📺 ♨ 🖥 A/C, cable TV w/movies. Some units w/terraces. **Services:** ✕ 🖾 🖘 Babysitting. **Facilities:** 🔗 🛆 🚘 🔲 ᕙ 1 rst, 1 beach (ocean), board surfing, games rm, washer/dryer. **Rates:** HS Dec–Apr $99–$119 S or D; from $150 ste. Extra person $10. Children under 18 stay free. Lower rates off-season. Spec packages avail. Pking: Outdoor, free. Maj CC.

🔳🔳 **Holiday Inn Jensen Beach**, 3793 NE Ocean Blvd, Jensen Beach, FL 34957; tel 407/225-3000 or toll free 800/992-4747; fax 407/225-1956. Its beachfront location is the main appeal.

Rooms: 181 rms, stes, and effic. CI 3pm/CO 11am. Nonsmoking rms avail. Well-maintained rooms. **Amenities:** 📺 ♨ A/C, satel TV w/movies, in-rm safe. All units w/terraces. **Services:** ✕ 🖾 🖘 Babysitting. **Facilities:** 🔗 🕹2 🚘 🎿 🔲 ᕙ 1 rst, 2 bars (1 w/entertainment), 1 beach (ocean), games rm, washer/dryer. Patio bar. **Rates:** HS Jan–Apr $100–$140 S or D; from $240 ste. Extra person $10. Children under 19 stay free. Min stay spec evnts. Lower rates off-season. Spec packages avail. Pking: Indoor/outdoor, free. Maj CC.

Motel

Hutchinson Inn, 9750 S Ocean Dr, Jensen Beach, FL 34957; tel 407/229-2000; fax 407/229-8875. 2 mi N of Jensen Beach Causeway. A quiet beachfront hideaway. Brick walkways lead to the pastel 2-story building, and the thick green lawns are dotted with white gazebos. The lobby, though tiny, is charming. Unrated. **Rooms:** 21 rms and effic. CI 2pm/CO 11am. Nonsmoking rms avail. Accommodations vary from a handful with queen-size beds to efficiencies with more space to a single apartment suite. Most units offer a view of the pool and limited ocean vistas. **Amenities:** 📺 ♨ 🖥 A/C, cable TV, refrig. Some units w/terraces. **Services:** 🖘 **Facilities:** 🔗 1 beach (ocean), washer/dryer. Good swimming beach. **Rates (CP):** HS Dec–Apr $90 S or D; from $145 effic. Extra person $10–$20. Children under 3 stay free. Min stay spec evnts. Lower rates off-season. Pking: Outdoor, free. Ltd CC.

Restaurants 🍽

Cafe Coconuts, in Island Shops, 4304 NE Ocean Blvd, Jensen Beach; tel 407/225-6006. Take Jensen Beach Causeway to Ocean Blvd and go 1 block north. **Seafood/Steak.** Casual, plant-filled restaurant. The early-bird dining specials offer terrific value. Surf-and-turf and baby-back ribs are mainstays. **FYI:** Reservations not accepted. Dancing/jazz/piano. Children's menu. **Open:** Sun–Thurs 11:30am–10pm, Fri–Sat 11:30am–11pm. Closed Dec 25. **Prices:** Main courses $7.95–$14.95. Ltd CC. 💟 ⅘

★ **Island Reef**, 10900 S Ocean Dr, Jensen Beach; tel 407/229-2600. 1 mi N of Jensen Beach Causeway. **Seafood/Steak.** A casual, tropical spot with great views, popular with locals and visitors alike. **FYI:** Reservations not accepted. Guitar. Children's menu. **Open:** Sun–Thurs 11:30am–9:30pm, Fri–Sat 11:30am–10pm. **Prices:** Main courses $9–$19. Maj CC. 🍱 🏞 💟 VP

JUNO BEACH

Map page M-9, D4

Attraction 📷

Marinelife Center of Juno Beach, 1200 US 1; tel 407/627-8280. Located in Loggerhead Park, a public beachfront park in Juno Beach, this combination ecology museum and nature trail focuses on South Florida's unique ecosystem. Hands-on exhibits, outdoor trails through dune vegetation, and live, endangered sea turtles. **Open:** Tues–Sat 10am–3pm, Sun 10am–noon. Free.

JUPITER

Map page M-9, C4

Motel 🛏

Wellesley Inn, 34 Fisherman's Wharf, Jupiter, FL 33477; tel 407/575-7201 or toll free 800/444-8888; fax 407/575-1169. Exit 59A off I-95. Just what the budget-minded motorist needs. **Rooms:** 105 rms and stes. CI 2pm/CO 11am. Nonsmoking rms avail. **Amenities:** 🕿 🔥 A/C, cable TV w/movies. **Services:** ✕ 🖃 ⊋ ⇦ **Facilities:** 🔥 15 ⅃ & Washer/dryer. **Rates (CP):** HS Dec 20–Apr 1 $75 S; $89 D; from $105 ste. Extra person $6. Children under 18 stay free. Lower rates off-season. Spec packages avail. Pking: Outdoor, free. Maj CC.

Resort

Jupiter Beach Resort, 5 N Fla A1A at Indiantown Rd, Jupiter, FL 33477; tel 407/746-2511 or toll free 800/228-8810; fax 407/744-1741. The local showplace, in a convenient location directly on the beach and near area attractions. Inside are some delightful public areas. **Rooms:** 197 rms and stes. CI 4pm/CO noon. Nonsmoking rms avail. Some rooms offer pretty panoramic views. **Amenities:** 🕿 🔥 A/C, cable TV w/movies. All units w/minibars, all w/terraces. **Services:** ✕ 🅅🅿 🚗 🖃 ⇦ Twice-daily maid svce, car-rental desk, babysitting. **Facilities:** 🔥 🚲 🕿 💪 500 & 2 rsts, 2 bars (1 w/entertainment), 1 beach (ocean), snorkeling, washer/dryer. **Rates:** HS Dec–Apr $181–$365 S or D; from $325 ste. Extra person $10. Children under 18 stay free. Lower rates off-season. Spec packages avail. Pking: Outdoor, free. Maj CC.

Restaurants 🍴

Backstage, in Reynolds Plaza, 1061 E Indiantown Rd, Jupiter; tel 407/747-9533. **American/Continental.** A local hangout owned by hometown boy Burt Reynolds. The crab cakes and the steak au poivre are popular. Seafood lovers can try the pecan-encrusted grouper. **FYI:** Reservations recommended. Band/jazz. Children's menu. **Open:** Lunch Mon–Fri 11:30am–2:30pm; dinner daily 5pm–2:30am. Closed Dec 25. **Prices:** Main courses $7.95–$26.95. Maj CC. 💟 &

Chili's Grill & Bar, in the Shops at Jupiter, 65 US 1, Jupiter; tel 407/575-6900. **American.** A fun, casual eatery with comfortable booths, serving good food at affordable prices. Enjoy a variety of salads, soups, or burgers for lunch, or opt for the fajitas at dinner. **FYI:** Reservations not accepted. Children's menu. **Open:** Sun–Thurs 11:15am–11:15pm, Fri–Sat 11:15am–12:15am. **Prices:** Main courses $4.95–$9.75. Maj CC. &

Harpoon Louie's, 1065 Fla A1A Service Rd, Jupiter; tel 407/744-1300. Across from the Jupiter Lighthouse. **American.** A tropically decorated, contemporary waterfront cafe serving Caribbean-inspired cuisine. The menu includes prime rib and a variety of seafood dishes. A good value for both lunch and dinner. **FYI:** Reservations not accepted. Children's menu. **Open:** Breakfast Sun 8–11am; lunch daily 11am–4pm; dinner Sun–Thurs 4:30–10pm, Fri–Sat 4:30–10:30pm. Closed Dec 25. **Prices:** Main courses $15.95–$19.95. Maj CC. 💟 &

Log Cabin Restaurant, 631 N Fla A1A, Jupiter; tel 407/746-6877. Between US 1 and Indiantown Rd. **Barbecue/Seafood/Steak.** A rustic eatery serving hearty fare in a relaxing atmosphere. The menu offers traditional fried and barbecued favorites like steaks, chicken, and spare ribs, as well as some seafood dishes. **FYI:** Reservations not accepted. Children's menu. **Open:** Daily 7am–10pm. **Prices:** Main courses $6.95–$18.95. Maj CC. 💟 &

Schooners, 1001 N Fla A1A, Jupiter; tel 407/746-7558. **Seafood.** A casual grill with a nautical motif. Appetizers include crabmeat-stuffed mushrooms; fresh fish entrees might be swordfish, salmon, or snapper. The fish can be ordered broiled, blackened, or grilled. **FYI:** Reservations not accepted. Children's menu. **Open:** Sun–Thurs 11am–9:30pm, Fri–Sat 11am–10:30pm. Closed some hols. **Prices:** Main courses $10.50–$15. Maj CC. 🍴 💟 &

Attractions 📷

Jupiter Inlet Lighthouse, US 1 and Alternate Fla A1A; tel 305/747-6639 (Loxahatchee Museum). Dating from 1860, this is the oldest structure still standing in Palm Beach County. The

Loxahatchee Historical Society sponsors tours every Sunday. There is a small museum at the base of the structure. **Open:** Sun 1–4pm only. Free.

Loxahatchee Historical Society Museum, 805 US 1N; tel 407/747-6639. In Burt Reynolds Park. Chronologically arranged exhibits in this museum relate to Jupiter and its vicinity, from Seminole utensils to Burt Reynolds's boots. **Open:** Tues–Fri 10am–4pm, Sat–Sun 1–4pm. $

Blowing Rocks Preserve, Fla A1A. This wonderfully picturesque beach on Jupiter Island owes its beauty to a cluster of large rock formations. Although not recommended for swimming, it is a popular fishing spot. The preserve is a 10-minute drive from downtown Jupiter.

Hobe Sound National Wildlife Refuge; tel 407/546-6141. Most of this 900-acre refuge is on the mainland, along US 1 near Hobe Sound, where visitors will find a museum and nature center. The remainder of the refuge covers the north end of Jupiter Island, which is accessible by car. Visitors to this portion of the refuge enjoy the island's 3 miles of undeveloped beach. Swimming, fishing, boating, hiking, nature trails. **Open:** Daily dawn–dusk. $$

KENNEDY SPACE CENTER

Map page M-7, C3

For lodging and dining, see Cocoa, Cocoa Beach, Indialantic, Melbourne, Merritt Island, Titusville

Located at Cape Canaveral on Fla 405, 12 miles east of Titusville (tel 407/452-2121). Spaceport USA, the visitor facility of the John F Kennedy Space Center, allows visitors to explore the past, present, and future of man's endeavors in space. Many exhibits, movie presentations, and 2 major tours make up a full-day itinerary designed to inform and entertain.

The **Red Tour**, a double-decker bus ride, includes stops at a simulated launch control room, where a liftoff is re-created; the Space Shuttle launch complex, including pads 39A and 39B where shuttles being prepared for launch can often be seen; the massive Vehicle Assembly building; and more. The **Blue Tour** highlights the history of space exploration, traveling through Cape Canaveral Air Force Station to visit the Air Force Space Museum and the mission control center for the Mercury and Gemini programs. Both tours last about 2 hours and depart at

regular intervals beginning at 9:45am, with the last tour departing 2 hours before dusk. Purchase tickets at the Ticket Pavilion as soon as you arrive.

Other features include "Satellites and You," a 50-minute voyage through a simulated space station explaining satellites and their uses; Explorer, a full-scale orbiter mock-up; the Galaxy Center, featuring 2 IMAX film presentations, a NASA art exhibit, and a walk-through model of the space station Freedom; Spaceport Theater; the Rocket Garden; and the Astronauts Memorial.

Also a part of the Space Center is the 140,000-acre **Merritt Island National Wildlife Refuge** (tel 407/861-0667), a pristine wilderness of dense woods, unspoiled beaches, and swampland that provides refuge for more than 500 species, many threatened or endangered. To find out about guided nature walks, interpretive programs, and self-guided hikes contact the Visitor Information Center, located 4 miles east of Titusville on Fla 402 (open Mon–Fri 8am–4:30pm, Sat to 5pm). Note: There won't be enough time to see the refuge and the Space Center all in 1 day.

For tickets to a launch call Spaceport USA for current launch information (ext 260 to make reservations or fax 407/454-3211). Tickets are $7 adults, $4 children 3–11, under 3 free. Tickets may be reserved up to 7 days before a launch but must be picked up at least 2 days defore launch. A special bus takes observers to a site just 6 miles from the launch pad.

KEY BISCAYNE

Map page M-11, B2

Restaurants 🍴

The Dragons, in Sonesta Beach Resort, 350 Ocean Dr, Key Biscayne; tel 305/361-2021. **Chinese.** Standard Chinese restaurant. Extensive menu. **FYI:** Reservations recommended. Children's menu. **Open:** Daily 5–11pm. **Prices:** Main courses $9.50–$18.75. Maj CC. 🅟 ⱴ🅿 ♿

Rusty Pelican, 3201 Rickenbacker Causeway, Key Biscayne; tel 305/361-3818. **Seafood/Steak.** A very romantic dining room with great ocean views. The menu offers seafood dishes, steaks, and an extensive wine selection. **FYI:** Reservations recommended. Children's menu. **Open:** Lunch Mon–Fri 11:30am–4pm; dinner Mon–Thurs 5–11pm, Fri–Sat 5pm–midnight, Sun 5–11pm; brunch Sun 10:30am–3pm. **Prices:** Main courses $18–$20. Maj CC. ♥ 🅟 ♿

Sundays on the Bay, 5420 Crandon Blvd, Key Biscayne; tel 305/361-6777. 3 mi E of toll plaza. **New American/Seafood.** An elegant, upscale eatery decorated in shades of pink. Dine on local favorites like grouper, tuna, or snapper or such classic shellfish dishes as oysters Rockefeller, lobster Fra Diavolo, or shrimp scampi. **FYI:** Reservations recommended. Band/blues. **Open:** Mon–Sat 11:30am–11:45pm, Sun 10:30am–11:45pm. **Prices:** Main courses $15–$19. Maj CC. 🖼 ♿

Attractions 🎦

Miami Seaquarium, 4400 Rickenbacker Causeway; tel 305/361-5705. A marine-life park offering 6 different animal shows each day as well as marine exhibits and aquariums. Shows feature killer whales, sea lions, ''man-eating'' sharks, and Flipper, the dolphin star of the old television series. Visitors can also see manatees, the American crocodile, sea turtles, exotic birds, and reptiles. **Open:** Daily 9:30am–6pm. $$$$

First Street Beach, Crandon Blvd, bottom of Ocean Drive. Crandon Blvd, at the bottom of Ocean Dr. One of the area's best surfing beaches. No lifeguard.

Crandon Park Beach, Crandon Blvd. Offers 3 miles of oceanfront beach and 493 acres of park, with barbecue grills and soccer and softball fields. There is also a public 18-hole golf course, a tennis center, and a marina. **Open:** 8am–sunset. $

Hobie Beach. Not really a beach, this area just along the causeway is actually a quiet inlet with calm winds and numerous windsurfer rental shops.

Bill Baggs Cape Florida State Park, 1200 S Crandon Blvd; tel 305/361-5811. On the south end of Key Biscayne. Barbecue grills and picnic tables, bicycle and nature trails. Adjacent, narrow soft-sand beach is home of Cape Florida Lighthouse, with re-created lightkeeper's residence (tours available, phone for schedule). $$

KEY LARGO

Map page M-11, D1

Hotels 🏨

≣≣≣ Holiday Inn Key Largo Resort & Marina, 99701 Overseas Hwy, MM 99.7, Key Largo, FL 33037; tel 305/451-2121 or toll free 800/843-5397; fax 305/451-5592. **Rooms:** 132 rms. CI 3pm/CO 11am. Nonsmoking rms avail. **Amenities:** 🛋 A/C, cable TV w/movies, voice mail. Some units w/minibars, some w/terraces. **Services:** ✗ 🖼 🍽 Babysitting. **Facilities:** 🔥 △ ▣ 🏊 ♿ 1 rst, 2 bars, games rm, snorkeling, whirlpool. **Rates:** HS Dec–Apr $139–$166 S or D. Extra person

$10. Children under 18 stay free. Min stay spec evnts. Lower rates off-season. Spec packages avail. Pking: Outdoor, free. Maj CC.

≣≣≣ Marina Del Mar Bayside Resort, 99500 Overseas Hwy, MM 99.5, PO Box 1050, Key Largo, FL 33037; tel 305/451-4450 or toll free 800/242-5229; fax 305/451-9650. This sibling of the Marina Del Mar Resort and Marina (see listing below) is set back from the highway in a 3-story, coral-colored building. **Rooms:** 56 rms and stes. CI 3pm/CO 11am. Nonsmoking rms avail. Standardized rooms with tropical decor; some have bayviews. **Amenities:** 🛋 A/C, cable TV. Some units w/terraces. **Services:** 🍽 **Facilities:** 🔥 ♿ 1 rst, 1 bar, 1 beach (bay), lawn games. Guests can use health club facilities and washers/dryers at nearby Marina Del Mar Resort and Marina. **Rates:** HS Dec–Apr $105–$160 S or D; from $225 ste. Children under 18 stay free. Min stay spec evnts. Lower rates off-season. Higher rates for spec evnts/hols. Spec packages avail. Pking: Outdoor, free. Maj CC.

≣≣ Marina Del Mar Resort and Marina, 527 Caribbean Dr, MM 94, Key Largo, FL 33037; tel 305/451-4107 or toll free 800/451-3483; fax 305/451-1891. Family-oriented 4-story property boasts the largest pool in the Upper Keys. **Rooms:** 76 rms and stes. CI 3pm/CO 11am. Nonsmoking rms avail. Studios have Murphy beds. **Amenities:** 🛋 🗄 🍽 A/C, cable TV, refrig. Some units w/terraces. **Services:** 🍽 **Facilities:** 🔥 △ 🏊 🍽 ▣ 1 rst, 2 bars (1 w/entertainment), snorkeling, whirlpool, washer/dryer. Open-air bar overlooks marina. **Rates (CP):** HS Dec–Apr $110–$130 S or D; from $160 ste. Children under 18 stay free. Min stay spec evnts. Lower rates off-season. Higher rates for spec evnts/hols. Spec packages avail. Pking: Outdoor, free. Maj CC.

Lodge

Jules' Undersea Lodge, Overseas Hwy MM 103.2, PO Box 3330, Key Largo, FL 33037; tel 305/451-2353; fax 305/451-4789. Attracts the diving enthusiast who wants to experience underwater living in a unique suite-style arrangement. Friendly service on the mainland will assist guests and potential guests with questions and specific needs. Book well in advance. Unrated. **Rooms:** 2 stes. CI 5pm/CO 11am. Nonsmoking rms avail. **Amenities:** 🛋 🗄 🍽 A/C, refrig, VCR, stereo/tape player. **Services:** Dinner is delivered to your door in a waterproof container. **Facilities:** Snorkeling, washer/dryer. **Rates (MAP):** From $195 ste. Spec packages avail. Pking: Outdoor, free. Ltd CC.

Resorts

≣≣≣ **Marriott's Key Largo Bay Beach Resort**, MM 103.5 103800 Overseas Hwy, Key Largo, FL 33037; tel 305/453-9393 or toll free 800/932-9332; fax 305/453-0093. **Rooms:** 145 rms and stes. CI 3pm/CO noon. Nonsmoking rms avail. **Amenities:** 🔒 🐾 🌡 A/C, cable TV w/movies, in-rm safe. All units w/minibars, some w/terraces, some w/Jacuzzis. **Services:** 🛎 Babysitting. **Facilities:** 🗗 🚴 ⚠ 🔲 [120] 🚹 2 rsts, 3 bars (1 w/entertainment), 1 beach (ocean), games rm, snorkeling, spa, whirlpool, washer/dryer. **Rates:** HS Dec–Apr $129–$235 S or D; from $275 ste. Extra person $25. Children under 18 stay free. Lower rates off-season. Higher rates for spec evnts/hols. Spec packages avail. Pking: Indoor/outdoor, free. Maj CC.

≣≣≣≣ **Ocean Reef Club**, 31 Ocean Reef Dr, Key Largo, FL 33037; tel 305/367-5923 or toll free 800/741-REEF; fax 305/367-2224. 4,000 acres. A massive, self-contained resort complex with a variety of accommodations and strict security. An ideal family vacation spot. Nonmember guests may be sponsored for their first visit by the hotel's membership department, but subsequent visits must be at the sponsorship of a member. **Rooms:** 199 rms, stes, and effic; 112 ctges/villas. CI 3pm/CO noon. Nonsmoking rms avail. **Amenities:** 🔒 🐾 🌡 🌡 A/C, cable TV w/movies, refrig, stereo/tape player. All units w/minibars, all w/terraces, some w/Jacuzzis. **Services:** ✕ 🗝 VP 🚗 🛄 🛎 Car-rental desk, masseur, babysitting. **Facilities:** 🗗 🚴 ⚠ 🔲 ▶ 36 🎿 🍹 ⛳ 🏌 💆 [250] 🚹 5 rsts, 3 bars (2 w/entertainment), 1 beach (ocean), lifeguard, board surfing, games rm, lawn games, snorkeling, whirlpool, beauty salon, day-care ctr, playground, washer/dryer. Manmade beach. Fishing village. **Rates:** HS Dec–Apr $290–$340 S or D; from $510 ste; from $350 effic; from $500 ctge/villa. Extra person $20. Children under 16 stay free. Min stay HS. Lower rates off-season. Higher rates for spec evnts/hols. AP and MAP rates avail. Spec packages avail. Pking: Indoor/outdoor, free. Maj CC.

≣≣≣ **Sheraton Key Largo Resort**, 97000 S Overseas Hwy MM 97, Key Largo, FL 33037; tel 305/852-5553 or toll free 800/826-1006; fax 305/852-8669. 12½ acres. A stylish facility that blends in with the natural surroundings and offers spectacular sunset views. **Rooms:** 200 rms and stes. CI 3pm/CO 11am. Nonsmoking rms avail. Upper floors offer the best sunset views. **Amenities:** 🔒 🐾 🌡 A/C, cable TV w/movies. All units w/minibars, all w/terraces, some w/Jacuzzis. **Services:** ✕ 🚗 🛄 🛎 Children's program, babysitting. **Facilities:** 🗗 🚴 ⚠ 🍹 🏌 💆 [250] 🚹 2 rsts, 4 bars (1 w/entertainment), 1 beach (ocean), games rm, spa, whirlpool, beauty salon. **Rates:** HS Jan–Apr $180–$255 S or D; from $410 ste. Extra person $15. Children under 17 stay free. Lower rates off-season. Higher rates for spec evnts/hols. Spec packages avail. Pking: Outdoor, free. Maj CC.

Attractions 💼

Seven-Mile Bridge, Overseas Hwy, MM 40-47. The Keys' most celebrated span rests on 546 concrete piers and rises to a 72-foot crest, the highest point in the Keys. The first bridge was constructed here in 1910, built to carry Henry Flagler's railroad track, which ran all the way to Key West. Most of the bridge was destroyed by a hurricane in 1935, but you can still see portions of the original track bed running for miles alongside the modern span that was constructed 10 years later.

John Pennekamp Coral Reef State Park, US 1, MM 102.5; tel 305/451-1202. The Key's largest and most popular park. The visitor center houses a 30,000-gallon saltwater marine aquarium surrounded by various educational exhibits and screens movies about the area's natural resources and the coral reef. There are 2 small, manmade beach areas; a concessionaire operates glass-bottom boat tours and snorkeling and scuba trips to the reef. Swimming, sailboat and canoe rentals, nature trails, camping. **Open:** Daily 8am–dusk. $$

KEYSTONE HEIGHTS

Map page M-5, D2

Attraction 💼

Mike Roess Gold Head Branch State Park, 6239 Fla 21; tel 904/473-4701. There are several small lakes within this 2,000-acre park. A wildlife refuge lies adjacent. Swimming, fishing, boating, canoe rentals, hiking, camping, nature trails. $$

KEY WEST

Map page M-10, E2

Hotels 🏨

≣≣ **Bayside Key West Resort Hotel**, 3444 N Roosevelt Blvd, Key West, FL 33040; tel 305/296-7593 or toll free 800/888-3233; fax 305/294-5246. US 1 to Roosevelt Blvd. Close to a public beach, this upbeat facility features rooms, suites and penthouses. **Rooms:** 64 rms and stes. CI 2pm/CO 11am. Nonsmoking rms avail. Rooms are moderately sized and adequately furnished, with Key West decor and ceiling fans. Some have views of the gulf. **Amenities:** 🔒 🐾 A/C, cable TV, in-rm safe. Some units w/minibars, some w/terraces. **Services:** 🛄 🛎 Babysitting. **Facilities:** 🗗 [20] 🚹 **Rates (CP):** $99–$149 D; from

$149 ste. Children under 16 stay free. Min stay spec evnts. Lower rates off-season. Higher rates for spec evnts/hols. Spec packages avail. Pking: Outdoor, free. Maj CC.

≣≣≣ The Gardens Hotel, 526 Angela St, Key West, FL 33040; tel 305/294-2661 or toll free 800/526-2664; fax 305/292-1007. 1 block N of Duval St. A secluded, gracious hotel contained in a walled enclave in the historic district. Deserves high marks for its beautifully and tastefully styled accommodations, which are some of the finest in Key West. **Rooms:** 17 rms and stes. CI 3pm/CO noon. Lovely rooms are individually styled with such details as leather-topped desks. **Amenities:** 🛎 🕹 🎯 🎙 A/C, cable TV, in-rm safe. All units w/minibars, all w/terraces, all w/Jacuzzis. **Services:** 🖐 🛆 Twice-daily maid svce, babysitting. **Facilities:** 🛐 🕹 1 bar, spa, whirlpool. **Rates (CP):** HS Dec–May $225–$315 S or D; from $385 ste. Extra person $20. Lower rates off-season. Higher rates for spec evnts/hols. Pking: Outdoor, free. Maj CC.

≣≣ Holiday Inn Beachside, 3841 N Roosevelt Blvd, Key West, FL 33040; tel 305/294-2571 or toll free 800/HOLIDAY; fax 305/296-5659. A pleasant facility consisting of a 2-story section that wraps a landscaped pool, and a 4-story building that faces the water and houses deluxe rooms. **Rooms:** 222 rms and stes. CI 3pm/CO noon. Express checkout avail. Nonsmoking rms avail. **Amenities:** 🛎 🕹 A/C, cable TV, in-rm safe. Some units w/terraces. **Services:** ✕ 🛆 🗘 Car-rental desk. **Facilities:** 🛐 🕹 △ 🏠 👫 600 🕹 1 rst, 1 bar, 1 beach (bay), snorkeling, whirlpool, washer/dryer. **Rates:** HS Feb–Apr $105–$225 S or D; from $215 ste. Children under 19 stay free. Lower rates off-season. Higher rates for spec evnts/hols. Spec packages avail. Pking: Outdoor, free. Maj CC.

≣≣ Holiday Inn La Concha Hotel, 430 Duval St, Key West, FL 33040; tel 305/296-2991 or toll free 800/745-2191; fax 305/294-3283. Standard for the chain, notable only for location in city's historic section. **Rooms:** 160 rms and stes. CI 3pm/CO 11am. **Amenities:** 🛎 🕹 A/C, cable TV w/movies. Some units w/terraces. **Services:** ✕ 🖐 🛆 🗘 Babysitting. **Facilities:** 🛐 300 🕹 2 rsts, 4 bars. **Rates:** HS Dec–Apr $160–$325 S or D; from $190 ste. Extra person $15. Children under 16 stay free. Lower rates off-season. Higher rates for spec evnts/hols. Pking: Outdoor, free. Maj CC.

≣≣≣ Hyatt Key West, 601 Front St, Key West, FL 33040; tel 305/296-9000 or toll free 800/233-1234; fax 305/292-1038. Ideally located on the waterfront, this hotel has lushly landscaped, though limited, grounds and a small man-made beach. Wonderful sunset views. **Rooms:** 120 rms and stes. CI 4pm/CO noon. Nonsmoking rms avail. Tastefully appointed rooms. **Amenities:** 🛎 🕹 🎙 A/C, cable TV w/movies, in-rm safe, bathrobes. All units w/minibars, all w/terraces, some w/Jacuzzis.

Services: 🍽 🖐 VP 🚗 🛆 🗘 Twice-daily maid svce, masseur, babysitting. **Facilities:** 🛐 🚲 △ 🏠 👫 60 🕹 3 rsts, 3 bars (1 w/entertainment), 1 beach (ocean), snorkeling, whirlpool. **Rates:** HS Dec–Apr $265–$370 S or D; from $435 ste. Extra person $45. Children under 18 stay free. Lower rates off-season. Higher rates for spec evnts/hols. Spec packages avail. Pking: Outdoor, free. Maj CC.

≣≣≣ Marriott's Reach Resort, 1435 Simonton St, Key West, FL 33040; tel 305/296-5000 or toll free 800/874-4118; fax 305/296-2830. Near Marriott's Casa Marina Resort, on its own nice section of beach, this tropically inspired establishment has the better rooms of the two. **Rooms:** 150 rms and stes. CI 4pm/CO 11am. Nonsmoking rms avail. **Amenities:** 🛎 🕹 🎯 🎙 A/C, cable TV w/movies, refrig. All units w/minibars, all w/terraces, some w/Jacuzzis. **Services:** ✕ 🖐 VP 🚗 🛆 🗘 Masseur, babysitting. **Facilities:** 🛐 △ 🏖 👫 80 🕹 3 rsts, 3 bars (1 w/entertainment), 1 beach (ocean), snorkeling, sauna, steam rm. **Rates:** HS Dec–Apr $270–$325 S or D; from $300 ste. Extra person $25. Children under 18 stay free. Lower rates off-season. Spec packages avail. Pking: Indoor/outdoor, free. Maj CC.

≣≣ Ocean Key House Suite Resort and Marina, Zero Duval St, Key West, FL 33040 (Old Town); tel 305/296-7201 or toll free 800/328-9815; fax 305/292-7685. In a prime location, this is ideal for those who appreciate independent living in an upscale environment. A good family offering. **Rooms:** 100 rms and stes. CI 4pm/CO noon. Many units have ocean views. **Amenities:** 🛎 🕹 🎯 🎙 A/C, cable TV, refrig, VCR, bathrobes. Some units w/minibars, some w/terraces, some w/Jacuzzis. **Services:** ✕ 🖐 🛆 🗘 Babysitting. **Facilities:** 🛐 🏠 30 🕹 1 bar (w/entertainment), snorkeling. **Rates:** HS Dec–Apr $135 S or D; from $325 ste. Extra person $25. Children under 21 stay free. Min stay wknds. Lower rates off-season. Higher rates for spec evnts/hols. Spec packages avail. Pking: Indoor/outdoor, free. Maj CC.

≣≣≣ The Pier House, 1 Duval St, Key West, FL 33040 (Old Town); tel 305/296-4600 or toll free 800/327-8340; fax 305/296-7569. In a prime waterfront location in the midst of the historic sector. One of the better Key West hotels, popular for its restaurants and bars, which offer good food and views. **Rooms:** 142 rms and stes. CI 4pm/CO noon. Nonsmoking rms avail. Rooms vary from simple business-class to luxurious. About 2 dozen overlook the pool. **Amenities:** 🛎 🕹 A/C, cable TV w/movies. All units w/minibars, all w/terraces, some w/fireplaces. **Services:** ✕ 🖐 🛆 🗘 🍷 Masseur, babysitting. **Facilities:** 🛐 🚲 👫 200 🕹 3 rsts, 5 bars (2 w/entertainment), 1 beach (ocean), spa, sauna, steam rm, whirlpool, beauty salon. **Rates:** HS Dec–Apr $275–$345 S or D; from $400 ste. Extra person $20. Children under 12 stay free. Lower rates off-season. Higher rates for spec evnts/hols. Spec packages avail. Pking: Outdoor, free. Maj CC.

≣≣≣ **Sheraton Suites Key West**, 2001 S Roosevelt Blvd, Key West, FL 33040; tel 305/292-9800 or toll free 800/325-3535; fax 305/294-6009. The area's newest hotel, located opposite Key West's best swimming beach and away from downtown district. Beautifully landscaped grounds and outdoor dining courtyard. Architecture is attempt at turn-of-the-century Key West look. **Rooms:** 184 stes. CI 3pm/CO 11am. Nonsmoking rms avail. All are 2-room suites, with tropical decor and upscale appointments. **Amenities:** 🛅 🐧 📺 🍴 A/C, cable TV w/movies. All units w/minibars, some w/terraces, some w/Jacuzzis. **Services:** ✗ 🍴 🚐 🏖 🛎 Social director, babysitting. Free shuttle to Old Town. Free newspaper daily. **Facilities:** 🏋 🎿 🏊 ⬆ 1 rst, 2 bars, whirlpool, washer/dryer. Atmospheric dining room decorated in fishmarket motif. **Rates (BB):** HS Dec–Apr from $235 ste. Extra person $25. Children under 18 stay free. Lower rates off-season. Spec packages avail. Pking: Outdoor, free. Maj CC.

Motels

≣ **Best Western Key Ambassador Resort Inn**, 3755 S Roosevelt Blvd, Key West, FL 33040; tel 305/296-3500 or toll free 800/432-4315; fax 305/296-9961. Pleasant lowrise with spacious grounds, located opposite the seawall and away from the downtown crush. **Rooms:** 100 rms. CI 3pm/CO noon. Standard budget rooms. **Amenities:** 🛅 🐧 A/C, cable TV w/movies, refrig. All units w/minibars, all w/terraces. **Services:** 🛎 **Facilities:** 🏋 Washer/dryer. **Rates (CP):** HS Dec–Mar $180–$195 S or D. Extra person $10. Children under 18 stay free. Lower rates off-season. Higher rates for spec evnts/hols. Spec packages avail. Pking: Outdoor, free. Maj CC.

≣≣ **Comfort Inn**, 3824 N Roosevelt Blvd, Key West, FL 33040; tel 305/294-3773 or toll free 800/695-5150; fax 305/294-3773. Neatly landscaped facility offering comfortable rooms. Short drive to historic district; convenient to restaurants. **Rooms:** 100 rms. CI 1pm/CO 11am. Nonsmoking rms avail. **Amenities:** 🛅 🐧 A/C, cable TV w/movies, refrig, in-rm safe. **Services:** 🛎 Babysitting. **Facilities:** 🏋 ⬆ Games rm, washer/dryer. **Rates (CP):** HS Dec–Apr $109–$130 S or D. Extra person $10. Children under 18 stay free. Min stay spec evnts. Lower rates off-season. Higher rates for spec evnts/hols. Pking: Outdoor, free. Maj CC.

≣≣ **Econo Lodge Resort of Key West**, 3820 N Roosevelt Blvd, Key West, FL 32040; tel 305/294-5511 or toll free 800/999-7277; fax 305/296-1939. Budget property. Rooms were

recently renovated. **Rooms:** 145 rms, stes, and effic. CI 3pm/CO 11am. Nonsmoking rms avail. The decor is better than you'd expect from a motel in this price category. **Amenities:** 🛅 🐧 A/C, cable TV. **Services:** 🛎 **Facilities:** 🏋 ⬆ 1 bar (w/entertainment), washer/dryer. **Rates:** HS Dec–Apr $145–$325 S or D. Extra person $10. Children under 18 stay free. Min stay spec evnts. Lower rates off-season. Pking: Outdoor, free. Maj CC.

≣≣ **Fairfield Inn by Marriott**, 2400 N Roosevelt Blvd, Key West, FL 33040; tel 305/296-5700 or toll free 800/843-5888; fax 305/292-9840. US 1 S to Roosevelt Blvd. Smart, attractive accommodations on nicely landscaped grounds. **Rooms:** 125 rms and stes. CI 3pm/CO 11am. Nonsmoking rms avail. **Amenities:** 🛅 🐧 A/C, cable TV. **Services:** 🛎 Babysitting. **Facilities:** 🏋 ⬆ 1 bar, washer/dryer. **Rates (CP):** HS Dec 22–Apr 17 $149 S; from $173 ste. Extra person $10. Children under 12 stay free. Min stay spec evnts. Lower rates off-season. Pking: Outdoor, free. Maj CC.

≣≣ **Hampton Inn**, 2801 N Roosevelt Blvd, Key West, FL 33040; tel 305/294-2917 or toll free 800/394-1634; fax 305/296-0211. Reliable accommodations overlooking the Gulf, with limited services and facilities. **Rooms:** 158 rms and stes. CI 3pm/CO noon. Nonsmoking rms avail. **Amenities:** 🛅 A/C, cable TV w/movies. 1 unit w/Jacuzzi. **Services:** 🏖 🛎 🚐 Continental breakfast buffet. **Facilities:** 🏋 🎿 ⬆ 1 bar (w/entertainment), whirlpool, washer/dryer. **Rates (CP):** HS Mid-Dec–Apr $95–$149 S or D; from $180 ste. Min stay spec evnts. Lower rates off-season. Higher rates for spec evnts/hols. Pking: Indoor/outdoor, free. Maj CC.

≣≣ **Key Wester Resort Inn & Villas**, 3675 S Roosevelt Blvd, Key West, FL 33040; or toll free 800/477-8888; fax 305/296-5671 Ext 419. US 1 S to Roosevelt Blvd. An array of lowrise buildings sprinkled roadside, near a public beach area. Limited landscaping. **Rooms:** 93 rms and effic; 12 ctges/villas. CI 2pm/CO 11am. Nonsmoking rms avail. **Amenities:** 🛅 A/C, cable TV. **Services:** 🛎 **Facilities:** 🏋 🎿 1 rst, 1 bar, games rm, sauna, washer/dryer. **Rates:** HS Dec–May $69–$149 S or D; from $125 effic; from $155 ctge/villa. Extra person $10. Children under 17 stay free. Min stay spec evnts. Lower rates off-season. Higher rates for spec evnts/hols. Spec packages avail. Pking: Outdoor, free. Maj CC.

≣≣ **Quality Inn of Key West**, 3850 N Roosevelt Blvd, Key West, FL 33040; tel 305/294-6681 or toll free 800/533-5024; fax 305/294-5618. A solid middle-grade operation. Gleaming lobby has lots of sunlight. **Rooms:** 148 rms, stes, and effic. CI 3pm/CO 11am. Nonsmoking rms avail. Units with kitchens are favored by self-sufficient guests and those staying longer than a weekend. **Amenities:** 🛅 🐧 📺 A/C, cable TV. **Services:** ✗ 🛎 **Facilities:** 🏋 ⬆ 1 rst, 1 bar, washer/dryer. **Rates:** HS Dec 26–

Mar 28 $90 S or D; from $189 ste; from $145 effic. Extra person $10–$20. Children under 18 stay free. Min stay spec evnts. Lower rates off-season. Higher rates for spec evnts/hols. Spec packages avail. Pking: Outdoor, free. Maj CC.

≣≣ **Ramada Inn at Key's Inn**, 3420 N Roosevelt Blvd, Key West, FL 33040; tel 305/294-5541 or toll free 800/330-5541; fax 305/294-7932. US 1 to Roosevelt Blvd. A lowrise hotel on a commercial strip, convenient to historic district and restaurants. **Rooms:** 104 rms, stes, and effic. CI 3pm/CO 11am. Nonsmoking rms avail. **Amenities:** 🛎 A/C, cable TV. **Services:** ✗ ⤴ ⬧ Babysitting. **Facilities:** 🔥 ⬜ ⬛ 1 rst, 1 bar (w/entertainment), playground, washer/dryer. Tiki bar in large pool area. **Rates:** HS Dec 25–Apr $149 D; from $209 ste; from $229 effic. Extra person $10. Children under 18 stay free. Min stay spec evnts. Lower rates off-season. Higher rates for spec evnts/hols. Spec packages avail. Pking: Outdoor, free. Maj CC.

≣≣ **Santa Maria Motel**, 1401 Simonton St, Key West, FL 33040; tel 305/296-5678 or toll free 800/821-5397; fax 305/294-0010. An art deco motel, just a half-block to the beach and handy to restaurants. Spacious lobby. **Rooms:** 50 rms and effic. CI 2:30pm/CO noon. Units are cool and comfortable. **Amenities:** 🛎 A/C, cable TV. Some units w/terraces. **Services:** ⤴ Babysitting. **Facilities:** 🔥 ⬛ 1 bar. **Rates:** HS Dec–Apr $135–$155 S or D; from $145 effic. Extra person $20. Children under 12 stay free. Min stay spec evnts. Lower rates off-season. Higher rates for spec evnts/hols. Pking: Outdoor, free. Maj CC.

≣≣ **South Beach Oceanfront Motel**, 508 South St, Key West, FL 33040; tel 305/296-5611 or toll free 800/354-4455; fax 305/294-8272. A beachside property popular among the younger crowd. Beach affords good swimming. **Rooms:** 47 rms, stes, and effic. CI 1pm/CO 11am. Nonsmoking rms avail. **Amenities:** 🛎 ⬛ A/C, cable TV, refrig, in-rm safe. Some units w/terraces. **Services:** ⬛ ⤴ Babysitting. **Facilities:** 🔥 ⬌ 1 beach (ocean), snorkeling. 150-foot pier for sunbathing. **Rates:** HS Dec–Apr $89–$197 S; $104–$197 D; from $167 ste; from $177 effic. Extra person $15. Children under 12 stay free. Min stay spec evnts. Lower rates off-season. Higher rates for spec evnts/hols. Spec packages avail. Pking: Outdoor, free. Maj CC.

≣≣ **Southernmost Motel in the USA**, 1319 Duval St, Key West, FL 33040; tel 305/296-6577 or toll free 800/354-4455; fax 305/294-8272. Handsomely outfitted, near the beach. **Rooms:** 127 rms and effic. CI 1pm/CO 11am. Nonsmoking rms avail. Fine accommodations; some open to pool. **Amenities:** 🛎 ⬧ A/C, cable TV, in-rm safe. Some units w/terraces. **Services:** 🔌 ⬛ ⤴ Babysitting. **Facilities:** 🔥 ⬌ ⬜ ⬛ 1 bar, whirlpool. **Rates:** HS Dec–Apr $99–$175 S or D; from $185 effic. Extra person $10. Children under 12 stay free. Min stay wknds. Lower rates off-season. Pking: Outdoor, free. Maj CC.

Inns

≣≣ **The Curry Mansion Inn**, 511 Caroline St, Key West, FL 33040; tel 305/294-5349 or toll free 800/253-3466; fax 305/294-4093. ½ block N of Duval St. This former mansion, listed on the National Register of Historic Places, is a popular sightseeing attraction (*see also* "Attractions" below) as well as a notable bed-and-breakfast. The inn is furnished with antiques in the main inn and wicker pieces in the annex; the lobby has beautiful hardwood floors and a tiled fireplace. Within walking distance of historic attractions, shopping, Mallory Square. **Rooms:** 29 rms and stes. CI 2pm/CO 11am. The few original mansion guest rooms are preferable to the annex rooms. **Amenities:** 🛎 ⬧ A/C, cable TV, refrig. Some units w/terraces, some w/Jacuzzis. **Services:** ⬛ Wine/sherry served. **Facilities:** 🔥 ⬛ Whirlpool, washer/dryer, guest lounge. Guests receive passes to Casa Marina's beach or to Pier House Beach Club, a block away. **Rates (CP):** HS Dec–Apr $150–$200 S or D; from $220 ste. Extra person $25. Children under 16 stay free. Min stay spec evnts. Lower rates off-season. Higher rates for spec evnts/hols. Pking: Outdoor, free. Ltd CC.

≣≣ **Heron House**, 512 Simonton St, Key West, FL 33040; tel 305/294-9227 or toll free 800/294-1644; fax 305/294-5692. 1 block E of Duval St. These 4 homes, set around a brick courtyard with a lush pool, date back to 1856. Unsuitable for children under 12. **Rooms:** 23 rms. CI 1pm/CO 11am. Many rooms open onto the courtyard. **Amenities:** 🛎 ⬧ A/C, cable TV, refrig. Some units w/terraces, 1 w/Jacuzzi. **Facilities:** 🔥 ⬛ Guest lounge. Breakfast bar. **Rates (BB):** HS Dec–Apr $125–$185 S or D. Extra person $20. Min stay spec evnts. Lower rates off-season. Higher rates for spec evnts/hols. Ltd CC.

≣≣ **Island City House Hotel**, 411 William St, Key West, FL 33040; tel 305/294-5702 or toll free 800/634-8230; fax 305/294-1289. 3 blocks E of Duval St. Consists of 3 guest houses dating back to the 1880s. Lush tropical gardens. **Rooms:** 24 stes. CI 2pm/CO 11am. All suites, some with marble baths, are furnished with antiques, hardwood floors, and paddle fans. **Amenities:** 🛎 ⬛ A/C, cable TV, refrig. Some units w/terraces. **Services:** ⤴ Breakfast buffet served on courtyard patio. **Facilities:** 🔥 ⬌ Whirlpool. **Rates (CP):** HS Dec–Apr from $165 ste. Extra person $20. Children under 12 stay free. Min stay spec evnts. Lower rates off-season. Higher rates for spec evnts/hols. Ltd CC.

≣≣ **La Mer**, 506 South St, Key West, FL 33040; tel 305/296-5611; fax 305/294-8272. An early-1900s Victorian clapboard home on the beach, this is a lovely, upscale property. No children under 16. **Rooms:** 58 rms, stes, and effic. CI 1pm/CO 11am. Pleasant, spacious country inn–style rooms with ceiling fans and attractive appointments. **Amenities:** 🛎 ⬧ ⬛ A/C, cable

TV, in-rm safe. All units w/minibars, some w/terraces. **Services:** 🖾 Afternoon tea and wine/sherry served. **Facilities:** 1 beach (ocean), guest lounge. Guests have access to pools at Southernmost Motel and South Beach Oceanfront Motel. **Rates (CP):** HS Dec–Apr $175–$210 S or D; from $175 ste; from $185 effic. Extra person $10. Min stay spec evnts. Lower rates off-season. Higher rates for spec evnts/hols. Spec packages avail. Pking: Outdoor, free. Ltd CC.

≡≡≡≡ **The Marquesa Hotel**, 600 Fleming St, Key West, FL 33040; tel 305/292-1919 or toll free 800/869-4631; fax 305/294-2121. Located 1 block east of Duval St. Luxurious, finely restored clapboard Victorian home with plush furnishings. Charming and delightful. **Rooms:** 27 rms and stes. CI 3pm/CO noon. Each room or suite is different, most with gilded mirrors, original art, and fresh flowers. **Amenities:** 📻 🗘 A/C, cable TV w/movies, in-rm safe, bathrobes. All units w/minibars, some w/terraces. **Services:** ✕ 𝖵𝖯 🖾 Twice-daily maid svce, wine/sherry served. **Facilities:** 🖫 1 rst (*see also* "Restaurants" below), 1 bar, guest lounge. First-rate restaurant. **Rates:** HS Dec–Apr $175–$200 D; from $235 ste. Extra person $15. Min stay wknds. Lower rates off-season. Higher rates for spec evnts/hols. Spec packages avail. Pking: Outdoor, free. Ltd CC.

≡≡≡ **Simonton Court Historic Inn and Cottages**, 320 Simonton St, Key West, FL 33040; tel 305/294-6386 or toll free 800/944-2687; fax 305/293-8446. 1 block E of Duval St. Unsuitable for children under 18. **Rooms:** 17 rms, stes, and effic; 6 ctges/villas. CI 2pm/CO 11am. **Amenities:** 📻 🗘 🗖 🍷 A/C, cable TV, refrig, in-rm safe. All units w/terraces, 1 w/Jacuzzi. **Services:** 🖾 Twice-daily maid svce. **Facilities:** 🖫 Whirlpool. **Rates (CP):** HS Dec–Apr $150 S or D; from $175 ste; from $150 effic; from $280 ctge/villa. Extra person $10. Min stay HS and spec evnts. Lower rates off-season. Pking: Outdoor, $5. Ltd CC.

≡ **Wicker Guesthouse**, 913 Duval St, Key West, FL 33040; tel 305/296-4275 or toll free 800/880-4275; fax 305/294-7240. Casual, low-key lodging in an atmospheric, cream-colored clapboard house. Well-priced. **Rooms:** 20 rms and effic (9 w/shared bath). CI 2pm/CO 11am. Some rooms share living space and kitchen. Rooms are appropriately appointed with lots of wicker furnishings. **Amenities:** A/C. No phone or TV. Some units w/terraces. Only some rooms with TV. **Services:** 🛏 Babysitting. **Facilities:** 🖫 🕭 Guest lounge w/TV. Some rooms open to pool. **Rates:** HS Dec–Apr $63–$75 S or D w/shared bath, $95 S or D w/private bath; from $125 effic. Extra person $10. Children under 12 stay free. Min stay HS and spec evnts. Lower rates off-season. Pking: Outdoor, free. Ltd CC.

Resort

≡≡≡ **Marriott's Casa Marina Resort**, 1500 Reynolds St, Key West, FL 33040; tel 305/296-3535 or toll free 800/228-9290, 800/626-0777, 800/235-4837 in FL; fax 305/296-9960. At Flagler Ave. 8 acres. This historic property, built in the 1920s by railroad tycoon Henry Flagler, is one of the Keys' most enduring and romantic spots. It is set on a huge swath of oceanfront and has some of the most charming public areas south of Miami, though guest rooms are fairly ordinary. **Rooms:** 312 rms and stes. CI 4pm/CO 11am. Nonsmoking rms avail. **Amenities:** 📻 🗘 🍷 A/C, cable TV w/movies, in-rm safe, bathrobes. All units w/minibars, all w/terraces. **Services:** ✕ 🍽 𝖵𝖯 🚗 🖾 🛏 Social director, masseur, children's program, babysitting. **Facilities:** 🖫 🚴 ⚠ 🗒 🖎 🛶 🍴 🔤 🕭 2 rsts, 2 bars (1 w/entertainment), 1 beach (ocean), spa, sauna, whirlpool, beauty salon. **Rates:** HS Dec–Apr $250–$325 S or D; from $325 ste. Extra person $25. Children under 18 stay free. Lower rates off-season. Higher rates for spec evnts/hols. Spec packages avail. Pking: Outdoor, free. Maj CC.

Restaurants 🍴

Antonia's, 615 Duval St, Key West; tel 305/294-6464. **Northern Italian.** Dark wood and crisp white linen adorn the interior of this romantic northern Italian. **FYI:** Reservations recommended. Beer and wine only. **Open:** Daily 6–11pm. **Prices:** Main courses $12.50–$22. Maj CC. 💗 🕭

Bagatelle, 115 Duval St, Key West; tel 305/296-6609. **Caribbean.** Gingerbread-style architectural details ornament this casually elegant eatery. The menu features fresh local seafood prepared with a tropical flair, such as sautéed grouper with macadamia crust in a mango-butter sauce. Expansive veranda. **FYI:** Reservations recommended. Piano. **Open:** Lunch daily 11:30am–4:30pm; dinner daily 6–10:30pm. Closed some hols. **Prices:** Main courses $9.95–$20. Maj CC.

Café des Artistes, 1007 Simonton St, Key West; tel 305/294-7100. **French.** A lovely cafe with contemporary works of art covering its walls. The house specialty is Lobster Tango Mango. An extensive wine list is available. **FYI:** Reservations recommended. **Open:** Daily 6–11pm. **Prices:** Main courses $18–$24. Maj CC. 💗 🍷

💗 ⭐ **Café Marquesa**, in the Marquesa Hotel, 600 Fleming St, Key West; tel 305/292-1244. 1 block E of Duval St. **New American/Eclectic.** A smart, colorful, sophisticated cafe with a formal atmosphere and menu. A local favorite. **FYI:** Reservations recommended. No smoking. **Open:** HS Dec–Apr daily 6–11pm. Reduced hours off-season. **Prices:** Main courses $18–$25. Maj CC. 💗

⑤ **Croissants de France**, 816 Duval St, Key West; tel 305/294-2624. **French/Middle Eastern.** A wonderful French cafe with its own pastry shop, serving breakfast, lunch, and dinner. The menu offers continental breakfast with cappuccino or café au lait, salads, entrees like lobster à l'américaine, and 10 flavors of homemade ice cream. Out-of-the-oven french bread is served. **FYI:** Reservations not accepted. Beer and wine only. **Open:** Breakfast Thurs–Tues 7:30–11am; dinner Thurs–Tues 6:00–10:30pm. Closed Labor Day. **Prices:** Main courses $10–$15. Ltd CC. ♥ ☎ 🎴 ⑤

⑤ ★ **Half Shell Raw Bar**, 231 Margaret St, Key West; tel 305/294-7496. **Seafood.** This appealing place, catering to tourists and locals alike, is decorated with license plates from all 50 states. You can sit at a picnic table and enjoy the catch of the day or oysters on the half-shell. **FYI:** Reservations not accepted. Children's menu. **Open:** Mon–Sat 11am–10pm, Sun noon–10pm. **Prices:** Main courses $5–$20. Ltd CC. ☎ 🖼

Jimmy Buffet's Margaritaville Cafe, 500 Duval St, Key West; tel 305/292-1435. **New American.** A collegiate-style eatery frequented by a generally young crowd. The menu includes salads, burgers, fish sandwiches, and the catch of the day, prepared deep-fried or grilled. Ben & Jerry's ice cream is available for dessert. **FYI:** Reservations not accepted. Band. **Open:** Sun–Thurs 11am–2am, Fri–Sat 11am–4am. **Prices:** Main courses $3.95–$12.95. Maj CC.

Jupiter Crab Co, in Sheraton Suites Key West, 2001 S Roosevelt Blvd, Key West; tel 305/293-9792. **American/Seafood.** A popular seafood spot with tropical decor featuring an aquarium and exotic birds. Dining offered outdoors by the pool. **FYI:** Reservations accepted. Guitar/singer. Children's menu. **Open:** Breakfast daily 6:30–10:30am; lunch daily 11:30am–5pm; dinner daily 5–11:30pm. **Prices:** Main courses $2.50–$20.95. Maj CC. 🎴 ⑤

Kelly's Caribbean Bar and Grill and Brewery, 301 Whitehead St, Key West; tel 305/293-8484. **Caribbean.** The only microbrewery in the Florida Keys. Indoor tables are available, but most patrons seem to prefer the tree-shaded outdoor dining area. The lunch menu includes cold curried seafood salad with mango chutney. Dinner entrees might include grilled jerk chicken breast with tamarind sweet-and-sour sauce. **FYI:** Reservations not accepted. Guitar/piano. Children's menu. **Open:** Daily 11am–1am. **Prices:** Main courses $6.95–$18.95. Maj CC. ☎ ⑤

La-Te-Da's, 1125 Duval St, Key West; tel 305/296-6706. **Seafood/Steak.** A beautiful, colorful little cafe with a great bar. Steaks, pastas, seafood dishes. Intimate outdoor dining available. **FYI:** Reservations accepted. **Open:** Lunch Mon–Sat 8am–3pm; dinner Mon–Sat 6–11pm. **Prices:** Main courses $11.95–$16.95. Maj CC. ☎ ⑤

★ **Louie's Backyard**, 700 Waddell Ave, Key West; tel 305/294-1061. **Caribbean/Eclectic.** This appealing open-air waterfront cafe is perfect for a casual lunch, a romantic dinner, or just a nightcap. The creative menu includes New Zealand venison, grouper, and wonderful salads. **FYI:** Reservations recommended. Jazz. Dress code. **Open:** HS Oct–Aug daily 11:30am–10pm. Reduced hours off-season. **Prices:** Main courses $25–$30. Maj CC. ■ ☎ 🏔

Papa's Banyan Tree Cafe, 217 Duval St, Key West; tel 305/293-0555. **New American.** A huge gumbo-limbo tree provides shade at this outdoor cafe. The simple lunch menu includes pizzas and burgers. For dinner, surf-and-turf and the catch of the day, served blackened, baked, or jerk-style, are available. **FYI:** Reservations not accepted. Children's menu. Beer and wine only. **Open:** Daily 11:30am–11pm. **Prices:** Main courses $9.95–$23.95. Maj CC. ☎ ▼ ⑤

Square One, in Duval Square, 1075 Duval St, Key West; tel 305/296-4300. **New American.** A beautiful, elegant dining room filled with floral murals and live piano music. Before dinner, you can enjoy cocktails at a fountainside table. Fresh fish and pasta are featured on the contemporary menu. **FYI:** Reservations recommended. Piano. **Open:** HS Oct–June daily 6:30pm–midnight. Reduced hours off-season. **Prices:** Main courses $14–$21. Maj CC. ♥ ⑤

Yo Saké, 722 Duval St, Key West; tel 305/294-2288. **Japanese.** Delicate lighting and cool, lively ambience. Favorites include seafood combo, beef Yakiniku, and sushi. **FYI:** Reservations accepted. Beer and wine only. **Open:** Daily 6–11pm. Closed Dec 25. **Prices:** Main courses $10–$18. Maj CC.

Attractions 🖼

Ernest Hemingway House Museum, 907 Whitehead St; tel 305/294-1575. The Nobel Prize–winning author owned this beautiful Spanish colonial house from 1931 to 1961. It was here that he wrote such novels as *For Whom the Bell Tolls, Death in the Afternoon,* and *To Have and Have Not,* and the short stories "The Snows of Kilimanjaro" and "The Short, Happy Life of Francis Macomber." Built in 1851, the house was one of the first in Key West to be fitted with indoor plumbing. It was opened to the public in 1963, 2 years after Hemingway's death, and contains many personal possessions as well as dozens of 6-toed cats, said by some to be descendants of a feline family that was here in Hemingway's day. **Open:** Daily 9am–5pm. Closed some hols. $$$

Little White House, 111 Front St; tel 305/294-9911. Built in 1890 as the residence of the naval base commandant, the house has been restored to its 1940s appearance. President Harry

Truman spent 11 working vacations here, which is how the house came by its name. Guided tours include a look at original Truman furnishings and memorabilia. **Open:** Daily 9am–5pm. $$$

Audubon House and Gardens, 205 Whitehead St; tel 305/294-2116. The restored 3-story house, surrounded by lush tropical gardens, features the master artist's original etchings and a large collection of lithographs. The house also holds a collection of porcelain birds and period furnishings. **Open:** Daily 9:30am–5pm. $$$

Curry Mansion, 511 Caroline St; tel 305/294-5349. Built in 1855 for William Curry, Florida's first millionaire, this "conch-style" house is a tribute to the early days of Key West and is listed in the National Register of Historic Places. Inside are an eclectic mix of stylish furnishings (including a Frank Lloyd Wright–designed lamp), Tiffany glass, mahogany paneling, and Audubon prints. Part of the mansion operates as a bed-and-breakfast. **Open:** Daily 10am–5pm. $$

East Martello Museum and Gallery, 3501 S Roosevelt Blvd; tel 305/296-3913. Housed in a pre–Civil War fort, the museum's various exhibits and artifacts illustrate Key West's history of shipwrecks, pirates, sponging, and cigar-making. Works of local artists are also displayed. **Open:** Daily 9am–5pm. $$

Key West Lighthouse Museum, 938 Whitehead St; tel 305/294-0012. Built in 1847, this historic brick lighthouse has 88 steps leading to the top lead to the observation level, where visitors have a panoramic view of Key West and the Florida Keys. **Open:** Daily 9:30am–5pm. $$

Mallory Pier Sunset Celebration. Every evening, just before sunset, locals and visitors alike gather at the docks to celebrate the day gone by. Numerous street-theater performers, such as magicians, jugglers, acrobats, and mimes, entertain.

Key West Cemetery, Margaret and Angela Sts. This decidedly unsolemn cemetery of above-ground vaults (a high water table and rocky soil prevent traditional below-ground interment) is worth a stroll. Many memorials are marked with amusing nicknames or tongue-in-cheek epitaphs like "I told you I was sick" or one widow's "At least I know where he's sleeping tonight."

Mel Fisher's Treasure Museum, 200 Greene St; tel 305/294-2633. Some of the $400 million in treasure from the sunken Spanish galleons *Atocha* and *Santa Margarita* are displayed. Although many of the doubloons, emeralds, and solid gold bars are copies, there are authentic cannons, historic weapons, and other artifacts for viewing. **Open:** Daily 9:30am–5pm. $$

KISSIMMEE

Map page M-7, D2

Hotels 🛏

≣≣ **Best Western Eastgate**, 5565 W Irlo Bronson Memorial Pkwy, Kissimmee, FL 34746; tel 407/396-0707 or toll free 800/223-5361; fax 407/396-6644. Exit 25A off I-4. A good family value, it's set back from the road and fronted by a small pond. Central courtyard has pool and whirlpool. **Rooms:** 403 rms. CI 4pm/CO noon. Nonsmoking rms avail. The choicest units are those facing the courtyard, but they tend to be more noisy. **Amenities:** 🛏 🔥 A/C, cable TV. **Services:** 🖦 🚗 🖼 🍴 ⚓ Car-rental desk, babysitting. **Facilities:** 🏋 🍹 🔥 1 rst, games rm, whirlpool, playground. **Rates:** HS Christmas/Feb–Apr/June–Aug $61 S; $71 D. Extra person $10. Children under 18 stay free. Lower rates off-season. Higher rates for spec evnts/hols. Spec packages avail. Pking: Outdoor, free. Maj CC.

≣≣ **Days Inn Maingate West**, 7980 W Irlo Bronson Memorial Hwy, Kissimmee, FL 34747; tel 407/396-8000 or toll free 800/327-9173, 800/432-9926 in FL; fax 407/396-6542. 18 mi S of Orlando, exit 25B off I-4. **Rooms:** 304 rms and stes. CI 3pm/CO 11am. Nonsmoking rms avail. **Amenities:** 🛏 🔥 A/C, cable TV. **Services:** 🚗 🖼 🍴 ⚓ Car-rental desk, babysitting. **Facilities:** 🏋 🍹 🔥 1 rst, games rm, playground, washer/dryer. **Rates:** HS June–Aug $35–$55 S or D; from $65 ste. Children under 18 stay free. Lower rates off-season. Higher rates for spec evnts/hols. Spec packages avail. Pking: Outdoor, free. Maj CC.

≣≣ **Holiday Inn Maingate East**, 5678 Irlo Bronson Memorial Hwy, Kissimmee, FL 32804; tel 407/396-4488 or toll free 800/FON-KIDS; fax 407/396-8915. 13 mi W of downtown Kissimmee, exit 25A off I-4. 3 mi E of Walt Disney World Resort. One of the more routine local Holiday Inns, although it does offer lots of activities for kids. **Rooms:** 670 rms. CI 3pm/CO 11am. Nonsmoking rms avail. Poolside units offer direct access to courtyard. **Amenities:** 🛏 🔥 📺 A/C, cable TV, refrig, VCR, in-rm safe. **Services:** ✕ 🖦 🚗 🖼 🍴 ⚓ Car-rental desk, children's program, babysitting. **Facilities:** 🏋 🍹 🔥 2 rsts, 2 bars, games rm, lawn games, whirlpool, day-care ctr, playground, washer/dryer. **Rates (BB):** HS Feb–Apr/June–Aug/Dec $75–$119 S or D. Children under 18 stay free. Lower rates off-season. Higher rates for spec evnts/hols. Spec packages avail. Pking: Outdoor, free. Maj CC.

≣≣ **Holiday Inn Maingate Resort Hotel**, 7300 Irlo Bronson Memorial Hwy, Kissimmee, FL 34747; tel 407/396-7300 or toll free 800/621-9378; fax 407/396-7555. 16 mi W of Orlando, exit 25B off I-4. Sprawling hotel that is a mecca for children, with its swimming pools, playground, and other recreational facilities. **Rooms:** 529 rms. CI 4pm/CO 11am. Nonsmoking rms avail. **Amenities:** 🛏 🕭 🕮 A/C, cable TV w/movies, in-rm safe. Some units w/minibars. **Services:** ✗ 🍽 🚍 🎨 🖉 Car-rental desk, children's program, babysitting. **Facilities:** 🏠 🍳 🕭 3 rsts, 1 bar, games rm, whirlpool, playground, washer/dryer. **Rates:** HS June–Sept $79–$109 S or D. Children under 18 stay free. Lower rates off-season. Higher rates for spec evnts/hols. Spec packages avail. Pking: Outdoor, free. Maj CC.

≣≣ **Holiday Inn Maingate West**, 7601 Black Lake Rd, Kissimmee, FL 34747; tel 407/240-7100 or toll free 800/ENJOY FL; fax 407/396-0689. Exit 25B off I-4. From I-4 take the Disney World exit (25B). Proceed 2½ miles west and turn right at first light. Draws many families, who come for the varied facilities and the kids-under-12-eat-free policy. Glittering atrium lobby. **Rooms:** 287 rms. CI 4pm/CO 11am. Nonsmoking rms avail. **Amenities:** 🛏 🕭 A/C, cable TV, VCR, in-rm safe. **Services:** ✗ 🍽 🚍 🎨 🖉 Car-rental desk, babysitting. **Facilities:** 🏠 🚲 💯 1 rst, 1 bar, games rm, lawn games, washer/dryer. **Rates:** HS June–Sept $95–$105 S or D. Children under 18 stay free. Lower rates off-season. Higher rates for spec evnts/hols. AP rates avail. Spec packages avail. Pking: Outdoor, free. Maj CC.

≣≣ **Howard Johnson Fountain Park Plaza Hotel**, 5150 W Irlo Bronson Memorial Hwy, Kissimmee, FL 34746; tel 407/396-1111 or toll free 800/327-9179; fax 407/396-1607. A range of accommodations housed in both midrise and highrise buildings, with attractive public areas and lovely manicured grounds. **Rooms:** 400 rms. CI 4pm/CO 11am. Nonsmoking rms avail. **Amenities:** 🛏 🕭 🕮 A/C, cable TV w/movies, VCR. Some units w/minibars, all w/terraces. **Services:** ✗ 🚍 🎨 🖉 Car-rental desk, babysitting. **Facilities:** 🏠 ⚠ 📱 💯 🕭 1 rst, 1 bar, games rm, lawn games, sauna, whirlpool, playground, washer/dryer. **Rates:** HS Feb–Apr/June–Aug $69–$99 S or D. Children under 18 stay free. Lower rates off-season. Spec packages avail. Pking: Outdoor, free. Maj CC.

≣≣ **Howard Johnson Maingate Hotel**, 7600 W Irlo Bronson Memorial Hwy, Kissimmee, FL 34747; tel 407/396-2500 or toll free 800/432-4335; fax 407/396-2096. 12 mi W of Orlando, exit 25B off I-4. Does not quite measure up to its sibling up the road, the Fountain Park Plaza (see above), but is nonetheless a fairly popular rest stop for families playing at Disney World. Its scaled-down facilities are more basic than those offered at hotels costing just a few dollars more. **Rooms:** 206 rms. CI 4pm/CO noon. Nonsmoking rms avail. **Amenities:** 🛏 🕭 A/C, satel TV, in-rm safe. Some units w/terraces. **Services:** 🚍 🎨 🖉 Car-rental desk, babysitting. **Facilities:** 🏠 🕭 1 rst, games rm, lawn games,

washer/dryer. **Rates:** HS Feb–Apr/June–Aug $68–$89 S or D. Extra person $10. Children under 17 stay free. Lower rates off-season. Pking: Outdoor, free. Maj CC.

≣≣≣ **Hyatt Orlando**, 6375 W Irlo Bronson Hwy, Kissimmee, FL 34747; tel 407/396-1234 or toll free 800/233-1234; fax 407/396-5024. Exit 25 off I-4. 56 acres. Situated on expansive grounds in an area of many hotels and restaurants, this complex offers an attractive package of facilities, services, and recreational diversions. This is a suburban version of a Hyatt hotel: comfortable and subdued. **Rooms:** 922 rms and stes. CI 4pm/CO noon. Nonsmoking rms avail. **Amenities:** 🛏 🕭 A/C, cable TV w/movies, in-rm safe. All units w/terraces. **Services:** ✗ 🍽 🅥🅟 🚍 🎨 🖉 Car-rental desk, children's program, babysitting. **Facilities:** 🏠 🎾 🍳 🏓 🔟 🕭 4 rsts, 1 bar, games rm, lawn games, whirlpool, beauty salon, playground, washer/dryer. **Rates:** HS Jan–Mar/June–July $119–$134 S or D; from $180 ste. Extra person $20. Children under 18 stay free. Lower rates off-season. Higher rates for spec evnts/hols. Spec packages avail. Pking: Outdoor, free. Maj CC.

≣≣≣ **Orlando/Kissimmee Gateway Hilton Inn**, 7470 US 192 W, Kissimmee, FL 34747; tel 407/396-4400 or toll free 800/327-9170; fax 407/396-4320. 1 mi W of Walt Disney World, exit 25B off I-4. One of the area's favorites, providing good value for families. **Rooms:** 500 rms and stes. CI 3pm/CO noon. Nonsmoking rms avail. **Amenities:** 🛏 🕭 A/C, cable TV w/movies, in-rm safe. Some rooms have microwaves. **Services:** ✗ 🚍 🎨 🖉 Car-rental desk. **Facilities:** 🏠 🏓 🔟 🕭 1 rst, 3 bars (1 w/entertainment), games rm, lawn games, washer/dryer. **Rates:** HS Jan–Mar/June–July $80–$110 S or D; from $160 ste. Extra person $15. Children under 18 stay free. Lower rates off-season. Higher rates for spec evnts/hols. AP rates avail. Spec packages avail. Pking: Indoor/outdoor, free. Maj CC.

≣≣ **Quality Inn Maingate**, 7675 W Irlo Bronson Memorial Hwy, Kissimmee, FL 34747; tel 407/396-4000 or toll free 800/568-3352; fax 407/396-0714. Exit 25B off I-4. 1 mi from the Walt Disney World Resort. Popular choice for families. **Rooms:** 199 rms, stes, and effic. CI 3pm/CO 11am. Nonsmoking rms avail. **Amenities:** 🛏 🕭 A/C, cable TV w/movies, VCR, in-rm safe. Kitchen units are equipped with stove, refrigerator, coffeemaker, microwave, and wet bar. **Services:** 🍽 🚍 🎨 🖉 Car-rental desk, babysitting. **Facilities:** 🏠 🔢 🕭 1 rst, 1 bar, games rm, washer/dryer. **Rates:** HS May–Oct $49–$69 S or D; from $59 ste; from $59 effic. Children under 18 stay free. Lower rates off-season. Higher rates for spec evnts/hols. Pking: Outdoor, free. Maj CC.

≣≣ **Radisson Inn Maingate**, 7501 W Irlo Bronson Hwy, Kissimmee, FL 34747; tel 407/396-1400 or toll free 800/333-3333; fax 407/396-0660. 15 mi W of Orlando, exit 25B off

I-4. The 2 modern 7-story buildings are connected by a restaurant and registration area, and offer more style than similarly priced hotels nearby. Located near Disney's main gate area, where there are a number of fast food eateries. **Rooms:** 580 rms and stes. CI 3pm/CO noon. Nonsmoking rms avail. **Amenities:** ⬚ ⬚ ⬚ A/C, cable TV, in-rm safe. Some units w/minibars, some w/Jacuzzis. **Services:** ✗ ⬚ ⬚ ⬚ ⬚ Car-rental desk, babysitting. **Facilities:** ⬚ ⬚ ⬚ ⬚ ⬚ 2 rsts, 2 bars, games rm, lawn games, whirlpool, washer/dryer. Courtyard. **Rates:** HS Jan–Apr/July/Dec $75–$85 S or D; from $125 ste. Extra person $10. Children under 18 stay free. Lower rates off-season. Spec packages avail. Pking: Outdoor, free. Maj CC.

≣≣ **Ramada Resort Maingate**, 2950 Reedy Creek Blvd, Kissimmee, FL 34747; tel 407/396-4466 or toll free 800/ENJOY FL; fax 407/396-6418. Exit 25B off I-4. Pleasant family hotel with a functional, contemporary lobby. Another middle-grade choice in the jumble of hotels clustered around Disney World's main gate. **Rooms:** 391 rms and stes. CI 4pm/CO noon. Nonsmoking rms avail. **Amenities:** ⬚ ⬚ A/C, cable TV, VCR, in-rm safe. **Services:** ✗ ⬚ ⬚ ⬚ Car-rental desk, babysitting. **Facilities:** ⬚ ⬚ ⬚ ⬚ 1 rst, 2 bars, games rm, washer/dryer. **Rates:** HS Feb–Aug $69–$99 S or D; from $150 ste. Extra person $10. Children under 18 stay free. Lower rates off-season. Higher rates for spec evnts/hols. Spec packages avail. Pking: Outdoor, free. Maj CC.

≣≣ **Residence Inn by Marriott on Lake Circle**, 4786 W Irlo Bronson Memorial Hwy, Kissimmee, FL 34746; tel 407/396-2056 or toll free 800/468-3027; fax 407/396-2906. US 192 exit off I-4. Set on a pretty lake, these family-oriented accommodations afford privacy and style as well as some wonderful views. **Rooms:** 159 rms. CI 4pm/CO 11am. Nonsmoking rms avail. Each unit has a fully equipped kitchen, including dishwasher and utensils. **Amenities:** ⬚ ⬚ ⬚ A/C, cable TV, refrig, in-rm safe. All units w/terraces, some w/fireplaces. **Services:** ⬚ ⬚ Twice-daily maid svce, car-rental desk, babysitting. **Facilities:** ⬚ ⬚ ⬚ ⬚ ⬚ ⬚ ⬚ 1 bar, games rm, lawn games, whirlpool, playground, washer/dryer. **Rates (CP):** HS June–Sept/Dec–Apr from $84 ste. Children under 18 stay free. Lower rates off-season. Pking: Outdoor, free. Maj CC.

≣≣≣ **Sheraton Inn Lakeside**, 7769 W Irlo Bronson Memorial Hwy, Kissimmee, FL 34747; tel 407/396-2222 or toll free 800/848-0801; fax 407/239-2650. 20 mi S of Orlando, exit 25B off I-4. One of the area's more attractive properties, helped by regular renovations. Close to Disney World's main gate but away from the hyper-commercialism of the neon strip, its lakeside locale helps create a soothing atmosphere. **Rooms:** 651 rms. CI 4pm/CO 11am. Nonsmoking rms avail. Comfortable rooms in pleasing designs are warm and restful. **Amenities:** ⬚ ⬚ A/C,

cable TV, refrig, in-rm safe. Some units w/terraces. **Services:** ✗ ⬚ ⬚ ⬚ ⬚ ⬚ Car-rental desk, children's program, babysitting. **Facilities:** ⬚ ⬚ ⬚ ⬚ ⬚ ⬚ ⬚ 2 rsts, 1 bar, games rm, playground, washer/dryer. **Rates:** HS Feb–Apr/June–Aug/Dec $72–$125 S or D. Extra person $12. Children under 18 stay free. Lower rates off-season. Pking: Outdoor, free. Maj CC.

Sol Orlando Village Resort Hotel, 4787 W Irlo Bronson Memorial Hwy, Kissimmee, FL 34746; tel 407/397-0555 or toll free 800/292-9765; fax 407/397-1968. This delightful complex of self-contained, 2-level townhouses is a solid choice for families that require more space than a traditional hotel room affords. Unrated. **Rooms:** 150 ctges/villas. CI 3pm/CO 11am. Nonsmoking rms avail. **Amenities:** ⬚ ⬚ ⬚ ⬚ A/C, cable TV, refrig. All units w/terraces. **Services:** ⬚ ⬚ Babysitting. **Facilities:** ⬚ ⬚ ⬚ ⬚ ⬚ ⬚ 1 rst, 1 bar, games rm, lawn games, racquetball, squash, whirlpool, washer/dryer. A mini-grocery store stocks essentials; supermarkets are nearby. **Rates:** HS Dec 19–Apr from $120 ctge/villa. Lower rates off-season. Pking: Outdoor, free. Maj CC.

Motels

≣ **Colonial Motor Lodge**, 1815 W Vine St, Kissimmee, FL 34741; tel 407/847-6121 or toll free 800/325-4348, 800/432-3052 in FL; fax 407/847-0728. A family-run enterprise that's been in business for nearly a quarter-century. **Rooms:** 83 rms and stes. CI 1pm/CO 11am. Nonsmoking rms avail. Rooms were last renovated in 1992. **Amenities:** ⬚ A/C, cable TV w/movies, in-rm safe. **Services:** ⬚ ⬚ Car-rental desk. **Facilities:** ⬚ ⬚ Washer/dryer. **Rates:** HS Feb–Apr/June–Aug/Dec $29–$59 S or D; from $54 ste. Extra person $5. Children under 18 stay free. Lower rates off-season. Higher rates for spec evnts/hols. Spec packages avail. Pking: Outdoor, free. Maj CC.

≣≣ **Comfort Inn Maingate**, 7571 W Irlo Bronson Memorial Hwy, Kissimmee, FL 34747; tel 407/396-7500 or toll free 800/432-0887, 800/223-1628 in FL; fax 407/396-7497. Exit 25B off I-4. Clean, spiffy-looking standard motel accommodations in 2-story peach stucco buildings. Restaurant serves low-priced buffets and à la carte meals. **Rooms:** 281 rms. CI 4pm/CO 11am. Nonsmoking rms avail. Garden rooms face a lawn with a gazebo. **Amenities:** ⬚ ⬚ A/C, TV. **Services:** ⬚ ⬚ ⬚ Car-rental desk. **Facilities:** ⬚ ⬚ 1 rst, 1 bar, games rm, playground, washer/dryer. **Rates:** HS Jan–Apr/July–Dec $54–$84 S or D. Children under 18 stay free. Lower rates off-season. Higher rates for spec evnts/hols. Spec packages avail. Pking: Outdoor, free. Maj CC.

≣≣ **Econo Lodge Maingate Hawaiian Resort**, 7514 W Irlo Bronson Memorial Hwy, Kissimmee, FL 34717; tel 407/396-2000 or toll free 800/365-6935; fax 407/396-1295. Exit

25B off I-4. Budget lodging. **Rooms:** 445 rms. CI 4pm/CO 11am. Nonsmoking rms avail. Routine rooms done in pastels. **Amenities:** 🛏 🐾 A/C, cable TV, VCR, in-rm safe. Some units w/terraces. **Services:** 📞 🍽 🄰 🛎 Car-rental desk, babysitting. Staff provides minimal assistance. **Facilities:** 🔧 ⅖ 1 rst, 2 bars (1 w/entertainment), games rm, whirlpool, playground, washer/dryer. **Rates:** HS Feb–Apr/June–Aug/Dec 21–31 $49–$74 S or D. Children under 17 stay free. Lower rates off-season. Higher rates for spec evnts/hols. Pking: Outdoor, free. Maj CC.

≣≣ **Howard Johnson Inn Maingate**, 6051 W Irlo Bronson Memorial Hwy, Kissimmee, FL 34747; tel 407/396-1748 or toll free 800/288-4678; fax 407/649-8642. Exit 25A off I-4. A 5-story family hotel offering reasonable comfort in plain surroundings for a fair price. **Rooms:** 367 rms and stes. CI 4pm/CO noon. Nonsmoking rms avail. **Amenities:** 🛏 🐾 A/C, cable TV w/movies. **Services:** 📞 🍽 🄰 🛎 Car-rental desk. **Facilities:** 🔧 ⅖ 1 bar, games rm, whirlpool, playground, washer/dryer. **Rates:** HS Christmas/Feb–Apr/June–Aug $75 D; from $105 ste. Extra person $6. Children under 18 stay free. Lower rates off-season. Spec packages avail. Pking: Outdoor, free. Maj CC.

≣≣ **Ramada Resort Maingate at the Parkway**, 2900 Parkway Rd, Kissimmee, FL 34747; tel 407/396-7000 or toll free 800/634-4774; fax 407/396-6792. Exit 25 off I-4 W. Some nice architectural touches provide a look that's less routine than many comparable properties. **Rooms:** 718 rms and stes. CI 3pm/CO noon. Nonsmoking rms avail. **Amenities:** 🛏 🐾 A/C, cable TV, in-rm safe. **Services:** ✕ 🄰 🛎 Car-rental desk. **Facilities:** 🔧 ⛹ 🛝 ⅖ 1 rst, 2 bars, games rm, lawn games, sauna, whirlpool, playground, washer/dryer. **Rates:** HS June–Aug/Dec 21–31 $67–$95 S or D; from $165 ste. Children under 18 stay free. Lower rates off-season. Higher rates for spec evnts/hols. MAP rates avail. Spec packages avail. Pking: Outdoor, free. Maj CC.

≣≣ **Rodeway Inn Eastgate**, 5245 W 192, Kissimmee, FL 34746; tel 407/396-7700 or toll free 800/423-3864; fax 407/396-0293. Budget motel with a family restaurant and adjoining lounge. Blends in inconspicuously with the neon glow of the commercial strip. **Rooms:** 200 rms. CI 4pm/CO 11am. Nonsmoking rms avail. **Amenities:** 🛏 🐾 A/C, TV, in-rm safe. **Services:** 📞 🍽 🄰 🛎 🛟 Car-rental desk. **Facilities:** 🔧 ⅖ 1 rst, 1 bar, games rm, lawn games, playground, washer/dryer. **Rates:** HS Jan/Mar–Apr/June–Aug/Dec $45 D. Children under 18 stay free. Lower rates off-season. Higher rates for spec evnts/hols. Spec packages avail. Pking: Outdoor, free. Maj CC.

Resort

≣≣≣ **Orange Lake Country Club**, 8505 W Irlo Bronson Memorial Hwy, Kissimmee, FL 34747; tel 407/239-0000 or toll free 800/877-6522; fax 407/239-5119. A low-key spread set in a rural-like setting; makes an ideal choice for families who want everything under one roof but still need to stay on budget. The colorful main clubhouse building houses the registry, dining facilities, and many activities. **Rooms:** 50 stes. CI 4pm/CO 10am. Express checkout avail. **Amenities:** 🛏 🐾 📺 A/C, cable TV, VCR, voice mail. Some units w/minibars. **Services:** ✕ 📞 🍽 🄰 🛎 Car-rental desk, social director, children's program, babysitting. **Facilities:** 🔧 ⛷ ⛰ ▶27 ⚓6 🏊10 ⅖ 🎣 60 3 rsts, 2 bars (1 w/entertainment), 1 beach (lake shore), games rm, racquetball, sauna, beauty salon, playground, washer/dryer. **Rates:** HS Jun–Aug/Feb–Apr from $120 ste. Children under 18 stay free. Lower rates off-season. Pking: Outdoor, free. Maj CC.

Attractions 🏛

Flying Tigers Warbird Air Museum, 231 N Hoagland Blvd; tel 407/933-1942. This "working museum" focuses on the restoration of vintage aircraft to flying condition. Most aircraft are from the World War II era, with a few more modern and some antique planes as well; one plane dates from 1929. Guided tours include the restoration area, where visitors can watch work in progress. **Open:** Mon–Sat 9am–5:30pm, Sun 9am–5pm. $$$

Florida Splendid China, 3000 Splendid China Blvd; tel 407/396-7111. Located off US 192, 12 miles southwest of Orlando. Opened in late 1993, this 76-acre cultural theme park re-creates elements of the land and culture of China. It is a near duplicate of the original Splendid China near Hong Kong, which debuted in 1989. There are reproductions of more than 60 of China's most famous historic sites, all built to various scales using authentic materials and adorned with painstaking detail. More than 100 Chinese artisans spent 2 years working in Florida to complete the project. Among the sites are the half-mile-long scale replica of the Great Wall, made up of 6.5 million hand-laid miniature bricks; the Forbidden City and its 9,999-room Imperial Palace; a 35-foot-tall version of the Leshan Grand Buddha; and more than 1,000 miniature copies of the 6,000-odd "Terra Cotta Warriors" that were unearthed in China in 1974.

Suzhou Gardens, the park's entrance area, replicates the main street of this eastern China urban area known as the "water city" or "the Venice of China," as it was in 1300. Here visitors can view a 13-minute orientation film. Throughout the park, Chinese acrobats, folk dancers, singers, and other traditional performers entertain; martial arts and Mongolian wrestling are also demonstrated. Chinese silk-makers, tapestry weavers, and other artisans create their wares. Afternoon performances are staged hourly in the 1,000-seat Temple of Light amphitheater. A parade steps off at 6:30pm and a finale performance is staged at Suzhou Gardens to close out the day. **Open:** Daily 9:30am–9:30pm. $$$$

Water Mania, 6073 W Irlo Bronson Memorial Hwy (US 192); tel 407/396-2626. This 38-acre water park offers a variety of aquatic thrill rides and attractions. Body-surf in the Whitecaps continuous wave pool or dare to try the the Wipe Out surfing ride; plummet down spiraling water slides and steep flumes; or enjoy a whitewater tubing adventure. Small children have pint-size slides and pools to frolic in. Adjoining miniature golf course and wooded picnic area with arcade games, beach, and volleyball. **Open:** Daily. Hours vary seasonally, phone ahead. Closed Nov 29–Dec 25. $$$$

Green Meadows Farm, Poinciana Blvd; tel 407/846-0770. Two-hour guided tours bring visitors in close contact with more than 200 farm animals, including pigs, cows, goats, sheep, donkeys, turkeys, and geese. Geared toward children of all ages, the farm also has a milking cow, pony rides, and a tractor-drawn hayride. Picnic area; snack and souvenir shop. **Open:** Daily 9:30am–4pm. Closed some hols. $$$$

LAKE BUENA VISTA

Map page M-7, D2

Hotels 🏨

≡≡ Comfort Inn Lake Buena Vista, 8442 Palm Pkwy, Lake Buena Vista, FL 32830; tel 407/239-4300 or toll free 800/999-7300; fax 407/239-7740. Exit 27 off I-4. Two V-shaped buildings rising 5 stories contain numerous rooms for the vacationing family on a budget. Sturdy and functional rooms and public areas; some renovating is underway. **Rooms:** 640 rms. CI 3pm/CO 11am. Nonsmoking rms avail. **Amenities:** 🛗 A/C, cable TV, in-rm safe. **Services:** 🚐 🚗 🛆 🖎 🍴 Car-rental desk, babysitting. **Facilities:** 🛝 🛆 1 rst, 1 bar, games rm, washer/dryer. **Rates:** HS Dec 24–Jan 2/Feb–Apr/June–Aug $65 D. Children under 18 stay free. Lower rates off-season. Higher rates for spec evnts/hols. Spec packages avail. Pking: Outdoor, free. Maj CC.

≡≡ Days Inn Resort & Suites, 12205 Apopka Vineland Rd, Lake Buena Vista, FL 32836; tel 407/239-0444 or toll free 800/325-2525; fax 407/239-1778. Exit 27 off I-4. **Rooms:** 490 rms and stes. CI 4pm/CO 11am. Nonsmoking rms avail. **Amenities:** 🛗 A/C, cable TV w/movies, in-rm safe. All units w/terraces. **Services:** 🍴 🚐 🚗 🛆 🍴 Children's program, babysitting. **Facilities:** 🛝 300 🛆 1 rst, 1 bar, games rm, playground, washer/dryer. **Rates:** HS Jan–Apr/June–Aug $76–$86 D; from $106 ste. Extra person $10. Children under 18 stay free. Lower rates off-season. Higher rates for spec evnts/hols. Spec packages avail. Pking: Outdoor, free. Maj CC.

≡≡ Disney's All-Star Sports Resort, 3499 W Buena Vista Dr, PO Box 10100, Lake Buena Vista, FL 32830; tel 407/939-5000; fax 407/939-7333. US 192 exit off I-4; follow signs for Disney Resorts. One of Disney's newest entries in the hotel scene, this sports-themed hotel is part of a budget complex that also includes the partially completed All-Star Music Resort. Rooms are housed in 10 buildings with baseball, basketball, football, surfing, and tennis themes. **Rooms:** 1,920 rms. CI 3pm/CO 11am. Express checkout avail. Nonsmoking rms avail. Some rooms are a hike from the parking lot. **Amenities:** 🛗 🗗 A/C, cable TV w/movies, refrig, voice mail, in-rm safe. **Services:** 🍴 🚐 🛆 🍴 Twice-daily maid svce, social director, babysitting. **Facilities:** 🛝 🛆 2 bars, lifeguard, games rm, playground, washer/dryer. One pool has a surfing theme and two 38-foot shark fins; the other is shaped like a baseball diamond with an "outfield" sun deck. Guests receive preferred tee times at Disney golf courses elsewhere. **Rates:** HS Dec 24–Jan 1/Feb–Apr/June–Aug $69–$79 S or D. Extra person $8. Children under 17 stay free. Lower rates off-season. Spec packages avail. Pking: Outdoor, free. Maj CC.

≡≡≡ Disney's Caribbean Beach Resort, 900 Cayman Way, PO Box 10100, Lake Buena Vista, FL 32830-0100; tel 407/934-3400; fax 407/934-3288. US 192 exit off I-4; follow signs for Disney Resorts. Each of the 5 clusters of attractive, coral-colored 2-story buildings surrounding the large, duck-filled lake is designed with its own Caribbean island theme. Custom House lobby is decked with potted palms and overhead fans. **Rooms:** 2,112 rms. CI 3pm/CO 11am. Nonsmoking rms avail. Many rooms offer lake views. **Amenities:** 🛗 🗗 🖥 A/C, cable TV w/movies, voice mail. All units w/minibars, some w/terraces. **Services:** 🍴 🚐 🛆 🛒 🍴 Babysitting. **Facilities:** 🛝 🚲 🛆 🖎 🛆 1 rst, 2 bars, 7 beaches (lake shore), lifeguard, games rm, whirlpool, playground, washer/dryer. Marina. Guests receive preferred tee times at Disney's 4 championship golf courses; fees are $85 including cart. **Rates:** HS Dec 24–Jan 1/Feb–Apr/June–Aug $89–$121 S or D. Extra person $12. Children under 17 stay free. Lower rates off-season. Higher rates for spec evnts/hols. AP rates avail. Spec packages avail. Pking: Outdoor, free. Maj CC.

≡≡≡ Disney's Dixie Landings Resort, 1251 Dixie Dr, PO Box 10100, Lake Buena Vista, FL 32830; tel 407/934-6000; fax 407/934-5777. Family complex with the look of an Old South plantation. Its landscaping is quite elaborate, and there's a fun, colorful outdoor area. Linked to other Disney resorts by a launch. **Rooms:** 2,048 rms. CI 3pm/CO 11am. Express checkout avail. Nonsmoking rms avail. Cleverly conceived rooms with log beds and other cute design elements create a wholesome look. **Amenities:** 🛗 🗗 A/C, cable TV w/movies, voice mail, in-rm safe. **Services:** 🚐 🚗 🛆 🍴 Babysitting. **Facilities:** 🛝 🚲 🛆 🖎 🖎 🛆 2 rsts (see also "Restaurants" below), 1 bar (w/entertainment), lifeguard, games rm, whirlpool, playground, washer/dryer. Guests receive preferred tee times at Disney's 4 championship golf courses; fees are $85 including cart. Dining choices are arranged like a food court. **Rates:** HS Feb–Aug $89–$121 S or D. Extra person $12. Children under 18 stay free. Lower rates off-season. Spec packages avail. Pking: Outdoor, free. Maj CC.

≣≣≣ Disney's Port Orleans Resort, 2201 Orleans Dr, PO Box 10100, Lake Buena Vista, FL 32830; tel 407/824-2900; fax 407/354-1866. US 192 exit off I-4; follow signs for Disney Resorts. A cluster of 3-story pastel buildings decked out in French Quarter motif. **Rooms:** 1,008 rms. CI 3pm/CO 11am. Nonsmoking rms avail. Accommodations, though not as posh as those at the more expensive Disney resorts, are comfortable. **Amenities:** 🔟 🖪 A/C, cable TV w/movies, voice mail. Some units w/terraces. **Services:** 🖪 🖪 🖪 🖪 Babysitting. Boats escort guests to Pleasure Island and other Disney spots from the dock. **Facilities:** 🖪 🖪 🖪 🖪 1 rst (*see also* "Restaurants" below), 2 bars, 1 beach (lake shore), lifeguard, games rm, whirlpool, playground, washer/dryer. Guests receive preferred tee times at Disney's 4 championship golf courses; fees are $85 including cart. **Rates:** HS Dec 24–Jan 1/June–Aug $89–$119 S or D. Extra person $12. Children under 17 stay free. Lower rates off-season. Higher rates for spec evnts/hols. AP and MAP rates avail. Spec packages avail. Pking: Outdoor, free. Maj CC.

≣≣≣≣ Disney's Wilderness Lodge, 901 W Timberline Dr, Lake Buena Vista, FL 32830; tel 407/824-3200; fax 407/824-3232. A wonderful new Disney hotel evocative of those grand turn-of-the-century lodges found in North American national parks. Design incorporates beautiful chandeliers, totem poles, and an 80-foot fireplace depicting the sedimentary rock layers of the Grand Canyon. The grounds feature beautiful 340-acre Bay Lake, replicas of Yellowstone fossils, volcanic craters, spewing geysers, and a waterfall. **Rooms:** 728 rms and stes. CI 3pm/CO 11am. Nonsmoking rms avail. Rooms re-create lodge atmosphere; walls are adorned with Native American tribal friezes and landscape paintings. **Amenities:** 🔟 🖪 A/C, cable TV w/movies, voice mail, in-rm safe. All units w/terraces. **Services:** ✗ 🖪 🖪 🖪 🖪 Car-rental desk, social director, children's program, babysitting. **Facilities:** 🖪 🖪 🖪 🖪 🖪 🖪 2 rsts (*see also* "Restaurants" below), 2 bars, 1 beach (lake shore), lifeguard, games rm, lawn games, whirlpool, day-care ctr, washer/dryer. Watersports on lake. Solid range of dining options will please gourmet, parent, and late-night snacker. **Rates:** HS Dec–Apr $149–$195 S or D; from $295 ste. Extra person $15. Children under 18 stay free. Lower rates off-season. Spec packages avail. Pking: Outdoor, free. Maj CC.

≣≣ Doubletree Club Hotel, 8688 Palm Pkwy, Lake Buena Vista, FL 32830; tel 407/239-8500 or toll free 800/228-2846; fax 407/239-8591. An artfully designed building with attractive landscaping. **Rooms:** 167 rms and stes. CI 3pm/CO 11am. Nonsmoking rms avail. **Amenities:** 🔟 🖪 A/C, cable TV. **Services:** ✗ 🖪 🖪 🖪 🖪 Car-rental desk, babysitting. Free shuttle operates to Magic Kingdom. **Facilities:** 🖪 🖪 🖪 🖪 1 rst, games rm, playground, washer/dryer. **Rates:** HS Jan–Apr/June–Aug $69–$109 D; from $99 ste. Children under 18 stay free. Lower rates off-season. Higher rates for spec evnts/hols. Spec packages avail. Pking: Outdoor, free. Maj CC.

≣≣≣ Embassy Suites Resort–Lake Buena Vista, 8100 Lake Ave, Lake Buena Vista, FL 32836; tel 407/239-1144 or toll free 800/257-8483; fax 407/239-1718. Exit 27 off I-4. One of the chain's newest area hotels, this peach-shaded building is constructed around an atrium, where breakfast and social-hour cocktails are served on granite tables. **Rooms:** 280 rms and stes. CI 4pm/CO 11am. Nonsmoking rms avail. Airy decor. **Amenities:** 🔟 🖪 🖪 🖪 A/C, cable TV w/movies, refrig, VCR, in-rm safe. Some units w/terraces. **Services:** ✗ 🖪 🖪 🖪 🖪 🖪 Car-rental desk, social director, children's program, babysitting. **Facilities:** 🖪 🖪 🖪 🖪 🖪 🖪 1 rst, 3 bars, games rm, lawn games, spa, sauna, steam rm, whirlpool, day-care ctr, playground, washer/dryer. **Rates (BB):** HS Dec 24–31/Mid-Feb–mid-Apr/Mid-June–mid-Aug from $169 ste. Children under 18 stay free. Lower rates off-season. Higher rates for spec evnts/hols. Spec packages avail. Pking: Outdoor, free. Maj CC.

≣≣≣ Grosvenor Resort at Walt Disney World Village, 1850 Hotel Plaza Blvd, Lake Buena Vista, FL 32830; tel 407/828-4444 or toll free 800/624-4109; fax 407/828-8192. Exit 27 off I-4. One of the older addresses in the area, it offers fresh and attractive accommodations and a seasoned staff. **Rooms:** 626 rms and stes. CI 3pm/CO 11am. Nonsmoking rms avail. **Amenities:** 🔟 🖪 🖪 🖪 A/C, cable TV, refrig, VCR, in-rm safe. All units w/minibars, some w/Jacuzzis. Irons and ironing boards. **Services:** ✗ 🖪 🖪 🖪 🖪 Car-rental desk, social director, children's program, babysitting. **Facilities:** 🖪 🖪 🖪 🖪 🖪 2 rsts, 3 bars (1 w/entertainment), games rm, lawn games, racquetball, squash, whirlpool, playground, washer/dryer. **Rates:** HS Dec/Feb–Apr/June–Aug $120–$160 S or D; from $295 ste. Children under 18 stay free. Lower rates off-season. Spec packages avail. Pking: Outdoor, free. Maj CC.

≣≣≣ Guest Quarters Suite Resort–Walt Disney World Village, 2305 Hotel Plaza Blvd, Lake Buena Vista, FL 32830; tel 407/934-1000 or toll free 800/424-2900; fax 407/934-1008. Exit 27 off I-4. Attractive hotel with marble lobby. **Rooms:** 229 stes. CI 4pm/CO 11am. Nonsmoking rms avail. Floral upholstery. **Amenities:** 🔟 🖪 🖪 🖪 A/C, cable TV w/movies, refrig. Some units w/terraces. **Services:** ✗ 🖪 🖪 🖪 🖪 Twice-daily maid svce, car-rental desk, masseur, children's program, babysitting. **Facilities:** ⚐ ⚐² ⚐ ⚐ ⚐ ⚐ 2 rsts, 2 bars, games rm, whirlpool, playground, washer/dryer. **Rates:** HS Jan–Apr/Dec from $129 ste. Extra person $20. Children under 18 stay free. Min stay HS. Lower rates off-season. MAP rates avail. Spec packages avail. Pking: Outdoor, free. Maj CC.

≣≣≣ **Hilton at Walt Disney World Village**, 1751 Hotel Plaza Blvd, Lake Buena Vista, FL 32830 (Walt Disney World Village); tel 407/827-4000 or toll free 800/782-4414; fax 407/827-6369. Exit 27 off I-4. This sleek contemporary hotel is a leader in this resort hotel district. Its public areas are adorned with marble and rich fabrics. Within walking distance to village shops and Pleasure Island activities. **Rooms:** 814 rms and stes. Exec-level rms avail. CI 3pm/CO 11am. Nonsmoking rms avail. All units are in top form. Alcove guest rooms are ideal for families who need a crib or playpen area. **Amenities:** ⚐ ⚐ ⚐ A/C, cable TV w/movies. All units w/minibars, some w/terraces. **Services:** ✗ ⚐ ⚐ ⚐ ⚐ ⚐ Car-rental desk, children's program, babysitting. **Facilities:** ⚐ ⚐ ⚐ ⚐ ⚐ ⚐ ⚐ 4 rsts, 3 bars, games rm, lawn games, sauna, steam rm, whirlpool, beauty salon, playground, washer/dryer. Guests receive preferred tee times at Disney's 4 championship golf courses; fees are $85 including cart. **Rates:** HS Feb 13–Apr 16/Dec 21–31 $215–$245 S or D; from $459 ste. Extra person $20. Children under 18 stay free. Lower rates off-season. Higher rates for spec evnts/hols. Spec packages avail. Pking: Outdoor, free. Ltd CC.

≣≣≣ **Holiday Inn–Sun Spree Lake Buena Vista**, 13351 Fla 535, Lake Buena Vista, FL 32821; tel 407/239-4500 or toll free 800/FON-MAXX; fax 407/239-7713. Exit 27 off I-4. Gated hotel is always busy with families with small children, who seemingly overtake the public areas and terrace. Many activities for kids. **Rooms:** 507 rms. CI 3pm/CO 11am. Nonsmoking rms avail. Oversize guest rooms, all done with a sturdy but cheerful decor, are big enough for children to play in. **Amenities:** ⚐ ⚐ ⚐ ⚐ A/C, cable TV, refrig, VCR, in-rm safe. **Services:** ✗ ⚐ ⚐ ⚐ Car-rental desk, social director, children's program, babysitting. Special children's programs permit parents to leave the hotel for some time alone. **Facilities:** ⚐ ⚐ ⚐ 2 rsts, 1 bar, games rm, whirlpool, day-care ctr, playground. **Rates:** HS Dec–Apr/June–Aug $70–$160 S or D. Children under 19 stay free. Lower rates off-season. Higher rates for spec evnts/hols. Spec packages avail. Pking: Outdoor, free. Maj CC.

≣≣ **Hotel Royal Plaza**, 1905 Hotel Plaza Blvd, Lake Buena Vista, FL 32830 (Walt Disney World Village); tel 407/828-2828 or toll free 800/248-7890; fax 407/827-6338. This 17-story hotel has just completed a major renovation and upgrade that has added 2 executive floors and a concierge level and refurbished all accommodations and public areas. **Rooms:** 396 rms and stes. CI 3pm/CO 11am. Nonsmoking rms avail. **Amenities:**

⚐ ⚐ A/C, cable TV w/movies, in-rm safe. Some units w/minibars, all w/terraces. Refrigerators available on request. **Services:** ✗ ⚐ ⚐ Car-rental desk. Free transport to and from all Walt Disney World parks. **Facilities:** ⚐ ⚐ ⚐ ⚐ 1 rst, 2 bars (w/entertainment), games rm, spa, sauna, whirlpool, beauty salon, playground, washer/dryer. **Rates:** HS Feb 18–Apr 9 $147–$177 S or D; from $404 ste. Children under 18 stay free. Lower rates off-season. Higher rates for spec evnts/hols. Spec packages avail. Pking: Outdoor, free. Maj CC.

≣≣ **Howard Johnson Park Square Inn and Suites**, 8501 Palm Pkwy, Lake Buena Vista, FL 32830; tel 407/239-6900 or toll free 800/635-8684; fax 407/239-1287. Exit 27 off I-4. **Rooms:** 222 rms and stes. CI 3pm/CO 11am. Nonsmoking rms avail. **Amenities:** ⚐ ⚐ ⚐ A/C, cable TV w/movies, refrig, in-rm safe. Some units w/terraces. **Services:** ✗ ⚐ ⚐ ⚐ ⚐ Car-rental desk, babysitting. **Facilities:** ⚐ ⚐ ⚐ 1 rst, 1 bar, games rm, whirlpool, playground, washer/dryer. **Rates:** HS Jan–Apr/June–Sept $65–$85 D; from $85 ste. Extra person $10. Children under 18 stay free. Lower rates off-season. Higher rates for spec evnts/hols. Spec packages avail. Pking: Outdoor, free. Maj CC.

≣≣≣ **Howard Johnson Resort Hotel**, 1805 Hotel Plaza Blvd, Lake Buena Vista, FL 32830 (Walt Disney World Village); tel 407/828-8888 or toll free 800/223-9930; fax 407/827-4623. **Rooms:** 323 rms and stes. CI 4pm/CO 11am. Nonsmoking rms avail. **Amenities:** ⚐ ⚐ A/C, cable TV w/movies, VCR, in-rm safe. Some units w/terraces. **Services:** ✗ ⚐ ⚐ ⚐ ⚐ Car-rental desk, babysitting. **Facilities:** ⚐ ⚐ ⚐ ⚐ 1 rst, 1 bar, games rm, spa, whirlpool, playground, washer/dryer. **Rates:** HS June–Sept $75–$145 S or D; from $179 ste. Children under 18 stay free. Lower rates off-season. Higher rates for spec evnts/hols. Spec packages avail. Pking: Outdoor, free. Maj CC.

≣≣≣ **Travelodge Hotel Walt Disney World Village**, 2000 Hotel Plaza Blvd, Lake Buena Vista, FL 32830; tel 407/824-2424 or toll free 800/348-3765; fax 407/828-8933. Exit 27 off I-4. Spiffy and immaculate lakefront property, far better than most in the chain (it's the flagship hotel). Designed to evoke a Caribbean plantation manor house. A solid and reliable choice. **Rooms:** 325 rms and stes. CI 3pm/CO 11am. Nonsmoking rms avail. Many accommodations offer views of Lake Buena Vista from furnished terraces. **Amenities:** ⚐ ⚐ ⚐ ⚐ A/C, cable TV w/movies, in-rm safe. All units w/minibars, all w/terraces. Free newspaper delivered to room weekdays. **Services:** ✗ ⚐ ⚐ ⚐ ⚐ ⚐ Car-rental desk, babysitting. Free transport to and from all Walt Disney World parks. **Facilities:** ⚐ ⚐ ⚐ 2 rsts, 2 bars (1 w/entertainment), games rm, playground, washer/dryer. **Rates:** HS Jan/Mar–Apr/Jun/Aug/Dec $139–$169 S or D; from

$199 ste. Children under 18 stay free. Lower rates off-season. Higher rates for spec evnts/hols. AP rates avail. MAP rates avail. Spec packages avail. Pking: Outdoor, free. Maj CC.

≡≡≡≡ Walt Disney World Dolphin, 1500 Epcot Resorts Blvd, Lake Buena Vista, FL 32830 (Epcot Resort); tel 407/934-4000 or toll free 800/325-3535; fax 407/934-4884. US 192 exit off I-4. Follow signs for Epcot Resorts. Larger-than-life and whimsically designed, from architect Michael Graves. The coral and turquoise facade is centered on a 27-story pyramid, which is flanked by 11-story wings topped by 56-foot twin dolphin sculptures. There are cascading fountains throughout the property and numerous works of art in the colorful, if sometimes dizzying, public areas. **Rooms:** 1,509 rms and stes. Exec-level rms avail. CI 3pm/CO 11am. Nonsmoking rms avail. Playful decor and many comforts of a near-luxury hotel. **Amenities:** A/C, cable TV w/movies, refrig, in-rm safe. All units w/minibars, some w/terraces. **Services:** Car-rental desk, social director, masseur, children's program, babysitting. **Facilities:** 7 rsts (see also "Restaurants" below), 4 bars (1 w/entertainment), lifeguard, games rm, lawn games, spa, sauna, whirlpool, beauty salon, day-care ctr, playground, washer/dryer. Guests receive preferred tee times at Disney's 4 championship golf courses; fees are $85 including cart. **Rates:** HS Feb 14–Apr 16/Dec 21–Jan 1 $220–$335 S or D; from $450 ste. Extra person $15. Children under 18 stay free. Lower rates off-season. Higher rates for spec evnts/hols. Spec packages avail. Pking: Outdoor, free. Maj CC.

≡≡≡≡ Walt Disney World Swan, 1200 Epcot Resorts Blvd, Lake Buena Vista, FL 32830 (Epcot Resort); tel 407/934-3000 or toll free 800/248-7926; fax 407/934-1399. Managed by Westin Hotels, this hard-to-miss, glamorous highrise with giant swans atop its roof is a big hit. Designed by Michael Graves, it allow both large groups and individuals to coexist in harmony, and the crack staff works hard to ensure that goal is achieved. Restaurants range from simple and functional to elegant and stylish. **Rooms:** 758 rms and stes. CI 3pm/CO 11am. Express checkout avail. Nonsmoking rms avail. Flashy, innovatively designed rooms. **Amenities:** A/C, cable TV w/movies, voice mail, in-rm safe. All units w/minibars, some w/terraces, 1 w/Jacuzzi. **Services:** Car-rental desk, social director, masseur, children's program, babysitting. **Facilities:** 4 rsts (see also "Restaurants" below), 3 bars (1 w/entertainment), 1 beach (lake shore), lifeguard, games rm, sauna, whirlpool, beauty salon, playground. Guests receive preferred tee times at Disney's 4 championship golf courses; fees are $85 including cart. **Rates:** HS Feb–Apr $260–$350 S or D; from $350 ste. Extra person

$25. Children under 18 stay free. Lower rates off-season. Higher rates for spec evnts/hols. Spec packages avail. Pking: Outdoor, free. Maj CC.

Resorts

≡≡≡≡ Buena Vista Palace–Walt Disney World Village, 1900 Buena Vista Dr, Lake Buena Vista, FL 32830; tel 407/827-2727 or toll free 800/327-2990; fax 407/827-6034. Exit 27 off I-4. A dazzling multi-winged highrise that soars above Walt Disney World Village like no other. Arriving guests will not be disappointed as they approach the impressive circular drive entry and the dozen-story atrium that sparkles with polished surfaces. Well-heeled families and foreigners make up much of the business. **Rooms:** 1,028 rms and stes. CI 3pm/CO 11am. Nonsmoking rms avail. Tasteful accommodations offer views of Lake Buena Vista or the vast Disney complex. **Amenities:** A/C, cable TV w/movies, in-rm safe. All units w/minibars, all w/terraces, some w/Jacuzzis. Some units have in-room safes and coffeemakers. **Services:** Twice-daily maid svce, car-rental desk, masseur, children's program, babysitting. The eager-to-please staff scurries to assist arrivals. **Facilities:** 5 rsts (see also "Restaurants" below), 4 bars (3 w/entertainment), games rm, whirlpool, beauty salon, playground, washer/dryer. Guests receive preferred tee times at Disney's 4 championship golf courses; fees are $85 including cart. **Rates:** HS Feb–Apr/June–Aug/Dec $150–$250 S or D; from $290 ste. Extra person $15. Children under 18 stay free. Lower rates off-season. Spec packages avail. Pking: Outdoor, free. Maj CC.

≡≡≡ Disney's Beach Club Resort, 1800 Epcot Resorts Blvd, PO Box 10100, Lake Buena Vista, FL 32830 (Epcot Resort); tel 407/934-8000; fax 407/934-3850. US 192 exit off I-4; follow signs for Disney Resorts. This Victorian-inspired complex faced with clapboard is positioned around a lake and accessed via a palm-lined drive. The sun-dappled lobby is graced with wicker and rattan furnishings amid tall potted palms. Within walking distance of Epcot. **Rooms:** 584 rms and stes. CI 3pm/CO 11am. Charming rooms furnished in bleached woods. **Amenities:** A/C, cable TV w/movies, voice mail, in-rm safe. All units w/minibars, some w/terraces, some w/Jacuzzis. **Services:** Children's program, babysitting. **Facilities:** 5 rsts (see also "Restaurants" below), 5 bars, 1 beach (lake shore), lifeguard, games rm, whirlpool, beauty salon, day-care ctr, playground, washer/dryer. Guests receive preferred tee times at Disney's 4 championship golf courses; fees are $85 including cart. Guests share some facilities with the Disney Yacht Club Resort next door. **Rates:** HS Dec 24–Jan 1/Feb–Apr/June–Aug $205–$290 S or D; from $390 ste. Extra person $15. Children under 17 stay free. Lower rates off-season. Higher rates for spec evnts/hols. AP and MAP rates avail. Spec packages avail. Pking: Outdoor, free. Maj CC.

Disney's Contemporary Resort, 4600 N World Dr, PO Box 10100, Lake Buena Vista, FL 32830 (Magic Kingdom Resort); tel 407/824-1000; fax 407/824-3539. US 192 exit off I-4; follow signs for Disney Resorts. One of Disney's original Magic Kingdom offerings and still very popular, this architecturally interesting double-sloped highrise is suitable for any Disney junkie. It's on the monorail line; trains pass through the center atrium. **Rooms:** 1,053 rms and stes. CI 3pm/CO 11am. Express checkout avail. Nonsmoking rms avail. Rooms decorated in desert tones, with art deco furnishings. **Amenities:** A/C, cable TV w/movies, voice mail. Some units w/terraces. **Services:** Children's program, babysitting. **Facilities:** 4 rsts (see also "Restaurants" below), 5 bars, 1 beach (lake shore), lifeguard, games rm, lawn games, sauna, beauty salon, day-care ctr, playground, washer/dryer. The concierge level enjoys private lakeview lounge. Guests receive preferred tee times at Disney's 4 championship golf courses; fees are $85 including cart. **Rates:** HS Dec 24–Jan 1/Feb–Apr/June–Aug $195–$270 S or D; from $245 ste. Extra person $15. Children under 17 stay free. Lower rates off-season. Higher rates for spec evnts/hols. AP and MAP rates avail. Spec packages avail. Pking: Outdoor, free. Maj CC.

Disney's Grand Floridian Beach Resort, 4401 Floridian Way, PO Box 10100, Lake Buena Vista, FL 32830 (Magic Kingdom Resort); tel 407/824-3000; fax 407/824-3186. US 192 exit off I-4; follow signs for Disney Resorts. The choicest of the Disney hotels, designed with much flair and imagination in turn-of-the-century style and without the heavy-handed commercialism of some of the other Disney properties. The lobby is nothing short of stunning and is staffed by a spirited team of Disney troupers who glide guests through registration. **Rooms:** 925 rms and stes. Exec-level rms avail. CI 3pm/CO 11am. Nonsmoking rms avail. Graciously styled, luxuriously furnished accommodations. Rooms facing away from the courtyard and toward the lagoon are quietest. **Amenities:** A/C, cable TV w/movies, voice mail, bathrobes. All units w/minibars, some w/terraces. **Services:** Social director, masseur, children's program, babysitting. **Facilities:** 5 rsts, 4 bars, 1 beach (lake shore), lifeguard, games rm, lawn games, whirlpool, beauty salon, day-care ctr, playground, washer/dryer. Guests receive preferred tee times at Disney's 4 championship golf courses; fees are $85 including cart. **Rates:** HS Christmas/Feb–Apr/June–Aug $245–$440 S or D; from $490 ste. Extra person $15. Children under 17 stay free. Lower rates off-season. Higher rates for spec evnts/hols. AP rates avail. Spec packages avail. Pking: Outdoor, free. Maj CC.

Disney's Polynesian Resort, 1600 Seven Seas Dr, PO Box 10100, Lake Buena Vista, FL 32840 (Magic Kingdom Resort); tel 407/824-2000; fax 407/824-3174. US 192 exit off I-4; follow signs for Disney Resorts. Polynesian-themed facility filled with gardens and lagoons and tropical foliage; one of the original Magic Kingdom properties. It's linked to Epcot and the Magic Kingdom by monorail. **Rooms:** 853 rms and stes. Exec-level rms avail. CI 3pm/CO 11am. Nonsmoking rms avail. Fine selection of accommodations may offer lagoon or garden views. **Amenities:** A/C, cable TV w/movies, voice mail. Some units w/terraces. **Services:** Children's program, babysitting. **Facilities:** 3 rsts (see also "Restaurants" below), 4 bars, 1 beach (lake shore), lifeguard, games rm, lawn games, beauty salon, day-care ctr, playground, washer/dryer. Guests receive preferred tee times at Disney's 4 championship golf courses; guest fees are $85 including cart. **Rates:** HS Dec 24–Jan 1/Feb–Apr/June–Aug $210–$325 S or D; from $340 ste. Extra person $15. Children under 17 stay free. Lower rates off-season. Higher rates for spec evnts/hols. AP and MAP rates avail. Spec packages avail. Pking: Outdoor, free. Maj CC.

Disney's Village Resort, 1901 Buena Vista Dr, PO Box 10100, Lake Buena Vista, FL 32830 (Walt Disney World Village); tel 407/827-1100; fax 407/934-2741. Exit 27 off I-4. A great choice for golfers and families. Sprawled over 265 acres of woodland, lakes, and streams; grounds include towering pines, cypress, magnolias, and live oaks draped with Spanish moss. Peacocks roam about. **Rooms:** 585 effic. CI 4pm/CO 11am. Express checkout avail. Nonsmoking rms avail. Accommodations are in octagonal Treehouse Villas, elevated on stilts; Fairway Villas, 2-bedroom cedar townhouses overlooking the golf course; inexpensive 1-bedroom Club Suites, bordering a lake; 1- and 2-bedroom Vacation Villas, in 2-story townhouses with big picture windows overlooking woodlands or waterways; and luxurious 2- and 3-bedroom Grand Vista homes, with full kitchens and 2 screened porches. **Amenities:** A/C, cable TV w/movies, refrig, voice mail. Some units w/terraces. **Services:** Car-rental desk, babysitting. **Facilities:** 1 rst, 1 bar, games rm, whirlpool, playground, washer/dryer. Par-72 championship golf course; 7 children's playgrounds. Disney Village Marketplace restaurants are adjacent via footbridge. **Rates:** HS Feb–Apr/June–Aug $200–$825 S or D; from $200 effic. Children under 17 stay free. Lower rates off-season. Higher rates for spec evnts/hols. AP and MAP rates avail. Spec packages avail. Pking: Outdoor, free. Maj CC.

Disney's Yacht Club Resort, 1700 Epcot Resorts Blvd, PO Box 10100, Lake Buena Vista, FL 32830 (Epcot Resort); tel 407/934-7000; fax 407/934-3450. US 192 exit off I-4; follow signs for Disney Resorts. This large and impressive resort, which shares its 25-acre lake, facilities, and gorgeous landscaping with the adjacent Beach Club (see listing above), evokes a luxurious turn-of-the-century New England yacht club. The 5-story, gray-clapboard building houses a magnificent, plush lobby. **Rooms:** 635 rms and stes. Exec-level rms avail. CI 3pm/ CO 11am. Nonsmoking rms avail. Handsome nautical decor and quality furnishings. French doors open onto porches and balconies. **Amenities:** 🛏 🖫 🍷 A/C, cable TV w/movies, voice mail, in-rm safe. All units w/minibars, some w/terraces, some w/Jacuzzis. **Services:** ✕ 🖛 VP 🚗 🖼 🍽 Children's program, babysitting. **Facilities:** 🛝 🛆 🕹 🐟 🖭 🏊 💻 🛗 5 rsts (see also "Restaurants" below), 5 bars (2 w/entertainment), 1 beach (lake shore), lifeguard, games rm, whirlpool, playground, washer/dryer. Bar has its own fireplace. Guests receive preferred tee times at Disney's 4 championship golf courses; guest fees are $85 including cart. **Rates:** HS Dec 24–Jan 1/Feb–Apr/June–Aug $205–$385 S or D; from $390 ste. Extra person $15. Children under 17 stay free. Lower rates off-season. Higher rates for spec evnts/hols. AP and MAP rates avail. Spec packages avail. Pking: Outdoor, free. Maj CC.

Restaurants 🍴

Ariel's, in Disney's Yacht and Beach Club Resort, 1700 Epcot Resorts Blvd, Lake Buena Vista; tel 407/934-1279. **Seafood.** This restaurant, decorated in cool hues of seafoam green, peach, and coral, offers elegant dining in a room adorned with crisp, white table linens, seashell-motif china, and attractively shaded lamps. Popular dishes include Maine lobster sautéed with shiitake mushrooms, lemon, and garlic, served on angel hair pasta. **FYI:** Reservations accepted. Children's menu. No smoking. **Open:** Daily 6–10pm. **Prices:** Main courses $17–$28. Maj CC. VP 🛗

♣ **Arthur's 27**, in Buena Vista Palace Hotel, 1900 Buena Vista Dr, Lake Buena Vista (Walt Disney World Village); tel 407/827-3450. **International.** This elegant restaurant, located at the top of the hotel, offers spectacular views of Walt Disney World Village in addition to renowned international cuisine. Specialties include fillet of beef with glazed shallots, pecans, and a roquefort-port sauce. A daily selection of fresh fish and lobster is prepared each evening. **FYI:** Reservations accepted. Piano/singer. Dress code. **Open:** Daily 6–10:30pm. **Prices:** Main courses $23–$35. Maj CC. ♥ VP 🛗

Artist's Point, in Disney's Wilderness Lodge, 901 W Timberline Dr, Lake Buena Vista; tel 305/824-3200. **Regional American.** One of Disney's most popular new dining spots. Windows overlook Bay Lake and western murals adorn the walls. Grilled steak, seafood, wild game. **FYI:** Reservations accepted. Children's menu. No smoking. **Open:** Breakfast daily 7:30am–noon; dinner daily 5:30–10:30pm. **Prices:** Main courses $17–$21. Maj CC. 🆒 🚹 VP 🛗

Boatwrights Dining Hall, in Disney's Dixie Landings Resort, 1251 Dixie Dr, Lake Buena Vista; tel 407/934-6000. **Cajun/ Seafood/Steak.** Dine in a 19th-century maritime atmosphere. The interior has 2 large fireplaces and is decorated with antique boatbuilding tools. Patrons can enjoy slowly roasted prime rib, blackened chicken sandwich, or blackened shrimp, scallops, or catfish, all served over brown-buttered pasta in creamy garlic sauce. **FYI:** Reservations accepted. Comedy/guitar/singer. Children's menu. No smoking. **Open:** Breakfast daily 6–11:30am; dinner daily 5–10pm. **Prices:** Main courses $6.95–$13.95. Maj CC. 🚹 VP 🛗

Bon Famille's Cafe, in Disney's Port Orleans Resort, 2201 Orleans Dr, Lake Buena Vista; tel 407/934-5000. Off Bonnet Creek Pkwy. **American/Cajun.** A family-oriented restaurant serving breakfast and dinner only. Notable selections from the menu are the family salad, spicy seafood kabobs, and grilled breast of chicken Creole. The Scat Cats Club offers musical entertainment in the evening. **FYI:** Reservations accepted. Piano. Children's menu. No smoking. **Open:** Breakfast daily 7–10:30am; dinner daily 5–10pm. **Prices:** Main courses $8.95–$15.95. Maj CC. VP 🛗

Cape May Cafe, in Disney's Beach Club Resort, 1700 Epcot Resorts Blvd, Lake Buena Vista; tel 407/934-8000. **Seafood.** A fun family restaurant with a menu offering lots of great values, including an appetizing seafood buffet. Kids can enjoy breakfast with their favorite Disney characters and are provided crayons with which to draw on the paper tablecloths. **FYI:** Reservations not accepted. Children's menu. No smoking. **Open:** Breakfast daily 7:30–11am; dinner daily 5:30–9:30pm. **Prices:** Main courses $8.50–$17.95. Maj CC. 🚹 VP 🛗

Chef Mickey's, Walt Disney World Village, Lake Buena Vista; tel 407/828-3859. **New American.** Where else can you have Mickey Mouse prepare your lunch? The children's menu offers a variety of dishes for young ones, all at $4.95; grown-ups might enjoy the rib-eye steak, barbecue ribs, or king crab legs. **FYI:** Reservations accepted. Children's menu. No smoking. **Open:** Breakfast daily 9–11:30am; lunch daily 11:30am–2pm; dinner daily 5–10pm. **Prices:** Main courses $11.50–$22.95. Maj CC. 🚹 🛗

$ **Contemporary Cafe**, in Disney's Contemporary Resort, 4600 N World Dr, Lake Buena Vista; tel 407/824-1000. **Buffet.** A bright, casual, buffet-style eatery with umbrella-covered tables and indoor gardens. The extensive buffet includes prime rib, seafood, a salad bar, and desserts. Popular with families for its festive atmosphere and good value. Kids will enjoy the daily breakfasts with Disney characters. **FYI:** Reservations not accepted. Children's menu. No smoking. **Open:** Breakfast daily 8–11am; dinner daily 5:30–9:30pm. **Prices:** PF dinner $4.95–$14.50. Maj CC. VP &

♠ **The Empress Room**, in Walt Disney World Village, Buena Vista Dr, Lake Buena Vista; tel 407/828-3900. Aboard the Empress Lilly. **French.** An elegant dining room with a menu featuring entrees such as strip steak in cognac cream sauce, and roasted rack of baby lamb. A great restaurant for a memorable evening. **FYI:** Reservations recommended. Jacket required. No smoking. **Open:** Daily 6:30–9:30pm. **Prices:** Main courses $26–$34. Maj CC. ▪ &

Fireworks Factory, 1630 Buena Vista Dr, Lake Buena Vista; tel 407/934-8989. On Pleasure Island. **Regional American.** A casual eatery with exposed brick, neon lights, and booth seating. Video games will entertain the young ones while you wait for your table. Dine on dishes such as Vermont pork chops, applewood-smoked baby-back ribs, Pacific shrimp salad. **FYI:** Reservations recommended. Children's menu. **Open:** Daily 11:30am–2:30am. **Prices:** Main courses $13.95–$19.95. Maj CC. &

Fisherman's Deck, in the Empress Lilly, Walt Disney World Village, Lake Buena Vista; tel 407/828-3900. **Seafood.** A casual seafood restaurant overlooking Lake Buena Vista. Every table has a lovely view. **FYI:** Reservations accepted. Children's menu. No smoking. **Open:** Lunch daily 11:30am–2pm; dinner daily 5:30–10pm. **Prices:** Main courses $15–$45. Maj CC. ▲ &

Garden Grove Cafe, in the Walt Disney World Swan, 1200 Epcot Resorts Blvd, Lake Buena Vista; tel 407/934-1618. **Seafood/Steak.** A comfortable restaurant with wicker furniture, potted palms, and a domed ceiling. House specialties are prime rib, baked stuffed Maine lobster, and broiled salmon fillet with hollandaise sauce. Dine with your favorite Disney characters on Monday and Thursday evenings, or breakfast with them on Wednesday and Saturday mornings. **FYI:** Reservations accepted. Children's menu. **Open:** Breakfast daily 6:30–11:30am; lunch daily 11:30am–2pm; dinner daily 5:30–11pm. **Prices:** Main courses $8–$11. Maj CC. ♥ VP &

⑤ **Jungle Jim's**, in Walt Disney World Village, PO Box 22821, Lake Buena Vista; tel 407/827-1257. **New American.** A fun, safari-themed bar and restaurant with stools shaped like elephant feet and murals of jungle animals. The fare includes hamburgers, salads, chicken burgers, and spare ribs. **FYI:** Reservations not accepted. Children's menu. **Open:** Daily 11am–2am. Closed Dec 25. **Prices:** Main courses $6–$15. Maj CC. &

JW Steakhouse, in Marriott's Orlando World Center, 8701 World Center Dr, Lake Buena Vista; tel 407/239-4200. **Steak.** This casual, clubhouse-like dining room offers steaks and seafood. The jumbo shrimp and the pan-seared crabcakes are favorite appetizers. **FYI:** Reservations accepted. **Open:** Lunch daily 11am–5pm; dinner daily 6–10pm; brunch Sat–Sun 7–11am. **Prices:** Main courses $17.25–$22.50. Maj CC. VP &

★ **Papeete Bay Verandah**, in Polynesian Resort, 1600 Seven Seas Dr, Lake Buena Vista; tel 407/824-1391. **Polynesian.** Curiously decorated Polynesian-style dining room. Breakfast is attended by Minnie Mouse and other Disney characters. **FYI:** Reservations accepted. Children's menu. No smoking. **Open:** Breakfast Sun 7:30–11am, Mon–Sat 7:30–10:30am; dinner daily 5:30–10pm. **Prices:** Main courses $10.95–$16.95. Maj CC. VP &

★ **Pebbles**, in Crossroads Shopping Center, 12551 Fla 535, Lake Buena Vista; tel 407/827-1111. **New American/Californian.** A casual, tropical restaurant offering a creative menu. The bar features live entertainment Thursday, Friday, and Saturday nights. A local favorite. **FYI:** Reservations not accepted. Children's menu. **Open:** Sun–Thurs 11am–midnight, Fri–Sat 11am–1am. Closed some hols. **Prices:** Main courses $9.95–$19.95. Maj CC. &

Portobello Yacht Club, 1650 Buena Vista Dr, Lake Buena Vista; tel 407/934-8888. On Pleasure Island. **Northern Italian.** Another soon-to-be classic Disney restaurant. The menu offers a variety of Italian-inspired specialties, including crispy thin-crust pizza, jumbo Alaskan red king crab served with pasta, and boneless chicken breast marinated in olive oil, garlic, and fresh rosemary. **FYI:** Reservations not accepted. Children's menu. **Open:** Daily 11:30am–midnight. **Prices:** Main courses $13.95–$22.95. Maj CC. ▲ ▲ &

Watercress Cafe, in Buena Vista Palace in Walt Disney World Village, 1900 Buena Vista Dr, Lake Buena Vista; tel 407/827-3440. **American.** A casual eatery in one of the area's best hotels, where you can enjoy views of Lake Buena Vista while you dine. A dinner buffet is available for $12.95; kids eat for $5.95. Disney characters make regular appearances here on Sundays 8–10am. The bakery operates around the clock. **FYI:** Reservations not accepted. Children's menu. **Open:** Daily 6am–midnight. **Prices:** Main courses $8–$15. Maj CC. VP &

Whispering Canyon Cafe, in Disney's Wilderness Lodge, 901 W Timberline Dr, Lake Buena Vista; tel 305/824-3200. **Regional American.** A fun, relaxed restaurant with a prix-fixe, all-you-can-eat menu. Dine at a large table with an oversized lazy susan at its center that spins food in your direction. The prix-fixe dinner for children is $6.50. **FYI:** Reservations not accepted.

Children's menu. No smoking. **Open:** Breakfast daily 7–11am; lunch daily 11:30am–3:30pm; dinner daily 4:30–10pm. **Prices:** PF dinner $6.50–$15.75. Maj CC. 📷 👶 VP ♿

Yachtsman Steakhouse, in Disney's Yacht Club Resort, 1700 Epcot Resorts Blvd, Lake Buena Vista; tel 407/934-3415. **Steak.** Wood floors, a beamed ceiling, and an open kitchen help to create a warm, comfortable atmosphere. Beef is the specialty; there's even a beef-aging room in which you can watch the chef cut the high-quality meats. The chef offers a few seafood specialties as well. Extensive wine list. **FYI:** Reservations accepted. Children's menu. No smoking. **Open:** Daily 6–10pm. **Prices:** Main courses $16–$25; PF dinner $42. Maj CC. 📷 ♿

Attractions 🧳

WALT DISNEY WORLD

About the Park. One of the world's most famous vacation spots, Walt Disney World sprawls across 43 square miles of central Florida just southwest of Orlando, at I-4 and Fla 535. In addition to its 3 main theme parks, Magic Kingdom, Epcot Center and Disney–MGM Studios, visitors can check out the night life at Pleasure Island, the waves at Typhoon Lagoon, or the shops at Disney Village Marketplace; sing around a campfire at Fort Wilderness; or experience a number of other varied amusements. Both within and around the parks, there are manmade beaches, tranquil lakes, 5 golf courses, dinner shows, conservation areas, and several elegant and imaginative hotels designed around a central theme. Disney characters make scheduled appearances all over Walt Disney World, but have also been known to pop up unannounced.

Disney offers a variety of ticket options: a 1-day, 1-park ticket (Magic Kingdom, Epcot Center, or Disney–MGM Studios); a 4-day pass, with unlimited admission on any 4 nonconsecutive days to any major park; and a 5-day pass, offering unlimited admission on any 5 nonconsecutive days to any major park, plus admission to Pleasure Island, Typhoon Lagoon, River Country, and Discovery Island for 7 consecutive days. For general information contact Walt Disney World (tel 407/824-4321), PO Box 10000, Lake Buena Vista, FL 32830. For reservations at Disney hotels, call 407/W-DISNEY or write to PO Box 10100, Lake Buena Vista, FL 32830.

Magic Kingdom. Centered around Cinderella Castle and its medieval spires, the Magic Kingdom consists of 7 "'lands'": **Main Street USA,** a Disney-style depiction of a small town street at the turn of the century; **Adventureland,** an exotic, jungle-like setting; **Frontierland,** celebrating America's frontier origins; **Liberty Square,** recalling colonial times; **Fantasyland,** an area of fairy tales brought to life; **Mickey's Starland,** featuring the cartoony hometown of Mickey Mouse; and **Tomorrowland,** a

futuristic land focusing on outer space. Among the most popular rides and attractions here are Space Mountain (Tomorrowland), a popular and frenetic indoor rollercoaster ride; Splash Mountain (Frontierland), a log flume ride based on the Disney film *Song of the South;* and Pirates of the Caribbean (Adventureland), an indoor boat ride through a series of tableaux depicting a pirate raid on a coastal village.

EPCOT Center. Emblemized by the 17-story geodesic sphere known as Spaceship Earth (which contains a ride by that name), the world's fair–like park is divided into 2 sections. The first is **Future World,** a collection of 10 themed pavilions dedicated to the past, present, and future of human technology. Some of the pavilions are: **The Living Seas,** built around a 5.6 million-gallon saltwater aquarium populated by several thousand undersea creatures; **Wonders of Life,** which includes Body Wars, a flight simulator-based trip through the human body; **Spaceship Earth,** a "time-travel" ride examining the history of human communication; and **Universe of Energy,** featuring a visit to a prehistoric forest filled with Audio-Animatronic dinosaurs, bubbling lava pits, and rumbling thunderstorms.

The rest of EPCOT Center comprises **World Showcase,** a representation of cultures from around the world. Exacting replications of each culture's architecture are the backdrop for art exhibits, native performers, and innovative films, rides, and attractions. Shops and restaurants offer authentic goods and cuisine, and employees in each enclave are natives of the country represented. **IllumiNations,** a laser, pyrotechnic, and water show set to music, is very popular; it takes place every night around World Showcase Lagoon, just before closing time.

Disney–MGM Studios. Opened in 1989, Disney's third major theme park invites visitors into the magical realms of the cinema, blending amusement park elements with actual working TV and movie production facilities. Attractions include adventure rides, stage shows (featuring *Beauty and the Beast* and *The Voyage of the Little Mermaid*), and a backstage studio tour that winds up in the middle of an earthquake, an oil fire, and a flash flood, all courtesy of **Catastrophe Canyon.**

Other highlights are **Star Tours,** which combines high-tech film and flight simulation technology; the **Indiana Jones Stunt Spectacular,** demonstrating movie stunt work; **The Magic of Disney Animation,** where guests learn about animation and get to watch real animators at work; and the new **Twilight Zone Tower of Terror,** a combination of special effects and thrill ride during what is ostensibly a tour through an abandoned—and haunted—Sunset Boulevard grand hotel. **Aladdin's Royal Caravan,** a spectacular parade based on the Disney movie, takes place once or twice a day, depending on the season, and includes a 26-foot genie riding a bejeweled float, scimitar dancers, and an appearance by Prince Ali and Princess Jasmine.

Pleasure Island. A 6-acre conglomeration of 7 nightclubs, several eateries and shops, and a 10-theater movie complex. Visitors under age 18 must be accompanied by an adult after 7pm, when the clubs open for the night. Dance clubs at Pleasure Island are: **Mannequins Dance Palace** (under 21 not admitted), a glitzy, high-tech club; **8 TRAX** (under 21 not admitted), a 1970s-themed club; and the **Rock & Roll Beach Club,** with live bands performing oldies and current pop tunes. In addition, guests can enjoy the **Pleasure Island Jazz Company,** with live jazz and blues music; the **Neon Armadillo Music Saloon,** a country & western establishment; the **Comedy Warehouse,** featuring top name comedians and a resident improvisational troupe; and the **Adventurers Club,** a theatrically stuffy English gentlemen's club offering improvisational comedy shows in the main salon and cabaret performances in the library. In addition, live bands perform nightly at the outdoor **West End Stage.**

Typhoon Lagoon. This large water park features water slides, streams, rapids, tidal pools, waterfalls, and an enormous manmade lagoon equipped with a powerful wave generator. Preceded by a foghorn blast, 6-foot waves surge across the length of the lagoon, but are engineered to dissipate quickly as they approach the shoreline. **Castaway Creek** is a meandering, 2,000-foot river for tubing; **Shark Reef** provides free snorkeling equipment and instruction for a 15-minute swim through a 362,000-gallon simulated coral reef; and **Ketchakiddie Creek** is a section of mini-slides, pools, and fountains reserved for small children.

River Country. River Country was Disney's first water park. Smaller than Typhoon Lagoon, it was based on the theme of a rural swimming hole. It features 2 corkscrew slides, ropes and booms to swing from, manmade boulders serving as diving platforms, and a tubing stream. A 350-yard boardwalk nature trail winds through a cypress swamp.

Discovery Island. A lush, 11-acre island conservation area and zoological sanctuary, Discovery Island offers nature trails, an enormous, walk-through aviary, and 3 live shows featuring birds of prey, trained exotic birds, and reptiles native to Florida. Specimens cared for range from exotic birds and miniature deer to alligators. Plants and trees along the trails are marked with explanatory placards. Access to Discovery Island is by boat from Frontierland (Magic Kingdom).

LAKE CITY

Map page M-5, C1

Hotel ⌂

Holiday Inn, US 90 at I-75, PO Box 1239, Lake City, FL 32056; tel 904/752-3901 or toll free 800/HOLIDAY; fax 904/775-1027. Exit 82 off I-75. Basic, familiar motel with the traditional look of the chain. **Rooms:** 227 rms and stes. CI 3pm/CO noon. Express checkout avail. Nonsmoking rms avail. **Amenities:** A/C, cable TV. **Services:** X ⌂ ⌂ ⌂ **Facilities:** ⌂ ⌂ 1 rst, 1 bar, washer/dryer. **Rates:** HS June–Aug $53–$58 S or D; from $75 ste. Lower rates off-season. Higher rates for spec evnts/hols. Spec packages avail. Pking: Outdoor, free. Maj CC.

LAKELAND

Map page M-6, E4

Hotels ⌂

Holiday Inn-South, 3405 S Florida Ave, Lakeland, FL 33803; tel 813/646-5731 or toll free 800/833-4902; fax 813/646-5215. Updated facility is top-notch for the chain. Attracts many families, but business clientele will find many amenities suited to their needs. **Rooms:** 171 rms and stes. CI 3pm/CO noon. Nonsmoking rms avail. **Amenities:** A/C, cable TV w/movies. Some units w/minibars. **Services:** X ⌂ ⌂ Children's program, babysitting. **Facilities:** ⌂ ⌂ 1 rst, 1 bar (w/entertainment), whirlpool. **Rates (CP):** HS Jan–May $68–$78 S or D; from $78 ste. Extra person $10. Children under 18 stay free. Lower rates off-season. Spec packages avail. Pking: Outdoor, free. Maj CC.

Ramada Inn Northpointe, 3260 US 98 N, Lakeland, FL 33809; tel 813/688-8080 or toll free 800/272-6232; fax 813/688-8080 ext 152. Exit 18 off I-4. Standard Ramada attracting a mainly business clientele. **Rooms:** 157 rms and stes. CI 3pm/CO noon. **Amenities:** A/C, cable TV w/movies. Some units w/minibars, some w/Jacuzzis. **Services:** X ⌂ ⌂ ⌂ **Facilities:** ⌂ ⌂ ⌂ 1 rst, 1 bar, washer/dryer. **Rates:** $69 S or D; from $120 ste. Children under 18 stay free. Spec packages avail. Pking: Outdoor, free. Maj CC.

Sheraton Inn & Conference Center, 4141 S Florida Ave, Lakeland, FL 33813; tel 813/647-3000 or toll free 800/325-3535; fax 813/644-0467. Exit 18 off I-4. Modern facility with adjacent multi-level parking garage. **Rooms:** 140 rms and stes. CI 2pm/CO 11am. Nonsmoking rms avail. **Amenities:** 🛏️🗄️ A/C, cable TV w/movies, VCR. Some units w/minibars. **Services:** ✗ VP 🖼️ 🔔 **Facilities:** 🔲 🛢️ 480 ⚓ 1 rst, 1 bar (w/entertainment), sauna, steam rm, whirlpool. Top-floor conference room offers grand views. **Rates:** HS Jan–Apr $88–$90 S or D; from $105 ste. Extra person $10. Children under 18 stay free. Lower rates off-season. Pking: Indoor/outdoor, free. Maj CC.

LAKE WALES

Map page M-7, E1

Hotel 🏨

🏛️🏛️ **Chalet Suzanne Country Inn**, 3800 Chalet Suzanne Dr, Lake Wales, FL 33853; tel 813/676-6011 or toll free 800/433-6011; fax 813/676-1814. A handful of pastel-colored buildings accented with some gingerbread details, arranged to provide views of the small lake, rose garden, or courtyard. The inn is most noted for its gourmet restaurant. **Rooms:** 30 rms, stes, and effic. CI 2pm/CO noon. **Amenities:** 🛏️🗄️ A/C, cable TV. Some units w/terraces, some w/Jacuzzis. **Services:** ✗ 🔔 🐾 Babysitting. **Facilities:** 🔲 ⚓ 1 rst (*see also* "Restaurants" below), 1 bar (w/entertainment). **Rates (BB):** HS Dec–Apr $125–$185 S or D; from $185 ste; from $145 effic. Extra person $12. Children under 5 stay free. Lower rates off-season. Spec packages avail. Pking: Outdoor, free. Maj CC.

Restaurants 🍽️

♣ **Chalet Suzanne**, in Chalet Suzanne Country Inn, 3800 Chalet Suzanne Dr, Lake Wales; tel 813/676-6011. 4 mi N of Lake Wales. **American.** This eclectic restaurant has received many kudos for service, quality, and style. The gourmet soups, which can be bought canned to take home, particularly stand out. **FYI:** Reservations recommended. Piano. Children's menu. Jacket required. **Open:** HS Nov–May breakfast daily 8–11am; lunch daily noon–5pm; dinner Sun–Thurs 5:30–8pm, Fri–Sat 5:30–9pm. Reduced hours off-season. **Prices:** PF dinner $52.50–$70. Maj CC. 💚 🏺

Vinton's, 229 E Stuart Ave, Lake Wales; tel 813/676-8242. 1.5 mi W of US 27. **Regional American/French.** The Creole-inspired menu outshines the decor at this popular family-owned restaurant. Try the shrimp jambalaya or one of the other southern-style seafood dishes. **FYI:** Reservations recommended. Dress code. **Open:** HS Dec–Apr lunch Mon–Fri 11:30am–2pm; dinner Mon–Sat 6–10pm. Reduced hours off-season. Closed some hols. **Prices:** Main courses $15.50–$19.50. Maj CC. 💚 ⚓

Attraction 🎟️

Bok Tower Gardens, 115 Tower Blvd; tel 813/676-1408. The focal point of the gardens is its 205-foot tower, which contains a 57-bell carillon. The resident carillonneur performs on it twice an hour, and there is a 45-minute recital daily at 3pm. The tower itself is closed to the public, but the visitor center presents a 10-minute video on the interior and contains historical exhibits, including an example of a carillon keyboard. Formal gardens and paths, nature trails, picnic area, restaurant. Guided tours daily, Jan–Apr at noon and 2pm. **Open:** Daily 8am–5pm. $

LAKE WORTH

Map page M-9, D4

Restaurant 🍽️

Abbey Road, 7306 Lake Worth Rd, Lake Worth; tel 407/967-4852. **American/Steak.** A comfortable grill with a library theme, done in lots of brick and wood. The menu includes prime rib, hamburgers, and other casual dishes; specials are offered daily. **FYI:** Reservations accepted. Band. Children's menu. **Open:** Lunch Mon–Fri noon–2pm; dinner Mon–Thurs 4–10pm, Fri–Sat 4–11pm, Sun 1–9pm. **Prices:** Main courses $9–$26. Maj CC. 💟⚓

LANTANA

Map page M-9, D4

Restaurant 🍽️

Anchor Inn, 2412 Floral Rd, Lantana; tel 407/965-4794. Exit 45 off I-95. ½ mi W of I-95. **Seafood/Steak/Pasta.** A casual, nautically styled seafood palace where you can watch the sun set over Lake Osborne as you dine. The menu includes the ocean catch of the day, a variety of seafood platters, and steaks. A good value. **FYI:** Reservations accepted. Children's menu. **Open:** Daily 5–9:30pm. Closed some hols. **Prices:** Main courses $10–$23. Maj CC. 🖼️ 💟⚓

LARGO

Map page M-6, E2

Attraction ■

Heritage Park, 11909 125th St N; tel 819/582-2123. This 21-acre, turn-of-the-century historical park features 20 of Pinellas County's oldest existing historic homes and buildings, which have been moved here from their original sites. There are periodic demonstrations of crafts such as rug-hooking, wool-spinning, flax-making, and weaving on a loom. **Open:** Tues–Sat 10am–4pm, Sun 1–4pm. Free.

LAUDERDALE-BY-THE-SEA

Map page M-11, A2

Motels ⊟

≣≣ Holiday Inn Lauderdale-by-the-Sea, 4116 N Ocean Blvd, Lauderdale-by-the-Sea, FL 33308; tel 305/776-1212 or toll free 800/465-4329; fax 305/776-1212 ext 600. ¼ mi S of Commercial Blvd. Two 5-story buildings with private beach access across the street. **Rooms:** 187 rms and effic. CI 3pm/CO noon. Nonsmoking rms avail. **Amenities:** 🛏 🖴 A/C, cable TV w/movies. Some units w/terraces. **Services:** ✕ 🗝 🛆 ↺ Car-rental desk, babysitting. **Facilities:** 🏊 ♿ 🎱 ⬛ ♿ 1 rst, 1 bar, 1 beach (ocean), lawn games, snorkeling, washer/dryer. **Rates:** HS Dec 16–Apr 24 $99–$120 S or D; from $135 effic. Extra person $10. Children under 18 stay free. Lower rates off-season. Pking: Outdoor, free. Maj CC.

≣ Santa Barbara Motel, 4301 El Mar Dr, Lauderdale-by-the-Sea, FL 33308; tel 305/491-5211. An owner-managed motel that tries hard to offer contemporary styling at competitive rates. **Rooms:** 13 rms, stes, and effic. CI noon-2pm/CO 11am. Full kitchens with microwaves and stoves. **Amenities:** 🛏 🖴 A/C, cable TV, refrig. Some units w/terraces. **Services:** ↺ Babysitting. **Facilities:** 🏊 **Rates:** HS Jan–Apr $42 S or D; from $88 ste; from $75 effic. Extra person $8. Lower rates off-season. Pking: Outdoor, free. Maj CC.

≣≣ Villas-by-the-Sea, 4456 El Mar Dr, Lauderdale-by-the-Sea, FL 33308; tel 305/772-3550 or toll free 800/247-8963; fax 305/772-3835. Affords good privacy and features a delightful pool area; close to beach and shopping. **Rooms:** 144 ctges/villas.

CI 3pm/CO 11am. Upbeat decor with designer appointments. Large units may have 3 TVs. **Amenities:** 🛏 🖴 A/C, cable TV, refrig. Some units w/terraces. **Services:** 🗝 🚐 ↺ Babysitting. **Facilities:** 🏊 ♿ 🎱 ⬛ 🏋 🎾 1 rst, 1 beach (ocean), lawn games, whirlpool, washer/dryer. **Rates (CP):** HS Feb–Apr from $110 ctge/villa. Extra person $8. Children under 12 stay free. Lower rates off-season. Spec packages avail. Pking: Outdoor, free. Maj CC.

Restaurants ▯▯▯

Aruba Beach Cafe, 1 Commercial Blvd, Lauderdale-by-the-Sea; tel 305/776-0001. **Caribbean.** An extremely popular open-air eatery with pier views. The Caribbean-inspired menu includes such dishes as grouper fingers and Baja black-bean chili. **FYI:** Reservations not accepted. Children's menu. **Open:** Mon–Sat 11am–2am, Sun 8am–2am. **Prices:** Main courses $9–$12. Maj CC. 🏞 🆅🅿 ♿

Country Ham n' Eggs, 4405 El Mar Dr, Lauderdale-by-the-Sea; tel 305/776-1666. **Coffeehouse.** Conveniently located close to the pier. Bright yellow booths, Formica tables. Serving meatloaf, burgers, sandwiches. **FYI:** Reservations not accepted. Children's menu. Beer and wine only. **Open:** Daily 6:30am–9pm. **Prices:** Main courses $2.50–$6.50. No CC.

Pier Restaurant, 2 E Commercial Blvd, Lauderdale-by-the-Sea; tel 305/776-1690. **American.** A popular '50s-style coffee shop with a nautical theme. A complete breakfast is available for $2.99. **FYI:** Reservations not accepted. No liquor license. **Open:** Daily 7am–4pm. **Prices:** Lunch main courses $3–$8. No CC. 🏞

LEESBURG

Map page M-6, B4

Motel ⊟

≣ Shoney's Inn, 1308 N 14th St, Leesburg, FL 34748; tel 904/787-1210 or toll free 800/222-2222; fax 904/365-0163. At jct US 27 and US 441. Variety of accommodations set amongst palm trees. Bahia Honda State Park is 10 miles away. **Rooms:** 130 rms. CI 3pm/CO 11am. Nonsmoking rms avail. **Amenities:** 🛏 A/C, cable TV w/movies. **Services:** 🚐 🛆 ↺ **Facilities:** 🏊 🏋 🎱 ♿ 1 bar, washer/dryer. Boat ramp and dock. **Rates:** HS Nov–Mar $38 S; $42 D. Children under 18 stay free. Lower rates off-season. Pking: Outdoor, free. Maj CC.

Restaurant 🍴

Vic's Embers, 7940 US 441, Leesburg; tel 904/728-8989. 4½ miles SE of jct US 27. **Seafood/Steak.** The atmosphere is casual and a bit rustic. Dishes include a variety of beef entrees, chops, pasta, and fish of the day. Early bird specials are a good value. **FYI:** Reservations not accepted. Guitar/piano. Children's menu. **Open:** Dinner Mon–Sat 4:30pm–2am, Sun 4:30–9:30pm; brunch Sun 11:30am–2:30pm. Closed some hols. **Prices:** Main courses $9.95–$13.95. Ltd CC. ▣ ▣ ⅄

LEHIGH ACRES

Map page M-8, D4

Resort 📷

▤▤▤ **Admiral Lehigh Golf Resort**, 225 E Joel Blvd, Lehigh Acres, FL 33936; tel 813/369-2121 or toll free 800/843-0971; fax 813/368-1660. Exit 22 off I-75. 500 acres. A holiday for the sporting crowd. An ideal spot for families in search of recreation. **Rooms:** 130 rms; 157 ctges/villas. CI 2pm/CO noon. Nonsmoking rms avail. Rooms overlook the courtyard or fairways. **Amenities:** 📷 ⅃ A/C, cable TV. Some units w/terraces. **Services:** ⅃ ⅃ Car-rental desk, social director, masseur, children's program, babysitting. **Facilities:** ⅃ ⅃ ⅃ ⅃ ⅃₃₆ ⅃ ⅃ ⅃ ⅃₂₂₀ ⅃ 3 rsts, 3 bars (1 w/entertainment), games rm, lawn games, beauty salon, playground. 9-hole miniature golf course. Fishing in the nearby lake. **Rates:** $78–$83 S or D; from $95 ctge/villa. Extra person $6. Children under 18 stay free. Lower rates off-season. Higher rates for spec evnts/hols. Spec packages avail. Pking: Outdoor, free. Maj CC.

LIDO BEACH

Map page M-8, B2

Hotels 📷

▤▤ **Harley Sandcastle**, 1540 Ben Franklin Dr, Lido Beach, FL 34236; tel 813/388-2181 or toll free 800/321-2323; fax 813/388-2655. A lowrise family-style property located directly on Lido Beach; enjoys a fine reputation both as a family spot and a romantic haven for couples. **Rooms:** 179 rms and stes. CI 3pm/CO 11am. **Amenities:** 📷 ⅃ ⅃ A/C, cable TV, refrig, in-rm safe. Some units w/terraces, some w/Jacuzzis. **Services:** ✗ ⅃ ⅃ Social director, babysitting. **Facilities:** ⅃ ⅃ ⅃ ⅃ ⅃₂₂₅ ⅃ 1 rst, 2 bars (1 w/entertainment), 1 beach (ocean), board surfing, games rm, washer/dryer. **Rates:** HS Jan–May $135–$205 S or D; from

$275 ste. Extra person $15. Children under 18 stay free. Lower rates off-season. Spec packages avail. Pking: Outdoor, free. Maj CC.

▤▤ **Holiday Inn–Lido Beach**, 233 Ben Franklin Dr, Lido Beach, FL 34236; tel 813/388-3941 or toll free 800/HOLIDAY; fax 813/388-4321. Exit 39 off I-75. At the northern end of Longboat Key, this atypical lowrise establishment with an innovative interior courtyard serves up fun and games to supplement the beach frontage. **Rooms:** 140 rms and stes. CI 3pm/CO noon. Nonsmoking rms avail. Some rooms with ocean views; others may face the Holidome. **Amenities:** 📷 ⅃ A/C, cable TV w/movies. Some units w/minibars, all w/terraces, some w/Jacuzzis. **Services:** ✗ ⅃ ⅃ Babysitting. **Facilities:** ⅃ ⅃₇₀ ⅃ 1 rst, 2 bars (1 w/entertainment), washer/dryer. **Rates:** HS Dec–May $159–$184 S or D; from $199 ste. Extra person $10. Children under 17 stay free. Lower rates off-season. Pking: Outdoor, free. Ltd CC.

Motels

▤▤ **Azure Tides**, 1330 Ben Franklin Dr, Lido Beach, FL 34236; tel 813/388-2101. 2½ mi S of Ringling Causeway. A pleasant low-key operation, located right on the beach. Near St Armands Circle and all its cafes. **Rooms:** 34 effic. CI 3pm/CO noon. **Amenities:** 📷 ⅃ A/C, cable TV w/movies, refrig, voice mail. Some units w/terraces. **Services:** ⅃ ⅃ Babysitting. **Facilities:** ⅃ 1 bar, 1 beach (ocean). The outdoor beach bar is open to guests as well as other beachgoers. **Rates:** HS Dec–May from $175 effic. Lower rates off-season. Pking: Outdoor, free. Maj CC.

▤▤▤ **Half Moon Beach Club**, 2050 Ben Franklin Dr, Lido Beach, FL 34236; tel 813/388-3694 or toll free 800/358-3245; fax 813/388-1938. Exit 39 off I-75. A beachside establishment catering to the comfort of beachgoers. Guests enjoy magnificent sunsets from the beach deck and private balconies. **Rooms:** 85 rms and stes. CI 3pm/CO 11am. **Amenities:** 📷 ⅃ ⅃ ⅃ A/C, cable TV w/movies, refrig. All units w/minibars, all w/terraces. **Services:** ✗ ⅃ ⅃ Babysitting. Beach attendant offers towels, beverages, and ice cream. **Facilities:** ⅃ ⅃₅₀ ⅃ 1 rst, 1 bar (w/entertainment), 1 beach (ocean), washer/dryer. **Rates:** HS Feb–Apr $110–$155 S or D; from $175 ste. Extra person $15. Children under 17 stay free. Lower rates off-season. Spec packages avail. Pking: Outdoor, free. Maj CC.

▤▤ **Hampton Inn**, 5000 N Tamiami Trail, Lido Beach, FL 34234; tel 813/351-7734 or toll free 800/336-9335; fax 813/351-8820. ¼ mi S of University Pkwy. Good for those seeking a dependable, short-stay option. **Rooms:** 97 rms. CI 2pm/CO 11am. Nonsmoking rms avail. **Amenities:** 📷 ⅃ ⅃ A/C, cable TV w/movies. Rooms furnished with dehumidifiers. **Services:** ![icon] ![icon] ![icon] **Facilities:** ![icon] ![icon] ![icon] ![icon] Washer/dryer. **Rates (CP):** HS Jan–Apr $84–$96 S or D. Extra person $10. Children under 18 stay free. Lower rates off-season. Spec packages avail. Pking: Outdoor, free. Maj CC.

Restaurant ![icon]

Carmichael's Beachside, in Lido Beach Inn, 1234 Ben Franklin Dr, Lido Beach; tel 813/388-3837. **Cafe/Deli.** A new roadside spot outfitted with plastic patio furniture and a jungle of potted plants, offering light fare to beachgoers. The menu includes a selection of sandwiches and pasta dishes, and Häagen-Dazs ice cream for dessert. **FYI:** Reservations not accepted. **Open:** Daily 8am–10pm. **Prices:** Main courses $5.50–$7.95. Maj CC. ![icon]

LIGHTHOUSE POINT

Map page M-11, A2

Restaurants ![icon]

Cafe Arugula, in 3110 Plaza, 3110 N Federal Hwy, Lighthouse Point; tel 305/785-7732. ¼ mi S of Sample Rd on US 1. **Regional American.** An innovative restaurant that prepares many items on its oak grill. Specialties include salmon fillet with arugula-butter sauce. **FYI:** Reservations recommended. Dress code. Beer and wine only. **Open:** Sun–Thurs 5:30–10pm, Fri–Sat 5:30–10:30pm. Closed some hols. **Prices:** Main courses $16–$30. Maj CC. ![icon]

Cafe Grazia, 3850 N Federal Hwy, Lighthouse Point; tel 305/942-7207. 1 block N of Sample Road on US 1. **Italian.** A traditional eatery that is truly Italian in both flavor and decor. The dining room is filled with red tablecloths, wine bottles, and Italian music. The menu includes pasta dishes, pizzas, bean and pasta soup, and lasagna. **FYI:** Reservations accepted. Piano/singer. Children's menu. **Open:** Lunch Mon–Fri 11:30am–2:30pm; dinner Sun–Thurs 4:30–10pm, Fri–Sat 4:30–11pm. **Prices:** Main courses $10–$15; PF dinner $13–$16. Maj CC. ![icon] ![icon]

★ **Cap's Place Island**, in Lighthouse Point Marina, 2765 NE 28th Court, Lighthouse Point; tel 305/941-0418. The restaurant's launch takes guests from Cap's Dock, next to the marina. **American.** There's no other place like this in Florida. The appealing shanty, with a simple, rustic decor and marina views, offers fresh seafood and other items; however, it is most noted for its fresh hearts of palm straight from the log. The restaurant, located on the National Register of Historic Places, is reached via

a launch that is on call to bring guests from the marina. Call ahead. **FYI:** Reservations recommended. Children's menu. **Open:** Sun–Thurs 5:30–10pm, Fri–Sat 5:30–11pm. Closed some hols. **Prices:** Main courses $13–$25. Maj CC. ![icon] ![icon]

LITTLE TORCH KEY

Map page M-10, D3

Resort ![icon]

![icon] **Little Palm Island**, Overseas Hwy MM 28.5, PO Box 1036, Little Torch Key, FL 33042; tel 305/872-2524 or toll free 800/843-8567; fax 305/872-4843. 5 acres. Romantic and secluded on its own private island, this is an exclusive, affluent adult sanctuary featuring top-of-the-line suites well hidden from view. Children under 12 not permitted. **Rooms:** 30 stes. CI 3pm/CO 11am. All units have outdoor showers. **Amenities:** ![icon] A/C, refrig. No phone or TV. All units w/minibars, all w/terraces. **Services:** ![icon] ![icon] ![icon] ![icon] Masseur. Hourly launch operates 7:30am–10:30 pm. **Facilities:** ![icon] ![icon] ![icon] ![icon] ![icon] ![icon] 2 rsts, 1 beach (ocean), snorkeling, sauna. Restaurant is open to public (except children under 12). **Rates:** HS Dec 21–Apr from $495 ste. Lower rates off-season. AP and MAP rates avail. Spec packages avail. Pking: Outdoor, free. Maj CC.

LIVE OAK

Map page M-4, C4

Attraction ![icon]

Suwannee River State Park; tel 904/362-2746. This tranquil, 1,800-acre park is at the halfway point of the Suwannee River Canoe Trail, which begins in Georgia. Within the park are earthworks remaining from a Confederate fortification overlooking the river. Fishing, boating, hiking, camping, nature trails. $

LONGBOAT KEY

Map page M-8, B1

Hotels ![icon]

![icon] **Harbour Villa Club at the Buccaneer**, 615 Dream Island Rd, Longboat Key, FL 34228; tel 813/383-9544 or toll free 800/433-5298; fax 813/383-8028. 8 mi N of St Armands Circle on Gulf Dr. Overlooking Sarasota Bay is this complex of tastefully designed 2-bedroom units. **Rooms:** 38 effic. CI 4pm/

CO noon. Nonsmoking rms avail. **Amenities:** 🔒⛱️📺 A/C, cable TV, refrig, VCR. All units w/terraces. **Services:** 🛗 🍴 Babysitting. **Facilities:** 🏊 Whirlpool, washer/dryer. On-site marina. **Rates:** HS Dec–May from $175 effic. Min stay. Lower rates off-season. Pking: Indoor/outdoor, free. Maj CC.

🏳️🏳️ **Holiday Inn–Longboat Key**, 4949 Gulf of Mexico Dr, Longboat Key, FL 34228; tel 813/383-3771 or toll free 800/HOLIDAY; fax 813/383-7871. Exit 42 off I-75. Opposite a public beach and within walking distance to St Armand's Circle shops and cafes. **Rooms:** 146 rms and stes. CI 3pm/CO noon. Nonsmoking rms avail. Rooms decorated in fresh tropical style; many offer views of the ocean. **Amenities:** 🔒⛱️ A/C, cable TV, bathrobes. Some units w/terraces, some w/Jacuzzis. **Services:** ✕ 🛗 🍴 Babysitting. **Facilities:** 🏊⛵🚲💻🎾🏌️ ♿ 3 rsts, 2 bars (1 w/entertainment), 1 beach (ocean), sauna, whirlpool. **Rates:** HS Jan–Apr $167–$194 S; $177–$204 D; from $206 ste. Extra person $10. Children under 18 stay free. Lower rates off-season. Higher rates for spec evnts/hols. Spec packages avail. Pking: Outdoor, free. Maj CC.

🏳️🏳️🏳️ **Longboat Key Hilton Beach Resort**, 4711 Gulf of Mexico Dr, Longboat Key, FL 34228; tel 813/383-2451 or toll free 800/282-3046; fax 813/383-7979. At St Armands Circle, drive north on Gulf Dr. Arranged in a handful of architecturally pleasing buildings standing parallel to the beach. Natural woods used both inside and out; surrounded by manicured landscaping. **Rooms:** 102 rms and stes. CI 3pm/CO 11am. Nonsmoking rms avail. **Amenities:** 🔒⛱️📺 🍷 A/C, cable TV w/movies, in-rm safe. All units w/minibars, all w/terraces. **Services:** ✕ 🛗 🍴 Twice-daily maid svce, babysitting. **Facilities:** 🏊🚲⛵🎾💻♿ 1 rst, 2 bars (w/entertainment), 1 beach (ocean), board surfing, lawn games. **Rates:** HS Oct–Apr $159–$249 S or D; from $235 ste. Extra person $25. Children under 18 stay free. Lower rates off-season. MAP rates avail. Spec packages avail. Pking: Outdoor, free. Maj CC.

Resorts

🏳️🏳️🏳️ **The Colony Beach & Tennis Resort**, 1620 Gulf of Mexico Dr, Longboat Key, FL 34228; tel 813/383-6464 or toll free 800/4 COLONY; fax 813/383-7549. At St Armands Circle drive north on Gulf Dr. 18 acres. Beach lovers will relish their stay in this gated enclave of taste and simplicity. So will families, who seem to get special attention. The large, super-friendly staff seems like it was hand-picked from Disney. **Rooms:** 235 stes. CI 4pm/CO 11am. **Amenities:** 🔒⛱️📺 🍷 A/C, cable TV w/movies, refrig, in-rm safe. Some units w/terraces, all w/Jacuzzis. **Services:** ✕ 🛗 📹🚗 🛗 🍴 Car-rental desk, social director, masseur, children's program, babysitting. **Facilities:** 🏊🚲 △ 🎾19 ⛵💻🎾 ♿ 2 rsts, 2 bars (1 w/entertainment), 1 beach

(ocean), lifeguard, board surfing, snorkeling, spa, sauna, steam rm, whirlpool, day-care ctr, playground, washer/dryer. **Rates:** HS Oct–Apr from $255 ste. Extra person $16. Children under 18 stay free. Min stay spec evnts. Lower rates off-season. Higher rates for spec evnts/hols. Spec packages avail. Pking: Outdoor, free. Maj CC. Units priced according to proximity to beach.

🏳️🏳️🏳️ **Resort at Longboat Key Club**, 301 Gulf of Mexico Dr, PO Box 15000, Longboat Key, FL 34228; tel 813/383-8821 or toll free 800/237-8821; fax 813/383-0359. St Armand's Circle to Gulf Dr N. 443 acres. An upmarket choice catering to the country club set. Resort encompasses a marina, beach area, fairways, and accommodations of varying sizes and shapes. **Rooms:** 225 rms, stes, and effic. CI 3pm/CO 11am. Nonsmoking rms avail. **Amenities:** 🔒⛱️📺 🍷 A/C, cable TV w/movies, refrig, in-rm safe. All units w/minibars, all w/terraces. **Services:** ✕ 📹 🛗 🍴 Twice-daily maid svce, car-rental desk, masseur, babysitting. Professional staff addresses guests needs adequately and with good cheer. **Facilities:** 🏊🚲 △ 🎾45 ♿🎾32 ⛵ 💻🎾 ♿ 5 rsts, 5 bars (1 w/entertainment), 1 beach (ocean), board surfing, snorkeling, spa, whirlpool, washer/dryer. **Rates:** HS Mar–Apr $195–$290 S or D; from $280 ste; from $315 effic. Extra person $15. Children under 18 stay free. Min stay spec evnts. Lower rates off-season. Higher rates for spec evnts/hols. Spec packages avail. Pking: Outdoor, free. Maj CC.

Restaurants 🍴

The Chart House, 210 Gulf of Mexico Dr, Longboat Key; tel 813/383-5593. **Seafood/Steak.** The open kitchen, the large, comfortable bar area, the wicker furnishings, and the terrific ocean view unite to create a charming, casual atmosphere. Besides steak and prime rib, there's lobster tail, swordfish, mahimahi, stone crab, and salmon. Salad bar. **FYI:** Reservations recommended. **Open:** Dinner daily 5–10pm. **Prices:** Main courses $17–$24. Maj CC. 🏔️ ♿

Moore's Stone Crab, 800 Broadway, Longboat Key; tel 813/383-1748. At Gulf of Mexico Dr at north end of Longboat Key. **Seafood.** A casual restaurant and bar overlooking Sarasota Bay. Popular menu items are scallops, shrimp, oysters, Florida lobster, and stone crab claws. **FYI:** Reservations not accepted. Children's menu. **Open:** Sun–Thurs 11:30am–9pm, Fri–Sat 11:30am–9:30pm. Closed some hols; May 16–Oct 14. **Prices:** Main courses $6.95–$23.95. Ltd CC. 🏔️ ♿

LONG KEY
Map page M-11, E1

Attraction 💼

Long Key State Recreation Area, Overseas Hwy, MM 68; tel 305/664-4815. This 1,000-acre park features a specially marked canoe trail to guide explorers through some of its wetlands. There is also a beach and several picnic areas, as well as swimming, fishing, canoe rentals, hiking, beachfront camping, nature trails. $$

MADEIRA BEACH
Map page M-8, A1

Hotels 🏨

≡≡ Holiday Inn–Madeira Beach, 15208 Gulf Blvd, Madeira Beach, FL 33708; tel 813/392-2275 or toll free 800/HOLIDAY; fax 813/392-2275. At 150th Ave. A welcome break from this high traffic area. Preferred among repeat guests for its ample beach frontage and waterfront activities. **Rooms:** 148 rms and stes. CI 4pm/CO 11am. Nonsmoking rms avail. **Amenities:** 🛍 ⏰ A/C, cable TV w/movies. Some units w/terraces. **Services:** ✕ 🖨 🍴 Babysitting. Car rentals and sightseeing are arranged by the staff. **Facilities:** 🏋 🏊 ⅔ 1 rst, 2 bars (1 w/entertainment), 1 beach (ocean), lifeguard, games rm, washer/dryer. Beach cabanas and boats available, as are nearby fishing charters. Poolside bar. **Rates:** HS Mar–Apr $105 S; $165 D; from $235 ste. Extra person $10. Children under 12 stay free. Lower rates off-season. Higher rates for spec evnts/hols. Spec packages avail. Pking: Outdoor, free. Maj CC.

≡ Shoreline Island Resort Motel, 14200 Gulf Blvd, Madeira Beach, FL 33708; tel 813/397-6641 or toll free 800/635-8373; fax 813/393-9157. Exit 15 off I-275 S. An all-adult resort community. **Rooms:** 69 rms and effic. CI 3pm/CO 11am. Nonsmoking rms avail. **Amenities:** 🛍 ⏰ 🖥 A/C, cable TV w/movies, refrig. Some units w/terraces. Gulf-front units have companion recliners. **Facilities:** 🏊 1 beach (ocean), washer/dryer. **Rates:** HS Jan 26–Apr 26 $80 S; $80–$146 D; from $136 effic. Lower rates off-season. Pking: Outdoor, free. Maj CC.

Restaurant 🍴

Friendly Fisherman, 150 128th Ave, Madeira Beach; tel 813/391-6025. At Gulf Blvd. **Seafood.** Before you dine, sample one of this waterfront eatery's drink specials, like the melon breezer or the lime freeze. For dinner, you can dive into barbecued ribs, Cajun shrimp, grouper nuggets, or deviled crab. **FYI:** Reservations not accepted. Band. Children's menu. **Open:** Daily 7am–10pm. Closed Dec 25. **Prices:** Main courses $6.45–$14.95. Ltd CC. ✅ ⅙

Attractions 💼

John's Pass Village and Boardwalk, 12901 Gulf Blvd; tel 813/397-9494. This rustic Florida fishing village lies on the southern edge of Madeira Beach, where the waters of Boca Ciega Bay meet the gulf. More than 100 merchants ply their wares here, but the focal point is the large fishing pier and marina, where you can watch commercial and charter fishing boats unloading their daily catch, or sign up for a day's fishing trip on a party boat. **Open:** Daily 9am–6pm for most shops and activities, 8am–11pm for most restaurants. Free.

Capt Hubbard's Marina, 150 128th Ave; tel 813/393-1947 or 392-0167. Known as a "fish famous" spot, the marina is the focal point of John's Pass, a huge recreational village perched on pilings where Boca Ciega Bay meets the gulf. Sailings daily: half-day trips, 8am–1pm and 1–6pm; full-day trips, 8am–6pm; overnight trips, Tues and Fri departing 8pm. $$$$

MAITLAND
Map page M-7, C2

Restaurants 🍴

Antonio's Lafiamma, 611 S Orlando Ave, Maitland; tel 407/645-5523. At Maitland Ave. **Northern Italian.** A stylishly contemporary Italian restaurant with floor-to-ceiling windows overlooking Lake Lily. A variety of pasta dishes, such as bow-tie pasta with scallops tossed in homemade pesto, is available. The deli downstairs offers outdoor dining. **FYI:** Reservations accepted. **Open:** Lunch Mon–Fri 11:30am–2:30pm; dinner Mon–Thurs 5–10pm, Fri–Sat 5–11pm. Closed some hols. **Prices:** Main courses $8.95–$27.95. Maj CC. ⅙

Bubble Room, 1351 S Orlando Ave, Maitland; tel 407/628-3331. Between Maitland Ave and Lee Rd. **New American.** A fun, eclectic restaurant filled with eye-catching memorabilia from the 1930s and '40s. The desserts are popular. A great children's menu is available. **FYI:** Reservations not accepted. Children's menu. **Open:** Lunch Mon–Fri 11:30am–2:30pm, Sat–Sun 11:30am–4pm; dinner Mon–Thurs 5:30–10pm, Fri 5:30–11pm, Sat 5–11pm, Sun 5–10pm. Closed Dec 25. **Prices:** Main courses $11–$27. Maj CC. ⅙

Jordan's Grove, 1300 S Orlando Ave, Maitland; tel 407/ 628-0020. Between Maitland Ave and Lee Rd. **Regional American.** A renowned, eclectic restaurant set in a restored historic home surrounded by giant oaks. One popular dish is grilled yellowfin tuna. The wine list is quite extensive and includes many hard-to-find vintages. The dessert menu includes home-style classics like old-fashioned bread pudding, as well as more exotic offerings such as macadamia nut torte. **FYI:** Reservations recommended. Beer and wine only. No smoking. **Open:** Lunch Tues–Fri 11:30am–2:30pm; dinner Tues–Sun 6–10pm; brunch Sun 11:30am–2:30pm. Closed Dec 25. **Prices:** Main courses $15.95–$25.95. Maj CC. ⬚

MANALAPAN

Map page M-9, D4

Resort ⬚

⬚⬚⬚⬚⬚ **The Ritz-Carlton Palm Beach**, 100 S Ocean Blvd, Manalapan, FL 33462; tel 407/533-6000 or toll free 800/ 241-3333; fax 407/588-4202. 8 mi S of downtown Palm Beach, exit 46 off I-95. Go east on Lantana Blvd to Ocean Blvd (Fla A1A). 7 acres. Designed in a 6-story, Mediterranean-style double-U facing the ocean, topped with faux bell towers. Furnished in true Ritz-Carlton fashion with polished wood paneling, museum-caliber art, and high-ceilinged salons with crystal chandeliers and elegantly draped windows. **Rooms:** 270 rms and stes. Exec-level rms avail. CI 3pm/CO noon. Express checkout avail. Nonsmoking rms avail. Rooms are gracious, refined, and comfortable; best bets for families are ground-floor "minimum" rooms opening directly to a quiet, green courtyard. Extra-large, marble-clad bathrooms with twin vanities. **Amenities:** ⬚ ⬚ ⬚ A/C, cable TV, refrig, in-rm safe, bathrobes. All units w/minibars, all w/terraces. Terraces have dining table and chairs. All rooms have 2-line phones. **Services:** ⬚ ⬚ ⬚ ⬚ ⬚ ⬚ Twice-daily maid svce, car-rental desk, masseur, children's program, babysitting. Brisk, competent, professional service. Outstanding Ritz Kids programs (with club room and tennis clinics). **Facilities:** ⬚ ⬚ ⬚ ⬚ ⬚ ⬚ ⬚ ⬚ ⬚ 3 rsts, 3 bars (1 w/entertainment), 1 beach (ocean), lifeguard, spa, sauna, steam rm, whirlpool, beauty salon, day-care ctr. Sculpted pool area with private cabanas. Golf privileges at nearby courses. Lifeguard at the adjoining state beach park. **Rates:** HS Dec 13–May 1 $310–$600 S or D; from $870 ste. Children under 18 stay free. Lower rates off-season. Spec packages avail. Pking: Indoor/outdoor, $12. Maj CC. Rates vary by room location (e.g., rooms with direct beach view are higher) and floor.

MARATHON

Map page M-10, E4

Hotels ⬚

⬚⬚⬚ **Banana Bay Resort & Marina**, 4590 Overseas Hwy, MM 49.5, Marathon, FL 33050; tel 305/743-3500 or toll free 800/226-2621; fax 305/743-2670. A resorty place with handsome accommodations. **Rooms:** 60 rms. CI 3pm/CO 11am. Rooms are decorated with plants, wicker wing chairs, ceiling fans, shutters, bed ruffles, and matching fabrics. **Amenities:** ⬚ ⬚ ⬚ A/C, cable TV, refrig. Some units w/terraces. **Services:** ⬚ ⬚ Babysitting. **Facilities:** ⬚ ⬚ ⬚ ⬚ ⬚ 2 ⬚ ⬚ ⬚ ⬚ 1 rst, 2 bars (w/entertainment), 1 beach (ocean), lawn games, snorkeling, whirlpool, washer/dryer. Small man-made beach. Parasailing offered seasonally. **Rates (CP):** HS Dec–Apr $95–$175 S or D. Extra person $10. Children under 5 stay free. Min stay HS, wknds, and spec evnts. Lower rates off-season. Higher rates for spec evnts/hols. Spec packages avail. Pking: Outdoor, free. Maj CC.

⬚⬚⬚ **Faro Blanco Marine Resort**, Overseas Hwy MM 48.5, Marathon, FL 33050; tel 305/743-9018 or toll free 800/ 759-3276; fax 305/743-2918. Unique, commendable offering comprising cottages, rooms in a 2-story barge docked in the marina, 3-bedroom condominiums, and 2 apartments in a lighthouse on the pier. **Rooms:** 95 stes and effic; 30 ctges/villas. CI 2pm/CO 11am. **Amenities:** ⬚ A/C, cable TV, refrig. Some units w/terraces. **Services:** ⬚ ⬚ ⬚ Babysitting. **Facilities:** ⬚ ⬚ ⬚ ⬚ ⬚ ⬚ 4 rsts, 4 bars (1 w/entertainment), 1 beach (ocean), playground, washer/dryer. **Rates:** HS Dec–Apr from $145 ste; from $69 effic; from $65 ctge/villa. Extra person $10. Children under 12 stay free. Min stay spec evnts. Lower rates off-season. Pking: Outdoor, free. Maj CC.

Resorts

⬚⬚⬚ **Hawk's Cay Resort & Marina**, Overseas Hwy, MM 61, Marathon, FL 33050; tel 305/743-7000 or toll free 800/ 432-2242; fax 305/743-5215. 10 mi N of Marathon Airport. 60 acres. A good family facility; operates a dolphin research program on the premises with 14 dolphins and daily shows offered free to guests and visitors. **Rooms:** 176 rms and stes; 17 ctges/ villas. CI 3pm/CO 11am. Nonsmoking rms avail. **Amenities:** ⬚ ⬚ A/C, cable TV w/movies, refrig. Some units w/minibars, all w/terraces, some w/fireplaces, some w/Jacuzzis. **Services:** ⬚ ⬚ ⬚ Car-rental desk, children's program, babysitting. **Facilities:** ⬚ ⬚ ⬚ ⬚ ⬚ ⬚ ⬚ 350 ⬚ 3 rsts, 2 bars (1 w/entertainment), 1 beach (cove/inlet), games rm, snorkeling, spa, whirlpool, playground. **Rates (BB):** HS Dec–Apr $205–

$365 S or D; from $380 ste; from $400 ctge/villa. Extra person $40. Children under 12 stay free. Lower rates off-season. Higher rates for spec evnts/hols. Spec packages avail. Pking: Outdoor, free. Maj CC.

≣≣≣ **Sombrero Resort & Lighthouse Marina**, 19 Sombrero Blvd, Marathon, FL 33050; tel 305/743-2250 or toll free 800/433-8660; fax 305/743-2998. Modern, well-maintained facility. **Rooms:** 122 stes and effic. CI 2pm/CO 11am. Nonsmoking rms avail. Gray and blue decor, formica-covered furniture. Large showers with seats. **Amenities:** 🛗🖲 A/C, cable TV, refrig, voice mail. All units w/terraces. **Services:** 🛎 **Facilities:** 🔧🏊🍸2 🏖 🎱 1 rst, 2 bars (1 w/entertainment), games rm, snorkeling, sauna, washer/dryer. Golf across the street. Sunny pool has inviting bar. **Rates (CP):** HS Dec–Apr from $125 ste; from $160 effic. Extra person $10. Children under 12 stay free. Lower rates off-season. Spec packages avail. Pking: Outdoor, free. Maj CC.

Attractions 🖼

Museum of Natural History, 5550 Overseas Hwy, MM 50.5; tel 305/743-9100. This small museum displays dozens of local historical artifacts, including shell tools and pottery from pre-Columbian native tribes and booty from one of America's oldest shipwrecks. Other exhibits focus on the Keys' natural habitats, including a coral reef tank that holds sharks, lobsters, and tropical fish, and a "touch" tank, where visitors can handle rays, starfish, and other safe sea creatures. Outside, visitors are encouraged to explore the museum's quarter-mile nature trail, which winds through rare tropical palm hammock. **Open:** Mon–Sat 9am–5pm, Sun noon–5pm. $$

Dolphin Research Center, Overseas Hwy, MM 59 (in Marathon Shores); tel 305/289-0002. A nonprofit organization that runs regularly scheduled tours to help visitors learn about and interact with dolphins and other sea creatures. The more in-depth (and much more expensive) DolphinInsight program includes a guided tour of the facility and open-air workshops on dolphin physiology and basic training techniques. Visitors are given the opportunity to touch and communicate with dolphins using a variety of hand signals. The center also operates a swim-with-the-dolphins program called Dolphin Encounter (reservations required up to a month in advance). Basic tours run daily at 10am, 12:30pm, 2pm, and 3:30pm. $$$

MARCO ISLAND

Map page M-10, B2

Hotels 🏨

≣≣ **Eagle's Nest Beach Resort**, 410 S Collier Blvd, Marco Island, FL 33927; tel 813/237-8906; fax 813/642-1599. Exit 15 off I-75. Unpretentious condo complex offering daily and weekly rentals. Outlying units to supplement the 12-story tower, where most guests stay. **Rooms:** 96 effic. CI 3pm/CO 10am. **Amenities:** 🛗🖲🍷 A/C, cable TV w/movies, refrig, VCR. No phone. All units w/terraces, all w/Jacuzzis. **Services:** 🛎 Children's program, babysitting. **Facilities:** 🔧🎱🏋20 1 beach (ocean), games rm, racquetball, spa, sauna, whirlpool, washer/dryer. Barbecue grills. **Rates:** HS Dec–Apr from $260 effic. Children under 18 stay free. Min stay. Lower rates off-season. Pking: Indoor/outdoor, free. Ltd CC.

≣≣≣ **Marco Bay Resort**, 1001 N Barfield Dr, Marco Island, FL 33937; tel 813/394-8881 or toll free 800/228-0661; fax 813/394-8909. Exit 15 off I-75. Go south on Fla 951 to the island and make a right at the first traffic light. A major condo complex drawing snowbirds who come for more than just a few days and desire a self-sufficient arrangement, while still being just a mile to shopping. Tends to receive more seasoned travelers than the chain names. **Rooms:** 109 effic. CI 4pm/CO 11am. Nonsmoking rms avail. **Amenities:** 🛗🖲🖲 A/C, cable TV w/movies, refrig. All units w/terraces. **Services:** 🛎 **Facilities:** 🔧🎱2 🏊200 ⚓ 2 rsts, 1 bar, whirlpool, washer/dryer. On-site marina. **Rates:** HS Jan–Apr from $130 effic. Children under 18 stay free. Lower rates off-season. Higher rates for spec evnts/hols. Pking: Indoor/outdoor, free. Maj CC.

≣≣≣ **Radisson Suite Beach Resort**, 600 S Collier Blvd, Marco Island, FL 33937; tel 813/394-4100 or toll free 800/333-3333; fax 813/394-0419. Exit 15 off I-75. A colorful, first-rate operation with luscious landscaped grounds, an attractive pool area, and a good selection of dining and recreational options. **Rooms:** 268 rms and stes. CI 4pm/CO noon. Nonsmoking rms avail. **Amenities:** 🛗🖲🖲 A/C, cable TV w/movies, refrig. All units w/terraces. **Services:** ✕🗝🧺🛎 Social director, children's program, babysitting. **Facilities:** 🔧🚲⚠ 🎱🚣🏊400 ⚓ 2 rsts, 2 bars (1 w/entertainment), 1 beach (ocean), games rm, racquetball, whirlpool, playground, washer/dryer. **Rates:** HS Feb–Apr $185 S or D; from $235 ste. Lower rates off-season. Higher rates for spec evnts/hols. Spec packages avail. Pking: Indoor/outdoor, free. Maj CC.

Resorts

≣≣≣ **Marco Island Hilton Beach Resort**, 560 S Collier Blvd, Marco Island, FL 33937; tel 813/394-5000 or toll free 800/445-8667; fax 813/394-5251. Exit 15 off I-75. 23 acres. A leader among the beachfront hotels, this shining facility boasts trend-setting design and excellent maintenance. **Rooms:** 290 rms and stes. CI 3pm/CO noon. Nonsmoking rms avail. **Amenities:** 🛏 👁 📺 🍽 A/C, cable TV w/movies, refrig, in-rm safe. All units w/minibars, all w/terraces. **Services:** ✕ ➔ VP ⌲ ⊐ Social director, masseur, children's program, babysitting. **Facilities:** 🔥 ⚠ 🏌 ⛵ 🏊 🏓 💯 ⊟ ⚿ 3 rsts, 2 bars (1 w/entertainment), 1 beach (ocean), board surfing, games rm, sauna, steam rm, whirlpool. **Rates:** HS Dec–Apr $175–$300 S or D; from $350 ste. Extra person $15. Children under 18 stay free. Lower rates off-season. Higher rates for spec evnts/hols. Spec packages avail. Pking: Outdoor, free. Maj CC.

≣≣≣ **Marriott's Marco Island Resort and Golf Club**, 400 S Collier Blvd, Marco Island, FL 33937; tel 813/394-2511 or toll free 800/228-9290; fax 813/642-2672. Exit 15 off I-75. Take Fla 951 to bridge; hotel 2.5 miles ahead. 12 acres. The largest resort on Florida's Gulf Coast, this deluxe establishment has two 9-story towers and two A-frame public wings that form beachfront courtyards. Popular with couples, families, and groups. **Rooms:** 738 rms and stes. CI 3pm/CO noon. Nonsmoking rms avail. All units have gulf views. **Amenities:** 🛏 👁 📺 A/C, cable TV w/movies, refrig, in-rm safe. All units w/minibars, all w/terraces. **Services:** ✕ ➔ VP ⌲ ⊐ Twice-daily maid svce, car-rental desk, social director, masseur, children's program. **Facilities:** 🔥 🚴 ⚠ ▶₁₈ ⛳₁₆ 🏊 🏌 ⛵ 🏓 💯 ⊟ ⚿ 4 rsts (see also "Restaurants" below), 4 bars (3 w/entertainment), 1 beach (ocean), board surfing, games rm, whirlpool, beauty salon, washer/dryer. Miniature golf course. Mall with chic boutiques. **Rates:** HS Jan–Apr $240–$350 D; from $520 ste. Children under 17 stay free. Lower rates off-season. Higher rates for spec evnts/hols. Spec packages avail. Pking: Outdoor, free. Maj CC.

Restaurants 🍴

Cafe Calusa, 527 Bald Eagle Dr, Marco Island; tel 813/394-5200. 2 blocks N of Collier Blvd. **Seafood.** A casual spot with an inspired menu. Dishes include stuffed crab cakes; calusa-bronzed grouper with Caribbean spices, cilantro, and lime; and grilled lamb chops. **FYI:** Reservations accepted. **Open:** Mon–Sat 5:30–10pm. **Prices:** Main courses $13.95–$18.95. Maj CC. ⚿

Cafe de Marco, in Port of Marco Shopping Village, 244 Palm St, Marco Island; tel 813/394-6262. **Seafood.** A garden-style cafe with wicker appointments, mint-colored tablecloths, and a fresh spring ambiance. Enjoy the giant prawns or one of the fresh fish dishes served from the daily menu. Outdoor dining is available on the brick patio. **FYI:** Reservations recommended. Children's menu. Beer and wine only. **Open:** Lunch Wed–Fri 11:30am–2:30pm; dinner daily 5–10pm. Closed some hols. **Prices:** Main courses $15–$25. Maj CC. 🍽

Captain's Corner Restaurant & Lounge, in Chamber of Commerce Plaza, 1106½ N Collier Blvd, Marco Island; tel 813/394-8887. **Seafood.** Dine indoors or on the enclosed porch overlooking Cedar Bay and the marina. The casual, comfortable eatery offers a lobster buffet and lots of local seafood. **FYI:** Reservations recommended. Dancing/piano. Children's menu. **Open:** Lunch daily noon–2:30pm; dinner daily 4:30–10pm. **Prices:** Main courses $13–$21. Maj CC. 🚗 ⚿

The Dining Room at Heritage Square, 1000 N Collier Blvd, Marco Island; tel 813/394-2221. **French.** A small, offbeat, romantic eatery in which the kitchen opens to the dining room. Chilled curried apple soup, fish of the day, and breast of chicken with grapes in wine sauce are featured. **FYI:** Reservations accepted. Beer and wine only. **Open:** Mon–Sat 5:30–10pm. **Prices:** Main courses $16.95–$23.95. Maj CC. ♥

Olde Marco Inn, 100 Palm St, Marco Island; tel 813/394-3131. **New American.** Established in 1883, this antiquated inn once rented rooms for $1 per day. Today, you can enjoy fine dining here amid 150-year-old Audubon prints and other period antiques, including the 2,000-piece prism-and-cranberry-glass chandelier. **FYI:** Reservations accepted. **Open:** Lunch daily 11:30am–2:30pm; dinner daily 5:30–10pm. **Prices:** Main courses $12.95–$24.95. Maj CC.

Snook Inn, 1215 Bald Eagle Dr, Marco Island; tel 813/394-3313. On the corner of Palm St and Bald Eagle Dr. **Seafood.** Rustic Florida setting. The grouper sandwich is the house specialty. **FYI:** Reservations not accepted. Children's menu. **Open:** HS Dec–May daily 11am–10pm. Reduced hours off-season. Closed some hols. **Prices:** Main courses $6.95–$16.95. Maj CC. 🚗 🚙 ⚿

★ **Stan's Idle Hour Seafood Restaurant**, downtown Goodland, Marco Island; tel 813/394-3041. **Seafood/Steak.** Enjoy fresh ocean treats at this fun and funky '60s-inspired eatery. (Stan, the owner, looks as if that era was mighty good to him.) Sample grilled shrimp and the softshell crabs. The outdoor bar shouldn't be missed. The patio hosts a party and show on Sundays. **FYI:** Reservations accepted. Band. Children's menu. **Open:** Tues–Sun 11am–10pm. Closed some hols; Aug. **Prices:** Main courses $10–$18. Ltd CC. 🚗 ⚿

Voyager Steak & Seafood, in Marriott's Marco Island Resort and Golf Club, 400 S Collier Blvd, Marco Island; tel 813/394-2511. **Seafood/Steak.** This restaurant serves what many consider the best brunch on the island, and at reasonable cost. The regular menu offers salads, seafood, beef, pasta, and fresh breads. **FYI:** Reservations recommended. Piano. Children's menu. **Open:** Dinner daily 5–10pm; brunch Sun 10am–2pm. **Prices:** Main courses $9.95–$18.95. Maj CC. ▨ ▦ ▧ &

Attraction ▣

Ted Smallwood's Store; tel 813/695-2989. Located on Chololoskee Island, just south of Everglades City, this is one of southwestern Florida's oldest buildings, dating back to pioneer days. It has been converted to a museum and gift shop. The rustic store was also once a Native American trading post. **Open:** Dec–Apr, daily 10am–5pm; schedule varies rest of year. $

MARIANNA

Map page M-3, A2

Motel ▣

▥▥ **Marianna Holiday Inn**, US 90 E, PO Box 979, Marianna, FL 32446; tel 904/526-3251 or toll free 800/HOLIDAY; fax 904/482-6223. Exit 21 off I-10. Standard, affordable lodging. **Rooms:** 80 rms. CI 2pm/CO noon. Nonsmoking rms avail. **Amenities:** ▨ & A/C, cable TV w/movies. **Services:** ✗ ▨ ↩ ↩ **Facilities:** ▨ ▨ ▨ & 1 rst, washer/dryer. Restaurant serves beer and wine coolers only. **Rates:** $44–$59 S; $46–$61 D. Extra person $5. Children under 19 stay free. Spec packages avail. Pking: Outdoor, free. Maj CC.

Attraction ▣

Florida Caverns State Park; tel 904/482-9598. An intriguing series of caves 65 feet underground decorated with stalagmites, limestone stalactites, columns, and other striking formations. Chambers include the Waterfall Room, the Cathedral Room, and the Wedding Room, so-called for its ornate wedding cake appearance. Guided ranger tours cover about a half-mile of illuminated passageways.

    Besides the caverns, the park offers swimming, fishing, horseback-riding (stables are available), and camping. The 50-mile Chipola River Canoe Trail begins in the park. **Open:** Daily 8am–sunset. $$

MARINELAND

Map page M-5, D4

Hotel ▣

▥▥▥ **Quality Inn–Marineland**, 9507 Ocean Shore Blvd, Marineland, FL 32086; tel 904/471-1222 or toll free 800/228-5151; fax 904/471-3352. Exit 93E off I-95 S. A beachfront family hotel located at the entrance to Marineland park. **Rooms:** 125 rms and stes. CI 3pm/CO 11am. Nonsmoking rms avail. **Amenities:** ▨ A/C, cable TV. Some units w/terraces. **Services:** ↩ Babysitting. **Facilities:** ▨ ▨ ▨ & 1 rst, 2 bars (1 w/entertainment), 1 beach (ocean), lawn games, playground, washer/dryer. Pool with neighboring kiddie pool receives sun throughout the day. Tennis courts across the street. **Rates:** HS Feb–Apr/May–Aug $69–$99 S or D; from $104 ste. Extra person $5. Children under 18 stay free. Lower rates off-season. Higher rates for spec evnts/hols. Spec packages avail. Pking: Outdoor, free. Maj CC.

Attraction ▣

Marineland of Florida, 9507 Ocean Shore Blvd (Fla A1A); tel 904/471-1111. The first marinelife park to successfully maintain dolphins in a manmade environment and achieve a successful birth in captivity, this was, in pre-Disney days, Florida's most popular attraction. Dolphins and California sea lions perform for crowds in the huge circular oceanarium. Also on view are sharks, moray eels, barracudas, and many other saltwater and freshwater fish; rare and beautiful sea shells are displayed in the Margaret Herrick Shell Museum. A 3-D film called *Sea Dream* is shown throughout the day at the Aquarius Theater. Restaurant and snack bars on premises. **Open:** Daily 9am–5pm. $$$$

MATLACHA

Map page M-6, C2

Restaurant ▣

Snook Harbour Inn, at the foot of Matlacha Bridge, Matlacha; tel 813/283-1131. **Seafood.** Dine indoors or out in a relaxing setting offering great views of the water. The weekend seafood buffet is a good value. Desserts are made on the premises. **FYI:** Reservations not accepted. Children's menu. Beer and wine only. **Open:** Daily 11am–10pm. **Prices:** Main courses $4–$15. No CC. ▧ ▨ &

MELBOURNE

Map page M-7, D4

Hotels 🛏

≝≝ **Courtyard by Marriott**, 2101 W New Haven Ave, Melbourne, FL 32904; tel 407/724-6400; fax 407/984-4006. Exit 71 off 95. Attractive hotel featuring neatly landscaped grounds and an attentive, friendly staff. A good value. **Rooms:** 146 rms and stes. Exec-level rms avail. CI 3pm/CO noon. Express checkout avail. Nonsmoking rms avail. **Amenities:** 🛎 ⚡ 🖭 A/C, cable TV w/movies. Some units w/terraces. **Services:** 🚗 🖾 🍴 Babysitting. **Facilities:** 🗔 🎾 🚷 🚹 1 bar, whirlpool, washer/dryer. **Rates:** HS Dec–Apr $49–$74 S or D; from $99 ste. Children under 18 stay free. Lower rates off-season. Spec packages avail. Pking: Outdoor, free. Maj CC.

≝≝≝ **Melbourne Hilton at Rialto Place**, 200 Rialto Place, Melbourne, FL 32901; tel 407/768-0200 or toll free 800/437-8010; fax 407/984-2528. Exit 71 off I-95. A classy place with a smart, modern style. The glass-and-concrete highrise is not on the beach, but it offers many of the facilities of a first-class hotel. **Rooms:** 240 rms and stes. CI 3pm/CO noon. Express checkout avail. Nonsmoking rms avail. **Amenities:** 🛎 ⚡ A/C, cable TV w/movies. Some units w/minibars, some w/terraces, some w/Jacuzzis. **Services:** ✕ 🖎 🚗 🖾 🍴 Car-rental desk, babysitting. **Facilities:** 🗔 🚹 🎾 🏊 🚹 1 rst, 2 bars, games rm, whirlpool, playground, washer/dryer. The sports bar is immensely popular. **Rates:** HS Jan–Apr $109–$139 S or D; from $225 ste. Children under 18 stay free. Lower rates off-season. Spec packages avail. Pking: Outdoor, free. Maj CC.

≝≝≝ **Radisson Suite Hotel Oceanside**, 3101 N Fla A1A, Melbourne, FL 32903; tel 407/773-9260 or toll free 800/333-3333; fax 407/777-3190. Exit 71 off 95. An oceanfront highrise. **Rooms:** 79 stes. CI 4pm/CO noon. Nonsmoking rms avail. Some rooms have bunk beds for families. **Amenities:** 🛎 🖭 A/C, cable TV, refrig, VCR, voice mail, in-rm safe. All units w/terraces. Suites have whirlpool tubs. **Services:** ✕ 🖾 🍴 Children's program, babysitting. **Facilities:** 🗔 🚹 🚹 1 rst, 2 bars (1 w/entertainment), 1 beach (ocean), board surfing, whirlpool, washer/dryer. Dinner and breakfast buffets. **Rates:** HS Jan–May from $99 ste. Extra person $10. Children under 18 stay free. Lower rates off-season. MAP rates avail. Spec packages avail. Pking: Outdoor, free. Maj CC.

≝≝ **Ramada Inn Riverfront**, 964 S Harbour City Blvd, Melbourne, FL 32901; tel 407/724-4422 or toll free 800/722-7462; fax 407/951-9974. Exit 71 off I-95. This hotel next to the airport is in need of updating. **Rooms:** 125 rms and stes. CI 3pm/CO noon. Nonsmoking rms avail. **Amenities:** 🛎 🖭 A/C, cable TV, voice mail. **Services:** 🚗 🖾 🍴 Babysitting. **Facilities:** 🗔 🚹 🚹 1 rst, 1 bar (w/entertainment), games rm, washer/dryer. Japanese restaurant; comedy club. **Rates:** HS Jan–Mar $49–$59 S or D; from $79 ste. Children under 18 stay free. Lower rates off-season. Spec packages avail. Pking: Outdoor, free. Maj CC.

Motels

≝≝ **Comfort Inn**, 8298 N Wickham Rd, Melbourne, FL 32940; tel 407/255-0077 or toll free 800/554-5188; fax 407/259-9633. Exit 73 off I-95. A superior selection in this chain. Hotel receives many guests from the nearby performing arts center. Close to zoo and Florida Marlins spring training camp. **Rooms:** 135 rms and stes. CI 3pm/CO 11am. Nonsmoking rms avail. **Amenities:** 🛎 A/C, cable TV w/movies, voice mail. **Services:** ✕ 🚗 🖾 🍴 Babysitting. **Facilities:** 🗔 🚹 🚹 1 bar, washer/dryer. Sandwich shop next door delivers to room. **Rates (CP):** $55–$85 S or D; from $65 ste. Extra person $10. Children under 18 stay free. Lower rates off-season. Spec packages avail. Pking: Outdoor, free. Maj CC.

≝≝ **Holiday Inn West**, 4500 W New Haven Ave, Melbourne, FL 32904; tel 407/724-2050 or toll free 800/HOLIDAY; fax 407/723-2040. Exit 71 off I-95. Standard accommodations. **Rooms:** 100 rms. CI 11am/CO 11am. Express checkout avail. Nonsmoking rms avail. **Amenities:** 🛎 ⚡ A/C. All units w/terraces. **Services:** ✕ 🖾 🍴 🐾 **Facilities:** 🗔 🚹 🚹 1 rst, 1 bar (w/entertainment), washer/dryer. **Rates:** HS Jan–May $65–$85 S or D. Extra person $8. Children under 18 stay free. Lower rates off-season. Pking: Outdoor, free. Maj CC.

Restaurants 🍴

Cooker Bar and Grille, 1510 W New Haven Ave, Melbourne; tel 407/727-8448. 2 blocks E of Wickam Rd and W New Haven Ave. **Regional American.** A dark wood-trimmed dining room and a cozy sports bar with 2 TV screens. The menu offers steaks, ribs, and prime rib; specialties include Cajun catfish fillet. **FYI:** Reservations accepted. Children's menu. **Open:** Mon–Thurs 11am–10:30pm, Fri–Sat 11am–11:30pm, Sun 11am–10pm. Closed some hols. **Prices:** Main courses $5.75–$14.95. Maj CC. 💟 🚹

Kipling's, 1114 E Palmetto Ave, Melbourne; tel 407/676-4024. 1 block N of US 1 and US 192. **American/Continental.** Cozy, 2-story converted home. Extensive wine list; wine shop on premises. **FYI:** Reservations recommended. Children's menu.

Beer and wine only. No smoking. **Open:** Lunch Mon–Fri 11am–2pm; dinner Thurs–Sat 5:30–9:30pm. Closed some hols. **Prices:** Main courses $14–$17. Maj CC.

Shells, 1490 W New Haven Ave, Melbourne; tel 407/722-1122. **Seafood.** Popular seafood eatery with nautical decor accented with fish logos and neon lights around the bar. **FYI:** Reservations not accepted. Children's menu. **Open:** Mon–Thurs 4–10pm, Fri–Sat 4–11pm, Sun noon–10pm. Closed some hols. **Prices:** Main courses $4.95–$12.95. Maj CC. &

Strawberry Mansion, 1218 E New Haven Ave, Melbourne; tel 407/724-8627. At Strawbridge and New Haven Aves. **American.** Housed in an elegant, restored Victorian home. The old-fashioned setting is an ideal one in which to enjoy traditional continental cuisine. Classical music wafts through the several dining rooms as you dine. Menu highlights include the fresh fish of the day, crab cakes, steak Oscar, and a variety of veal dishes. **FYI:** Reservations accepted. **Open:** Daily 5–10pm. **Prices:** Main courses $12.95–$16.50. Maj CC.

Attractions 📷

Brevard Art Center and Museum (BACAM), 1463 Highland Ave; tel 407/242-0737. This "community-oriented" museum offers classes, lectures, and workshops on a variety of topics. Galleries with frequently changing exhibits cover a range of visual arts from painting to neon. Items from the center's permanent collection include unique works by local and regional artists, some antiquities, and decorative arts. **Open:** Tues–Sat 10am–5pm, Sun 1–5pm. Closed some hols. $

Space Coast Science Center, 1510 Highland Ave; tel 407/259-5572. A "playground" of hands-on exhibits dealing with science and technology. Exhibits, which are changed every few months, have included "Invaders," dealing with exotic flora and fauna in Florida, and "The Art of Design," exploring the boundaries between science and art. A nature room has local animals on view. **Open:** Tues–Sat 10am–5pm, Sun noon–5pm. Closed some hols. $

MERRITT ISLAND

Map page M-7, D3

Hotel 🛏

≣≣ Holiday Inn–Merritt Island, 260 E Merritt Island Causeway, Merritt Island, FL 32952; tel 407/452-7711 or toll free 800/HOLIDAY. Exit 75 off I-95. Casual, attractive lodging. **Rooms:** 128 rms. CI 3pm/CO noon. Express checkout avail.

Nonsmoking rms avail. **Amenities:** 🛏 🕭 A/C, cable TV. **Services:** ✗ 🚗 🖨 🕭 Car-rental desk. **Facilities:** 🎣 🍴 🏊 ᖴ 1 rst, 1 bar (w/entertainment). **Rates:** HS Feb–Apr/July–Aug $59 S; $59–$85 S or D. Extra person $8. Children under 18 stay free. Lower rates off-season. Higher rates for spec evnts/hols. AP and MAP rates avail. Spec packages avail. Pking: Outdoor, free. Maj CC.

MIAMI

Map page M-11, B2

See also Bal Harbour, Coral Gables, Fisher Island, Homestead, Key Biscayne, Miami Beach, Miami Lakes, Miami Springs, North Miami, Surfside, Sunny Isles

TOURIST INFORMATION

Greater Miami Convention and Visitors Bureau, 701 Brickell Ave, Suite 2700 (tel 305/539-3063 or 800/283-2707 for recorded information). Open Mon–Fri 8:30am–5pm.

Miami Design Preservation League, 1001 Ocean Dr, in the Ocean Front Auditorium at 10th St (tel 305/672-2014). Open Mon–Sat 10am–7pm. Free guide to the art deco district available.

PUBLIC TRANSPORTATION

Metrorail Operates 6am–12:40am. Runs north–south between downtown Miami and city's southern suburbs, including Coral Gables and Coconut Grove. Fare $1.25. For information call 305/638-6700.

Metromover Operates 6am–12:40am. Single-train car connects with Metrorail at Government Center and circles city's downtown area. Travels through Miami's most important office locations. Fare 25¢. For information call 305/638-6700 or 375-5675.

Hotels 🛏

≣≣ Airport Regency Hotel, 1000 NW LeJeune Rd, Miami, FL 33126; tel 305/441-1600 or toll free 800/367-1039, 800/432-1192 in FL; fax 305/443-0766. 1 mi S of airport terminal entrance. Mostly a layover hotel for both passengers and airline crews, with a mishmash of decor and some spotty housekeeping. **Rooms:** 176 rms. CI noon/CO noon. Nonsmoking rms avail. Room decor runs the gamut from the Kennedy Administration to the Reagan years. **Amenities:** 🛏 A/C, cable TV w/movies. All units w/terraces. **Services:** ✗ 🚗 🖨 🕭 Car-rental desk, babysitting. Security cameras ensure safety. **Facilities:** 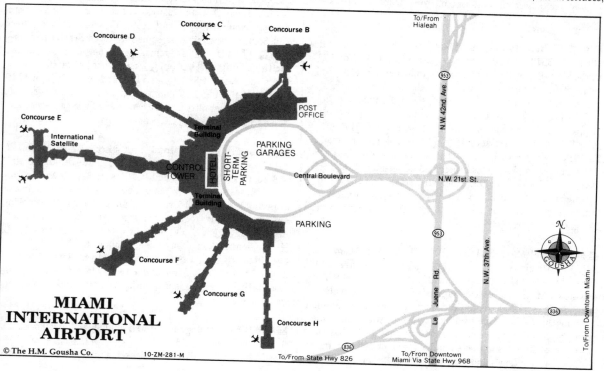 1 rst, 2 bars (1 w/entertainment), games rm, washer/dryer. **Rates:** HS Dec–Apr $85–$95 S or D. Extra person $10. Children under 16 stay free. Lower rates off-season. Higher rates for spec evnts/hols. Spec packages avail. Pking: Outdoor, free. Maj CC.

Biscayne Bay Marriott Hotel & Marina, 1633 N Bayshore Dr, Miami, FL 33132; tel 305/374-3900 or toll free 800/228-9290; fax 305/375-0597. A deluxe highrise with commanding views from most rooms of downtown Miami, Miami Beach, or the Port of Miami. Its public areas are glossy and sleek. **Rooms:** 603 rms and stes. Exec-level rms avail. CI 4pm/CO noon. Express checkout avail. Nonsmoking rms avail. Beautifully decorated rooms in sophisticated tones and patterns. **Amenities:** A/C, cable TV w/movies. Some units w/minibars, some w/terraces. **Services:** Car-rental desk. **Facilities:** 2 rsts, 2 bars, games rm, whirlpool, beauty salon. **Rates:** HS Dec–Apr $145–$155 S or D; from $400 ste. Children under 18 stay free. Lower rates off-season. Spec packages avail. Pking: Indoor, $7. Maj CC.

Days Inn–Miami Airport, 3401 NW LeJeune Rd, Miami, FL 33142; tel 305/871-4221 or toll free 800/325-2525; fax 305/871-3933. Renovation underway as new owners put their own brand on this property. **Rooms:** 155 rms. CI noon/CO noon. Nonsmoking rms avail. Rooms to be updated, but present condition is adequate. **Amenities:** A/C, cable TV w/movies. **Services:** Children's program. **Facilities:** 1 rst. **Rates:** HS Dec 15–Apr 15 $69–$89 S or D. Extra person $10. Children under 18 stay free. Lower rates off-season. Higher rates for spec evnts/hols. Spec packages avail. Pking: Outdoor, free. Maj CC.

Grand Bay Hotel, 2669 S Bayshore Dr, Miami, FL 33133 (Coconut Grove); tel 305/858-9600 or toll free 800/327-2788; fax 305/859-2026. 5 mi SW of downtown Miami. Striking hotel with Aztec pyramid architecture and stepped balconies overlooking Biscayne Bay. The lobby is lavishly done in marble and gleaming wood paneling and furnished with antiques and elaborate chandeliers. Located close to the Grove's restaurants, shops, and nightlife. **Rooms:** 184 rms and stes. CI 2pm/CO noon. Express checkout avail. Nonsmoking rms avail. Some rooms have uninspired layouts and furnishings, but redecorating and refurbishing was taking place at time of inspection. Spacious suites, some with grand pianos, are individually designed with exotic themes (e.g., Mandarin, Marrakech, Safari). **Amenities:** A/C, cable TV w/movies, VCR, in-rm safe, shoe polisher, bathrobes. All units w/minibars, all w/terraces,

MIAMI INTERNATIONAL AIRPORT

© The H.M. Gousha Co.
10-ZM-281-M

some w/Jacuzzis. Some rooms with faxes; bathroom TVs in suites. **Services:** |O| ▭ VP 🚗 ⌷ ↻ Twice-daily maid svce, masseur, children's program, babysitting. Guests are "introduced" to reception staff by bellmen and offered fresh orange juice or champagne. **Facilities:** ⌂ ⛳ ▦ ⌷ ♿ 2 rsts (*see also* "Restaurants" below), 2 bars (1 w/entertainment), lifeguard, spa, sauna, whirlpool, beauty salon. Poolside grill on rooftop. **Rates:** HS Aug 1–Apr 30 $275–$325 S or D; from $340 ste. Extra person $. Min stay spec evnts. Lower rates off-season. Spec packages avail. Pking: Indoor, $8. Maj CC.

≣≣≣ **HJ Occidental Plaza Hotel**, 100 SE 4th St, Miami, FL 33131; tel 305/374-5100 or toll free 800/521-5100; fax 305/381-9826. at 1st Ave SE. Located downtown near the Hyatt is this all-suites highrise with an impressive marbled lobby and other stylish public areas. **Rooms:** 134 rms and stes. CI 3pm/CO noon. Nonsmoking rms avail. Suites come in an assortment of configurations and have the conveniences to make business executives—the primary patrons—happy. Impressive marbled lobby; stylish public areas. **Amenities:** ☎ ⚘ ☙ A/C, cable TV w/movies, in-rm safe. Some units w/minibars. **Services:** ✗ ▭ VP 🚗 ⌷ ↻ Babysitting. **Facilities:** ⌂ ⛳ ▦ ⌷ ♿ 1 rst, 2 bars (1 w/entertainment), whirlpool. **Rates:** HS Jan–Apr $105–$150 S or D; from $150 ste. Extra person $20. Children under 12 stay free. Lower rates off-season. Pking: Outdoor, $10. Maj CC.

≣≣≣ **Holiday Inn LeJeune Centre**, 950 NW Le Jeune Rd, Miami, FL 33126; tel 305/446-9000 or toll free 800/428-9582; fax 305/441-0725. 1 mi S of airport terminal entrance. A good value that is smart, attractive, and reliable. The responsive management keeps this place looking sharp. **Rooms:** 304 rms and stes. Exec-level rms avail. CI 2pm/CO noon. Express checkout avail. Nonsmoking rms avail. **Amenities:** ☎ ⚘ A/C, cable TV w/movies. **Services:** ✗ 🚗 ⌷ ↻ Children's program. **Facilities:** ⌂ ⛳ ▦ ♿ 1 rst, 1 bar, sauna, steam rm, washer/dryer. Fenced-in parking lot is patrolled by security. **Rates:** HS Dec 1–Apr 15 $99 S; $109 D; from $201 ste. Extra person $10. Children under 19 stay free. Min stay spec evnts. Lower rates off-season. Higher rates for spec evnts/hols. Spec packages avail. Pking: Outdoor, free. Maj CC.

≣≣≣ **Hotel Mayfair House**, 3000 Florida Ave, Miami, FL 33133 (Coconut Grove); tel 305/441-0000 or toll free 800/433-4555, 800/341-0809 in FL; fax 305/447-9173. 5 mi SW of downtown Miami. An upscale fantasyland. The hotel, with its phantasmagoric facade, is an integral part of a 3-story atrium shopping mall, although a newer mall across the street is now the center of action in Coconut Grove. Grotto-like lobby has sit-down reception desks to the left and a cozy lounge to the right furnished with antiques and decorative glass. **Rooms:** 182 stes.

CI Open/CO 1pm. Express checkout avail. Nonsmoking rms avail. Rooms, which are lined up on open corridors around the atrium (picking up some extraneous noises), have spacious, off-center layouts and feature carved mahogany trim, Tiffany-style glass, and art deco furnishings. Many suites have antique grand pianos. **Amenities:** ☎ ⚘ ☙ A/C, cable TV w/movies, refrig, VCR. All units w/minibars, all w/terraces, all w/Jacuzzis. TV in bathrooms; central stereo system with 3 music channels. Japanese kimonos. **Services:** |O| ▭ VP 🚗 ⌷ Twice-daily maid svce, masseur, babysitting. 24-hour "in-suite restaurant service." Complimentary orange juice and champagne in reception area. **Facilities:** ⌂ ▦ ♿ 1 rst, 2 bars (1 w/entertainment), lifeguard, sauna, whirlpool, beauty salon. Rooftop garden has pool w/lifeguard, spa, sundeck, and bar is more urban than tropical. **Rates:** HS Dec 16–Apr 30 $230–$270 S or D; from $330 ste. Extra person $35. Children under 12 stay free. Min stay spec evnts. Lower rates off-season. Pking: Indoor, $10. Ltd CC.

≣≣≣ **Hotel Sofitel Miami**, 5800 Blue Lagoon Dr, Miami, FL 33126; tel 305/264-4888 or toll free 800/258-4888; fax 305/261-7871. Take Dolphin Expressway (Fla 836) west to NW 57th Ave. Turn right on Blue Lagoon Dr. This highrise establishment brings a distinctive, French look to the airport hotel community. Beautifully adorned public areas exhibit a flair for the dramatic. A seasoned staff brings everything together. **Rooms:** 281 rms and stes. CI 3pm/CO noon. Express checkout avail. Nonsmoking rms avail. **Amenities:** ☎ ☙ A/C, cable TV w/movies, refrig, voice mail. Some units w/minibars, some w/terraces. **Services:** |O| ▭ VP 🚗 ⌷ ↻ ✈ Car-rental desk, masseur, babysitting. **Facilities:** ⌂ ⛳ ▦ ⛳ ▦ ♿ 2 rsts, 1 bar (w/entertainment), games rm. **Rates:** HS Oct–Apr $179–$189 S or D; from $219 ste. Extra person $50. Children under 12 stay free. Lower rates off-season. Higher rates for spec evnts/hols. Spec packages avail. Pking: Outdoor, free. Maj CC. Romance packages available.

≣≣ **Howard Johnson Hotel**, 1100 Biscayne Blvd, Miami, FL 33132; tel 305/358-3080 or toll free 800/654-2000; fax 305/358-3080 ext 1613. Exit 5 off I-95. Close to Bayside Market, this 7-story property was undergoing extensive renovations at time of inspection. **Rooms:** 115 rms. CI 3pm/CO noon. Nonsmoking rms avail. Front rooms are larger and better furnished. **Amenities:** ☎ ⚘ A/C, TV. All units w/terraces. **Services:** ✗ ⌷ ↻ Car-rental desk, babysitting. Shuttle to Port of Miami. **Facilities:** ⌂ ▦ ♿ 1 rst, 1 bar, washer/dryer. **Rates:** HS Dec–Apr $69 S; $79 D. Children under 18 stay free. Lower rates off-season. Higher rates for spec evnts/hols. Pking: Indoor/outdoor, free. Maj CC.

≣≣≣≣ **Hyatt Regency Miami**, 400 SE 2nd Ave, Miami, FL 33131; tel 305/358-1234 or toll free 800/233-1234; fax 305/358-0529. On the river, this sleek highrise is a staple in the convention market; it adjoins the convention center. Soaring atrium is polished up for a clean, efficient look. **Rooms:** 615 rms and stes. Exec-level rms avail. CI 3pm/CO noon. Express checkout avail. Nonsmoking rms avail. **Amenities:** 🔒 ⊘ 📶 A/C, cable TV w/movies, in-rm safe, bathrobes. Some units w/minibars, all w/terraces. **Services:** 🍽 ➖ VP 🚐 ⊠ ↩ Car-rental desk, babysitting. City's water taxi stops at hotel's dock. **Facilities:** 🛗 1.5k 💻 ⅙ 2 rsts, 2 bars (1 w/entertainment). Restaurants get overtaxed during big events. **Rates:** HS Dec–Apr $145–$160 S; $155–$170 D; from $175 ste. Extra person $20. Children under 18 stay free. Lower rates off-season. Spec packages avail. Pking: Indoor/outdoor, $10. Maj CC.

Marina Park Hotel Miami, 340 Biscayne Blvd, Miami, FL 33132; tel 305/371-4400 or toll free 800/526-5655; fax 305/372-2862. Exit 5 off I-95. Pleasant, middle-grade accommodations near access to cruise ships. **Rooms:** 198 rms, stes. CI 3pm/CO noon. Nonsmoking rms avail. **Amenities:** 🔒 ⊘ A/C, cable TV, in-rm safe. **Services:** ✕ ⊠ ↩ Babysitting. **Facilities:** 🛗 ⅙ 1 rst, 1 bar. **Rates:** HS Dec–Feb $85 S; $95 D; from $105 ste. Extra person $10. Children under 12 stay free. Lower rates off-season. Pking: Outdoor, $8. Maj CC.

Miami Airport Marriott, 1201 NW LeJeune Rd, Miami, FL 33126; tel 305/649-5000 or toll free 800/228-9290; fax 305/642-3369. A first-rate operation, accessible via a security-controlled gate. A variety of dining options and recreational diversions helps keep layover guests and others here for longer stays content. **Rooms:** 782 rms and stes. Exec-level rms avail. CI 3pm/CO noon. Express checkout avail. Nonsmoking rms avail. **Amenities:** 🔒 ⊘ 📶 A/C, cable TV, voice mail, bathrobes. **Services:** ✕ ➖ 🚐 ⊠ ↩ 🐾 Babysitting. **Facilities:** 🛗 🎾 ●2 💧8 🏓 360 ⅙ 2 rsts, 2 bars (1 w/entertainment), lifeguard, games rm, racquetball, spa, whirlpool, beauty salon, washer/dryer. **Rates:** HS Sept–May $145–$150 S or D; from $225 ste. Children under 19 stay free. Lower rates off-season. Higher rates for spec evnts/hols. Spec packages avail. Pking: Outdoor, free. Maj CC.

Miami International Airport Hotel, NW 20th St and Le Jeune Rd, PO Box 997510, Miami, FL 33299; tel 305/871-4100 or toll free 800/327-1276; fax 305/871-0800. Part of the airport terminal, a hectic location at the best of times and a nightmare for anyone arriving by car. Best suited for those requiring moderate lodging close to gates for early-morning departures or late-night arrivals. **Rooms:** 263 rms and stes. Exec-level rms avail. CI 3pm/CO noon. Express checkout avail. Nonsmoking rms avail. Half the rooms overlook the runways and tarmac. **Amenities:** 🔒 ⊘ 📶 A/C, cable TV w/movies, bathrobes. Some units w/Jacuzzis. **Services:** ✕ ⊠ ↩ **Facilities:** 🛗 🎾 🏓 🌊400 💻 ⅙ 2 rsts, 2 bars (1 w/entertainment), racquetball, sauna,

steam rm, whirlpool. **Rates:** HS Sept–Feb $109–$159 S; $129–$179 D; from $195 ste. Extra person $10. Children under 12 stay free. Lower rates off-season. Spec packages avail. Pking: Outdoor, $6. Maj CC.

Radisson Mart Plaza Hotel, 711 NW 72nd Ave, Miami, FL 33126; tel 305/261-3800 or toll free 800/333-3333; fax 305/261-7665. A smart, attractive hotel with a capable staff, attached to the Merchandise Mart. **Rooms:** 334 rms and stes. Exec-level rms avail. CI 3pm/CO noon. Express checkout avail. Nonsmoking rms avail. **Amenities:** 🔒 A/C, cable TV w/movies. Some units w/minibars. **Services:** ✕ ➖ VP 🚐 ⊠ ↩ 🐾 Car-rental desk, babysitting. **Facilities:** 🛗 🎾 🌊 🏓 2k 💻 ⅙ 2 rsts, 2 bars (1 w/entertainment), sauna, whirlpool, beauty salon. **Rates:** HS Jan–Apr $149–$159 S or D; from $169 ste. Extra person $20. Children under 18 stay free. Min stay spec evnts. Lower rates off-season. Higher rates for spec evnts/hols. Spec packages avail. Pking: Outdoor, free. Maj CC.

Ramada Hotel Miami International Airport, 3941 NW 22nd St, Miami, FL 33142 (Miami Int'l Airport); tel 305/871-1700 or toll free 800/272-6232; fax 305/871-4830. **Rooms:** 265 rms and stes. CI 9/CO noon. Nonsmoking rms avail. **Amenities:** 🔒 ⊘ 📶 A/C, satel TV. Some units w/terraces, 1 w/Jacuzzi. **Services:** ✕ 🚐 ⊠ ↩ 🐾 Car-rental desk. **Facilities:** 🛗 300 ⅙ 1 rst, 1 bar, games rm, sauna, steam rm, whirlpool. **Rates:** HS Mar 1–Apr 15 $89–$109 S; $99–$119 D; from $129 ste. Extra person $10. Children under 18 stay free. Lower rates off-season. Higher rates for spec evnts/hols. Spec packages avail. Pking: Indoor/outdoor, free. Maj CC.

Residence Inn by Marriott, 1212 NW 82nd Ave, Miami, FL 33126; tel 305/591-2211 or toll free 800/331-3131; fax 305/591-0902. Suitable for long-stay guests. **Rooms:** 112 stes. CI 3pm/CO noon. Nonsmoking rms avail. **Amenities:** 🔒 ⊘ 📶 A/C, satel TV, refrig. All units w/terraces, some w/fireplaces. **Services:** 🚐 ⊠ ↩ 🐾 Babysitting. **Facilities:** 🛗 40 ⅙ Whirlpool, washer/dryer. **Rates (CP):** HS Jan 1–Apr 15 from $139 ste. Children under 12 stay free. Lower rates off-season. Higher rates for spec evnts/hols. Spec packages avail. Pking: Outdoor, free. Maj CC.

Sheraton River House, 3900 NW 21st St, Miami, FL 33142 (Miami Int'l Airport); tel 305/871-3800 or toll free 800/325-3535; fax 305/871-0447. Located in a modern, elongated building; it's due respect for its attention to maintenance and housekeeping. **Rooms:** 408 rms and stes. Exec-level rms avail. CI 3pm/CO noon. Express checkout avail. Nonsmoking rms avail. Colorful accommodations are popular with business folk, who usually book the upper floors where rooms are equipped with extra phones, irons and boards, and coffeemakers. **Amenities:** 🔒 ⊘ 📶 A/C, cable TV w/movies. Some units

w/Jacuzzis. **Services:** 🍽 🔑 VP 🚗 ⛱ 🛎 🔊 Babysitting.
Facilities: 🏋 🎿 ⛳ 🎾 700 💻 ♿ 1 rst, 1 bar (w/entertainment), games rm, sauna, steam rm, whirlpool. **Rates:** HS Jan–Mar $110 S; $120 D; from $500 ste. Children under 19 stay free. Lower rates off-season. Higher rates for spec evnts/hols. Spec packages avail. Pking: Indoor/outdoor, free. Maj CC.

Motel

≣≣ **Howard Johnson Lodge**, 1980 NW Le Jeune Rd, Miami, FL 33126; tel 305/871-4370 or toll free 800/446-4656; fax 305/871-4370 ext 135. Caters to layovers and business guests. Standard. **Rooms:** 64 rms. CI 2pm/CO noon. Nonsmoking rms avail. **Amenities:** 🔒 🌡 A/C, cable TV w/movies. **Services:** 🚗 🔊 🔊 **Facilities:** 🏋 ♿ 1 rst. **Rates:** HS Nov–Apr $59–$99 S or D. Extra person $10. Children under 18 stay free. Lower rates off-season. Higher rates for spec evnts/hols. Pking: Outdoor, free. Maj CC.

Resort

≣≣≣ **Doral Resort & Country Club**, 4400 NW 87th Ave, Miami, FL 33178; tel 305/592-2000 or toll free 800/327-6334, 800/367-2826 in FL; fax 305/594-4682. 7 mi W of Miami Int'l Airport. 2,400 acres. A golfer's paradise and a tennis buff's demi-paradise, but otherwise an ordinary spot for everyone else (just 1 swimming pool). With its location, low-flying jets can at times mar the tranquility. The resort is popular for business meetings. **Rooms:** 650 rms and stes. CI 4pm/CO 11am. Express checkout avail. Nonsmoking rms avail. Rooms are spacious but motel-like, though renovation was in the works. Some have views of only other rooms or pathways. Second-floor rooms are best bets (higher ceilings, more security). **Amenities:** 🔒 🌡 📞 A/C, cable TV w/movies, refrig, voice mail, shoe polisher. Some units w/minibars, some w/terraces. Some rooms have refrigerators. **Services:** 🍽 🔑 VP 🚗 ⛱ 🔊 Twice-daily maid svce, car-rental desk, social director, masseur, children's program, baby-sitting. Shuttle to Doral at Miami Beach. **Facilities:** 🏋 🚴 ▶ 99 🎿 ⚓11 ⛳ 🎾 12K 💻 ♿ 4 rsts, 2 bars (1 w/entertainment), lifeguard, games rm, spa, sauna, steam rm, whirlpool, beauty salon, playground. European-style spa, Doral Saturnia, a short walk away through landscaped gardens. Well-equipped business center. **Rates:** HS Dec 18–Apr 30 $210–$295 S or D; from $340 ste. Extra person $20. Children under 17 stay free. Lower rates off-season. Higher rates for spec evnts/hols. Spec packages avail. Pking: Outdoor, $8.95. Maj CC. There are 4 rate categories; choicest and priciest lodgings are in Doral Saturnia.

Restaurants 🍴

Cafe Europa, 3159 Commodore Plaza, Miami (Coconut Grove); tel 305/448-5723. **Continental/French.** A traditional French creperie where you can dine outdoors or inside the casual, softly toned cafe. **FYI:** Reservations accepted. Singer. **Open:** Mon–Thurs 5pm–1am, Fri–Sun noon–2am. **Prices:** Main courses $9–$20. Maj CC. 🍰

Casa Juancho, 2436 SW 8th St, Miami; tel 305/642-2452. **Spanish.** Traditional Spanish appointments as well as nightly performing Spanish musicians give this eatery an authentic flavor. The menu offers mixed seafood in vinaigrette, fresh shrimp in hot garlic sauce, and fried calamari rings. **FYI:** Reservations recommended. Piano/singer. Dress code. **Open:** Mon–Fri noon–midnight, Sat–Sun noon–1am. **Prices:** Main courses $11.95–$26.95. Maj CC. ♥ VP ♿

The Chart House, 51 Chart House Dr, Miami (Coconut Grove); tel 305/856-9741. Off Bayshore Dr near the Grand Bay Hotel. **Seafood/Steak.** Great food, service, and views are available at this solid oceanside eatery. **FYI:** Reservations recommended. **Open:** Mon–Thurs 5:30pm–11, Fri–Sat 5:30–11:30pm, Sun 5:30–10pm. **Prices:** Main courses $15.95–$24.95. Maj CC. 🏞 VP ♿

The Crab House, 1551 79th Street Causeway, Miami; tel 305/868-7085. **Seafood.** Enjoy lovely views of Biscayne Bay while you feast on selections from the fresh seafood bar. At lunchtime, the seafood bar is $9.95. **FYI:** Reservations not accepted. Children's menu. **Open:** Mon–Thurs 11:30am–11pm, Fri 11:30am–midnight, Sat noon–midnight, Sun noon–11pm. Closed Thanksgiving. **Prices:** Main courses $10.95–$19.95. Maj CC. 🏞 ♥ VP ♿

Crocodile Cantina, in Bayside Marketplace, 401 Biscayne Blvd, Miami; tel 305/374-7417. **Southwestern.** A casual, family-oriented dining spot with a festive atmosphere. Standard Mexican fare like chili, nachos, salads, and burritos is served at basic wooden tables, either indoors or out. **FYI:** Reservations accepted. Children's menu. **Open:** Sun–Thurs 11am–midnight, Fri–Sat 11am–midnight. **Prices:** Main courses $2.95–$13.95. Maj CC. 🎪 ♿

East Coast Fisheries, 360 W Flagler St, Miami; tel 305/377-2529. **Seafood.** This combination fish market/restaurant has a rustic atmosphere, an open kitchen, an extensive seafood menu, and views of the river. Rock lobster and lobster tails are house specialties. **FYI:** Reservations accepted. Beer and wine only. **Open:** Sun–Thurs 11:30am–10pm, Fri–Sat 11:30am–11pm. **Prices:** Main courses $8.95–$23.95. Maj CC. 🏞 🎪

$ **Fish Bone Grille**, 650 S Miami Ave, Miami; tel 305/530-1915. **Seafood.** Basic, unpretentious eatery serving great seafood at outstanding prices. The chef's specialty is classic cioppino with homemade cornbread. **FYI:** Reservations accepted. Island music. Beer and wine only. **Open:** HS Dec–Apr Mon–Thurs 11:30am–10pm, Fri 11:30am–11pm, Sat 5:30–11pm. Reduced hours off-season. Closed some hols. **Prices:** Main courses $7.95–$12.95. Maj CC. &

$ **Fish Peddler**, 8699 Biscayne Blvd, Miami; tel 305/757-0648. At 87th St. **American.** Relaxed restaurant with a maritime theme specializing in seafood and steaks. Both the food and the service enjoy excellent reputations. Specialties include grilled Florida swordfish, grilled marinated veal chops, and rack of lamb. The menu also features a variety of pizzas and pastas. Counter service available. **FYI:** Reservations not accepted. Children's menu. **Open:** Daily 10am–11pm. Closed some hols. **Prices:** Main courses $11.50–$17. Maj CC. ● &

★ **Flemming**, 8611 SW 136th St, Miami; tel 305/232-6444. **Danish.** A simple, warm restaurant with glass block walls. Dishes include swordfish, Norwegian salmon, and Grandfather's Duck Danoise. **FYI:** Reservations recommended. Dress code. **Open:** Tues–Sun 5:30–10:30pm. Closed July 4; Mid-July–mid-Aug. **Prices:** Main courses $8–$17. Maj CC. &

Fuddruckers, in Mayfair Shops, 3444 Main Hwy, Miami (Coconut Grove); tel 305/442-8164. **Burgers.** An open, self-serve establishment catering to families and seniors. The menu offers burgers and fish; lots of toppings are available to dress up your selection. **FYI:** Reservations not accepted. Children's menu. **Open:** Fri–Sat 11am–2am, Sun–Thurs 11am–midnight. Closed some hols. **Prices:** Main courses $2.95–$8.95. Maj CC.

♥ **Grand Cafe**, in Grand Bay Hotel, 2669 S Bayshore Dr, Miami (Coconut Grove); tel 305/858-9600. **New American/Seafood.** Accented with pink linen and soft piano music, this lovely restaurant is a special place for a romantic interlude. Entrees include seared Pacific salmon served with Japanese Ikura salmon caviar, annatto-marinated breast of chicken, and spiced tenderloin of beef with grilled wild mushrooms and crispy foie gras. The chef can prepare most entrees to dietary specifications. **FYI:** Reservations recommended. Jacket required. **Open:** Breakfast daily 7–11am; lunch daily 11am–3pm; dinner Sun–Thurs 6–11pm, Fri–Sat 6–11:30pm; brunch Sun 11:30am–3pm. **Prices:** Main courses $19–$34. Maj CC. ♥ VP &

Green Street Cafe, 3468 Commodore Plaza, Miami (Coconut Grove); tel 305/444-0244. **American/Italian.** Light, airy restaurant outfitted with French doors and ceiling fans. The menu includes pizzas from the wood-burning oven, pastas, and black-ened mahimahi. A great people-watching spot. **FYI:** Reservations not accepted. **Open:** Sun–Thurs 7am–midnight, Fri–Sat 7am–1:30am. **Prices:** Main courses $7–$14. Maj CC. ● &

★ **Hard Rock Cafe**, in Bayside Market Place, 401 Biscayne Blvd, Miami; tel 305/377-3160. **New American.** This festive international chain restaurant, housed in a distinctive circular building with a vintage pink Cadillac suspended over its entryway, offers spectacular views of downtown Miami, beautiful Biscayne Bay, and the popular Bayside Marketplace. The menu features substantial burgers, barbecued chicken, smoked ribs, fajitas, vegetarian entrees, salads, soups, and desserts, all at moderate prices. **FYI:** Reservations not accepted. Rock. Children's menu. **Open:** Daily 11am–2am. **Prices:** Main courses $2.95–$16.95. Maj CC. ⊞ VP &

Janjo's, 3131 Commodore Plaza, Miami; tel 305/445-5030. **Californian/Caribbean.** A busy, appealing eatery with colorful, tropical decor and open-air dining. The menu includes sea bass and roast salmon. A sidewalk table here is a great spot for people-watching. **FYI:** Reservations accepted. Band/blues/jazz/piano/rock. **Open:** Daily 6–10:30pm, Tues–Thurs 11:30am–10:30pm, Fri–Sat 11:30am–12am, Sun 9am–10:30pm. Closed some hols. **Prices:** Main courses $13–$25. Maj CC. ● VP

★ **Johnny Rockets Hamburgers**, 3036 Grand Ave, Miami (Coconut Grove); tel 305/444-1000. **Diner.** A fun, popular diner-style joint. This is a branch of the original Johnny Rockets located on Melrose Avenue in Los Angeles. Burgers, fries, shakes, and malts are staples; you can even order a peanut butter and jelly sandwich. **FYI:** Reservations not accepted. Rock. No liquor license. No smoking. **Open:** Sun–Wed 11am–1am, Thurs–Sat 11am–3am. **Prices:** Main courses $2.25–$4.55. Maj CC. ▲ &

Kaleidoscope, 3112 Commodore Plaza, Miami; tel 305/446-5010. **American/Caribbean.** An engaging, attractive cafe furnished in white wrought iron and wicker. Its location, overlooking a bustling street, makes it a great people-watching spot. The eclectic menu offers a wide variety of dishes, including cassoulet of duck, Jamaican jerk pork, and linguine with smoked salmon. The grilled swordfish with fried leeks and jalapeño butter is a favorite. **FYI:** Reservations recommended. **Open:** Lunch daily 11:30am–3pm; dinner daily 6–11pm; brunch Sun 11:30am–3pm. **Prices:** Main courses $13–$20. Maj CC. ⊞ ▲

Langosta Beach Restaurant, 1279 NE 79th St Causeway, Miami; tel 305/751-1200. Next to the Pelican Harbor Park and Marina. **Seafood.** A nautically themed eatery with great water and marina views as well as pleasant outdoor dining. The menu features lots of seafood and poultry, and a few pastas. The sunset menu, which includes salad, soup, entree, and dessert, all for a single price, is offered 5–6:45pm. **FYI:** Reservations recommended. Piano. Children's menu. **Open:** Sun 5–10:30pm, Mon–Thurs 5–10:30pm, Fri–Sat 5–11pm, Sat 5–11:30pm. Closed Dec 25. **Prices:** Main courses $9.95–$19.95. Maj CC. ◨ VP ⚹

Las Tapas, in Bayside Market Place, 401 Biscayne Blvd, Miami; tel 305/372-2737. **Spanish.** Authentic Spanish artifacts, fabrics, and furniture adorn this attractive restaurant serving Spanish cuisine with a South Florida twist. Diners can sample many of the house specialties by ordering a variety of appetizer-size portions. The relaxing outdoor terrace has full bar and food service. **FYI:** Reservations accepted. Singer. **Open:** Sun–Thurs 11:30am–midnight, Fri–Sat 11:30am–1am. **Prices:** Main courses $2.95–$19.95. Maj CC. ♨ ⚹

Los Ranchos, in Bayside Marketplace, 401 Biscayne Blvd, Miami; tel 305/375-8188. **Steak/Nicaraguan.** A Nicaraguan chain restaurant with floor-to-ceiling windows overlooking the port of Miami. It has garnered awards for its cuisine, which features mostly Central American beef dishes. **FYI:** Reservations accepted. Singer. Children's menu. **Open:** Daily 11:30am–11:30pm. Closed Thanksgiving. **Prices:** Main courses $9–$25. Maj CC. ◪ ◨ ⚹

Mike Gordon's, 1201 NE 79th St, Miami; tel 305/751-4429. **Seafood.** A landmark Miami restaurant with a beautiful waterfront location. Enjoy views of the waterfowl and boats while you dine on any one of a variety of pastas and seafood dishes. **FYI:** Reservations not accepted. Children's menu. **Open:** Daily noon–10pm. Closed Thanksgiving. **Prices:** Main courses $13.95–$19.95. Maj CC. ◨ VP ⚹

Qui du Crepes, 3115 Commodore Plaza, Miami (Coconut Grove); tel 305/446-7964. **French.** A fun, French-accented eatery with a young, energetic staff. A typical dish is roasted chicken with cream sauce. You can top off your meal with a banana split. **FYI:** Reservations not accepted. Guitar/jazz/singer. Beer and wine only. **Open:** Mon–Fri 11am–midnight, Sat–Sun 9am–2am. **Prices:** Main courses $4–$6.95. Maj CC. ♨

Señor Frog's, 3008 Grand Ave, Miami (Coconut Grove); tel 305/448-0990. **Mexican.** Twentysomethings regularly converge at this fun, lively spot. Choose among 14 varieties of chili, along with traditional Mexican-American entrees, all served with rice or beans. **FYI:** Reservations accepted. **Open:** Sun–Wed 11:30am–1am, Thurs–Sat 11:30am–2am. **Prices:** Main courses $5.90–$10.90. Maj CC. ◨ ⚹

Snappers Bar and Grill, in Bayside Market Place, 401 Biscayne Blvd N110, Miami; tel 305/379-0605. **Seafood.** Enjoy lovely ocean views at this pleasant, laid-back seafood eatery. **FYI:**

Reservations not accepted. Rock. Children's menu. **Open:** Sun–Thurs 10:30am–11pm, Fri–Sat 10:30am–1am. **Prices:** Main courses $8.95–$19.95. Maj CC. ◪ ◨ ⚹

The Terrace Cafe, in the Omni International Hotel, Biscayne Blvd at 16th St, Miami; tel 305/374-0000. **New American.** An upbeat, tropical atmosphere sets the tone for you to enjoy fresh seafood, attractive fruit platters, oriental salad, or more hearty dishes like grilled pork loin and shrimp scampi. **FYI:** Reservations accepted. **Open:** Breakfast daily 7–11:30am; lunch Mon–Fri 11:30am–5pm, Sat 11:30am–5pm; dinner daily 5:30–10pm; brunch Sun 11:30am–3pm. **Prices:** Main courses $6.50–$17.75. Maj CC. ◨ VP ⚹

Tuscany Trattoria, 3484 Main Hwy, Miami (Coconut Grove); tel 305/445-0022. Next to Coconut Grove Playhouse. **Italian.** Attractive, brick-accented interior with fireplace. Pasta and fish dishes. **FYI:** Reservations accepted. Beer and wine only. **Open:** Daily 11:30am–midnight. **Prices:** Main courses $7–$17. Maj CC. ♨ ▣ VP

Ⓢ **Versailles**, 3535 SW 8th St, Miami; tel 305/444-0240. **Cuban.** This casual Latin restaurant, specializing in fried fish and Cuban dishes, sparkles with crystal, chandeliers, and mirrors. **FYI:** Reservations accepted. Children's menu. **Open:** Mon–Thurs 8am–2am, Fri 8am–3:30am, Sat 8am–4:30am, Sun 9am–2am. **Prices:** Main courses $5.95–$14.95. Maj CC. ◨ ◨ ⚹

Refreshment Stop 🍵

Joffrey's Coffee & Tea Co, 3434 Main Hwy, Miami (Coconut Grove); tel 305/448-0848. **Coffeehouse.** A fun, artsy coffeehouse with live entertainment. Teas, coffees, coffee coolers, and desserts are available. Popular sweets include Banana Nut Chantilly, German apple torte, and the Heavenly Beast. **Open:** Sun–Tues 7:30am–midnight, Wed–Thurs 7:30am–1am, Fri–Sat 7:30am–2am. Closed some hols. Maj CC.

Attractions ▦

Miami Museum of Science and Space Transit Planetarium, 280 S Miami Ave (Coconut Grove); tel 305/854-4247 (museum) or 854-2222 (planetarium). Features over 150 hands-on exhibits exploring the mysteries of the universe. The adjacent Space Transit Planetarium presents astronomy and rock music laser shows. The in-house observatory is free and open to the public on weekend evenings. **Open:** Museum, daily 10am–6pm; Planetarium shows, hourly noon–4pm, Sun 10am–5pm. Closed some hols. $$$

Historical Museum of Southern Florida, 101 W Flagler St; tel 305/375-1492. Part of the Metro-Dade Cultural Center, which also houses the Center for Fine Arts and the Dade County Public Library, this museum's primary exhibit is "Tropical Dreams," a state-of-the-art, chronological history of the past 10,000 years in South Florida. Hands-on displays, audio-visual presentations, and hundreds of artifacts. **Open:** Mon–Wed and Fri–Sat 10am–5pm, Thurs 10am–9pm, Sun noon–5pm. Closed some hols. $$

Spanish Monastery Cloisters, 16711 W Dixie Hwy (at 167th St); tel 305/945-1462. First erected in 1141 in Segovia, Spain, the monastery was purchased by newspaper magnate William Randolph Hearst and shipped overseas in crates where it remained in a New York warehouse until after Hearst's death. In 1954 Miami developers had it reassembled on its present site as a tourist attraction. It is now an Episcopal church. Lush formal garden. **Open:** Mon–Sat 10am–5pm, Sun noon–5pm. Closed some hols. $$

Villa Vizcaya, 3251 South Miami Ave; tel 305/579-2708. Italian Renaissance-style villa (1916) surrounded by 10 acres of beautiful formal gardens. Antiques adorn 34 of the 70 rooms, which are filled with examples of decorative art from the 15th to 19th centuries. Outside, the gardens are accented with statuary, fountains, balustrades and decorative urns, and front an enormous swath of Biscayne Bay. **Open:** Daily 9:30am–4:30pm; gardens open until 5:30pm. $$$

The Barnacle, 3485 Main Hwy (Coconut Grove); tel 305/448-9445. The former home of naval architect and early settler Ralph Middleton Munroe, this is now a museum in the heart of Coconut Grove. The house was built in 1891 and occupied by the family until 1973. The furnishings are mostly original and date from the 1920s. Some of Munroe's ship drawings can be seen. Tours Thurs–Mon at 10:30am, 1pm, and 2:30pm. Schedule may vary. $

Cuban Museum of Arts and Culture, 1300 SW 12th Ave (at SW 13th St); tel 305/858-8006. This unique museum displays significant works reflecting the main historical currents in Cuban art. Paintings and drawings add up to only about 200, but they are well selected and representative of a very wide range of styles. **Open:** Tues–Fri 11am–5pm, Sat–Sun 1–5pm. Closed some hols. $

American Police Hall of Fame and Museum, 3801 Biscayne Blvd; tel 305/573-0202. More than 10,000 items relating to police work, ranging from weapons and uniforms to squad cars and execution devices. Guests may study a "crime scene" for clues and are awarded a certificate if they solve the crime. A memorial lists the names of more than 5,000 US police officers killed in the line of duty. **Open:** Daily 10am–5pm. Closed Dec 25. $$$

Miami Metrozoo, 12400 SW 152nd St (at SW 124th Ave); tel 305/251-0400 or 251-0401. This huge 290-acre complex is completely cageless; animals are separated from people by moats. Highlights include 2 rare white Bengal tigers, a 1.5-acre free-flight tropical aviary, a monorail "safari," and one of the few koala bear exhibits in America. There's a newly designed petting zoo as well. **Open:** Daily 9:30am–5:30pm. $$

Parrot Jungle and Gardens, 11000 SW 57th Ave; tel 305/666-7834. This 50-year-old park features birds of nearly every description, as well as alligators, tortoises, and iguanas. Continuous shows in Parrot Bowl Theater star performing parrots, roller-skating cockatoos, and card-playing macaws. Other attractions include a wildlife show, "Primate Experience," and a children's playground and petting zoo. **Open:** Daily 9:30am–6pm. $$$$

Monkey Jungle, 14805 SW 216th St; tel 305/235-1611. There are no cages to restrain the antics of monkeys, gorillas, and chimpanzees, but screened-in trails that wind through acres of "jungle" give visitors ample protection. Four different shows that feature performing primates rotate on a 30-minute cycle. Also on view are such species as golden lion tamarins and Asian macaques. **Open:** Daily 9:30am–6pm. $$$$

Club Nautico of Coconut Grove, 2560 S Bayshore Dr (in Coconut Grove); tel 305/858-6258. Rental of high-quality power boats for fishing, waterskiing, diving, and cruising on the bay or ocean. All boats are equipped with Coast Guard–approved VHF radios and safety gear. Half- and full-day rentals. **Open:** Mon–Fri 9am–5pm, Sat–Sun 8am–5pm. Closed some hols. $$$$

Heritage Miami II Topsail Schooner, Bayside Marketplace Marina, 401 Biscayne Blvd; tel 305/442-9697. This relaxing ride aboard Miami's only tall ship is a fun way to see the city. Two-hour cruises pass by Villa Vizcaya, Coconut Grove, and Key Biscayne, and put you in sight of Miami's spectacular skyline. Cruises are offered September through May only. **Open:** Trips: Mon–Fri, 1:30pm, 4pm, and 6:30pm, Sat & Sun also 11am & 9pm. $$$$

Dade County Auditorium, 2901 W Flagler St; tel 305/545-3395. This intimate, 2,500-seat facility, home to the Greater Miami Opera, also stages productions of the Miami Ballet Company and the Concert Association of Greater Miami. **Open:** Varies.

Miami Arena, 721 NW 1st Ave; tel 305/577-HEAT. The NBA's Miami Heat hold court here from November to April. $$$$

Joe Robbie Stadium, 2269 NW 199th St; tel 305/620-5000. The Miami Dolphins (NFL) play their home games here from August to December. $$$$

Flagler Greyhound Track, 401 NW 38th Court (at NW 33rd St); tel 305/649-3000. Some of the nation's top dogs are featured at this high-stakes track, which hosts the $110,000 International Classic. Racing season is usually May–June and September–October; call ahead for exact dates. Post times: 7:30pm daily and 12:30pm Tues, Thurs, Sat, and some hols. $

Miami Jai Alai Fronton, 3500 NW 37th Ave (at NW 35th St); tel 305/633-6400. This is America's oldest jai alai fronton, built in 1926. Approximately 13 matches are scheduled every evening. $

MIAMI BEACH

Map page M-11, B2

See also Bal Harbour, Fisher Island, Surfside

Hotels 🛏

The Alexander All-Suite Luxury Hotel, 5225 Collins Ave, Miami Beach, FL 33140; tel 305/865-6500 or toll free 800/327-6121; fax 305/864-8525. A luxury address, featuring beautifully decorated public areas with fine sculptures, paintings, and antiques, and panoramic views from the upper floors. **Rooms:** 170 stes. CI 3pm/CO noon. Expertly outfitted accommodations are some of the largest in Miami Beach. **Amenities:** 🛅 ⚴ 🎛 📶 A/C, cable TV w/movies, refrig, shoe polisher. All units w/terraces, some w/Jacuzzis. **Services:** ✕ ⛏ 🆅🅿 📠 📥 ⚙ Social director, masseur. Chefs will cook for guests privately in suites. **Facilities:** 🔁 △ 🏌 📶 300 🚹 2 rsts (*see also* "Restaurants" below), 1 bar, 1 beach (ocean), lifeguard, sauna, steam rm, whirlpool, beauty salon, washer/dryer. **Rates:** HS Dec 15–Apr 30 from $310 ste. Extra person $25. Children under 17 stay free. Lower rates off-season. Spec packages avail. Pking: Indoor, $4.50.

Avalon Hotel, 700 Ocean Dr, Miami Beach, FL 33139 (South Beach); tel 305/538-0133 or toll free 800/933-3306; fax 305/534-0258. Visually striking, with classic art deco look. Modest lobby. Situated in the center of glamorous South Beach, near many trendy restaurants. **Rooms:** 108 rms. CI 3pm/CO 11am. Rooms with familiar art deco style. **Amenities:** 🛅 ⚴ A/C, cable TV, VCR, stereo/tape player, in-rm safe. **Services:** 🆅🅿 📠 📥 **Facilities:** 40 🚹 1 rst, 1 bar, day-care ctr. Atmospheric outdoor cafe. Playground for children across the street. **Rates (CP):** HS Dec 23–Apr 3 $110–$160 S or D. Extra person $10. Children under 3 stay free. Min stay spec evnts. Lower rates off-season. Spec packages avail. Pking: Outdoor, $12. Ltd CC.

Bel-Aire Hotel, 6515 Collins Ave, Miami Beach, FL 33141; tel 305/866-6511 or toll free 800/327-0553; fax 305/866-5881. Exit 9 off I-95. Tries to make the most of its grounds with a tiered fountain along walkway to the courtyard. Facade is scheduled for renovation. **Rooms:** 110 rms and effic. CI noon/CO noon. Small rooms with simple appointments. Dehumidifier would help in some rooms. **Amenities:** 🛅 A/C, TV, refrig. Some units w/terraces. **Services:** ✕ Car-rental desk. **Facilities:** 🔁 24 1 bar, 1 beach (ocean), lifeguard, beauty salon. Live entertainment during winter season. **Rates:** HS Dec–Apr $26–$29 S; $51–$57 D; from $63 effic. Extra person $3. Lower rates off-season. Higher rates for spec evnts/hols. Pking: Outdoor, free. Maj CC.

Boulevard Hotel & Cafe, 740 Ocean Dr, Miami Beach, FL 33139 (South Beach); tel 305/532-0376; fax 305/674-8179. Blends well with the art deco delights, with accommodations dressed in pastel, of course. **Rooms:** 37 rms and stes. CI 2pm/CO 11am. **Amenities:** 🛅 A/C, cable TV, refrig, in-rm safe. 1 unit w/Jacuzzi. Fireplaces will be added to suites in 1995. **Services:** ✕ 🆅🅿 📠 Social director. **Facilities:** 40 🚹 1 rst. Playground across the street, gym nearby. **Rates:** HS Dec 15–May 15 $125 S or D; from $225 ste. Children under 17 stay free. Lower rates off-season. Pking: Outdoor, $6–12. Maj CC.

Cardoza Hotel, 1300 Ocean Dr, Miami Beach, FL 33139 (South Beach); tel 305/535-6500 or toll free 800/782-6500; fax 305/532-3563. One of the art deco district's sharpest and most notable properties. Prime location. Owned by pop star Gloria Estéfan. **Rooms:** 42 rms and stes. CI 3pm/CO noon. Room decor features bright jazzy colors. Spacious suites have cedar closets; some have 2 baths. **Amenities:** 🛅 A/C, cable TV, refrig, VCR, stereo/tape player, voice mail, in-rm safe. All units w/minibars, some w/Jacuzzis. **Services:** ✕ 🆅🅿 📠 📥 🍴 **Facilities:** 1 rst, 1 bar (w/entertainment). **Rates (CP):** $110–$135 S or D; from $195 ste. Children under 12 stay free. Pking: Outdoor, $4. Maj CC.

Casa Grande Suite Hotel, 834 Ocean Dr, Miami Beach, FL 33139 (South Beach); tel 305/672-7003 or toll free 800/688-7678; fax 305/673-3669. One of the top hotels in South Beach, it offers stylish, large accommodations. **Rooms:** 32 stes. CI 3pm/CO noon. Nonsmoking rms avail. Units have full kitchens, beautifully tiled baths, large closets, mahogany beds, and interesting art. **Amenities:** 🛅 ⚴ 🎛 📶 A/C, cable TV w/movies, refrig, VCR, stereo/tape player, in-rm safe, bathrobes. All units w/minibars. **Services:** ✕ 🆅🅿 📥 🍴 Twice-daily maid svce, babysitting. **Facilities:** 🚹 1 rst (*see also* "Restaurants" below), 1 bar (w/entertainment). **Rates:** HS Dec–Apr from $175 ste. Extra person $15. Children under 18 stay free. Min stay wknds. Lower rates off-season. Pking: Outdoor, $14. Maj CC.

▤▤▤ **Castle Beach Club**, 5445 Collins Ave, Miami Beach, FL 33140; tel 305/865-1500 or toll free 800/352-3224; fax 305/ 861-3430. Exceptionally well-decorated lobby with marble entrance, raised oak paneling, and artwork. Piano is sometimes enlisted for entertainment. Excellent value. **Rooms:** 250 rms. CI 3pm/CO noon. Express checkout avail. Tastefully appointed rooms with sinks in dressing area, walk-in closets. Views of Intracoastal Waterway and ocean. Renovation underway. **Amenities:** ▦ A/C, cable TV w/movies, voice mail. Some units w/terraces. **Services:** ✗ ▣ VP ▦ ⤙ Babysitting. **Facilities:** ▦ ▨ ▨ ▦ 1 rst, 1 beach (ocean), games rm, lawn games, whirlpool, washer/dryer. Beach cabanas and outdoor showers. Tennis club across the street. **Rates:** HS Dec 16–May 31 $125– $205 S or D. Extra person $15. Children under 19 stay free. Lower rates off-season. Spec packages avail. Pking: Indoor, $8. Maj CC.

▤▤ **Cavalier Hotel**, 1320 Ocean Dr, Miami Beach, FL 33139; tel 305/534-2135 or toll free 800/338-9076; fax 305/531-5543. Historic hotel (built in 1936) that was among the first Ocean Drive art deco properties to undergo extensive renovation. This architectural gem has beautifully restored period furnishings and an ultra-contemporary style. Located on the best strip on the beach. **Rooms:** 44 rms and stes. CI 3pm/CO noon. Nonsmoking rms avail. **Amenities:** ▦ ▨ A/C, cable TV, refrig, VCR, stereo/ tape player, in-rm safe. **Services:** ▦ ⤙ Babysitting. Newspaper provided daily. **Facilities:** ▣ **Rates:** HS Oct–Apr $135 S or D; from $180 ste. Extra person $15. Children under 18 stay free. Lower rates off-season. Higher rates for spec evnts/hols. Spec packages avail. Maj CC.

▤ **The Clay Hotel and International Hostel**, 1438 Washington Ave, Miami Beach, FL 33139; tel 305/534-2988; fax 305/ 673-0346. Suggested for the young and young-at-heart on a budget. Public areas always bustling with activity. Walking distance to beach, bars, and restaurants. **Rooms:** 238 rms. CI 1pm/CO noon. Nonsmoking rms avail. Very basic and frill-less rooms. **Amenities:** ▦ A/C, refrig. Some units w/terraces. **Services:** ▣ ▦ **Facilities:** ▨ 1 rst, washer/dryer. Inexpensively priced restaurant is usually busy. **Rates:** HS Dec 15–Apr 15 $24–$28 S; $32–$36 D. Extra person $8. Children under 6 stay free. Lower rates off-season. Ltd CC.

▤▤ **Dezerland Surfside Beach Hotel**, 8701 Collins Ave, Miami Beach, FL 33154; tel 305/865-6661 or toll free 800/ 331-9346 in the US, 800/331-9347 in Canada; fax 305/ 866-2630. A fun hotel with a 1950s-automobile theme in a tropical setting. Mint-condition cars are scattered about the floors. **Rooms:** 227 rms. CI 3pm/CO noon. Nonsmoking rms avail. Rooms take their name from classic cars and are comfortable and in good condition. **Amenities:** ▦ ▨ A/C, cable TV

w/movies. Some units w/terraces. **Services:** ✗ ⤙ ⤙ Babysitting. **Facilities:** ▦ ▨ ▣ 1 rst, 3 bars, 1 beach (ocean), lifeguard, games rm, whirlpool, washer/dryer. Fishing and scuba diving can be arranged. **Rates:** HS Dec 16–Apr 15 $80–$125 S or D. Extra person $9. Children under 18 stay free. Lower rates off-season. Spec packages avail. Pking: Outdoor, free. Maj CC.

▤▤▤ **Doral Ocean Beach Resort**, 4833 Collins Ave, Miami Beach, FL 33140; tel 305/532-3600 or toll free 800/233-6725; fax 305/534-7409. The beachside sibling to the redoubtable Doral Resort and Country Club, offering a wide range of facilities for the sports enthusiast. **Rooms:** 422 rms and stes. CI 3pm/CO noon. Express checkout avail. Nonsmoking rms avail. Rooms are decorated in pastel seashore colors. **Amenities:** ▦ ▨ ▦ A/C, cable TV w/movies, voice mail. All units w/minibars, some w/Jacuzzis. **Services:** ✗ ▣ VP ▦ ⤙ ⤙ Car-rental desk, social director, masseur, children's program, babysitting. Chilled champagne awaits arrivals. Housekeeping routinely ask guests if they desire afternoon service. Shuttle bus goes to other Doral properties for golf. **Facilities:** ▦ ▨ ▨ ▨ ▦ ▦ ▦ ▦ ▦ ▨ 2 rsts, 3 bars, 1 beach (ocean), games rm, snorkeling, whirlpool, beauty salon. Beach cabanas. **Rates:** $230–$300 S or D; from $335 ste. Extra person $20–$40. Children under 13 stay free. Lower rates off-season. Spec packages avail. Pking: Indoor, $9. Maj CC.

▤▤ **The Dorchester**, 1850 Collins Ave, Miami Beach, FL 33139 (South Beach); tel 305/534-6971 or toll free 800/ 327-4739; fax 305/673-1006. Convenient to SoBe beach, activities, and nightlife. **Rooms:** 94 rms, stes, and effic. CI 2pm/CO noon. Rooms are quieter than at many art deco district hotels. **Amenities:** ▦ ▦ A/C, TV, refrig. Some units w/terraces, 1 w/Jacuzzi. Efficiencies will have microwaves shortly. **Services:** ⤙ Car-rental desk. **Facilities:** ▦ ▨ Games rm, day-care ctr, washer/dryer. A coffeeshop is planned. **Rates:** HS Nov–mid-Apr $50–$65 S; $65–$85 D; from $85 ste; from $60 effic. Children under 14 stay free. Lower rates off-season. Pking: Outdoor, $5. Maj CC.

▤▤ **Eden Roc Resort and Spa**, 4525 Collins Ave, Miami Beach, FL 33140; tel 305/531-0000 or toll free 800/327-8337; fax 305/531-6959. N of I-95 at Arthur Godfrey Rd. Showy 1950s charmer, with a fanciful pink pastel, Morris Lapidus–designed lobby. Offers unusually spacious accommodations that are priced better than those of nearby deluxe hotels. **Rooms:** 350 rms and stes. CI 3pm/CO noon. Nonsmoking rms avail. Some units have 1½ baths and extra-large closets. **Amenities:** ▦ ▨ A/C, cable TV w/movies, in-rm safe. All units w/minibars, some w/terraces, some w/Jacuzzis. **Services:** ✗ ▣ VP ▣ ▦ ⤙ Car-rental desk. **Facilities:** ▦ ▨ ▦ ▦ 1 rst (see also "Restaurants" below), 2 bars, 1 beach (ocean). Porch Restaurant affords diners underwater view through glass sides of the adjacent swimming pool. **Rates:** HS Dec 15–Apr $195–$350 S or D; from $500 ste. Extra person $20. Children under 18 stay free. Lower rates off-season. Spec packages avail. Pking: Indoor, $8.50. Maj CC.

▤▤ **Edison Hotel**, 960 Ocean Dr, Miami Beach, FL 33139 (South Beach); tel 305/531-2744. Situated in the midst of beach action, on prime real estate. Was undergoing renovations to restaurant and pool at press time. **Rooms:** 62 rms. CI 1pm/CO 1pm. Sparse, clean accommodations. Work to interiors is still necessary. **Amenities:** 🛏 A/C, cable TV. **Services:** 🆅🅿 **Facilities:** Guests have use of facilities at the Cleveland Hotel. **Rates:** HS Oct–Apr $65 S; $65 D. Children under 21 stay free. Min stay spec evnts. Lower rates off-season. Higher rates for spec evnts/hols. Pking: Outdoor, $6–$10. Maj CC.

▤▤ **Essex House Hotel**, 1001 Collins Ave, Miami Beach, FL 33139 (South Beach); tel 305/534-2700 or toll free 800/553-7739; fax 305/532-3827. Plush, romantic South Beach art deco hotel, located 1 block from the beach. Tastefully done lobby is outfitted with leather appointments, piano, Oriental vases, and silk flower arrangements. Relaxing courtyard encircled by stucco wall, with palms and plants. **Rooms:** 57 rms and stes. CI 3pm/CO noon. Nonsmoking rms avail. Solid oak furnishings, fine linens, and pastel colors make rooms cool and inviting. **Amenities:** 🛏 A/C, cable TV. **Services:** 🅰 Car-rental desk, babysitting. **Rates (CP):** HS Dec–May $125 S or D; from $300 ste. Extra person $20. Min stay spec evnts. Lower rates off-season. Maj CC.

501 Miami Beach, 3925 Collins Ave, Miami Beach, FL 33140; tel 305/531-3534 or toll free 800/531-3534; fax 305/531-1765. Exit 7 off I-95. Impressive lobby full of flair, with vibrant colors and neon. A waterfall flows into a small indoor pond. Unrated. **Rooms:** 271 rms. CI 3pm/CO noon. **Amenities:** 🛏 A/C, cable TV w/movies, refrig, in-rm safe. Some units w/minibars, some w/fireplaces. **Services:** 🔑 🆅🅿 🅰 🍽 Babysitting. **Facilities:** 🗗 🍽 💯 ⅙ 2 rsts, 2 bars, 1 beach (ocean), games rm, beauty salon, washer/dryer. **Rates:** HS Dec–Apr $75–$100 S or D. Extra person $15. Children under 18 stay free. Lower rates off-season. Higher rates for spec evnts/hols. Spec packages avail. Pking: Outdoor, $6. Maj CC.

▤▤ **Golden Sands**, 6901 Collins Ave, Miami Beach, FL 33141; tel 305/866-8734 or toll free 800/932-0333 in the US, 800/423-5170 in Canada; fax 305/866-0187. Good value. Smallish lobby is redeemed by the attractive guest rooms. **Rooms:** 98 rms and effic. CI 11am/CO noon. Nonsmoking rms avail. Pastel decor, airy appointments, new wallpaper. Some rooms have ocean views. **Amenities:** 🛏 A/C, cable TV, refrig. **Services:** ✕ 🅰 🍽 Car-rental desk, babysitting. Staff will arrange sports activities. **Facilities:** 🗗 🚲 🛆 🗗 🎿 🛶 🍽 1 rst,

2 bars (w/entertainment), 1 beach (ocean), games rm, snorkeling, beauty salon. Cozy restaurant has pool views. **Rates:** HS Dec 20–Apr 5 $67–$77 S or D; from $80 effic. Children under 18 stay free. Lower rates off-season. Higher rates for spec evnts/hols. Spec packages avail. Pking: Indoor/outdoor, $5. Maj CC.

▤▤ **The Governor Hotel**, 435 21st St, Miami Beach, FL 33139 (South Beach); tel 305/532-2100 or toll free 800/542-0444; fax 305/532-9139. In a quiet neighborhood close to the beach action. The modest accommodations are fine for those with minimal expectations. **Rooms:** 126 rms. CI 2pm/CO 11am. Nonsmoking rms avail. **Amenities:** 🛏 A/C, cable TV w/movies. Some units w/terraces. **Services:** ✕ 🅰 🍽 🐕 Car-rental desk, babysitting. **Facilities:** 🗗 1 rst, 1 bar, washer/dryer. Lounge area in lobby has piano and pool table. **Rates:** HS Dec 20–Apr 10 $85–$125 S or D. Extra person $10. Children under 17 stay free. Lower rates off-season. Spec packages avail. Pking: Outdoor, free. Maj CC.

▤▤▤ **Holiday Inn Newport Pier Resort**, 16701 Collins Ave, Miami Beach, FL 33160 (Oceanside); tel 305/949-1300 or toll free 800/327-5476, 800/826-5319 in FL; fax 305/956-2733. Tropical-themed property offering an abundance of activities. Super-friendly staff. **Rooms:** 355 rms and stes. CI 3pm/CO noon. Nonsmoking rms avail. Crisp, newly renovated rooms. **Amenities:** 🛏 🛁 A/C, cable TV, refrig, in-rm safe. Some units w/terraces. **Services:** ✕ 🔑 🆅🅿 🅰 🍽 🐕 Car-rental desk, social director, masseur, children's program, babysitting. **Facilities:** 🗗 🛆 🗗 🍽 💯 ⅙ 4 rsts, 4 bars (2 w/entertainment), 1 beach (ocean), lifeguard, board surfing, games rm, snorkeling, spa, whirlpool, beauty salon, washer/dryer. **Rates:** HS Dec–Apr 15 $135–$185 S or D; from $275 ste. Extra person $10. Children under 19 stay free. Lower rates off-season. Higher rates for spec evnts/hols. AP and MAP rates avail. Spec packages avail. Pking: Indoor/outdoor, $4. Maj CC.

▤▤▤ **Holiday Inn–Oceanside (Convention Inn)**, 2201 Collins Ave, Miami Beach, FL 33139 (South Beach); tel 305/534-1511 or toll free 800/356-6902; fax 305/532-1403. Popular for its oceanfront location, this full-service, 12-story hotel fronts the boardwalk and is a popular rendezvous for both convention delegates and avid beachgoers. **Rooms:** 357 rms and stes. CI 3pm/CO noon. Express checkout avail. Nonsmoking rms avail. Some rooms have ocean views. **Amenities:** 🛏 🛁 A/C, cable TV w/movies. **Services:** ✕ 🅰 🍽 Car-rental desk. **Facilities:** 🗗 🏊 💯 ⅙ 1 rst, 2 bars (1 w/entertainment), 1 beach (ocean), games rm, whirlpool, washer/dryer. **Rates:** HS Dec–Apr $114–$129 S or D; from $185 ste. Extra person $15. Children under 10 stay free. Lower rates off-season. Pking: Indoor, $6. Maj CC.

▤▤ **The Indian Creek Hotel**, 2727 Indian Creek Dr, Miami Beach, FL 33140; tel 305/531-2727; fax 305/531-5651. At 28th

St. A small, friendly hotel; handy to the Intracoastal Waterway. Ongoing improvements being made. **Rooms:** 61 rms and stes. CI noon/CO noon. Nonsmoking rms avail. **Amenities:** 🏨 💧 A/C, TV. **Services:** ✗ ⛱ **Facilities:** 🔥 🏊 ⛴ 1 rst. **Rates:** HS May–Oct $100 S; $110 D; from $190 ste. Extra person $10. Min stay spec evnts. Lower rates off-season. Maj CC.

▐▌▐▌ Kenmore Hotel, 1050 Washington Ave, Miami Beach, FL 33139 (South Beach); tel 305/674-1930; fax 305/534-6591. Traditional art deco hotel that is a mecca for South Beach beautiful people. **Rooms:** 60 rms and stes. CI 3pm/CO noon. Clean, sparsely decorated rooms have some period furnishings in 1930s style; rooms with pool and patio views are best. **Amenities:** 🏨 A/C, satel TV, refrig. **Services:** 🚗 Babysitting. **Facilities:** 🔥 🏊 Washer/dryer. **Rates:** HS Nov 15–May 1 $59–$79 S or D; from $99 ste. Extra person $10. Lower rates off-season. Maj CC.

▐▌▐▌ Kent Hotel, 1131 Collins Ave, Miami Beach, FL 33139 (South Beach); tel 305/531-6771; fax 305/531-0720. Comfortable art deco hotel, though not fancy, in a fine location. Garden setting with trees, plants, and umbrella tables. Security bars protect the ground floor. **Rooms:** 52 rms, stes, and effic. CI 2pm/CO noon. Cozy pastel colors used throughout. Efficiencies have double sinks, 2-burner stoves. **Amenities:** 🏨 A/C, TV, refrig. **Services:** 🚗 Car-rental desk. **Facilities:** 🏊 **Rates (CP):** HS Oct 15–May 1 $65 S or D; from $140 ste; from $70 effic. Extra person $10. Lower rates off-season. Spec packages avail. Maj CC.

▐▌▐▌ The Leslie, 1244 Ocean Dr, Miami Beach, FL 33139 (South Beach); tel 305/534-2135 or toll free 800/338-9076; fax 305/531-5543. One of the district's most popular historic hotels, it was among the first Ocean Drive properties to undergo extensive renovation. Small and quiet, with a distinct art deco design on the outside and an art nouveau interior. Within walking distance of some of the best restaurants and clubs. **Rooms:** 43 rms and stes. CI 3pm/CO noon. Suites with ocean views have lots of windows to take in Ocean Drive color. **Amenities:** 🏨 A/C, cable TV w/movies, VCR, stereo/tape player, in-rm safe. Minibars are being added to suites. **Services:** 🅥🅟 ⛱ Babysitting. **Facilities:** 1 rst, 1 bar. Outdoor cafe. **Rates:** HS Oct–Apr $105–$135 S or D; from $225 ste. Extra person $15. Min stay spec evnts. Lower rates off-season. Pking: Outdoor, $10. Maj CC.

▐▌▐▌ The Marlin, 1200 Collins Ave, Miami Beach, FL 33139 (South Beach); tel 305/673-8770 or toll free 800/338-9076; fax 305/673-9609. Garners much local attention for its rock-and-roll clientele. Beautifully lit, powder blue exterior, but relatively simple rooms. **Rooms:** 12 stes. CI 3pm/CO noon. **Amenities:** 🏨 A/C, cable TV w/movies. All units w/minibars. **Services:** ✗

🅥🅟 ⛱ 🚗 🍴 Masseur, babysitting. **Facilities:** 🍽 1 rst, 1 bar. Caribbean restaurant. Guests receive discounts at nearby health club. **Rates (CP):** From $200 ste. Extra person $15. Children under 5 stay free. Min stay spec evnts. Pking: Outdoor, $10. Maj CC.

▐▌▐▌ Marseilles Hotel, 1741 Collins Ave, Miami Beach, FL 33139 (South Beach); tel 305/538-5711 or toll free 800/327-4739; fax 305/673-1006. Well priced, basic lodging in a good people-watching location in the heart of the art deco district. **Rooms:** 115 rms. CI noon/CO noon. Pastel colors, rattan appointments. **Amenities:** 🏨 A/C, cable TV, refrig. **Services:** 🍴 **Facilities:** 🔥 2 rsts, 1 bar, 1 beach (ocean), games rm, washer/dryer. Outdoor bar. **Rates:** HS Dec 16–Apr 15 $75–$105 S or D. Extra person $5. Children under 8 stay free. Lower rates off-season. Higher rates for spec evnts/hols. Pking: Outdoor, $5. Maj CC. Oceanfront units $8 extra, kitchens $5 extra, junior suites $10 extra.

▐▌▐▌ Park Central Hotel, 640 Ocean Dr, Miami Beach, FL 33139 (South Beach); tel 305/538-1611 or toll free 800/727-5236; fax 305/534-7520. Pretty art deco hotel harks back to 1937, when it was built. It is still in need of some improvement, but it has the right idea for a solid start. The lobby is decorated with black-and-white photos from the 1930s. South Beach atmosphere makes up for relative lack of facilities. **Rooms:** 117 rms and stes. CI 3pm/CO noon. Rooms are pleasant and simple. **Amenities:** 🏨 💧 A/C, cable TV, refrig, in-rm safe. **Services:** ✗ 🅥🅟 🚐 ⛱ Masseur, babysitting. **Facilities:** 🔥 🏋 🏊 1 rst, 1 bar. Contemporary French cuisine served in restaurant. **Rates:** HS Oct 15–May 15 $120–$165 S or D; from $175 ste. Children under 12 stay free. Lower rates off-season. Spec packages avail. Pking: Outdoor, $7. Maj CC.

▐▌▐▌ Park Washington Hotel, 1020 Washington Ave, Miami Beach, FL 33139 (South Beach); tel 305/532-1930; fax 305/672-6706. Geared toward tourists, the Park Washington is one of the better values in South Beach. The hotel is one part of a major effort intended to create a resort-style complex covering an entire block. Three hotels and several restaurants are planned, with a shared pool, all amid tropical landscaping. **Rooms:** 30 rms and stes. CI 3pm/CO noon. Express checkout avail. Clean, comfortable rooms. **Amenities:** 🏨 A/C, TV, refrig. 1 unit w/minibar. **Services:** Free coffee and danish served mornings in lobby. **Facilities:** 🔥 **Rates (CP):** HS Nov–May $49 S; $59 D; from $129 ste. Extra person $10. Children under 18 stay free. Lower rates off-season. Spec packages avail. Maj CC.

▐▌▐▌▐▌ Quality Shawnee Beach Resort, 4343 Collins Ave, Miami Beach, FL 33140; tel 305/532-3311 or toll free 800/832-8332; fax 305/531-5296. Green wicker furniture dresses up the tropical lobby, which also sports a fountain and raised seating area. **Rooms:** 475 rms and stes. CI 3pm/CO noon. Nonsmoking rms avail. Rooms have light woods and soothing colors. **Amenities:** ⬚ ⬚ A/C, cable TV, voice mail. Some units w/terraces. **Services:** ✗ [VP] ⬚ ⬚ Social director, masseur, babysitting. **Facilities:** ⬚ ⬚ ⬚ ⬚ ⬚ ⬚ 3 rsts, 3 bars, 1 beach (ocean), lifeguard, lawn games, whirlpool, beauty salon, washer/dryer. Tennis pro shop. **Rates:** HS Dec–Apr $99–$149 S or D; from $229 ste. Extra person $20. Children under 16 stay free. Lower rates off-season. Spec packages avail. Pking: Outdoor, $7. Maj CC.

⬚⬚ **Ritz Plaza Hotel**, 1701 Collins Ave, Miami Beach, FL 33139; tel 305/534-3500 or toll free 800/522-6400; fax 305/531-6928. A better-than-average art deco hotel and a prime address for beach action. You might see models posing in the hotel's backyard. **Rooms:** 132 rms and stes. CI 2pm/CO noon. **Amenities:** ⬚ A/C, cable TV, in-rm safe. **Services:** ✗ [VP] ⬚ ⬚ **Facilities:** ⬚ ⬚ 2 rsts, 2 bars, 1 beach (ocean), washer/dryer. **Rates:** HS Dec–Apr $135–$165 S or D; from $395 ste. Children under 17 stay free. Lower rates off-season. Pking: Outdoor, $6. Maj CC.

⬚⬚ **The Shelborne Beach Hotel**, 1801 Collins Ave, Miami Beach, FL 33139 (South Beach); tel 305/531-1271 or toll free 800/327-8757; fax 305/531-2206. A one-time headquarters for beauty pageants in the 1940s and '50s, the hotel has retained its original look, including a very appealing marbled entry and a curved staircase in the lobby. **Rooms:** 225 rms, stes, and effic. CI 3pm/CO noon. Suites offer exceptional decor, black leather sofas, full kitchens, dining areas with glass-block partitions, den, and bedroom. Balconies provide views of SoBe, downtown, or the beach. **Amenities:** ⬚ ⬚ A/C, cable TV, refrig. Some units w/minibars, some w/terraces. **Services:** ✗ ⬚ [VP] ⬚ ⬚ **Facilities:** ⬚ ⬚ 1 rst, 1 bar, 1 beach (ocean), beauty salon, washer/dryer. **Rates:** HS Dec–Apr $105–$150 S; $115–$160 D. Extra person $10. Children under 17 stay free. Lower rates off-season. Spec packages avail. Pking: Outdoor, free. Maj CC.

⬚⬚ **The Surfcomber**, 1717 Collins Ave, Miami Beach, FL 33139 (South Beach); tel 305/532-7715 or toll free 800/336-4264 in the US, 800/446-4264 in Canada; fax 305/532-7280. A friendly staff welcomes guests at this art deco district standby. Ongoing renovations to rooms. **Rooms:** 194 rms and effic. CI 2pm/CO noon. Traditional art deco colors. **Amenities:** ⬚ A/C, cable TV, in-rm safe. Some units w/terraces. **Services:** ⬚ [VP] ⬚ Car-rental desk. **Facilities:** ⬚ ⬚ ⬚ 3 rsts (see also "Restaurants" below), 1 bar, 1 beach (ocean), lifeguard, washer/dryer. **Rates:** HS Dec 15–Apr 15 $70–$110 S or D; from $75 effic. Extra person $5. Children under 15 stay free. Lower rates off-season. Spec packages avail. Pking: Outdoor, $5. Maj CC.

⬚⬚ **Waldorf Towers Hotel**, 860 Ocean Dr, Miami Beach, FL 33139 (South Beach); tel 305/531-7684 or toll free 800/933-2332; fax 305/672-6836. Classic local styling, with wicker ceiling fans and potted tropical plants in the lobby. **Rooms:** 45 rms and stes. CI 3pm/CO noon. Rooms decorated in seascape colors with light, comfortable furnishings. **Amenities:** ⬚ ⬚ A/C, cable TV w/movies. **Services:** [VP] ⬚ ⬚ Masseur, babysitting. **Facilities:** ⬚ 1 rst (see also "Restaurants" below), 1 bar. Nearby health club offers discount. **Rates:** HS Dec 15–Apr 15 $109–$149 S or D; from $199 ste. Extra person $10. Children under 12 stay free. Min stay spec evnts. Lower rates off-season. Pking: Outdoor, $12. Maj CC.

Motels

⬚ **The New Waterside Inn**, 2360 Collins Ave, Miami Beach, FL 33139; tel 305/538-1951; fax 305/531-3217. Just outside the official art deco district, it provides comfortable rooms without fanfare. Popular with European tourists. **Rooms:** 80 rms. CI 11am/CO 11am. Nonsmoking rms avail. **Amenities:** ⬚ A/C, cable TV. **Services:** ⬚ ⬚ Car-rental desk. Continental breakfast ($2.50) served poolside. **Facilities:** ⬚ ⬚ Washer/dryer. Fax machine in lobby for guest use. Boat rentals available on Intracoastal Waterway. Food market across the street. **Rates:** HS Dec 15–Apr 15 $50 S; $60 D. Extra person $10. Children under 12 stay free. Lower rates off-season. Spec packages avail. Pking: Outdoor, free. Maj CC.

⬚ **Paradise Inn Motel**, 8520 Harding Ave, Miami Beach, FL 33141; tel 305/865-6216; fax 305/865-9028. Exit 13 off I-95. One of the area's original motels, intended for budget-minded guests who want basic, clean accommodations close to the beach. **Rooms:** 96 rms and effic. CI open/CO noon. **Amenities:** ⬚ ⬚ A/C, cable TV w/movies, refrig, in-rm safe. **Services:** ⬚ ⬚ Coffee available mornings. Uniformed security patrols at night. **Facilities:** ⬚ Washer/dryer. **Rates:** HS Dec–Apr $42 S; $48 D; from $54 effic. Extra person $3. Children under 12 stay free. Lower rates off-season. Pking: Outdoor, free. Maj CC.

Resort

⬚⬚ **Fountainebleau Hilton Resort & Spa**, 4441 Collins Ave, Miami Beach, FL 33140; tel 305/538-2000 or toll free 800/548-8886; fax 305/673-5351. 20 acres. A magnet for the old and new in-crowd and a staple of the beach scene, this elaborate, always bustling complex harks back to the forgotten heyday of 1950s Miami Beach. Often a stop for tourists even if they're not staying here. **Rooms:** 1,207 rms and stes. CI 3pm/CO 11am. Express checkout avail. Nonsmoking rms avail. Handsome rooms. **Amenities:** ⬚ ⬚ A/C, cable TV w/movies, refrig. Some units w/minibars, some w/terraces. **Services:** ✗ ⬚ [VP] ⬚ ⬚

Car-rental desk, masseur, children's program, babysitting. Business center operates 6 days per week. Secretarial services available. **Facilities:** 🔲 🔺 🔳 🔲 🔲 🔲 🔲 🔲 🔲 🔲 9 rsts (*see also* "Restaurants" below), 2 bars (w/entertainment), 1 beach (ocean), lifeguard, board surfing, games rm, lawn games, spa, sauna, steam rm, whirlpool, beauty salon, playground. **Rates:** HS Nov–May $185–$265 S; $210–$290 D; from $405 ste. Extra person $20. Children under 18 stay free. Lower rates off-season. Spec packages avail. Pking: Indoor, $9. Maj CC. Pets under 20 pounds permitted for $20 per day.

Restaurants 🍴

A Fish Called Avalon, in Avalon Hotel, 700 Ocean Dr, Miami Beach; tel 305/538-0133. **Seafood.** Pastel colors, white table linen, and huge windows create a casual setting in which to enjoy inventive cuisine. The menu changes nightly but always includes fresh local seafood served with creative seasonal sauces; steak, chicken, stone crabs, and pasta dishes are also available. **FYI:** Reservations recommended. Guitar. Children's menu. **Open:** Sun–Thurs 6:30pm–midnight, Fri–Sat 6:30pm–1am. **Prices:** Main courses $7.95–$20.50; PF dinner $19.75. Maj CC. ♥ 🔲 VP

A Mano, in the Betsy Ross Hotel, 1440 Ocean Dr, Miami Beach; tel 305/531-6266. **Regional American/Caribbean.** A romantic hideaway (whose name means "by hand" in Spanish) often frequented by celebrities. The extensive, eclectic tropical-French-accented menu includes a variety of creative seafood and lamb dishes. **FYI:** Reservations recommended. Jazz. **Open:** Daily 6–11pm. Closed some hols. **Prices:** Main courses $8.95–$32.95. Maj CC. ♥ VP 🔲

The Beacon Cafe, in the Beacon Hotel, 720 Ocean Dr, Miami Beach; tel 305/672-7360. **American.** A casual art deco restaurant overlooking the esplanade; outdoor umbrella-covered tables allow you to people-watch while you dine. The menu includes a variety of salads and sandwiches. **FYI:** Reservations accepted. **Open:** Daily 7am–midnight. **Prices:** Main courses $11–$22. Maj CC. 🔲 VP

Caffe Milano, 850 Ocean Dr, Miami Beach (South Beach); tel 305/532-0707. **Italian.** Dine either outside or indoors under whirling ceiling fans. Specialties include penne pomodoro, swordfish and salmon. **FYI:** Reservations accepted. **Open:** Wed–Mon noon–midnight, Tues 5pm–midnight. **Prices:** Main courses $12–$25. Maj CC. 🔲 🔲 🔲 VP

Casona De Carlitos, 2236 Collins Ave, Miami Beach; tel 305/534-7013. **South American/Steak.** A casual dining room with an Argentine-Italian menu published in various languages. Entrees include baked fish in bleu-cheese sauce, chicken oreganato

in wine, and a number of grilled meats. **FYI:** Reservations not accepted. Combo. Beer and wine only. **Open:** Sun–Thurs noon–12:30am, Fri–Sat noon–1:30am. **Prices:** Main courses $9.95–$20.95. Maj CC. 🔲 🔲

Colony Bistro, in Colony Hotel, 736 Ocean Ave, Miami Beach; tel 305/673-6776. **New American/Caribbean.** A sophisticated, romantic bistro. One of South Beach's top hot spots. **FYI:** Reservations recommended. **Open:** Lunch daily 11:30am–3:00pm; dinner Mon–Fri 6–11pm, Sat–Sun 6:00pm–midnight. **Prices:** Main courses $11.75–$27.50. Maj CC. ♥ VP 🔲

Compass Cafe & Market, in Waldorf Towers Hotel, 860 Ocean Dr, Miami Beach (South Beach); tel 305/673-5890. **American.** An outdoor corner cafe with umbrella-covered tables, serving stir-fry, pizza, burgers, and pastas. In the basement you'll find a wine shop as well as a market selling magazines and deli sandwiches. **FYI:** Reservations not accepted. **Open:** Daily 8am–1am. **Prices:** Main courses $8–$20. Maj CC. 🔲 🔲 🔲 VP

★ **Crawdaddy's**, 1 Washington Ave, Miami Beach; tel 305/673-1708. ½ mi S of Fla A1A in South Pointe Park. **New American/Seafood.** A casual waterfront restaurant with great views and affordable prices. The early-bird dinner specials and the luncheon buffet both offer particularly good values. **FYI:** Reservations accepted. Children's menu. **Open:** Lunch Mon–Fri 11am–3pm; dinner Mon–Thurs 5–11pm, Fri–Sat 5pm–midnight, Sun 5–10pm; brunch Sun 11am–3:30pm. Closed Dec 25. **Prices:** Main courses $21–$30. Maj CC. 🔲 🔲 🔲

Dining Galleries, in Fontainebleau Hilton Hotel, 4441 Collins Ave, Miami Beach; tel 305/538-2000. **Continental.** A romantic, very elegant, antique-filled restaurant serving fine cuisine. Known for its attentive service, its seafood and beef entrees, and an impressive Sunday brunch. **FYI:** Reservations recommended. Piano. Children's menu. **Open:** Daily 6:30pm–2am. **Prices:** Main courses $19–$27. Maj CC. VP 🔲

♣ **Dominique's**, in The Alexander Hotel, 5225 Collins Ave, Miami Beach; tel 305/861-5252. **Continental/French.** An opulent oceanside restaurant serving adventurous, French-inspired cuisine. Dine among antiques, Persian rugs, and lush foliage, on selections including buffalo sausage, alligator scaloppine, and fresh rattlesnake salad. The less adventurous might choose one of the steaks or the rack of lamb. One of the finest restaurants in Miami Beach. **FYI:** Reservations recommended. Combo/piano. Jacket required. **Open:** Daily 7am–11pm. **Prices:** Main courses $20–$30; PF dinner $21.95. Maj CC. ♥ 🔲 VP 🔲

Escopazzo, 1311 Washington Ave, Miami Beach; tel 305/674-9450. **Italian.** A cozy, romantic Italian restaurant featuring a distinguished menu and wine list. **FYI:** Reservations recommended. Beer and wine only. **Open:** Tues–Sun 6pm–midnight. **Prices:** Main courses $15–$25. Maj CC. ♥ VP

Fashion Cafe, in Casa Grande Suite Hotel, 834 Ocean Dr, Miami Beach (South Beach); tel 305/674-1330. **Italian.** Dine indoors or out at this Italianate art deco restaurant with butter-yellow walls and a sophisticated menu. **FYI:** Reservations accepted. Jazz/piano/singer. **Open:** Sun–Thurs noon–midnight, Fri–Sat noon–4am. **Prices:** Main courses $7–$19. Maj CC. ▮ ⏏ ▲ VP

♣ **The Forge**, 432 Arthur Godfrey Rd, Miami Beach; tel 305/538-8533. **American.** An elegant restaurant of several rooms adorned with oak paneling and artwork. The chef prepares fish, veal, poultry and beef specialties, many on the oak grill. **FYI:** Reservations accepted. Piano. **Open:** Sun–Thurs 5–11:30pm, Fri–Sat 5pm–1am. **Prices:** Main courses $18–$25. Maj CC. ♥ VP &

★ **Joe's Stone Crab**, 227 Biscayne St, Miami Beach; tel 305/673-0365. 6 blocks S of Fla A1A. **Regional American/Seafood.** A simply decorated landmark eatery whose stone crabs have been drawing crowds for decades. Other fish and seafood dishes, all prepared to order, are also available. **FYI:** Reservations not accepted. **Open:** Lunch Tues–Sat 11:30am–2pm; dinner Sun–Thurs 5–10pm, Fri–Sat 5–11pm. Closed Thanksgiving; May 15–Oct 15. **Prices:** Main courses $4.95–$29.95. Maj CC. ▦ VP &

The Lazy Lizard, 646 Lincoln Rd, Miami Beach; tel 305/532-2809. At Euclid Ave. **Southwestern.** A good place to relax and enjoy southwestern-style potato skins, chicken wings, nachos, or similar fare. The menu also offers big burritos, fajitas, and green chile pie. Flavored margaritas are a specialty. Daily specials. **FYI:** Reservations not accepted. **Open:** Tues–Thurs 11:30am–11pm, Fri 11:30am–midnight, Sat–Sun 5pm–midnight. Closed some hols. **Prices:** Main courses $6.50–$14.95. Maj CC. ⏏

♣ **Mezzanotte**, 1200 Washington Ave, Miami Beach; tel 305/673-4343. **Italian.** An open, airy restaurant with tile floors and black lacquered chairs serving a traditional Italian menu. **FYI:** Reservations recommended. **Open:** Sun–Thurs 6pm–midnight, Fri–Sat 6pm–2am. Closed Thanksgiving. **Prices:** Main courses $18.95–$26.95. Maj CC. ▦ VP &

★ **News Cafe**, 800 Ocean Dr, Miami Beach; tel 305/538-6397. **New American/Cafe.** This trendy South Beach hangout, a favorite with locals, serves healthy entrees, a variety of green salads, both meat and cheese sandwiches, and a selection of coffee drinks. **FYI:** Reservations not accepted. Rock. No smoking. **Open:** Daily 24 hrs. **Prices:** Main courses $2.50–$8.75. Maj CC. ▮24▮

Pacific Time, 915 Lincoln Rd, Miami Beach; tel 305/534-5979. Between Jefferson and Michigan Aves. **Regional American/Thai.** Your senses will be dazzled with the flavors of the ocean at this inventive seafood eatery. Fish and chips take on new meaning here–tuna is prepared tartare and served with Idaho potato chips. Some poultry and beef selections are available. **FYI:** Reservations recommended. **Open:** Sun–Thurs 6–11pm, Fri–Sat 6–midnight. **Prices:** Main courses $16–$24; PF dinner $20. Maj CC. ♥ &

★ **Palace Bar & Grill**, 1200 Ocean Dr, Miami Beach; tel 305/531-9077. **Cafe.** Enjoy lovely views as you dine outdoors. The varied menu includes burgers, salads, sandwiches, and steaks. **FYI:** Reservations not accepted. Rock. **Open:** Sun–Thurs 8am–2am, Fri–Sat 8am–3am. **Prices:** Main courses $6.95–$14.95. Maj CC. ⏏ ▲

Pineapples, 530 Arthur Godfrey Rd, Miami Beach; tel 305/532-9731. **New American/Health/Spa.** Plain-looking health food restaurant serving sandwiches and fresh juices as well as meal-size salads, stir-fries, and such dishes as chicken with pineapple sauce, and mahimahi with kiwi sauce. **FYI:** Reservations not accepted. Beer and wine only. No smoking. **Open:** Daily 11am–10pm. **Prices:** Main courses $5–$13. Maj CC. ▼

ShaBeen, in the Marlin Hotel, 1200 Collins Ave, Miami Beach; tel 305/673-8373. **Caribbean.** Sharp, stylish restaurant with a fun atmosphere, catering to a young, hip crowd. Menu highlights include jerk chicken, Jamaican roti, oxtail with beans, and fillet of yellowtail snapper prepared Creole-style. **FYI:** Reservations accepted. Combo. **Open:** Sun–Thurs 2–11pm, Fri–Sat 2pm–midnight. **Prices:** Main courses $11–$18. Maj CC. ♥ ▼

★ **The Strand**, 671 Washington Ave, Miami Beach; tel 305/532-2340. **Regional American/French.** An old standby, with a large, open dining room and candlelit tables. Attracts a lively, fashionable crowd that comes for the boisterous bar scene and the comfort food prepared with a twist. **FYI:** Reservations recommended. **Open:** Sun–Thurs 6pm–midnight, Fri–Sat 6pm–1am. **Prices:** Main courses $7.25–$19.50. Maj CC. ♥ ▲ VP

Thai Toni, 890 Washington Ave, Miami Beach; tel 305/538-8424. **Thai.** Thai food prepared with a tropical twist is served in an attractive, informal setting at this trendy eatery. **FYI:** Reservations accepted. Beer and wine only. **Open:** Sun–Thurs 5:30–11pm, Fri–Sat 5:30pm–midnight. Closed some hols. **Prices:** Main courses $6.95–$18.95. Maj CC. ▦ VP &

Ⓢ **Toni's New Tokyo Cuisine**, 1208 Washington Ave, Miami Beach; tel 305/673-9368. **Japanese.** A relaxed, neon-lit eatery serving reliable Japanese. Specialties include sautéed pork with ginger sauce. Extensive sushi bar. Combination plates available. **FYI:** Reservations not accepted. Beer and wine only. **Open:** Mon–Thurs 6–11pm, Fri–Sat 6pm–midnight. **Prices:** Main courses $9.95–$17.95. Maj CC. ♿

Wolfie's, 2038 Collins Ave, Miami Beach; tel 305/538-6626. **American/Jewish.** This New York–based landmark Jewish deli has been serving the South Beach area around the clock since 1947. Cold smoked-fish platters, overstuffed sandwiches, chicken entrees, and special platters are good values. Patrons are provided a bowl of pickles, a basket of rolls, and a small danish in addition to their meal. **FYI:** Reservations not accepted. Children's menu. Beer and wine only. **Open:** Daily 24 hrs. **Prices:** Main courses $6.85–$13.75. Ltd CC. 🖼 🍴 💟 ♿

Yo-Si Peking, in Eden Roc Resort and Spa, 4525 Collins Ave, Miami Beach; tel 305/531-0000. **Chinese/Thai.** This new Kosher-Chinese eatery is a commendable effort by the rejuvenated art deco hotel. **FYI:** Reservations recommended. **Open:** Breakfast daily 7–11:30am; lunch Sat–Thurs 12–2:30pm, Fri 12–3pm; dinner Sun–Thurs 4–10:30pm. **Prices:** Main courses $11–$25. Maj CC. 🖼 VP

Attractions 📷

Lummus Park Beach, Ocean Dr. Runs along Ocean Drive from about 6th to 14th St in the art deco district of south Miami Beach. Free.

Bass Museum of Art, 2121 Park Ave; tel 305/673-7530. European paintings, sculptures, and tapestries from the Renaissance, baroque, rococo, and modern periods make up the bulk of the small but impressive permanent collection. Temporary exhibitions alternate between traveling shows and rotations of the Bass's stock. Built from coral rock in 1930, the museum sits in the middle of 6 landscaped, tree-topped acres. **Open:** Tues–Sat 10am–5pm, Sun 1–5pm; 2nd and 4th Wed of month 1–9pm. Closed some hols. $$

Art Deco District Tours; tel 305/672-2014. The Miami Design Preservation League sponsors tours of Miami Beach's famous art deco district, which encompasses about 800 buildings from the 1920s and 1930s. Many of the buildings were rescued from demolition, renovated and repainted in the bright pastel colors that have become characteristic of the area. The revitalized district now houses numerous shops, hotels, restaurants, and nightclubs. Walking and bicycle tours do not follow a specific route, but take in a number of noteworthy sights. Walking tours (90 minutes) depart Saturday at 10:30am from the Art Deco

Welcome Center at 1001 Ocean Dr. Bicycle tours depart Sunday 10:30am from the Cycles on the Beach Shop at 1421 Washington Ave; bikes can be rented. $$

Colony Theater, 1040 Lincoln Rd; tel 305/674-1026. Renovated to become the architectural showpiece of the art deco district, this 465-seat theater hosts performances by the Miami City Ballet, the Ballet Flamenco La Rosa, as well as various special events. **Open:** Varies.

Jackie Gleason Theater of the Performing Arts, 1700 Washington Ave; tel 305/673-7300. This newly renovated theater, which seats 2,700, provides a venue for big-budget Broadway shows, classical music concerts, opera, and dance performances. **Open:** Varies.

Kelley Fishing Fleet, Haulover Marina, 10800 Collins Ave (at 108th St); tel 305/945-3801. Half-day, full-day, and night fishing aboard diesel-powered "party boats" reaps fish like snapper, sailfish, and mackerel. Reservations recommended. **Open:** Daily; phone for details. $$$$

Charter Boat *Helen C*, Haulover Marina, 10800 Collins Ave; tel 305/947-4081. A 55-foot, twin-engine fishing charter equipped for "monster" fish, such as marlin, tuna, dolphin, and bluefish. Individual fishermen are put together to make a full boat.

MIAMI LAKES

Map page M-11, B2

Hotel 🏨

🟰🟰🟰 **Don Shula's Hotel & Golf Club**, Main St, Miami Lakes, FL 33014; tel 305/821-1150 or toll free 800/247-4852; fax 305/819-8298. Owned by Miami Dolphins coach Don Shula, it does a brisk business with athletic types and others who don't mind being 20 minutes out of the downtown loop. The facility is comprised of a main inn and other units at the golf course, where most of the athletic facilities are located. Traditional golfing attire is worn by some staff. **Rooms:** 301 rms and stes. Exec-level rms avail. CI 3pm/CO noon. Express checkout avail. Nonsmoking rms avail. **Amenities:** �⛱ A/C, cable TV w/movies, refrig. Some units w/minibars, some w/terraces. **Services:** ✕ 🖥 ⬛ 🍴 Car-rental desk, babysitting. **Facilities:** 🏌▶18 🎾⬛⬛ 🛥 500 🖥♿ 4 rsts, 3 bars (1 w/entertainment), racquetball, squash, spa, sauna, steam rm, whirlpool, playground. Restaurant and lounge have rows of TV monitors so diners and drinkers don't miss any of the football action. **Rates:** HS Jan 11–Feb 28 $154 S or D;

from $164 ste. Extra person $10. Children under 18 stay free. Lower rates off-season. Higher rates for spec evnts/hols. Spec packages avail. Pking: Outdoor, free. Maj CC.

MIAMI SPRINGS
Map page M-11, B2

Hotels 🛏

≣≣≣ Crown Sterling Suites, 3974 NW South River Dr, Miami Springs, FL 33142; tel 305/634-5000 or toll free 800/772-3787; fax 305/635-9499. ¾ mi N of airport terminal entrance on Fla 953 (LeJeune Rd). The sporty look of this all-suites arrangement is a nice alternative to some of the humdrum offerings an airport tends to attract. **Rooms:** 314 stes. CI 3pm/CO noon. Express checkout avail. Nonsmoking rms avail. **Amenities:** 🛏 🕰 🖭 A/C, cable TV w/movies, refrig, voice mail. All units w/terraces. Rooms are equipped with microwave ovens. **Services:** ✗ 🚐 🛆 ⌓ ⌓ **Facilities:** 🛗 🚇 🕰 1 rst, 1 bar, washer/dryer. **Rates (BB):** HS Feb from $189 ste. Extra person $10. Children under 12 stay free. Lower rates off-season. Higher rates for spec evnts/hols. Spec packages avail. Pking: Outdoor, free. Maj CC.

≣≣ Ramada Limited, 5125 NW 36th St, Miami Springs, FL 33166; tel 305/887-2153 or toll free 800/272-6232; fax 305/887-2151 ext 114. 2 mi NW of terminal entrance. New owners are continuing renovations. **Rooms:** 110 rms. CI noon/CO noon. Nonsmoking rms avail. **Amenities:** 🛏 🕰 A/C, cable TV. **Services:** 🚐 🛆 ⌓ ⌓ Babysitting. **Facilities:** 🚇 🕰 **Rates (CP):** HS Dec 15–Apr 15 $70–$80 S or D. Extra person $10. Children under 18 stay free. Lower rates off-season. Higher rates for spec evnts/hols. Spec packages avail. Pking: Outdoor, free. Maj CC.

NAPLES
Map page M-10, A2

Hotels 🛏

≣≣ Comfort Inn, 1221 5th Ave S, Naples, FL 33940; tel 813/649-5800 or toll free 800/382-7941; fax 813/619-0523. Exit 16 off I-75. From Pine Ridge Rd W turn left onto Goodlette Rd and proceed to 5th Ave. A waterfront lodging at an affordable price. Close to area beaches and shopping. **Rooms:** 101 rms. CI 3pm/CO noon. Nonsmoking rms avail. **Amenities:** 🛏 🕰 A/C, cable TV, refrig. Some units w/minibars. **Services:** 🚐 ⌓ Babysitting. **Facilities:** 🛗 🚇 🕰 Washer/dryer. **Rates (CP):** HS Dec 21–Apr

21 $99 S; $109 D. Extra person $5. Children under 18 stay free. Lower rates off-season. Higher rates for spec evnts/hols. Spec packages avail. Pking: Outdoor, free. Maj CC.

≣≣ Days Inn, 1925 Davis Blvd, Naples, FL 33942; tel 813/774-3117 or toll free 800/272-0106; fax 813/775-5333. A comfortable economy choice. **Rooms:** 158 rms and stes. CI 3pm/CO noon. Nonsmoking rms avail. **Amenities:** 🛏 A/C, cable TV, refrig, in-rm safe. Some units w/terraces. **Services:** ⌓ **Facilities:** 🚇 🕰 1 rst, lawn games, whirlpool, playground, washer/dryer. Picnic tables and grills for cooking outdoors. **Rates (CP):** HS Dec–Apr $90 S or D; from $115 ste. Extra person $5. Children under 18 stay free. Lower rates off-season. Higher rates for spec evnts/hols. Pking: Outdoor, free. Maj CC.

≣≣≣ Edgewater Beach Hotel, 1901 Gulf Shore Blvd N, Naples, FL 33940; tel 813/262-6511 or toll free 800/821-0196; fax 813/262-1243. 3½ mi N of Downtown Naples. A low-key deluxe offering sometimes overshadowed by the big names but nonetheless a top choice for those who don't require the luxury level of the Ritz. A fashionable address, at prices lower than you might expect. **Rooms:** 124 stes. CI 3pm/CO noon. Some suites in the lowrise section offer views of the tranquil courtyard. **Amenities:** 🛏 🕰 🖭 🕮 A/C, cable TV w/movies, refrig, in-rm safe. All units w/terraces, some w/Jacuzzis. **Services:** ✗ 🖛 🆅🅿 🛆 ⌓ Twice-daily maid svce, masseur, babysitting. **Facilities:** 🚇 🛆 🍴 🖇 🕰 🕰 2 rsts, 3 bars (1 w/entertainment), 1 beach (ocean), board surfing, games rm. Roof restaurant offers exquisite views. Enjoy lunch in the courtyard under an umbrella amidst gardens of impatiens. **Rates:** HS Dec–Apr from $205 ste. Children under 18 stay free. Lower rates off-season. Spec packages avail. Pking: Indoor/outdoor, free. Maj CC.

≣≣ Hampton Inn, 3210 Tamiami Trail N, Naples, FL 33940; tel 813/261-8000 or toll free 800/732-4667; fax 813/261-7802. Exit 16 off I-75. Handsome new construction; good, predictable accommodations. **Rooms:** 107 rms and stes. CI 2pm/CO noon. Nonsmoking rms avail. **Amenities:** 🛏 A/C, cable TV w/movies, refrig. **Services:** 🛆 ⌓ Free local calls and continental breakfast. **Facilities:** 🚇 🖇 🕰 🕰 **Rates (CP):** HS Dec–Apr $99–$129 S or D; from $160 ste. Extra person $10. Children under 18 stay free. Lower rates off-season. Spec packages avail. Pking: Outdoor, free. Maj CC.

≣≣≣ Inn of Naples, 4055 N Tamiami Trail, Naples, FL 33940; tel 813/649-5500 or toll free 800/237-8858; fax 813/649-5500. Exit 16 off I-75. A good value for those who don't require a beachfront location. Its architecture, featuring Spanish and Mediterranean accents, lends an appealing look. **Rooms:** 64 rms. CI 3pm/CO noon. Nonsmoking rms avail. **Amenities:** 🛏 🕰 🖭 A/C, cable TV w/movies, refrig, VCR, in-rm safe. All units w/minibars, all w/terraces. **Services:** ✗ 🛆 ⌓ **Facilities:** 🚇 🕰

🔥 1 rst, 1 bar, whirlpool. Guests have access to a nearby golf course and fitness club for a fee. **Rates (CP):** HS Jan–Apr $120–$146 S or D. Extra person $10. Children under 18 stay free. Lower rates off-season. Higher rates for spec evnts/hols. Pking: Outdoor, free. Maj CC.

≣≣≣ La Playa Beach & Racquet Inn, 9891 Gulf Shore Dr, Naples, FL 33963; tel 813/597-3123 or toll free 800/237-6883, 800/282-4423 in FL; fax 813/597-6278. Exit 17 off I-75. 6 mi W of I-75. Beachgoers will be proud to drop anchor here. A major renovation was completed in 1994. **Rooms:** 180 rms, stes, and effic. CI 2pm/CO 11am. Tropical appointments. **Amenities:** 🛅 A/C, cable TV. All units w/terraces. **Services:** ✕ 🗝 🖼 🖵 Babysitting. **Facilities:** 🗂 🏊6 🔲 🔥 2 rsts, 2 bars, 1 beach (ocean), washer/dryer. **Rates:** HS Dec–Apr $125–$145 S or D; from $240 ste; from $165 effic. Extra person $10. Children under 12 stay free. Lower rates off-season. Pking: Outdoor, free. Maj CC.

≣≣≣ Naples Beach Hotel and Golf Club, 851 Gulf Shore Blvd, Naples, FL 33940; tel 813/261-2222 or toll free 800/237-7600; fax 813/261-7380. Exit 16 off I-75. This old favorite hasn't quite kept up with the Joneses, but golfers still come here to enjoy their familiar stomping ground. Conventions and other groups also find this spot appealing. **Rooms:** 315 rms, stes, and effic. CI 4pm/CO noon. Nonsmoking rms avail. **Amenities:** 🛅 A/C, cable TV w/movies. All units w/minibars, some w/terraces. **Services:** ✕ 🗝 VP 🖼 🖵 Social director, children's program, babysitting. **Facilities:** 🗂 🏊 ⛳ ▶18 🏄4 🔲 🔥 3 rsts, 2 bars (1 w/entertainment), 1 beach (ocean), games rm, beauty salon, day-care ctr. Sundays are pool party day, and twice weekly a big band performs for dinner dances. **Rates:** HS Dec–Apr $165–$255 S or D; from $350 ste; from $225 effic. Extra person $15. Children under 12 stay free. Lower rates off-season. Spec packages avail. Pking: Outdoor, free. Maj CC.

≣≣ Park Shore Resort Hotel, 600 Neopolitan Way, Naples, FL 33940; tel 813/263-2222 or toll free 800/548-2077; fax 813/263-0946. 2 blocks W of US 41. Handsome 4-story complex. Wicker-furnished lobby has lodge-like atmosphere. **Rooms:** 156 effic. CI 3pm/CO 11am. All units have 2 baths, tropical-style furniture, and ceiling fans. **Amenities:** 🛅 🔧 🖵 A/C, cable TV, refrig. Some units w/minibars, all w/terraces. **Services:** ✕ 🖵 Children's program, babysitting. **Facilities:** 🗂 🏄4 🔥 1 rst, 1 bar, lawn games, racquetball, whirlpool, washer/dryer. **Rates:** HS Dec–Apr from $135 effic. Extra person $10. Children under 18 stay free. Lower rates off-season. Higher rates for spec evnts/hols. Pking: Outdoor, free. Maj CC.

≣≣≣ Port of the Islands Resort & Marina, 25000 E Tamiami Trail, Naples, FL ; tel 813/394-3101 or toll free 800/237-4173; fax 813/394-4335. 20 mi S of Naples. Boasts a spacious lobby with Spanish patterns, Mexican tile, potted palms, and a huge fireplace. **Rooms:** 187 rms, stes, and effic. CI 3pm/CO noon. Nonsmoking rms avail. **Amenities:** 🛅 🔧 🖵 A/C, cable TV w/movies. Ceiling fans in rooms. **Services:** ✕ 🖵 **Facilities:** 🗂 🚲 🔲 🏄4 🔫 🎣 🔲 🔥 2 rsts, 2 bars (1 w/entertainment), lawn games, playground, washer/dryer. **Rates:** HS Dec–Apr $95–$125 S or D; from $175 ste; from $110 effic. Extra person $10. Children under 16 stay free. Lower rates off-season. Pking: Outdoor, free. Maj CC.

≣≣≣ Quality Inn Golf & Country Club, 4100 Golden Gate Pkwy, Naples, FL 33999; tel 813/455-1010 or toll free 800/277-0017; fax 813/455-4038. Exit 15 off I-75. A golfing favorite; draws a sedate crowd. **Rooms:** 181 rms, stes, and effic. CI 3pm/CO noon. Nonsmoking rms avail. Cheerful rooms have platform beds; some overlook the golf course. **Amenities:** 🛅 A/C, cable TV w/movies. Some units w/terraces. **Services:** 🖼 🖵 **Facilities:** 🗂 ▶18 🏄2 🔲 1 rst, 2 bars (1 w/entertainment), whirlpool. **Rates:** HS Jan–Apr $79–$109 S or D; from $119 ste; from $89 effic. Extra person $8. Children under 18 stay free. Lower rates off-season. Higher rates for spec evnts/hols. Spec packages avail. Pking: Outdoor, free. Maj CC.

≣≣ Quality Inn Gulfcoast, 2555 N Tamiami Trail, Naples, FL 33940; tel 813/261-6046 or toll free 800/330-0046; fax 813/261-5742. Exit 16 off I-75. An inviting, updated facility with a popular pool bar and Japanese steak house. **Rooms:** 121 rms. CI 2pm/CO noon. Nonsmoking rms avail. **Amenities:** 🛅 🔧 🖵 A/C, cable TV w/movies, in-rm safe. **Services:** 🖵 Babysitting. **Facilities:** 🗂 🔲 🔥 2 rsts, 2 bars (1 w/entertainment), games rm. Pool bar under a thatched hut attracts locals and guests alike for its jukebox and wide-screen TV. **Rates (CP):** HS Jan–Apr $85–$90 S or D. Extra person $5. Children under 18 stay free. Lower rates off-season. Higher rates for spec evnts/hols. Spec packages avail. Pking: Outdoor, free. Maj CC.

≣≣ Vanderbilt Inn on the Gulf, 11000 Gulf Shore Dr N, Naples, FL 33963; tel 813/597-3157 or toll free 800/643-8654; fax 813/597-3099. Exit 17 off I-75. 5½ mi W of I-75. This otherwise plain offering is appealing for its beach locale and informality. **Rooms:** 147 rms and effic. CI 3pm/CO 11am. Nonsmoking rms avail. **Amenities:** 🛅 A/C, cable TV w/movies, in-rm safe. Some units w/terraces. **Services:** ✕ 🖵 **Facilities:** 🗂 ⛱ 🍹 🔲 🔥 1 rst, 2 bars (w/entertainment), 1 beach (ocean), washer/dryer. **Rates:** HS Feb–Apr $127–$173 S or D; from $259 effic. Extra person $10. Children under 18 stay free. Min stay HS. Lower rates off-season. Spec packages avail. Pking: Outdoor, free. Maj CC.

Motels

Best Western Naples Inn, 2329 9th Street N, Naples, FL 33940 (Old Naples); tel 813/261-1148 or toll free 800/243-1148; fax 813/262-4684. At US 41 N and Mooring Lane Dr. Only a short drive to area beaches; a reliable place to stay. **Rooms:** 80 rms. CI 3pm/CO 11am. Nonsmoking rms avail. All rooms have fully equipped kitchens. **Amenities:** 🛏 🕭 🖭 A/C, cable TV w/movies, refrig, VCR, in-rm safe. All units w/terraces. **Services:** 🛆 **Facilities:** 🛆 🛆 1 rst, washer/dryer. **Rates (CP):** HS Dec 20–Apr $79–$109 S or D; from $99 ste. Extra person $6. Children under 18 stay free. Min stay spec evnts. Lower rates off-season. Higher rates for spec evnts/hols. Spec packages avail. Pking: Outdoor, free. Maj CC.

Cove Inn Resort & Marina, 1191 8th St S, Naples, FL 33940; tel 813/262-7161 or toll free 800/255-4365; fax 813/261-6905. A waterfront resort and condominium complex where guests can stroll the marina docks or relax in the pool. **Rooms:** 75 rms and effic. CI 3pm/CO 11am. Nonsmoking rms avail. **Amenities:** 🛏 A/C, cable TV, refrig. All units w/terraces. **Services:** 🛆 🛆 Babysitting. **Facilities:** 🛆 🛆 3 rsts (see also "Restaurants" below), 3 bars, beauty salon, washer/dryer. Full-service marina. **Rates:** HS Dec 20–Apr 20 $99–$110 S or D; from $115 effic. Extra person $5–10. Children under 16 stay free. Lower rates off-season. Higher rates for spec evnts/hols. Pking: Outdoor, free. Maj CC.

Holiday Inn, 1100 9th St N, Naples, FL 33940 (Old Naples); tel 813/262-7146 or toll free 800/465-4329; fax 813/261-3809. A convenient location and the tropical pool area make this a well-chosen resting spot. **Rooms:** 137 rms. CI 4pm/CO noon. Nonsmoking rms avail. **Amenities:** 🛏 🕭 🖭 A/C, cable TV. **Services:** ✗ 🚗 🛆 🛆 🛆 Newspapers delivered daily to rooms. **Facilities:** 🛆 🛆 1 rst, 1 bar (w/entertainment), games rm. **Rates:** HS Dec 25–Apr $89 S; $101 D. Extra person $10. Children under 18 stay free. Min stay spec evnts. Lower rates off-season. Higher rates for spec evnts/hols. Spec packages avail. Pking: Outdoor, free. Maj CC.

Howard Johnson Lodge, 221 9th St S, Naples, FL 33940; tel 813/262-6181 or toll free 800/654-2000; fax 813/262-0318. Exit 16W off I-75. Recently renovated motel is an adequate home base for touring area attractions. **Rooms:** 101 rms and effic. CI 3pm/CO noon. Nonsmoking rms avail. Deluxe rooms are basically standards with refrigerators. **Amenities:** 🛏 🕭 A/C, cable TV, in-rm safe. All units w/terraces. **Services:** 🛆 🛆 Babysitting. **Facilities:** 🛆 🛆 1 rst, 2 bars (1 w/entertainment). **Rates:** HS Dec–Apr $95 S; $125 D; from $125 effic. Extra person $10. Children under 18 stay free. Lower rates off-season. Pking: Outdoor, free. Maj CC.

Trails End Motel, 309 9th St S, Naples, FL 33940; tel 813/262-6336 or toll free 800/247-5307; fax 813/262-3381. 1 mi N of Fla 84 on US 41. Very affordable, basic lodging. Walk to nearby shopping district. **Rooms:** 50 rms. CI noon/CO 11am. Nonsmoking rms avail. **Amenities:** 🛏 A/C, cable TV, refrig. **Services:** 🛆 🛆 🛆 **Facilities:** 🛆 🛆 Washer/dryer. **Rates (CP):** HS Dec–Apr $85 S; $100 D. Extra person $6. Children under 16 stay free. Lower rates off-season. Higher rates for spec evnts/hols. Spec packages avail. Pking: Outdoor, free. Maj CC.

Wellesley Inn, 1555 5th Ave S, Naples, FL 33942; tel 813/793-4646 or toll free 800/444-8888; fax 813/793-5248. 1 mi S on US 41 at jct Fla 84. A stylish and inviting lobby, but rooms are just standard. **Rooms:** 105 rms and stes. CI 1pm/CO 11am. Nonsmoking rms avail. **Amenities:** 🛏 🕭 A/C, cable TV. **Services:** ✗ 🛆 🛆 🛆 Babysitting. **Facilities:** 🛆 🛆 🛆 **Rates (CP):** HS Dec 20–Apr 26 $100 S; $110 D; from $140 ste. Children under 18 stay free. Lower rates off-season. Pking: Outdoor, free. Maj CC.

Resorts

Naples Bath & Tennis Club, 4995 Airport Rd N, Naples, FL ; tel 813/261-5777 or toll free 800/225-9692; fax 813/649-2050. ½ mi S of Pine Ridge. 23 acres. Expansive grounds and a multitude of tennis courts are good evidence this facility caters to the athletic guest. Security-controlled gate entrance. **Rooms:** 40 effic. CI 3pm/CO 11am. Nonsmoking rms avail. Tastefully decorated units are in excellent repair. **Amenities:** 🛏 🕭 🖭 A/C, cable TV w/movies, refrig. Some units w/terraces. **Services:** 🛆 🛆 Social director, masseur, babysitting. **Facilities:** 🛆 🛆28 🛆10 🛆 🛆 🛆 2 rsts, 2 bars, squash, spa, sauna, steam rm, whirlpool, washer/dryer. Poolside snack-bar. **Rates:** HS Dec–Apr from $135 effic. Children under 18 stay free. Min stay. Lower rates off-season. Higher rates for spec evnts/hols. Spec packages avail. Pking: Outdoor, free. Maj CC.

The Registry Resort, 475 Seagate Dr, Naples, FL 33940 (Pelican Bay); tel 813/597-3232 or toll free 800/247-9810; fax 813/597-3147. Exit 16 off I-75. 25 acres. Contemporary-styled 18-story tower, angled to the beach so that most balconies have a sea view. Set amongst gardens and a mangrove preserve. **Rooms:** 474 rms and stes; 50 ctges/villas. CI 3pm/CO 11am. Express checkout avail. Nonsmoking rms avail. Spacious but unremarkable. 9 suites in tower and 50 suites in Tennis Villas. **Amenities:** 🛏 🕭 🖳 A/C, refrig, in-rm safe, shoe polisher, bathrobes. All units w/minibars, all w/terraces, some w/Jacuzzis. **Services:** 🍽 🛆 🖭 🚗 🛆 🛆 Twice-daily maid svce, car-rental desk, masseur, children's program, babysitting. Shuttle tram to beach. **Facilities:** 🛆 🚴 🛆 🛆 🛆10 🛆 🛆 🛆 🛆 🖳 🛆 6 rsts, 3 bars (1 w/entertainment), 1 beach (bay), lifeguard, games rm, lawn games, spa, sauna, steam rm, whirlpool, beauty salon, day-care ctr. Great for tennis players; guests share tennis courts with local club members. Guaranteed tee times at nearby golf courses. 10-minute walk or 3-minute tram ride to beach. Canoes for paddling through mangrove preserve, which is home to egrets and roseate spoonbills. The tony Lafite restaurant serves a fine selection of seafood in stylish surroundings. Also ice cream parlor, snack bar on beach. Multi-level nightclub. **Rates:** HS Jan 15–Apr 15 $275–$355 S or D; from $375 ste. Extra person $25. Children under 18 stay free. Min stay HS and spec evnts. Lower rates off-season. Spec packages avail. Pking: Indoor/outdoor, $7. Maj CC. Rates vary by floor and view rather than size or amenities.

≡≡≡≡ **The Ritz-Carlton Naples**, 280 Vanderbilt Beach Rd, Naples, FL 33941 (Vanderbilt Beach); tel 813/598-3300 or toll free 800/241-3333; fax 813/598-6690. 9 mi N of downtown Naples, exit 17 off I-75. Go West to Vanderbilt Beach Road. 13 acres. A '90s version of '20s splendor. Located right on the edge of seemingly endless white beach, this pink palace is filled with original art, chandeliers, and lofty salons with sumptuous draperies. **Rooms:** 463 rms and stes. Exec-level rms avail. CI 3pm/CO noon. Express checkout avail. Nonsmoking rms avail. Spacious and efficient rooms with refined furnishings. Were being refurbished at time of inspection. **Amenities:** 🗄 🛁 🎣 A/C, cable TV, refrig, in-rm safe, shoe polisher, bathrobes. All units w/minibars, all w/terraces. **Services:** 🍽 🔑 VP 🚗 🛎 🐕 Twice-daily maid svce, car-rental desk, masseur, children's program, babysitting. Responsive, attentive service; staff-to-room ratio of 2 to 1. Popular, well-organized Ritz Kids activities. **Facilities:** 🏊 🚵 ⚠ 🏖 🎣 📞 🏸 📶 💻 🔥 4 rsts (*see also* "Restaurants" below), 3 bars (1 w/entertainment), 1 beach (bay), lifeguard, games rm, lawn games, sauna, steam rm, whirlpool, beauty salon, day-care ctr. First-rate tennis facility and fitness center/spa. Golf privileges at nearby clubs, with priority tee times. Elegant though expensive dining, offered indoors and out. **Rates:** HS Dec 11–Apr 30 $295–$540 S or D; from $795 ste. Extra person $15. Children under 15 stay free. Lower rates off-season. Spec packages avail. Pking: Indoor/outdoor, $15. Maj CC.

≡≡≡ **World Tennis Center & Resort**, 4800 Airport–Pulling Rd, Naples, FL 33942; tel 813/263-1900 or toll free 800/292-6663, 800/292-6663 in the US, 800/621-6665 in Canada; fax 813/649-7855. Exit 16 off I-75. An all-condo resort for the tennis enthusiast. Extensive grounds and modern facilities. **Rooms:** 148 effic. CI 3pm/CO 11am. **Amenities:** 🗄 🛁 📺 A/C, TV. All units w/terraces. **Services:** 🐕 🐾 Social director, children's program, babysitting. Daily maid service offered for fee. **Facilities:** 🏊 🏸6 🎾10 🏋40 🔥 1 rst, 1 bar (w/entertainment),

sauna, washer/dryer. **Rates:** HS Feb–Apr from $160 effic. Extra person $15. Lower rates off-season. Spec packages avail. Pking: Outdoor, free. Maj CC.

Restaurants 🍴

Backstage Tap & Grill, in WaterSide Shops, 5535 N Tamiami Trail, Naples; tel 813/598-1300. Exit 16 off I-75. At the corner of US 41 and Seagate Dr. **Burgers/Seafood.** This show-themed restaurant has a jazzy decor featuring stage lighting, director's chairs, and posters from Broadway musicals. Its equally jazzy menu features items like the Backstage Burger. Outdoor seating is available. Live classical jazz is featured Thursday, Friday, and Saturday nights. **FYI:** Reservations not accepted. Beer and wine only. **Open:** Mon–Sat 7:30am–midnight, Sun 7:30am–10pm. Closed some hols. **Prices:** Main courses $4.95–$9.95. Maj CC. 🍴 ⑂

Bayside, a Seafood Grill and Bar, in the Village on Venetian Bay, 4270 Gulfshore Blvd N, Naples; tel 813/649-5552. **Mediterranean.** Sky-blue wicker, white walls, lush plants, and water views at a tropical-style restaurant and bar. The lunch fare includes soups such as black bean with chorizo, as well as salads, sandwiches, and other specialties. The creative dinner menu includes oak-grilled salmon over wilted spinach salad with warm pancetta and balsamic vinaigrette, and breast of chicken with sauce chasseur and baked orzo mushroom timbale. **FYI:** Reservations accepted. Piano. **Open:** HS Jan/May daily 11:30am–11pm. Reduced hours off-season. **Prices:** Main courses $15.50–$23.95; PF dinner $30. Maj CC. 🍴 🖼 VP ⑂

Chardonnay, 2331 Tamiami Trail, Naples; tel 813/261-1744. **French.** Enjoy a romantic evening in this glass-enclosed dining room. A favorite dish is the duck pâté studded with pistachio nuts, the chef's special appetizer. **FYI:** Reservations recommended. Dress code. **Open:** HS Dec–Apr daily 5:30–10pm. Reduced hours off-season. Closed some hols. **Prices:** Main courses $16.50–$27.50. Maj CC. VP ⑂

★ **Chef's Garden/Truffles**, 1300 3rd St S, Naples; tel 813/262-5500. At 13th Ave. **New American.** Mirrors and wicker furnishings adorn this colorful, attractive dining room. Meals are served on the outdoor patio as well. The menu often includes yellowfin tuna, red snapper served with couscous, and special calzones. The dessert menu is extensive. **FYI:** Reservations recommended. Piano/singer. Children's menu. **Open:** Sun–Thurs 11:30am–10pm, Fri–Sat 11:30am–11pm. Closed some hols. **Prices:** Main courses $15–$25; PF dinner $19.94. Maj CC. 🍴 VP ⑂

Ciao, 835 4th Ave S, Naples; tel 813/263-3889. At 8th St. **Italian.** This bistro is well-known for its wonderful Italian cuisine. Try the pasta with lobster and baby shrimp sautéed in olive oil and garlic, or choose one of the specials, such as linguine with spinach. **FYI:** Reservations recommended. Beer and wine only. No smoking. **Open:** Daily 5:30–10pm. Closed some hols; July–Aug. **Prices:** Main courses $12–$26. Maj CC. &

Cove Inn Coffee Shop, 1191 8th St S, Naples; tel 813/262-7161. At Broad Ave and 9th St. **Coffeehouse.** A traditional coffee shop with the expected decor and menu. Counter service. **FYI:** Reservations not accepted. No liquor license. **Open:** Daily 7am–1:30pm. **Prices:** Main courses $1.25–$5.50. No CC. &

The Dining Room, in The Ritz-Carlton Naples, 280 Vanderbilt Beach Rd, Naples (Vanderbilt Beach); tel 813/598-3300. 9 mi N of downtown Naples; exit 17 off I-7. Go West on Vanderbilt Beach Road. **New American/Mediterranean/Seafood.** Elegant French provincial ambience, with low lighting. Terrine of Florida spiny lobster with leek and potato; scaloppine of monkfish and lobster medaillon with port wine sauce; steamed halibut filet on a bed of braised cabbage; banana gratin with rum sauce. **FYI:** Reservations recommended. Jazz/piano. Jacket required. **Open:** Daily 7–10pm. Closed some hols; mid-May–mid-Oct. **Prices:** Main courses $16–$38. Maj CC. ♥ VP &

The Dock at Crayton Cove, 12th Ave S on Naples Bay, Naples; tel 813/263-9940. **American.** A surf-and-turf restaurant located at the Naples City Dock. **FYI:** Reservations not accepted. Children's menu. **Open:** Daily 11:30am–midnight. Closed Dec 25. **Prices:** Main courses $5–$15. Maj CC. ⚓ ▲ &

The English Pub, 2408 Linwood Ave, Naples; tel 813/774-2408. **British/Pub.** British pub fare is served up in this traditionally styled tavern, decorated with hundreds of labels from beers of yesteryear. The menu includes fish and chips, steak pies, and Yorkshire pudding. A large array of imported beers is available. **FYI:** Reservations not accepted. Combo/sing along. Children's menu. Beer and wine only. **Open:** Mon–Sat 11am–midnight. Closed some hols. **Prices:** Main courses $9–$14. Maj CC. ▣ ▾

♥ **Lafite**, in the Registry Resort, 475 Seagate Dr, Naples; tel 813/597-3232 ext 5666. **Continental.** Feast on Wisconsin veal or seared prime filet mignon in one of several beautifully decorated dining rooms. If you're feeling extravagant, sample 50-year-old cognac for $100 per glass. A harpist entertains diners on the weekends. **FYI:** Reservations recommended. Jacket required. **Open:** HS Nov–May Fri–Mon 6–11:30pm, Tues–Thurs 6–10pm. Reduced hours off-season. **Prices:** Main courses $20–$35; PF dinner $35. Maj CC. ♥ VP &

L & N Seafood Grill, in Gateway of Naples, 2184 Tamiami Trail N, Naples; tel 813/649-1141. Golden Gate Pkwy at Tamiami

Trail. **Seafood.** A casual, 3-tiered restaurant with ceiling fans, nautical overtones, and great river views. The grilled catch of the day might be tuna, salmon, grouper, or halibut. **FYI:** Reservations not accepted. Children's menu. **Open:** Daily 11am–10pm, Fri–Sat 11am–11pm. Closed Dec 25. **Prices:** Main courses $7.95–$26. Maj CC. ▾ &

L'Auberge, 602 5th Ave S, Naples; tel 813/261-8148. **French.** A simple French cafe with a small kitchen and an intimate bar serving beer and wine. Casual for lunch, slightly more dressy for dinner. The menu includes a variety of chicken, veal, and lamb dishes. **FYI:** Reservations accepted. Dress code. Beer and wine only. **Open:** Lunch Mon–Fri 11am–2pm; dinner Mon–Sat 5:30pm–close. Closed July 4. **Prices:** Main courses $16.95–$21.95. Maj CC.

Margaux's Restaurant, 3080 N Tamiami Trail, Naples; tel 813/434-2773. **Country French.** Floral prints abound in this romantic dining room, which features a country-French menu and rich desserts. **FYI:** Reservations accepted. Children's menu. Beer and wine only. **Open:** Lunch Mon–Fri 11:30am–2pm; dinner daily 5:30–9pm. Closed some hols. **Prices:** Main courses $10.95–$18.95. Ltd CC. ▾

Mark & Mike's Grill, in Waterloo Station, 200 Goodlette Rd S, Naples; tel 813/263-8440. **Pub/Seafood.** Photos of Naples cover the walls. Prime rib, stuffed fish, and other seafood dishes. **FYI:** Reservations recommended. Children's menu. **Open:** Mon–Fri 11:30am–11pm, Sat 5–11pm, Sun 5–9pm. Closed Dec 25. **Prices:** Main courses $10.95–$19.95. Maj CC. ▦ ▾ &

Merriman's Wharf, in Old Marine Marketplace at Tin City, 1200 5th Ave S, Naples; tel 813/261-1811. At jct US 41 and Goodlett Road. **New American/Seafood/Steak.** Enjoy the friendly nautical atmosphere and views of the river while you dine. A variety of seafood is available, but the specialty here is prime rib. **FYI:** Reservations not accepted. Children's menu. **Open:** Mon–Sat 11am–10pm, Sun noon–10pm. **Prices:** Main courses $10.95–$17.95. Maj CC. ▲ &

Michelbob's, 371 Airport Rd, Naples; tel 813/843-RIBS. Opposite Naples Airport. **Barbecue.** The eating is hearty and the setting casual. Unfinished wood and early Coca-Cola advertisements decorate the room. Nationally celebrated for the quality of its ribs and other barbecued meats. Entertainment is offered on the patio in summer. **FYI:** Reservations not accepted. Guitar/singer. Children's menu. No smoking. **Open:** Fri–Sat 11am–10pm, Sun 8:30am–9pm, Mon–Thurs 11am–9pm. Closed Thanksgiving. **Prices:** Main courses $8–$19. Maj CC. ▾ &

Nick's on the Water, in Coconut Grove Marketplace and Marina, 1001 10th Ave S, Naples; tel 813/649-7770. **Italian.**

Enjoy the view from any table in this waterside restaurant. The high-ceilinged room has hanging light fixtures and plants. The varied menu ranges from spaghetti and meat balls to fancier dishes like veal marsala. **FYI:** Reservations recommended. Band. Children's menu. **Open:** Mon–Thurs 4–10pm, Fri 4–11pm, Sat 11:30am–11pm, Sun 11:30am–10pm. **Prices:** Main courses $6.95–$19.95. Maj CC. 🖼 💟 VP ♿

Old Naples Pub, in Robinson Court, 255 13th Ave S, Naples; tel 813/649-8200. **Burgers/Pub.** Dining tables surround the central bar at this tavern-style restaurant. Outdoor seating is under umbrellas. Popular dishes include caesar salad with chicken. Live jazz is performed on Sunday; during the week, you can enjoy board games or darts. **FYI:** Reservations not accepted. Piano. Beer and wine only. **Open:** Daily 11am–midnight. Closed some hols. **Prices:** Main courses $4.50–$6.95. Maj CC. 🍴 ♿

Peppino's Cafe, in Naples Plaza, 2041 9th St N, Naples; tel 813/263-4191. **Italian.** Old-world Italian-style eatery, with pictures of stars and the proprietor's family and friends adorning the walls. Standard Italian fare. **FYI:** Reservations not accepted. Beer and wine only. **Open:** Mon–Fri 11am–10pm, Sat–Sun 4–10pm. Closed some hols. **Prices:** Main courses $8.95–$16.95. Maj CC.

Plum's Cafe, 8920 Tamiami Trail N, Naples; tel 813/597-8819. Exit 16 off I-75. Go west on Pine Ridge Rd, then right onto US 41. **Cafe/Italian.** Sandwiches, salads, and other light fare are prepared in an open kitchen. **FYI:** Reservations not accepted. Children's menu. **Open:** HS Oct–Apr Sun 5–11pm, Mon–Sat 11:30am–11pm. Reduced hours off-season. Closed some hols. **Prices:** Main courses $12.50–$16.50. Maj CC. 💟 VP ♿

St George and the Dragon, 936 5th Ave, Naples; tel 813/262-6546. **New American.** Sumptuous club-like surroundings, with nautical antiques and exposed carved beams under a vaulted ceiling. Start off a lunch or dinner of prime rib, a thick steak, or grilled local fish with the famed conch chowder. After 4pm, no shorts are allowed and jackets are compulsory in the dining room; however, no jacket is required in the lounge. **FYI:** Reservations recommended. Beer and wine only. **Open:** HS Jan–Mar Mon–Sat 11am–10pm, Sun 5–9pm. Reduced hours off-season. Closed Dec 25. **Prices:** Main courses $10.50–$29.95. Maj CC. VP ♿

♥ **Sign of the Vine**, 980 Solana Rd, Naples; tel 813/261-6745. 1 mi S of Seagate Dr. **Eclectic.** The romantic ambience of this former private home, with vines wrapped in white lights and a porch furnished with white wicker, will become apparent even before you enter its doors. Inside, you'll find a lovely fireplace and an eclectic menu featuring the likes of duck, pasta, and salmon. The menu changes seasonally. **FYI:** Reservations recom-

mended. Dress code. Beer and wine only. **Open:** HS Jan–May Mon–Sat 6–10pm. Reduced hours off-season. Closed some hols; June–July. **Prices:** Main courses $26–$48. Ltd CC. ♥ ♿

Silver Spoon Cafe, in Waterside Shops at Pelican Bay, 5375 Tamiami Trail N Ste 210, Naples; tel 813/591-2123. **New American/Italian.** Clean cafe-style restaurant, decorated in a contemporary black-and-white scheme, overlooking the mall and its small waterfall. Sandwiches, salads, grilled fish of the day, chicken pot pie, delightful desserts. **FYI:** Reservations accepted. Children's menu. **Open:** Sun–Thurs 11am–10pm, Fri–Sat 11am–11pm. Closed some hols. **Prices:** Main courses $5–$13. Maj CC. ♿

Villa Pescatore, 8920 Tamiami Trail N, Naples; tel 813/597-8119. Exit 16 off I-75. **Italian/Seafood.** Enjoy pasta and fish dishes amid floral prints and wicker furniture. Soft music and lighting help to create a relaxed atmosphere. **FYI:** Reservations recommended. Children's menu. Dress code. **Open:** HS Oct–Apr daily 5:30–10pm. Reduced hours off-season. **Prices:** Main courses $15.95–$22.95. Maj CC. ♥ VP ♿

Attractions 💼

Jungle Larry's Zoological Park at Caribbean Gardens, 1590 Goodlette Rd; tel 813/262-5409. Acres of lush vegetation and lakes provide a natural home for a collection of endangered species from around the world. Visitors can take guided tram and boat tours through the park. Wild animal shows, petting zoo, elephant rides, and playground. Concessions, gift shop. **Open:** Daily 9:30am–5:30pm. Closed some hols. $$$$

Collier County Museum, 3301 Tamiami Trail E; tel 813/774-8476. A permanent exhibit hall traces the last 10,000 years in the history of Florida's largest county. The grounds include a re-created Seminole village, an archeological lab, and an antique steam locomotive. Special events include the 2-day Indian Days Festival and Southwest Florida Heritage Days Festival. **Open:** Mon–Fri 9am–5pm. Free.

Conservancy Nature Center, 14th Ave N; tel 813/262-0304. Located off Goodlette-Frank Rd, the center features the Natural Science Museum, with serpentarium, sea turtle tank, and daily presentations; an aviary with bald eagles and other birds; a wildlife rehabilitation center; 45-minute guided boat tours through a mangrove swamp; and nature trails. **Open:** Mon–Fri 9am–4:30pm; Oct–June also open Sat 9am–4:30pm; Jan–Mar also open Sun 1–5pm. $

Conservancy Briggs Nature Center, 401 Shell Island Rd; tel 813/775-8569. Situated within the Rookery Bay National Estuarine Research Reserve just south of Naples. Visitors can observe a great variety of birds and other wildlife in their natural habitat along the half-mile boardwalk. Arrangements can be made for canoe and boat tours. Hours vary, call ahead. $

Teddy Bear Museum, 2511 Pine Ridge Rd; tel 813/598-2711. Some 2,000 teddy bears from around the world are imaginatively and humorously displayed. There is a collection of antique stuffed bears as well. Adjoining gift shop. **Open:** Wed–Sat 10am–5pm, Sun 1–5pm. $$

Collier-Seminole State Park, 20200 E Tamiami Trail (US 41); tel 813/394-3397. More than 6,000 acres adjoining Big Cypress Swamp. Many species of birds inhabit the mangrove jungle. The interpretive center has complete information about the park. There is a small primitive camping area on the Blackwater River, which runs through the park; a boat tour of the river is offered. Swimming, fishing, boating, canoe rentals, hiking, nature trails. **Open:** Daily 8am–sunset. $$

Corkscrew Swamp Sanctuary, 375 Sanctuary Rd; tel 813/657-3771. Northeast of Naples, this natural preserve maintained by the National Audubon Society contains one of the largest ancient bald cypress forests in the United States. Alligators, wood storks and other wading and migratory birds, and ferns and orchids share the habitat. **Open:** Dec–Apr, daily 7am–5pm; May–Nov, daily 8am–5pm. $$$

NAVARRE BEACH

Map page M-2, B2

Hotel 🏨

Holiday Inn Navarre Beach, 8375 Gulf Blvd, Navarre Beach, FL 32569; tel 904/939-2321 or toll free 800/HOLIDAY; fax 904/939-4768. Built with the trademark Holidome indoor atrium, this facility offers courtyard dining and tropical gardens. **Rooms:** 254 rms. CI 3pm/CO 11am. Nonsmoking rms avail. **Amenities:** 🛁 A/C, cable TV, in-rm safe. Some units w/terraces. **Services:** ✕ 🖼 ↩ Social director, children's program, babysitting. **Facilities:** 🏋 ⛴ 🏐 🎱 ⚓ 2 rsts, 3 bars (1 w/entertainment), 1 beach (ocean), games rm, sauna, whirlpool, playground, washer/dryer. **Rates:** HS May–Sept $85–$120 S or D. Extra person $8. Children under 18 stay free. Min stay spec evnts. Lower rates off-season. Higher rates for spec evnts/hols. Spec packages avail. Pking: Outdoor, free. Maj CC.

NEW PORT RICHEY

Map page M-6, D2

Hotels 🏨

Holiday Inn Bayside, 5015 US 19, New Port Richey, FL 34652; tel 813/849-8551 or toll free 800/HOLIDAY. A bayside property in a quiet location. **Rooms:** 135 rms. CI 2pm/CO noon. Nonsmoking rms avail. Some rooms with bay views. **Amenities:** 🛁 A/C, cable TV w/movies. **Services:** ✕ 🖼 ↩ 🛎 **Facilities:** 🏋 ⚓ 🅿 ⚓ 1 rst, 1 bar (w/entertainment). The pool overlooks the marina and features regular live entertainment. **Rates:** HS Jan–Apr $64–$69 S or D. Extra person $5. Children under 12 stay free. Lower rates off-season. Higher rates for spec evnts/hols. Spec packages avail. Pking: Outdoor, free. Maj CC.

Sheraton Inn, 5316 US 19, New Port Richey, FL 34652; tel 813/847-9005 or toll free 800/282-1422; fax 813/847-9005 ext 350. Two-story property. **Rooms:** 160 rms and stes. CI 3pm/CO 11am. Express checkout avail. Nonsmoking rms avail. Cheerful rooms with colorful green accents. **Amenities:** 🛁 A/C, cable TV. **Services:** ✕ 🖼 ↩ 🛎 **Facilities:** 🏋 🅿 ⚓ 1 rst, 1 bar (w/entertainment), whirlpool, washer/dryer. **Rates:** HS Dec–Apr $69 S or D; from $149 ste. Extra person $8. Children under 18 stay free. Lower rates off-season. Pking: Outdoor, free. Maj CC.

NEW SMYRNA BEACH

Map page M-7, B3

Hotels 🏨

Islander Beach Resort, 1601 S Atlantic Ave, New Smyrna Beach, FL 32169; tel 904/427-3452; fax 904/426-5606. Exit 56 off I-4. This 7-story timeshare facility situated on the beach features self-contained accommodations ranging from studios to 1- and 2-bedroom units. **Rooms:** 114 effic. CI 4pm/CO 10am. **Amenities:** 🛁 A/C, cable TV, refrig, VCR. Some units w/terraces. **Services:** ↩ Car-rental desk, social director, children's program, babysitting. **Facilities:** 🏋 🏐 ⚓ 1 rst, 1 bar (w/entertainment), 1 beach (ocean), lifeguard, games rm, whirlpool, washer/dryer. Discounts available at nearby golf course. **Rates:** HS Dec–Apr/June–Aug from $70 effic. Children under 18 stay free. Min stay. Lower rates off-season. Higher rates for spec evnts/hols. Pking: Outdoor, free. Maj CC.

Oceania Suite Hotel, 421 S Atlantic Ave, New Smyrna Beach, FL 32169; or toll free 800/874-1931; fax 904/423-0254. Exit 56 off I-4. Go east to Fla A1A, then turn left on Atlantic Ave. The hotel was undergoing an extensive renovation to both accommodations and public areas at time of inspection. Unrated. **Rooms:** 65 stes. CI 3pm/CO 11am. **Amenities:** 🛏 🕹 🖭 A/C, cable TV, refrig. All units w/terraces. **Services:** 🖼 🔃 Children's program, babysitting. **Facilities:** 🔥 🖼 🕹 1 beach (ocean), games rm, washer/dryer. **Rates:** HS Feb–Aug from $99 ste. Children under 18 stay free. Lower rates off-season. Higher rates for spec evnts/hols. Spec packages avail. Pking: Outdoor, free. Ltd CC.

🏨 **Riverview Hotel**, 103 Flagler Ave, New Smyrna Beach, FL 32169; tel 904/428-5858 or toll free 800/945-7416; fax 904/423-8927. Nicely furnished lodge on the Indian River; a popular rendezvous for the boating crowd, who moor at the dock to dine in the restaurant. **Rooms:** 18 rms and stes. CI 2pm/CO noon. **Amenities:** 🛏 A/C, cable TV. All units w/terraces. **Services:** ✗ 🔃 Babysitting. **Facilities:** 🔥 🔳 1 rst, 1 bar (w/entertainment), washer/dryer. **Rates (CP):** $65–$150 S or D; from $150 ste. Extra person $10. Children under 6 stay free. Min stay spec evnts. Pking: Outdoor, free. Maj CC.

Motel

🏨 **Coastal Waters Inn**, 3509 S Atlantic Ave, New Smyrna Beach, FL 32169; tel 904/428-3800 or toll free 800/321-7882; fax 904/423-5002. Exit 56 off I-4. A pleasant facility on the beach, with both standard motel rooms and units with kitchens. **Rooms:** 40 rms and effic. CI 3pm/CO 11am. Express checkout avail. There are 3 rooms considered oceanfront. **Amenities:** 🛏 🕹 🖭 A/C, cable TV, refrig. Some units w/terraces. **Services:** 🔃 **Facilities:** 🔥 🕹 1 beach (ocean). **Rates:** HS Dec–Sept $65–$135 S or D; from $79 effic. Extra person $7.50. Children under 12 stay free. Lower rates off-season. Higher rates for spec evnts/hols. Pking: Outdoor, free. Maj CC.

Restaurants 🍴

★ **JB's Fish Camp**, 859 Pompano Ave, New Smyrna Beach; tel 904/427-5747. 5 mi S of New Smyrna Beach; exit 56 off I-4. **Regional American/Seafood.** This waterside restaurant offers a New Zealand scallops, fresh flounder, and lobster tails. Live band with vocalist entertains diners with quiet music. **FYI:** Reservations not accepted. **Open:** Sun–Thurs 11:30am–9:30pm, Fri–Sat 11:30am–10:30pm. Closed some hols. **Prices:** Main courses $7.25–$16.95. Maj CC. 🏞

♣ **Riverview Charlie's**, 101 Flagler Ave, New Smyrna Beach; tel 904/428-1865. New Smyrna exit off I-95. **American/Seafood.** A waterside restaurant with a traditional menu offering seafood dishes, pasta, and black Angus beef. You can sit on the patio and watch the sun set as you dine. **FYI:** Reservations

accepted. Band. Children's menu. **Open:** Sun–Thurs 11:30am–10pm Fri–Sat 11:30am–11pm. **Prices:** Main courses $11.95–$26.95. Maj CC. ♥ 🏞 ♥

NICEVILLE

Map page M-2, B3

Resort 🏨

🏨 **Bluewater Bay Resort**, 1950 Bluewater Blvd, Niceville, FL 32578; tel 904/897-3613 or toll free 800/874-2128; fax 904/897-2424. 2,000 acres. This bayfront resort complex has self-sufficient units ranging from efficiencies to 3-bedroom "homes." Units are located bayside, or on the fairways or gardens. **Rooms:** 100 effic. CI 3pm/CO 11am. Nonsmoking rms avail. **Amenities:** 🛏 🕹 🖭 A/C, cable TV, refrig, voice mail. Some units w/terraces, some w/fireplaces. **Services:** 🔃 Social director, children's program. **Facilities:** 🔥 🚲 △ 🖼 ►36 🎱21 🟦 🔳 1 rst, 1 bar, 1 beach (bay), washer/dryer. Deep-water marina; picnic areas. **Rates:** HS Mar–May/Oct from $85 effic. Children under 18 stay free. Min stay. Lower rates off-season. Spec packages avail. Pking: Indoor/outdoor, free. Maj CC.

Attraction 🏨

Rocky Bayou State Recreation Area; tel 904/833-2144. Located north of Destin, this park encompasses over 350 acres for swimming, fishing, boating, camping, and picnicking. **Open:** 8am–dusk. $

NORTH FORT MYERS

Map page M-8, D3

Hotel 🏨

🏨 **Best Western Robert E Lee Motor Inn**, 13021 N Cleveland Ave, North Fort Myers, FL 33903; tel 813/997-5511 or toll free 800/274-5511; fax 813/656-6962. Exit 27 off I-75. Some great river views from this property 1 mile from downtown. **Rooms:** 108 rms and stes. CI 3pm/CO 11am. Nonsmoking rms avail. Rooms are large. **Amenities:** 🛏 🕹 A/C, cable TV, refrig. All units w/terraces. **Services:** ✗ 🖼 🔃 **Facilities:** 🔥 🔳 🕹 1 rst, 1 bar (w/entertainment), whirlpool, washer/dryer. Lounge at the water's edge is a nice feature. **Rates:** HS Feb–Apr $75–$80 S; $100–$125 D; from $145 ste. Extra person $5. Lower rates off-season. Pking: Outdoor, free. Maj CC.

Motel

≣≣ **Hampton Inn–Riverfront**, 13000 N Cleveland Ave, North Fort Myers, FL 33903; tel 813/656-4000 or toll free 800/HAMPTON; fax 813/656-1612. Exit 26 off I-75. Standard, barebones accommodations offering pleasant surroundings. Close to shopping. **Rooms:** 123 rms. CI 3pm/CO noon. Nonsmoking rms avail. **Amenities:** 🔒 A/C, cable TV. Some units w/terraces. **Services:** ⊠ 🖒 **Facilities:** 🔂 🎱 ৬ Washer/dryer. **Rates (CP):** HS Dec–Apr $63–$70 S; $70–$90 D. Children under 18 stay free. Lower rates off-season. Spec packages avail. Pking: Outdoor, free. Maj CC. Senior discounts available.

NORTH LAUDERDALE
Map page M-11, A2

Restaurant 🍴

Tien Hong Chinese Restaurant, in Shoppes of McNab, 8006 W McNab Rd, North Lauderdale; tel 305/726-9916. 1 mi W of Rock Island Rd. **Chinese.** An attractive Asian restaurant serving healthy dishes and traditional Chinese specialties. The glass-block, mirrored interior is accented in soft blues and pinks. **FYI:** Reservations accepted. Children's menu. Beer and wine only. **Open:** Tues–Sat 11am–10pm, Sun 2–10pm. Closed some hols. **Prices:** Main courses $7–$12. Ltd CC. ⬛ ৬

NORTH MIAMI
Map page M-11, B2

Resort 🏨

≣≣≣≣ **Turnberry Isle Resort & Club**, 19999 W Country Club Dr, North Miami, FL 33180 (Aventura); tel 305/932-6200 or toll free 800/327-7028; fax 305/933-6554. 10 mi S of Ft Lauderdale, exit 26 off I-95. Between US 1 and Fla A1A via Aventura Blvd or Wm Lehman Causeway. 300 acres. A 3-part resort consisting of the Country Club, surrounded by 2 golf courses and featuring new 7-story wings and a Mediterranean-style courtyard; the Yacht Club and Marina, located beside the Intracoastal Waterway, with a circular 4-story hotel; and the Beach Club, situated on the Atlantic Ocean. **Rooms:** 340 rms and stes. CI 3pm/CO noon. Express checkout avail. Nonsmoking rms avail. Country Club rooms have clay tile floors, small balconies, and ceiling fans, for a cool, elegant Mediterranean flavor; they are convenient for golfers and tennis players. Yacht Club rooms, recently upgraded, have a no-nonsense 1960s ambience with a few contemporary touches and are popular with celebrities seeking seclusion and anonymity. **Amenities:** 🚪🛏🗝 A/C, cable TV w/movies, refrig, VCR, in-rm safe, bathrobes. All units w/minibars, all w/terraces. Country Club rooms have bath slippers and umbrella in closet, small TV in bathroom. Cellular phones can be rented. **Services:** 🍽 ⊶ 🅥🄿 🚗 ⊠ 🖒 Twice-daily maid svce, car-rental desk, masseur, babysitting. Free shuttle between hotels and Beach Club. **Facilities:** 🔂 ⛰ 🏖 ▶36 🏊🐟6 💇 🚣 🐎 🟰 💻 ৬ 5 rsts, 6 bars (2 w/entertainment), 1 beach (ocean), lifeguard, racquetball, spa, sauna, steam rm, whirlpool, beauty salon. Helipad on property. Cabanas at Beach Club, beverage service on beach. Tennis courts supervised by Fred Stolle; 2 golf courses designed by Robert Trent Jones. Marina for 117 boats up to 200 feet in length. Spa at Yacht Club includes healthy and relaxing treatments such as shiatsu and Dead Sea mud packs. **Rates:** HS Dec 20–Apr 30 $375–$395 S or D; from $450 ste. Extra person $30. Children under 18 stay free. Lower rates off-season. Spec packages avail. Pking: Outdoor, $8. Maj CC.

Restaurants 🍴

👤⭐ **Mark's Place**, 2286 NE 123rd St, North Miami; tel 305/893-6888. At Bay Shore Ave. **New American.** A bright, stylish, trendy restaurant with an open kitchen. The innovative daily menu is prepared from local fresh fish and produce. **FYI:** Reservations recommended. **Open:** Lunch Mon–Fri noon–2:30pm; dinner Mon–Thurs 6–10:30pm, Fri–Sat 6–11pm, Sun 6–10pm. Closed some hols. **Prices:** Main courses $35–$50. Maj CC. 🅥🄿 ৬

Outback Steakhouse, 3161 NE 163rd St, North Miami; tel 305/944-4329. Between Biscayne Blvd and Intracoastal Waterway. **Steak.** A casual, Australian-themed steakhouse with whirling ceiling fans, serving chicken, ribs, and steaks. **FYI:** Reservations not accepted. Children's menu. **Open:** Mon–Thurs 4–10:30pm, Fri–Sun 4–11pm. Closed some hols. **Prices:** Main courses $7.95–$16.95. Maj CC. ৬

Roadhouse Grill, 12599 Biscayne Blvd, North Miami; tel 305/893-7433. At NE 126th St. **Steak.** A bucket of peanuts awaits you when you arrive at your table in this neon-lit establishment. Steaks, ribs, chicken, salads. A butcher shop is on the premises. **FYI:** Reservations not accepted. Children's menu. **Open:** Daily 11am–11pm. Closed some hols. **Prices:** Main courses $4.79–$15.99. Maj CC. ৬

NORTH PALM BEACH
Map page M-9, D4

Restaurant

De Cesare's, 639 US 1, North Palm Beach; tel 407/848-1400. ¼ mile N of N Lake Blvd. **New American.** A casual eatery where the walls are decorated with photos of golf pros. Pastas and prime rib. A good value. **FYI:** Reservations not accepted. Children's menu. **Open:** Mon–Sat 11am–10pm, Sun noon–10pm. Closed Dec 25. **Prices:** Main courses $9.95–$16.95. Maj CC. ◆ VP &

Attraction ◼

John D MacArthur Beach State Park, 10900 N State Rd 703; tel 407/624-6950. This large day-use park off Fla A1A has about 2 miles of oceanfront beach. The nature center shows a movie about the park and has several exhibits on the flora and fauna of the area. Swimming, fishing, nature trails. **Open:** Nature center, Wed–Mon 9am–5pm. $$

NORTH REDINGTON BEACH
Map page M-8, A1

Hotels ▦

▦▦▦ **North Redington Beach Hilton Resort**, 17120 Gulf Blvd, North Redington Beach, FL 33708; tel 813/391-4000 or toll free 800/221-2424; fax 813/391-4000 ext 7777. 3 mi N of Treasure Island. The ocean laps up against this delightful first-class hotel. A fine upmarket choice. Neatly attired staff, too. **Rooms:** 125 rms and stes. CI 3pm/CO 11am. Nonsmoking rms avail. **Amenities:** ▦ ◑ ▦ A/C, cable TV w/movies, VCR. All units w/minibars, all w/terraces. **Services:** ✕ ▤ ▨ ↵ Babysitting. **Facilities:** ▦ △ ▨ & 1 rst, 2 bars (1 w/entertainment), 1 beach (ocean). New sand has made the beach as inviting as ever. **Rates:** HS Feb–Apr $150–$165 S or D; from $165 ste. Children under 18 stay free. Lower rates off-season. Pking: Indoor/outdoor, free. Maj CC.

▦▦ **Tides Hotel and Bath Club Resort**, 16700 Gulf Blvd, North Redington Beach, FL 33708; tel 813/391-9681 or toll free 800/255-3349; fax 813/397-2476. Exit 4 off I-275. This beachside sprawl of old-style buildings has hosted the likes of Marilyn Monroe and Joe DiMaggio in its '50s heyday. For a look at a bygone era, this is the place for couples or families. **Rooms:** 160 rms and effic; 8 ctges/villas. CI 2pm/CO noon. Nonsmoking rms avail. Somewhat plain accommodations run the gamut from simple rooms to units with cooking facilities. **Amenities:** ▦ A/C, cable TV. Some units w/terraces, 1 w/fireplace. **Services:** ↵ **Facilities:** ▦ ▨ ▨ 1 rst, 2 bars (1 w/entertainment), 1 beach (ocean), lawn games, washer/dryer. **Rates:** HS Feb–Apr $45–$65 S or D; from $100 effic; from $120 ctge/villa. Extra person $8. Children under 12 stay free. Min stay spec evnts. Lower rates off-season. Pking: Outdoor, free. Maj CC.

Restaurant ▦

The Wine Cellar, 17307 Gulf Blvd, North Redington Beach; tel 813/393-3491. 2 mi N of Treasure Island. **Continental.** Formal dining room, offering German-influenced continental cuisine. Seafood includes fresh salmon fillet, lobster tails, and Dover sole. The beef Wellington gets high marks. Popular early-bird specials. **FYI:** Reservations recommended. Children's menu. **Open:** Tues–Sat 4:30–11pm, Sun 4–11pm. **Prices:** Main courses $13.75–$19.50. Maj CC. ◆ VP &

OCALA
Map page M-6, B4

Hotels ▦

▦▦ **Holiday Inn West**, 3621 W Silver Springs Blvd, PO Box 3308, Ocala, FL 32678; tel 904/629-0381 or toll free 800/HOLIDAY; fax 904/629-0381 ext 51. Exit 69 off Fla 40. This modern hotel caters to business travelers and large groups and has good resources for staging business meetings and conventions. **Rooms:** 270 rms and stes. CI 2pm/CO noon. Express checkout avail. Nonsmoking rms avail. **Amenities:** ▦ A/C, cable TV w/movies. **Services:** ✕ ▤ ▨ ↵ ↵ **Facilities:** ▦ ▨ & 1 rst, 1 bar (w/entertainment), washer/dryer. **Rates:** HS Jan–Apr $49 S or D; from $79 ste. Children under 18 stay free. Lower rates off-season. Higher rates for spec evnts/hols. Pking: Outdoor, free. Maj CC. AARP discount rates available.

▦▦ **Howard Johnson Park Square Inn**, 3712 SW 38th Ave, Ocala, FL 32674; tel 904/237-8000 or toll free 800/821-8272; fax 904/237-0580. Exit 68 off I-75. The comfortable lounge, updated public areas, and courtyard are great places to rest after a long trip. **Rooms:** 176 rms and stes. CI 3pm/CO noon. Nonsmoking rms avail. **Amenities:** ▦ ◑ A/C, cable TV w/movies. Some units w/terraces, 1 w/Jacuzzi. **Services:** ▨ ↵ ↵ **Facilities:** ▦ ▨ 1 rst, 1 bar, whirlpool, washer/dryer.

Rates (CP): HS Jan–Mar $60–$95 S or D; from $125 ste. Extra person $6. Children under 18 stay free. Min stay spec evnts. Lower rates off-season. Higher rates for spec evnts/hols. Pking: Outdoor, free. Maj CC.

≣≣≣ **Ocala/Silver Springs Hilton**, 3600 SW 36th Ave, Ocala, FL 34474; tel 904/854-1400 or toll free 800/445-8667; fax 904/854-1400. Exit 68 off I-75. The premier hotel in Ocala. Marble floors, potted palms, and chandeliers grace the lobby. **Rooms:** 198 rms and stes. CI 3pm/CO 11am. Nonsmoking rms avail. **Amenities:** 🛏 🅱 🖥 A/C, cable TV w/movies. Some units w/terraces. **Services:** ✕ 🛇 🛆 Babysitting. **Facilities:** 🔗 ⛹ 🏊 ⅋ 1 rst, 1 bar, whirlpool. The lobby lounge with baby grand piano is a great place for an evening cocktail; there's an English-style pub, too. **Rates:** HS Jan–Mar 15 $109–$119 S or D; from $250 ste. Children under 18 stay free. Min stay spec evnts. Lower rates off-season. Pking: Outdoor, free. Maj CC.

≣≣ **Ramada Inn Steinbrenner's**, 3810 NW Blitchton Rd, Ocala, FL 32675; tel 904/732-3131 or toll free 800/2-RAMADA; fax 904/732-5692. At US 27 and I-75. Colonial-inspired design, smart layout, and lush landscaping. This moderately priced establishment offers a relaxed ambience for both businesspeople and vacationers. **Rooms:** 133 rms. CI 2pm/CO noon. Nonsmoking rms avail. **Amenities:** 🛏 🅱 A/C, cable TV. **Services:** ✕ 🛆 🛇 🛇 Babysitting. **Facilities:** 🔗 ⛹ 🏊 1 rst, 1 bar (w/entertainment), whirlpool, playground, washer/dryer. **Rates:** HS Jan–April $50–$65 S; $52–$65 D. Extra person $10. Children under 18 stay free. Lower rates off-season. Higher rates for spec evnts/hols. Pking: Outdoor, free. Maj CC.

Motels

≣≣ **Days Inn**, 3811 NW Blitchton Rd, Ocala, FL 34482; tel 904/629-7041 or toll free 800/325-2525; fax 904/629-1026. Exit 70 off US 27. Renovations were underway. **Rooms:** 64 rms and stes. CI 2pm/CO noon. Nonsmoking rms avail. **Amenities:** 🛏 🅱 A/C, cable TV w/movies. Some units w/terraces. **Services:** 🛇 🛇 **Facilities:** 🔗 🏊 ⅋ Washer/dryer. **Rates:** HS Jan–mid-Apr $40–$60 S; $45–$70 D; from $60 ste. Extra person $5. Children under 17 stay free. Lower rates off-season. Higher rates for spec evnts/hols. Pking: Outdoor, free. Maj CC.

≣≣ **Days Inn Ocala**, 3620 W Silver Springs Blvd, Ocala, FL 32674; tel 904/629-0091 or toll free 800/333-3333; fax 904/867-8399. A former Radisson Inn, it's now undergoing some cosmetic and behind-the-scenes changes. **Rooms:** 100 rms and stes. CI 3pm/CO noon. Express checkout avail. Nonsmoking rms avail. **Amenities:** 🛏 🅱 A/C, cable TV. All units w/terraces. **Services:** ✕ 🛆 🛇 🛇 **Facilities:** 🔗 🏊 ⅋ 1 rst, 1 bar,

playground, washer/dryer. **Rates:** HS Jan–Mar $39 S or D; from $79 ste. Children under 10 stay free. Lower rates off-season. Higher rates for spec evnts/hols. Pking: Outdoor, free. Maj CC.

≣≣ **Quality Inn**, 3767 NW Blichton Rd, Ocala, FL 32675; tel 904/732-2300 or toll free 800/221-2222; fax 904/351-0153. Exit 70 off I-75. An older but adequately maintained 2-story property, handy to the highway. **Rooms:** 120 rms. CI 1pm/CO 11am. Nonsmoking rms avail. **Amenities:** 🛏 A/C, cable TV. **Services:** ✕ 🛇 🛇 **Facilities:** 🔗 🏊 ⅋ 1 rst, 1 bar (w/entertainment), washer/dryer. **Rates:** HS Mid-Dec–Apr $45 S; $49 D. Lower rates off-season. Higher rates for spec evnts/hols. Pking: Outdoor, free. Maj CC.

OCHOPEE

Map page M-10, B3

Attraction 🖼

Big Cypress National Preserve; tel 813/695-4111 or 695-2000. This 2,000-square-mile chunk of protected land encompasses Big Cypress Swamp and helps to provide water to the Everglades. The preserve is a sanctuary for alligator, deer, panther, and many types of birds. During the 19th-century Seminole Wars, many Seminoles escaped to the swamp to avoid forced emigration to Oklahoma; their descendants live in Big Cypress Seminole Indian Reservation and Miccousukee Indian Village. Ranger-led programs Jan–Mar. Visitor center located on US 41 about 60 miles east of Naples. **Open:** Visitor center, daily 8:30am–4:30pm. Closed Dec 25. Free.

ORANGE CITY

Map page M-7, B2

Attraction 🖼

Blue Spring State Park, 2100 W French Ave; tel 904/775-3663. This 1,500-acre park is very popular between October and April; about 80 manatees winter here every year, enjoying the relatively warm waters of the spring. Swimming in the spring and fishing in St Johns River are allowed. Canoe rentals, camping, nature trails. **Open:** Daily 8am–sunset. $$

ORLANDO

Map page M-7, C2

For Walt Disney World, see **Lake Buena Vista.** *See also* **Altamonte Springs, Apopka, Clermont, Kissimmee, Maitland, Winter Garden, Winter Park**

TOURIST INFORMATION

Orlando/Orange County Convention and Visitors Bureau, 845 International Dr, in Mercado Shopping Village (tel 407/ 363-5871). Free "Magicard," good for 10—50% discounts on accommodations, attractions, car rentals and more. Open daily 8am–8pm. Closed Dec 25.

For information about Walt Disney World, contact the **Walt Disney World Company,** Box 10000, Lake Buena Vista, FL 32830-1000 (tel 407/824-4321).

PUBLIC TRANSPORTATION

Disney Shuttles Unlimited complimentary service via bus, monorail, ferry, and water taxi between all Disney resorts and official hotels and all 3 Disney parks from 2 hours before opening to 2 hours after closing. Also free to Disney Village Marketplace, Typhoon Lagoon, Pleasure Island, and Fort Wilderness. Disney properties also offer transport to other area attractions; fees vary.

Mears Transportation Group Buses To all major attractions, including Cypress Gardens, Kennedy Space Center, Universal Studios, Sea World, Busch Gardens in Tampa, and Church Street Station. Depart from most major hotels. 2-day advance reservation required; call 407/423-5566.

Hotels 🛏

≣≣ **Best Western Plaza International**, 8738 International Dr, Orlando, FL 32819; tel 407/395-8195 or toll free 800/ 654-7160; fax 407/352-8196. Exit 29 off I-4. Popular for its reasonable rates and wide variety of accommodations. **Rooms:** 672 rms, stes, and effic. CI 4pm/CO 11am. Nonsmoking rms avail. **Amenities:** 🛏 🅰 A/C, cable TV, VCR, in-rm safe. Some units w/Jacuzzis. **Services:** 🍽 🚗 🛄 🍸 Car-rental desk, babysitting. **Facilities:** 🏋 🅰 1 bar, games rm, whirlpool, washer/dryer. Spacious deck with lounge chairs. **Rates:** HS Feb– Apr/June–Aug $65–$80 S or D; from $85 ste; from $90 effic. Children under 18 stay free. Lower rates off-season. Spec packages avail. Pking: Outdoor, free. Maj CC.

≣≣≣ **Clarion Plaza Hotel**, 9700 International Dr, Orlando, FL 32819; tel 407/352-9700 or toll free 800/363-9700; fax 407/ 351-9111. Exit 29 off I-4. This large, busy hotel is designed for the masses and manages to keep things moving along with some consistency, despite often being over-burdened with arrivals and departures. **Rooms:** 810 rms and stes. CI 3pm/CO noon. Nonsmoking rms avail. Decor has some warm touches, such as bordered ceilings and bed ruffles. **Amenities:** 🛏 🅰 A/C, cable TV w/movies, in-rm safe. **Services:** ✗ 𝐕𝐏 🚗 🛄 🍸 Car-rental desk, babysitting. **Facilities:** 🏋 2.8K 🖥 🅰 3 rsts, 2 bars (w/entertainment), games rm, whirlpool, washer/dryer. Delicatessen does a hearty business, even in the wee hours. **Rates:** HS

Feb–Apr/June–July/Dec $125–$145 S or D; from $200 ste. Extra person $15. Children under 17 stay free. Lower rates off-season. Spec packages avail. Pking: Outdoor, free. Maj CC.

▤▤ Courtyard by Marriott International Drive, 8600 Austrian Court, Orlando, FL 32819; tel 407/351-2244 or toll free 800/321-2211; fax 407/351-1933. Exit 29 off I-4. Located in a secluded complex of hotels and restaurants off International Drive, the Courtyard occupies a tan stucco 4-story building with a green tile roof. Out front are lush tropical plantings; the expertly landscaped courtyard features a gazebo. **Rooms:** 151 rms and stes. CI 3pm/CO 11am. Nonsmoking rms avail. Tasteful accommodations furnished with mahogany pieces. **Amenities:** ▢ ♨ A/C, cable TV w/movies. Some units w/terraces. **Services:** ✕ ▬ ☞ ⚐ ⟲ Car-rental desk, babysitting. **Facilities:** ▥ ♨ ♿ Games rm, whirlpool, washer/dryer. **Rates:** HS Jan–Apr $94–$104 S; $104–$114 D; from $104 ste. Extra person $10. Children under 18 stay free. Lower rates off-season. Higher rates for spec evnts/hols. Spec packages avail. Pking: Outdoor, free. Maj CC.

▤▤ Courtyard by Marriott–Orlando Airport, 7155 N Frontage Rd, Orlando, FL 32812 (Orlando Int'l Airport); tel 407/240-7200 or toll free 800/321-2211; fax 407/240-8962. Chosen by many businesspeople for its proximity to the airport. **Rooms:** 149 rms and stes. CI 3pm/CO noon. Nonsmoking rms avail. **Amenities:** ▢ ♨ A/C, cable TV w/movies, refrig. Some units w/terraces. **Services:** ☞ ⚐ ⟲ Car-rental desk, babysitting. **Facilities:** ▥ ♨ 50 ♿ 1 rst, 1 bar, whirlpool, washer/dryer. The restaurant is open only for breakfast. Guests can receive passes for Bally's Fitness Center and can use the tennis courts and pool at the Orlando Airport Marriott. **Rates:** HS Jan–Apr $94 D; from $109 ste. Extra person $10. Children under 18 stay free. Lower rates off-season. Higher rates for spec evnts/hols. AP and MAP rates avail. Spec packages avail. Pking: Outdoor, free. Maj CC.

▤▤ Days Inn Civic Center, 9990 International Dr, Orlando, FL 32819; tel 407/352-8700 or toll free 800/224-5055; fax 407/363-3965. Exit 28 off I-4. **Rooms:** 223 rms. CI 4pm/CO noon. Nonsmoking rms avail. **Amenities:** ▢ ♨ A/C, cable TV w/movies, in-rm safe. **Services:** ⚐ ⟲ Babysitting. **Facilities:** ▥ 12 ♿ 1 rst, playground, washer/dryer. **Rates:** HS Feb–Apr/June–Aug/Dec $62–$110 S; $72–$120 D. Extra person $6. Children under 18 stay free. Lower rates off-season. Higher rates for spec evnts/hols. Spec packages avail. Pking: Outdoor, free. Maj CC.

▤▤ Days Inn International Drive, 7200 International Dr, Orlando, FL 32819; tel 407/351-1200 or toll free 800/224-5057; fax 407/363-1182. Exit 29 off I-4. Standard operation with rates a bit high for what is offered. **Rooms:** 243 rms. CI

4pm/CO noon. Nonsmoking rms avail. **Amenities:** ▢ ♨ A/C, cable TV w/movies, in-rm safe. **Services:** ☞ ⚐ ▬ ⟲ ⟲ Car-rental desk, babysitting. **Facilities:** ▥ 60 ♿ 1 rst, games rm, playground, washer/dryer. **Rates:** HS Christmas/Mar–Apr/July–Aug $68–$74 S; $74–$84 D. Extra person $6. Children under 13 stay free. Lower rates off-season. Spec packages avail. Pking: Outdoor, free. Maj CC.

▤▤▤ Delta Orlando Resort, 5715 Major Blvd, Orlando, FL 32819; tel 407/351-3340 or toll free 800/634-4763; fax 407/351-5117. A long-established facility offering an array of diversions for guests. **Rooms:** 805 rms and stes. CI 4pm/CO 11am. Express checkout avail. Nonsmoking rms avail. **Amenities:** ▢ ♨ ▢ A/C, cable TV w/movies, in-rm safe. All units w/terraces. Some rooms with coffeemakers. Refrigerators available on request. **Services:** ✕ ☞ ▬ ⚐ ⟲ ⟲ Car-rental desk, children's program, babysitting. **Facilities:** ▥ ♨ 800 ♿ 3 rsts, 3 bars (1 w/entertainment), games rm, sauna, whirlpool, playground, washer/dryer. Cafeteria; sports bar. **Rates:** HS Feb–Mar $108–$178 S or D; from $150 ste. Children under 18 stay free. Lower rates off-season. Spec packages avail. Pking: Outdoor, free. Maj CC.

▤▤▤ Embassy Suites Orlando Plaza International, 8250 Jamaican Court, Orlando, FL 32819; tel 407/345-8250 or toll free 800/327-9797; fax 407/352-1463. Exit 29 off I-4. ¼ mi S of Sand Lake Rd. Stands out from the lackluster offerings on this drive. Suite configuration surrounds atrium. **Rooms:** 246 stes. CI 3pm/CO noon. Nonsmoking rms avail. **Amenities:** ▢ ♨ ▢ A/C, cable TV, refrig, in-rm safe. **Services:** ✕ ☞ ▬ ⚐ ⟲ Car-rental desk, babysitting. Attentive service. **Facilities:** ▥ ♨ 280 ♿ 1 bar, games rm, sauna, steam rm, whirlpool, washer/dryer. **Rates (BB):** HS Dec–Apr/June–Aug from $159 ste. Lower rates off-season. Spec packages avail. Pking: Outdoor, free. Maj CC.

▤▤▤ Embassy Suites Orlando South, 8978 International Dr, Orlando, FL 32819; tel 407/352-1400 or toll free 800/EMBASSY; fax 407/363-1120. Exit 29 off I-4. Another in the chain of quality all-suites hotels, this one is housed in a Mediterranean-influenced, 8-floor building containing the trademark atrium. **Rooms:** 249 stes. CI 3pm/CO noon. Nonsmoking rms avail. **Amenities:** ▢ ♨ ▢ A/C, cable TV w/movies, refrig. **Services:** ✕ ▬ ⚐ ⟲ Car-rental desk, children's program, babysitting. Full breakfast and social-hour cocktails served in the atrium. **Facilities:** ▥ ♨ 400 ♿ 1 rst, 2 bars, games rm, spa, sauna, steam rm, whirlpool, washer/dryer. **Rates (BB):** HS Feb–Apr/Aug–Dec from $135 ste. Extra person $15. Children under 18 stay free. Lower rates off-season. Spec packages avail. Pking: Outdoor, free. Maj CC.

▤▤ Enclave Suites at Orlando, 6165 Carrier Dr, Orlando, FL 32819; tel 407/351-1155 or toll free 800/457-0077; fax 407/

352-7292. Exit 28 off I-4. A complex of 3 buildings offering a residential look; handy to International Drive restaurants and souvenir shopping. **Rooms:** 321 stes. CI 3pm/CO 11am. Nonsmoking rms avail. **Amenities:** 🛅 🅿 📺 A/C, cable TV w/movies, refrig, in-rm safe. All units w/minibars, all w/terraces. Units also equipped with microwaves, stoves, and other appliances, and utensils. **Services:** ✕ 🖭 🚐 🛄 ↵ Car-rental desk, babysitting. **Facilities:** 🛋 🏊 🏋 ⛳ 🏌 200 💻 ♿ 1 rst, 1 bar, 1 beach (lake shore), games rm, sauna, whirlpool, playground, washer/dryer. **Rates (CP):** HS Jan–Apr/June–Aug from $59 ste. Children under 18 stay free. Lower rates off-season. Spec packages avail. Pking: Outdoor, free. Maj CC.

≣≣≣ **Guest Quarters Orlando International Airport**, 7550 Augusta National Dr, Orlando, FL 32822; tel 407/240-5555 or toll free 800/424-2900; fax 407/240-1300. A fine alternative to Lake Buena Vista hotels when those are all booked by Disney-bound vacationers. Joggers can often be seen circling the attractive pond in front of the hotel. **Rooms:** 150 stes. CI 3pm/CO 11am. Nonsmoking rms avail. Breezily decorated 2-room suites. **Amenities:** 🛅 🅿 📺 A/C, cable TV, refrig. Some units w/terraces. **Services:** ✕ 🖭 🚐 🛄 ↵ Car-rental desk, babysitting. **Facilities:** 🛋 🏌 75 ♿ 1 rst, 1 bar, games rm, whirlpool, washer/dryer. Bakery on premises. **Rates:** HS Jan–Apr from $109 ste. Extra person $20. Children under 18 stay free. Lower rates off-season. Higher rates for spec evnts/hols. AP and MAP rates avail. Spec packages avail. Pking: Outdoor, free. Maj CC.

≣≣ **Hampton Inn–Universal Studios**, 7110 S Kirkman Rd, Orlando, FL 32819; tel 407/345-1112 or toll free 800/763-1100; fax 407/352-6591. Within driving but not walking distance to Universal Studios, this small, scaled-down hotel offers basic rooms and friendly service. **Rooms:** 170 rms and stes. CI 3pm/CO 11am. Nonsmoking rms avail. **Amenities:** 🛅 🅿 A/C, cable TV, refrig. Some units w/Jacuzzis. All rooms have microwaves. Some king rooms have whirlpools. **Services:** 🖭 🚐 🛄 Car-rental desk. **Facilities:** 🛋 🏌 35 ♿ Games rm, washer/dryer. **Rates (CP):** HS Christmas/June–Aug $70–$79 S or D; from $99 ste. Children under 18 stay free. Lower rates off-season. Higher rates for spec evnts/hols. Spec packages avail. Pking: Outdoor, free. Maj CC.

≣≣ **Hawthorn Suites Hotel**, 6435 Westwood Blvd, Orlando, FL 32821; tel 407/351-6600 or toll free 800/527-1133; fax 407/351-1977. Exit 28 off I-4. Offers generally attractive suites in an informal setting, with a sunny furnished deck around the pool. **Rooms:** 150 stes. CI 4pm/CO 11am. Nonsmoking rms avail. All units have microwaves, ovens, stoves, dishwashers, and ice-makers. **Amenities:** 🛅 🅿 📺 A/C, cable TV w/movies, refrig, VCR. **Services:** ✕ 🖭 🚐 🛄 ↵ Car-rental desk, babysitting.

Facilities: 🛋 🏌 35 ♿ Games rm, whirlpool, washer/dryer. **Rates (CP):** HS Dec/Feb–Apr $109–$145 S; $165–$185 D. Children under 18 stay free. Lower rates off-season. Higher rates for spec evnts/hols. Spec packages avail. Pking: Outdoor, free. Maj CC.

≣≣≣ **Holiday Inn International Dr**, 6515 International Dr, Orlando, FL 32819; tel 407/351-3500; fax 407/351-9196. Exit 30A off I-4. Placed squarely in the midst of the International Drive bustle, this large operation features an atrium soaring 14 floors and a tropical-accented lobby. **Rooms:** 650 rms and stes. CI 4pm/CO 11am. Nonsmoking rms avail. **Amenities:** 🛅 🅿 📺 A/C, cable TV w/movies, in-rm safe. Microwaves and refrigerators in some rooms. **Services:** ✕ 🖭 🚐 🛄 ↵ Twice-daily maid svce, car-rental desk, children's program, babysitting. The staff sometimes hosts barbecues on the pool terrace. **Facilities:** 🛋 🏌 12K ♿ 2 rsts, 2 bars (1 w/entertainment), games rm, lawn games, whirlpool, day-care ctr, playground, washer/dryer. **Rates:** HS Apr/June/Aug $89–$99 S or D; from $175 ste. Children under 19 stay free. Lower rates off-season. Spec packages avail. Pking: Outdoor, free. Maj CC.

≣≣≣ **Holiday Inn–Orlando International Airport**, 5750 T G Lee Blvd, Orlando, FL 32822 (Orlando Int'l Airport); tel 407/851-6400 or toll free 800/HOLIDAY; fax 407/240-3717. A subdued hotel with an upscale look. Marble lobby. **Rooms:** 290 rms and stes. CI 3pm/CO noon. Nonsmoking rms avail. Well-appointed guest rooms. **Amenities:** 🛅 🅿 📺 A/C, cable TV w/movies. **Services:** ✕ 🖭 VP 🚐 🛄 ↵ 🐾 Car-rental desk, babysitting. **Facilities:** 🛋 🏊 🏌 300 💻 ♿ 1 rst, 1 bar, games rm, lawn games, sauna, whirlpool, washer/dryer. **Rates:** HS Jan–Mar $94–$109 D; from $115 ste. Extra person $10. Children under 18 stay free. Lower rates off-season. Higher rates for spec evnts/hols. Spec packages avail. Pking: Outdoor, free. Maj CC.

≣≣ **Holiday Inn–Winter Park**, 626 Lee Rd, Orlando, FL 32810; tel 407/645-5600 or toll free 800/HOLIDAY; fax 407/740-7912. Exit 46 off I-4. This 5-story hotel with easy interstate access has recently completed guest room updating. **Rooms:** 200 rms. CI 3pm/CO noon. Nonsmoking rms avail. **Amenities:** 🛅 🅿 A/C, cable TV w/movies. **Services:** ✕ 🚐 🛄 ↵ Car-rental desk. **Facilities:** 🛋 🏌 75 1 rst, 1 bar, games rm, washer/dryer. Comedy club operates several nights per week. **Rates:** HS Jan–Apr $59 D. Extra person $5. Children under 19 stay free. Lower rates off-season. Higher rates for spec evnts/hols. Spec packages avail. Pking: Outdoor, free. Maj CC.

≣≣≣ **Hyatt Orlando International Airport**, 9300 Airport Blvd, Orlando, FL 32827; tel 407/825-1234 or toll free 800/233-1234; fax 407/856-1672. Airport exit off Fla 528. This hotel sparkles at every turn. Rooms are sophisticated and stylish; the staff is gracious and seasoned. This is just what Orlando needs, a civil spot to light where children probably won't be underfoot. **Rooms:** 446 rms. CI 3pm/CO noon. Nonsmoking rms avail. **Amenities:** 🔒 ⚗ 🔲 ☜ A/C, cable TV w/movies. All units w/terraces. New business floors have such extras as fax machines and coffeemakers. **Services:** 🍴 ☞ VP 🚗 ⬜ ⤴ Car-rental desk, masseur, babysitting. **Facilities:** 🏌 800 ⬜ ♿ 1 rst, 1 bar, games rm, whirlpool, beauty salon. **Rates:** HS Jan–Apr $145 D; from $200 ste. Extra person $25. Children under 18 stay free. Lower rates off-season. Higher rates for spec evnts/hols. AP and MAP rates avail. Spec packages avail. Pking: Indoor/outdoor, $11. Maj CC.

≋≋ **International Inn**, 6327 International Dr, Orlando, FL 32819; tel 407/351-4444 or toll free 800/999-6327; fax 407/352-5806. Exit 30A off I-4. Fairly large facility has not kept pace with the times, as reflected in the dated accommodations. **Rooms:** 315 rms and stes. CI 3pm/CO 11am. **Amenities:** 🔒 ⚗ A/C, TV, VCR, in-rm safe. **Services:** ⬜ ⤴ ⬇ Babysitting. **Facilities:** 🏌 90 ♿ 2 rsts, 1 bar, games rm, washer/dryer. Japanese-style steakhouse. **Rates:** HS Feb–Oct $49–$59 S or D; from $49 ste. Children under 18 stay free. Lower rates off-season. Pking: Outdoor, free. Maj CC.

≋≋ **La Quinta Inn International Drive**, 8300 Jamaican Court, Orlando, FL 32819; tel 407/351-1660 or toll free 800/531-5900; fax 407/351-9264. Exit 29 off I-4. A notch or two above the others in this chain; situated in the convenient and more desirable Plaza International section of International Drive. Reliable lodging. **Rooms:** 200 rms. CI 4pm/CO noon. Nonsmoking rms avail. **Amenities:** 🔒 ⚗ A/C, cable TV w/movies, refrig. **Services:** ✗ ☞ 🚗 ⬜ ⤴ ⬇ Car-rental desk, babysitting. **Facilities:** 🏌 ♿ 1 rst, 1 bar, whirlpool, washer/dryer. **Rates:** HS Jan–Apr $65–$84 S or D. Extra person $8. Children under 18 stay free. Lower rates off-season. Higher rates for spec evnts/hols. Spec packages avail. Pking: Outdoor, free. Maj CC.

≋≋ **Las Palmas Hotel**, 6233 International Dr, Orlando, FL 32819; tel 407/351-3900 or toll free 800/327-2114; fax 407/352-5597. Sand Lake Rd exit off I-4. In the thick of International Drive's vast commercial strip stands this routine 4-story budget hotel. **Rooms:** 262 rms and stes. CI 3pm/CO noon. Nonsmoking rms avail. **Amenities:** 🔒 ⚗ A/C, cable TV, in-rm safe. **Services:** ✗ ☞ 🚗 ⬜ ⤴ Car-rental desk, babysitting. **Facilities:** 🏌 250 ⬜ ♿ 1 rst, 1 bar, games rm, washer/dryer. Lounge sometimes offers entertainment. **Rates:** HS June–Aug $69–$79 S; $79–$89 D; from $150 ste. Extra person $5. Children under 17 stay free. Lower rates off-season. MAP rates avail. Spec packages avail. Pking: Outdoor, free. Maj CC.

≋≋≋ **Orlando Airport Marriott**, 7499 Augusta National Dr, Orlando, FL 32822 (Orlando Int'l Airport); tel 407/851-9000 or toll free 800/228-9290; fax 407/857-6211. Surrounded by neatly trimmed landscaping, this first-class hotel is fronted by a pond and offers guests a fresh look at traditional stylings in its public areas and rooms. **Rooms:** 484 rms and stes. CI 3pm/CO noon. Nonsmoking rms avail. **Amenities:** 🔒 ⚗ A/C, cable TV w/movies. **Services:** ✗ ☞ VP 🚗 ⬜ ⤴ Car-rental desk, babysitting. **Facilities:** 🏌 🎾 ⚲ ♿ 1.5K ⬜ ♿ 2 rsts, 3 bars, games rm, lawn games, sauna, steam rm, whirlpool, washer/dryer. **Rates:** HS Jan–Apr $109–$125 S or D; from $175 ste. Children under 18 stay free. Lower rates off-season. Higher rates for spec evnts/hols. AP and MAP rates avail. Spec packages avail. Pking: Outdoor, free. Maj CC.

≋≋≋ **Orlando Marriott**, 8001 International Dr, Orlando, FL 32819; tel 407/351-2420 or toll free 800/228-9290, 800/421-8001 in FL; fax 407/351-5016. Exit 29 off I-4. At Sand Lake Rd. This multi-building complex on extensive grounds is a haven for families. Its lowrise design provides an almost suburban feel, even though the surrounding area is unrelentingly commercial. **Rooms:** 1,054 rms and stes. CI 4pm/CO 11am. Nonsmoking rms avail. Fairly consistent accommodations. **Amenities:** 🔒 ⚗ ☜ A/C, cable TV w/movies, in-rm safe, shoe polisher. Some units w/terraces, some w/Jacuzzis. **Services:** ✗ ☞ 🚗 ⬜ ⤴ Car-rental desk, babysitting. More staff would help ease service glitches. **Facilities:** 🏌 🎾 ⚲ ♿ IX ⬜ ♿ 3 rsts, 2 bars, games rm, lawn games, whirlpool, beauty salon, playground, washer/dryer. **Rates:** $79–$120 S or D; from $110 ste. Children under 18 stay free. Pking: Outdoor, free. Maj CC.

≋≋≋ **Orlando Renaissance Hotel–International Airport**, 5445 Forbes Place, Orlando, FL 32812; tel 407/240-1000 or toll free 800/228-9898; fax 407/240-1005. Orlando Int'l Airport exit off Fla 528. **Rooms:** 300 rms and stes. CI 3pm/CO noon. Nonsmoking rms avail. **Amenities:** 🔒 ⚗ ☜ A/C, cable TV w/movies. All units w/minibars. **Services:** ✗ ☞ 🚗 ⬜ ⤴ Car-rental desk, babysitting. **Facilities:** 🏌 ♿ 450 ♿ 2 rsts, 1 bar, games rm, whirlpool. **Rates:** HS Jan–Apr $110–$145 D; from $190 ste. Extra person $15. Children under 18 stay free. Lower rates off-season. Higher rates for spec evnts/hols. AP and MAP rates avail. Spec packages avail. Pking: Outdoor, free. Maj CC.

≋≋≋≋ **The Peabody Orlando**, 9801 International Dr, Orlando, FL 32819; tel 407/352-4000 or toll free 800/42-DUCKS; fax 407/351-0073. A true tour de force, one of the most architecturally pleasing hotels in Orlando. This deluxe establishment pampers guests with gracious service and fine facilities. The skylit atrium lobby is a showcase for live orchids, palms, bamboo, ficus, and magnolia trees. The hotel is probably best known for the daily duck march to and from the lobby fountain, staged at 11am and 5pm. **Rooms:** 891 rms and stes. Exec-level rms avail. CI 3pm/CO noon. Express checkout avail. Nonsmoking rms avail. Luxurious rooms with bamboo and bleached wood furnishings. **Amenities:** 🔒 ⏲ 🦺 A/C, cable TV w/movies, voice mail, bathrobes. All units w/minibars, some w/terraces, some w/Jacuzzis. **Services:** 🍽 🍴 VP 🚗 🖨 🛏 Car-rental desk, masseur, babysitting. **Facilities:** 🏊 🛜 🛎 1K 🖥 ♿ 3 rsts (*see also* "Restaurants" below), 3 bars (1 w/entertainment), lifeguard, games rm, spa, sauna, steam rm, whirlpool, beauty salon. Luxurious rooms with bamboo and bleached wood furnishings. **Rates:** $210–$270 S or D; from $375 ste. Children under 12 stay free. Spec packages avail. Pking: Outdoor, free. Maj CC.

🟰🟰 **Quality Inn International Drive**, 7600 International Dr, Orlando, FL 32819; tel 407/351-1600 or toll free 800/825-7600; fax 407/352-5328. Exit 29 off I-4. Offers good location, well-maintained grounds, and adequate accommodations at very competitive rates. **Rooms:** 1,020 rms. CI 3pm/CO 11am. Nonsmoking rms avail. **Amenities:** 🔒 ⏲ A/C, cable TV w/movies. **Services:** 🚗 🖨 🛏 🦽 Car-rental desk, babysitting. **Facilities:** 🏊 80 ♿ 1 rst, 1 bar, games rm, washer/dryer. **Rates:** HS June–Aug $39–$53 S or D. Children under 18 stay free. Lower rates off-season. Spec packages avail. Pking: Outdoor, free. Maj CC.

🟰🟰 **Quality Inn Plaza**, 9000 International Dr, Orlando, FL 32819; tel 407/345-8585 or toll free 800/999-8585; fax 407/352-6839. Exit 29 off I-4. A huge complex with a city of rooms attracting an unending stream of families for its rates and simple comforts served up in a no-nonsense way. **Rooms:** 1,020 rms. CI 3pm/CO 11am. Nonsmoking rms avail. **Amenities:** 🔒⏲A/C, cable TV, in-rm safe. Refrigerators may be rented from an independent vendor. **Services:** ✗ 🚗 🖨 🛏 🦽 Car-rental desk, babysitting. **Facilities:** 🏊 🛎 ♿ 1 rst, 1 bar, games rm, washer/dryer. The restaurant, though nothing special, is priced right for families. **Rates:** HS June–Aug $59 S or D. Children under 18 stay free. Lower rates off-season. Spec packages avail. Pking: Outdoor, free. Maj CC.

🟰🟰 **Quality Suites International Drive Area**, 7400 Canada Ave, Orlando, FL 32819; tel 407/352-2598 or toll free 800/228-2027; fax 407/352-2598. 8 mi W of Orlando, exit 29 off I-4. Attractive suites, fine for families. **Rooms:** 154 stes. CI 3pm/CO 11am. Nonsmoking rms avail. **Amenities:** 🔒 ⏲ A/C, cable TV w/movies, refrig, VCR, stereo/tape player. Microwaves. **Services:** ✗ 🍴 🚗 🖨 🛏 Cocktail hour 5:30–7:30pm. TGI Fridays provides room service. **Facilities:** 🏊 🛎 75 ♿ Games rm, whirlpool, playground, washer/dryer. **Rates (BB):** HS Dec 20–31/Feb 11–Apr 16/Mid-June–Aug from $139 ste. Children under 18 stay free. Lower rates off-season. Higher rates for spec evnts/hols. Spec packages avail. Pking: Outdoor, free. Maj CC.

🟰🟰🟰 **Radisson Hotel Orlando Airport**, 5555 Hazeltine National Dr, Orlando, FL 32812; tel 407/856-0100 or toll free 800/333-3333; fax 407/855-7991. Orlando Int'l Airport exit off

Fla 528. Stylish commercial hotel receiving more business guests than families. **Rooms:** 350 rms and stes. CI 3pm/CO noon. Nonsmoking rms avail. **Amenities:** 🔒 ⏲ A/C, cable TV w/movies. Some units w/terraces. **Services:** ✗ 🍴 🚗 🖨 🛏 🦽 Car-rental desk, babysitting. **Facilities:** 🏊 🛎 1K ♿ 1 rst, 1 bar, games rm, whirlpool. **Rates:** HS Jan–Apr $109–$119 D; from $250 ste. Extra person $15. Children under 18 stay free. Lower rates off-season. Higher rates for spec evnts/hols. AP and MAP rates avail. Spec packages avail. Pking: Outdoor, free. Maj CC.

🟰🟰🟰 **Radisson Inn–Lake Buena Vista**, 8686 Palm Pkwy, Orlando, FL 32836; tel 407/239-8400 or toll free 800/333-3333; fax 407/239-8025. Exit 27 off I-4. Smartly styled hotel in fine shape, with an efficient staff. Good value. **Rooms:** 200 rms. CI 3pm/CO noon. Nonsmoking rms avail. **Amenities:** 🔒 ⏲ A/C, cable TV. Some units w/minibars, all w/terraces. **Services:** ✗ 🍴 🚗 🖨 🛏 🦽 Car-rental desk, babysitting. **Facilities:** 🏊 ♿ 1 rst, 1 bar, games rm, playground. **Rates:** HS Dec 24–31/June–Aug $119–$139 D. Lower rates off-season. Higher rates for spec evnts/hols. AP and MAP rates avail. Spec packages avail. Pking: Outdoor, free. Maj CC.

🟰🟰 **Radisson Inn on International Drive**, 8444 International Dr, Orlando, FL 32819; tel 407/345-0505 or toll free 800/304-8000; fax 407/352-5894. Exit 29 off I-4. Handsome 5-story structure with well-chosen appointments and a friendly staff. The impressive lobby and other public areas are presented with flair and imagination. **Rooms:** 299 rms and stes. CI 4pm/CO noon. Nonsmoking rms avail. **Amenities:** 🔒 ⏲ A/C, cable TV, refrig, in-rm safe. **Services:** ✗ 🚗 🖨 🛏 Car-rental desk, babysitting. **Facilities:** 🏊 🛜 🛎 600 ♿ 1 rst, 2 bars, games rm, lawn games, racquetball, squash, whirlpool, playground, washer/dryer. Pool bar. **Rates:** HS Dec–Apr/June–Aug $89 S; $99 D; from $178 ste. Extra person $10. Children under 12 stay free. Lower rates off-season. MAP rates avail. Spec packages avail. Pking: Outdoor, free. Maj CC.

🟰🟰🟰 **Radisson Plaza Hotel Orlando**, 60 S Ivanhoe Blvd, Orlando, FL 32804; tel 407/425-4455 or toll free 800/333-3333; fax 407/843-0262. Exit 42 off I-4. A downtown highrise receiving many commercial guests and convention delegates. Convenient parking adjacent. **Rooms:** 337 rms and stes. Exec-level rms avail. CI 3pm/CO 11am. Express checkout avail. Nonsmoking rms avail. **Amenities:** 🔒 ⏲ 🖥 🦺 A/C, cable TV w/movies, bathrobes. All units w/minibars. **Services:** ✗ 🍴 VP 🚗 🖨 🛏 Car-rental desk, babysitting. **Facilities:** 🏊 🛜 🛎 500 ♿ 1 rst, 1 bar (w/entertainment), lawn games, sauna, whirlpool. **Rates:** HS Jan–May $109–$134 S; $119–$144 D;

from $145 ste. Extra person $15. Children under 18 stay free. Lower rates off-season. Spec packages avail. Pking: Indoor, $5.50. Maj CC.

Residence Inn by Marriott, 8800 Meadow Creek Dr, Orlando, FL 32821; tel 407/239-7700 or toll free 800/331-3131; fax 407/239-7605. 20 mi S of Orlando, exit 27 off I-4 W. Popular facility provides all the at-home conveniences for self-sufficient living. **Rooms:** 688 stes. CI 4pm/CO 11am. **Amenities:** A/C, cable TV w/movies, refrig, in-rm safe. Some units w/terraces. Full kitchens. Dishwasher, microwave, utensils. **Services:** Car-rental desk, masseur, children's program, babysitting. **Facilities:** 1 rst, games rm, lawn games, squash, sauna, whirlpool, beauty salon, playground, washer/dryer. Sports court. **Rates:** HS Feb–Apr/June–Aug/Dec from $175 ste. Lower rates off-season. Higher rates for spec evnts/hols. Spec packages avail. Pking: Outdoor, free. Maj CC.

Residence Inn–Orlando Attraction Center, 7975 Canada Ave, Orlando, FL 32819; tel 407/345-0117 or toll free 800/227-3978; fax 407/352-2689. Exit 29 off I-4. These well-outfitted suites receive many guests for long stays. **Rooms:** 176 stes. CI 3pm/CO 11am. Nonsmoking rms avail. Attractive upholstery and appointments. **Amenities:** A/C, cable TV w/movies, refrig, in-rm safe. All units w/terraces, some w/fireplaces. **Services:** Car-rental desk, babysitting. **Facilities:** Lawn games, whirlpool, washer/dryer. **Rates (CP):** HS Christmas–Apr/July–Aug from $94 ste. Children under 12 stay free. Lower rates off-season. Higher rates for spec evnts/hols. Spec packages avail. Pking: Outdoor, free. Maj CC.

Sheraton Plaza Hotel at the Florida Mall, 1500 Sand Lake Rd, Orlando, FL 32809; tel 407/859-1500 or toll free 800/231-7883; fax 407/855-1585. Highrise features a food court. **Rooms:** 496 rms and stes. CI 3pm/CO noon. Nonsmoking rms avail. **Amenities:** A/C, cable TV w/movies. Some units w/terraces, some w/Jacuzzis. **Services:** Car-rental desk. **Facilities:** 2 rsts, 1 bar, games rm, spa, sauna, whirlpool, beauty salon. **Rates:** $112–$180 S or D; from $250 ste. Children under 17 stay free. Higher rates for spec evnts/hols. AP and MAP rates avail. Spec packages avail. Pking: Outdoor, free. Maj CC.

Sheraton World, 10100 International Dr, Orlando, FL 32821; tel 407/352-1100 or toll free 800/327-0363; fax 407/352-3679. Exit 28 off I-4. Nearly two dozen buildings spread out over extensive grounds, though none are too far from parking or the pool and courtyard areas. A highly satisfactory selection. **Rooms:** 788 rms and stes. CI 3pm/CO 11am. Nonsmoking rms avail. **Amenities:** A/C, cable TV w/movies, in-rm safe.

All units w/terraces. **Services:** Car-rental desk, masseur, children's program, babysitting. **Facilities:** 2 rsts, 3 bars (1 w/entertainment), games rm, lawn games, whirlpool, playground, washer/dryer. **Rates:** HS Jan–May $95–$125 S or D; from $125 ste. Extra person $10. Children under 17 stay free. Lower rates off-season. MAP rates avail. Spec packages avail. Pking: Outdoor, free. Maj CC.

Sonesta Villa Resort, 10000 Turkey Lake Rd, Orlando, FL 32819; tel 407/352-8051 or toll free 800/424-0708; fax 407/345-5384. Exit 29 off I-4. 97 acres. A luscious lakeside setting and fine accommodations provide the atmosphere of a private retreat that feels more remote than it is. The smart lobby has courtyard views. Close to Sea World. **Rooms:** 369 ctges/villas. CI 4pm/CO noon. Nonsmoking rms avail. **Amenities:** A/C, cable TV w/movies, refrig, in-rm safe. All units w/terraces. **Services:** Twice-daily maid svce, car-rental desk, children's program, babysitting. **Facilities:** 1 rst, 2 bars, 1 beach (lake shore), games rm, whirlpool, day-care ctr, playground, washer/dryer. **Rates:** HS Dec/June–Aug from $98 ctge/villa. Children under 18 stay free. Lower rates off-season. Higher rates for spec evnts/hols. Spec packages avail. Pking: Outdoor, free. Maj CC.

Stouffer Orlando Resort, 6677 Sea Harbor Dr, Orlando, FL 32821 (Sea World); tel 407/351-5555 or toll free 800/327-6677; fax 407/351-4994. Exit 28 off I-4. A grand offering in a striking setting opposite Sea World. Spectacular atrium is lush with tropical foliage, ponds, and meandering walkways. Large, helpful staff. **Rooms:** 780 rms and stes. CI 3pm/CO noon. Nonsmoking rms avail. Some rooms have French doors opening out to atrium. **Amenities:** A/C, cable TV w/movies, bathrobes. All units w/minibars, some w/terraces, 1 w/Jacuzzi. **Services:** Twice-daily maid svce, car-rental desk, social director, masseur, children's program, babysitting. **Facilities:** 5 rsts, 2 bars (1 w/entertainment), games rm, lawn games, spa, sauna, steam rm, whirlpool, beauty salon, day-care ctr, playground, washer/dryer. **Rates:** HS Jan–Apr $195–$235 S or D; from $390 ste. Children under 12 stay free. Lower rates off-season. Spec packages avail. Pking: Outdoor, free. Maj CC.

Summerfield Suites Hotel, 8480 International Dr, Orlando, FL 32806; tel 407/352-2400 or toll free 800/833-4353; fax 407/352-4631. Exit 27 off I-4. Fairly new, occupies a 5-story building with mission architectural overtones. **Rooms:** 146 stes. CI 4pm/CO noon. Nonsmoking rms avail. **Amenities:** A/C, cable TV w/movies, in-rm safe. **Services:** Car-rental desk, babysitting. Continental breakfast included. Coffee and tea available at all times in lobby. **Facilities:** 1 bar, games rm, whirlpool, washer/dryer. No full-service restaurant on premises but many are nearby. **Rates (CP):** HS Dec–Jan/Mar–Apr/June–Aug from $179 ste. Children under 18 stay free. Lower rates off-season. Spec packages avail. Pking: Outdoor, free. Maj CC.

≡≡≡ **Twin Towers Hotel and Convention Center**, 5780 Major Blvd, Orlando, FL 32819; tel 407/351-1000 or toll free 800/327-2110; fax 407/363-0106. Exit 30A off I-4. Large hotel located opposite Universal Studios. Public areas are spacious, and there are services here that are usually available only at more upscale hotels. **Rooms:** 740 rms and stes. CI 3pm/CO 11am. Nonsmoking rms avail. Accommodations are larger since balconies were eliminated and extra space added to rooms during a major overhaul in the early 1990s. **Amenities:** 🛏 🐾 A/C, cable TV w/movies. **Services:** 🍽 🔑 🅥🅟 🚗 🛅 🛎 Twice-daily maid svce, car-rental desk. **Facilities:** 🔂 🏌 🏊 🖥 🛗 2 rsts, 3 bars (2 w/entertainment), games rm, sauna, whirlpool, beauty salon, playground, washer/dryer. **Rates:** HS Jan–Apr $114–$150 D; from $350 ste. Extra person $15. Children under 17 stay free. Lower rates off-season. Spec packages avail. Pking: Outdoor, free. Maj CC.

Motels

≡ **Economy Inns of America**, 8222 Jamaican Court, Orlando, FL 32819; tel 407/345-1172 or toll free 800/826-0778; fax 407/352-2801. Exit 29 off I-4. Right on International Dr. Appeals to value-conscious families; close to area attractions and food outlets. **Rooms:** 121 rms. CI 4pm/CO 11am. Nonsmoking rms avail. **Amenities:** 🛏 A/C, cable TV w/movies, in-rm safe. **Services:** 🔑 🚗 🛅 🛎 🛎 Car-rental desk, babysitting. **Facilities:** 🔂 🛗 **Rates (CP):** HS Mar–Dec $49 S or D. Lower rates off-season. Higher rates for spec evnts/hols. Spec packages avail. Pking: Outdoor, free. Maj CC.

≡≡ **Fairfield Inn–International Dr**, 8342 Jamaican Court, Orlando, FL 32819; tel 407/363-1944; fax 407/363-1944. Exit 29 off I-4. Budget offering provides good value. **Rooms:** 150 rms. CI 3pm/CO noon. Nonsmoking rms avail. **Amenities:** 🛏 🐾 A/C, cable TV w/movies. **Services:** 🔑 🚗 🛅 🛎 Babysitting. **Facilities:** 🔂 🛗 **Rates (CP):** HS Dec/June–Aug $59–$64 D. Lower rates off-season. Higher rates for spec evnts/hols. Spec packages avail. Pking: Outdoor, free. Maj CC.

≡≡ **Heritage Inn Orlando**, 9861 International Dr, Orlando, FL 32819; tel 407/352-0008 or toll free 800/447-1890; fax 407/352-5449. Exit 28 off I-4. Located across from the Orange County Convention Center, this property deserves high praise for pleasant, homey surroundings. The country decor and the down-home hospitality are a pleasant change from the usual in this area. Among its fans are returning retirees and families.

Rooms: 150 rms. CI 3pm/CO noon. Nonsmoking rms avail. **Amenities:** 🛏 🐾 A/C, cable TV w/movies, refrig, in-rm safe. **Services:** ✕ 🚗 🛅 🛎 Car-rental desk, babysitting. **Facilities:** 🔂 🏊 🛗 1 rst, 1 bar, games rm, washer/dryer. **Rates:** HS Feb–Apr/June–July/Oct–Nov $89–$129 S or D. Children under 12 stay free. Lower rates off-season. Higher rates for spec evnts/hols. AP rates avail. Pking: Outdoor, free. Maj CC.

≡ **Red Roof Inn**, 9922 Hawaiian Court, Orlando, FL 32819; tel 407/352-1507 or toll free 800/THE-ROOF; fax 407/352-5550. Exit 28 off I-4. Next to the convention center. Economical, basic accommodations. **Rooms:** 134 rms. CI 3pm/CO 11am. Nonsmoking rms avail. **Amenities:** 🛏 🐾 A/C, cable TV w/movies. **Services:** 🛎 🛎 Babysitting. **Facilities:** 🔂 🛗 Whirlpool, washer/dryer. **Rates:** $53–$59 S or D. Children under 18 stay free. Higher rates for spec evnts/hols. Spec packages avail. Pking: Outdoor, free. Maj CC.

≡≡ **Wynfield Inns Westwood**, 6263 Westwood Blvd, Orlando, FL 32821; tel 407/396-2121; fax 407/396-1142. Exit 28 (Sea World) off I-4. Close to Sea World and the Plaza International action, this decent hotel offers good room quality, though nondescript, limited public areas. **Rooms:** 299 rms. CI 3pm/CO 11am. Nonsmoking rms avail. **Amenities:** 🛏 🐾 A/C, cable TV, in-rm safe. 1 unit w/minibar. **Services:** 🔑 🚗 🛅 🛎 🛎 Car-rental desk, children's program, babysitting. **Facilities:** 🔂 🛗 🛗 1 rst, 1 bar, games rm, washer/dryer. Many low- and medium-priced restaurants with familiar names are nearby, if not exactly walking distance. **Rates:** HS Feb–Apr/June–Aug $54–$66 S or D. Extra person $5. Children under 17 stay free. Lower rates off-season. Higher rates for spec evnts/hols. Spec packages avail. Pking: Outdoor, free. Ltd CC.

Inn

≡ **The Courtyard at Lake Lucerne**, 211 N Lucerne Circle E, Orlando, FL 32801; tel 407/648-5188 or toll free 800/444-5289; fax 407/246-1368. Exit 31 off I-4. A stylish downtown inn that incorporates an interesting mix of Victorian and art deco styles in its 3 separate buildings embracing a brick courtyard. **Rooms:** 22 rms, stes, and effic. CI 3pm/CO 11am. **Amenities:** 🛏 🐾 A/C, cable TV. Some units w/terraces, some w/Jacuzzis. **Services:** 🛎 **Facilities:** 🛗 🛗 Guest lounge. **Rates (CP):** $65–$85 S or D; from $100 ste; from $85 effic. Extra person $10. Children under 6 stay free. Spec packages avail. Pking: Outdoor, free. Ltd CC.

Resorts

≡≡≡≡ **Hyatt Regency Grand Cypress**, 1 Grand Cypress Blvd, Orlando, FL 32836; tel 407/239-1234 or toll free 800/

233-1234; fax 407/239-3800. Impressive resort with fantastic grounds and deluxe accommodations. The atrium lobby houses a mini–rain forest, with stone-bedded streams and live birds in cages. Outside are lovely flower beds, rock gardens, brooks, and sculpture, as well as scores of palm, cypress, oak, and pine trees; swans and sailboats grace a picturesque lake. **Rooms:** 750 rms and stes. Exec-level rms avail. CI 4pm/CO noon. Express checkout avail. Nonsmoking rms avail. Well-appointed rooms. Mediterranean-style villas have fully equipped kitchens and feature large picture windows overlooking the golf course. **Amenities:** 🛅 🕭 🖺 A/C, cable TV w/movies, voice mail, in-rm safe. All units w/minibars, all w/terraces, 1 w/Jacuzzi. **Services:** 🍽 🖴 VP 🚐 🖺 🕭 Car-rental desk, social director, masseur, children's program, babysitting. **Facilities:** 🛅 🚲 ⚠ ▶₄₅ 🅰 ⚓₇ 🆘 🕺 ⛳ 🍸 □ 5 rsts (see also "Restaurants" below), 5 bars (2 w/entertainment), lifeguard, racquetball, sauna, steam rm, whirl-pool, day-care ctr. Lagoon-like swimming pool with waterfalls and waterslides. Jack Nicklaus-designed golf course. Helipad. **Rates:** HS Dec–Apr $210–$400 S or D; from $600 ste. Extra person $25. Children under 18 stay free. Lower rates off-season. Higher rates for spec evnts/hols. Spec packages avail. Pking: Indoor/outdoor, free. Maj CC.

Marriott's Orlando World Center, 8701 World Center Dr, Orlando, FL 32821; tel 407/239-4200 or toll free 800/621-0638; fax 407/238-8777. This enormous, grand resort hotel is a city unto itself, with various towers and sections augmented by elaborate landscaping and surrounded by a golf course. Little wonder the resort is one of the top venues in Florida for meetings and conventions; it's also a great choice for tourists. Unrated. **Rooms:** 1,503 rms and stes. CI 4pm/CO 11am. Express check-out avail. Nonsmoking rms avail. **Amenities:** 🛅 🕭 🖃 🖺 A/C, cable TV w/movies, voice mail, in-rm safe. All units w/minibars, all w/terraces. **Services:** 🍽 🖴 VP 🚐 🖺 🕭 Car-rental desk, social director, masseur, children's program, babysitting. The legions of staff try hard but are sometimes overwhelmed, leading to inconsistent service. **Facilities:** 🛅 ▶₁₈ 🏊 🆘 🍸 🖼 5K □ & 6 rsts, 4 bars (1 w/entertainment), lifeguard, lawn games, sauna, steam rm, whirlpool, beauty salon, day-care ctr, washer/dryer. Vast public areas, and enough leisure diversions to make guests content to stay on the grounds. **Rates:** HS Dec–Apr $174–$209 S or D; from $225 ste. Extra person $20. Children under 18 stay free. Lower rates off-season. Higher rates for spec evnts/hols. Spec packages avail. Pking: Outdoor, free. Maj CC.

Restaurants 🍴

⑤ B-Line Diner, in The Peabody, 9801 International Dr, Orlando; tel 407/352-4000. Exit 29 off I-4. **Diner.** An old-time rock 'n' roll cafe, this stylish take on a '50s diner serves inventive food and terrific desserts all night long. The menu includes fountain favorites and blue plate specials. **FYI:** Reservations not accepted. Children's menu. **Open:** Daily 24 hrs. **Prices:** Main courses $6.95–$17.95. Maj CC. 🍽 VP &

★ Enzo's, in the Market Place Shopping Center, 7600 Dr Phillips Blvd, Orlando; tel 407/351-1187. **Italian.** A classic Italian trattoria with peach walls hung with fine art prints. Always bustling and extremely popular. **FYI:** Reservations accepted. Children's menu. Beer and wine only. **Open:** Lunch daily 11:30am–4pm; dinner Mon–Thurs 4:30–10pm, Fri–Sat 4:30–11pm. Closed some hols. **Prices:** Main courses $7.50–$12.50. Maj CC. &

❦ Hemingway, in Hyatt Regency Grand Cypress, 1 Grand Cypress Blvd, Orlando; tel 407/239-1234. **Seafood.** A beautiful dining room with a tropical atmosphere, lots of plants and flowers, and a great view from every table. An attentive staff serves dishes from the impressive seafood menu. The warm country apple pie à la mode is a popular postscript to an elegant meal. **FYI:** Reservations accepted. **Open:** Lunch Tues–Sun 11am–2:30pm; dinner daily 6–10:30pm. **Prices:** Main courses $25–$45. Maj CC. 🏔 VP &

⑤ L & N Seafood Grill, 4120 E Colonial Dr, Orlando; tel 407/897-7124. ¼ mi E of Fashion Square Mall. **Seafood.** The nautical decor is a bit overblown in this chain of seafood palaces. Also at: 1375 Fla 436, Casselberry (407/657-0201); 108 Markham Woods Rd, Longwood (407/774-4474). **FYI:** Reservations not accepted. Children's menu. **Open:** Mon–Fri 11:30am–2pm, Sat 11:30am–10pm, Sun noon–9pm. Closed some hols. **Prices:** Main courses $7.95–$16.95. Maj CC. ✅ &

La Normandie, 2021 E Colonial Dr, Orlando; tel 407/896-9976. Exit 41 off I-4. Between Bumby St and Mills St. **French.** Enjoy classic northern French cuisine in this attractive country-style restaurant named for its owners' homeland. There is a minimum charge of $8.95 per person. **FYI:** Reservations recommended. Dress code. **Open:** Lunch Mon–Fri 11:30am–2pm; dinner Mon–Sat 5–10pm, Sun 5–8pm; brunch Sun 11:30am–2pm. Closed some hols. **Prices:** Main courses $20–$35. Maj CC. ✅ &

★ Le Coq au Vin, 4800 S Orange Ave, Orlando; tel 407/851-6980. **French.** A comfortable, stylish cafe with a relaxed, home-like atmosphere serving country French cuisine prepared with a regional twist. The menu regularly includes Black Angus sirloin and blackened grouper as well as salmon and veal dishes. **FYI:** Reservations recommended. Beer and wine only. **Open:** Lunch Tues–Fri 11am–2pm; dinner daily 5:30–9:45pm. Closed Dec 25. **Prices:** Main courses $11–$20. Maj CC. &

Linda's Lacantina, 4721 E Colonial Dr, Orlando; tel 407/ 894-4491. At Humphrey Ave. **Steak.** The open dining room, outfitted with exposed brick, hanging plants, and red tablecloths, is a suitable environment in which to enjoy hearty fare from a conventional Italian-American menu. Satisfied customers have been coming back to Linda's for steaks and seafood for over 35 years. **FYI:** Reservations recommended. Children's menu. **Open:** Tues–Sat 4:30–11pm. Closed some hols. **Prices:** Main courses $8–$21. Ltd CC. 🔲 &

Mikado Japanese Steakhouse, in Marriott's Orlando World Center, 8701 World Center Dr, Orlando; tel 407/239-4200. Exit 26A off Fla 53. **Japanese/Steak.** An elegant Japanese steakhouse adorned with attractive foliage and artwork. Choose from fillet of salmon, lobster tails, or filet mignon, all prepared with a pan-Asian flair. **FYI:** Reservations accepted. Children's menu. **Open:** Daily 6–10pm. **Prices:** Main courses $13.95–$32. Maj CC. VP &

Ming Court, 9188 International Dr, Orlando; tel 407/ 351-9988. Exit 29 off I-4. **Chinese.** A casual restaurant preparing traditional east Asian cuisine at affordable prices. The variety of entrees ranges from curried chicken to the Szechuan platter with seasonal vegetables. **FYI:** Reservations accepted. Children's menu. **Open:** Lunch daily 11am–2:30pm; dinner daily 4:30pm–midnight. **Prices:** Main courses $2.95–$18.95. Maj CC. &

Straub's Fine Seafood, 5101 E Colonial Dr, Orlando; tel 407/ 273-9330. **Seafood.** A wide variety of fresh fish dishes served in a tropical dining room adorned with hanging shell lights. The early-bird specials offer good value. Also at: 5101 E Colonial Dr, Orlando (407/273-9330). **FYI:** Reservations recommended. Children's menu. **Open:** Mon–Thurs 4:30–10pm, Fri–Sat 4:30–11pm, Sun 4:30–10pm. Closed some hols. **Prices:** Main courses $10.95–$26.95. Maj CC. 🔲 &

Attractions 🧳

Universal Studios Florida, 1000 Universal Studios Plaza; tel 407/363-8000. A state-of-the-art theme park built around a working motion picture and TV production studio, Universal Studios Florida uses thrilling rides and cutting-edge special effects in 10 major attractions to introduce visitors to the world of movie-making. Major attractions are **ET Adventure,** which transports visitors to ET's home planet; **Back to the Future,** where riders join Doc Brown in pursuing the evil Biff through time; **Kongfrontation,** with an attack by the giant ape himself; and **Earthquake,** the Big One, replete with splitting sidewalks, bursting water mains and an exploding propane truck.

Other features include stage shows, filmings of movie and TV productions, and Hanna-Barbera cartoon characters. There are

over 25 shops and numerous restaurants, including Mel's Drive-In from the film *American Graffiti* as well as a Hard Rock Cafe. **Open:** Daily, 9am–7pm; extended hours hols and in summer. $$$$

Sea World, 7007 Sea World Drive; tel 407/351-3600. This popular, 175-acre marine life park explores the world of the deep, combining entertainment with promoting wildlife conservation awareness. Its landscaped grounds include a 17-acre lagoon and a lush tropical rain forest.

The newest of more than 10 major shows and attractions include **Mission: Bermuda Triangle,** a high-definition film coupled with flight simulator technology that takes visitors on an exciting underwater mission; **Monster Marsh,** a re-created Mesozoic swamp, complete with life-size, animated robotic dinosaurs, that teaches awareness of endangered species; **Shamu: Close Up!** , a multipurpose habitat and research facility that gives visitors a close look at how killer whales interact; **Big Splash Bash,** a fast-paced song-and-dance extravaganza with an aquatic theme; **Mermaids, Myths & Monsters,** a nighttime show combining music, fireworks, and laser graphic images projected onto a 60-foot "waterscreen"; and a **killer whale show,** highlighted by an underwater "ballet."

Other favorites include Hotel Clyde and Seamore, a comedy show starring sea lions, otters, and walruses; the Gold Rush Ski Show, with acrobatics set to hoedown music; Penguin Encounter, with hundreds of Arctic and Antarctic specimens; and Dolphin Community Pool, where guests can feed and pet bottlenose dolphins. There is also a revolving 400-foot Sky Tower, a Polynesian Luau Dinner, and guided behind-the-seas tours. **Open:** Daily, 9am–7pm. $$$$

Church Street Station, 129 W Church St; tel 407/422-2434. A popular downtown dining, shopping, and entertainment complex. A city block's worth of cobblestone streets and authentic turn-of-the-century buildings house a variety of Victorianesque establishments adorned with magnificent woodwork, stained glass, ornate chandeliers, and authentic antiques.

Highlights include **Rosie O'Grady's Good Time Emporium,** an 1890s-style gambling hall/saloon; **Cheyenne Saloon and Opera House,** a 3-tiered country-and-western dance hall; the **Orchid Garden Ballroom,** a setting of wrought iron and marble featuring rock-and-roll oldies; **Apple Annie's Courtyard,** evocative of a Victorian tropical garden; **Phineas Phogg's Balloon Works,** a high-energy dance club with an aviation theme; **Crackers Oyster Bar;** and **Lili Marlene's Aviator's Pub & Restaurant,** embellished with World War I memorabilia. There are 20 live shows featured nightly, from live bands to cancan girls. Also Commander Ragtime's Midway of Fun, Food and Games, with a huge video arcade, a food court, and 50 specialty shops in the Church Street Exchange. **Open:** Daily; clubs 11–2am, shops 11am–11pm. $$$$

Orlando Science Center, 810 E Rollins St; tel 407/896-7151. The center offers an entertaining exposure to various scientific principles and concepts, employing permanent and traveling exhibits, and live demonstrations and shows. Permanent features include Nature Works, showcasing Florida's unique environment (including a real "gator hole"); Water Works, geared toward younger children, which illustrates principles of water and water life; Weather Central; and Tunnel of Discovery, an "arcade" of the physical sciences. A planetarium has shows throughout the day. **Open:** Mon–Thurs and Sat 9am–5pm, Fri 9am–9pm, Sun noon–5pm. Closed some hols. $$$

Orlando Museum of Art, 2416 N Mills Ave (in Loch Haven Park); tel 407/896-4231. A permanent collection of 19th- and 20th-century American art, pre-Columbian artifacts, and African objects is presented on a rotating basis. Also available are guided tours, children's workshops, and gallery talks. **Open:** Tues–Sat 9am–5pm, Sun noon–5pm. $$

Terror on Church Street, 135 S Orange Ave; tel 407/649-FEAR or 649-1912. Housed in a converted old building in downtown Orlando, this attraction uses high technology, cinematic special effects, theatrical techniques, and even climate control to provide a terrifying journey through a maze of more than 20 elaborately detailed rooms, or "sets," each with its own horrific theme. The sets are populated by assorted monsters and chain-saw-wielding maniacs that can spring up almost anywhere—the actors are encouraged to improvise. People enter in groups of 8; the tour lasts about 25 minutes, but there are "chicken-out" exits for the faint of heart. **Open:** Tues–Thurs and Sun 7pm–midnight, Fri–Sat 7pm–1am; extended hours June 15–Aug 31. $$$$

Harry P Leu Gardens, 1730 N Forest Ave; tel 407/246-2620. This 56-acre botanical garden showcases a magnificent array of flowering trees, orchids, perennials, wildflowers, camelias, azaleas, roses, and more. There are also specialty gardens, such as the Xerophyte Garden and Mary Jane's Rose Garden, which contains more than 70 varieties. The Leu House Museum is a turn-of-the-century farmhouse, restored and furnished to reflect the 1910–1930 period; guided tours are available. **Open:** Daily 9am–5pm. Closed Dec 25. $

Gatorland, 14501 S Orange Blossom Trail (US 441); tel 407/855-5496. Founded in 1949 with a handful of alligators living in huts and pens, this facility has grown to accommodate 5,000 alligators and crocodiles on a 55-acre spread. A 2,000-foot boardwalk winds through a cypress swamp and a 10-acre breeding marsh with an observation tower. There are three

shows scheduled throughout the day: Gator Jumparoo, The Snakes of Florida, and Gator Wrestlin'. Picnic facilities, restaurant, gift shop. **Open:** Daily 8am–dusk. $$$$

Wet 'n' Wild, 6200 International Dr; tel 407/351-WILD. Among the highlights of this water park are Surf Lagoon, which sports 4-foot waves; Bomb Bay, a 76-foot vertical drop into a target pool; and Black Hole, a 500-foot, 2-person raft ride in total darkness propelled by a 1,000-gallon-per-minute blast of water. Elaborate children's playground as well. **Open:** Year-round. Hours vary seasonally, phone ahead. $$$$

Orlando Arena, 600 W Amelia St; tel 407/849-2020. The NBA's Orlando Magic play basketball here November–April, and the Tampa Bay Lightning hockey team has a few of its home games here as well.

ORMOND BEACH
Map page M-7, A2

Hotel 🏨

≣≣ Maverick Resort, 485 S Atlantic Ave, Ormond Beach, FL 32176; tel 904/672-3550. Exit 88 off US 40. Pleasant timeshare accommodations housed in a midrise building on the ocean. Popular with families. **Rooms:** 138 effic. CI 3pm/CO 10am. **Amenities:** 🛏 ♨ 🖵 A/C, cable TV, refrig. All units w/terraces. **Services:** ⊖ Children's program, babysitting. **Facilities:** 🛝 ⚓ 1 rst, 1 beach (ocean), lifeguard, games rm, spa, sauna, whirlpool, playground, washer/dryer. **Rates:** From $50 effic. Children under 18 stay free. Pking: Outdoor, free. Maj CC.

Motels

≣≣ Casa Del Mar, 621 S Atlantic Ave, Ormond Beach, FL 32176; tel 904/672-4550 or toll free 800/245-1590; fax 904/672-1418. Located just north of where college spring break is centered, this pleasant, modest facility receives many repeat guests. **Rooms:** 151 rms, stes, and effic. CI 3pm/CO 11am. Nonsmoking rms avail. Florida-tropical decor. Efficiencies on oceanfront are spacious. **Amenities:** 🛏 ♨ 🖵 A/C, cable TV, refrig, in-rm safe. All units w/terraces. **Services:** ✕ 🚗 🖂 ⊖ ♨ Children's program. **Facilities:** 🛝 🏊 ⚓ 1 rst, 2 bars, 1 beach (ocean), lifeguard, games rm, whirlpool, washer/dryer. Guests often gather in the sitting area of the lobby to converse or watch TV. **Rates:** HS Feb–Mar/June–Aug $90–$124 S or D; from $136 ste; from $124 effic. Extra person $10. Children under 16 stay free. Min stay spec evnts. Lower rates off-season. Higher rates for spec evnts/hols. Spec packages avail. Pking: Indoor/outdoor, free. Maj CC.

Granada Inn, 51 S Atlantic Ave, Ormond Beach, FL 32176; tel 904/672-7550 or toll free 800/228-8089, 800/237-6865 in Canada. A favorite among the senior set, who often come for long stays, it's low-key and folksy. Unrated. **Rooms:** 192 rms, stes, and effic. CI 4pm/CO 11am. Nonsmoking rms avail. Rooms come in 4 categories. Plain decor. **Amenities:** 📺 🛏 A/C, cable TV. All units w/terraces, all w/fireplaces. **Services:** ✕ 🚐 🍽 Children's program, babysitting. **Facilities:** 🏋 🏊 ᵭ 1 rst, 2 bars, 1 beach (ocean), lifeguard, games rm, whirlpool, washer/dryer. **Rates:** HS Feb 10–Apr 10 $98 S or D; from $166 ste; from $114 effic. Extra person $6. Children under 16 stay free. Min stay HS. Lower rates off-season. Pking: Outdoor, free. Maj CC.

▦▦ Ivanhoe Beach Resort, 205 S Atlantic Ave, Ormond Beach, FL 32176; tel 904/672-6711 or toll free 800/874-9910; fax 904/676-9494. On Fla A1A ½ mi S of jct Fla 40. A midrise hotel directly on the beach, noteworthy for its variety of accommodations. **Rooms:** 147 rms and effic. CI 2pm/CO 11am. Nonsmoking rms avail. Generally well-tended units are sometimes a mishmash of decor. **Amenities:** 📺 A/C, cable TV, refrig, in-rm safe. All units w/terraces. **Services:** 🚐 🛎 🍽 Children's program. **Facilities:** 🏋 🏊 ᵭ 1 rst, 1 bar, 1 beach (ocean), lifeguard, games rm, washer/dryer. **Rates:** HS July/Feb/Mar $75 S; $105 D; from $90 effic. Extra person $5. Children under 18 stay free. Min stay spec evnts. Lower rates off-season. Spec packages avail. Pking: Indoor/outdoor, free. Maj CC.

Restaurants 🍴

Bennigan's, 890 S Atlantic Ave, Ormond Beach; tel 904/673-3691. At Harvard Blvd. **American.** A simple American restaurant and bar with a casual atmosphere and a varied menu. You'll find potato skins, chicken fingers, salads, sandwiches, pastas, and steaks here. **FYI:** Reservations not accepted. Children's menu. **Open:** Mon–Thurs 11am–12:30am, Fri–Sat 11am–1:30am. **Prices:** Main courses $4.99–$14.99. Maj CC. ᵭ

Julian's, 88 S Atlantic Ave, Ormond Beach; tel 904/677-6767. 1 block S of Fla 40. **American.** You can choose from a variety of char-broiled poultry or beef entrees as well as from an extensive selection of seafood dishes. An organist entertains 6 nights a week. **FYI:** Reservations not accepted. Piano. **Open:** Daily 4–11pm. **Prices:** Main courses $7.95–$15.95. Maj CC. ᵭ

La Crepe en Haut, in Fountain Square Shops, 142 E Granada Blvd, Ormond Beach; tel 904/673-1999. At Vining Court. **French.** Attentive service is part of the fine dining experience here. Specialties include the Cajun sampler with chicken, shrimp, oysters, and sausage; and mushroom ravioli in cream sauce. **FYI:** Reservations recommended. **Open:** Lunch Tues–Fri 11:30am–2:30pm; dinner Tues–Sun 5:30–10pm. Closed some hols. **Prices:** Main courses $20–$30. Maj CC.

Sophie Kay's Coffee Tree Family Restaurant, 100 S Atlantic Ave, Ormond Beach; tel 904/677-0300. At Bosarvey Dr. **American.** This casual and old-fashioned coffee shop–style restaurant can serve patrons in booths or at the counter. Variety of items to choose from, including veal, beef, and seafood dishes. Special entrees and sandwiches are offered daily. **FYI:** Reservations not accepted. Children's menu. Beer and wine only. **Open:** Daily 7am–10pm. Closed Dec 25. **Prices:** Main courses $5–$9. Maj CC. ᵭ

Attractions 🧳

The Casements, 25 Riverside Dr; tel 904/676-3216. Guided tours are offered of this 3-story villa that was once the winter home of billionaire John D Rockefeller. The house presently serves as a cultural and civic center. With a Hungarian folk art and costume collection as well as an exhibit of Boy Scout memorabilia. Tours are Mon–Fri 10am–2:30pm, Sat 10–11:30am. Free.

Birthplace of Speed Museum, 160 E Granada Blvd; tel 904/672-5657. The history of beach racing is chronicled in this small but colorful collection featuring antique cars, automotive memorabilia, and photographs. **Open:** Tues–Sat 1–5pm. Closed some hols. $

OSPREY

Map page M-8, C2

Attraction 🧳

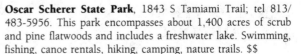

Oscar Scherer State Park, 1843 S Tamiami Trail; tel 813/483-5956. This park encompasses about 1,400 acres of scrub and pine flatwoods and includes a freshwater lake. Swimming, fishing, canoe rentals, hiking, camping, nature trails. $$

PALM BEACH

Map page M-9, D4

See also **Lake Worth, Lantana, Manalapan, North Palm Beach, Palm Beach Gardens, Palm Beach Shores, Riviera Beach, Singer Island**

Hotels

Brazilian Court Hotel, 301 Australian Ave, Palm Beach, FL 33480; tel 407/655-7740 or toll free 800/552-0335 in the US, 800/228-6852 in Canada; fax 407/655-0801. 2 blocks S of Royal Palm Way. A lovely old hotel still appreciated for its classic charm. The double courtyard with its flowering shrubs and flower beds is quite beautiful. **Rooms:** 134 rms and stes. CI 3pm/CO noon. Nonsmoking rms avail. Some of the rooms are cramped and a bit dated in places, but the overall look is still pleasing. **Amenities:** A/C, cable TV, refrig. Some units w/terraces. **Services:** Car-rental desk, babysitting. **Facilities:** 2 rsts, 1 bar (w/entertainment). **Rates:** HS Dec–Apr $185–$290 S or D; from $315 ste. Extra person $25. Lower rates off-season. MAP rates avail. Pking: Outdoor, $6. Maj CC.

Chesterfield Hotel Deluxe, 363 Coconut Row, Palm Beach, FL 33480; tel 407/659-5800 or toll free 800/243-7871; fax 407/659-6707. Between Australian St and Chilean St. A dignified yet stylish choice, with some whimsical touches inside. **Rooms:** 58 rms and stes. CI 4pm/CO noon. Nonsmoking rms avail. Individually decorated, functional rooms and suites. **Amenities:** A/C, cable TV w/movies, bathrobes. **Services:** Babysitting. **Facilities:** 1 rst, 1 bar (w/entertainment). **Rates:** HS Dec–Mar $175–$225 S or D; from $325 ste. Extra person $10. Children under 17 stay free. Lower rates off-season. Maj CC.

The Colony Hotel, 155 Hammon Ave, Palm Beach, FL 33480; tel 407/655-5430 or toll free 800/521-5525; fax 407/832-7318. Maintains a loyal following (including some celebrities) in this fashionable neighborhood. Attentive, respectful service. **Rooms:** 93 rms, stes, and effic; 7 ctges/villas. CI 4pm/CO noon. Nonsmoking rms avail. Some guest rooms are not up to par considering the rates, but the higher-end accommodations are well done, and suites are fitted with superior appointments. **Amenities:** A/C, cable TV w/movies, in-rm safe. Some units w/terraces. **Services:** Car-rental desk, masseur, babysitting. **Facilities:** 1 rst (see also "Restaurants" below), 2 bars (1 w/entertainment), spa, beauty salon. Live jazz in the bar is popular on weekends. **Rates:** HS

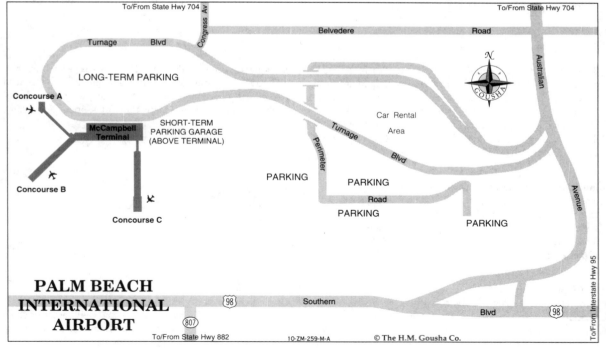

PALM BEACH INTERNATIONAL AIRPORT

To/From State Hwy 704
Belvedere Road
Turnage Blvd
Congress Av
LONG-TERM PARKING
Concourse A
McCampbell Terminal
SHORT-TERM PARKING GARAGE (ABOVE TERMINAL)
Concourse B
Concourse C
Car Rental Area
Turnage Blvd
Perimeter
PARKING
PARKING
PARKING
Road
PARKING
PARKING
To/From State Hwy 704
Australian
Avenue
To/From Interstate Hwy 95
Southern Blvd
To/From State Hwy 882
10-ZM-259-M-A
© The H.M. Gousha Co.

Dec–Apr $180–$275 S or D; from $325 ste; from $650 ctge/ villa. Extra person $20. Children under 16 stay free. Lower rates off-season. MAP rates avail. Spec packages avail. Pking: Outdoor, $6. Maj CC.

≣≣ **Heart of Palm Beach Hotel**, 160 Royal Palm Way, Palm Beach, FL 33480; tel 407/655-5600 or toll free 800/523-5377; fax 407/832-1201. Between S County Rd and Ocean Blvd. A 2- and 3-story building, within walking distance to the beach and 4 blocks north of Worth Ave shopping. **Rooms:** 88 rms and stes. CI 3pm/CO noon. Nonsmoking rms avail. Some rooms face the pool and deck area. **Amenities:** ☎ A/C, cable TV, refrig, voice mail. Some units w/terraces. **Services:** ✗ ☞ ⊠ ⇦ ⇦ Babysitting. **Facilities:** ⑮ ⚲ ⌷ 2 rsts, 1 bar. **Rates:** HS Dec 15–Apr 30 $99–$189 S or D; from $225 ste. Extra person $15. Children under 18 stay free. Lower rates off-season. Pking: Indoor/outdoor, free. Maj CC.

≣≣ **Howard Johnson Hotel**, 2870 S Ocean Blvd, Palm Beach, FL 33480; tel 407/582-2581 or toll free 800/654-2000; fax 407/ 582-7189. Exit 93 off Fla Tpk. Not on the beach, but it's an easy walk to it. There are some quite charming rooms that you might not expect in a place of this grade. **Rooms:** 98 rms and stes. CI 2pm/CO noon. Nonsmoking rms avail. **Amenities:** ☎ A/C, cable TV w/movies, in-rm safe. Some units w/terraces. **Services:** ✗ ⊠ ⇦ Babysitting. **Facilities:** ⑮ ⚲ ⌷ ⚹ 1 rst, 2 bars, washer/dryer. Well-lighted, ample parking. **Rates:** HS Dec–Apr $102–$120 S or D; from $250 ste. Extra person $10. Children under 12 stay free. Lower rates off-season. Spec packages avail. Pking: Outdoor, free. Maj CC.

≣≣ **Palm Beach Hawaiian Ocean Inn**, 3550 S Ocean Blvd, Palm Beach, FL 33480; tel 407/582-5631 or toll free 800/ 457-5631; fax 407/582-5631. 2 mi S of Lake Worth Bridge. A modest family operation with light Hawaiian touches. **Rooms:** 58 rms, stes, and effic. CI 2pm/CO 11am. Nonsmoking rms avail. **Amenities:** ☎ A/C, cable TV, refrig, in-rm safe. **Services:** ✗ ⊞ ⊠ ⇦ ⇦ Car-rental desk, babysitting. **Facilities:** ⑮ ⚲ ⚹ 1 rst, 1 bar (w/entertainment), 1 beach (ocean), games rm, washer/dryer. The patio and dining room can get hectic during peak times. **Rates:** HS Jan–Apr $98–$100 S or D; from $124 ste; from $109 effic. Extra person $5. Children under 18 stay free. Lower rates off-season. Pking: Outdoor, free. Maj CC.

≣≣ **Palm Beach Hilton**, 2842 S Ocean Blvd, Palm Beach, FL 33480; tel 407/586-6542 or toll free 800/433-1718; fax 407/ 585-0188. ½ mi N of Lake Worth Bridge. Upscale resort feel; makes efficient use of its limited grounds. **Rooms:** 134 rms and stes. CI 3pm/CO noon. Express checkout avail. Nonsmoking rms avail. **Amenities:** ☎ ⚹ ⚎ A/C, cable TV w/movies, refrig. All units w/minibars, some w/terraces, some w/Jacuzzis. **Services:** ✗ ☞ ⓋⓅ ⊠ ⇦ Car-rental desk, masseur, babysitting.

Facilities: ⑮ ⚲ △ ⚎⚎ ⌷₁₅₀ 2 rsts, 2 bars (1 w/entertainment), 1 beach (ocean), lifeguard, snorkeling, sauna, whirlpool. The pool is surrounded by the parking lot area. **Rates:** HS Dec–Apr $160– $295 S or D; from $650 ste. Extra person $25. Children under 18 stay free. Min stay spec evnts. Lower rates off-season. Higher rates for spec evnts/hols. Spec packages avail. Pking: Outdoor, $5. Maj CC.

≣≣≣ **Plaza Inn**, 215 Brazilian Ave, Palm Beach, FL 33480; tel 407/832-8666 or toll free 800/233-2632; fax 407/835-8776. 1 block S of Royal Palm Way at S County Rd. Located in an art deco building, this luxurious bed-and-breakfast exudes charm. Entrance hall contains antique writing table and grand piano. **Rooms:** 50 rms, stes. CI 2pm/CO noon. Nonsmoking rms avail. Accommodations in front are particularly attractive and roman- tic and are worth the extra cost. **Amenities:** ☎ A/C, cable TV, refrig. **Services:** ✗ ⊠ ⇦ Babysitting. **Facilities:** ⑮ ⌷₄₅ 1 bar, whirlpool. **Rates (BB):** HS Dec–Apr $125–$195 S or D; from $225 ste. Extra person $15. Children under 18 stay free. Min stay spec evnts. Lower rates off-season. Pking: Outdoor, free. Maj CC.

Motel

≣ **Beachcomber Sea Cay Motor Apartments**, 3024 S Ocean Blvd, Palm Beach, FL 33480; tel 407/585-4646. Three lowrise buildings set on landscaped grounds, with an attractive beach- side pool and sunning area. **Rooms:** 50 rms and effic. CI 1pm/ CO noon. Some rooms with showers only. Jalousie windows let in cool ocean breeze. **Amenities:** ☎ A/C, cable TV, refrig. Some units w/terraces. **Services:** ⇦ **Facilities:** ⑮ 1 beach (ocean), lawn games, washer/dryer. Pool is saltwater. Barbecue grills. **Rates:** HS Jan–Apr $75–$140 S or D; from $95 effic. Extra person $10. Children under 18 stay free. Lower rates off-season. Pking: Outdoor, free. Maj CC.

Resorts

≣≣≣≣ **The Breakers**, 1 S County Rd, Palm Beach, FL 33480; tel 407/655-6611 or toll free 800/833-3141; fax 407/ 659-8403. Exit 52A off I-95. 140 acres. The owners have done a commendable job preserving this historic 70-year-old beauty, with its palazzo-like facade and twin belvedere towers, by gently adapting the interiors to modern tastes—sometimes successfully (like adding 8 much-needed new elevators), sometimes by sacrificing grandeur. A popular rendezvous for business meet- ings, the hotel's innate graciousness is sometimes swamped by the hordes of temporary exhibits and omnipresent name tags. **Rooms:** 562 rms and stes. Exec-level rms avail. CI 4pm/CO noon. Express checkout avail. Nonsmoking rms avail. Brighter and sunnier after a recent renovation, lodgings vary considerably in size and view. **Amenities:** 🔐 ◖ 🍴 A/C, cable TV, refrig, in-rm safe, shoe polisher, bathrobes. All units w/minibars, some w/terraces. Guests with hearing problems will welcome the special beds with wakeup vibrating pads. **Services:** 🍽️ 🛎️ VP 🚐 ⛱️ 🛍️ Twice-daily maid svce, car-rental desk, social director, masseur, children's program, babysitting. Kids' program includes annual etiquette and money management camps. Personable staff sometimes overwhelmed by number of guests. **Facilities:** 🏋️ 🚴 ⚠️ ▶₃₆ 🎿 ●₁₅ 🏊 🍴 🛎️ 500 🖥️ 5 rsts, 4 bars (1 w/entertainment), 1 beach (ocean), lifeguard, games rm, lawn games, snorkeling, spa, sauna, whirlpool, beauty salon, day-care ctr, playground. Outstanding sports facilities, though beach is small for a luxury seaside resort. Pool and beach cabanas available. Fitness center offers such services as crania sacral massage and lymphodrain treatments. **Rates:** HS Dec 15–Apr 30 $285–$550 S or D; from $475 ste. Extra person $25. Children under 17 stay free. Min stay HS. Lower rates off-season. AP and MAP rates avail. Spec packages avail. Pking: Outdoor, $8. Maj CC. Some of the special packages offer exceptional values.

🌋🌋🌋🌋🌋 **Four Seasons Ocean Grand**, 2800 S Ocean Blvd, Palm Beach, FL 33480; tel 407/582-2800 or toll free 800/332-3442, 800/332-3442 in the US, 800/268-6282 in Canada; fax 407/547-1557. 5 mi S of downtown Palm Beach. 6 acres. The limited grounds and the 5-story condo facade belie a lobby lavishly coated with marble and a spacious lounge/library facing a patio with a fountain. Given the caliber of amenities and service, this hotel represents good value for the neighborhood. **Rooms:** 211 rms and stes. Exec-level rms avail. CI 4pm/CO noon. Express checkout avail. Nonsmoking rms avail. Efficiently laid-out rooms feature beachy colors and fine fabrics, as well as dazzlingly mirrored bathrooms. **Amenities:** 🔐 ◖ 🍴 A/C, refrig, in-rm safe, bathrobes. All units w/minibars, all w/terraces. Bathrooms with TV, telephone, and scale. **Services:** 🍽️ 🛎️ VP 🚐 ⛱️ 🛍️ 🍹 Twice-daily maid svce, car-rental desk, masseur, children's program, babysitting. Top-flight staff. **Facilities:** 🏋️ 🚴 ●₃ 🍴 500 ♿ 3 rsts (*see also* "Restaurants" below), 4 bars (1 w/entertainment), 1 beach (ocean), lifeguard, spa, sauna, steam rm, whirlpool, beauty salon, day-care ctr. Well-equipped clubroom for kids with professional staff. The Ocean Bistro has canopied, poolside terrace that recalls the French Riviera, while The Restaurant serves innovative cuisine in an elegant setting. **Rates:** HS Dec 17–Apr 15 $310–$580 S or D; from $780 ste. Extra person $30. Children under 17 stay free. Lower rates off-season. Spec packages avail. Pking: Indoor/outdoor, $6. Maj CC.

Restaurants 🍴

Au Bar, 336 Royal Ponciana Way, Palm Beach; tel 407/832-4800. **Continental.** An upscale eatery catering to the local jet set and young up-and-comers. Patrons come here as much to see and be seen as to eat and drink. Enjoy cocktails at the bar or dine on the continental cuisine. **FYI:** Reservations recommended. **Open:** Wed–Sun 5–11pm. **Prices:** Main courses $11–$22. Maj CC. VP ♿

Bice, 313½ Worth Ave, Palm Beach; tel 407/835-1600. **Northern Italian.** Cheery pastel-yellow tablecloths and bright flowers decorate the modern dining room of this upscale Milan-based chain. The daily menu includes pasta, veal, chicken, and seafood specialties. Outdoor dining overlooking posh Worth Avenue is available. **FYI:** Reservations recommended. Jacket required. **Open:** HS Sept–May lunch Mon–Sat noon–3pm; dinner daily 6–11pm. Reduced hours off-season. Closed Dec 25. **Prices:** Main courses $7–$28. Maj CC. VP ♿

Bistro, in the Brazilian Court Hotel, 301 Australian Ave, Palm Beach; tel 407/659-7840. Between Coconut Row and Hibiscus Ave. **New American.** Contemporary American cuisine, including the catch of the day, is served on marble-topped tables in this historic hotel dining room. Tropical prints and lush garden views abound. **FYI:** Reservations recommended. Piano. Children's menu. **Open:** Breakfast daily 7–11am; lunch daily 11am–2:30pm; dinner daily 6–10pm. **Prices:** Main courses $10–$18. Maj CC. VP ♿

Charley's Crab, 456 S Ocean Ave, Palm Beach; tel 407/659-1500. ⁴⁄₁₀ mi S of Royal Palm Way. **Seafood.** A tavern-style restaurant with beautiful ocean views. A good value for families, Sunday brunchers, and seafood lovers. **FYI:** Reservations recommended. Children's menu. **Open:** Lunch Mon–Sat 11:30am–4pm; dinner Sun–Thurs 4–10pm, Fri–Sat 4–11pm; brunch Sun 10:30am–2:30pm. **Prices:** Main courses $13.50–$25. Maj CC. 💳 VP ♿

Chuck & Harold's, 207 Royal Poinciana Way, Palm Beach; tel 407/659-1440. ⅓ mile E of Flagler Memorial Bridge on Fla A1A. **New American.** A fun, stylish cafe with a loyal clientele of both tourists and locals. Tuscan black bean soup, gazpacho for appetizers; fresh grilled or broiled fish, lobster, chicken, and pastas for main courses. Different lunch specials are offered daily. **FYI:** Reservations accepted. Children's menu. **Open:** Breakfast daily 7–11am; lunch daily 11:30am–4pm; dinner daily 4:30–11pm; brunch Sun 7:30–11am. **Prices:** Main courses $21–$30. Maj CC.

E R Bradley's Saloon, 111 Bradley Place, Palm Beach; tel 407/833-3520. At Bradley Place and Royal Palm Way. **American.** An intimate cafe with marble-topped tables, ceiling fans, and an outdoor patio. For lunch, there is caesar, conch, or basic house salad. The dinner menu includes grilled swordfish, sautéed chicken breast, and steaks. **FYI:** Reservations accepted. Children's menu. **Open:** Mon–Fri 11am–3am, Sat–Sun 10am–3am. **Prices:** Main courses $4.95–$17.95. Maj CC. �

♥★ **Florentine Room**, in the Breakers Hotel, 1 S County Rd, Palm Beach; tel 407/655-6611. 1 block S of Royal Poinciana Way. **New American.** One of America's great dining rooms, reaching a pinnacle of European style and elegance rarely attained in North American restaurants. The fluted marble columns and domed oval muraled ceiling of this grand old formal room are spectacular. Enjoy heart-healthy foods, fresh Florida seafood, or rack of lamb, and finish your meal with homemade rum-raisin ice cream. **FYI:** Reservations recommended. Band/piano. Children's menu. Jacket required. **Open:** Breakfast daily 7–11am; dinner daily 6:30–10pm. **Prices:** Main courses $19–$30. Maj CC. ♥ ▆ VP

Green's Pharmacy, 151 N County Rd, Palm Beach; tel 407/832-9171. **American.** A traditional black-and-white-tiled coffee shop with an open kitchen serving sandwiches, soups, and salads to patrons seated in booths or at the counter. **FYI:** Reservations not accepted. No liquor license. **Open:** Mon–Sat 7am–5pm, Sun 7am–2pm. **Prices:** Main courses $3–$5. Maj CC. ⅟

Jo's Restaurant, 200 Chilian Ave, Palm Beach; tel 407/659-6776. At County Rd. **French.** A cozy, antique-filled bistro, located in Palm Beach's historic district, serving a traditional menu. **FYI:** Reservations recommended. Beer and wine only. **Open:** Mon–Sat 6:30–9:30pm. **Prices:** Main courses $18.95–$26.95. Ltd CC. ⅟

Rendezvous Room, in the Colony Hotel, 155 Hammon Ave, Palm Beach; tel 407/655-5430. **Continental.** The look is lively but mannered, with white shutters and an elegant bar partially overlooking the pool. The menu includes lobster linguine, yellowtail snapper, and penne with vodka and prosciutto. **FYI:** Reservations recommended. Dancing/jazz. Jacket required. **Open:** HS Dec–Apr Sun–Wed 7am–midnight, Thurs–Sat 7am–1am. Reduced hours off-season. **Prices:** Main courses $17–$30. Maj CC. ♥ VP

♥★ **The Restaurant**, in at the Four Seasons Ocean Grand, 2800 S Ocean Blvd, Palm Beach; tel 407/582-2800. 5 mi S of Downtown Palm Beach. Go east on Southern Blvd across the Intracoastal Waterway. **Regional American.** Innovative cuisine served in a refined, pillared setting enhanced with antiques and chinoiserie. Much-lauded chef Hubert de Marais makes regular use of local produce and ingredients (like hearts of palm from a Seminole reservation and goat cheese from Loxahatchee). He even has his own orchard and herb garden on the premises. Typical dishes include stone-ground grits cake with ruby chard, yellowtail snapper with smoked tangelo sauce, fire-roasted ten-

derloin of beef with Oregon morels, and ginger-buttermilk wrap cake. Exceptional wine list; enthusiastic staff. **FYI:** Reservations recommended. Piano. Jacket required. **Open:** HS Dec–Apr daily 6–11pm. Reduced hours off-season. **Prices:** Main courses $19–$32. Maj CC. ♥ VP ⅟

Ta-boo, 221 Worth Ave, Palm Beach; tel 407/835-3500. **Southwestern.** A smart, casual, yet elegant grill with a southwestern-style menu. Grilled fish, veal, steaks, Maine lobster, and pasta. Try one of their trademark exotic cocktails. **FYI:** Reservations recommended. Dancing/piano. Jacket required. **Open:** Lunch daily 11:30am–5pm; dinner daily 5–11pm; brunch Sun 11:30am–2pm. **Prices:** Main courses $15–$25. Maj CC. VP ⅟

Testa's, 221 Royal Poinciana Way, Palm Beach; tel 407/832-0992. **Continental.** An upbeat eatery with outdoor dining overlooking Royal Poinciana Way. Freshwater fish, pasta, and seafood selections are offered daily. **FYI:** Reservations recommended. Children's menu. **Open:** Daily 7am–midnight. Closed Thanksgiving. **Prices:** Main courses $11.95–$24.95. Maj CC. ♥ VP ⅟

Attractions 🖼

Henry Morrison Flagler Museum, Coconut Row and White-hall Way; tel 407/655-2833. Henry Flagler, co-founder of the Standard Oil Company, probably had a greater influence on South Florida's development than any other individual. The museum that now bears his name was originally a mansion called Whitehall, built by Flagler in 1901 and restored to its original opulence in 1960. Also on display is Flagler's luxurious personal railroad car, "The Rambler," dating from 1886. **Open:** Tues–Sat 10am–5pm, Sun noon–5pm. $$

Society of the Four Arts, Four Arts Plaza; tel 407/655-7226. This cultural complex is made up of a museum, theater, library, and auditorium. Plays, movies, local art exhibits. **Open:** Mon–Sat 10am-5pm, Sun 2-5pm. Closed May-Nov. $

PALM BEACH GARDENS
Map page M-9, D4

Hotel 🧳

≣≣≣ **Radisson Suites PGA**, 4350 PGA Blvd, Palm Beach Gardens, FL 33410; tel 407/622-1000 or toll free 800/333-3333; fax 407/626-6254. PGA Blvd exit off I-95. Convenient to highways and local attractions. Stylish layout, including a soaring lobby. This is one of the more sophisticated all-suites properties on the market. **Rooms:** 160 stes. CI 3pm/CO noon.

Express checkout avail. Nonsmoking rms avail. **Amenities:** 📞 🛁 📺 🍷 A/C, cable TV w/movies, refrig. All units w/minibars, some w/Jacuzzis. **Services:** ✗ 🔑 🗺 🛏 🐟 Babysitting. **Facilities:** 🏋 🍽 500 ⛱ 🖥 ♿ 2 rsts, 1 bar, games rm, sauna, whirlpool, beauty salon, washer/dryer. **Rates (CP):** HS Dec–April from $169 ste. Extra person $10. Children under 18 stay free. Min stay. Lower rates off-season. Spec packages avail. Pking: Outdoor, free. Maj CC.

Resort

📘📘📘 **PGA National Resort and Spa**, 400 Ave of the Champions, Palm Beach Gardens, FL 33418; tel 407/627-2000 or toll free 800/633-9150; fax 407/672-0261. PGA Blvd exit off I-95. 2,600 acres. A massive and impressive resort complex whose grounds include a lake. The resort receives many groups and conventions, but also hosts its share of individual golfers and tennis enthusiasts. Cheerful staff. **Rooms:** 315 rms and stes; 100 ctges/villas. CI 3pm/CO noon. Nonsmoking rms avail. The variety of accommodations include cottage-like arrangements that provide extra space. Some rooms are a hike from the lobby. **Amenities:** 📞 🛁 🍷 A/C, cable TV w/movies, in-rm safe. All units w/minibars, all w/terraces. **Services:** ✗ 🔑 VP 🚐 🗺 🛏 Car-rental desk, masseur, children's program, babysitting. **Facilities:** 🏋 🚴 ⛳ 📷 90 📷 🏌 7 🎾 12 🍽 550 🖥 ♿ 3 rsts, 3 bars (1 w/entertainment), 1 beach (lake shore), games rm, lawn games, racquetball, spa, sauna, steam rm, whirlpool, beauty salon, washer/dryer. **Rates:** HS Dec–Apr $265–$300 S or D; from $280 ste; from $365 ctge/villa. Extra person $30. Children under 18 stay free. Lower rates off-season. Spec packages avail. Pking: Outdoor, $5. Maj CC.

Restaurants 🍴

Cafe Chardonnay, in Garden Square Shoppes, 4533 PGA Blvd, Palm Beach Gardens; tel 407/627-2662. **Regional American.** An casual, upscale cafe with funky decor and a comfortable bar area. The inventive contemporary menu concentrates on lighter fare and includes pasta, beef, and seafood dishes. **FYI:** Reservations recommended. Children's menu. Beer and wine only. **Open:** Lunch Mon–Fri 11:30am–2:30pm; dinner daily 5:30–10pm. Closed some hols. **Prices:** Main courses $14.95–$25.95. Maj CC. ♿

The Explorers, in the PGA National Resort and Spa, 400 Ave of the Champions, Palm Beach Gardens; tel 407/627-2000. Exit 57B off I-95. **Regional American.** Dine while seated in luxurious wingbacked leather chairs or a velvet-cushioned booth. Typical dishes include roasted half-duck, sautéed red snapper,

and beef tenderloin. **FYI:** Reservations recommended. **Open:** Tues–Sat 5:30–10pm. **Prices:** Main courses $15.95–$22.50. Maj CC. VP ♿

Parker's Lighthouse, in Harbor Financial Center, 180 Rue de la Mer, Palm Beach Gardens; tel 407/627-0000. At PGA Blvd and Prosperity Rd. **Seafood.** A lovely restaurant with a cool, casual atmosphere and an open kitchen. Choose the appetizing crab cakes or one of the other fresh seafood dishes prepared to order. **FYI:** Reservations recommended. Children's menu. **Open:** Lunch Mon–Sat 11:30am–2:30pm; dinner Mon–Thurs 4:30–10pm, Fri–Sat 4:30–10:30pm, Sun 4:30–9pm; brunch Sun 11am–2:30pm. **Prices:** Main courses $10.95–$17.95. Maj CC. 💳 VP ♿

Ristorante La Capannina, in Garden Square Shopping Center, 10971 N Military Trail, Palm Beach Gardens; tel 407/626-4632. **Northern Italian.** A taste of northern Italy in a south Florida strip-mall bistro. Great old-world Italian dishes are served, including veal, pasta, and seafood. **FYI:** Reservations recommended. **Open:** Lunch Mon–Sat 11:30am–2:30pm; dinner Mon–Sat 5–10:30pm. **Prices:** Main courses $16.75–$23.75. Maj CC. VP ♿

Waterway Cafe, 2300 PGA Blvd, Palm Beach Gardens; tel 407/694-1700. Between Prosperity Rd and US 1. **American.** An open-air, nautically themed restaurant located on the Intracoastal Waterway, serving a variety of beef, pasta, and seafood dishes. While the dining room is firmly planted on solid ground, the bar is located on an adjacent floating boat; in addition to cocktails, a limited bar menu, including chicken wings and burgers, is served there. **FYI:** Reservations recommended. Band. Children's menu. **Open:** Mon–Thurs 11:30am–midnight, Fri–Sat 11:30am–1am. **Prices:** Main courses $8.95–$17.95. Maj CC. 🏔 💳 VP ♿

PALM BEACH SHORES

Map page M-4, D9

Hotels 🏨

📘📘 **Best Western Seaspray Inn**, 123 Ocean Ave, Palm Beach Shores, FL 33404; tel 407/844-0233 or toll free 800/330-0233; fax 407/844-9885. Blue Heron Blvd exit off I-95. A pretty establishment on the oceanfront with a pleasant pool area. **Rooms:** 50 rms and effic. CI 2pm/CO 11am. Nonsmoking rms avail. **Amenities:** 📞 A/C, cable TV. Some units w/terraces. **Services:** 🛏 🐟 Babysitting. **Facilities:** 🏋 ♿ 2 rsts, 2 bars (1 w/entertainment), 1 beach (ocean). **Rates:** HS Feb 13–Apr 9

$80–$126 S; $90–$136 D; from $120 effic. Extra person $10. Children under 18 stay free. Lower rates off-season. Pking: Indoor/outdoor, free. Maj CC.

≣≣≣ **Embassy Suites Resort**, 181 Ocean Ave, Palm Beach Shores, FL 33404 (Singer Island); tel 407/863-4000 or toll free 800/328-2289; fax 407/845-3245. Blue Heron Blvd exit off I-95. Geared toward families and those who want a little spa pampering, instead of the business clientele who are the traditional market for this chain. The waterfront location allows for a multitude of activities, especially for children. **Rooms:** 254 stes. CI 3pm/CO noon. Nonsmoking rms avail. **Amenities:** 🛏🕏🎛🍹 A/C, cable TV w/movies, refrig, VCR, voice mail. **Services:** ✕ 🍽 🆅🅿 🖼 ⇦ Car-rental desk, social director, masseur, children's program, babysitting. Evening cocktail service and full breakfast included. **Facilities:** 🛠 🚲 🍽 [350] 🔥 1 rst, 2 bars (1 w/entertainment), 1 beach (ocean), lifeguard, games rm, sauna, whirlpool, day-care ctr, playground, washer/dryer. **Rates (BB):** HS Dec–Apr from $250 ste. Extra person $15. Children under 12 stay free. Lower rates off-season. Higher rates for spec evnts/hols. Spec packages avail. Pking: Outdoor, $5. Maj CC. Package plans include spa programs or golf.

PALM HARBOR

Map page M-6, D2

Resort 📇

≣≣≣≣ **Innisbrook Hilton Resort**, 36750 US 19 N, Palm Harbor, FL 34684; tel 813/942-2000 or toll free 800/456-2000; fax 813/942-5220. S of Klosterman Rd on US 19. 1,100 acres. An expansive and lush complex located in a gated community, with several restaurants and lounges. Golfers and others are drawn to its manicured greens and its lakes, pools, and lovely natural setting. **Rooms:** 1,258 effic. CI 3pm/CO noon. Express checkout avail. Nonsmoking rms avail. **Amenities:** 🛏🕏🎛 A/C, cable TV w/movies, refrig. All units w/minibars, all w/terraces. **Services:** ✕ 🍽 🚗🖼⇦🎿 Twice-daily maid svce, car-rental desk, social director, masseur, children's program, babysitting. **Facilities:** 🛠 🚲 ⛳▶63 🎿🎱 🍽 [2K] 🖥 🔥 4 rsts, 4 bars (1 w/entertainment), lifeguard, racquetball, spa, sauna, whirlpool, beauty salon, day-care ctr, playground, washer/dryer. **Rates:** HS Dec–Apr from $187 effic. Children under 18 stay free. Lower rates off-season. AP rates avail. Spec packages avail. Pking: Outdoor, free. Maj CC.

PANAMA CITY

Map page M-3, C1

Hotel 📇

≣≣ **The Sandpiper–Beacon**, 17403 Front Beach Rd, Panama City, FL 32413; tel 904/234-2154 or toll free 800/488-8828; fax 904/233-0278. A 3-story complex with accommodations ranging from motel-style rooms to 2-bedroom units sleeping up to 10 persons in 5 beds. Large beach. **Rooms:** 155 rms and stes. CI 4pm/CO 11am. Nonsmoking rms avail. **Amenities:** 🛏🎛 A/C, cable TV, refrig. Some units w/terraces. **Services:** ✕ 🖼⇦🎿 **Facilities:** 🛠 ⛱ 🐟 🔥 [40] 🔥 1 rst, 2 bars (1 w/entertainment), 1 beach (ocean), lifeguard, games rm, snorkeling, washer/dryer. Tiki beach bar. **Rates:** HS May–Aug $54–$69 S or D; from $84 ste. Children under 18 stay free. Min stay spec evnts. Lower rates off-season. Higher rates for spec evnts/hols. Spec packages avail. Pking: Outdoor, free. Maj CC.

Restaurants 🍴

Harbour House, in the Ramada Inn, 3001A W 10th St, Panama City; tel 904/785-9053. **New American.** This hotel dining room, outfitted with wicker chairs, chandeliers, and plants, offers a lovely view of St Andrews Bay. The standard menu includes seafood and steaks; there's also a salad bar. **FYI:** Reservations not accepted. Band. Children's menu. **Open:** Daily 6am–10pm. **Prices:** Main courses $8.95–$16.95. Maj CC. 🏔🔥

Pappy's German Restaurant and Oyster Bar, in St Andrew's Marina, 1000 Bayview Ave, Panama City; tel 904/785-6611. **German/Seafood. FYI:** Reservations not accepted. Children's menu. Beer and wine only. **Open:** Mon–Sat 11am–10pm, Sun 3–10pm. Closed some hols. **Prices:** Main courses $7–$10. Ltd CC.

Attraction 🏛

Junior Museum of Bay County, 1731 Jenks Ave; tel 904/769-6128. Exhibits include a Florida pioneer log cabin, a grist and cane mill, and Native American artifacts from nearby archeological digs. Also on site: a re-created 1880s farm where visitors can feed chickens and ducks, a nature trail with an elevated walkway, and science exhibits. **Open:** Tues–Fri 10am–4:30pm, Sat 10am–4pm. Closed some hols. Free.

PANAMA CITY BEACH

Map page M-3, C1

Hotels 🏖

≋ ≋ ≋ **Holiday Inn Sunspree Resort**, 11127 Front Beach Rd, Panama City Beach, FL 32407; tel 904/234-1111 or toll free 800/633-0266; fax 904/235-1907. This curved, 15-story beach hotel is one of the top Holiday Inns in the country. Its dramatic, tropical lobby has a waterfall. **Rooms:** 342 rms and stes. CI 4pm/CO 11am. Nonsmoking rms avail. Attractive, spacious rooms have gulf views from balconies. **Amenities:** 🔒 👁 📺 🍽 A/C, cable TV w/movies, refrig. All units w/terraces, some w/Jacuzzis. **Services:** ✗ 🍴 🛄 🛎 Social director, children's program, babysitting. **Facilities:** 🏋 ▶18 ⚓6 🏌 💺 🏊 👥 3 rsts, 2 bars, 1 beach (ocean), games rm, sauna, steam rm, whirlpool, playground, washer/dryer. Extra-large pool and lounge area. **Rates:** HS Mar–Sept $140 S or D; from $425 ste. Extra person $10. Children under 16 stay free. Min stay HS. Lower rates off-season. Higher rates for spec evnts/hols. Spec packages avail. Pking: Outdoor, free. Maj CC.

≋ ≋ ≋ **Ramada Inn Beachside Resort**, 12907 Beach Front Rd, Panama City Beach, FL 32407; tel 904/234-1700 or toll free 800/633-0266; fax 904/235-2700. On US 98, 3½ mi W of Hathaway Bridge. Modest facility catering to beachgoers. **Rooms:** 147 rms. CI 4pm/CO 11am. Nonsmoking rms avail. **Amenities:** 🔒 A/C, cable TV. All units w/terraces. **Services:** ✗ 🛎 **Facilities:** 🏋 🏌 🛗 👥 1 rst, 2 bars, 1 beach (ocean), games rm, sauna, steam rm. Waves lap against the tiki bar. **Rates:** HS Mar–Aug $109–$129 S or D. Children under 16 stay free. Min stay wknds. Lower rates off-season. Higher rates for spec evnts/hols. Spec packages avail. Pking: Outdoor, free. Maj CC.

Motels

≋ **Georgian Terrace**, 14415 Front Beach Rd (US 89A), Panama City Beach, FL 32413; tel 904/234-2144. **Rooms:** 28 effic. CI 2pm/CO 11am. **Amenities:** 🔒 📺 A/C, cable TV, refrig. **Services:** 🛎 **Facilities:** 1 beach (ocean), games rm. **Rates:** HS May–Sept from $69 effic. Children under 18 stay free. Min stay spec evnts. Lower rates off-season. Higher rates for spec evnts/hols. Pking: Outdoor, free. Maj CC.

≋ ≋ **La Brisa Inn**, 9424 Front Beach Rd, Panama City Beach, FL 32407; tel 904/235-1122 or toll free 800/523-4369. A good budget find for families, even if it's not on the beach. **Rooms:** 60 rms. CI 2pm/CO 11am. Nonsmoking rms avail. Many rooms have kitchenettes. **Amenities:** 🔒 A/C, cable TV. Morning coffee and donuts. **Facilities:** 🏋 👥 Washer/dryer. **Rates:** HS July–Aug

$85 S or D. Extra person $10. Children under 18 stay free. Min stay HS. Lower rates off-season. Higher rates for spec evnts/hols. Pking: Outdoor, free. Maj CC.

≋ **The Mark II**, 15285 Front Beach Rd, Panama City Beach, FL 32413; tel 904/234-8845 or toll free 800/234-8843. 2 mi E of US 79. A 4-story hotel on a well-trodden beach. **Rooms:** 80 rms. CI 4pm/CO 11am. Guest quarters are sparsely furnished, but roomy. All rooms have views of the gulf. **Amenities:** 🔒 A/C, cable TV. Some units w/terraces. **Facilities:** 🏋 **Rates:** HS Jan–Mar $89–$109 S or D. Children under 18 stay free. Lower rates off-season. Pking: Outdoor, free. Maj CC.

≋ ≋ **Rendezvous Beach Resort**, 17281 Front Beach Rd, Panama City Beach, FL 32407; tel 904/234-8841 or toll free 800/874-6617. ½ block W of US 79. All rooms face the beach at this 4-story hotel. **Rooms:** 72 rms, stes, and effic. CI 2pm/CO 11am. **Amenities:** 🔒 A/C, cable TV. **Services:** 🛎 🏄 **Facilities:** 🏋 ⚠ 🛗 1 rst, 1 bar, 1 beach (ocean), whirlpool, washer/dryer. **Rates:** HS Mar–Aug $50–$70 S; $58–$80 D; from $78 ste; from $68 effic. Extra person $5. Children under 12 stay free. Lower rates off-season. Pking: Outdoor, free. Maj CC.

≋ **Sunset Inn**, 8109 Surf Dr, Panama City Beach, FL 32408; tel 904/234-7370; fax 904/234-7370 ext 303. At Joan Ave. Family-oriented beachfront lodging. **Rooms:** 50 stes and effic. CI 2pm/CO 10am. Large, modestly furnished and decorated rooms. **Amenities:** 🔒 📺 A/C, cable TV, refrig. Some units w/terraces. **Services:** 🛎 Babysitting. **Facilities:** 🏋 1 beach (ocean), washer/dryer. **Rates:** HS May–Sept from $88 ste; from $60 effic. Children under 18 stay free. Min stay HS. Lower rates off-season. Pking: Outdoor, free. Maj CC.

Resorts

≋ ≋ ≋ **Edgewater Beach Resort**, 11212 Front Beach Rd, Panama City Beach, FL 32407; tel 904/235-4044. Large resort complex includes 3 high-rise towers as well as low condominium sections, half on the beautiful beach, half on the golf course. Spectacular beachfront swimming lagoon features cascading waterfalls and an island. Garden landscaping with palm trees. **Rooms:** 525 effic. CI 4pm/CO 10am. Express checkout avail. Nonsmoking rms avail. Spacious 1- to 3-bedroom apartments come with fully equipped kitchen and living and dining areas. **Amenities:** 🔒 👁 📺 A/C, cable TV w/movies, refrig, voice mail. All units w/terraces. Apartments have washers and dryers. **Services:** ✗ 🍴 🚗 🛎 Children's program, babysitting. **Facilities:** 🏋 ▶9 🏌 💺 🏊 👥 3 rsts, 2 bars (1 w/entertainment), 1 beach (ocean), games rm, whirlpool, beauty salon, washer/dryer.

Rates: HS May–Sept from $150 effic. Children under 18 stay free. Min stay spec evnts. Lower rates off-season. Spec packages avail. Pking: Outdoor, free. Maj CC.

≣≣≣≣ Marriott's Bay Point Resort, 4200 Marriott Dr, Panama City Beach, FL 32408; tel 904/234-3307 or toll free 800/874-7105; fax 904/233-1308. 1,100 acres. Bordered by St Andrew's Bay and Grand Lagoon, this top golf-and-tennis resort serves as a respite from the honky-tonk beachside community nearby. The outstanding coral stucco hotel is surrounded by gardens, palm trees, oaks, and magnolias. A window wall in the 3-story lobby looks out to pretty water views. **Rooms:** 355 rms and stes. CI 4pm/CO 11am. Express checkout avail. Nonsmoking rms avail. Spacious, well-maintained guest rooms. **Amenities:** 🛁 🔌 📺 🖥 A/C, cable TV w/movies, refrig, voice mail. All units w/terraces, some w/Jacuzzis. **Services:** ✕ 🔑 VP 🚗 🖼 🐾 Social director, masseur, children's program, babysitting. **Facilities:** 🏊 🚴 ⛴ 🏕 ▶36 🎱14 🏌 🚤 🍽 900 🍴 4 rsts, 4 bars (2 w/entertainment), 1 beach (bay), games rm, snorkeling, sauna, whirlpool, beauty salon, day-care ctr, playground, washer/dryer. The Terrace Court, overlooking Bay Point Marina, offers romantic, candlelit (and expensive) dinners. **Rates:** HS Mar–Aug $175–$195 S or D; from $215 ste. Extra person $20. Children under 17 stay free. Min stay spec evnts. Lower rates off-season. Spec packages avail. Pking: Outdoor, free. Maj CC.

Restaurants 🍽

Angelo's Steak Pit, 9527 Front Beach Rd, Panama City Beach; tel 904/234-2531. **Steak.** This busy, family-oriented eatery provides video games to keep the young ones occupied while you wait for your table or booth. Separate lounge and a gift shop on the premises. Chicken and fish dishes are on the menu, but beef is the specialty. **FYI:** Reservations not accepted. Children's menu. **Open:** HS June–Sept Mon–Sat 5–10pm. Reduced hours off-season. Closed Oct–Mar. **Prices:** Main courses $9.75–$18.50. Maj CC. ⅄

Ⓢ **Billy's**, 3000 Thomas Dr, Panama City Beach; tel 904/235-2349. **Seafood.** You can write whatever you wish on the dollar bills that cover the walls and ceiling of this casual establishment. What's more, you'll get your money's worth of Maine lobster, oysters, Florida blue crab, and sandwiches. **FYI:** Reservations not accepted. Beer and wine only. **Open:** Daily 11am–9:30pm. Closed Dec 25. **Prices:** Main courses $3.50–$13.95. Maj CC. ☑ ⅄

★ **Boar's Head Restaurant**, 17290 Front Beach Rd, Panama City Beach; tel 904/234-6628. **New American.** The pub-style decor of this comfortable establishment, complete with fireplace, sets the stage for a British-inspired menu. Specialties include prime rib of beef with Yorkshire pudding on the side. Extensive wine list. A local favorite for over 15 years. **FYI:** Reservations accepted. Children's menu. **Open:** HS Apr–Sept Sun–Thurs 4:30–9:30pm, Fri–Sat 4:30–10pm. Reduced hours off-season. Closed some hols; Dec 14–30. **Prices:** Main courses $10.95–$22.95. Maj CC. ☑ ⅄

Cajun Inn, in Edgewater Beach Resort Shopping Center, 477 Beckrich Rd, Panama City Beach; tel 904/235-9987. **Cajun/Seafood.** A fun, casual spot with seating at booths amid a jungle of plants. Menu offers boiled crayfish and other seafood dishes prepared Cajun-style. A variety of sandwiches and specials are available at lunch. **FYI:** Reservations not accepted. Children's menu. Beer and wine only. **Open:** Daily 11am–10pm. Closed Dec 25. **Prices:** Main courses $3.95–$11.95. Ltd CC. ⅄

Captain Anderson's Restaurant, 5551 N Lagoon Dr, Panama City Beach; tel 904/234-2225. **Seafood/Steak.** Come early to see the fishing boats unload their catch. You can dine indoors at a table made from an old World War II Liberty Ship hatch cover, or outdoors on the rooftop deck. A variety of seafood dishes, steaks, and pastas are available. **FYI:** Reservations not accepted. Children's menu. **Open:** HS June–Aug daily 4–10pm. Reduced hours off-season. Closed some hols; Nov–Jan. **Prices:** Main courses $11–$27. Maj CC. 🍽 🖼 ⅄

Captain Davis Dockside Restaurant, 5550 N Lagoon Dr, Panama City Beach; tel 904/234-3608. **Seafood/Steak.** A casual, nautically themed, waterside seafood eatery where the catch of the day is served fried, broiled, or char-broiled. **FYI:** Reservations not accepted. Children's menu. **Open:** Mon–Tues 5–9:30pm, Thurs–Fri 5–9:30pm, Sat–Sun 4–10pm. Closed some hols; mid-Nov–mid-Feb. **Prices:** Main courses $9.95–$23.95. Maj CC. 🖼 ⅄

JP's Restaurant and Bar, 617 Azalea St, Panama City Beach; tel 904/234-7147. **New American.** Families and seniors should appreciate this open, airy restaurant. The menu offers seafood dishes, steaks, and pastas at affordable prices. Both lunch and early-bird dinner specials are available. **FYI:** Reservations accepted. Jazz. Children's menu. **Open:** Mon–Sat 11am–10:30pm. **Prices:** Main courses $7.95–$18.95. Maj CC. ☑ ⅄

Ⓢ **Mariner Restaurant**, 9104 Front Beach Rd, Panama City Beach; tel 904/234-8450. 2 mi W of Hathaway Bridge. **Seafood/Buffet.** Quite a find for budget-minded diners. This basic dining room offers an all-you-can-eat buffet at $14.95 for adults, $6.50 for children; it's free for kids under 3. **FYI:** Reservations not accepted. Children's menu. **Open:** Lunch daily 11am–2:30pm; dinner daily 5–10pm. **Prices:** Main courses $7–$18.95. Maj CC. 🍴 ⅄

Montego Bay Seafood House and Oyster Bar, 4920 Thomas Dr, Panama City Beach; tel 904/234-8686. **Seafood/Steak.** A fun, colorful, active, beach-themed eatery that's popular with families. The Captain's Catch is a favorite among patrons. **FYI:** Reservations not accepted. Children's menu. Beer and wine only. **Open:** HS Apr–Aug daily 11am–11pm. Reduced hours off-season. Closed some hols. **Prices:** Main courses $9–$13. Maj CC. ■

The Terrace Court, in Marriott's Bay Point Resort, 100 Delwood Beach Rd, Panama City Beach; tel 904/235-6914. **Continental.** Elegant, romantic dining in a room outfitted with a grand piano, lovely flowers, and glittering chandeliers. The menu offers chateaubriand for two and rack of lamb as well as fresh seafood and veal entrees. **FYI:** Reservations accepted. Piano. Jacket required. **Open:** Dinner Wed–Sat 6–10pm. **Prices:** Main courses $14–$24. Maj CC. ♥ &

Attractions ■

Museum of Man in the Sea, 17314 Back Beach Rd; tel 904/235-4101. Among the diving-related exhibits are artifacts recovered from shipwrecks, including items from the Spanish galleon *Atocha* (a 25-minute video chronicles its discovery) and relics from the early days of scuba diving. Also displays on oceanography, marine life, and underwater archeology. **Open:** Daily 9am–5pm. Closed some hols. $$

Gulf World, 15412 Front Beach Rd; tel 904/234-5271. Set in a landscaped tropical garden, this marine park has continuously running shows starring porpoises, sea lions, and parrots, and is home to penguins, sea turtles, alligators, and other creatures. Visitors can also witness shark feedings, scuba demonstrations, and underwater shows. **Open:** Mem Day–Labor Day, daily 9am–7pm, rest of year 9am–3pm. Closed some hols. $$$$

Zoo World Zoological & Botanical Park, 9008 Front Beach Rd (Fla 98); tel 904/230-0096. More than 100 species live here in re-created natural habitats, including many rare and endangered animals. Visitors can see orangutans and other primates, big cats, and reptiles. **Open:** Daily 9am–sunset. $$$

Miracle Strip Amusement Park, 12000 Front Beach Rd; tel 904/234-5810. A family-oriented park with 9 acres of rides and attractions, food concessions, and a full-service snack bar. **Open:** Mid-Mar–May, Fri– Sat 1–11:30pm; June–Labor Day, Mon–Fri 6–11:30pm, Sat 1–11:30pm, Sun 3–11:30pm. $$$$

Shipwreck Island Water Park, 12000 Front Beach Rd; tel 904/234-0368. A 6-acre water park built around a tropical theme.

Highlights include 1,600-foot river for tubing, Speed Slide, White Water Tube Trip, and wave pool. Children's area, lifeguard. **Open:** April–Sept, daily 10:30am–5:30pm. $$$$

Shell Island. Accessible only by boat, this 7½-mile long, 1-mile-wide barrier island is off the coast of St Andrews State Recreation Area (see below). The uninhabited natural preserve offers terrific opportunities for shell collecting, swimming, and sunbathing on the brilliant white sand beach. Several boats offer day-trip excursions to Shell Island boat from Panama City Beach marinas. One of the most popular is the double-decker sailing daily at 9am and 1pm from **Captain Anderson's Marina**, 1550 Thomas Dr, at Grand Lagoon Dr (tel 914/234-3435). $$$

St Andrews State Recreation Area, 4415 Thomas Dr; tel 904/233-5140. Located between the Gulf of Mexico and St Andrews Bay, 3 miles east of Panama City Beach, are over 1,000 acres of dazzling beaches topped by towering sand dunes. The area also features pine woodlands and the Grand Lagoon. Activities include swimming, scuba diving, boating, fishing from piers and jetties, picnicking, and camping. Nature trails, boat trips to Shell Island (see above). **Open:** Daily 8am-sunset. $$

PENSACOLA
Map page M-2, B2

See also Gulf Breeze, Navarre Beach, Pensacola Beach

Hotels ■

≡≡ **Days Inn Downtown**, 710 N Palafox St, Pensacola, FL 32501; tel 904/438-4922 or toll free 800/329-7466; fax 904/438-7999. Cervantes St exit off I-110. An economically priced, well-kept older facility, close to the historic district. **Rooms:** 156 rms. CI 3pm/CO noon. Nonsmoking rms avail. **Amenities:** ■ A/C, satel TV w/movies, in-rm safe. **Services:** ✗ ⌂ ⌀ ⌁ **Facilities:** ⌂ ⌂ 1 rst, 1 bar, washer/dryer. Outdoor pool was under renovation. **Rates:** HS Easter–Labor Day $60–$65 S; $65–$80 D. Extra person $5. Children under 18 stay free. Min stay spec evnts. Lower rates off-season. Higher rates for spec evnts/hols. Spec packages avail. Pking: Outdoor, free. Maj CC.

≡≡ **New World Landing**, 600 S Palafox St, Pensacola, FL 32501; tel 904/432-4111; fax 904/435-8939. Garden St exit off I-110. Attractive hotel designed with natural woods and brick and overseen by a dedicated staff. **Rooms:** 16 rms and stes. CI 2pm/CO noon. Nonsmoking rms avail. Rooms are individually decorated. **Amenities:** ■ ⌀ ⌁ A/C, cable TV. **Services:** ✗ ⌂ ⌀ **Facilities:** ⌂ & 1 rst (*see also* "Restaurants" below), 1 bar. The restaurant is well-known throughout the region. Pub-style lounge with wooden bar. **Rates:** $70 S; $80 D; from $125 ste. Extra person $10. Children under 18 stay free. Pking: Outdoor, free. Maj CC.

≣≣≣ **Pensacola Grand Hotel**, 200 E Gregory St, Pensacola, FL 32501; tel 904/433-3336 or toll free 800/348-3336; fax 904/432-7572. Garden St exit off I-110. Unique hotel in the Seville Historic District on the site of the former L & N Train Depot, built in 1912. The beautifully restored grand lobby, which incorporates the antiquated station, contains an ornate railroad clock, the original oak stair rails, mosaic tile floors, and antique furniture. The 2-story glass galleria links the historic depot to the modern 15-floor tower housing guest rooms. **Rooms:** 212 rms and stes. CI 3pm/CO 1pm. Express checkout avail. Nonsmoking rms avail. Executive floors have city views. **Amenities:** 🛏 🅰 🖵 ♟ A/C, cable TV. Some units w/minibars, some w/Jacuzzis. **Services:** ✗ 🚗 🖾 🛎 🖐 Car-rental desk, babysitting. **Facilities:** 🖼 ⛳️ 600 ♿ 1 rst, 2 bars, games rm. **Rates:** $80–$90 S; $90–$100 D; from $150 ste. Extra person $10. Min stay. Spec packages avail. Pking: Outdoor, free. Maj CC.

≣≣ **Residence Inn**, 7230 Plantation Rd, Pensacola, FL 32504; tel 904/479-1000 or toll free 800/331-3131; fax 904/477-3399. Exit 5 off I-110. Residential-style living; units have kitchens and living and sleeping areas. Handy to the interstate and University Mall. **Rooms:** 64 stes. CI noon/CO noon. **Amenities:** 🛏 🅰 🖵 A/C, cable TV, refrig. 1 unit w/minibar, some w/terraces, all w/fireplaces. **Services:** ✗ 🖾 🛎 🖐 Babysitting. **Facilities:** 🖼 40 ♿ Sauna, washer/dryer. **Rates (CP):** From $85 ste. Children under 18 stay free. Spec packages avail. Pking: Outdoor, free. Maj CC.

Motels

≣≣ **Comfort Inn**, 13585 Perdido Key Dr, Pensacola, FL 32507 (Perdido Key); tel 904/492-2755 or toll free 800/554-8879; fax 904/492-9587. Close to the gulf, near Johnson Beach, this mid-range offering is a standard-bearer for families. **Rooms:** 99 rms. CI 4pm/CO 11am. Nonsmoking rms avail. **Amenities:** 🛏 A/C, cable TV. **Services:** 🛎 🖐 Fishing charters can be arranged. **Facilities:** 🖼 ♿ Games rm. Restaurants nearby. **Rates (CP):** HS May–Aug $63–$65 S; $65–$75 D. Extra person $10. Children under 18 stay free. Min stay spec evnts. Lower rates off-season. Higher rates for spec evnts/hols. Spec packages avail. Pking: Outdoor, free. Maj CC. Golf packages available.

≣≣ **Hampton Inn–University Mall**, 7330 Plantation Rd, Pensacola, FL 32504; tel 904/477-3333 or toll free 800/426-7866; fax 904/477-3333 ext 503. 3 mi N of Pensacola, exit 5 off I-10. Behind University Mall. Fairly priced middle-grade

choice. Mall and restaurants are within walking distance. **Rooms:** 124 rms and effic. CI 3pm/CO noon. Nonsmoking rms avail. **Amenities:** 🛏 🅰 A/C, cable TV w/movies. Some units w/minibars. **Services:** 🚗 🖾 🛎 🖐 Babysitting. **Facilities:** 12 ♿ Washer/dryer. Guests have access to the pool at the Holiday Inn nearby. **Rates (CP):** HS Easter–Labor Day $53 S; $60 D. Min stay spec evnts. Lower rates off-season. Higher rates for spec evnts/hols. Spec packages avail. Pking: Outdoor, free. Maj CC.

≣≣ **Holiday Inn Express**, 6501 Pensacola Blvd, Pensacola, FL 32505; tel 904/476-7200 or toll free 800/HOLIDAY; fax 904/476-7200. Exit 3A off I-10. Basic motel. Offers rates lower than traditional Holiday Inns. **Rooms:** 178 rms. CI 3pm/CO noon. Express checkout avail. Nonsmoking rms avail. **Amenities:** 🛏 🅰 ♟ A/C, satel TV w/movies. 1 unit w/minibar. **Services:** 🖾 🛎 🖐 **Facilities:** 🖼 200 ♿ Washer/dryer. **Rates (CP):** HS May–Sept $45–$55 S or D. Extra person $6. Children under 18 stay free. Lower rates off-season. Spec packages avail. Pking: Indoor, free. Maj CC.

≣≣≣ **Holiday Inn University Mall**, 7200 N Plantation Rd, Pensacola, FL 32504; tel 904/474-0100 or toll free 800/465-4329. Exit 5 off I-110. Located some 5 miles north of downtown Pensacola, 2 miles from University of Western Florida and near the University Mall complex. **Rooms:** 152 rms and stes. CI noon/CO noon. Nonsmoking rms avail. **Amenities:** 🛏 🅰 ♟ A/C, cable TV w/movies. **Services:** ✗ 🚗 🖾 🛎 🖐 **Facilities:** 🖼 350 ♿ 1 rst, 2 bars (w/entertainment), washer/dryer. Comedy club 3 times a week. **Rates (AP):** HS Apr–Aug $65–$75 S; $69–$83 D; from $132 ste. Extra person $6. Children under 17 stay free. Lower rates off-season. Spec packages avail. Pking: Outdoor, free. Maj CC.

≣≣ **Ramada Inn Bayview**, 7601 Scenic Hwy, Pensacola, FL 32504; tel 904/477-7155 or toll free 800/282-1212. Exit 6 off I-10. **Rooms:** 150 rms and stes. CI 3pm/CO noon. Express checkout avail. Nonsmoking rms avail. **Amenities:** 🛏 🅰 ♟ A/C, cable TV w/movies. Some units w/minibars, all w/terraces. **Services:** ✗ 🚗 🖾 🛎 🖐 **Facilities:** 🖼 ⛳️ 100 ♿ 1 rst, 1 bar (w/entertainment), games rm, whirlpool. **Rates:** HS Apr–Aug 15 $59–$77 S or D; from $89 ste. Extra person $6. Children under 18 stay free. Min stay spec evnts. Lower rates off-season. Spec packages avail. Pking: Outdoor, free. Maj CC.

≣≣ **Ramada Inn North**, 6550 Pensacola Blvd, Pensacola, FL 32505; tel 904/477-0711 or toll free 800/228-2828; fax 904/477-0711 ext 602. Good, no-nonsense accommodations. **Rooms:** 106 rms and stes. CI 2pm/CO noon. Express checkout avail. Nonsmoking rms avail. **Amenities:** 🛏 🅰 🖵 ♟ A/C, cable TV, voice mail, shoe polisher. Some units w/minibars, some w/terraces. **Services:** ✗ 🚗 🖾 🛎 Babysitting. **Facilities:** 🖼 50 ♿ 1 rst, 1 bar, washer/dryer. **Rates:** HS Apr–Sept $49–$53 S;

$55–$59 D; from $99 ste. Extra person $5. Children under 18 stay free. Min stay spec evnts. Lower rates off-season. Spec packages avail. Pking: Outdoor, free. Maj CC.

≣ **Red Roof Inn**, 7340 Plantation Road, Pensacola, FL 32504; tel 904/476-7960 or toll free 800/THE-ROOF. Exit 5 off I-110. Relatively new budget motel with clean, simple rooms. **Rooms:** 108 rms. CI 3pm/CO noon. Nonsmoking rms avail. **Amenities:** 🛁 A/C, cable TV. **Services:** 🛏 🛎 **Facilities:** ⬆ **Rates:** HS May–Sept $38–$43 S; $44–$49 D. Extra person $6. Children under 18 stay free. Lower rates off-season. Higher rates for spec evnts/hols. Spec packages avail. Pking: Outdoor, free. Maj CC.

≣≣ **Seville Inn**, 223 E Garden St, Pensacola, FL 32501; tel 904/433-8331 or toll free 800/277-7275; fax 904/432-6849. Garden St exit off I-110. Renovated in 1993. Downtown location is convenient for commercial travelers as well as families. **Rooms:** 125 rms. CI 3pm/CO 11am. Nonsmoking rms avail. **Amenities:** 🛁 🍽 A/C, cable TV. **Services:** 🚐 🖼 🛏 🛎 **Facilities:** 🎣 💯 ⬆ Washer/dryer. **Rates:** HS May–Aug $30–$49 S; $36–$59 D. Extra person $10. Children under 18 stay free. Min stay spec evnts. Lower rates off-season. Spec packages avail. Pking: Outdoor, free. Maj CC.

≣ **Shoney's Inn**, 8086 N Davis Hwy, Pensacola, FL 32504; tel 904/484-8070 or toll free 800/222-2222; fax 904/484-3853. Exit 5 off I-110. Satisfactory for a short stay. **Rooms:** 115 rms, stes, and effic. CI 3pm/CO noon. Express checkout avail. Nonsmoking rms avail. **Amenities:** 🛁 ⚙ 📺 A/C, satel TV w/movies, refrig. Some units w/minibars. **Services:** ✕ 🚐 🖼 🛏 Babysitting. **Facilities:** 🎣 💯 ⬆ 1 rst, washer/dryer. **Rates:** HS May 28–Sept 6 $59–$71 S or D; from $71 ste; from $71 effic. Extra person $6. Children under 18 stay free. Min stay spec evnts. Lower rates off-season. Pking: Outdoor, free. Maj CC.

Restaurants 🍴

★ **Boy on a Dolphin**, 400 Pensacola Beach, Pensacola; tel 904/932-7949. Chase St exit off I-110. **Greek.** Floor-to-ceiling windows provide views of the bay and docks while you dine on Greek specialties and such classic seafood dishes as oysters Rockefeller. **FYI:** Reservations recommended. Guitar/singer. Children's menu. **Open:** Mon–Sat 4–11pm, Sun 11am–11pm. Closed some hols. **Prices:** Main courses $5.95–$21.95. Maj CC. 🍽 🖼 ⬆

⑤ **Hopkin's Boarding House**, 900 N Spring St, Pensacola; tel 904/438-3979. Cervantes St exit off I-110. **American.** A friendly, cozy eatery serving traditional, homestyle meals and favorite regional dishes. **FYI:** Reservations not accepted. No liquor license. No smoking. **Open:** Breakfast Tues–Sun 7–9:30am; lunch Tues–Sun 11am–2pm; dinner Tues–Sun 5–7:30pm. Closed Dec 25. **Prices:** Main courses $6.50–$6.50. No CC. 📷

♥ **Jamie's**, 424 E Zaragoza St, Pensacola; tel 904/434-2911. Garden St exit off I-110. **French.** An elegant, romantic French dining room in the Seville Historic District. **FYI:** Reservations recommended. Guitar. Dress code. Beer and wine only. **Open:** Lunch Tues–Sat 11:30am–2:30pm; dinner Mon–Sat 6–10pm. Closed some hols. **Prices:** Main courses $17.50–$21.75. Maj CC. ♥ 🍴

★ **McGuire's Irish Pub & Brewery**, 600 E Gregory St, Pensacola (East Hill); tel 904/433-6789. Cervantes or Gregory St exit off I-110. **Seafood/Steak.** A Gaelic-style tavern where you'll find steak, seafood dishes, and pub fare at fair prices. **FYI:** Reservations not accepted. Guitar/sing along/singer. Children's menu. **Open:** Mon–Sat 11am–11pm, Sun 11am–4pm. Closed some hols. **Prices:** Main courses $13.95–$18.95. Maj CC. 🍴 🍷 📷

♥ **New World Landing Restaurant**, 600 S Palafox St, Pensacola; tel 904/434-7736. Garden St exit off I-110. **Regional American/Seafood/Steak.** Charming restaurant in an old brick building, with dining rooms recalling different periods in Pensacola's colorful history. Chandeliers, antique furnishings, and rich wood paneling enhance the setting. Dine on seafood in wine or butter sauce, or on prime rib, steak, or veal. **FYI:** Reservations recommended. Children's menu. **Open:** Lunch Tues–Fri 11am–2pm; dinner Tues–Sat 5:30–9:30pm. Closed some hols. **Prices:** Main courses $9.99–$19.99. Maj CC. ♥ 🍷 ⬆

♥ **Skopelos on the Bay**, 670 Scenic Hwy, Pensacola; tel 904/432-6565. Cervantes St exit off I-110. **Seafood/Steak.** One of the area's finest dining experiences, featuring Greek-inspired seafood dishes. **FYI:** Reservations accepted. Children's menu. **Open:** dinner Tues–Sat 5–10:30pm. Closed some hols. **Prices:** Main courses $12.95–$17.95. Maj CC. ♥ 🖼 ⬆

★ **Strega Nona's Bakery & Cafe**, 1010 N 12th Ave, Tower East, Pensacola (East Hill); tel 904/433-3055. Brent Lane exit off I-110. **Coffeehouse/Vegetarian.** A coffeehouse that attracts a hip, health-conscious crowd. Vegetarian dishes featured. **FYI:** Reservations recommended. Guitar/singer. Beer and wine only. No smoking. **Open:** Sun–Mon 7am–4pm, Tues–Thurs 7am–midnight. Closed some hols. **Prices:** Main courses $3–$7.95. Ltd CC.

★ **The Yacht Restaurant and Lounge**, in Pitt Slip Marina, 600 S Barracks St, Slip No 1, Pensacola (Seville Historic District); tel 904/432-3707. Chase St exit off I-110. **Regional American/Seafood/Steak.** Seafood and steaks are served in a nautically themed restaurant overlooking the marina. **FYI:** Reservations recommended. Children's menu. **Open:** Dinner Tues–Sun 5–10pm; brunch, Sun 11am–2pm. Closed some hols. **Prices:** Main courses $8.95–$16.95. Maj CC. ♥ ▨

★ **Ye Olde Beef & Ale House**, in Harbour Village at Pitt Slip Marina, 600 S Barracks St, Pensacola; tel 904/435-9719. Garden St exit off I-110. **American.** An old-style tavern serving burgers, steaks, and a selection of interesting beers. **FYI:** Reservations accepted. Band/rock. Children's menu. **Open:** Daily 11am–1am. **Prices:** Main courses $8.95–$18.95. Maj CC. ▦ ▨ &

Attractions ▦

HISTORIC PENSACOLA VILLAGE

Seville Historic District and Historic Pensacola Village; tel 904/444-8905. Listed on the National Register of Historic Places, the downtown district, which includes Seville Square, has some of Florida's oldest homes, along with charming boutiques and restaurants. Among the landmarks to visit in the 4-block area of **Historic Pensacola Village** are the Museum of Industry, which contains a working sawmill, and the Museum of Commerce, with many of the storefronts and shop-fittings of turn-of-the-century Pensacola; the French Creole Charles Lavalle House; the elegant Victorian Dorr House; and the French colonial–Creole Quina House. The 1809 **Julee Cottage Black History Museum** records the life and deeds of Julee Panton, a "free-woman of color" who owned her own land and business and loaned money to slaves so they could buy their own freedom. Also in the area are **St Michael's Cemetery,** which has been in use since the 1780s, and **Old Christ Church,** which houses the Pensacola Historical Museum (see below).

Combination tickets to Historic Pensacola Village and the TT Wentworth, Jr, Florida State Museum (see below) are good for an entire week and can be purchased at the museum or at the Ticket Information Center, 205 E Zaragoza St. **Open:** Mon–Sat 10am–4pm. $$$

Pensacola Historical Museum, 405 S Adams St; tel 904/433-1559. Located in the landmark Old Christ Church building (1832), used by Union troops during the Civil War as a hospital and barracks. Exhibits trace Pensacola's history from earliest times and feature Native American artifacts, photography, and a 2,000-volume library. **Open:** Mon–Sat 9am–4:30pm; Dec–Feb, Mon–Sat 10am–4:30pm. Closed some hols. $

T T Wentworth, Jr, Florida State Museum, 330 S Jefferson St; tel 904/444-8586. Originally the city hall, this 1907 landmark Renaissance revival building contains an eclectic collection of objects and memorabilia pertaining to the art, archeology, and

history of western Florida. Discovery Museum for children on 3rd floor has hands-on exhibits. **Open:** Open: Daily 10am–4pm. Closed Sun and some hols. $$

OTHER ATTRACTIONS

Pensacola Museum of Art, 407 S Jefferson St; tel 904/432-6247. Housed in a 2-story mission revival building that was once used as the city jail, the museum features permanent and changing exhibits ranging from European masters to the avant-garde. **Open:** Tues–Fri 10am–5pm, Sat 10am–4pm, Sun 1–4pm. Free.

Civil War Soldiers Museum, 108 S Palafox Place; tel 904/469-1900. Life-size dioramas, paintings, and artifacts dealing with the Civil War. The bookstore features more than 500 titles, as well as art prints, period music, and such souvenirs as Confederate soldiers' caps. **Open:** Mon–Sat 10am–4:30pm. Closed some hols. $$

National Museum of Naval Aviation, 1750 Radford Blvd, Suite C; tel 904/452-3604. One of the world's largest air and space museums and located at the world's largest air station, this major attraction traces the history and development of Navy, Marine Corps, and Coast Guard aviation. Nearly 100 historic aircraft are on display, from biplanes and blimps to such space-age craft as the Skylab command module and an F-14 Tomcat fighter plane. The museum is also home to memorabilia, scale models, and high-tech photography. **Open:** Daily 9am–5pm. Free.

Palafox Historic District; tel 904/444-8905. Formerly Old Pensacola's harborfront commercial center, this area features fine Spanish Renaissance–style buildings. At one time the area had such outstanding hotels as the San Carlos, at Palafox and Garden Sts, once considered one of the South's finest but closed for many years. Other structures have been restored, though, including the ornate **Saenger Theater,** with wrought-iron balconies, now the base of the Pensacola Symphony Orchestra. **Plaza Ferdinand VII,** part of Pensacola's first settlement, is a National Historic Landmark. At a ceremony here in 1821 Gen Andrew Jackson formally accepted Florida into the United States. His statue commemorates the event.

North Hill Preservation District; tel 904/444-8905. Located just north of the Palafox Historic District, this 50-block district contains more than 500 homes built for Pensacola's professional classes between 1870 and 1930. Homes in this fashionable, tree-studded area reflect a wide variety of architectural styles—Tudor revival, neoclassical, Queen Anne, Victorian, and art moderne are just some. Free.

Bay Bluffs Park, Scenic Hwy (US 90) and Summit. Part of the Scenic Highway, where US 90 heads northeast to Tallahassee, the park offers 20 acres of nature trails and boardwalks. An elevated boardwalk descends stunning red bluffs, which afford spectacular views of Pensacola Bay.

PENSACOLA BEACH

Map page M-2, C2

Hotels

Best Western Pensacola Beach, 16 Via de Luna Dr, Pensacola Beach, FL 32561; tel 904/934-3300 or toll free 800/934-3301; fax 904/934-4366. Chase St exit off I-110. A beach location for budget-minded families. **Rooms:** 123 rms and stes. CI 2pm/CO 11am. Nonsmoking rms avail. **Amenities:** A/C, cable TV w/movies, refrig. **Services:** Babysitting. **Facilities:** 1 rst, 1 bar, 1 beach (ocean), playground, washer/dryer. Cabana bar on beach. **Rates:** HS Apr–Sept $95–$105 S or D; from $95 ste. Extra person $10. Children under 12 stay free. Min stay spec evnts. Lower rates off-season. Spec packages avail. Pking: Outdoor, free. Maj CC.

Clarion Suites Resort & Convention Center, 20 Via de Luna Dr, Pensacola Beach, FL 32561; tel 904/932-4300 or toll free 800/874-5303; fax 904/934-9112. Chase St exit off I-110. This beach hotel is well suited for groups and families. **Rooms:** 86 stes. CI 3pm/CO 11am. Express checkout avail. Nonsmoking rms avail. All suites have water views. **Amenities:** A/C, cable TV, refrig, shoe polisher. Some units w/terraces. **Services:** Babysitting. **Facilities:** 1 beach (ocean), washer/dryer. **Rates:** HS Mem Day–Labor Day from $105 ste. Extra person $10. Children under 18 stay free. Min stay spec evnts. Lower rates off-season. Spec packages avail. Pking: Outdoor, free. Maj CC.

The Dunes, 333 Fort Pickens Rd, Pensacola Beach, FL 32561; tel 904/932-3536 or toll free 800/83-DUNES; fax 904/932-7088. Chase St exit off I-10. An attractive lodging in 2 buildings. **Rooms:** 140 rms and stes. CI 3pm/CO 11am. Nonsmoking rms avail. Routine room decor. **Amenities:** A/C, cable TV w/movies, in-rm safe. Some units w/terraces, some w/Jacuzzis. **Services:** Car-rental desk, social director, children's program, babysitting. **Facilities:** 1 rst, 1 bar, 1 beach (ocean). The beach and pools are in superior condition. **Rates:** HS Apr–Labor Day $75–$239 S or D; from $215 ste. Extra person $10. Children under 18 stay free. Min stay HS. Lower rates off-season. Spec packages avail. Pking: Outdoor, free. Maj CC.

Holiday Inn Pensacola Beach, 165 Fort Pickens Rd, Pensacola Beach, FL 32561; tel 904/932-5361 or toll free 800/HOLIDAY; fax 904/932-7121. Chase St exit off I-110. Situated between the bay and the beach, this beach-lover's hotel has many repeat guests. **Rooms:** 150 rms and stes. CI 3pm/CO 11am. Express checkout avail. Nonsmoking rms avail. **Amenities:** A/C, cable TV, refrig, in-rm safe. All units w/terraces. **Services:** Babysitting. **Facilities:** 1 rst, 2 bars, 2 beaches (ocean, bay), games rm, washer/dryer. Rooftop lounge offers panoramic views. Seafood restaurant has waterview dining. **Rates:** HS Apr–Sept $90–$110 S or D; from $160 ste. Extra person $10. Children under 19 stay free. Min stay HS and spec evnts. Lower rates off-season. Higher rates for spec evnts/hols. Spec packages avail. Pking: Outdoor, free. Maj CC.

Motel

Five Flags Motel, 299 Fort Pickens Rd, Pensacola Beach, FL 32561; tel 904/932-3586. Chase St exit off I-110. A 2-story family motel on the beach. **Rooms:** 49 rms. CI 3pm/CO 11am. **Amenities:** A/C, cable TV. All units w/terraces. **Services:** **Facilities:** 1 beach (ocean). Pool heated in winter. **Rates:** HS May–Sept $69 S or D. Min stay HS and wknds. Lower rates off-season. Pking: Outdoor, free. Maj CC.

Resort

Beachside Resort & Conference Center, 14 Via de Luna Dr, Pensacola Beach, FL 32561; tel 904/932-5331 or toll free 800/232-2416; fax 904/932-3011. Chase St exit off I-110. 5 acres. A beach offering popular with a mix of families, couples, and small groups. **Rooms:** 115 rms, stes, and effic. CI 3pm/CO 11am. Nonsmoking rms avail. **Amenities:** A/C, cable TV w/movies. All units w/terraces. **Services:** Babysitting. **Facilities:** 1 rst, 1 bar, 1 beach (ocean), games rm, playground, washer/dryer. **Rates:** HS May–Sept $75–$150 S or D; from $125 ste; from $125 effic. Extra person $10. Children under 18 stay free. Min stay spec evnts. Lower rates off-season. Spec packages avail. Pking: Outdoor, free. Maj CC.

Restaurant

Jubilee Restaurant, 400 Quietwater Beach Rd, Pensacola Beach; tel 904/934-3108. Garden St exit off I-110. **Seafood/Steak.** Beachside restaurant complex, complete with Island Bar and cocktail lounge, offering casual dining. The Sunday brunch attracts quite a crowd. **FYI:** Reservations accepted. Band/guitar. Children's menu. **Open:** Mon–Sat 11am–midnight, Sun 9am–3pm. Closed some hols. **Prices:** Main courses $16.95–$24.95. Maj CC.

PINE ISLAND

Map page M-6, C2

See **Bokeelia, Malacha, St James City**

Restaurant 🍴

Waterfront Restaurant and Marina, 2131 Oleander St, Pine Island; tel 813/283-0592. **Seafood.** Dine overlooking the marina. Beef, chicken, and seafood are among the offerings. **FYI:** Reservations not accepted. Beer and wine only. **Open:** Daily 11am–8pm. **Prices:** Main courses $7–$20. Ltd CC. 🍽 🖼 ⚹

PLANTATION

Map page M-11, A2

Restaurants 🍴

Brasserie Max, in the Fashion Mall, 321 N University Dr, Plantation; tel 305/424-8000. 1 block N of Broward Blvd. **Regional American.** A cozy cafe with dark wood in the dining room and a brick wall in the appealing lounge. The menu offers such items as oak-grilled chicken and New York strip steak. A good value. **FYI:** Reservations not accepted. Jazz. Children's menu. **Open:** Mon–Thurs 11:30am–10pm, Fri–Sat 11:30am–11pm, Sun 11am–10pm. Closed some hols. **Prices:** Main courses $7.95–$14.95. Maj CC. ⚹

Outback Steakhouse, 1823 N Pine Island Rd, Plantation; tel 305/370-9956. **Steak.** Enjoy ribs, chicken, or the daily fish grilled to order as you relax in a spacious booth at this casual, comfortable eatery. Also at: 650 Riverside Dr, Coral Springs (305/345-5965). **FYI:** Reservations not accepted. Children's menu. **Open:** Mon–Thurs 4:30–10:30pm, Fri–Sat 4–11:30pm, Sun 4:30–10:30pm. Closed Dec 25. **Prices:** Main courses $7.95–$17.95. Maj CC. ⚹

POINT WASHINGTON

Map page M-2, B4

Attraction 🏛

Eden State Gardens and Mansion; tel 904/231-4214. A restored late 19th–century Greek revival manor. The white-columned, 2-story Wesley Mansion contains period architectural details and is furnished with 18th-century antiques, among other items. The mansion stands amid huge moss-draped oaks, and the gardens are filled with azaleas, camellias, and other typical southern flowers. Mansion tours given hourly Thurs–Mon 9am–4pm. **Open:** Park, daily 8am–sunset. $

POMPANO BEACH

Map page M-11, A2

Hotels 🏨

≣≣≣ **Beachcomber Hotel and Villas**, 1200 S Ocean Blvd, Pompano Beach, FL 33062; tel 305/941-7830 or toll free 800/231-2423; fax 305/942-7680. Exit 34A off I-95. Set on lush, tropical oceanside grounds, with a relaxed atmosphere enhanced by rattan-furnished lobby with fountain. **Rooms:** 138 rms, stes, and effic; 9 ctges/villas. CI 3pm/CO 11am. Nonsmoking rms avail. Generally large rooms, with ocean views, tropical colors, dust ruffles, and large baths. **Amenities:** 🛗 🌂 📺 ☎ A/C, cable TV w/movies, refrig, in-rm safe. Some units w/terraces. **Services:** ✕ 🖼 🍴 Car-rental desk. **Facilities:** 🔧 🏊 ⚹ 1 rst, 2 bars (1 w/entertainment), 1 beach (ocean), lawn games, playground, washer/dryer. **Rates:** HS Jan 16–Apr 15 $87–$182 S or D; from $182 ste; from $152 effic; from $185 ctge/villa. Extra person $10. Children under 12 stay free. Min stay spec evnts. Lower rates off-season. Higher rates for spec evnts/hols. AP rates avail. Spec packages avail. Pking: Outdoor, free. Maj CC.

≣≣ **Holiday Inn Pompano Beach**, 1350 S Ocean Blvd, Pompano Beach, FL 33062; tel 305/941-7300 or toll free 800/332-2735; fax 305/941-7300 ext 7793. ¾ mi S of Atlantic Blvd (Fla 814). Pleasant lodging straddles both sides of Fla A1A. **Rooms:** 112 rms, stes, and effic; 21 ctges/villas. CI 2pm/CO 11am. Express checkout avail. Nonsmoking rms avail. **Amenities:** 🛗 🌂 A/C, cable TV w/movies, refrig. All units w/terraces. **Services:** ✕ 🔑 🖼 🍴 Social director, children's program, babysitting. Water taxi stops at Intracoastal Highway dock. **Facilities:** 🔧 🏊 ⛵3 ⚓ 🎣 🍴 ⚹ 1 rst, 2 bars (1 w/entertainment), 1 beach (ocean), board surfing, games rm, lawn games, snorkeling, day-care ctr, washer/dryer. Guests receive discounts for nearby Gold's Gym. **Rates:** HS Dec–Apr $115–$165 S or D; from $275 ste; from $130 effic; from $155 ctge/villa. Extra person $10. Children under 19 stay free. Lower rates off-season. AP and MAP rates avail. Spec packages avail. Pking: Outdoor, free. Maj CC.

≣≣ **Howard Johnson's Pompano Beach Resort Inn**, 9 N Pompano Beach Blvd, Pompano Beach, FL 33062; tel 305/781-1300 or toll free 800/223-5844; fax 305/782-5585. Centrally located for the beach, shopping, and attractions. A fishing pier is up the street. **Rooms:** 104 rms and effic. CI 3pm/CO noon. Nonsmoking rms avail. Pastel decor and wicker headboards. Most rooms offer ocean views. **Amenities:** ☎ ⚲ A/C, cable TV w/movies. Some units w/terraces. Refrigerators available from front desk for $3 a day. **Services:** ✗ 🚗 🖼 🕭 Free coffee and newspapers are provided in lobby every morning. **Facilities:** 🔂 1 rst, 1 bar, 1 beach (ocean), lifeguard, washer/dryer. **Rates:** HS Feb 1–Apr 9 $110–$130 S or D; from $140 effic. Extra person $10. Children under 18 stay free. Lower rates off-season. Spec packages avail. Pking: Indoor/outdoor, free. Maj CC.

Resort

▆▆▆ **Palm-Aire Spa, Resort & Club**, 2601 Palm-Aire Dr N, Pompano Beach, FL 33069; tel 305/972-3300 or toll free 800/272-5624; fax 305/968-2744. 1,500 acres. A stylish, elaborate resort with lush landscaping. Extensive recreational facilities. **Rooms:** 191 rms, stes, and effic. CI 3pm/CO noon. Nonsmoking rms avail. Soft-toned, plush accommodations are spacious and amply furnished. Many have double baths and closets. **Amenities:** ☎ ⚲ A/C, cable TV w/movies, bathrobes. All units w/terraces. **Services:** ✗ 🗝 🆅🅿 🖼 🕭 Car-rental desk, social director, masseur, babysitting. **Facilities:** 🔂 ♐ ▶94 🖼 ☜31 🏌 🏸 ⛳ 3 rsts, 2 bars (w/entertainment), lifeguard, racquetball, squash, spa, sauna, steam rm, whirlpool, beauty salon, washer/dryer. Spa measures 40,000 square feet and is tended by 80 staffers. **Rates:** HS Dec 13–Mar 31 $338 S; $576 D; from $190 ste; from $165 effic. Extra person $35. Children under 12 stay free. Lower rates off-season. Higher rates for spec evnts/hols. AP and MAP rates avail. Spec packages avail. Pking: Outdoor, free. Maj CC.

Restaurants 🍴

Cafe Maxx, 2601 E Atlantic Blvd, Pompano Beach; tel 305/782-0606. **Regional American/Caribbean.** An inventive new American restaurant outfitted with fine woods, stylish appointments, iron ice cream parlor–style chairs, and an open kitchen. The menu includes sweet onion–crusted yellowtail snapper, lamb, and fillet of veal. There is a bar on the premises. **FYI:** Reservations recommended. Dress code. Beer and wine only. **Open:** Sun–Thurs 5:30–10:30pm, Fri–Sat 5:30–11pm. Closed July 4. **Prices:** Main courses $18–$31. Maj CC. 🆅🅿

Fisherman's Wharf, 222 Pompano Beach Blvd, Pompano Beach; tel 305/941-5522. At Pompano Pier. **New American/Seafood.** A nautically themed haven for seafood lovers, with a big, bustling bar that invites you to linger. The separate dining room has ocean and pier views. Daily specials are offered on 3 separate chalkboards. Outdoor bar. **FYI:** Reservations not ac-

cepted. Band/piano. Children's menu. **Open:** Sun–Thurs 10:30am–midnight, Fri–Sat 10:30am–1am. **Prices:** Main courses $9–$17. Maj CC. 🍽 🖼 ☑ ⛑

Attractions 🖼

Butterfly World, 3600 W Sample Rd (in Coconut Creek); tel 305/977-4400. Amid 3 acres of tropical gardens are thousands of brilliantly colored, exotic butterflies in all stages of life. Visitors can watch butterflies emerge from their cocoons. With an insectarium, butterfly museum, and gift shop. **Open:** Mon–Sat 9am–5pm, Sun from 1 pm. Closed some hols. $$$

Goodyear Blimp Base, 1500 NE Fifth Ave; tel 305/946-8300. Base for the airship *Stars and Stripes,* which visitors may view when the ship is moored. Free.

PONCE INLET
Map page M-7, B3

Attraction 🖼

Ponce de León Inlet Lighthouse, 4931 S Peninsula Dr; tel 904/761-1821. This 175-foot-tall brick lighthouse dates from the mid-1880s and was in operation until 1970. It has since been restored and is now listed in the National Register of Historic Places. The head lighthouse keeper's cottage houses exhibits on navigational aids, marine biology, and ocean exploration. A climb to the top of the lighthouse provides a fantastic panoramic view. **Open:** May–Aug, daily 10am–9pm; Sept–Apr, daily 10am–5pm. Closed Dec 25. $

PONTE VEDRA BEACH
Map page M-5, C4

Resorts 🛏

▆▆▆▆ **The Lodge and Bath Club at Ponte Vedra Beach**, 607 Ponte Vedra Blvd, Ponte Vedra Beach, FL 32082; or toll free 800/243-4304; fax 904/285-9934. In a beautiful location on the ocean. Elaborately decorated deluxe facility with Spanish mission accents. Public areas are delightful venues for relaxing and appreciating the ocean vistas. **Rooms:** 66 rms and stes. CI 4pm/CO noon. Express checkout avail. Nonsmoking rms avail. Handsome accommodations with some very fine appointments. **Amenities:** ☎ ⚲ 🖥 ⚲ A/C, cable TV w/movies, refrig, in-rm safe, bathrobes. All units w/minibars, all w/terraces, some w/fireplaces. **Services:** 🍽 🗝 🆅🅿 🚗 🖼 🕭 Twice-daily maid svce, car-rental desk, social director, masseur, children's program, babysitting. Expert staff. **Facilities:** ⛵ 🚴 ⛰ 🏠 ⚓ 🎾 🏊 ⛳ 2 rsts, 2 bars (1 w/entertainment), 1 beach (ocean), lifeguard, board surfing, spa, sauna, steam rm, whirlpool, day-care ctr. Restaurant and lounge are romantic settings at night. **Rates:** HS Mar–May $189–$229 S or D; from $279 ste. Extra person $20. Children under 16 stay free. Lower rates off-season. AP and MAP rates avail. Spec packages avail. Pking: Indoor/outdoor, free. Maj CC.

▣▣▣▣ **Marriott at Sawgrass Resort**, 1000 TPC Blvd, Ponte Vedra Beach, FL 32082; tel 904/285-7777 or toll free 800/457-GOLF; fax 904/285-0906. 4 mi S of J Turner Butler Blvd on Fla A1A. 25 acres. One of Marriott's prized resort facilities, and with good reason. Its manicured acres contain gorgeous golf greens, waterfalls, lakes, and lagoons spanned by graceful wooden bridges, while the hotel's deluxe lobby is a towering skylit atrium with a waterfall and lush tropical garden. Also, terrific recreational facilities. **Rooms:** 525 rms and stes; 13 ctges/villas. CI 4pm/CO noon. Express checkout avail. Nonsmoking rms avail. Luxurious 1- to 3-bedroom beachfront villas have huge kitchens, living rooms with fireplaces, full dining rooms, and screened wooden decks. **Amenities:** 🏧 ⚏ A/C, cable TV w/movies, refrig. All units w/minibars, all w/terraces. **Services:** ✕ ⌨ ⓋⓅ 🍴 🖼 🛎 🐕 Car-rental desk, social director, masseur, children's program, babysitting. **Facilities:** ⛵ 🚴 ⛰ 🏠 ⛳₉₉ ⚓ 🏊 ⚓₁₀ 🎾 ⬜₅₀₀ 🖥 ⛳ 2 rsts (*see also* "Restaurants" below), 3 bars (1 w/entertainment), 1 beach (ocean), lifeguard, board surfing, snorkeling, spa, sauna, steam rm, whirlpool, day-care ctr, washer/dryer. **Rates:** HS Mar–May $189 S; $209 D; from $500 ste; from $225 ctge/villa. Extra person $20. Children under 18 stay free. Lower rates off-season. Higher rates for spec evnts/hols. Spec packages avail. Pking: Outdoor, free. Maj CC.

▣▣▣▣ **Ponte Vedra Inn & Club**, 200 Ponte Vedra Blvd, Ponte Vedra Beach, FL 32082; tel 904/285-1111 or toll free 800/234-7842; fax 904/285-2111. Bulter Blvd exit off I-95. 300 acres. A wonderful, sprawling country club and spa in the area's high-rent shoreline district. Elegance abounds, from the manicured front lawn that doubles as a putting green to the charming lobby and adjoining Great Lounge, which features overstuffed sofas and armchairs and massive fireplaces all under a beamed cypress ceiling. **Rooms:** 202 rms and stes. Exec-level rms avail. CI 3pm/CO noon. Express checkout avail. Nonsmoking rms avail. Spacious, lovely rooms, some with 4-poster or sleigh beds. **Amenities:** 🏧 ⚏ 📺 🍴 A/C, cable TV, refrig, in-rm safe, bathrobes. All units w/minibars, all w/terraces, some w/fireplaces, some w/Jacuzzis. **Services:** 🍽 ⌨ ⓋⓅ 🍴 🖼 🐕 Twice-daily maid svce, social director, masseur, children's program, babysitting. **Facilities:** ⛵ 🚴 ⛰ 🏠 ⛳₃₆ ⚓₈ 🏊 🎾 🏊 ⬜₄₀₀ 🖥 ⛳

4 rsts, 5 bars (1 w/entertainment), 1 beach (ocean), lifeguard, board surfing, lawn games, spa, sauna, whirlpool, beauty salon, day-care ctr, playground, washer/dryer. Dining rooms range from casual to formal. **Rates:** HS Mar–May $175–$295 S or D; from $265 ste. Children under 18 stay free. Lower rates off-season. AP and MAP rates avail. Pking: Outdoor, free. Maj CC.

Restaurant 🍴

The Augustine Room, in the Marriott at Sawgrass Resort, 1000 TPC Blvd, Ponte Vedra Beach; tel 904/285-7777. Exit 101 off I-95. **New American.** Fresh roses as well as fine linen, china, crystal, and silver set the tone for the elegant dining experience to come. Specialties include hazelnut snapper, rack of lamb; sumptuous desserts. **FYI:** Reservations recommended. Dress code. **Open:** Tues–Sat 6:30am–10pm. **Prices:** Main courses $22.95–$38.95. Maj CC. ♥ ⓋⓅ ⛳

PORT EVERGLADES

Map page M-11, A2

Restaurant 🍴

Burt & Jack's, Berth 23, Port Everglades; tel 305/522-5225. At the Port Everglades cruise ship terminal. **American.** A club-like restaurant with water views from all sides due to its location on Port Everglades Peninsula. Prime-cut steaks, baked veal chops with seasoned honey-wheat crumbs, Maine lobster, and pork chops with baked apples are all favorites. **FYI:** Reservations recommended. Piano. Jacket required. **Open:** Sun–Thurs 4:30–10pm, Fri–Sat 4:30–11pm. Closed Dec 25. **Prices:** Main courses $15–$25. Maj CC. ⓋⓅ ⛳

PORT ST JOE

Map page M-3, D2

Attraction 🏛

St Joseph Peninsula State Park; tel 904/227-1327. One of Florida's major scallop-gathering spots. Scallops can be found by snorkeling in the gulf or they can be harvested along the beaches. Swimming, fishing, boating, hiking, camping, nature trails. **Open:** Daily 8am–sunset. $$

PORT ST LUCIE

Map page M-9, B3

Hotels

Best Western Port St Lucie, 7900 US 1 S, Port St Lucie, FL 34952; tel 407/878-7600 or toll free 800/528-1234; fax 407/340-0422. Exit 142 off Fla Tpk. A modest offering on the highway, next door to a chain steak house. **Rooms:** 98 stes. CI 2pm/CO 11am. Nonsmoking rms avail. Guest rooms are oversized and have with a sitting area separate from the bedroom. **Amenities:** A/C, cable TV w/movies. **Services:** Twice-daily maid svce, babysitting. **Facilities:** Whirlpool, washer/dryer. **Rates (CP):** HS Dec–Apr from $59 ste. Extra person $5. Children under 18 stay free. Lower rates off-season. Pking: Outdoor, free. Maj CC.

Holiday Inn Port St Lucie, 10120 S Federal Hwy, Port St Lucie, FL 34952; tel 407/337-2200 or toll free 800/HOLIDAY; fax 407/335-7872. Former Radisson Hotel offers modest rooms. Not on the beach, but convenient to island activities. **Rooms:** 142 rms and stes. CI 3pm/CO noon. Nonsmoking rms avail. Rooms were recently renovated. **Amenities:** A/C, cable TV w/movies. Some units w/Jacuzzis. **Services:** Babysitting. Small staff is friendly and accommodating. **Facilities:** 1 rst, 1 bar, whirlpool, washer/dryer. **Rates:** HS Jan–Apr $89 S or D; from $99 ste. Extra person $10. Children under 12 stay free. Lower rates off-season. Higher rates for spec evnts/hols. Spec packages avail. Pking: Outdoor, free. Maj CC.

Resort

Club Med–The Sandpiper, 3500 Morningside Blvd, Port St Lucie, FL 34952; tel 407/335-4400 or toll free 800/CLUB MED; fax 407/335-9497. Off US Rte 1. 1,000 acres. This large, all-inclusive family getaway offers plenty of sports and activities as well as programs for children. **Rooms:** 332 rms. CI 2pm/CO 11am. **Amenities:** A/C, cable TV, refrig, in-rm safe. All units w/terraces. **Services:** Car-rental desk, social director, children's program, babysitting. All-you-can-eat buffets served in the main dining room 3 times a day. **Facilities:** 4 rsts, 2 bars (w/entertainment), games rm, playground, washer/dryer. River beach. Full-service marina. **Rates (AP):** HS Dec–Apr $210–$380 D. Lower rates off-season. Higher rates for spec evnts/hols. Spec packages avail. Pking: Outdoor, free. Maj CC.

PUNTA GORDA

Map page M-8, C3

Hotels

Days Inn Punta Gorda, 26560 N Jones Loop Rd, Punta Gorda, FL 33950; tel 813/637-7200 or toll free 800/325-2525; fax 813/639-0848. Exit 28 off I-75. Best for overnight stays while on the move. Next door to fast-food outlets. **Rooms:** 76 rms and stes. CI 3pm/CO noon. Nonsmoking rms avail. **Amenities:** A/C, cable TV w/movies. **Services:** **Facilities:** Whirlpool, washer/dryer. **Rates:** HS Dec–Apr $64 S; $65–$69 D; from $95 ste. Children under 12 stay free. Lower rates off-season. Spec packages avail. Pking: Outdoor, free. Maj CC.

Holiday Inn, 300 Retta Esplanada, Punta Gorda, FL 33950; tel 813/639-1165 or toll free 800/525-1022; fax 813/639-8116. Exit 29 off I-75. A well-regarded establishment in the heart of town. **Rooms:** 183 rms and stes. CI 3pm/CO noon. Nonsmoking rms avail. **Amenities:** A/C, cable TV w/movies. Some units w/terraces, some w/Jacuzzis. **Services:** Babysitting. Daily activity information is posted on the lobby video monitor. Romantic sunset dinner cruise departs from the hotel's pier. **Facilities:** 1 rst, 2 bars (1 w/entertainment), whirlpool, washer/dryer. Pool looks over the private harborside pier. **Rates (CP):** HS Jan–Apr $81 S; $86 D; from $138 ste. Extra person $5. Children under 18 stay free. Lower rates off-season. Spec packages avail. Pking: Outdoor, free. Maj CC.

Howard Johnson Lodge, 33 Tamiami Trail, Punta Gorda, FL 33950; tel 813/639-2167 or toll free 800/654-2000; fax 813/639-1707. Exit 29 off I-75. Conveniently located, with panoramic views of Charlotte Harbor. **Rooms:** 100 rms. CI 3pm/CO noon. Nonsmoking rms avail. Some rooms are only a few feet from the water's edge. **Amenities:** A/C, cable TV w/movies. All units w/terraces. **Services:** **Facilities:** 1 rst, 1 bar (w/entertainment), washer/dryer. **Rates:** HS Dec–Apr $69–$74 S or D. Extra person $5. Children under 12 stay free. Lower rates off-season. Higher rates for spec evnts/hols. Pking: Outdoor, free. Maj CC.

Restaurants

Captain's Table, in Fishermen's Village, 1200 W Retta Esplanade, Punta Gorda; tel 813/637-1177. Exit 29 off I-75. **American/Seafood.** An upscale but casual restaurant offering spectacular sunset views, the best from Fisherman's Village Wharf. The menu features poultry, veal, fish, and Italian dishes. **FYI:** Reservations recommended. Piano. Children's menu. **Open:** HS Oct–May Sun–Thurs 7am–9pm, Fri–Sat 7am–10pm. Reduced hours off-season. **Prices:** Main courses $9–$26. Maj CC. 🏞 💟 ⚹

Village Oyster Bar, in Fishermen's Village, 1200 W Retta Esplanade, Punta Gorda; tel 813/637-1212. Exit 29 off I-75. **Burgers/Seafood.** This casual waterside stop on the Fisherman's Village Wharf pedestrian mall specializes in seafood. Food can be served at the outside bar. **FYI:** Reservations recommended. Piano. **Open:** Mon–Thurs 11:30am–8pm, Fri–Sat 11:30am–9pm, Sun noon–8pm. Closed some hols. **Prices:** Main courses $6.95–$22. Maj CC. 🍽 🏞 💟 ⚹

Attraction 📷

Babcock Wilderness Adventures, 8000 Fla 31; tel 813/338-6367 or 489-3911 (reservations). A 90-minute swamp-buggy tour through Telegraph Cypress Swamp and the surrounding woodlands of a 90,000-acre working ranch, conducted by an experienced naturalist. Passengers can see alligators, bison, panthers, wild boars, birds, and other wildlife in their natural habitat. Reservations are essential. Picnic facilities available. $$$$

REDINGTON SHORES

Map page M-8, A1

Restaurants 🍽

Lobster Pot, 17814 Gulf Blvd, Redington Shores; tel 813/391-8592. ½ mi S of Park Blvd. **Seafood.** This romantic lobster house with a nautical motif is widely known for the quality of its fare. Choose from a variety of seafood entrees. **FYI:** Reservations recommended. Children's menu. **Open:** Mon–Sat 4:30–10pm, Sun 4–10:30pm. Closed some hols. **Prices:** Main courses $9.25–$23.50. Maj CC. 🏞 💟 ⚹

Shells, 17855 Gulf Blvd, Redington Shores; tel 813/393-8990. Just north of 175th St. **Seafood.** This waterfront restaurant offers diners a casual, nautical atmosphere and lovely views. Fish dishes may be ordered blackened, fried, or char-grilled. A great value for large groups or families. Tuesday is Lobster Night. **FYI:** Reservations not accepted. Children's menu. **Open:** Sun–Thurs 11:30am–10pm, Fri–Sat 11:30am–11pm. **Prices:** Main courses $5.95–$16.95. Maj CC. 🏞 ⚹

Attraction 📷

Redington Long Pier, 17490 Gulf Blvd (at 175th Ave); tel 813/391-9398. Extending 1,021 feet into the Gulf of Mexico, the pier is popular with fisherman and sightseers alike. There are rod rentals, bait and tackle, fish-cleaning facilities, and a snack bar. **Open:** Daily 24 hours. $$

RIVIERA BEACH

Map page M-9, D4

See also **Singer Island**

Hotels 🏨

■■ **Days Inn Oceanfront Resort**, 2700 Ocean Dr, Riviera Beach, FL 33404 (Singer Island); tel 407/848-8661 or toll free 800/325-2525; fax 407/844-0999. A decent choice right on the ocean, a half-block from Ocean Mall. For those not-particularly-demanding guests who appreciate casual surroundings where the kids roam freely. **Rooms:** 163 rms and effic. CI 4pm/CO noon. Nonsmoking rms avail. **Amenities:** 🛗 A/C, cable TV, in-rm safe. All units w/terraces. **Services:** ✗ 🖼 🛏 🛎 Babysitting. **Facilities:** 🛗 🛗 ⚹ 1 rst, 2 bars (1 w/entertainment), 1 beach (ocean), whirlpool, washer/dryer. **Rates:** HS Dec–Apr $84–$139 S or D; from $89 effic. Extra person $10. Children under 12 stay free. Lower rates off-season. Higher rates for spec evnts/hols. Pking: Outdoor, free. Maj CC.

■■■ **Holiday Inn Sunspree Resort**, 3700 N Ocean Dr, Riviera Beach, FL 33404 (Singer Island); tel 407/848-3888 or toll free 800/443-4077; fax 407/845-9754. N of Blue Heron Causeway. An 8-story establishment right on the beach, with a sunny pool area flanked on one side by palm trees and fronted by the beach. **Rooms:** 222 rms and stes. CI 3pm/CO noon. Nonsmoking rms avail. **Amenities:** 🛗 🛗 🛗 A/C, cable TV w/movies, refrig. All units w/terraces. **Services:** ✗ 🖼 🛏 Masseur, children's program, babysitting. **Facilities:** 🛗 🚲 🛝 🛗 ⚹ 1 rst, 2 bars (1 w/entertainment), 1 beach (ocean), lifeguard, board surfing, games rm, snorkeling, spa, washer/dryer. **Rates:** HS Dec–Apr $139–$199 S or D; from $310 ste. Children under 12 stay free. Lower rates off-season. Higher rates for spec evnts/hols. Spec packages avail. Pking: Outdoor, free. Maj CC.

■■■ **Quality Resort**, 3800 N Ocean Dr, Riviera Beach, FL 33404; tel 407/848-5502 or toll free 800/765-5502; fax 407/863-6560. 8 mi NE of West Palm Beach. A 3- and 4-story property affording angled views of the ocean. **Rooms:** 125 rms and stes. CI 3pm/CO noon. Nonsmoking rms avail. **Amenities:**

🏨 ▣ A/C, cable TV, stereo/tape player. All units w/terraces. **Services:** ✗ 🔑 🖥 ♫ Babysitting. Complimentary beverages evenings. Staff will shuttle guests to local shops. **Facilities:** 🗄 🚲 🎿 🛶 🛥 🎱 ⚓ 1 rst, 2 bars (1 w/entertainment), 1 beach (bay), lifeguard, games rm, lawn games, snorkeling, spa, sauna, whirlpool. **Rates:** HS Feb–Apr $99–$149 S or D; from $179 ste. Extra person $10. Children under 18 stay free. Min stay spec evnts. Lower rates off-season. Spec packages avail. Pking: Outdoor, free. Maj CC.

SAFETY HARBOR

Map page M-6, E2

Resort 🏨

▤▤▤ **Safety Harbor Spa and Fitness Center**, 105 N Bayshore Dr, Safety Harbor, FL 34695; tel 813/726-1161 or toll free 800/237-0155. Take US 60 to Bayshore Dr and drive 3 miles north. 32 acres. Not far from either Tampa or Clearwater, this facility receives guests who want to follow a fitness regimen in a lovely setting. It operates much like a hotel, but many activities are geared to those here for a purpose. **Rooms:** 182 rms. CI 2pm/CO noon. Nonsmoking rms avail. **Amenities:** 🏨 A/C, cable TV w/movies. Some units w/terraces. **Services:** ✗ VP 🚗 🖥 ♫ Masseur. **Facilities:** 🗄 🚲 ⚓ 🎱 🛥 🛶 250 ⚓ 1 rst, 3 bars (1 w/entertainment), spa, sauna, steam rm, whirlpool, beauty salon, washer/dryer. **Rates (AP):** HS Dec–Mar $226–$312 S; $338–$464 D. Children under 2 stay free. Lower rates off-season. Spec packages avail. Pking: Outdoor, free. Maj CC.

Attraction 🎒

Safety Harbor Museum of Regional History, 329 S Bayshore Blvd; tel 813/726-1668. This small museum focuses on local history, with particular emphasis on the 16th century, when Hernando De Soto discovered 5 mineral springs here. Also displayed are local Native American artifacts and photographs of Safety Harbor around the turn of the century, when visitors flocked to the mineral springs. **Open:** Tues–Fri 10am–4pm, Sat–Sun 1–4pm. $

ST AUGUSTINE

Map page M-5, D4

See also Marineland, Ponte Vedra Beach

Hotels 🏨

▤▤ **Comfort Inn**, 1111 Ponce de Leon Blvd, St Augustine, FL 32084; tel 904/824-5554 or toll free 800/221-2222; fax 904/829-2222. Exit 95 off I-95. In a quiet locale, minutes from area attractions. Spiffy rooms are housed in a 2-story, tan stucco building with a mission-style facade and terra cotta roof. **Rooms:** 85 rms and stes. CI 2pm/CO 11am. Express checkout avail. Nonsmoking rms avail. **Amenities:** 🏨 A/C, cable TV. **Services:** 🔑 🖥 ♫ ⚓ **Facilities:** 🗄 25 ⚓ 1 bar, whirlpool, washer/dryer. **Rates (CP):** HS June–Aug $69–$125 S or D; from $95 ste. Children under 18 stay free. Lower rates off-season. Spec packages avail. Pking: Outdoor, free. Maj CC.

▤▤ **Holiday Inn–Downtown**, 1300 Ponce de Leon Blvd, St Augustine, FL 32084; tel 904/824-3383 or toll free 800/HOLI-DAY; fax 904/829-0668. Fla 16 exit off I-95. A well-tended establishment located in the old Spanish Quarter of St Augustine. **Rooms:** 122 rms. CI 3pm/CO noon. Express checkout avail. Nonsmoking rms avail. **Amenities:** 🏨 ♨ A/C, cable TV. **Services:** ✗ 🔑 🖥 ♫ Car-rental desk. **Facilities:** 🗄 300 ⚓ 1 rst, 1 bar. The family-style restaurant is very reasonably priced. **Rates:** HS June–Aug $76–$81 S or D. Children under 18 stay free. Lower rates off-season. Higher rates for spec evnts/hols. Spec packages avail. Pking: Outdoor, free. Maj CC.

▤▤ **Holiday Inn–St Augustine Beach**, 3250 S Fla A1A, St Augustine, FL 32084; tel 904/471-2555 or toll free 800/465-4329; fax 904/461-8450. Exit 93 off I-95. Beachfront hotel near area attractions. **Rooms:** 151 rms. CI 3pm/CO noon. Nonsmoking rms avail. Ocean views from balconies. **Amenities:** 🏨 A/C, cable TV, VCR. All units w/terraces. **Services:** ✗ 🖥 ♫ ⚓ Car-rental desk, babysitting. **Facilities:** 🗄 100 ⚓ 1 rst, 2 bars (1 w/entertainment), 1 beach (ocean), lawn games, washer/dryer. Beachfront tiki bar. Extra-large pool surrounded by lounge chairs is steps from the beach. **Rates:** HS June–Aug $73–$130 S or D. Extra person $5. Children under 18 stay free. Lower rates off-season. Spec packages avail. Pking: Outdoor, free. Maj CC.

▤▤ **Howard Johnson Resort Hotel**, 2050 Fla A1A, St Augustine, FL 32084; tel 904/471-2575 or toll free 800/752-4037; fax 904/471-1247. Fla 206E exit off I-95. A 2-story oceanfront facility set on spacious grounds. **Rooms:** 144 rms. CI 3pm/CO 11am. Express checkout avail. Nonsmoking rms avail. **Amenities:** 🏨 A/C, cable TV w/movies. **Services:** ✗ 🖥 ♫ ⚓

Car-rental desk. **Facilities:** 🏠 🅿️ ♿ 1 rst, 1 bar (w/entertainment), 1 beach (ocean), games rm, lawn games, whirlpool, playground, washer/dryer. Playground on beach. Volleyball court. **Rates:** HS June–Aug $60–$115 S or D. Children under 18 stay free. Lower rates off-season. Higher rates for spec evnts/hols. Spec packages avail. Pking: Outdoor, free. Maj CC.

≡≡≡ **Ponce de León Golf & Conference Resort**, 4000 US 1N, St Augustine, FL 32095; tel 904/824-2821 or toll free 800/228-2821; fax 804/824-8254. Exit 95 off I-95. Set on minimally landscaped but extensive grounds, with a beautiful championship golf course. **Rooms:** 193 rms and stes. CI 3pm/CO noon. Express checkout avail. Nonsmoking rms avail. Traditionally furnished accommodations; may be a bit of a hike from the registration lobby. **Amenities:** 🏠 🅰️ 📺 A/C, cable TV. All units w/terraces. **Services:** ✕ 🚐 🚗 🖼️ 🍽️ Twice-daily maid svce, car-rental desk, social director, masseur, children's program, babysitting. **Facilities:** 🏠 ⛳18 ⛳ ♦6 🏊450 ♿ 1 rst, 2 bars (1 w/entertainment), lawn games, washer/dryer. **Rates:** HS Feb–Apr/June–Aug $85–$145 S; $95–$155 D; from $145 ste. Extra person $10. Children under 18 stay free. Lower rates off-season. Higher rates for spec evnts/hols. AP and MAP rates avail. Spec packages avail. Pking: Outdoor, free. Maj CC.

≡≡ **Quality Inn Alhambra**, 2700 Ponce de Leon Blvd, St Augustine, FL 32084; tel 904/824-2883 or toll free 800/223-4153; fax 904/825-0976. Exit Fla 16 off I-95. Designed in an architectural style imitative of nearby historic buildings. The warm lobby features chandeliers and a vaulted ceiling. **Rooms:** 77 rms and stes. CI 3pm/CO noon. Nonsmoking rms avail. **Amenities:** 🏠 🅰️ A/C, cable TV. Some units w/Jacuzzis. **Services:** ✕ 🍽️ Car-rental desk. **Facilities:** 🏠 ♿ 1 rst, 1 bar, whirlpool. Restaurant is pancake house. **Rates:** HS Feb–Apr $60–$95 S or D; from $125 ste. Extra person $5. Children under 18 stay free. Lower rates off-season. Higher rates for spec evnts/hols. Spec packages avail. Pking: Outdoor, free. Maj CC.

Motels

≡≡ **Howard Johnson**, 137 San Marco Ave, St Augustine, FL 32084; tel 904/824-6181 or toll free 800/654-2000; fax 904/825-2774. Exit 95 off I-95. A downtown motel offering basic amenities. Acceptable for its location and rates. **Rooms:** 77 rms and stes. CI 3pm/CO 11am. Nonsmoking rms avail. **Amenities:** 🏠 A/C, cable TV. Some units w/Jacuzzis. **Services:** 🚗 🍽️ Car-rental desk. **Facilities:** 🏠 🅿️ ♿ 1 rst, 1 bar, whirlpool, washer/dryer. Ample parking for large vehicles. **Rates (CP):** HS June–Aug $59–$99 S or D; from $129 ste. Children under 18 stay free. Lower rates off-season. Pking: Outdoor, free. Maj CC.

≡ **La Fiesta Oceanside Inn**, 3050 Fla A1A, St Augustine, FL 32084; tel 904/471-2220 or toll free 800/852-6390; fax 904/471-0186. Cheerful 2-story beachfront property, with tan stucco walls and terra cotta roof. **Rooms:** 37 rms. CI 3pm/CO 11am. Some rooms have ocean views. The 2 ocean-view bridal suites have king-size beds and extra-large tubs. **Amenities:** 🏠 🅰️ A/C, cable TV, refrig. Some units w/terraces. **Services:** Babysitting. **Facilities:** 🏠 1 rst, 1 beach (ocean), lifeguard, games rm, playground, washer/dryer. Bright, sunny cafe serves breakfast only. **Rates:** HS Feb 10–Sept 10 $60–$119 S or D. Extra person $5. Min stay spec evnts. Lower rates off-season. Higher rates for spec evnts/hols. Pking: Outdoor, free. Maj CC.

≡≡ **Ramada Inn**, 116 San Marco Ave, St Augustine, FL 32084; tel 904/824-4352 or toll free 800/272-6232; fax 904/824-2745. Exit 95 off I-95. At Old Mission Rd. Standard motel units housed in a 5-story mission-style stucco building with arched entranceway and terra cotta roof. Close to historic district. **Rooms:** 100 rms. CI 2pm/CO 11am. Express checkout avail. Nonsmoking rms avail. **Amenities:** 🏠 A/C, cable TV. **Services:** ✕ 🖼️ 🍽️ 🛎️ **Facilities:** 🏠 ♿ 1 rst, 1 bar, whirlpool. **Rates:** HS June–Aug $50–$110 S or D. Extra person $7. Children under 18 stay free. Lower rates off-season. Higher rates for spec evnts/hols. Spec packages avail. Pking: Outdoor, free. Maj CC.

Inn

≡≡ **The Kenwood Inn**, 38 Marine St, St Augustine, FL 32084; tel 904/824-2116; fax 904/824-1684. Exit SR16 off I-95S. This old Victorian woodframe house, painted in pale peach with white trim, has served as a boarding house or inn since the late 19th century; it's listed on the National Register of Historic Places. Offers gracious southern style and hospitality. Unsuitable for children under 8. **Rooms:** 14 rms and stes. CI 2pm/CO 11am. No smoking. Each room uniquely and beautifully decorated, some with mahogany canopied beds. **Amenities:** 🅰️ A/C, cable TV. No phone. Some units w/terraces. **Services:** Babysitting, afternoon tea and wine/sherry served. Continental breakfast can be taken in a parlor with lace-curtained bay windows and a fireplace; in a wicker-furnished sun room; or on the front porch. **Facilities:** 🏠 Guest lounge w/TV. Secluded garden courtyard with fishpond, flower beds, and pecan tree. Small swimming pool with sun deck planted with hibiscus. **Rates (CP):** HS Feb–Sept $65–$75 D; from $95 ste. Min stay wknds. Lower rates off-season.

Restaurants 🍴

Anthony's Fine Foods, 4265 Fla A1A S, St Augustine; tel 904/471-7415. At Dondaville Rd. **Italian.** A cozy Italian-style restaurant where the accent is on food rather than decor. The dining room has a big-screen TV. Specials are available nightly. **FYI:** Reservations not accepted. Children's menu. Beer and wine only. **Open:** Sun–Thurs 7am–9pm, Fri–Sat 7am–3am. Closed Dec 25. **Prices:** Main courses $5.50–$10.95. Ltd CC. 🔲 ♿

Creekside Dinery, 160 Nix Boat Yard Rd, St Augustine; tel 904/829-6113. **Regional American.** A lovely restaurant with a cedar-lined interior augmented with plants and brightly colored table linens. The screened patio overlooks a creek and boats. Seafood includes pan-broiled oysters, crab cakes, scallops, and the catch of the night. **FYI:** Reservations not accepted. **Open:** Daily 5–10pm. Closed some hols. **Prices:** Main courses $7.99–$12.99. Ltd CC. 🖼️ ♿

Fiddler's Green, 2750 Anahma Dr, St Augustine; tel 904/824-8897. **Seafood.** A rustically elegant dining room with cedar paneling, beamed, knotty pine ceilings, and 2 stone fireplaces. Most tables have a view of both the marsh and the ocean beyond. The fresh catch of the day could be snapper, grouper, or tuna. All entrees include vegetables and a starchy side. A specialty is the roasted breast of chicken with sherry, apple, and pecan stuffing, glazed with a raspberry port sauce. **FYI:** Reservations recommended. **Open:** Daily 5–10pm. Closed some hols. **Prices:** Main courses $8.95–$14.95. Maj CC. 🖼️ 🖼️ ♿

Florida Cracker Cafe, 81 St George St, St Augustine (Historic District); tel 904/829-0397. **Regional American.** A breezy, light cafe with French doors leading to an outdoor dining patio. The house specialties include crab cakes, coconut-fried shrimp, and the fish platter, served blackened or broiled. **FYI:** Reservations not accepted. Guitar/singer. Beer and wine only. **Open:** Lunch daily 11am–4pm; dinner Wed–Thurs 5–9pm, Fri–Sat 5–10pm, Sun 5–9pm. Closed Dec 25. **Prices:** Main courses $8.50–$14. Ltd CC. 🍴 ♿

Gypsy Cab Company, 828 Anastasia Blvd, St Augustine; tel 904/824-8244. Between White and Comares Sts. **Eclectic.** A funky eatery serving original "urban cuisine." **FYI:** Reservations not accepted. Children's menu. Beer and wine only. **Open:** Lunch Mon–Sat 11–3pm; dinner Sun–Thurs 5:30–10pm, Fri–Sat 5:30–11pm; brunch Sun 10:30am–3pm. Closed some hols. **Prices:** Main courses $8.99–$15.99. Maj CC. ♿

La Parisienne, 60 Hypolita St, St Augustine; tel 904/829-0055. 3 blocks W of Avenida Menendez. **French.** An intimate, Euro-style dining room situated in the heart of the historic district. The charming setting and gourmet French menu help create a delightful dining experience. Duck salad with raspberry vinaigrette is a special appetizer, shrimp scampi a favorite entree. Steaks are prepared with selection of sauces. **FYI:** Reservations recommended. Beer and wine only. **Open:** Breakfast Sat–Sun 9–

11am; lunch Tues–Sun 11am–3pm; dinner Tues–Sun 5:30–9pm. Closed some hols; Sept 1–21. **Prices:** Main courses $12.50–$16.95. Maj CC. 🔲 ♿

Oscar's Old Florida Grill, 614 Euclid Ave, St Augustine; tel 904/829-3794. **Seafood.** A very casual restaurant with pine-planked floors and a pitched ceiling, housed in an old fish camp. Dine inside or at riverside picnic tables outdoors. Fresh specialties include fried shrimp, crab patties, or the catch of the day; all are served with fries, coleslaw, and homemade sauces. **FYI:** Reservations not accepted. Beer and wine only. **Open:** Wed–Thurs 5–9pm, Fri 5–10pm, Sat noon–10pm, Sun noon–9pm. Closed some hols. **Prices:** Main courses $3.95–$10.95. Ltd CC. 🍴 ♿

Raintree, 102 San Marco Ave, St Augustine; tel 904/824-7211. At Bernard St. **Eclectic.** This 1879 converted Victorian home, a cozy restaurant with a lovely garden, is one of the city's most romantic eateries. Popular dishes include beef Wellington, veal Oscar, and live Maine lobster, prepared steamed or broiled. More then 300 wines are available. A courtesy car provides transportation from local hotels. **FYI:** Reservations accepted. Children's menu. **Open:** Daily 5–9:30pm. Closed some hols. **Prices:** Main courses $8.95–$19.95. Maj CC. 💛 🔲 ♿

Salt Water Cowboy's, 299 Dondanville Rd, St Augustine; tel 904/471-2332. **Barbecue/Seafood.** Arrive early and watch the sun set over the saltwater marsh as you dine. In addition to the wonderful variety of seafood dishes, barbecued specialties are available. **FYI:** Reservations not accepted. **Open:** Daily 5–10pm. Closed some hols; Dec 12–25. **Prices:** Main courses $7.95–$13.95. Maj CC. 🖼️ 🔲 ♿

Schmagel's Bagels, 69 Hypolita St, St Augustine; tel 904/824-4444. 2 blocks W of St George St. **Deli.** A basic coffee shop with only 4 booths inside. The shaded patio tables are perfect for enjoying a fresh bagel and a cup of coffee outside. Twelve bagel varieties are usually available; sandwiches are prepared on homemade bread or on the bagel of your choice. **FYI:** Reservations not accepted. No liquor license. No smoking. **Open:** Mon–Sat 8am–3pm, Sun 9am–2pm. Closed some hols. **Prices:** Main courses $1–$4.50. No CC. 🍴 ♿

Attractions 💼

HISTORIC DISTRICT

Restored Spanish Quarter, Entrance at 29 St George St; tel 904/825-6830. A 2-block area south of the City Gate that is the city's most comprehensive historic section. Under the auspices of the Historic St Augustine Preservation Board, the houses, workshops, and gardens have been reconstructed to reflect their mid-18th century appearance. Houses have been named for prominent occupants. **Open:** Daily 9am–5pm. Closed Dec 25. $$

Triay House. This Spanish colonial house—with its highly pitched shingle gable roof and grape arbor overhanging the patio—belonged to Minorcan settlers, Francisco and Maria Triay. The property remained in their family through 1834. Today it serves as an orientation center, where visitors can learn about area history and archeological studies and view many of the artifacts uncovered in local digs.

Gómez House. This was the home of Lorenzo Gómez, a footsoldier, and his Native American wife, Catalina. They lived in this sparsely furnished one-room cypress A-frame with 3 children, and supplemented Lorenzo's meager income by operating a store and part-time tavern on the premises. Some of the types of items they would have sold, such as wine, blankets, and fabrics, rosin (used heated for caulking), beans, jars of olives, and tobacco, can be seen here. The sleeping loft upstairs is where the children slept in cold weather, on straw-filled mattresses.

In the yard outdoors is a square coquina well (the family's water source) and a vegetable garden that would be typical of one from the era.

Gallegos House. Built in 1720, this was the home of Martín Martínez Gallegos and his wife, Victoria, who lived here with 3 children and Juan Garcia, a retired infantryman. The Gallegos family was more affluent than the Gómez family. Martín was an officer—an artillery sergeant stationed at the Castillo. Their 2-room tabby (oyster-shell concrete) home has a built-in interior masonry stove, though most cooking was still done outside over a wood fire. A thatch-roofed pole shed over this outdoor fire protected the cooking space from the elements. An outdoor wooden trough served as a sink, washing machine, and bathtub, with whelk shells for dippers. Note the swinging rat shelf, used to store food, over the table; its motion was intended to scare rats away. Outside is a *matate,* used for grinding corn, made from volcanic rock.

Blacksmith Shop. Near the Gallegos House is the blacksmith shop, where a craftsman turns out hand-wrought hardware using 18th-century methods. He tells about his work, his life (he lives above the shop), and the everyday expressions rooted in blacksmithing, such as "strike while the iron is hot."

Gonzáles House. The rectangular Gonzáles House, home of cavalryman Bernardo Gonzáles, is larger than those that belonged to many of his neighbors. The architecture is typical of the first Spanish Period, with a flat roof constructed of hand-hewn boards laid across hand-hewn rafters. The house is used for spinning and weaving demonstrations using a 1797 loom.

Natural yarn colors were created from berries, carrots, onion skins, marigolds, indigo, and even crushed insects. The vegetable garden is supplemented by plants used for dyes.

Geronimo de Hita y Salazar House. This tabby house belonged to a soldier with a large family. Here a woodworker demonstrates how typical items—furniture, kitchen implements, and religious artifacts—were made in the 18th century, using a manual lathe to turn the wood.

De Mesa–Sanchéz House. Two historical periods are represented within this house. Two rooms date to the residence of shore guard Antonio de Mesa in the late 1700s, while a second story was added in the 19th century. Furnishings reflect the comfortable lifestyle of Charles and Mary Jane Loring, who lived here during the American Territorial Period (1821–45). They even had a bathtub in the kitchen, the practice of bathing having recently come into vogue. The house is made of coquina, which has been plastered over and painted white.

José Peso de Burgo and Francisco Pellicer House. A wooden structure dating from the British Period (1763–83), this house was shared by 2 families. Peso de Burgo, a Corsican, was a merchant and shopkeeper; Francisco Pellicer, a Minorcan carpenter. The families had separate kitchens. Today a shop occupies the house, selling books and other gift items relating to the period.

MUSEUMS AND HISTORIC SITES

Mission of Nombre De Dios, San Marco Ave and Old Mission Rd; tel 904/824-2809. Believed to be the site of the first Indian mission in the United States, founded in 1565. A 208-foot stainless-steel cross (which is lit up at night) marks the site of the founding of St Augustine. The mission is a popular destination of religious pilgrimages. Also on the grounds is a charming old mission-style chapel, Our Lady of La Leche (1915). **Open:** Daily 7am–6pm. Free.

Castillo de San Marcos National Monument, Castillo Dr and Avenida Menendez; tel 904/829-6506. This massive stone fortress overlooking Matanzas Bay was completed by the Spanish in 1695 to defend against British advances on St Augustine. Constructed of a native shell stone called coquina, the symmetrical fort was designed with diamond-shaped ramparts at each corner for maximum firepower, a double-drawbridge entrance over a 40-foot moat, and walls 33 feet high and 14 feet thick at the base. The Castillo was never captured in battle and its walls did not crumble when pounded by enemy artillery. Today the old storerooms house exhibits documenting the history of the fort. Visitors can tour the vaulted powder-magazine room, a dank prison cell, the chapel, and guard rooms, as well as the upper-level gun deck. Free guided tours daily. **Open:** Daily 8:45am–4:45pm. Closed Dec 25. $

Zorayda Castle, 83 King St; tel 904/824-3097. A replica of 1 wing of the Alhambra, a famous Spanish castle. The interior reflects the lifestyle of Moorish kings. Self-guided tours. **Open:** Daily 9am–5pm. Closed Dec 25. $$

Oldest House, 14 St Francis St; tel 904/824-2872. Also known as the Gonzales-Alvarez House, the area's oldest colonial home evolved from a 2-room coquina dwelling built between 1702 and 1727. Rooms are furnished to reflect periods of Spanish, British, and American ownership, and artifacts from each are displayed. Admission also entitles you to explore the adjacent Museum of Florida's Army and the exhibits in the Manucy Museum of St Augustine History. Tours depart on the hour and half-hour. **Open:** Daily 9am–5pm. Closed Dec 25. $$

Oldest Store Museum, 4 Artillery Lane; tel 904/829-9729. The C F Hamblen General Store was St Augustine's one-stop shopping center from 1835 to 1960, and the museum on its premises today depicts the emporium at the turn of the century. Among the more than 100,000 items on display are a piston-operated vacuum cleaner, patent medicines, gramophones, an 1899 typewriter, and an 1885 steam tractor. Gift shop. **Open:** Mon–Sat 9am–5pm, Sun noon–5pm. Closed Dec 25. $$

Oldest Wooden Schoolhouse, 14 St George St; tel 904/824-0192 or 800/428-0222. This red cedar and cypress structure, held together by wooden pegs and handmade nails, is more than 2 centuries old; its hand-wrought beams are still intact. The house served as a private residence and schoolhouse before the Civil War. **Open:** Daily 9am–5pm. Closed Dec 25. $

Authentic Old Jail, 167 San Marco Ave; tel 904/829-3800. This Victorian brick prison dating from 1890 was recently restored, and fascinating tours are conducted throughout the day by costumed guides. Exhibits include photographs of all the county's sheriffs from 1845 to the present, documentation of a 1908 hanging, early 20th-century newspaper articles, weapons seized from criminals, restraining devices, and an exact replica of the electric chair still used today in Florida. **Open:** Daily 8:30am–5pm. Closed some hols. $$

Government House Museum, 48 King St; tel 904/825-5033. Built on the site of a 16th-century Spanish colonial governor's office, the museum offers visitors an overview of St Augustine's history from native settlement to the Flagler era using state-of-the-art audio and visual media. Displays highlight the struggles of the first Spanish settlement, the construction of the Castillo de San Marcos, and the various inhabitants who have lived here throughout the centuries. **Open:** Daily 10am–4pm. Closed Dec 25. $

Florida Heritage Museum, 167 San Marco Ave; tel 904/829-3800. This new museum documents state and local history in exhibits focusing on the colorful life of Henry Flagler and his Florida and East Coast Railroad and Hotel Company, which played a key role in the development of Florida tourism; the Civil War; and the Seminole Wars. Visitors can also see a replica of a Spanish galleon, and displays of actual gold, silver, and jewelery recovered from galleons sunk off Florida's coast. **Open:** Daily 8:30am–5pm. Closed some hols. $$

Lightner Museum, 75 King St; tel 904/824-2874. The vast collection of Victoriana housed in the former Alcazar Hotel (1888) includes 18th- and 19th-century European porcelains, Victorian cut glass, Tiffany lamps, antique music boxes, and more. The Victorian Science and Industry room displays shells, minerals, and Native American artifacts in beautiful turn-of-the-century cases. Demonstration of Victorian mechanical musical instruments daily at 11am and 2pm. **Open:** Daily 9am–5pm. Closed Dec 25. $$

Museum of Weapons and Early American History, 81-C King St; tel 904/829-3727. An eclectic assortment of historic artifacts and weapons from 1500 to 1900 is displayed in this small private museum, located between Sevilla and Cordova Sts. Exhibits include Native American war clubs, spears, and arrowheads; 19th-century firearms; and items from the Civil War, including Confederate weapons, money, and buttons. Adjoining gift shop. **Open:** Daily 9:30am–5pm. Closed Dec 25. $

Potter's Wax Museum, 17 King St; tel 804/829-9056. More than 170 wax figures, each carefully researched and authentically costumed, are displayed. Portrayed are key players in local Florida history, as well as international historical figures. A 12-minute film is shown continuously throughout the day, and a workshop in front allows visitors to watch a wax sculptor at work. **Open:** Daily 9am–5pm; call ahead for summer hours. Closed Dec 25. $$

Ripley's Believe It or Not! Museum, 19 San Marco Ave; tel 904/824-1606. Housed in a converted 1887 Moorish revival residence are hundreds of examples of the "oddities" collected by Robert Ripley in the course of his travels around the world. Videos and films at various points. **Open:** Daily 9am–6pm; later summer hours. $$$

OTHER ATTRACTIONS

Fountain of Youth, 155 Magnolia Ave; tel 904/829-3168. A 14-acre archeological park purported to be the Native American village visited by Ponce de León upon his arrival in the New World in 1513. The legendary fountain itself flows from an underground stream located in the springhouse, which contains a coquina stone cross believed to date from the Spanish explorer's visit. Tableaux depict a Timucuan village and the arrival of Ponce de León. All guests receive a sample of water from the spring. Guided tours begin with a planetarium show about 16th-century celestial navigation. **Open:** Daily 9am– Closed Dec 25. $$

Cross and Sword, St Augustine Amphitheatre, Fla A1A; tel 904/471-1965. Written by historical dramatist Paul Green, the official state play of Florida recounts the founding of America's oldest city in 1565 and its turbulent early history. It features spectacular battles, elaborate choreography, and a symphonic musical score, all presented on a large outdoor stage. Performances held July–late Aug, Wed–Sun at 8:30pm. $$$

St Augustine Alligator Farm, 999 Anastasia Blvd (Fla A1A); tel 904/824-3337. Houses the world's most complete collection of crocodilians, a category that includes alligators, crocodiles, caimans, and gavials. Major attractions include "The Land of Crocodiles," with specimens of all 22 species of crocodilians, and Gomek, the largest captive crocodile in the western hemisphere (1,700 pounds and almost 18 feet long). Other creatures on the farm include geckos, snakes, tortoises, and tropical birds. Petting zoo. **Open:** Daily 9am–5pm. $$$

ST MARKS

Map page M-4, C1

Attractions 📼

St Marks National Wildlife Refuge; tel 904/925-6121. Bordering Ochlockonee Bay and the Gulf of Mexico, this wildlife refuge encompasses more than 60,000 acres of varied terrain. Stop first at the visitor center for an orientation, and to view the bird, waterfowl, and wildlife habitat displays. **Open:** Park, daily sunrise–sunset; visitor center, Mon–Fri 8:15am–4:15pm, Sat–Sun 10am–5pm. Closed some hols. $$

San Marcos De Apalachee State Historic Site, Canal St; tel 904/925-6216. This site was visited by Spanish explorer Panfilo de Narvaez in 1528 and then by Hernando de Soto in 1539 after he followed de Narvaez's overland route. Ruins of a stone fort used by the Spanish, British, and Civil War Confederates can be toured. The visitor center has historic exhibits and artifacts excavated nearby. Picnic facilities, nature trails. **Open:** Thurs–Mon 9am–5pm. Closed some hols. Free.

ST PETERSBURG

Map page M-8, A1

See also **Belleair Beach, Indian Rocks, Indian Shores Beach, Isle of Capri, Madeira Beach, North Redington Beach, Redington Shores, St Petersburg Beach, Treasure Island**

TOURIST INFORMATION

St Petersburg/Clearwater Convention and Visitors Bureau, 1 Stadium Dr, Suite A, at St Petersburg ThunderDome (tel 813/892-7892). Open Mon–Fri 8:30am–5pm.

St Petersburg Chamber of Commerce, 100 2nd Ave N (tel 813/821-4069). Open Mon–Fri 8:30am–5pm.

Visitors Center on the Pier, 800 2nd Ave N (tel 813/821-6164). Open Mon–Sat 10am–8pm, Sun 11am–6pm.

PUBLIC TRANSPORTATION

Pinellas Suncoast Transit Authority/PSTA Buses Operate throughout St Petersburg. Hours vary, depending upon route. Fare 90¢. For information call 813/530-9911.

BATS City Transit Buses Operate along St Petersburg Beach strip. Fare 95¢. For information call 813/367-3086.

Treasure Island Transit System Buses Operate along Treasure Island strip. Fare $1. For information call 813/360-0811.

Clearwater Beach Trolley Free service in Clearwater Beach area. For information call 813/530-9911.

Hotels 🛏

🏢🏢 Days Inn Marina Beach Resort, 6800 34th St S, St Petersburg, FL 33711; tel 813/867-1151 or toll free 800/227-8045; fax 813/864-4494. Exit 3 off I-275. A well-tended hotel with enticing views of Tampa Bay. Close to area attractions. **Rooms:** 157 rms, stes, and effic. CI 2pm/CO 11am. Nonsmoking rms avail. **Amenities:** 🎁 A/C, cable TV, in-rm safe. Some units w/terraces. **Services:** ✗ 🖂 ⮐ Babysitting. **Facilities:** 🗂 ⚠ 🏠 💦 🛳 & 2 rsts, 2 bars (w/entertainment), 1 beach (ocean), games rm, playground, washer/dryer. Private marina; on-site sailing school. **Rates:** HS Feb–Apr $79–$117 S or D; from $190 ste; from $98 effic. Extra person $10. Children under 18 stay free. Lower rates off-season. Higher rates for spec evnts/hols. Pking: Outdoor, free. Maj CC.

▤▤▤ The Heritage Holiday Inn, 234 3rd Ave N, St Petersburg, FL 33701; tel 813/822-4814 or toll free 800/HOLIDAY. Exit 10 off I-275. A historic hotel. The lobby is filled with antique furnishings and has hardwood floors, oriental rugs, and a fireplace. Arriving guests are greeted with classical music. **Rooms:** 71 rms and stes. CI 3pm/CO noon. Nonsmoking rms avail. Nicely appointed rooms have 1920s furnishings. **Amenities:** 🛁 🛎 A/C, cable TV. Some units w/minibars. **Services:** ✗ ⚒ 🛎 **Facilities:** 🛋 300 🛎 1 rst, 1 bar, whirlpool. The bar was once a fixture in Gen. Andrew Jackson's home. **Rates:** HS Feb–Apr $89 S; $94 D. Extra person $10. Children under 18 stay free. Min stay spec evnts. Lower rates off-season. Pking: Outdoor, free. Maj CC.

▤▤ Holiday Inn–Stadium, 4601 34th St S, St Petersburg, FL 33711; tel 813/867-3131 or toll free 800/HOLIDAY; fax 813/867-2025. Exit 4 off I-275. With its central location, this makes a fine jumping-off point for touring area attractions. **Rooms:** 134 rms. CI 2pm/CO noon. Nonsmoking rms avail. **Amenities:** 🛁 🛎 A/C, cable TV w/movies. **Services:** ⚒ 🛎 **Facilities:** 🛋 125 🛎 1 bar (w/entertainment), games rm, washer/dryer. Families will appreciate the extra-large pool. **Rates:** HS Feb–Apr $74–$84 S or D. Extra person $10. Children under 18 stay free. Lower rates off-season. Pking: Outdoor, free. Maj CC.

▤▤ Howard Johnson Hotel, 3600 34th St S, St Petersburg, FL 33711; tel 813/867-6070 or toll free 800/221-4335; fax 813/867-6591. Exit 6 off I-275. A basic hotel with spacious rooms and public areas. **Rooms:** 170 rms and stes. CI 3pm/CO noon. Nonsmoking rms avail. **Amenities:** 🛁 🛎 A/C, cable TV w/movies, shoe polisher. **Services:** ⚒ 🛎 **Facilities:** 🛋 🏊 1K 🛎 1 rst, 1 bar (w/entertainment), games rm. Poolside bar. **Rates (CP):** HS Feb–Apr $68–$74 S or D; from $90 ste. Extra person $6. Children under 18 stay free. Lower rates off-season. Higher rates for spec evnts/hols. Pking: Outdoor, free. Maj CC.

▤▤▤ Presidential Inn, 100 2nd Ave S PO Box 57306, St Petersburg, FL 33701; tel 813/821-7117; fax 813/821-7818. Exit 10 off I-275. Located on 5th floor of Northern Trust Bldg. Geared toward businesspeople. **Rooms:** 29 rms and stes. CI 3pm/CO noon. Nonsmoking rms avail. Individually decorated with dark woods and artwork. **Amenities:** 🛁 🍷 A/C, cable TV. Some bathrooms are equipped with whirlpool jets in tubs. **Services:** ✗ ⚒ 🛎 **Facilities:** 13 🛎 Guests have full access to the next-door Hilton's exercise and leisure facilities. **Rates (CP):** HS Dec–May $85 S or D; from $105 ste. Extra person $10. Children under 18 stay free. Lower rates off-season. Pking: Indoor/outdoor, free. Maj CC.

▤▤▤ St Petersburg Hilton and Towers, 333 1st St S, St Petersburg, FL 33701; tel 813/894-5000 or toll free 800/944-5500; fax 813/894-7655. Exit 9 off I-275. Top-flight hotel offering excellent facilities for businesspeople and others. Public areas are spacious and appealing. **Rooms:** 333 rms and stes. CI 3pm/CO noon. Nonsmoking rms avail. **Amenities:** 🛁 🛎 A/C, cable TV w/movies. **Services:** ✗ 🖙 VP ⚒ 🛎 Car-rental desk, babysitting. **Facilities:** 🛋 🏊 1K 🛎 2 rsts, 1 bar, games rm, whirlpool. Tennis and golf are nearby. Restaurant has cathedral ceiling and large windows providing expansive pool views. **Rates:** HS Feb–Apr $104–$124 S; $114–$134 D; from $239 ste. Extra person $10. Children under 18 stay free. Lower rates off-season. Spec packages avail. Pking: Outdoor, free. Maj CC.

▤▤ Suncoast Executive Inn Athletic Center, 3000 34th St S, St Petersburg, FL 33711; tel 813/867-1111 or toll free 800/458-8671; fax 813/867-7068. Exit 6 off I-275. This 3-story hotel, a good choice for tennis enthusiasts, offers easy access to downtown and the beaches. **Rooms:** 120 rms and stes. CI 3pm/CO 11am. Nonsmoking rms avail. **Amenities:** 🛁 A/C, cable TV. Some units w/terraces. **Services:** ⚒ 🛎 🐕 Babysitting. **Facilities:** 🛋 🏊10 🛎 🖳 🛎 Beauty salon, day-care ctr, washer/dryer. **Rates:** $60 S; $65 D; from $85 ste. Extra person $5. Children under 18 stay free. Lower rates off-season. Pking: Outdoor, free. Maj CC.

Resort

▤▤▤▤ Stouffer Renaissance Vinoy Resort, 501 5th Ave NE, St Petersburg, FL 33701; tel 813/894-1000 or toll free 800/HOTELS 1; fax 813/822-2785. At Beach Dr. 114 acres. A landmark placed on the National Register, featuring a magnificently restored ballroom and palatial public areas. If you can't stay at this grand hotel, at least stop in the restaurant for a drink. **Rooms:** 360 rms and stes. CI 3pm/CO noon. Nonsmoking rms avail. Smallish standard rooms have well-equipped baths and designer decor. **Amenities:** 🛁 🛎 🍷 A/C, cable TV w/movies, bathrobes. All units w/minibars, some w/terraces, some w/Jacuzzis. Special spa rooms offer private whirlpools on patios. **Services:** 🍴 🖙 VP 🚗 ⚒ 🛎 Twice-daily maid svce, social director, masseur, babysitting. **Facilities:** 🛋 ▶18 🏊 14 🛎 300 🛎 5 rsts, 4 bars (2 w/entertainment), lawn games, spa, sauna, steam rm, whirlpool, beauty salon. On-site marina. **Rates:** HS Dec–Apr $229 S or D; from $349 ste. Extra person $20. Children under 18 stay free. Lower rates off-season. Higher rates for spec evnts/hols. Spec packages avail. Pking: Indoor/outdoor, free. Maj CC.

Restaurants 🍴

Apropos, 300 2nd Ave NE, St Petersburg; tel 813/823-8934. **New American/Eclectic.** A small but popular restaurant overlooking the marina. Wine tastings every Thursday evening. Live jazz on the deck on Sundays. **FYI:** Reservations recommended. Jazz. **Open:** Tues–Sat 7:30am–midnight, Sun 8:30am–midnight. Closed Thanksgiving. **Prices:** Main courses $8.95–$15.95. Ltd CC. 🍷 📷 &

♟ **Basta's Cantina D'Italia Ristorante**, 1625 4th St S, St Petersburg; tel 813/894-7880. **Northern Italian.** An elegant, old-world restaurant with tuxedoed waiters and an elaborate menu featuring more than 300 dishes. Specialties include seafood Porto Fino, veal saltimbocca, shrimp scampi, and rack of lamb. **FYI:** Reservations recommended. Dress code. Beer and wine only. **Open:** Daily 5–11pm. Closed some hols. **Prices:** Main courses $13.95–$24.95. Maj CC. ♥ VP &

Cha Cha Coconuts, 1241 Gulf Blvd, St Petersburg; tel 813/822-6655. **New American/Caribbean.** A fun restaurant with a relaxed atmosphere. Watch the sun set over the Gulf of Mexico from the outdoor patio as you enjoy tasty burgers, sandwiches, soups, salads, or munchies. **FYI:** Reservations not accepted. Band. Children's menu. **Open:** Mon–Thurs 11am–midnight, Fri–Sat 11am–1am, Sun noon–11pm. **Prices:** Main courses $3.95–$8. Maj CC.

Maria's Family Restaurant, 5571 4th St N, St Petersburg; tel 813/526-7070. Exit 10 off I-275. **Greek/Italian.** Casual eatery, with traditional seafood and unremarkable decor. Offers families a good value. **FYI:** Reservations not accepted. Beer and wine only. **Open:** Mon–Sat 7am–9pm, Sun 7am–2pm. **Prices:** Main courses $3.50–$7.50. Ltd CC. 📷 &

Mulligan's Sunset Grille, 9524 Blind Pass Rd, St Petersburg; tel 813/367-6680. 5th Ave exit N off I-275, ½ block S of Blind Pass Bridge. **Seafood/Steak.** An attractive waterfront eatery with nautical decor. From the deck, watch the Florida sun set over the picturesque marina nearby. Maine lobster and local seafood dishes are specialties. **FYI:** Reservations not accepted. Children's menu. **Open:** Mon–Fri 11am–midnight, Sat–Sun 11am–1am. Closed Thanksgiving. **Prices:** Main courses $8.95–$29.95. Maj CC. 🍷 📷 &

★ **Ted Peter's Famous Smoked Fish**, 1350 Pasadena Ave S, St Petersburg; tel 813/381-7931. 22nd Ave S exit off I-275. **Burgers/Seafood.** A family-owned and tourist-friendly operation offering smoked fish dinners at covered outdoor picnic tables. Takeout is sold by the pound. **FYI:** Reservations not accepted. Beer and wine only. **Open:** Wed–Mon 11:30am–7:30pm. Closed some hols. **Prices:** Main courses $3.60–$12.95. No CC. 🍷 📷 &

The Waterfront Steak House, 8800 Bay Pines Blvd N, St Petersburg; tel 813/345-5335. Exit 13 off I-275. **Seafood/Steak.** Enjoy wonderful views from the booths of this oceanfront restaurant. The varied menu is popular with seniors, especially at lunch. **FYI:** Reservations not accepted. Children's menu. **Open:** Daily 11:30am–10pm. Closed some hols. **Prices:** Main courses $7.95–$19.95. Maj CC. 📷 ♥ &

Attractions 📷

St Petersburg Historical and Flight One Museum, 335 Second Ave NE; tel 813/894-1052. This museum chronicles local and state history, with exhibits ranging from the city's founding to the world's first scheduled commercial flight, which departed from St Petersburg in 1914. **Open:** Mon–Sat 10am–5pm, Sun 1–5pm. $$

Salvador Dali Museum, 1000 Third St S; tel 813/823-3767. Contains the world's largest collection of works by the renowned Spanish surrealist, including 94 oil paintings, over 100 watercolors and drawings, and 1,300 graphics, plus posters, photos, sculptures, objets d'art, and a 2,500-volume library. Museum store offers over 100 reproductions, plus jewelry, books, and gift items. **Open:** Tues–Sat 9:30am–5:30pm, Sun–Mon noon–5:30pm. Closed some hols. $$

Museum of Fine Arts, 255 Beach Dr NE; tel 305/896-2667. Resembling a Mediterranean waterfront villa, this museum houses a permanent collection of European, American, pre-Columbian, and Far Eastern art, with works by such artists as Fragonard, Monet, Renoir, Cezanne, and Gauguin. Also displayed are period rooms, a gallery of Steuben crystal, and rotating exhibits. Guided tours are available. **Open:** Tues–Sat 10am–5pm, Sun 1–5pm; third Thurs of each month 10am–9pm. $$

Great Explorations, 1120 Fourth St S; tel 813/821-8885. Offers a wide variety of entertaining hands-on exhibits that are geared toward children. Kids can explore a long, dark tunnel; shoot a game of laser pinball; and paint a picture with sunlight, among other activities. **Open:** Mon–Sat 10am–5pm, Sun 1–5pm. $$

Sunken Gardens, 1825 Fourth St N; tel 813/896-3186 (recorded info) or 896-3187. A 5-acre tropical garden park containing a vast array of plants, flowers, and trees, as well as an aviary with almost 500 rare birds. There are performing bird shows throughout the day. A wax museum depicts biblical figures. Huge gift shop. **Open:** Daily 9am–5pm. $$$$

The Pier, 800 Second Ave NE; tel 813/821-6164. The center of sightseeing, entertainment, and shopping in St Petersburg, this festive waterfront complex extends a quarter-mile into Tampa Bay. In addition to panoramic views of the bay, the marina, and the city's skyline, it offers 5 levels of shops and restaurants, plus an aquarium, nightclub, observation deck, catwalks for fishing, boat rides and docks, a small beach, miniature golf, and watersports rentals. A free trolley service runs between the Pier entrance and nearby parking lots. Adjacent to the Pier is scenic Straub Park, 36 acres of waterfront running along Beach Drive. **Open:** Most shops, Mon–Sat 10am–9pm, Sun noon–6pm; aquarium, Mon and Wed–Sat 10am–8pm, Sun noon–6pm. Free.

Fort De Soto Park, Fla 679; tel 815/866-2484. One of the oldest sections of St Petersburg, this is the largest and most diverse park in the area. A public park for over 25 years, it also offers fishing piers, shaded picnic sites, a bird and animal sanctuary, and 235 campsites. **Open:** Daily, sunrise–sunset. Free.

Sunshine Skyway Bridge, I-275 and US 19; tel 823-8804. Florida's first suspension bridge connects Pinellas and Manatee Counties and the city of St Petersburg with the Bradenton/Sarasota area. It rises 183 feet above the bay and is 4.1 miles long. **Open:** Open: Daily 24 hours. $

Boyd Hill Nature Park, 1101 Contry Club Way S; tel 813/893-7326. Located at the south end of Lake Maggiore, this 216-acre park has scenic trails and boardwalks lined with subtropical flora. Visitors can observe birds, young reptiles, and other native species as they walk along the paths. There is also a library and nature center, aquariums, a beehive, as well as a picnic area and children's playground. **Open:** Daily 9am–5pm. $

Lady Anderson **Cruises**, 3400 Pasadena Ave S; tel 813/367-7804 or toll free 800/533-2288. Cruises are operated at lunch and dinner times aboard this 3-deck boat, with buffet meal service and dance music, as well as cocktail service. Boarding is half-hour before departure. Lunch cruise 11:30am–2pm; dinner cruise 7–10pm. Oct–May. $$$$

ThunderDome, 1 Stadium Dr; tel 813/825-3100. Opened in 1990, this $110-million stadium features a translucent roof that is the first cable-supported dome of its kind in the United States and one of the largest of its type in the world. The Tampa Bay Lightning hockey team plays home games here October–April. Guided tours available on non-event days. **Open:** Box office, Mon–Fri 10am–5pm, Sat (event days only) 10am–2pm.

Al Lang Stadium, 180 Second Ave SE; tel 813/822-3384. The winter home of the St Louis Cardinals and (at least temporarily) the Baltimore Orioles. Both teams hold their spring training here,

with exhibition games held in March. Following the major league exhibition season, the St Petersburg Cardinals, a Class A minor league team, play their home games here (Apr–Sept). $$

ST PETERSBURG BEACH

Map page M-8, A1

Hotels 🏨

≡≡ **Best Western Sirata Beach Resort**, 5390 Gulf Blvd, St Petersburg Beach, FL 33706; tel 813/367-2771 or toll free 800/344-5999; fax 813/360-6799. Exit 4 off I-275 S. A family-style beach resort set on 350 feet of private white sand beach. **Rooms:** 155 stes and effic. CI 4pm/CO 11am. **Amenities:** 🛁 ♨ 🖥 ☎ A/C, cable TV w/movies, refrig, in-rm safe. Some units w/terraces. **Services:** ✕ 🚗 🖨 🛎 Babysitting. **Facilities:** 🏋 🛶 🏖 ♿ 1 rst, 1 bar, 1 beach (ocean), games rm, whirlpool, playground, washer/dryer. Poolside bar, restaurant, and cocktail lounge serve as pre- and post-beach gathering spots. **Rates:** HS Jan–Apr from $154 ste; from $220 effic. Extra person $10. Children under 12 stay free. Min stay spec evnts. Lower rates off-season. Spec packages avail. Pking: Outdoor, free. Maj CC.

≡≡≡ **Holiday Inn St Petersburg Beach**, 5300 Gulf Blvd, St Petersburg Beach, FL 33706; tel 813/360-6911 or toll free 800/HOLIDAY; fax 813/360-6172. Exit 4 off I-275. **Rooms:** 148 rms and stes. CI 3pm/CO 11am. Nonsmoking rms avail. **Amenities:** 🛁 ♨ A/C, cable TV, bathrobes. Some units w/terraces. **Services:** ✕ 🖨 🛎 Babysitting. **Facilities:** 🏋 🎱 ♿ 2 rsts, 3 bars (1 w/entertainment), 1 beach (ocean), games rm, washer/dryer. **Rates:** HS Feb–Apr $88–$95 S; $94–$101 D; from $129 ste. Extra person $6. Children under 18 stay free. Lower rates off-season. Higher rates for spec evnts/hols. Spec packages avail. Pking: Outdoor, free. Maj CC.

≡≡≡ **Radisson Sandpiper Beach Resort**, 6000 Gulf Blvd, St Petersburg Beach, FL 33706; tel 813/360-5551 or toll free 800/333-3333; fax 813/360-0417. Exit 4 off I-275. Located on the beach, this satisfactory full-service facility caters to many families. A good bet. **Rooms:** 159 rms and stes. CI 4pm/CO noon. Nonsmoking rms avail. Many units with ocean views; some with microwaves and an extra TV. **Amenities:** 🛁 ♨ 🖥 A/C, cable TV, refrig, bathrobes. Some units w/terraces. **Services:** ✕ 🖨 🛎 Car-rental desk, children's program, babysitting. **Facilities:** 🏋 🎱 🍴 ♿ 2 rsts, 2 bars, 1 beach (ocean), games rm, racquetball, washer/dryer. **Rates:** $129–$174 S or D; from $189 ste. Extra person $15. Children under 17 stay free. Spec packages avail. Pking: Indoor/outdoor, free. Maj CC.

≣≣≣ **St Petersburg Beach Hilton Inn**, 5250 Gulf Blvd, St Petersburg Beach, FL 33706; tel 813/360-1811 or toll free 800/221-2424; fax 813/360-6919. Exit 4 off I-275. A one-time beach leader, it still offers a wide variety of facilities for couples and families. **Rooms:** 151 rms and stes. CI 3pm/CO 11am. Nonsmoking rms avail. **Amenities:** 🛁 🕹 A/C, cable TV w/movies, in-rm safe. All units w/terraces, 1 w/Jacuzzi. **Services:** ✗ 🖼 ⤳ Babysitting. **Facilities:** 🛖 250 1 rst, 2 bars (1 w/entertainment), 1 beach (ocean), washer/dryer. Revolving roof lounge provides a romantic setting. **Rates:** HS Feb–Apr $100–$160 S or D; from $195 ste. Extra person $10. Children under 18 stay free. Lower rates off-season. Higher rates for spec evnts/hols. Spec packages avail. Pking: Indoor/outdoor, free. Maj CC.

Motels

≣≣ **Colonial Gateway Inn**, 6300 Gulf Blvd, St Petersburg Beach, FL 33706; tel 813/367-3711 or toll free 800/237-8918; fax 813/367-7068. Exit 4 off I-275. Take Pinellas Bayway W 2½ miles to Gulf Blvd. Lowrise property with lovely gardens and beach. **Rooms:** 200 rms and effic. CI 2pm/CO 11am. **Amenities:** 🛁 🕹 A/C, cable TV w/movies. **Services:** ✗ 🖼 ⤳ 🚗 Car-rental desk. Tours available to area attractions. **Facilities:** 🛖 200 1 rst, 2 bars (1 w/entertainment), 1 beach (ocean), games rm. Beach bar. **Rates:** HS Feb–Apr $91–$108 S or D; from $99 effic. Extra person $6. Children under 12 stay free. Lower rates off-season. Pking: Outdoor, free. Maj CC.

≣≣ **Days Inn Island Beach Resort**, 6200 Gulf Blvd, St Petersburg Beach, FL 33706; tel 813/367-1902 or toll free 800/544-4222; fax 813/367-4422. 2 mi N of Pinellas Bayway on Fla 699. Well-kept establishment with private beach; offers a variety of activities. **Rooms:** 102 rms and effic. CI 4pm/CO 11am. Nonsmoking rms avail. **Amenities:** 🛁 A/C, cable TV. Some units w/terraces. **Services:** 🖼 ⤳ Babysitting. **Facilities:** 🛖 2 bars (1 w/entertainment), 1 beach (ocean), games rm. Sports bar with wide-screen TV and complimentary hors d'oeuvres. Beach bar with nightly live entertainment. **Rates:** HS Feb–Apr $128–$148 S or D; from $128 effic. Lower rates off-season. Pking: Outdoor, free. Maj CC.

≣≣ **Dolphin Beach Resort**, 4900 Gulf Blvd, St Petersburg Beach, FL 33706; tel 813/360-7011 or toll free 800/237-8916; fax 813/367-5909. Exit 4 off I-275 S. Beachfront resort catering to both families and couples. **Rooms:** 173 rms and effic. CI 4pm/CO 11am. **Amenities:** 🛁 A/C, satel TV. Some units w/terraces. **Services:** ✗ 🚗 🖼 ⤳ Car-rental desk, babysitting. Tours

arranged by the knowledgeable staff depart from the lobby. **Facilities:** 🛖 300 🕹 1 rst, 2 bars (1 w/entertainment), 1 beach (ocean), games rm, washer/dryer. **Rates:** HS Feb–Apr $98–$118 S or D; from $110 effic. Min stay spec evnts. Lower rates off-season. Spec packages avail. Pking: Outdoor, free. Maj CC.

≣≣ **Howard Johnson Lodge**, 6100 Gulf Blvd, St Petersburg Beach, FL 33706; tel 813/360-7041 or toll free 800/231-1419; fax 813/360-8941. 2 mi N of Pinellas Bayway. This 4-story beachfront property is popular among families. **Rooms:** 136 rms and effic. CI 3pm/CO noon. Nonsmoking rms avail. **Amenities:** 🛁 🕹 A/C, cable TV, refrig. Some units w/terraces. **Facilities:** 🛖 🕹 1 beach (ocean). Comedy club with nightly acts. **Rates:** $92–$118 S or D; from $102 effic. Extra person $10. Children under 18 stay free. Lower rates off-season. Higher rates for spec evnts/hols. Pking: Outdoor, free. Maj CC.

Passe-A-Grille Beach Motel, 709 Gulf Way, St Petersburg Beach, FL 33706; tel 813/367-4726 or toll free 800/537-3269. Located across from the beach. A good candidate for the budget-conscious. Unrated. **Rooms:** 25 effic. CI 3pm/CO 11am. Nonsmoking rms avail. Basic, comfortable furnishings. **Amenities:** 🛁 🕹 A/C, cable TV, refrig. **Services:** ⤳ **Facilities:** 1 rst, 1 bar (w/entertainment), 1 beach (ocean), washer/dryer. **Rates:** HS Late Dec–mid-Apr from $52 effic. Extra person $5. Min stay spec evnts. Lower rates off-season. Higher rates for spec evnts/hols. Spec packages avail. Pking: Outdoor, free. Ltd CC. Extended-stay and senior discounts available.

Resorts

≣≣≣ **The Don Cesar Beach Resort**, 3400 Gulf Blvd, St Petersburg Beach, FL 33706; tel 813/360-1881 or toll free 800/282-1116; fax 813/367-6952. 15 mi SW of St Petersburg, exit 4 off I-275. At the end of US 19 and Fla 693, across the Pinellas Bayway. Another of Florida's golden oldies, the striking pink structure in faux-Moorish style has been well maintained, retaining much of its 1920s sparkle and glitter. It was said to have been a playground for Al Capone and F Scott and Zelda Fitzgerald, but today the clientele is more likely to be groups of insurance salesmen and specialists in medical paraphernalia. The endless beach, shared with private homes and condos, is the resort's main attraction. **Rooms:** 275 rms and stes. CI 4pm/CO noon. Express checkout avail. Nonsmoking rms avail. Aside from a few duds facing the courtyard (room 272, with its cubbyhole closet, should be avoided), the lodgings are adequate, with few glimmerings of decorating flair evident. **Amenities:** 🛁 🕹 🍷 A/C, cable TV. Some units w/terraces. **Services:** 🍴 🔑 VP 🚗 🖼 ⤳ Twice-daily maid svce, masseur, children's program, babysitting. Young, gung-ho staff. **Facilities:** 🛖 △ 🖼 🕹 ⚓ 🎾 500 🎱 🕹 4 rsts, 3 bars (2 w/entertainment), 1 beach (bay), lifeguard, spa, sauna, steam rm, whirlpool, beauty salon, day-care ctr, washer/dryer. Efficient, well-equipped business center; new fitness center. The classic King Charles dining room on the 5th floor is now reserved for weekend brunch; the other 2 restaurants are hardly worth a detour. **Rates:** HS Dec 23–Apr 30 $235–$265 S or D; from $285 ste. Extra person $15. Children under 18 stay free. Lower rates off-season. Spec packages avail. Pking: Outdoor, free. Maj CC.

≣≣≣ **Tradewinds**, 5500 Gulf Blvd, St Petersburg Beach, FL 33706; tel 813/367-6461 or toll free 800/237-0707; fax 813/367-4567. 18 acres. Clearly the size leader on the beach, this offers an excellent selection of accommodations. Lacking the style and class of the Don Cesar, it's more the Disney-like choice on the beach scene. With so many rooms and buildings spread along the shore, it's easy to get lost in the tropical setting. Families will thrive here. **Rooms:** 577 rms, stes, and effic. CI 4pm/CO noon. Nonsmoking rms avail. Some rooms with views of the lagoon or ocean. **Amenities:** 🛁 🄰 🖬 A/C, cable TV w/movies, refrig. All units w/terraces. **Services:** �🍽 🔑 VP 🖂 🍽 Car-rental desk, social director, masseur, children's program, babysitting. Large staff is attentive and smartly dressed. **Facilities:** 🎲 🛆 🆀 🍴 🚤 🛶 965 🖳 ⅄ 5 rsts, 3 bars (w/entertainment), 1 beach (ocean), board surfing, games rm, lawn games, racquetball, snorkeling, spa, sauna, steam rm, whirlpool, beauty salon, day-care ctr, playground, washer/dryer. **Rates:** HS Feb–Apr $179–$217 S or D; from $249 ste; from $189 effic. Extra person $15. Children under 12 stay free. Lower rates off-season. Spec packages avail. Pking: Indoor/outdoor, free. Maj CC.

Restaurants 🍴

Crabby Bill's Seafood Restaurant, 5100 Gulf Blvd, St Petersburg Beach; tel 813/360-8858. 38th St N exit off I-275. **Burgers/Seafood/Steak.** Very casual beach-house-style restaurant with terrific views of the gulf. Known for its many types of crabs and crab dishes: steamed blue crabs, garlic crabs, soft-shell crabs, stone crab claws, crab cakes. Also available are clams, mussels, and oysters, and shrimp, mahimahi, and catfish. **FYI:** Reservations not accepted. Children's menu. **Open:** Mon–Thurs 11:30am–10pm, Fri–Sat 11:30am–11pm, Sun noon–10pm. Closed some hols; Christmas week. **Prices:** Main courses $3.50–$16.95. Ltd CC. 🍽 🏖 🍱 ⅄

Hurricane, 807 Gulf Way, St Petersburg Beach; tel 813/360-9558. **New American.** Informal, 3-level indoor/outdoor restaurant specializing in Florida black grouper, which is prepared many ways. Also available are crab legs, shrimp, swordfish, and barbecued ribs and steaks. **FYI:** Reservations not accepted. Children's menu. **Open:** Daily 8pm–1:30am. **Prices:** Main courses $8.95–$17.95. Ltd CC. 🍽 🏖 ⅄

Leverock's Seafood House, 10 Corey Ave, St Petersburg Beach; tel 813/367-4588. **Seafood.** A fun, tidy, tropical eatery overlooking Boca Ciega Bay. Fresh seafood dishes served in a cheerful setting for affordable prices attract large crowds, particularly families. **FYI:** Reservations not accepted. Children's menu. **Open:** Daily 11:30am–10pm. Closed some hols. **Prices:** Main courses $6.95–$19.95. Maj CC. 🍱 ⅄

Silas Dent's, 5501 Gulf Blvd, St Petersburg Beach; tel 813/360-6961. Across from the Tradewinds Resort. **Seafood.** Seafood linguine, fried catfish, surf and turf, and filet mignon are served in a tropical atmosphere. Chicken Silas, with Spanish rice and spicy tomato pepper salsa, is the specialty. **FYI:** Reservations accepted. Children's menu. **Open:.** **Prices:** Main courses $8–$22. Ltd CC. ⅄

Woody's Waterfront, 7308 Sunset Way, St Petersburg Beach; tel 813/360-9265. **New American.** A popular beachgoers' hangout decorated in 1960s style, with colorful surfboards on display. Serving hot dogs, chicken wings, and some more substantial fare like grouper and other fresh fish. **FYI:** Reservations not accepted. Guitar. **Open:** Mon–Sat 11am–2am, Sun noon–1am. **Prices:** Main courses $4–$7. No CC. 🏖 ⅄

SANFORD
Map page M-7, C2

Hotel 🏨

≣≣≣ **Marina Hotel**, 530 N Palmetto Ave, Sanford, FL 32771; tel 407/323-6500 or toll free 800/290-1910; fax 407/322-7076. Exit 52 off I-4. A 2-story offering on Lake Monroe. **Rooms:** 100 rms. CI noon/CO 4pm. Express checkout avail. Nonsmoking rms avail. Rooms with lake, marina, or pool views. **Amenities:** 🛁 🄰 🖬 🕾 A/C, cable TV w/movies. **Services:** ✗ 🖂 🍽 ⅏ Babysitting. **Facilities:** 🎲 150 ⅄ 2 rsts, 2 bars (1 w/entertainment), lifeguard, washer/dryer. Pianist plays in restaurant 5 nights a week. **Rates:** HS Feb–May $59–$109 S or D. Extra person $10. Children under 18 stay free. Lower rates off-season. Higher rates for spec evnts/hols. Spec packages avail. Pking: Outdoor, free. Maj CC.

Motel

≣≣ **Days Inn**, 4650 W Fla 46, Sanford, FL 32771; tel 407/323-6500 or toll free 800/325-2525; fax 407/323-2962. Exit 52 off I-4. Economy lodging with easy interstate access midway between Daytona and Walt Disney World. **Rooms:** 120 rms. CI noon/CO noon. Nonsmoking rms avail. Highest priced rooms are on Intracoastal Waterway. **Amenities:** ☎ A/C, cable TV. **Services:** ⫫ ⫬ **Facilities:** 🏠 ⚃ 1 rst, washer/dryer. **Rates:** HS Jan 15–Apr $37–$78 S; $45–$78 D. Children under 18 stay free. Lower rates off-season. Higher rates for spec evnts/hols. Pking: Outdoor, free. Maj CC.

SANIBEL ISLAND
Map page M-8, E3

Hotels 🏨

▤▤ **Ramada Inn Resort**, 1231 Middle Gulf Dr, Sanibel Island, FL 33957; tel 813/472-4123 or toll free 800/443-0909; fax 813/472-0930. On a fine shorefront location, the 4-story property handles a brisk business in season. Some rooms could do with renovation. **Rooms:** 101 rms, stes, and effic. CI 3pm/CO 11am. Nonsmoking rms avail. **Amenities:** ☎ ⚃ A/C, cable TV, refrig, in-rm safe. **Services:** ✕ ⫫ **Facilities:** 🏠 ⚵ ⚃2 ▣40 ⚃ 1 rst, 2 bars (1 w/entertainment), 1 beach (ocean), washer/dryer. **Rates:** HS Dec–Apr $168–$215 S or D; from $215 ste; from $215 effic. Extra person $10. Children under 18 stay free. Lower rates off-season. Spec packages avail. Pking: Outdoor, free. Maj CC.

▤▤ **Song of the Sea**, 863 E Gulf Dr, Sanibel Island, FL 33957; tel 813/472-2220 or toll free 800/231-1045; fax 813/472-8569. A small, intimate establishment, with self-contained units. Architecture is a nice mix of country French and mission styles. **Rooms:** 30 effic. CI 3pm/CO 11am. **Amenities:** ☎ ⚃ ⚑ A/C, cable TV, refrig, VCR, in-rm safe. All units w/terraces. **Services:** ⫫ Babysitting. **Facilities:** 🏠 ⚵ ⚃ 1 beach (ocean), whirlpool, washer/dryer. **Rates (CP):** HS Feb–Apr from $259 effic. Extra person $10. Min stay HS and spec evnts. Lower rates off-season. Spec packages avail. Pking: Outdoor, free. Maj CC.

▤▤ **West Wind Inn**, 3345 W Gulf Dr, Sanibel Island, FL 33957; tel 813/472-1541 or toll free 800/824-0476, 800/282-2831 in FL; fax 813/472-8134. An enticing oceanfront resort with a relaxed atmosphere. **Rooms:** 104 rms and effic. CI 2pm/CO 11am. Nonsmoking rms avail. **Amenities:** ☎ ⚃ A/C, cable TV w/movies, refrig, in-rm safe. All units w/terraces. **Services:** ☞ ⫫ Babysitting. Attentive service throughout, even on the beach. **Facilities:** 🏠 ⚵ △ ⚓2 ▣50 ⚃ 1 rst, 2 bars, 1 beach (ocean), washer/dryer. Shell-cleaning hut for beachcombers. **Rates:** HS Dec–Apr $175–$193 S or D; from $198 effic. Extra person $17. Lower rates off-season. Pking: Outdoor, free. Maj CC.

Motels

▤ **Gallery Motel**, 541 E Gulf Dr, Sanibel Island, FL 33957; tel 813/472-1400 or toll free 800/831-7384; fax 813/472-6518. Exit 22 off I-75. A basic, beachfront family establishment. **Rooms:** 32 rms and effic. CI 2pm/CO 11am. **Amenities:** ☎ A/C, TV. Some units w/terraces. **Services:** ⫫ **Facilities:** 🏠 ⚵ 1 beach (ocean), washer/dryer. **Rates:** HS Feb–Apr $159 S or D; from $198 effic. Extra person $10. Min stay HS and wknds. Lower rates off-season. Higher rates for spec evnts/hols. Spec packages avail. Pking: Outdoor, free. Ltd CC.

▤ **Kona Kai**, 1539 Periwinkle Way, Sanibel Island, FL 33957; tel 813/472-1001; fax 813/472-4821. Exit 22 off I-75. Tropical garden setting. Located next to a popular seafood eatery. **Rooms:** 16 rms and effic. CI 3pm/CO 10am. Nonsmoking rms avail. **Amenities:** ☎ ▣ A/C, cable TV. **Services:** ⫫ **Facilities:** 🏠 **Rates:** HS Dec/Feb–Apr $86–$96 S or D; from $108 effic. Extra person $7. Children under 12 stay free. Lower rates off-season. Higher rates for spec evnts/hols. Spec packages avail. Pking: Outdoor, free. Maj CC.

Resorts

▤▤▤ **Casa Ybel Resort**, 2255 W Gulf Dr, Sanibel Island, FL 33957; tel 813/472-3145 or toll free 800/448-2736; fax 813/472-2109. 30 acres. In top form, this resort on the beach occupies more than a dozen 3-story buildings housing handsome condo-style accommodations. Lush, painstakingly maintained landscaping. **Rooms:** 114 effic. CI 3pm/CO 10am. **Amenities:** ☎ ⚃ ▣ A/C, cable TV, refrig, VCR. All units w/terraces. **Services:** ⫫ Social director, children's program, babysitting. **Facilities:** 🏠 ⚵ △ ⚓6 ⚑ 2 rsts (see also "Restaurants" below), 2 bars (1 w/entertainment), 1 beach (ocean), lawn games, whirlpool, playground, washer/dryer. **Rates:** HS Dec–Apr from $350 effic. Extra person $10. Children under 16 stay free. Min stay HS. Lower rates off-season. Higher rates for spec evnts/hols. Spec packages avail. Pking: Outdoor, free. Ltd CC.

▤▤ **Pointe Santo de Sanibel**, 2445 W Gulf Dr, Sanibel Island, FL 33957; tel 813/472-9100 or toll free 800/824-5442; fax 813/472-0487. A seaside condominium resort, set on a white sand beach with tall palms and lush greenery. **Rooms:** 22 effic. CI 3pm/CO 10am. All units have ocean views and tropical Florida decor. **Amenities:** ☎ ⚃ ▣ A/C, satel TV, refrig. All units w/terraces. **Services:** ⫫ Children's program, babysitting. **Facilities:** 🏠 ⚓2 1 beach (ocean), whirlpool, washer/dryer. Outdoor barbecue and dining under tiki huts. **Rates:** HS Dec/Feb–Apr from $235 effic. Children under 18 stay free. Min stay. Lower rates off-season. Higher rates for spec evnts/hols. Spec packages avail. Pking: Outdoor, free. Maj CC.

≡≡≡ **The Sanibel Inn**, 937 Gulf Dr, Sanibel Island, FL 33957; tel 813/472-3181 or toll free 800/237-1491; fax 873/472-5234. 14 mi SW of Ft Meyers, exit 21 off I-75. 8 acres. Enjoying a resurgence of popularity—the result of ambitious renovation—this friendly family place is neatly packaged on modestly landscaped grounds and has a fine beach. **Rooms:** 96 rms, stes, and effic. CI 3pm/CO 11am. Nonsmoking rms avail. Larger 2-bedroom units have double screened-in furnished porches and 2 full baths. **Amenities:** 🛅 🍷 📺 🍴 A/C, cable TV w/movies, refrig. All units w/terraces. **Services:** 🛎 🍽 Social director, children's program, babysitting. **Facilities:** 🛗 🚲 ⛺ ▶18 🎱2 🏊 📖 2 rsts, 2 bars (1 w/entertainment), 1 beach (ocean), washer/dryer. **Rates:** HS Feb–Apr 16 $225–$275 S or D; from $355 ste; from $245 effic. Extra person $10. Children under 12 stay free. Lower rates off-season. Spec packages avail. Pking: Outdoor, free. Maj CC.

≡≡≡ **Sundial Beach and Tennis Resort**, 1451 Middle Gulf Dr, Sanibel Island, FL 33957; tel 813/472-4151 or toll free 800/237-4184; fax 813/472-1809. 10 mi SW of Fort Meyers. via causeway connecting mainland at Runta Rasio. 20 acres. Affiliated with the Sanibel Inn (see above) and located on modestly landscaped beachfront, this full-service property attracts repeat visitors escaping the Northeast winter. Spacious public areas. **Rooms:** 300 effic. CI 3pm/CO 11am. Nonsmoking rms avail. One third of the units have been recently renovated. **Amenities:** 🛅 🍷 📺 A/C, cable TV, refrig. All units w/terraces. **Services:** ✗ 🛎 🍽 Social director, children's program, babysitting. **Facilities:** 🛗 🚲 ⛺ ▶18 🎱12 🏊 🎳 📖 ♿ 3 rsts (see also "Restaurants" below), 2 bars (1 w/entertainment), 1 beach (ocean), games rm, whirlpool, washer/dryer. Basketball court. **Rates:** HS Feb–Apr from $270 effic. Extra person $15. Children under 14 stay free. Lower rates off-season. AP and MAP rates avail. Spec packages avail. Pking: Indoor/outdoor, free. Maj CC.

Restaurants 🍴

Calamity Jane's Cafe, in Olde Sanibel, 630 Tarpon Bay Rd, Sanibel Island; tel 813/472-6622. At the west end of Periwinkle Way. **New American.** A western-style cafe with a fascinating post card collection decorating the ceiling. A great spot for families or anyone else looking for good home-style cooking. Soup du jour, New England clam chowder, grouper sandwich, and award-winning key lime pie. **FYI:** Reservations not accepted. Children's menu. Beer and wine only. **Open:** Breakfast Mon–Sat 8–11am; lunch Mon–Sat 11:30am–3pm; dinner Mon–Sat 5–9pm; brunch Sun 8am–noon. Closed some hols. **Prices:** Main courses $7.95–$13.95. Maj CC. 💟 ♿

Harbor House, 1244 Periwinkle Way, Sanibel Island; tel 813/472-1242. **Seafood/Steak.** The oldest restaurant on the island lives up to its name—its nautical theme is carried through in every detail, right down to the lighthouse candle at each table. A selection of well-priced seafood and steaks make this a good value. Try the key lime pie, which is made from limes picked right outside the door. **FYI:** Reservations not accepted. Children's menu. Beer and wine only. **Open:** HS Feb–Apr lunch Mon–Fri 11:30am–2pm; dinner daily 5–9:30pm. Reduced hours off-season. Closed some hols. **Prices:** Main courses $9–$15. Maj CC. ⬛ 💟

Jean-Paul's French Corner, 708 Tarpon Bay Rd, Sanibel Island; tel 813/472-1493. Next door to post office. **French.** Fine dining at an attractive French cafe. Selections such as roast duckling in fruit sauce, mixed seafood in a pastry shell, and the daily fresh seafood suggestion are available. **FYI:** Reservations accepted. Beer and wine only. **Open:** HS Nov–Apr open only Mon–Sat 6–10pm. Reduced hours off-season. Closed some hols; May–Oct. **Prices:** Main courses $19–$25. Ltd CC. 💟

Lighthouse Cafe, in Seahorse Shops, 362 Periwinkle Way, Sanibel Island; tel 813/472-0303. **New American.** A beacon for those in search of good food at great prices. Who can pass up eggs Benedict for $4.95? **FYI:** Reservations not accepted. Children's menu. Beer and wine only. **Open:** HS Christmas–Easter breakfast daily 7am–3pm; lunch daily 11am–3pm; dinner daily 5–9pm. Reduced hours off-season. Closed Labor Day–Sept 15. **Prices:** Lunch main courses $3.85–$5.75. Ltd CC. ♿

The Mad Hatter, 6460 Sanibel Captiva Rd, Sanibel Island; tel 813/472-0033. **New American/Seafood.** Located between the dunes and the beach, both the sitting and dining rooms offer beach views. Roasted sterling salmon is a special dish. **FYI:** Reservations recommended. Dress code. Beer and wine only. No smoking. **Open:** Mon–Sat 5–9:30pm. Closed some hols; Labor Day–Mid Sept. **Prices:** Main courses $16.50–$29.95. Maj CC. 💟 ♿

♣ **Thistle Lodge Waterfront Restaurant**, in Casa Ybel Resort, 2255 W Gulf Dr, Sanibel Island; tel 813/472-9200. **New American.** Inventive specialties include Florida seafood strudel with scallops, grouper, and lobster wrapped and roasted in lavender-scented phyllo, set on green Thai curry sauce; and goat cheese–crusted rack of Colorado lamb with Gilroy garlic. A wide selection of wines from all over the world are available. **FYI:** Reservations recommended. Jazz. Children's menu. **Open:** HS Jan–Apr daily 5:30–10pm. Reduced hours off-season. **Prices:** Main courses $21.95–$32.95. Maj CC. 💟 🏞 ♿

★ **Timbers Restaurant and Fish Market**, 703 Tarpon Bay Rd, Sanibel Island; tel 813/472-3128. Across from the post office. **Seafood/Steak.** The fish doesn't get much fresher than this—the fish market from which it comes is located right on the premises. You may be the one who ages a bit, though, as you wait to get in to this popular local hot spot. **FYI:** Reservations not accepted. Children's menu. **Open:** Daily 4:30–10pm. **Prices:** Main courses $13.95–$19.95. Maj CC. ♿

Windows on the Water, in Sundial Beach and Tennis Resort, 1451 Middle Gulf Dr, Sanibel Island; tel 813/472-5151. **Regional American/Cajun.** Here is an airy, casual restaurant overlooking the sea and an active pool area. Enjoy a glass of wine with smoked salmon, caesar salad, or shrimp cocktail. Penne Diablo is one of the most popular dishes on the menu. **FYI:** Reservations not accepted. Children's menu. No smoking. **Open:** Breakfast Mon–Sat 7:30–10:30am; lunch Mon–Sat 11:30am–3pm; dinner Sun–Thurs 5:30–9:30pm, Fri–Sat 5:30–10pm; brunch Sun 7:30–10am. **Prices:** Main courses $14–$20. Maj CC. ▦ ♥ ♿

Attractions 🖼

Sanibel/Captiva Conservation Foundation, 3333 Sanibel-Captiva Rd; tel 813/472-2329. A library, exhibits, guest lecturers, and a variety of brochures help explain the island's unusual ecosystem. Native plants, birdhouses, books, and nature-oriented gifts for sale. Guided and self-guided tours let visitors observe wildlife and native vegetation. The 247-acre wetlands tract features a 4-mile nature trail along the Sanibel River. **Open:** Winter, Mon–Sat 9am–4pm; summer, Mon–Fri 9am–3pm. Closed some hols. $

Sealife Learning Center, Wing Surf and Sport Center, 2353 Periwinkle Way; tel 813/472-8680. The center features a 450-gallon touch tank, 230-gallon shark tank, 18 other aquariums, and other sea animal displays to introduce nature enthusiasts to sea life in the Gulf of Mexico. Hourly guided program includes slide show and discussion. A 3½-hour van tour explores the flora and fauna of secluded beach areas of the island. **Open:** Sept–May, daily 9am–8pm; for other months, phone ahead. $$

J N "Ding" Darling National Wildlife Refuge, 1 Wildlife Dr; tel 813/472-1100. Over 5,000 protected acres of vibrant wildlife habitat. Along the 5-mile-long Wildlife Drive through undisturbed mangrove swamp, visitors have the chance to observe some of the hundreds of species of birds and migratory waterfowl that populate the refuge, including roseate spoonbills, white ibis, blue herons, snowy egrets, and ospreys. Also in abundance are alligators, otters, and raccoons. Hiking and winding canoe trails provide for fascinating viewing, as does the observation tower. The visitor center offers regularly scheduled slide shows. **Open:** Sat–Thurs dawn-dusk. $$

SANTA ROSA BEACH
Map page M-2, B4

Attraction 🖼

Grayton Beach State Recreation Area; tel 904/231-4210. Part of the Beaches of South Walton district, this outstanding park has a self-guided, 1.5-mile nature trail that traverses salt marsh, 40-foot-high sand dunes, and natural Florida scrub. The park also contains pine forests and the scenic Western Lake, with boat ramp. Swimming, fishing, camping, and picnicking permitted. For information write to PO Box 6600, Santa Rosa Beach, FL 32459. **Open:** 8am–sundown. $$

SARASOTA
Map page M-8, B2

See also Anna Maria Island, Bradenton, Bradenton Beach, Cortez, Longboat Key, Siesta Key

Hotels 🏨

▤▤▤ **Hyatt Sarasota**, 1000 Blvd of the Arts, Sarasota, FL 34236; tel 813/366-9000 or toll free 800/233-1234; fax 813/952-1987. The longstanding choice for businesspeople who enjoy access to the adjacent marina and beaches during their free time. **Rooms:** 297 rms and stes. CI 3pm/CO noon. Nonsmoking rms avail. Sharp guest accommodations are in top form. **Amenities:** 🛁 ♨ A/C, cable TV w/movies. Some units w/terraces. **Services:** ✕ VP 🚗 🗄 ⌂ Car-rental desk, babysitting. **Facilities:** 🛝 ⚲ 🛳 350 ♿ 2 rsts, 2 bars (1 w/entertainment). **Rates:** HS Jan–Apr $180–$205 S or D; from $350 ste. Extra person $25. Children under 16 stay free. Lower rates off-season. Spec packages avail. Pking: Outdoor, free. Maj CC.

▤▤▤ **Ramada Inn Airport**, 8440 N Tamiami Trail, Sarasota, FL 34243 (Sarasota-Bradenton Airport); tel 813/355-7771 or toll free 800/272-6232, 800/272-6232 in the US, 800/854-7854 in Canada; fax 813/351-7411. N of University Pkwy on US 41. Handy for those in town for a 1-day meeting or those who cannot find accommodations in the beach area. **Rooms:** 105 rms and stes. CI 3pm/CO 11am. Nonsmoking rms avail. **Amenities:** 🛁 📺 A/C, cable TV w/movies. **Services:** ✕ 🚐 🗄 ⌂ ⚐ **Facilities:** 🛝 350 ♿ 1 rst, 1 bar (w/entertainment), washer/dryer. Comedy Club operates Thursday through Sunday. **Rates (CP):** HS Mar–May $65 S; $85 D; from $95 ste. Extra person $5. Children under 18 stay free. Lower rates off-season. Pking: Outdoor, free. Maj CC.

≡≡ **Wellesley Inn**, 1803 N Tamiami Trail, Sarasota, FL 34234; tel 813/366-5128 or toll free 800/444-8888; fax 813/953-4322. 1 mile N of Fruitville Road. Located adjacent to a marina. **Rooms:** 106 rms and stes. CI 2pm/CO 11am. Nonsmoking rms avail. **Amenities:** 🏠 🐾 A/C, cable TV w/movies. **Services:** 🚗 📠 🛎 🐾 **Facilities:** 🏋 🍴 ⚖ **Rates (CP):** HS Jan–Apr $90–$100 S or D; from $119 ste. Extra person $6. Children under 17 stay free. Lower rates off-season. Higher rates for spec evnts/hols. Pking: Outdoor, free. Maj CC.

Motel

≡≡ **Comfort Inn**, 4800 N Tamiami Trail, Sarasota, FL 34234; tel 813/355-7091 or toll free 800/228-5150; fax 813/359-1639. ¼ mile S of University Pkwy. A comfortable spot for budget-minded travelers who want clean, pleasant surroundings. **Rooms:** 81 rms, stes, and effic. CI 2pm/CO 11am. Nonsmoking rms avail. **Amenities:** 🏠 🐾 A/C, cable TV w/movies. Some units w/Jacuzzis. **Services:** 📠 🐾 🐾 **Facilities:** 🏋 ⚖ Whirlpool, washer/dryer. **Rates (CP):** HS Dec–May $70 S; $90 D; from $140 ste; from $110 effic. Extra person $5. Children under 18 stay free. Lower rates off-season. Higher rates for spec evnts/hols. Spec packages avail. Pking: Outdoor, free. Maj CC.

Restaurants 🍴

Bijou Cafe, 1287 1st St, Sarasota; tel 813/366-8111. 2 blocks E of US 41 N; across the street from the Opera House. **New American/Continental.** A charming, stylish little cafe with a wonderful menu and wine list. Daily offerings may include roast duckling, veal, and New Orleans crabcakes. **FYI:** Reservations recommended. **Open:** Lunch Mon–Fri 11:30am–2pm; dinner Sun–Thurs 5–9:30pm, Fri–Sat 5–10:30pm. Closed some hols. **Prices:** Main courses $12.95–$21. Maj CC. 💟 ⚖

The Buttery, 470 John Ringling Circle, Sarasota (St Armands Key); tel 813/388-1523. **New American.** Choose either a counterside seat or a comfortable booth at this clean, small cafe. Breakfast, lunch, and dinner are served around the clock. The menu includes various sandwiches, salads, burgers, and dinner specials. **FYI:** Reservations not accepted. Beer and wine only. **Open:** Daily 24 hrs. **Prices:** Main courses $4–$9.95. Ltd CC. 🏧

Cafe l'Europe, 431 St Armands Circle, Sarasota (St Armands Key); tel 813/388-4415. **Continental/French.** A cozy French cafe with exposed brick in the bar area. Dining is also available on the patio. The menu offers rack of lamb, crab dijon, roast duckling, pork piccata, and a variety of beef and seafood dishes. **FYI:** Reservations accepted. Piano. **Open:** Lunch Mon–Sat 11am–4pm; dinner Mon–Sat 5–11pm, Sun 5–10pm. **Prices:** Main courses $16–$22. Maj CC. ⚖

Cafe St Louie, in Bay Plaza, 1258 N Palm Ave, Sarasota; tel 813/955-8550. 1 block E of US 41. **Steak.** Save $3 on all entrees if you arrive 4:30–5:30pm. Choices include the fresh catch of the day, salmon, pasta dishes, and St Louis chicken. **FYI:** Reservations recommended. Children's menu. No smoking. **Open:** Dinner daily 4:30–10pm. **Prices:** Main courses $12.95–$23.95; PF dinner $50. Maj CC. 💟 VP ⚖

Caragiulos, 69 S Palm Ave, Sarasota; tel 813/951-0866. Between Ringling Blvd and Main St. **Italian/Pizza.** A small cafe near the theater district offering pizzas and pastas along with soups, salads, and sandwiches. Outdoor streetside table service is available. **FYI:** Reservations not accepted. Guitar. Beer and wine only. **Open:** Mon–Thurs 11am–10pm, Fri–Sat 11am–11pm, Sun 5–10pm. Closed some hols. **Prices:** Main courses $5.95–$13.95. Maj CC. 🍴 🍷 📺 💟 ⚖

Charley's Crab, 420 St Armands Circle, Sarasota (St Armands Key); tel 813/388-3964. **Seafood.** After a stroll around the circle, stop into this tavern-style restaurant for one of the pasta or fish selections. The setting is comfortable and the service attentive. **FYI:** Reservations accepted. Piano. Children's menu. **Open:** Lunch Mon–Sat 11:30am–2:30pm, Sun noon–2:30pm; dinner Sun–Sat 5–10pm. **Prices:** Main courses $10–$21. Maj CC. ⚖

Coasters Seafood Bistro, 1500 Stickney Point Rd, Sarasota; tel 813/923-4848. Just E of Stickney Point Bridge. **Regional American.** Both the floor-to-ceiling windows and the outside deck offer lovely views of the Intracoastal Waterway. Specialties include mahimahi with pineapple sweet-and-sour glaze. **FYI:** Reservations accepted. Combo. Children's menu. **Open:** Lunch daily 11:30am–3:45pm; dinner Sun–Thurs 4–10pm, Fri–Sat 4–11pm. Closed some hols. **Prices:** Main courses $12.95–$18.95. Maj CC. VP ⚖

The Columbia, 411 St Armands Circle, Sarasota (St Armands Key); tel 813/388-3987. **Spanish.** The newest branch of this popular Spanish-Cuban chain couldn't be in a more appealing location. The menu includes meat, chicken, and seafood dishes, including 3 types of spicy paellas. A favorite starter is the "Original 1905 Salad," prepared tableside. Lunch specials are a great value. **FYI:** Reservations accepted. **Open:** Mon–Sat 11am–11pm, Sun noon–10pm. **Prices:** Main courses $16–$20. Maj CC. ⚖

Hemingway's, 325 John Ringling Blvd, St Armands Circle, Sarasota; tel 813/388-3948. **New American.** This family-style restaurant may appeal to a less discerning crowd. Seafood and meat dishes are supplemented by soups and salads on the standard menu. **FYI:** Reservations accepted. Children's menu.

Open:. Lunch Sun–Sat 11:30am–4pm; dinner Sun–Thurs 4–10pm, Fri–Sat 4–11pm. **Prices:** Main courses $10.95–$24.95. Maj CC. 🍽 📷 📹 ♿

$ **Mrs. Appleton's Family Buffet**, in Palm Plaza, 4458 Bee Ridge Rd, Sarasota; tel 813/378-1177. Exit 38 off I-75. **Buffet.** Mrs. Appleton can satisfy almost any craving with her massive smorgasbord. This cafeteria-style dining room is quite a find for hungry families. **FYI:** Reservations not accepted. Children's menu. No liquor license. **Open:** Breakfast Sat–Sun 8–10:30am; lunch Mon–Sat 11am–3:30pm, Sun 11am–4pm; dinner daily 4pm–8:30. **Prices:** PF dinner $6.95. Ltd CC. 📷 ♿

Nick's on the Water, 230 Sarasota Quay, Sarasota; tel 813/954-3839. **Italian.** A comfortable waterside restaurant serving dishes such as pizza, pasta, steak pizzaiola, and the chef's special veal medallions. Terrace diners can watch boats come and go from the nearby marina. **FYI:** Reservations accepted. **Open:** Sun–Thurs 11:30am–10pm, Fri–Sat 11:30am–11pm. **Prices:** Main courses $8.95–$16.95. Maj CC. 🍽 📹 ♿

Old Hickory, 5100 N Tamiami Trail, Sarasota; tel 813/355-8757. At Mecca St near Ringling Museum. **Barbecue.** A comfortable, casual restaurant and lounge. Enjoy Old Hickory's famous homemade barbecue sauce on beef, pork, baby back ribs, or chicken. All items are hickory-smoked. **FYI:** Reservations not accepted. **Open:** Mon–Sat 11:30am–10:30pm. Closed Dec 25. **Prices:** Main courses $5.95–$12.95. Ltd CC. 📹

Patrick's, 1442 Main St, Sarasota; tel 813/952-1170. **New American.** A casual sports bar and restaurant with a black-and-white tile floor and a veritable jungle of plants. Seafood, poultry, pasta, and burgers populate the dinner menu; sandwiches and salads are offered at lunch. **FYI:** Reservations not accepted. **Open:** Sun–Thurs 11am–midnight, Fri–Sat 11am–1am. Closed Dec 25. **Prices:** Main courses $6.95–$16.95. Maj CC. 📹 ♿

Ristorante Bellini, 1551 Main St, Sarasota; tel 813/365-7380. Between Orange and Lemon Aves. **Northern Italian.** A comfortable, romantic Italian bistro with a menu featuring chicken cacciatore and a variety of pasta dishes. Highlights also include scaloppine Bellini (veal topped with asparagus and mozzarella cheese) and sautéed snapper. **FYI:** Reservations accepted. Beer and wine only. **Open:** Lunch Mon–Fri 11:30am–2pm; dinner Mon–Sat 6–10pm. **Prices:** Main courses $10–$22. Ltd CC. ♥ ♿

Shells, 7253 S Tamiami Trail, Sarasota; tel 813/924-2568. 2 mi S of Downtown Sarasota. **Seafood/Steak.** A local favorite with a cheerful staff. Choose either one of the many seafood selections or the vegetable stir-fry. A good value. **FYI:** Reservations not

accepted. Children's menu. **Open:** Sun–Thurs 4–10pm, Fri–Sat 4–11pm. Closed some hols. **Prices:** Main courses $3.95–$16.95. Maj CC. ♿

Yoder's, 3434 Bahia Vista St, Sarasota; tel 813/955-7771. 3 mi E of downtown Sarasota. **Regional American/Amish.** A restaurant offering home-style atmosphere along with its home-cooked food. Full breakfasts are available for $2.95. Burgers and sandwiches are available at lunch. Mom's meatloaf with gravy and the chicken pot pie are dinnertime favorites. **FYI:** Reservations not accepted. Children's menu. No liquor license. No smoking. **Open:** Mon–Sat 6am–8pm. Closed some hols. **Prices:** Main courses $4.95–$9.95. No CC. 📷 ♿

Refreshment Stop 🥤

Garaways Gourmet Coffee, 367 St Armands Circle Ste 2A, Sarasota (St Armands Key); tel 813/388-4225. **Coffeehouse.** Enjoy your choice of coffees, espressos, and cappuccinos here—25 different kinds of beans are roasted on the premises. Beverages and desserts are served both indoors and out. **Open:** Mon–Thurs 9am–11pm, Fri–Sat 9am–midnight, Sun 10am–10pm. Closed some hols. Maj CC.

Attractions 💼

Ringling Museum Complex, 5401 Bay Shore Rd; tel 813/359-5700 or 813/351-1660 (recorded info). This 66-acre site overlooking Sarasota Bay is the former estate of circus entrepreneur John Ringling. Its 4 attractions include the John and Mable Ringling Museum of Art, Florida's official state art museum, which contains a major exhibit of baroque art; the 30-room Ringling Mansion Ca' d'Zan ('House of John"), the winter residence that was modeled after a Venetian palace; the Circus Museum, devoted to circus memorabilia; and the Asolo Theater. The grounds also contain restaurants and shops. **Open:** Daily 10am–5:30pm. Closed some hols. $$$

Mote Marine Science Aquarium, 1600 Thompson Pkwy; tel 813/388-4441. This facility, located on City Island, focuses on local marine life. Displays include a living mangrove swamp and seagrass environment, a 135,000-gallon shark tank, loggerhead turtles and their eggs, dolphins, manatees, and an extensive shell collection. Also, "research exhibits" on red tide, aquaculture enhancement, cancer in sharks, and effects of pesticide and petroleum pollution on the coast. **Open:** Daily 10am–5pm. Closed some hols. $$

Marie Selby Botanical Gardens, 811 S Palm Ave; tel 813/366-5730. A 17-acre museum of living plants that is home to more than 20,000 exotic plants, including over 6,000 orchids.

Also featured are a waterfall garden, cactus garden, fernery, hibiscus garden, palm grove, tropical food garden, and bamboo pavilion. **Open:** Daily 10am–5pm. Closed Dec 25. $$$

Bellm's Cars & Music of Yesterday, 5500 N Tamiami Trail (US 41); tel 813/355-6228. This museum displays over 200 classic and antique autos, from Rolls-Royces to Pierce Arrows. There are also over 1,200 antique music machines, from miniature music boxes to a 30-foot Belgian organ. **Open:** Daily 9:30am–5:30pm. $$$

Myakka River State Park, 13207 Fla 72; tel 813/361-6511. The Myakka River has been designated a National Wild and Scenic River within Sarasota County. The park, located off Fla 72, covers more than 28,000 acres of dry prairie, pine flatwoods, and numerous small wetlands. Fishing, canoe rentals, hiking, camping, nature trails. $$

SEASIDE

Map page M-2, C4

Resort 🏨

Seaside Cottage Rental Agency, County Rd 30A, PO Box 4730, Seaside, FL 32459; tel 904/231-4224 or toll free 800/277-TOWN; fax 904/231-2219. Take US 98 to Fla 283, proceed 2 miles and turn east onto County Rd 30A into Seaside. Handles rentals for a set of impressive, well-designed shoreline accommodations that range from beautifully furnished homes to hideaway cottages. Unrated. **Rooms:** 12 rms and effic; 166 ctges/villas. CI 4pm/CO noon. Nonsmoking rms avail. **Amenities:** 🛆 🐾 🖥 A/C, cable TV, refrig, VCR, stereo/tape player. All units w/terraces, some w/fireplaces, some w/Jacuzzis. **Services:** ✗ 🖚 🛆 🍴 Twice-daily maid svce, social director, children's program. **Facilities:** 🐚 🚲 🏊 🎱 8 🏓 100 🖥 8 rsts, 2 bars (w/entertainment), 1 beach (ocean), board surfing, lawn games, playground, washer/dryer. **Rates:** HS June–Sept $105 S or D; from $220 effic; from $167 ctge/villa. Children under 18 stay free. Min stay HS. Lower rates off-season. Spec packages avail. Pking: Outdoor, free. Maj CC.

Restaurant 🍴

Shades, Seaside Center, Seaside; tel 904/231-1950. **Seafood.** The rustic interior of this seafood place has hardwood floors and a fireplace. Festive atmosphere on the patio. **FYI:** Reservations not accepted. Guitar/singer. Children's menu. **Open:** Daily 11am–10pm. Closed some hols; Jan 1–14. **Prices:** Main courses $3.50–$16.95. Ltd CC. 🛆 💟 🛆

SEBRING

Map page M-8, B4

Hotel 🏨

🇪🇪 **Holiday Inn**, 6525 US 27 N, Sebring, FL 33870; tel 813/385-4500 or toll free 800/HOLIDAY; fax 813/382-4793. 80 mi SE of Tampa. US 27 exit off I-4. Basic lodging on the highway. **Rooms:** 148 rms and stes. CI 4pm/CO noon. Nonsmoking rms avail. **Amenities:** 🛍 A/C, cable TV w/movies. **Services:** ✗ 🛆 🍴 Masseur. **Facilities:** 🐚 🏓 500 🛆 1 rst, 1 bar (w/entertainment), washer/dryer. **Rates:** HS Nov–Apr $55–$65 S; $60–$70 D; from $95 ste. Extra person $5. Children under 18 stay free. Lower rates off-season. Higher rates for spec evnts/hols. Pking: Outdoor, free. Maj CC.

Attraction 💼

Highlands Hammock State Park; tel 813/386-6094. This is one of Florida's original state parks, which were built by the New Deal–era Civilian Conservation Corps. Its 3,800 tranquil acres encompass a hardwood hammock and a cypress swamp. Hiking, nature trails, camping. $$

SIESTA KEY

Map page M-8, B2

Hotel 🏨

🇪🇪 **Crescent View Beach Club**, 6512 Midnight Pass Rd, Siesta Key, FL 34242; tel 813/349-2000 or toll free 800/344-7171; fax 813/349-9748. ¼ mi S of Stickney Point Rd. A condominium-style complex, with tropical decor throughout. **Rooms:** 26 effic. CI 3pm/CO 11am. **Amenities:** 🛍 🛆 🖥 A/C, cable TV w/movies, refrig. Some units w/terraces. All rooms have ceiling fans and washers and dryers. **Services:** 🍴 Babysitting. **Facilities:** 🐚 1 beach (ocean), whirlpool, washer/dryer. **Rates:** HS Feb–Apr from $175 effic. Lower rates off-season. Spec packages avail. Pking: Outdoor, free. Maj CC.

Motels

🇪🇪 **Best Western Siesta Beach Resort**, 5311 Ocean Blvd, Siesta Key, FL 34242; tel 813/349-3211 or toll free 800/223-5786; fax 813/349-7915. Exit 38 off I-75. 2 miles N of Stickney Point Rd. Comfortable, unpretentious atmosphere, good for families. Handy to local attractions. **Rooms:** 53 rms, stes, and effic. CI 3pm/CO 11am. Nonsmoking rms avail.

Amenities: A/C, cable TV. **Services:** ✕ 🖼 🗊 Complimentary morning coffee. Free passes offered on the Siesta Key trolley. **Facilities:** Whirlpool, washer/dryer. **Rates:** HS Feb–Mar $99–$115 S or D; from $155 ste; from $135 effic. Extra person $8. Children under 18 stay free. Lower rates off-season. Higher rates for spec evnts/hols. Spec packages avail. Pking: Outdoor, free. Maj CC.

Gulf Sun Motel, 6722 Midnight Pass Rd, Siesta Key, FL 34242; tel 813/349-2442 or toll free 800/653-6753; fax 813/349-7141. 1 mi S of Stickney Point Rd. For budget-minded families with young children. Beach access. **Rooms:** 17 rms and effic. CI 2pm/CO 10am. Nonsmoking rms avail. **Amenities:** A/C, cable TV, refrig. Gas grills, beach umbrellas, and kiddie toys are available to guests. **Services:** 🗊 **Facilities:** Washer/dryer. **Rates:** HS Jan–Apr $90 S or D; from $115 effic. Extra person $10. Children under 2 stay free. Min stay HS. Lower rates off-season. Pking: Outdoor, free. Ltd CC.

Restaurant 🍴

Turtle's, 8875 Midnight Pass Rd, Siesta Key; tel 813/346-2207. 5 mi S of Sarasota. **Seafood/Steak.** Dine along the water's edge at this marina-side restaurant. The menu features grouper in potato crust, sautéed Dungeness crab cakes, rack of lamb, and ribs. A good spot for late-night dining. **FYI:** Reservations recommended. Singer. Children's menu. **Open:** Daily 11:30am–11:30pm. **Prices:** Main courses $10.95–$17.95. Maj CC. 🍷🖼 💺🕊

SILVER SPRINGS
Map page M-6, A4

Motels 🛏

Holiday Inn, 5751 E Silver Springs Blvd, PO Box 156, Silver Springs, FL 32688; tel 904/236-2575 or toll free 800/HOLIDAY; fax 904/236-2575 ext 163. 1 mi E of Ocala. Located at the entrance to Silver Springs; suited for families. **Rooms:** 103 rms and stes. CI 2pm/CO noon. Express checkout avail. Nonsmoking rms avail. **Amenities:** A/C, cable TV w/movies, in-rm safe. **Services:** ✕ 🖼 🗊 **Facilities:** 🕊 1 rst, 1 bar. **Rates:** HS Feb–Apr/June–Aug $40–$50 S; $50–$60 D; from $94 ste. Extra person $6. Children under 18 stay free. Lower rates off-season. Higher rates for spec evnts/hols. Pking: Outdoor, free. Maj CC.

Howard Johnson Lodge, 5565 E Silver Springs Blvd, PO Box 475, Silver Springs, FL 34489; tel 904/236-1941 or toll free 800/I GO HOJO; fax 904/236-1941. Exit 69 off I-75. Its two 2-story buildings lie opposite Wild Waters water park and within walking distance of Silver Springs. **Rooms:** 89 rms. CI 11am/CO noon. Nonsmoking rms avail. **Amenities:** A/C, cable TV. **Services:** 🗊 🍽 **Facilities:** 🕊 Italian restaurant next door offers discounts to guests and delivers to rooms. **Rates:** $35–$39 S or D. Extra person $8. Children under 18 stay free. Pking: Outdoor, free. Maj CC.

Attraction

Silver Springs; tel 904/236-1212 or 800/234-7458. Located just off I-75. Venerated by Native Americans since ancient times, the springs have produced half a billion gallons of water daily for the past 100,000 years. Glass-bottom boats ply the waters of this 350-acre site, making 4 tours that highlight the area's 7 major springs. In addition, the **Jungle Cruise** passes through a waterway lined with habitats containing 25 species of exotic animals from across the globe, while the **Lost River Voyage** traverses untouched areas. A stop is made on this tour for a presentation at the wildlife outpost, where injured animals are brought and nursed back to health. **Safari trams** wind through jungle habitats where visitors can see roaming zebras, deer, monkeys, and even the occasional tapir or sloth. With petting zoo and animal shows. A recent addition is the **Touch of Garlits** antique and race car museum. **Open:** Daily 9am–5:30pm; extended hours during hols and summer. $$$$

SINGER ISLAND
Map page M-9, D4

See also Riviera Beach

Hotel 🛏

Sheraton Ocean Inn, 3200 N Ocean Dr, Singer Island, FL 33404; tel 407/842-6171 or toll free 800/327-0522; fax 407/848-6842. Floor-to-ceiling windows in the tropically decorated units ensure guests won't miss a sunrise. **Rooms:** 202 rms and stes. CI 3pm/CO noon. Nonsmoking rms avail. **Amenities:** A/C, cable TV w/movies. All units w/terraces. **Services:** ✕ 🚐 🖼 🗊 **Facilities:** 🕊 1 rst, 3 bars (1 w/entertainment), 1 beach (ocean), games rm, washer/dryer. Sports bar opens in afternoons for pizza and happy hour drinks. **Rates:** HS Dec–Apr $140–$180 S or D; from $180 ste. Children under 18 stay free. Lower rates off-season. Higher rates for spec evnts/hols. Pking: Outdoor, free. Maj CC.

Motel

▤▤ **Rutledge Inn**, 3730 Ocean Dr, Singer Island, FL 33404; tel 407/848-6621 or toll free 800/348-7946; fax 407/840-1787. Blue Heron Blvd exit off I-95. Comfortable oceanfront accommodations in a seaside setting. Good beach. **Rooms:** 60 rms, stes, and effic. CI 2pm/CO noon. **Amenities:** 🛗 A/C, cable TV, refrig. All units w/terraces. **Services:** ▦ 🍴 **Facilities:** 🛗 1 bar, 1 beach (ocean), washer/dryer. Eye-level wall blocks sunbathers on the deck from strong breezes. **Rates:** HS Feb–Mar $80–$86 S or D; from $200 ste; from $90 effic. Extra person $6. Children under 18 stay free. Lower rates off-season. Higher rates for spec evnts/hols. Pking: Outdoor, free. Maj CC.

SOUTH MIAMI
Map page M-11, B2

Restaurant 🍴

LB's Eatery, 5813 Ponce de Leon Blvd, South Miami; tel 305/661-7091. At Hurricane Dr, near Univ of Miami Stadium. **American.** A casual, cafeteria-style eatery with basic decor. You can create your own sandwiches on a variety of breads, and have them with your choice of salad. The dinner menu offers selections such as lasagna, roast beef, and vegetarian entrees. **FYI:** Reservations not accepted. No liquor license. **Open:** Mon–Thurs 11am–10pm, Fri–Sat 11am–11:30pm. Closed Dec 25. **Prices:** Main courses $5–$8. Ltd CC. ♿

SPRING HILL
Map page M-6, C3

Attraction 🏛

Weeki Wachee Spring, 6131 Commercial Way; tel 904/596-2062 or 800/678-9335. "The City of Mermaids" has been drawing visitors to its underwater performances since 1947, when a former US Navy frogman taught underwater breathing techniques to a few young women, dressed them in mermaid outfits, and began staging shows 16 feet below the surface of the clear waters of Weeki Wachee ("winding waters") Spring. Guests watch the show through thick plate glass windows. Shows take place several times daily on 2 underwater "stages" (featuring Hans Christian Andersen's *The Little Mermaid*). Shows on dry land include the Birds of Prey show, with free-flying eagles, falcons, hawks, and owls, and the Exotic Bird Show, with trained parrots, macaws, and other birds. There is also a petting zoo.

The **Wilderness River Cruise** is a boat tour down a waterway filled with native foliage and wildlife. One highlight is Pelican Preserve, a refuge that treats and releases injured birds.

Adjacent is **Buccaneer Bay** (separate admission), the only Florida water park that uses water from a natural spring. Features include water slides, Lazy River tube ride, beach volleyball, and a children's area. **Open:** Daily 9:30am–5:30pm; extended summer hours. $$$$

STUART
Map page M-9, C3

Motels 🏨

▤▤ **Holiday Inn–Downtown**, 1209 S Federal Hwy, PO Box 566, Stuart, FL 34995; or toll free 800/HOLIDAY; fax 407/287-6200 ext 100. Although located on a busy commercial road, guests have access to the beach through the nearby Holiday Inn Surfside. Caribbean island theme; Custom House lobby is decked with potted palms and overhead fans. **Rooms:** 126 rms and stes. CI 1pm/CO noon. Express checkout avail. Nonsmoking rms avail. Executive suite features its own whirlpool and dry bar. **Amenities:** 🛗 ♨ A/C, cable TV w/movies. **Services:** ✗ ▦ 🍴 **Facilities:** 🛗 🏊 ⚓ 100 ♿ 1 rst, 1 bar, sauna, washer/dryer. **Rates:** HS Oct–Mar $87 S or D; from $160 ste. Children under 12 stay free. Lower rates off-season. Pking: Outdoor, free. Maj CC.

▤▤ **Howard Johnson Lodge**, 950 S Federal Hwy, Stuart, FL 34994; or toll free 800/I GO HOJO; fax 407/220-3594. ½ mi S of jct Fla 76 on US 1. This centrally located, 2-story motel is fine for families not requiring beach frontage. **Rooms:** 82 rms. CI 2pm/CO noon. Nonsmoking rms avail. **Amenities:** 🛗 A/C, cable TV. Some units w/terraces. **Services:** ✗ ▦ 🍴 **Facilities:** 🛗 🏊 140 ♿ 1 rst, 1 bar (w/entertainment), washer/dryer. Attractive landscaped pool area with lounge chairs. **Rates (CP):** HS Jan–May $75 S or D. Min stay spec evnts. Lower rates off-season. Spec packages avail. Pking: Outdoor, free. Maj CC.

Resort

▤▤▤ **Indian River Plantation Beach Resort**, 555 NE Ocean Blvd, Stuart, FL 34996; tel 407/225-3700 or toll free 800/444-3389; fax 407/225-0003. Exit 61 or 67 off I-95. 200 acres. Occupying a former pineapple plantation, this resort is by far the largest of its kind on Hutchinson Island. It offers lush surroundings and a white lattice-and-wicker lobby filled with plants. The numerous activities available to both adults and children make this an excellent choice for families. **Rooms:** 306 rms, stes, and effic. CI 3pm/CO 11am. Nonsmoking rms avail. Larger accommodations offer complete kitchen facilities. Standard units have 2-poster beds and trendy color combinations. **Amenities:** 🔒 ☕ 🍽 A/C, cable TV w/movies, refrig. All units w/terraces. **Services:** 🍴 ⛟ 🆅🅿 🚗 🖼 ⤵ 🛎 Car-rental desk, social director, children's program, babysitting. **Facilities:** 🛗 🚲 ⛰ 🛍 ⛳18 🏊 🏌6 🎾 ⚓ 🚴 🛶 🏄 🎱 5 rsts, 4 bars (3 w/entertainment), 2 beaches (ocean, bay), board surfing, games rm, snorkeling, whirlpool, playground, washer/dryer. **Rates:** HS Apr–May/Sept–Oct $160 S or D; from $230 ste; from $160 effic. Extra person $25. Children under 17 stay free. Lower rates off-season. Higher rates for spec evnts/hols. AP and MAP rates avail. Spec packages avail. Pking: Indoor/outdoor, free. Maj CC.

Restaurants 🍴

★ **Ashley Restaurant**, 61 SW Osceola St, Stuart; tel 407/221-9476. **Regional American/French.** Delightful art deco styling, inventive cuisine. Popular menu selections include duck à l'orange and steak pizzaiola. **FYI:** Reservations not accepted. Band/guitar. **Open:** Lunch daily 11:30am–2:30pm; dinner daily 5–10pm. Closed some hols; Sept. **Prices:** Main courses $7–$15. Maj CC. 💟 ♿

China Star, 1501 S Federal Hwy, Stuart; tel 407/283-8378. 1 mile S of Colorado Ave. **Chinese.** Decor featuring Asian murals and handsome lacquered furniture set the tone in this cool, pleasant eatery. Extensive menu. **FYI:** Reservations recommended. Beer and wine only. **Open:** Daily 11am–10pm. Closed Thanksgiving. **Prices:** Main courses $5.25–$10.95; PF dinner $9.25. Maj CC. ♿

Flagler Grill, 47 SW Flagler Ave, Stuart; tel 407/221-9517. **Eclectic.** A casual eatery where crayons are provided for doodling on the paper tablecloths. Patrons can watch their meals being prepared in the open kitchen. **FYI:** Reservations recommended. Beer and wine only. No smoking. **Open:** Daily 5:30–9:30pm. Closed some hols. **Prices:** Main courses $12–$18. Maj CC. 💟 ♿

Nature's Way Cafe, 25 SW Osceola St in the Post Office Arcade, Stuart; tel 407/220-7306. **Deli/Health/Spa.** A casual yet lively place attracting a hip, health-conscious crowd. You can create your own salad or choose one of the tropical fruit salads on the menu. Young, energetic staff. **FYI:** Reservations not accepted. No liquor license. **Open:** Mon–Fri 10am–4pm, Sat 11am–3pm. Closed some hols. **Prices:** Lunch main courses $4–$6. No CC. ♿

Refreshment Stop ☕

Osceola Bakery, 38 W Osceola St, Stuart; tel 407/287-BAKE. **Deli.** A fun, casual place filled with enticing aromas. Wide variety of delectable desserts and pastries. **Open:** Mon–Fri 8am–5pm, Sat 9am–3pm. Closed some hols. No CC.

Attractions 🎭

Elliott Museum, 825 NE Ocean Blvd; tel 407/225-1961. Built in honor of the inventor Sterling Elliott, this museum packed with early Americana illustrates life from the Revolutionary War to the Civil War. An apothecary, a barbershop, a blacksmith forge, and a clock and watch shop are among the the life-size dioramas on view. The highlight of the museum is the display of some of Elliott's many inventions, including the first envelope-addressing machine, a mechanical knot-tier, and a quadricycle. **Open:** Daily 11am–4pm. Closed some hols. $

Gilbert's Bar House of Refuge, 301 SE MacArthur Blvd; tel 407/225-1875. Dating from 1875, the oldest structure in this area was originally a refuge center for shipwrecked sailors. Convincingly restored, today it functions as a historical museum, with displays of marine artifacts, life-boat equipment, ships' logs, and other interesting objects. **Open:** Tues–Sun 11am–4:15pm. Closed some hols. $

SUGAR LOAF KEY

Map page M-10, E3

Motel 🏨

🛏 **Sugarloaf Lodge**, Overseas Hwy, MM 17, PO Box 148, Sugar Loaf Key, FL 33044; tel 305/745-3211; fax 305/745-3389. More motel than lodge, with a few extras. Grounds need work. **Rooms:** 55 rms and effic. CI 1pm/CO 11am. Inexpensively furnished rooms with 1960s look. **Amenities:** 🔒 A/C, cable TV, refrig. All units w/terraces. **Services:** ✕ ⤵ 🛎 Babysitting. **Facilities:** 🛗 ⛰ 🛍 🎱2 1 rst (see also "Restaurants" below), 1 bar (w/entertainment), 1 beach (bay), lawn games, snorkeling, washer/dryer. Dolphin show 3 times daily. Three-thousand foot airstrip available. Small beach is grassy and weedy. **Rates:** HS Dec–Apr $90 S or D; from $100 effic. Extra person $10. Children under 12 stay free. Min stay spec evnts. Lower rates off-season. Pking: Outdoor, free. Maj CC.

Restaurants 🍴

Mangrove Mama's Restaurant, Overseas Hwy, MM 20, Sugar Loaf Key; tel 305/745-3030. **Seafood/Vegetarian.** Casablanca-style fans whirl overhead in this very casual, homestyle restaurant, an open-air eatery that is a staple among locals. The menu features shrimp and fish tempura. The key lime pie shouldn't be missed. **FYI:** Reservations accepted. Guitar. Children's menu. **Open:** Daily 11:30am–10pm. Closed Dec 25; June. **Prices:** Main courses $13.50–$20.50. Ltd CC. ♨ 🖼

Maximillions Diner, in Sugarloaf Lodge, Overseas Hwy, MM 17, Sugar Loaf Key; tel 305/745-3741. **American.** The decor may be mundane, but the sunset views are decidedly not. Popular menu items include prime rib, blackened chicken breast, and barbecued baby-back Canadian ribs. **FYI:** Reservations accepted. **Open:** Breakfast daily 7:30–11am; lunch daily 11am–2:15pm; dinner daily 5–9pm. **Prices:** Main courses $9–$17. Maj CC. ⛰

SUMMERLAND KEY

Map page M-10, E3

Restaurant 🍴

Monte's, Overseas Hwy, MM 25, Summerland Key; tel 305/745-3731. **Seafood.** No decor or atmosphere, but excellent fresh fish. The day's catch might include shark, tuna, lobster, and stone crabs. Clam chowder, spiced crayfish pie. **FYI:** Reservations not accepted. Beer and wine only. **Open:** Tues–Sat 10am–10pm, Sun 11am–9pm. Closed some hols. **Prices:** Main courses $11–$14. No CC.

SUNNY ISLES

Map page M-11, B2

Hotels 🛏

Marco Polo Resort Hotel, 19201 Collins Ave, Sunny Isles, FL 33160; tel 305/932-2233 or toll free 800/327-6363, 800/432-3664 in FL; fax 305/935-5009. A large hotel catering to older couples who come for the fun-and-games atmosphere. Dated appearance doesn't deter regulars. **Rooms:** 508 rms, stes, and effic. CI 3pm/CO noon. Some odd color combinations. **Amenities:** 🛏 A/C, cable TV, refrig, in-rm safe. Some units w/terraces. **Services:** ✗ 🖬 VP ⚲ ↻ Staff can be disorganized at times. **Facilities:** 🛗 500 ⚅ 4 rsts, 4 bars (2 w/entertainment), 1 beach (ocean), lifeguard, games rm, beauty salon, washer/dryer. Dinner theater is very popular. Arcade of shops. **Rates:** $50–$74 S or D; from $84 ste; from $54 effic. Extra person $10. Children under 12 stay free. Higher rates for spec evnts/hols. Spec packages avail. Pking: Outdoor, $5. Maj CC.

Pan American Ocean Resort, 17875 Collins Ave, Sunny Isles, FL 33160; tel 305/932-1100 or toll free 800/327-5678; fax 305/935-2769. Curved stucco walls and fountain at entry lead to this 3-story oceanfront hotel. Close to exclusive Bal Harbour shops. **Rooms:** 146 rms and stes. CI 4pm/CO noon. Nonsmoking rms avail. Good-quality accommodations employ pastel color schemes and have dark rattan furniture. Most rooms have ocean view. **Amenities:** 🛏 ⚲ A/C, cable TV w/movies, refrig, in-rm safe. All units w/minibars, some w/terraces. **Services:** ✗ VP ⚲ ⚄ ↻ Car-rental desk, social director, masseur, children's program, babysitting. Afternoon tea served at 3:30pm. Manager's cocktail party Mondays. **Facilities:** 🛗 △ ⚅ ⚲ 🎳 250 ⚏ ⚅ 2 rsts, 2 bars (w/entertainment), 1 beach (ocean), games rm, lawn games, beauty salon, washer/dryer. **Rates:** HS Dec 22–Apr 30 $149–$189 S or D; from $195 ste. Extra person $15. Children under 17 stay free. Lower rates off-season. Pking: Outdoor, free. Maj CC.

Suez Oceanfront Resort, 18215 Collins Ave, Sunny Isles, FL 33160; tel 305/932-0661 or toll free 800/327-5278, 800/327-5278, 800/432-3661 in FL; fax 305/937-0058. Built in the 1950s glamour days, this facility is definitely more impressive inside than outside. Courtyard with fountains and pool are set on manicured grounds. **Rooms:** 196 rms, stes, and effic. CI 3pm/CO noon. Nonsmoking rms avail. Some rooms and baths under renovation. **Amenities:** 🛏 ⚲ ⚄ A/C, cable TV, refrig, stereo/tape player. All units w/terraces, 1 w/Jacuzzi. **Services:** ✗ 🖬 ↻ Twice-daily maid svce, social director, babysitting. **Facilities:** 🛗 ⚅ ⚲ 🎳 1 rst, 1 bar (w/entertainment), 1 beach (ocean), lawn games, sauna, playground, washer/dryer. Fenced-in area good for children at play. **Rates:** HS Dec 20–Jan 3 $62–$93 S or D; from $195 ste; from $78 effic. Extra person $10. Children under 16 stay free. Lower rates off-season. MAP rates avail. Pking: Outdoor, free. Maj CC.

Motels

Desert Inn, 17201 Collins Ave, Sunny Isles, FL 33160; tel 305/947-0621 or toll free 800/327-6361; fax 305/944-7050. A complex of motel rooms and condominiums that are privately owned and decorated with some individuality. Shops and restaurants across the street. **Rooms:** 100 rms and effic. CI 2pm/CO noon. Many units have Murphy beds. **Amenities:** 🛏 A/C, cable TV, refrig. Some units w/terraces. **Services:** ↻ Babysitting. **Facilities:** 🛗 ⚅ 1 rst, 1 bar (w/entertainment), 1 beach (ocean), washer/dryer. Card room upstairs. **Rates:** HS Feb–Apr $69–$90 S or D; from $79 effic. Extra person $10. Children under 13 stay free. Lower rates off-season. Higher rates for spec evnts/hols. Pking: Outdoor, free. Ltd CC.

≣≣ Driftwood Resort Motel, 17121 Collins Ave, Sunny Isles, FL 33160 (Sunny Isles Beach); tel 305/944-5141 or toll free 800/327-1263; fax 305/945-0763. A traditional motel with clean, basic rooms. **Rooms:** 114 effic. CI noon/CO noon. **Amenities:** 🗚 A/C, cable TV. **Services:** ✗ ⌂ Babysitting. **Facilities:** 🛢 ᴄ 1 rst, 1 bar (w/entertainment), 1 beach (ocean), lawn games, playground, washer/dryer. **Rates:** HS Dec–Mar from $45 effic. Lower rates off-season. Pking: Outdoor, free. Maj CC.

≣≣ Monaco Oceanfront Resort, 17501 Collins Ave, Sunny Isles, FL 33160; tel 305/932-2100 or toll free 800/227-9006; fax 305/931-5519. Opposite a grocery store and 24-hour chain restaurant, this large, well-maintained family motel caters to parents with children in tow. **Rooms:** 113 rms, stes, and effic. CI 2pm/CO noon. **Amenities:** 🗚 A/C, cable TV w/movies, refrig. Some units w/terraces. **Services:** ✗ ⌂ ⌂ **Facilities:** 🛢 ᴄ ⌂ 1 rst, 1 bar (w/entertainment), 1 beach (ocean), games rm, lawn games, sauna, washer/dryer. **Rates:** HS Jan 1–Apr 3/Dec 18–Jan 6 $80–$90 S or D; from $130 ste; from $87 effic. Extra person $7. Children under 15 stay free. Min stay spec evnts: Lower rates off-season. Pking: Outdoor, Maj CC.

≣≣ Ocean Roc, 19505 Collins Ave, Sunny Isles, FL 33160; tel 305/931-7600 or toll free 800/327-0553; fax 305/866-5881. Basic accommodations are satisfactory but lack warmth or style. Painting and general repairs are needed. **Rooms:** 100 rms and effic. CI noon/CO noon. Nonsmoking rms avail. **Amenities:** 🗚 A/C, TV w/movies, refrig. Some units w/terraces. **Services:** ✗ 🚐 ⌂ ⌂ Car-rental desk, social director, babysitting. **Facilities:** 🛢 ⌂ ⌂ ⌂ ⌂ ⌂ ᴄ ⌂ ⌂ 1 rst, 1 beach (ocean), lifeguard, board surfing, games rm, lawn games, racquetball, snorkeling, playground, washer/dryer. **Rates:** HS Dec–Apr $48–$68 S or D; from $55 effic. Children under 12 stay free. Lower rates off-season. Pking: Outdoor, free. Maj CC.

SUNRISE

Map page M-11, A2

Hotel 🛏

≣≣≣ Sunrise Hilton Inn, 3003 N University Dr, Sunrise, FL 33322; tel 305/748-7000 or toll free 800/533-9555; fax 305/572-0799. Spiffy interior to this first-class hotel of glass and concrete. Lavender and seafoam-green blend nicely in public areas. **Rooms:** 297 rms and stes. CI 3pm/CO noon. Nonsmoking rms avail. **Amenities:** 🗚 A/C, cable TV w/movies, voice mail. Some units w/minibars, some w/terraces. **Services:** ✗ 🚐 ⌂ ⌂ Car-rental desk, babysitting. **Facilities:** 🛢 ⌂ ⌂ ᴄ 1 rst, 1 bar (w/entertainment), sauna, whirlpool. **Rates (CP):** HS Dec 20–

Apr 15 $99–$109 S or D; from $119 ste. Extra person $10. Lower rates off-season. Higher rates for spec evnts/hols. AP rates avail. Spec packages avail. Pking: Outdoor, free. Maj CC.

Restaurant 🍽

Stacey's Buffet, 4121 Pine Island Rd, Sunrise; tel 305/749-1521. At 44th St. **Buffet.** A cafeteria-style dining room with country-style decor. Popular menu items include roast turkey and roast prime rib; the buffet includes a variety of salads and soups. Large choice of desserts, ice cream. Great value, particularly for families. **FYI:** Reservations not accepted. Children's menu. No liquor license. **Open:** Mon–Fri 11am–8pm, Sat–Sun 11am–8:30pm. Closed Dec 25. **Prices:** Main courses $4.99–$6.99. Ltd CC. 🖭 ᴄ

SURFSIDE

Map page M-11, B2

Hotels 🛏

≣≣ Coronado Hotel, 9501 Collins Ave, Surfside, FL 33154; tel 305/866-1625; fax 305/861-1881. There's a quiet, relaxed atmosphere in this 2-story budget hotel sandwiched between highrises. Has managed to retain its original charm. **Rooms:** 41 rms and effic. CI 3pm/CO 11am. Pastel-colored rooms. **Amenities:** 🗚 A/C, cable TV, refrig. Some units w/terraces. **Services:** ✗ 🚐 ⌂ Car-rental desk. **Facilities:** 🛢 ⌂ 1 rst, 1 beach (ocean). Newly opened restaurant. **Rates (CP):** HS Dec–Mar $79–$125 S or D; from $93 effic. Extra person $8. Children under 18 stay free. Min stay spec evnts. Lower rates off-season. Higher rates for spec evnts/hols. Spec packages avail. Pking: Indoor, free. Maj CC.

≣≣ The Palms, 9449 Collins Ave, Surfside, FL 33154; tel 305/865-3551 or toll free 800/327-6644 in the US, 800/843-6974 in Canada; fax 305/861-6596. Basic rooms on the ocean. Friendly staff persevering through continuing renovations to public areas and rooms. Many guests here are retired vacationers. **Rooms:** 170 rms and stes. CI 3pm/CO noon. Nonsmoking rms avail. **Amenities:** 🗚 A/C, cable TV w/movies, refrig, in-rm safe. Some units w/terraces. **Services:** ✗ ⌂ Twice-daily maid svce, social director, babysitting. **Facilities:** 🛢 ᴄ 1 rst, 1 bar, 1 beach (ocean), lifeguard, games rm, whirlpool, washer/dryer. **Rates (AP):** HS Dec 16–Feb 21 $115–$135 S or D; from $160 ste. Extra person $12. Children under 18 stay free. Lower rates off-season. Spec packages avail. Pking: Outdoor, free. Maj CC.

Motel

≡ **Hilyard Manor Motel and Apartments**, 9541 Collins Ave, Surfside, FL 33154; tel 305/866-7351 or toll free 800/327-1413; fax 305/864-3045. A no-frills operation in need of repair. Landscaping, corridors, and general overall look need help. Hotel does receive many long-term guests, however, for its suites. Does not rent to those under age 25. **Rooms:** 30 rms and stes. CI 3pm/CO 11am. Kitchen appliances need to be replaced in some cases. **Amenities:** 🛢 🖭 A/C, TV, refrig. 1 unit w/terrace. **Services:** 🖵 **Facilities:** 🔏 1 beach (ocean), washer/dryer. **Rates:** HS Jan 18–Mar 20 $66 S or D; from $76 ste. Extra person $7. Lower rates off-season. Spec packages avail. Pking: Outdoor, free. Maj CC.

TALLAHASSEE

Map page M-4, B1

See also **Spring Hill**

Hotels 🖼

≡≡ **Holiday Inn University Center Downtown**, 316 W Tennessee St, Tallahassee, FL 32301; tel 904/222-8000 or toll free 800/HOLIDAY; fax 904/681-8578. 4 blocks from the capitol. Octagonal tower patronized by business travelers and others. **Rooms:** 174 rms. CI 3pm/CO 11am. Nonsmoking rms avail. **Amenities:** 🛢 🖭 A/C, cable TV w/movies, voice mail, in-rm safe. **Services:** ✕ 🚗 🖾 🖵 🛳 **Facilities:** 🔏 300 🔏 1 rst, 2 bars. Upscale restaurant with good views. **Rates:** $79–$95 S; $89–$105 D. Children under 18 stay free. Higher rates for spec evnts/hols. Pking: Outdoor, free. Maj CC.

≡≡ **Killearn Country Club and Inn**, 100 Tyron Circle, Tallahassee, FL 32308; tel 904/893-2186 or toll free 800/476-4101; fax 904/688-7637. Exit 30 off I-10. This golf and tennis facility set in an area of luxury homes is host to several golf tournaments. **Rooms:** 39 rms and stes. CI 2pm/CO noon. Nonsmoking rms avail. Guest rooms modest by resort standards. **Amenities:** 🛢 🖭 🍴 A/C, cable TV, refrig. Some units w/minibars, all w/terraces. **Services:** ✕ 🖾 🖵 Twice-daily maid svce. **Facilities:** 🔏 ⏺27 🏌 🥐4 🚤 🛶 250 2 rsts, 2 bars, sauna. **Rates (CP):** $69–$89 S or D; from $95 ste. Extra person $10. Children under 16 stay free. Min stay spec evnts. Higher rates for spec evnts/hols. Spec packages avail. Pking: Outdoor, free. Maj CC.

≡≡ **Radisson Hotel**, 415 N Monroe St, Tallahassee, FL 32301; tel 904/224-6000 or toll free 800/333-3333; fax 904/224-6000 ext 4118. Located just beyond the shadow of the capitol building, this is one of the best choices in the downtown

sector. A warm residential ambience radiates from both public areas and guest rooms. **Rooms:** 116 rms and stes. CI 3pm/CO noon. Express checkout avail. Nonsmoking rms avail. **Amenities:** 🛢 🖭 A/C, cable TV w/movies. Some units w/Jacuzzis. **Services:** ✕ 🆅🅿 🚗 🖾 🖵 Babysitting. **Facilities:** 🛳 350 🔏 1 rst, 1 bar (w/entertainment), sauna. The young and friendly staff makes a special effort to please guests. **Rates:** HS Feb–Apr $87 S; $97 D; from $129 ste. Extra person $10. Children under 18 stay free. Min stay spec evnts. Lower rates off-season. Higher rates for spec evnts/hols. Spec packages avail. Pking: Outdoor, free. Maj CC.

≡≡≡ **Ramada Inn Tallahassee**, 2900 N Monroe St, Tallahassee, FL 32303; tel 904/386-1027 or toll free 800/2-RAMADA; fax 904/422-1023. Exit 29 off I-10. A business-class hotel in contemporary style. **Rooms:** 198 rms and stes. CI 2pm/CO noon. Nonsmoking rms avail. **Amenities:** 🛢 🖭 🍴 A/C, cable TV w/movies, refrig, voice mail. **Services:** ✕ 🚗 🖾 🖵 Babysitting. **Facilities:** 🔏 🛳 300 🖳 🔏 2 rsts, 2 bars (1 w/entertainment). Lounge offers blues and jazz and weekend comedy shows. **Rates:** HS Feb–May/Sept–Nov $78 S; $80 D; from $125 ste. Extra person $5. Children under 18 stay free. Lower rates off-season. Higher rates for spec evnts/hols. Spec packages avail. Pking: Outdoor, free. Maj CC.

≡≡≡ **Sheraton Tallahassee Hotel**, 101 S Adams St, Tallahassee, FL 32301; tel 904/224-5000 or toll free 800/325-3535; fax 904/224-1168. In the commercial district, near the capitol, this property caters largely to government business and other non-leisure clientele. **Rooms:** 244 rms and stes. CI 3pm/CO noon. Nonsmoking rms avail. **Amenities:** 🛢 🖭 A/C, cable TV w/movies. Some units w/minibars. **Services:** ✕ 🚗 🖾 🖵 Babysitting. **Facilities:** 🔏 350 🔏 1 rst, 1 bar. Access to nearby health club. **Rates:** HS Feb–Apr $99–$150 S or D; from $250 ste. Children under 12 stay free. Min stay spec evnts. Lower rates off-season. Higher rates for spec evnts/hols. Spec packages avail. Pking: Indoor, free. Maj CC.

Motels

≡ **Best Western Pride Inn**, 2016 Apalachee Pkwy, Tallahassee, FL 32301; tel 904/656-6312 or toll free 800/827-7390; fax 904/942-4312. A small 2-story property best suited for undemanding motorists. **Rooms:** 78 rms and stes. CI 2pm/CO 11am. Nonsmoking rms avail. **Amenities:** 🛢 🖭 A/C, cable TV. **Services:** 🖾 🖵 🛳 **Facilities:** 🔏 50 🔏 Washer/dryer. **Rates (CP):** $41 S; $46 D; from $51 ste. Extra person $5. Children under 12 stay free. Pking: Outdoor, free. Maj CC.

≡≡ **Cabot Lodge East**, 1653 Raymond Diehl Rd, Tallahassee, FL 32308; tel 904/386-7500 or toll free 800/255-6343; fax 904/

386-1136. Exit 30 off I-10. Modeled after a New England country inn, geared toward the business traveler. **Rooms:** 134 rms and stes. CI 1pm/CO 11am. Nonsmoking rms avail. Rooms are large, with plenty of seating and a sizeable desk. **Amenities:** 🛏🔥 A/C, cable TV, voice mail. 1 unit w/Jacuzzi. **Services:** ✗🖨 🛍 Continental breakfast and cocktail hour are complimentary. **Facilities:** 🍽🅿♿ 1 bar, washer/dryer. Lending library. **Rates (CP):** HS Feb–Mar/Sept–Nov $61 S; $71 D; from $175 ste. Extra person $10. Children under 15 stay free. Lower rates off-season. Pking: Outdoor, free. Maj CC.

🟰🟰 **Cabot Lodge North**, 2735 N Monroe St, Tallahassee, FL 32303; tel 904/386-8850 or toll free 800/223-1964; fax 904/386-4254. This New England–style inn caters to business clientele. **Rooms:** 160 rms. CI 2pm/CO noon. Nonsmoking rms avail. **Amenities:** 🛏🔥 A/C, cable TV w/movies. **Services:** 🖨🛍 Evening cocktails and popcorn. **Facilities:** 🍽♨🈂♿ **Rates:** $55 S; $61 D. Extra person $6. Children under 18 stay free. Higher rates for spec evnts/hols. Pking: Outdoor, free. Maj CC.

🟰🟰 **Hampton Inn**, 3210 N Monroe St, Tallahassee, FL 32303; tel 904/562-4300 or toll free 800/222-3210; fax 904/562-6735. Basic, no-frills rooms. **Rooms:** 93 rms. CI 3pm/CO noon. Nonsmoking rms avail. **Amenities:** 🛏 🔥 A/C, cable TV. **Services:** 🚐 🖨 🛍 Babysitting. Continental breakfast. **Facilities:** 🍽♨♿ **Rates:** $46 S; $54–$56 D. Children under 18 stay free. Higher rates for spec evnts/hols. Pking: Outdoor, free. Maj CC.

🟰🟰 **Holiday Inn Parkway**, 1302 Apalachee Pkwy, Tallahassee, FL 32301; tel 904/877-3141 or toll free 800/HOLIDAY. Moderately priced small-scale motel. Nearby shopping and restaurants. **Rooms:** 165 rms and stes. CI 1pm/CO 11am. Nonsmoking rms avail. **Amenities:** 🛏 🔥 A/C, cable TV, voice mail. **Services:** 🍽 🛍 Twice-daily maid svce, children's program. **Facilities:** 🍽♨♿ 1 rst, 1 bar. Complimentary pass offered for YMCA. **Rates:** HS Feb–Apr/Sept–Nov $54 S; $64 D; from $85 ste. Extra person $10. Children under 16 stay free. Lower rates off-season. Spec packages avail. Pking: Outdoor, free. Maj CC.

🟰🟰 **Quality Inn & Suites**, 2020 Apalachee Pkwy, Tallahassee, FL 32301; tel 904/877-4437 or toll free 800/553-4787; fax 904/878-9964. Capitol-area lowrise. **Rooms:** 96 rms and stes. CI 2pm/CO noon. Nonsmoking rms avail. **Amenities:** 🛏 📺 A/C, cable TV, refrig. **Services:** ✗🖨🛍 Babysitting. **Facilities:** 🍽♨♨♿ Pool under construction at time of inspection. **Rates:** HS Sept–Nov $60 S; $65 D; from $120 ste. Extra person $5. Children under 18 stay free. Lower rates off-season. Pking: Outdoor, free. Maj CC.

Inn

🟰🟰🟰 **Governors Inn**, 209 S Adams St, Tallahassee, FL 32301; tel 904/681-6855 or toll free 800/342-7717; fax 904/222-3105. 1 block north of the capitol complex. Elegant, award-winning hotel opened in 1984 by the son of Florida Gov Lawton Chiles. The building, at one time a livery stable, retains part of its original architecture, including the handsome wood beams. **Rooms:** 40 rms and stes. CI 3pm/CO noon. Furnished with 4-poster beds, black oak writing desks, maple armoires, and antique accoutrements. Sumptuous suites. **Amenities:** 🛏🔥 A/C, cable TV w/movies, bathrobes. Some units w/terraces, some w/fireplaces, some w/Jacuzzis. **Services:** ✗ 🅅🄿 🚐 🖨 🛍 Babysitting, wine/sherry served. Same-day laundry service. **Facilities:** ♨ ♿ 1 bar, guest lounge. Breakfast and evening cocktails served in beautiful, pine-paneled Florida Room. **Rates (CP):** HS Feb–Apr $139–$149 S or D; from $179 ste. Extra person $10. Children under 18 stay free. Min stay spec evnts. Lower rates off-season. Higher rates for spec evnts/hols. Spec packages avail. Pking: Outdoor, free. Ltd CC.

Restaurants 🍴

Andrew's 2nd Act, 228 S Adams St, Tallahassee; tel 904/222-2759. 1 block W of Monroe St. **Continental.** The basement location gives this basic eatery a dark, rather intimate ambience. The French-inspired menu offers New York strip steak, rack of lamb, and filet of grouper. **FYI:** Reservations accepted. Dress code. **Open:** Lunch Mon–Fri 11:30am–11:30pm; dinner Mon–Thurs 6–10pm, Fri–Sat 6–11pm, Sun 6–9:30pm. Closed some hols. **Prices:** Main courses $17–$22; PF dinner $19.94. Maj CC. 🅅🄿

Andrew's Upstairs, 228 S Adams St, Tallahassee; tel 904/222-3446. 1 block W of Monroe St. **New American.** A simple, casual grill offering soups, a salad bar, burgers, chicken, steak sandwiches, pastas, fajitas, and lasagne. **FYI:** Reservations accepted. Band. **Open:** Lunch Mon–Fri 11:30am–2pm; dinner Mon–Thurs 6–10pm, Fri–Sat 6–11pm. Closed some hols. **Prices:** Main courses $8–$14. Maj CC.

Anthony's, in Betton Place, 1950 Thomasville Rd, Tallahassee; tel 904/224-1447. **Italian.** A dark, casual restaurant adorned with plants and antiques. The northern Italian–inspired menu includes shrimp scampi, fresh salmon, and New York strip steak. **FYI:** Reservations accepted. **Open:** Mon–Sat 5:30–10pm, Sun 5–9pm. Closed some hols. **Prices:** Main courses $11.95–$19.95. Maj CC. ♿

⑤ **Food Glorious Food**, in Betton Place, 1950-C Thomasville Rd, Tallahassee; tel 904/224-9974. **International.** Small black-and-white-tiled cafe with open kitchen and a constantly changing menu. Salads, pastas, sandwiches, muffins, and cakes are always fresh and interesting. **FYI:** Reservations not accepted. Beer and wine only. No smoking. **Open:** Mon–Sat 11am–8pm. Closed Dec 25. **Prices:** Main courses $3.95–$9.50. Maj CC.

Lucy Ho's Bamboo Garden, 2814 Apalachee Pkwy, Tallahassee; tel 904/878-3366. Off US 27 N. **Japanese.** Fans of Asian food will love Lucy Ho's. They can enjoy the Chinese lunch spread, the sushi bar, or the extensive menu filled with Chinese and Japanese favorites. A great place for those who are on the go to make a quick stop for a pleasing meal. **FYI:** Reservations accepted. **Open:** Mon–Thurs 11:30am–10pm, Fri 11:30am–11pm, Sat 5–11pm, Sun noon–10pm. Closed some hols. **Prices:** Main courses $5.25–$10. Maj CC. &

The Melting Pot, 1832 N Monroe St, Tallahassee; tel 904/386-7440. **Chinese/Japanese.** A dark, plainly decorated eatery offering an array of unusual fondues, which can be enjoyed with chicken, steak, seafood, and vegetables. **FYI:** Reservations accepted. Beer and wine only. **Open:** Sun–Thurs 6–10:30pm, Fri–Sat 6–11:30pm. Closed some hols. **Prices:** Main courses $7.95–$16.50. Maj CC.

★ **Mill Bakery, Eatery and Brewery**, 2329 Apalachee Pkwy, Tallahassee; tel 904/565-2867. **New American/Vegetarian.** A clean, airy, cafeteria-style hangout that caters to the college crowd. Endless entree choices are supplemented by excellent salads, fresh baked goods, and tasty desserts. **FYI:** Reservations not accepted. Children's menu. **Open:** Sun–Thurs 6:30am–11pm, Fri–Sat 6:30–midnight. **Prices:** Main courses $4.95–$8.95. Maj CC. &

Silver Slipper, 531 Scotty's Lane, Tallahassee; tel 904/386-9366. **New American.** You and your sweetheart can dine in easy splendor under the sparkling chandelier in the main room, or you can opt for one of the private dining rooms. Inventive seafood dishes and steaks are among the menu selections. **FYI:** Reservations accepted. Children's menu. **Open:** Daily 5–11pm. Closed some hols. **Prices:** Main courses $9–$20. Maj CC. &

Attractions

New Capitol Building, Duval St; tel 904/488-6167 (tour info) or 681-9200. Built in 1977 to replace the Old Capitol, the 22-story skyscraper offers a spectacular view from the top-floor observatory. The chambers of the House and Senate have public viewing galleries; the legislature convenes from early February to early April. Guided tours are given Mon–Fri at 9, 10, and 11am, and 1, 2, and 3pm; Sat–Sun, hourly 9am–4pm. **Open:** Mon–Fri 8am–5pm. Closed some hols. Free.

Old Capitol Building, Monroe St and Apalachee Pkwy; tel 904/487-1902. Restored to its original beauty, the strikingly white former capitol building with playful red and white awnings and a majestic dome now serves as a museum. An 8-room exhibit details Florida's fascinating political history. Visitors can also view turn-of-the-century furnishings, cotton gins, and other interesting artifacts. **Open:** Mon–Fri 9am–4:30pm, Sat 10am–4:30pm, Sun noon–4:30pm. Free.

The Columns, 100 N Duval St; tel 904/224-8116. This 3-story, white-columned brick mansion is the city's oldest surviving building, dating from the 1830s. It has been restored and furnished with antiques, and now serves as the office of the Chamber of Commerce. **Open:** Mon–Fri 9am–5pm. Free.

Governor's Mansion, 700 N Adams St; tel 904/488-4661. The Florida governor's residence is an impressive Georgian-style mansion, with a portico patterned after the Hermitage, Andrew Jackson's columned antebellum home. The lawns are enhanced by giant magnolia trees. Visitors can tour 5 of the rooms, which are furnished with antiques and adorned by paintings by Renoir, Modigliani, and others. Schedule varies; phone ahead. Free.

Brokaw–McDougall House, 329 N Meridian; tel 904/488-3901. This magnificent house, built in 1856, possesses elements of both Italianate and classical revival architecture; landscaping conforms to the original design. **Open:** Mon–Fri 8am–5pm. Closed some hols. Free.

Union Bank Building, 295 Apalachee Pkwy; tel 904/487-3803. Situated a block south from the Capitol Complex is Florida's oldest surviving bank, built in 1841. It once served as a "planters' bank" for cotton plantation owners and then as a freedman's bank for newly emancipated slaves; it now presents the history of territorial-period banking. **Open:** Tues–Fri 10am–1pm; by appointment Sat–Sun 1–4pm. Free.

Tallahassee Museum of History and Natural Science, 3945 Museum Dr; tel 904/576-1636 or 575-8684. Formerly the Tallahassee Junior Museum, this attraction features native Florida animals, including the endangered Florida panther and red wolf, in a natural woodland setting; a re-creation of an 1880s farm; science and history displays; the restored plantation home of Princess Murat; and a restored one-room schoolhouse, grist-mill, old church, and railroad caboose. Special programs demonstrate butter-churning, syrup-making, blacksmithing, sheep-shearing, spinning, weaving, and quilt-making. **Open:** Mon–Sat 9am–5pm, Sun 12:30–5pm. $$

Museum of Florida History, RA Gray Building, 500 S Bronough St; tel 904/488-1484 or 488-1673. Florida's history from the paleolithic era to the present. Visitors can see ancient Native

American artifacts, a mastodon skeleton 12 feet high, treasures from sunken Spanish galleons, war relics, and a reconstructed steamboat. Guided tours, gift shop. **Open:** Mon–Fri 9am–4:30pm, Sat 10am–4:30pm, Sun noon–4:30pm. Closed some hols. Free.

Black Archives Research Center and Museum, Florida A&M University; tel 904/599-3020. Located on the campus of Florida Agricultural and Mechanical University between Gaines St and Orange Ave, this illuminating center displays one of the most extensive collections of African-American historical artifacts in the United States. On view are items ranging from leg irons from slavery times to letters and memorabilia of such figures as Booker T Washington, Martin Luther King, Jr, Mary McLeod Bethune, and Zora Neale Hurston. There's also a 500-piece Ethiopian cross collection. **Open:** Mon–Fri 9am–4pm. Closed some hols. Free.

Foster Tanner Fine Arts Gallery, Florida A&M University; tel 904/599-3161. Focuses on works by African-American artists, with a variety of paintings, sculptures, and more. Exhibits change monthly. **Open:** Mon–Fri 9am–5pm. Closed some hols. Free.

LeMoyne Art Foundation, 125 N Gadsden St; tel 904/222-8800. Housed in a restored 1852 antebellum home, the collection features displays by local artists, traveling exhibits, sculpture, pottery, and photography. Gardens with old-fashioned gazebo. Call in advance for the current schedule. **Open:** Tues–Sat 10am–5pm, Sun 2–5pm. Closed some hols. Free.

Florida State University Museum of Fine Arts, 250 Fine Arts Building, at Copeland and W Tennesse Sts; tel 904/644-6836. The permanent collection features 16th-century Dutch paintings, 20th-century American paintings, Japanese prints, pre-Columbian artifacts, and much more. Touring exhibits. **Open:** Mon–Fri 9am–5pm, Sat–Sun 1–4pm. Schedule may vary; phone ahead. Free.

Knott House Museum, 301 E Park Ave; tel 904/922-2459. Anchoring the Park Avenue Historic District, this museum is a capsule of state history. Built in 1843 by a free black builder, the mansion was the site of the emancipation of the North Florida slaves in 1865. It was also the laboratory for Florida's first black physician, and the home of Supreme Court justices and key state political figures. Today it is best known as "the House that Rhymes," for the whimsical rhymes written by its last mistress, Luella Pugh Knott, and attached with satin ribbons to her Victorian furnishings. **Open:** Open: Wed–Fri 1–4pm, Sat 10am–4pm. $

Maclay State Gardens, 3540 Thomasville Rd (US 319); tel 904/487-4115. The former winter retreat of New York financier

Alfred B Maclay, an amateur gardener who, along with his wife, planted these spectacular gardens of azaleas, camellias, pansies, and dogwood and redbud trees. Over 200 varieties of flowers in all. The surrounding park has nature trails and picnicking, along with canoe rentals, boating, picnicking, swimming, and fishing. **Open:** Park, daily 8am–sunset; gardens, daily 9am–5pm; Maclay House, Jan–Apr, daily 9am–5pm. $$

First Presbyterian Church, 110 N Adams St; tel 904/222-4504. Tallahassee's oldest church (1838). Townspeople took refuge beneath the church steeple during the Seminole raids of 1838. Slaves were welcome to worship here as independent members. Visitors may request keys to the sanctuary at the church office during business hours. **Open:** Mon–Thurs 8:30am–5pm, Fri 8:30am–1pm. Free.

Old City Cemetery and Episcopal Cemetery, Park Ave and Bronough St; tel 904/545-5842. These adjacent cemeteries contain the graves of Prince Achille Murat, Napoleon's nephew, and Princess Catherine Murat, his wife and George Washington's grandniece. Also buried here are 2 governors and numerous Confederate and Union soldiers who died at the Battle of Natural Bridge during the Civil War. A number of slaves and the first African-American Florida A&M University graduates are also among those buried here.

Natural Bridge Battlefield State Historic Site, Natural Bridge Rd; tel 904/922-6007. This park and monument 15 miles southeast of Tallahassee commemorate the site of a battle in the closing days of the Civil War won by a small group of Confederate soldiers against a much larger contingent of Union troops. Although the Confederate victory prevented the Florida capital from falling to the Union, the war ended only several weeks later. **Open:** Daily 8am–sunset. Free.

Lake Jackson Mounds State Archeological Site, 1313 Crowder Rd; tel 904/562-0042. Artifacts such as copper breastplates and ritual figures suggest that this was the site of an important Native American ceremonial center. Visitors can see 6 earthen temple mounds and a burial mound. **Open:** Daily 8am–sundown. Free.

River Bluff Picnic Site; tel 904/922-6007. Located off Fla 20 about 20 miles west of Tallahassee. Visitors can enjoy fishing, boating and picnicking amid thick pine forest, deep ravines, and rolling hills. Abundant wildlife along the nature trail. **Open:** Daily 8am–sunset. Free.

De Soto Archeological and Historical Site, 1022 DeSoto Park Dr; tel 904/922-6007 or 925-6216. An archeologist searching for Spanish mission ruins in 1986 discovered the de Soto encampment site. In December a colorful pageant-drama reenacting the first Christmas is presented, beginning at 9am and continuing to 8pm. Check ahead for the exact date and program schedule. The admission is free. Because the archeological site is being excavated and the home is under restoration, only the Christmas pageant is open to the public at present.

San Luis Archeological and Historic Site, 2020 W Mission Rd; tel 904/487-3711. This 50-acre site located on a hilltop west of downtown Tallahassee was once an important Apalachee settlement and, later, a Spanish mission and town. Visitors can observe the annual spring excavation; exhibits along the trails explain the San Luis story. **Open:** Mon–Fri 9am–4:30pm, Sat 11am–4:30pm, Sun noon–4:30pm. Closed some hols. Free.

Apalachicola National Forest; tel 904/926-3561, 681-7265 or 670-8644. Located on US 319, with the closest entrance approximately 20 miles south of Tallahassee, this is the largest of Florida's 3 national forests. It is a varied woodland with lakes and streams encompassing about 600,000 acres, which include parts of 4 Panhandle counties. The canoe trails along the Sopchoppy and Ochlockonee rivers are popular. Boating and camping are permitted. Nature trails, bike paths.

TAMPA

Map page M-6, E3

See also St Petersburg

TOURIST INFORMATION

Tampa/Hillsborough Convention and Visitors Association, Inc (THCVA), 111 Madison St, Suite 110 (tel 813/223-1111 or 800/44-TAMPA). Open Mon–Sat 9am–5pm.

PUBLIC TRANSPORTATION

Hillsborough Area Regional Transit/HARTline Buses Local and express service between downtown Tampa and surrounding suburbs. Local fare $1, express fare $1.50. Local fares half-price for children, seniors, and passengers with disabilities. Exact change required. For information call 813/254-HART.

The People Mover Motorized tram on elevated tracks connecting downtown Tampa with Harbour Island. Operates Mon–Sat 7am–midnight, Sun 8am–midnight. Departs from 3rd level of Fort Brooke Parking Garage, on Whiting St between Franklin Ave and Florida St. Fare 25¢.

Hotels

Colony Hotel and Conference Center, 820 E Busch Blvd, Tampa, FL 33612; tel 813/933-4011 or toll free 800/288-4011; fax 813/932-1784. Exit 33 off I-275. Formerly under Ramada ownership; offers something of a retreat from the amusement park atmosphere nearby. **Rooms:** 255 rms and stes. CI 4pm/CO noon. Nonsmoking rms avail. **Amenities:** A/C, cable TV w/movies. Some units w/terraces. **Services:** Car-rental desk. **Facilities:** 1 rst, 1 bar, games rm, sauna, steam rm, washer/dryer. **Rates:** HS Jan–Apr $49–$69 S; $59–$79 D; from $159 ste. Children under 18 stay free. Lower rates off-season. Spec packages avail. Pking: Outdoor, free. Maj CC.

Courtyard by Marriott, 3805 W Cypress St, Tampa, FL 33607; tel 813/874-0555 or toll free 800/321-2211; fax 813/870-0685. Exit 23B off I-275. At US 92. Solid hotel providing reliable service and a comfortable stay. **Rooms:** 145 rms and stes. CI 3pm/CO noon. Nonsmoking rms avail. **Amenities:** A/C, cable TV w/movies. Free in-room coffee. **Services:** Babysitting. **Facilities:** 1 rst, 1 bar, sauna, whirlpool, washer/dryer. **Rates:** $56–$84 S or D; from $95 ste. Extra person $10. Children under 18 stay free. Pking: Outdoor, free. Maj CC.

Crown Sterling Suites Hotel–USF/Busch Gardens, 11310 N 30th St, Tampa, FL 33612; tel 813/971-7690 or toll free 800/433-4600; fax 813/972-5525. Exit 33 off I-275. A quiet spot in an otherwise bustling area. The lobby, with wicker furnishings and floral patterns, opens to a lush courtyard pool with abutting waterfall. **Rooms:** 129 stes. CI 3pm/CO noon. Express checkout avail. Nonsmoking rms avail. **Amenities:** A/C, cable TV w/movies, refrig, voice mail. All suites with wet bar and microwave. **Services:** Babysitting. Complimentary beverages served 5:30-7:30pm daily. Free shuttle to area attractions. **Facilities:** Whirlpool, washer/dryer. **Rates (BB):** HS Jan–Apr $104 S; $114 D. Extra person $10. Children under 12 stay free. Lower rates off-season. Spec packages avail. Pking: Outdoor, free. Maj CC.

Days Inn–Downtown Tampa, 515 E Cass St, Tampa, FL 33602; tel 813/229-6431 or toll free 800/329-7466; fax 813/228-7534. At Mairon St. Located in the hub of the financial district, this downtown hotel is fine for a business trip. Unrated. **Rooms:** 90 rms. CI 2pm/CO noon. Nonsmoking rms avail. **Amenities:** A/C, cable TV. **Services:** **Facilities:** 1 rst, washer/dryer. Banquet facilities. Distinctive rooftop pool has splendid views. **Rates:** $39–$54 S or D. Extra person $5. Children under 12 stay free. Higher rates for spec evnts/hols. Pking: Indoor, free. Maj CC.

≡≡ Days Inn–Rocky Point, 7627 Courtney Campbell Causeway, Tampa, FL 33607; tel 813/281-0000 or toll free 800/237-2555; fax 813/281-1067. Exit 20 off I-275. 2 mi W of Tampa Int'l Airport. Clustered with other hotels near the causeway in a high-rent district. **Rooms:** 144 rms and stes. CI 2pm/CO noon. Nonsmoking rms avail. **Amenities:** 🛁 A/C, cable TV w/movies, in-rm safe. **Services:** 🚐 🖼 🛎 Free shuttle to area restaurants and shopping. **Facilities:** 🏋 △ 🏊 🛥 🎱 1 rst, 1 bar (w/entertainment), 1 beach (bay), games rm, playground, washer/dryer. Game room with wide-screen TV, 2 pool tables, jukebox, and video games. **Rates:** HS Nov–Apr $65–$85

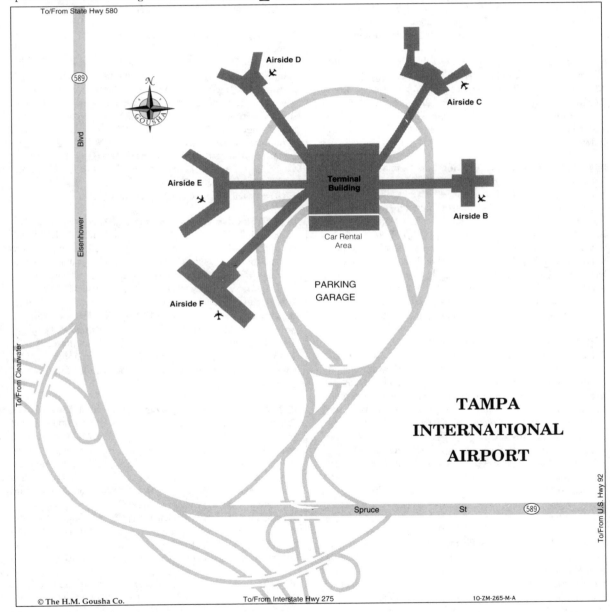

TAMPA INTERNATIONAL AIRPORT

© The H.M. Gousha Co.

S or D; from $125 ste. Extra person $5. Children under 12 stay free. Lower rates off-season. Spec packages avail. Pking: Outdoor, free. Maj CC.

≣ ≣ ≣ **Embassy Suites Hotel**, 555 N Westshore Blvd, Tampa, FL 33609 (Tampa Int'l Airport); tel 813/875-1555 or toll free 800/362-2779; fax 813/287-3664. 2.5 mi S of the airport. Westshore Blvd exit off I-275. Sophisticated appeal, designed for the business traveler. Lobby with vaulted ceiling. **Rooms:** 221 stes. CI 3pm/CO noon. Express checkout avail. Nonsmoking rms avail. **Amenities:** ☎ ☖ ▣ ☜ A/C, cable TV w/movies, refrig. All units w/minibars, some w/terraces. **Services:** ✕ VP ☛ ☒ ☝ ◁ Babysitting. Shuttle service within a 3-mile radius. **Facilities:** ☖ ☝ 230 ঌ 1 rst, 1 bar, sauna, whirlpool, washer/dryer. **Rates (BB):** HS Dec–Mar from $149 ste. Extra person $10. Children under 18 stay free. Lower rates off-season. Pking: Indoor/outdoor, free. Maj CC.

≣ ≣ ≣ **Guest Quarters Suite Hotel on Tampa Bay**, 3050 N Rocky Point Dr W, Tampa, FL 33607; tel 813/888-8800 or toll free 800/424-2900; fax 813/888-8743. Exit 20 off I-75. A sleek establishment offering varied fitness facilities, located just off the causeway to Clearwater. **Rooms:** 203 stes. CI 3pm/CO noon. Nonsmoking rms avail. **Amenities:** ☎ ☖ ▣ ☜ A/C, cable TV w/movies, refrig. All units w/minibars, some w/terraces. **Services:** ✕ ☛ ☒ ☝ ◁ Car-rental desk, children's program, babysitting. **Facilities:** ☖ ☝ 100 ☐ ঌ 1 rst, 1 bar, spa, sauna, whirlpool, washer/dryer. **Rates (CP):** HS Jan–Apr from $119 ste. Extra person $20. Children under 18 stay free. Lower rates off-season. Spec packages avail. Pking: Outdoor, free. Maj CC.

≣ ≣ ≣ **Guest Quarters Suites Hotel**, 4400 W Cypress St, Tampa, FL 33607; tel 813/873-8675; fax 813/879-7196. Exit 22 off I-275. A well-respected all-suites hotel situated in the dense off-airport hub of hotels, near a shopping mall. Mediterranean touches in its architecture inside and out. Atrium lobby. **Rooms:** 260 stes. CI 3pm/CO noon. Express checkout avail. Nonsmoking rms avail. Living rooms separated by French doors. Fine upholstery. **Amenities:** ☎ ☖ ▣ A/C, cable TV w/movies, refrig, voice mail. All units w/terraces. **Services:** ✕ ☛ ☝ ◁ Babysitting. **Facilities:** ☖ ☝ 450 ঌ 1 rst, 2 bars (1 w/entertainment), sauna, steam rm, whirlpool, washer/dryer. **Rates (BB):** HS Dec–Apr from $99 ste. Extra person $10. Children under 12 stay free. Lower rates off-season. Spec packages avail. Pking: Outdoor, free. Maj CC.

≣ ≣ **Holiday Inn–Ashley Plaza**, 111 W Fortune St, Tampa, FL 33602; tel 813/223-1351 or toll free 800/ASK-VALU; fax 813/221-2000. Exit 25 off I-275. Handy to convention center functions and downtown businesses, this commercial hotel is the economical alternative to the bigger Hyatt and more posh Wyndham. **Rooms:** 312 rms and stes. CI 3pm/CO 11am.

Nonsmoking rms avail. Executive floor rooms have coffeemakers. **Amenities:** ☎ ☖ ☜ A/C, cable TV w/movies. Some units w/minibars. **Services:** ✕ ☛ ☝ ◁ Car-rental desk, babysitting. **Facilities:** ☖ ☝ 650 ঌ 1 rst, 1 bar, whirlpool, washer/dryer. **Rates:** HS Jan–Apr $90 S or D; from $164 ste. Extra person $10. Children under 18 stay free. Lower rates off-season. Spec packages avail. Pking: Outdoor, free. Maj CC.

≣ ≣ **Holiday Inn–Busch Gardens**, 2701 E Fowler Ave, Tampa, FL 33612 (Busch Gardens); tel 813/971-4710 or toll free 800/99-BUSCH; fax 813/977-0155. Exit 34 off I-275. This complex of 2-story buildings does a brisk business for both salesmen and tourists visiting nearby Busch Gardens. Parents will appreciate the courtyard with pool, good for children. **Rooms:** 396 rms and stes. CI 3pm/CO noon. Nonsmoking rms avail. **Amenities:** ☎ ☖ A/C, cable TV w/movies. Some units w/minibars, some w/Jacuzzis. **Services:** ✕ ☛ ☝ ◁ ◁ Car-rental desk, babysitting. **Facilities:** ☖ ☝ 400 ঌ 1 rst, 3 bars, washer/dryer. **Rates:** HS Jan–Apr $79 S; $89 D; from $120 ste. Children under 18 stay free. Lower rates off-season. Spec packages avail. Pking: Outdoor, free. Maj CC.

≣ ≣ ≣ **Holiday Inn Crowne Plaza**, 700 N Westshore Blvd, Tampa, FL 33609; tel 813/289-8200 or toll free 800/HOLIDAY; fax 813/289-9166. Westshore Blvd exit off I-275. Long a favorite of the business set as the Omni Tampa Hotel, it is now under the upscale Crowne Plaza umbrella. **Rooms:** 272 rms and stes. CI 3pm/CO noon. Express checkout avail. Nonsmoking rms avail. Whether an executive level will be offered under the new banner remains to be seen. **Amenities:** ☎ ☖ ☜ A/C, cable TV w/movies. **Services:** ✕ ☛ ☝ ◁ ◁ Babysitting. **Facilities:** ☖ ☝ 650 ঌ 1 rst, 1 bar (w/entertainment), sauna, whirlpool. **Rates:** $130–$145 S; $145–$160 D; from $225 ste. Extra person $10. Children under 18 stay free. Spec packages avail. Pking: Indoor/outdoor, free. Maj CC.

≣ ≣ ≣ **Holiday Inn Crowne Plaza–Sabal Park**, 10221 Princess Palm Ave, Tampa, FL 33610; tel 813/623-6363 or toll free 800/HOLIDAY; fax 813/621-7224. Exit 52 off I-75. Situated in an office park; will appeal mainly to business travelers. Stylish design. **Rooms:** 265 rms and stes. CI 3pm/CO noon. Express checkout avail. Nonsmoking rms avail. Smart, sophisticated decor. **Amenities:** ☎ ☖ ☜ A/C, cable TV w/movies. Some units w/terraces, some w/Jacuzzis. **Services:** ✕ ☛ VP ☛ ☝ ◁ Car-rental desk, babysitting. **Facilities:** ☖ ☒ ☝ 500 ঌ 2 rsts, 1 bar (w/entertainment), whirlpool, beauty salon. **Rates:** $120–$140 S or D; from $130 ste. Extra person $10. Children under 19 stay free. Spec packages avail. Pking: Outdoor, free. Maj CC.

≣ ≣ **Holiday Inn Express–Stadium-Airport Area**, 4732 N Dale Mabry Hwy, Tampa, FL 33614; tel 813/877-6061 or toll free 800/898-4484; fax 813/876-1531. Exit 23A off I-275. Hotel underwent a full renovation in 1994, including the construction of additional facilities. **Rooms:** 200 rms. CI 3pm/CO noon. Nonsmoking rms avail. **Amenities:** 🛏 A/C, cable TV w/movies, bathrobes. **Services:** 🍴 🖃 🗗 🌮 Babysitting. **Facilities:** 🛗 🏊 ♿ Washer/dryer. **Rates (CP):** $62 S; $72 D. Extra person $10. Children under 19 stay free. Higher rates for spec evnts/hols. Pking: Outdoor, free. Maj CC.

≡≡≡ Holiday Inn Tampa International Airport at Westshore, 4500 W Cypress St, Tampa, FL 33607; tel 813/879-4800 or toll free 800/HOLIDAY; fax 813/874-2036. Westshore Blvd exit off I-275. Clustered with other hotels not far from the airport, this middle-grade choice has a 10-story tower as its focal point. Marble lobby makes a nice first impression. **Rooms:** 500 rms and stes. CI 3pm/CO noon. Nonsmoking rms avail. **Amenities:** 🛏 🏊 A/C, cable TV w/movies. All units w/terraces. **Services:** ✗ 🍴 🖃 🗗 Babysitting. **Facilities:** 🛗 🏊 🏋 ♿ 2 rsts, 2 bars, games rm, whirlpool. **Rates:** HS Jan–Apr $89–$120 S or D; from $200 ste. Children under 18 stay free. Lower rates off-season. Spec packages avail. Pking: Outdoor, free. Maj CC.

≡≡≡ Hyatt Regency Tampa, 2 Tampa City Center, Tampa, FL 33602; tel 813/225-1234 or toll free 800/233-1234; fax 813/273-0234. At Tampa and Jackson Sts. The local glossy highrise, this slick and inviting mainstay offers all the features of a major convention and business hotel. **Rooms:** 518 rms and stes. CI 3pm/CO noon. Express checkout avail. Nonsmoking rms avail. **Amenities:** 🛏 🏊 📺 A/C, cable TV w/movies. **Services:** 🍴 ☎ 🆅🅿 🍴 🖃 🗗 Car-rental desk, masseur, babysitting. **Facilities:** 🛗 🏊 🏋 🖥 ♿ 2 rsts (*see also* "Restaurants" below), 1 bar (w/entertainment), steam rm, whirlpool, washer/dryer. **Rates:** $169 S; $194 D; from $265 ste. Extra person $25. Children under 18 stay free. Spec packages avail. Pking: Indoor/outdoor, $7. Maj CC.

≡≡≡≡ Hyatt Regency Westshore, 6200 Courtney Campbell Causeway, Tampa, FL 33607; tel 813/874-1234 or toll free 800/233-1234; fax 813/281-9168. Airport exit off I-275. One of the city's best hotels, a world-class operation with a top-notch staff and facilities to support its rates. With lush landscaping and palm-lined entry. **Rooms:** 397 rms and stes; 48 ctges/villas. CI 3pm/CO noon. Express checkout avail. Nonsmoking rms avail. Rooms done in sophisticated designs. Marble baths. Corner rooms have particularly nice views. **Amenities:** 🛏 🏊 🍴 A/C, cable TV w/movies. All units w/minibars, some w/terraces, some w/Jacuzzis. **Services:** 🍴 ☎ 🆅🅿 🍴 🖃 🗗 🌮 Masseur, babysitting. **Facilities:** 🛗 🏊 🏋 🖥 ♿ 3 rsts (*see also* "Restaurants" below), 3 bars (2 w/entertainment), 1 beach (bay), sauna, steam rm, whirlpool, beauty salon. **Rates:** HS Jan–Mar $169–$194 S; $194–$219 D; from $390 ste; from $179

ctge/villa. Extra person $25. Children under 18 stay free. Lower rates off-season. Higher rates for spec evnts/hols. Spec packages avail. Pking: Indoor/outdoor, free. Maj CC.

≡≡ La Quinta–Airport, 4730 W Spruce St, Tampa, FL 33607; tel 813/287-0440 or toll free 800/531-5900; fax 813/286-7399. Exit 21 off I-275. Super-clean establishment designed with Spanish-style accents. Recent renovations to grounds and public areas. **Rooms:** 122 rms and stes. CI 2pm/CO noon. Nonsmoking rms avail. **Amenities:** 🛏 🏊 A/C, cable TV w/movies. Free local calls. **Services:** 🍴 🖃 🗗 🌮 **Facilities:** 🛗 🏊 ♿ Family restaurant is open 24 hours. **Rates (CP):** HS Jan–Apr $62–$69 S; $70–$79 D; from $105 ste. Extra person $7. Children under 18 stay free. Lower rates off-season. Pking: Outdoor, free. Maj CC.

≡≡ Quality Hotel Riverside, 200 N Ashley Dr, Tampa, FL 33602; tel 813/223-2220; fax 813/273-0839. Exit 25 off I-275. **Rooms:** 286 rms and stes. CI 3pm/CO noon. Express checkout avail. Nonsmoking rms avail. **Amenities:** 🛏 🏊 A/C, cable TV. Some units w/minibars, some w/terraces. **Services:** ✗ 🍴 🖃 🗗 Babysitting. **Facilities:** 🛗 🏊 🏋 ♿ 1 bar (w/entertainment), games rm, sauna. **Rates (CP):** $75–$85 S or D; from $220 ste. Extra person $10. Children under 18 stay free. Spec packages avail. Pking: Indoor, $4.50. Maj CC.

≡≡ Quality Suites–Busch Gardens, 3001 University Center Dr, Tampa, FL 33612; tel 813/971-8930 or toll free 800/786-7446; fax 813/971-8935. Exit 33 off I 275. Often fully booked because of its convenient location and pleasing amenities. The lobby is draped with memorabilia from the many sports teams that have stayed here. **Rooms:** 15 stes. CI 3pm/CO noon. Express checkout avail. Nonsmoking rms avail. **Amenities:** 🛏 🏊 📺 A/C, cable TV w/movies, refrig, VCR, voice mail. Some units w/terraces. All rooms with microwaves. **Services:** 🖃 🗗 Complimentary breakfast buffet and evening cocktails. The front desk rents videos and also dispenses snacks and frozen dinners. **Facilities:** 🛗 🏊 ♿ Whirlpool, washer/dryer. **Rates (BB):** HS Feb–Mar $62–$159 S or D. Extra person $5. Children under 18 stay free. Lower rates off-season. Higher rates for spec evnts/hols. Spec packages avail. Pking: Outdoor, free. Maj CC.

≡≡≡ Radisson Bay Harbor Inn, 7700 Courtney Campbell Causeway, Tampa, FL 33607 (Tampa Int'l Airport); tel 813/281-8900 or toll free 800/333-3333; fax 813/281-0189. Airport exit off I-275. Close to the airport and overlooking the bay, this fine hotel receives many business travelers and conventioneers drawn by its beachfront location, a tough find in Tampa. **Rooms:** 257 rms and stes. CI 3pm/CO noon. Express checkout avail. Nonsmoking rms avail. **Amenities:** 🛏 🏊 A/C, cable TV w/movies. Some units w/minibars, all w/terraces. **Services:** ✗ 🆅🅿 🍴 🖃 🗗 Twice-daily maid svce, babysitting. **Facilities:** 🛗

1 rst, 1 bar (w/entertainment), 1 beach (ocean), games rm, beauty salon, washer/dryer. **Rates:** HS Jan–Apr $105–$120 S or D; from $225 ste. Extra person $10. Children under 18 stay free. Lower rates off-season. Spec packages avail. Pking: Outdoor, free. Maj CC.

Residence Inn by Marriott, 3075 N Rocky Point Dr, Tampa, FL 33607; tel 813/281-5677 or toll free 800/331-3131. Exit 20 off I-75. Small village of home-away-from-home-style apartments in a quiet bayside location. **Rooms:** 176 effic. CI 3pm/CO noon. Express checkout avail. Nonsmoking rms avail. Fully equipped kitchens. **Amenities:** A/C, cable TV. Some units w/terraces, some w/fireplaces. **Services:** Babysitting. Complimentary breakfast and morning newspaper. Free shuttle service serving surrounding area. Staff will shop for groceries. **Facilities:** Whirlpool, washer/dryer. **Rates (CP):** From $102 effic. Extra person $10. Children under 18 stay free. Pking: Outdoor, free. Maj CC.

Sailport Resort, 2506 Rocky Point Dr, Tampa, FL 33607; tel 813/281-9599 or toll free 800/255-9599, 800/321-9599 in Canada; fax 813/281-9510. This on-the-bay all-suites resort, with its fully equipped units, is perfect for lengthy stays or family vacations. Beautiful bay views and nearby area attractions bring repeat business. **Rooms:** 212 stes. CI 1pm/CO 11am. Nonsmoking rms avail. **Amenities:** A/C, cable TV, refrig. All units w/terraces. **Services:** Car-rental desk, babysitting. **Facilities:** Washer/dryer. Fishing pier; barbecue grills. **Rates (CP):** HS Jan–Apr from $97 ste. Extra person $5. Children under 12 stay free. Lower rates off-season. Spec packages avail. Pking: Outdoor, free. Maj CC.

Sheraton Grand Hotel, 4860 W Kennedy Blvd, Tampa, FL 33607; tel 813/286-4400 or toll free 800/325-3535; fax 813/286-4053. Exit 21 off I-275. This smoked-glass hotel is a favorite address for businesspeople, and it's close to shops and restaurants. Subdued and attractive lobby. **Rooms:** 124 rms and stes. CI 3pm/CO noon. Nonsmoking rms avail. **Amenities:** A/C, cable TV w/movies. **Services:** X Babysitting. **Facilities:** 2 rsts, 2 bars, beauty salon. **Rates:** HS Jan–Apr $109–$129 S or D; from $149 ste. Extra person $10. Children under 18 stay free. Lower rates off-season. Spec packages avail. Pking: Indoor, free. Maj CC.

Sheraton Inn Tampa & Conference Center, 7401 E Hillsborough Ave, Tampa, FL 33610; tel 813/626-0999 or toll free 800/325-3535; fax 813/622-7893. Exit 6 off I-4. Standard Sheraton made up of both low- and mid-rise buildings. Value pricing for tourists. **Rooms:** 276 rms and stes. CI 3pm/CO noon. Nonsmoking rms avail. Rooms in tower have been updated more recently than others. **Amenities:** A/C, cable TV w/movies. Some units w/terraces. **Services:** X Babysitting.

Facilities: 2 rsts, 2 bars, whirlpool. **Rates:** HS Jan–Mar $115 S; $120 D; from $180 ste. Extra person $10. Children under 19 stay free. Lower rates off-season. Higher rates for spec evnts/hols. Spec packages avail. Pking: Outdoor, free. Maj CC.

Tampa Airport Hilton at Metro Center, 2225 N Lois Ave, Tampa, FL 33607; tel 813/877-6688 or toll free 800/445-8667; fax 813/879-3264. Exit 22 off I-275. Lofty 2-story lobby makes a fine entrance to this business hotel close to the airport. Better suited to commercial needs than to tourists', although weekend rates may be attractive to families. **Rooms:** 238 rms and stes. CI 3pm/CO noon. Express checkout avail. Nonsmoking rms avail. **Amenities:** A/C, cable TV w/movies. Some units w/terraces. **Services:** X Babysitting. **Facilities:** 1 rst, 1 bar, whirlpool. **Rates:** HS Jan–Apr $125–$130 S; $135–$140 D; from $150 ste. Extra person $10. Children under 18 stay free. Lower rates off-season. Spec packages avail. Pking: Outdoor, free. Maj CC.

Tampa Airport Marriott, Tampa International Airport, Tampa, FL 33607; tel 813/879-5151 or toll free 800/228-9290, 800/228-9290; fax 813/873-0945. Airport exit off I-275. This well-run Marriott connected to the airport terminal is designed to handle its large capacity and is outfitted with ample staff. Spacious public areas. Revolving rooftop restaurant. **Rooms:** 295 rms and stes. CI 3pm/CO 1pm. Express checkout avail. Nonsmoking rms avail. **Amenities:** A/C, cable TV w/movies, voice mail. All units w/terraces. **Services:** X VP Babysitting. **Facilities:** 2 rsts (see also "Restaurants" below), 2 bars. **Rates:** HS Nov–Apr $134–$149 S; $149–$164 D; from $250 ste. Children under 18 stay free. Lower rates off-season. Spec packages avail. Pking: Indoor/outdoor, free. Maj CC.

Tampa Marriott Westshore, 1001 N Westshore Blvd, Tampa, FL 33607; tel 813/287-2555 or toll free 800/228-9290; fax 813/289-5464. Exit 21 off I-75. This major operation in the center of the Westshore hotel cluster is a staple in the area and is well received by business travelers. **Rooms:** 311 rms and stes. CI 4pm/CO 1pm. Express checkout avail. Nonsmoking rms avail. **Amenities:** A/C, cable TV w/movies, voice mail. Some units w/terraces. **Services:** X Babysitting. **Facilities:** 2 rsts, 3 bars, games rm, sauna, whirlpool, washer/dryer. **Rates:** HS Jan–June $134–$149 S or D; from $200 ste. Children under 18 stay free. Lower rates off-season. Spec packages avail. Pking: Outdoor, free. Maj CC.

Travelodge at Busch Gardens, 9202 N 30th St, Tampa, FL 33612; tel 813/935-7855 or toll free 800/578-7878; fax 813/935-7958. Exit 33 off I-275. An affordable hotel offering few amenities; the plus is its central location for taking in the area sights and attractions. **Rooms:** 146 rms and stes. CI 3pm/CO

11am. Nonsmoking rms avail. **Amenities:** 🕾 A/C, cable TV. **Services:** 🔄 🔌 **Facilities:** 🛗 🅿 ⛇ Games rm, washer/dryer. **Rates:** HS Feb–Apr $40–$45 S; $45–$55 D; from $65 ste. Extra person $4. Children under 18 stay free. Lower rates off-season. Higher rates for spec evnts/hols. Spec packages avail. Pking: Outdoor, free. Maj CC.

═══ Wyndham Harbour Island Hotel, 725 S Harbour Island Blvd, Tampa, FL 33602; tel 813/229-5000 or toll free 800/822-4200, 800/822-4200 in the US, 800/631-4200 in Canada; fax 813/229-5322. Exit Ashley St off I-275. Cross the bridge to Harbour Island; hotel is adjacent to Tampa Convention Center. A rather elaborate hotel with a dignified, stately look and style. A frontrunner in town. **Rooms:** 300 rms and stes. CI 3pm/CO noon. Express checkout avail. Nonsmoking rms avail. Classic guest rooms decorated in posh style; all have views of the water. **Amenities:** 🕾 🕭 📻 A/C, cable TV w/movies. All units w/minibars, some w/terraces. **Services:** ✗ 🔑 VP 🚗 🖂 🔄 Car-rental desk, babysitting. **Facilities:** 🛗 🅿 💻 ⛇ 1 rst, 1 bar (w/entertainment). 50 boat slips. **Rates:** HS Dec–Mar $139–$179 S; $159–$199 D; from $500 ste. Children under 18 stay free. Lower rates off-season. Spec packages avail. Pking: Indoor/outdoor, $6. Maj CC.

Motels

══ Comfort Inn, 2106 E Busch Blvd, Tampa, FL 33612; tel 813/931-3313 or toll free 800/221-2222; fax 813/933-8140. Offering the basics, this is a favored site for tourists for its proximity to Busch Gardens. **Rooms:** 50 rms and effic. CI 2pm/CO 11am. Nonsmoking rms avail. **Amenities:** 🕾 A/C, cable TV w/movies. **Services:** 🔄 **Facilities:** 🛗 ⛇ Whirlpool. **Rates:** $34–$49 S; $39–$54 D; from $54 effic. Extra person $5. Children under 18 stay free. Pking: Outdoor, free. Maj CC.

═ John Henry's Econo Lodge, 1701 E Busch Blvd, Tampa, FL 33612; tel 813/933-7681 or toll free 800/783-7681; fax 813/935-3301. 1 mi W of Busch Gardens, exit 33 off I-275 N. Serves its purpose as a place to rest your head. Popular only for its proximity to Busch Gardens. **Rooms:** 238 rms. CI 11am/CO 11am. Nonsmoking rms avail. **Amenities:** 🕾 A/C, cable TV. **Services:** 🔄 🔌 **Facilities:** 🛗 🅿 1 rst, 1 bar, washer/dryer. **Rates:** HS Feb–Aug $33–$48 S; $38–$52 D. Extra person $5. Children under 18 stay free. Lower rates off-season. Pking: Outdoor, free. Maj CC.

Restaurants 🍽

♛ Armani's, in the Hyatt Regency Westshore, 6200 Courtney Campbell Causeway, Tampa; tel 813/281-9165. Exit 20 B off I-275. **Northern Italian.** The views are breathtaking from this lovely, stylish room, located on the top floor of the world-class Hyatt Regency Westshore. Seafood and northern Italian dishes are highlights, as is the vast antipasto bar. **FYI:** Reservations recommended. Piano. Jacket required. **Open:** Mon–Thurs 6–10pm, Fri–Sat 6–11pm. Closed some hols. **Prices:** Main courses $7.75–$25.75. Maj CC. ♥ ▲ VP ⛇

♛ Bern's Steak House, 1208 S Howard Ave, Tampa; tel 813/251-2421. **Steak.** This stalwart one-of-a-kind Tampa institution features 7 rooms and a separate dessert lounge. Wonderful, aged steaks come with onion soup, salad, baked potato, garlic toast, and onion rings. Encylopedic wine list. **FYI:** Reservations accepted. **Open:** Daily 5–11pm. Closed Dec 25. **Prices:** Main courses $21–$30. Maj CC. VP ⛇

The Castaway, 7720 Courtney Campbell Causeway, Tampa; tel 813/281-0770. **Seafood.** Popular with the locals, this dimly lit eatery has a casual atmosphere, fresh seafood, and a superb view of the ocean. **FYI:** Reservations accepted. Children's menu. **Open:** Lunch Mon–Fri 11am–4pm; dinner Mon–Fri 5–10pm, Sat 5pm–midnight, Sun 5–10pm; brunch Sat 10am–3:30pm, Sun 9:30am–2:30pm. **Prices:** Main courses $13–$20. Maj CC. ▼ VP ⛇

CK's, in the Tampa Airport Marriott, Tampa International Airport, Tampa; tel 813/879-5178. **Continental/Steak.** Tampa's only revolving restaurant has terrific views as well as appetizing steaks, veal, lamb, salmon, and caesar salad. **FYI:** Reservations accepted. Children's menu. **Open:** Lunch Mon–Sat 11:30am–2:30pm; dinner Sun–Thurs 5–10pm, Fri–Sat 5–11pm; brunch Sun 10:30am–2:30pm. **Prices:** Main courses $17–$23. Maj CC. ▲ ▼ VP ⛇

The Colonnade, 3401 Bayshore Blvd, Tampa; tel 813/839-7558. **Seafood/Steak.** This restaurant has been satisfying customers with its fabulous food for over 60 years. Order the fresh grouper sandwich or choose one of their many platter specials, and top it off with a slice of coconut cream or key lime pie. **FYI:** Reservations not accepted. Children's menu. **Open:** Sun–Thurs 11am–10pm, Fri–Sat 11am–11pm. Closed some hols. **Prices:** Main courses $6.95–$12.95. Maj CC. ▲ ▼ ⛇

The Columbia, 601 S Harbour Island Blvd, Tampa; tel 813/229-2992. **Spanish.** Crisp black and white decor, traditional Spanish cuisine, outdoor dining, and a lovely view of Tampa Bay make this casual spot a winner. Also at: 2117 7th Ave E, Ybor City (813/248-4961). **FYI:** Reservations recommended. Children's menu. Dress code. **Open:** Sun 11am–9pm, Mon–Thurs 11am–10pm, Fri–Sat 11am–11pm. **Prices:** Main courses $9.95–$14.95. Maj CC. 🛥 ▼ ⛇

Crabby Tom's Old Time Oyster Bar and Seafood Restaurant, 3120 W Hillsborough Ave, Tampa; tel 813/870-1652. **Seafood.** The name isn't the only amazing mouthful at this seafood palace. Enjoy a variety of tasty ocean treats at red-tableclothed picnic tables. **FYI:** Reservations accepted. Children's menu. Beer and wine only. **Open:** Mon–Thurs 11am–10pm, Fri–Sat 11am–11pm, Sun 4–9pm. Closed some hols. **Prices:** Main courses $4.95–$15.95. Maj CC.

Crawdaddy's, 2500 Rocky Point Dr, Tampa; tel 813/281-0407. **Regional American/Seafood.** Enjoy down-home cooking and beautiful bay views at this romantic, antique-filled Victorian dining room. **FYI:** Reservations accepted. Band. Children's menu. **Open:** Lunch Mon–Fri 11am–3pm; dinner Sun–Thur 5–11pm, Fri–Sat 5pm–midnight. **Prices:** Main courses $11–$20. Maj CC.

Donatello, 232 N Dale Mabry Hwy, Tampa; tel 813/875-6660. **Northern Italian.** Soft lights, lovely decor, and an attentive tuxedoed staff make this a place for romance. Try the Maine lobster over linguine, the breast of duck, or a well-prepared Italian dish. **FYI:** Reservations accepted. **Open:** Lunch Mon–Fri 11:30am–2:30pm; dinner daily 6–11pm. Closed some hols. **Prices:** Main courses $15.95–$23.95. Maj CC.

JB Winberie, in Olde Hyde Park Village, 1610 W Swann Ave at Dakota St, Tampa; tel 813/253-6500. **New American.** A fun, casual eatery with a menu featuring award-winning chili. Also available are stir-fries, pasta primavera, sandwiches, and burgers. Sunday brunch is popular. **FYI:** Reservations accepted. Children's menu. **Open:** Daily 11am–11pm. **Prices:** Main courses $2.95–$11.95. Maj CC.

★ **Le Bordeaux**, 1502 S Howard Ave, Tampa; tel 813/254-4387. 1 block north of Bayshore Ave. **French.** The rotating daily menu features a selection of duck, fish, pork, and chicken dishes prepared Provençal-style. Setting is reminiscent of a French country tavern. **FYI:** Reservations recommended. Singer. Dress code. **Open:** Mon–Fri 5:30–10pm, Sat–Sun 5–11pm. Closed Dec 25. **Prices:** Main courses $7.95–$14.95; PF dinner $9–$19. Maj CC.

Ⓢ **Mel's Hot Dogs**, 4136 E Busch Blvd, Tampa; tel 813/985-8000. **American.** Great family fun and value. Choose from a variety of franks, or try a beef burger or the fried chicken basket. **FYI:** Reservations not accepted. Children's menu. Beer and wine only. **Open:** Sun 11am–9pm, Mon–Sat 10am–10pm. Closed some hols. **Prices:** Main courses $1–$6. No CC.

★ **Mise en Place**, 420 W Kennedy Blvd, Tampa; tel 813/254-5373. **New American.** A casual, contemporary bistro serving hearty fare with a healthy twist. Entrees might include roast duck with wild strawberry sauce or grilled swordfish with melon and mint salsa. **FYI:** Reservations not accepted. **Open:** Lunch Mon–Fri 11am–3pm; dinner Tues–Thurs 5:30–10pm, Fri–Sat 5:30–11pm. Closed some hols. **Prices:** Main courses $10.95–$16.95. Maj CC.

★ **Oystercatchers**, in the Hyatt Regency Westshore, 6200 Courtney Campbell Causeway, Tampa; tel 813/281-9116. **Seafood.** Dine while overlooking Tampa Bay from either indoor booths or outdoor tables. Menu includes the catch of the day, steaks, lamb, and nightly specials. **FYI:** Reservations recommended. **Open:** Lunch Mon–Fri 11:30am–2:30pm, Sun 10:30am–3pm; dinner Sun–Thurs 6–10:30pm, Fri–Sat 6–11pm. **Prices:** Main courses $13–$21. Maj CC.

Parker's Lighthouse, 601 S Harbour Island Blvd, Tampa; tel 813/223-3101. **Seafood.** A seafood restaurant with great water views from both indoor and outside tables. Brunch is a great value. **FYI:** Reservations accepted. Band. Children's menu. **Open:** Lunch Mon–Fri 11:30am–2pm, Sat noon–3pm; dinner Mon–Thurs 5–10pm, Fri–Sat 5–10:30pm, Sun 5–10pm; brunch Sun 10:30am–2:30pm. **Prices:** Main courses $10.95–$19.95. Maj CC.

Rumpelmayer's Restaurant, in the Ambassador Square Shopping Center, 4812 E Busch Blvd, Tampa; tel 813/989-9563. 8 blocks E of Busch Gardens at 48th St. **German.** Walk through the doors of this whimsical eatery and straight into the heart of Europe. Flemish shrimp, beef stroganoff, chicken cordon bleu, and a variety of German dishes highlight the menu. More than 60 imported beers are available. **FYI:** Reservations recommended. Sing along/singer. Children's menu. Beer and wine only. **Open:** Sun–Sat 11am–11pm. **Prices:** Main courses $7.50–$16.50; PF dinner $29.95. Maj CC.

Saltwaters Bar and Grille, in Hyatt Regency Tampa, 2 City Center, Tampa; tel 813/225-1234. **New American/Seafood.** While the kitchen recently closed here, patrons can still order from the menu of the Hyatt Regency Tampa's other in-house restaurant, the City Center Cafe. **FYI:** Reservations recommended. Jazz. Children's menu. **Open:** Daily 11:30am–midnight. **Prices:** Main courses $8.50–$11.50. Maj CC.

Selena's, in Olde Hyde Park, 1623 Snow Ave, Tampa; tel 813/251-2116. **Creole/Italian.** Patrons can dine either in the casual, comfortable Antique Room, or in the more formal Queen Anne Room, with its lace and linen. The Creole-inspired menu offers new twists on pasta, shrimp scampi, and chicken parmagiana. A low-fat menu is available. **FYI:** Reservations recommended. Children's menu. **Open:** Lunch daily 11am–4:30pm; dinner

Sun–Wed 4:30–9pm, Thurs 4:30–11pm, Fri–Sat 4:30pm–midnight; brunch Sun 11am–3pm. **Prices:** Main courses $8.95–$19.95. Maj CC. ⛴ ⛇

Shells, 202 S Dale Mabry Hwy, Tampa; tel 813/875-3467. **Seafood.** A basic and affordable eatery particularly suitable for families. While seafood is the primary offering, some beef and chicken dishes are offered as well. Also at: 11010 N 30th St (813/977-8456). **FYI:** Reservations not accepted. Children's menu. **Open:** Sun–Thurs 5–10pm, Fri–Sat 5–11pm. Closed some hols. **Prices:** Main courses $4.95–$12.95. Maj CC. ⛇

Villanova by Lauro, 3915 Henderson Blvd, Tampa; tel 813/281-2100. 2 blocks W of Dale Mabry Hwy. **Northern Italian.** Classic decor, soft music, tuxedoed waiters. Specialties include several veal dishes, grilled marinated shrimp, and chicken with eggplant, mozzarella, and a touch of tomato. **FYI:** Reservations recommended. **Open:** Lunch Mon–Fri 11:30am–2:30pm; dinner Mon–Sat 6–11pm. **Prices:** Main courses $10.50–$22.50. Maj CC. **VP** ⛇

The Wine Exchange, in Olde Hyde Park Village, 1611 W Swann Ave, Tampa; tel 813/254-9463. **International.** Great outdoor dining in a lively bistro setting. Enjoy innovative pizzas, pastas, sandwiches, and more. **FYI:** Reservations not accepted. Beer and wine only. **Open:** Mon–Thurs 11:30am–10:30pm, Fri–Sat 11:30am–11:30pm, Sun 11:30am–10:30pm. **Prices:** Main courses $7.95–$12.95. Ltd CC. ⛴ ⛇

Refreshment Stop ☕

Joffrey's Coffee & Tea Co, in Old Hyde Park, 1628 W Snow Circle, Tampa; tel 813/251-3315. **Coffeehouse.** Brick floors, track lighting, and glass-topped tables help to create a cool, contemporary feel. Wide assortment of appetizing desserts and pastries. This is a great post-shopping stop for coffee, tea, or cappuccino; you can even purchase coffee by the pound to take home with you. **Open:** Mon–Wed 7:30am–11pm, Thurs–Fri 7:30am–midnight, Sat 8am–midnight, Sun 9am–11pm. Closed some hols. Maj CC. ⛇

Attractions 🖼

Henry B Plant Museum, 401 W Kennedy Blvd; tel 813/254-1891. This landmark was modeled after the Alhambra Palace in Spain. It was built as the 511-room Tampa Bay Hotel in 1891, at the outrageous cost (for those days) of $2 million. The facility showcases original furnishings and art pieces (chosen by Plant for the hotel) in historic room settings. In December the museum is festively decorated during the Victorian Christmas Stroll. **Open:** Tues–Sat 10am–4pm, Sun noon–4pm. $

Busch Gardens, 3000 E Busch Blvd; tel 813/987-5000 or 987-5082 (recorded info). This 300-acre theme park has grown to become the most popular attraction on Florida's west coast. The park contains one of the largest collections of free-roaming wild animals in the United States, as well as dozens of rides, live entertainment, restaurants, and shops. It's divided into 8 sections, among them **Timbuktu**, featuring African artisans at work, a shopping bazaar, dolphin shows, and a 1,200-seat German-style dining hall with music and dancing; **Serengeti Plain**, home to hippos, buffalo, impala, gazelles, giraffes, rhinos, elephants, and ostriches; **Nairobi**, with a baby-animal nursery and petting zoo; and **Morocco**, a walled city featuring crafts demonstrations, a sultan's tent with snake charmers, and an ice show. Crown Colony, the newest area of the park, is home to a team of Clydesdale horses and is the location of Questor, a flight simulator–based ride.

The park also offers the **Anheuser-Busch brewery tour** to observe the beer-making process and get a chance to sample the famous brews. Air-conditioned monorail, open-air skyride, and train all circle the park. **Open:** Daily 9am–7:30pm; extended hours summer and hols. $$$$

Adventure Island, 4545 Bougainvillea Ave; tel 813/987-5660. Adjacent to Busch Gardens, this separate 23-acre outdoor water theme park has pools, water slides, an arcade, and picnic areas. **Open:** Apr–Oct, daily 10am–5pm; hours extended in summer. $$$$

Lowry Park Zoo, 7530 North Blvd; tel 813/935-8552. This 24-acre zoo houses animals in settings that closely resemble their natural habitats. Highlights include an aviary in a subtropical forest setting; a wildlife center showcasing Florida's native animals and plants; and a Florida at Night building, featuring rare, nocturnal animals. The manatee center has 2 large viewing tanks and facilities for the treatment and rehabilitation of injured manatees. There's also a children's petting zoo. **Open:** Apr–Aug, daily 9:30am–6pm; Sept–Mar, daily 9:30am–5pm. Closed Dec 25. $$$

Fun Forest at Lowry Park, 7520 North Blvd (at Sligh Ave); tel 813/935-5503. An old-fashioned theme park offering a dozen traditional kiddie rides, including a Ferris wheel, a merry-go-round, and bumper cars. **Open:** Mon–Sat 11am–5pm, Sun noon–6pm. $$$

Museum of Science and Industry (MOSI), 4801 E Fowler Ave; tel 813/985-5531. Located a mile north of Busch Gardens, MOSI has permanent and changing exhibits that focus on industry, technology, and the physical and natural sciences. It includes a ham radio station, communications gallery, power plant model, and weather station. Other attractions are the *Challenger* Center, a memorial to the 7 *Challenger* astronauts, which features a simulated space shuttle mission; and the Back Woods, a 40-acre wooded area that contains nature trails, a planetarium, an interactive butterfly garden, and a fossil garden. **Open:** Sun–Thurs 9am–4:30pm, Fri–Sat 9am–9pm. $$$

Tampa Museum of Art, 600 N Ashley Drive; tel 813/274-8130. This visual arts complex offers 7 galleries with changing exhibits ranging from Greek and Roman antiquities to German expressionism and contemporary American photography. Tours Wed, Sat, and Sun at 1pm. **Open:** Tues and Thurs–Sat 10am–5pm, Wed 10am––pm, Sun 1–5pm. $$

Museum of African-American Art, 1308 N Marion St; tel 813/272-2466. This museum is the first of its kind in Florida, and one of only 10 in the United States. It houses the Barnett-Aden African-American art collection, valued at $7.5 million and considered to be the country's foremost collection of African-American art. More than 80 artists are represented in the collection, which includes 32 pieces of sculpture and 106 paintings. **Open:** Tues–Sat 10am–4:30pm, Sun 1–4:30pm. $

Florida Center for Contemporary Art, 1513 E Eighth Ave; tel 813/248-1171. A gallery for alternative visual arts within a growing creative community in Ybor City, emphasizing Florida artists. Many exhibitors at this nonprofit space offer their works for sale. **Open:** Wed–Sat 11am–5pm (hours may vary, phone ahead). Free.

USF Contemporary Art Museum, Building FAM 101, University of South Florida, 4202 E Fowler Ave; tel 813/974-2849. This 10,000-square-foot facility spotlights contemporary artworks from around the world. Exhibits change approximately every 6–8 weeks. In particular, there are valuable collections of pre-Columbian and African artifacts, as well as contempoary prints from the southeastern United States. **Open:** Mon–Fri 10am–5pm, Sat 1–4pm. Closed some hols. Free.

Ybor City State Museum, 1818 Ninth Ave; tel 813/247-6323. The focal point of Ybor City, this museum is housed in the former Ferlita Bakery (1896–1973). Exhibits depict the political, social, and cultural influences that shaped this section of Tampa, with a particular emphasis on the once-flourishing cigar industry. The museum includes a collection of cigar memorabilia and works by local artisans. Adjacent to the park is Preservation Park, the site of 3 renovated cigar workers' cottages with original furnishings from the turn of the century. Cottage tours are offered twice daily, in the morning and afternoon. **Open:** Tues–Sat 9am–noon and 1–5pm. $

Seminole Indian Village, 5221 N Orient Rd; tel 813/620-3077. Located on Tampa's Seminole Reservation, this museum traces the history of the Seminoles in the area. Visitors can watch skilled Seminole craftspeople as they practice beadwork, wood carving, basketmaking, and patchwork sewing. More lively demonstrations include alligator-wrestling and snake-handling. The grounds also serve as a natural habitat for Florida black bears, panthers, otters, bobcats, and deer. There is a gift shop with handmade crafts. Tours available every hour on the half-hour, with last tour at 3:30pm. **Open:** Mon–Sat 9am–5pm, Sun noon–5pm. Closed some hols. $$

Children's Museum of Tampa, 7550 North Blvd; tel 813/935-8441. Geared for children 2–10, this museum's interactive exhibits are designed to increase curiosity and imagination. Activities range from grocery shopping to blowing giant bubbles to papermaking. Safety Village is Tampa in miniature, a place for kids to learn the rules of safety, with miniature traffic lights, buildings, and paved streets. **Open:** Mon–Thurs 9am–4:30pm, Sat 10am–5pm, Sun 1–5pm. $

Gondola Getaway Cruises, Waterwalk (Harbour Island); tel 813/855-8518. See the skyscrapers and other downtown highlights as you float across the waters of Tampa Bay and the lower Hillsborough River in an authentic 70-year-old Venetian gondola. Each 30-foot gondola is capable of carrying up to 4 passengers. Ice bucket and glasses can be supplied for passengers bringing wine. Cruises offered Mon–Sat 6pm–midnight, Sun noon–9pm; other times by appointment. Reservations accepted 9am–7pm. $$$$

Tampa Stadium, 4201 N Dale Mabry Hwy; tel 813/872-7977. Home base for the Tampa Bay Buccaneers football team and the Tampa Bay Rowdies soccer team, this 74,296-capacity stadium also hosts a wide variety of sporting events, shows, and concerts. Call in advance for information on games and events or reserve through Ticketmaster outlets.

TARPON SPRINGS

Map page M-6, D2

See also **Palm Harbor**

Hotels 🛏

≣≣ Best Western Tahitian Resort, 2337 US 19, Tarpon Springs, FL 34691; or toll free 800/528-1234; fax 813/937-3806. A well-maintained facility with fresh decor and a small but capable staff. Set on modestly landscaped grounds. **Rooms:** 140 rms and effic. CI 3pm/CO 11am. Nonsmoking rms avail. **Amenities:** 🛋 🗄 A/C, cable TV w/movies. **Services:** ✕ 🛎 🐾 **Facilities:** 🖼 🔥 1 rst, 1 bar (w/entertainment), washer/

dryer. **Rates:** HS Feb–Apr $61–$76 S or D; from $61 effic. Extra person $5. Children under 13 stay free. Lower rates off-season. Pking: Outdoor, free. Maj CC.

≣≣ **Quality Inn Resort**, 38724 US 19 N at Klosterman Rd, Tarpon Springs, FL 34689; tel 813/934-5781 or toll free 800/ 682-7766; fax 813/934-1755. Basic, unpretentious accommodations. **Rooms:** 115 rms, stes, and effic. CI 1pm/CO noon. Nonsmoking rms avail. **Amenities:** 🛎 ⚬ A/C, cable TV w/movies. All units w/terraces. **Services:** ✗ 🖼 ⌟ **Facilities:** 🛆 ⚑ 🔟 ⚿ 1 rst, 1 bar, sauna, steam rm, whirlpool, playground, washer/dryer. Terraced poolside sitting area and upper-level sun deck. **Rates:** HS Jan–Apr $63 S; $68 D; from $89 ste; from $71 effic. Extra person $5. Children under 18 stay free. Lower rates off-season. Pking: Outdoor, free. Maj CC.

Attractions 💼

Konger Coral Sea Aquarium, 850 Dodecanese Blvd; tel 813/ 938-5378. This aquarium features a wide collection of fish indigenous to the Gulf of Mexico and the Caribbean Sea, including lemon sharks, angel fish, puffers, and stingrays. Feeding shows every 90 minutes beginning at 10:30am. **Open:** Daily 10am–5pm. Closed some hols. $$

Spongeorama, 510 Dodecanese Blvd; tel 813/942-3771. The exhibits in this museum/theater trace the history of the city's sponge industry and its Greek settlers. There's a film demonstrating sponge diving. **Open:** Daily 10am–6pm. Free.

TEQUESTA

Map page M-9, C4

Restaurant 🍴

Cobblestone Cafe, in Gallery Square North, 383 Tequesta Dr, Tequesta; tel 407/747-4419. **New American.** This cozy, country-style cafe offers a variety of seafood dishes, from the fresh catch of the day to sautéed crab cakes. The regularly changing menu may also include grilled leg of lamb or veal medallions. **FYI:** Reservations accepted. Children's menu. Beer and wine only. No smoking. **Open:** Lunch Mon–Fri 11:30am–2:30pm; dinner Mon–Sat 5:30–9:30pm. Closed some hols. **Prices:** Main courses $13.95–$20.95. Maj CC. ◼ ⚿

THONOTOSASSA

Map page M-6, E3

Attraction 💼

Hillsborough River State Park, 15402 US 301N; tel 813/ 987-6771. The Hillsborough River runs through this 3,000-acre park, located off US 301, with a string of rapids and a swinging bridge spanning its banks. A small museum contains memorabilia from Fort Foster, built in 1847 during the Second Seminole War. Guided tours of a reconstruction of the fort. Swimming (Mem Day–Labor Day), fishing, canoe rentals, hiking, camping, nature trail. $

TITUSVILLE

Map page M-7, C3

See also **Kennedy Space Center**

Hotels 🛏

≣≣ **Holiday Inn Titusville**, 4951 S Washington Ave, Titusville, FL 32780; tel 407-269-2121 or toll free 800/355-6655; fax 407/267-4739. Exit 79 off I-95. The hotel closest to the Kennedy Space Center, it overlooks the launch site as well as the Intracoastal Waterway. US Space Camp is 2 miles away. **Rooms:** 117 rms and stes. CI 3pm/CO noon. Nonsmoking rms avail. Standard guest rooms are in fresh condition. **Amenities:** 🛎 ⚬ A/C, cable TV. **Services:** ✗ 🚐 🖼 ⌟ Car-rental desk, babysitting. **Facilities:** 🛆 🔟 🔟 ⚿ 1 rst, 1 bar (w/entertainment), games rm, lawn games, washer/dryer. **Rates:** HS Jan–Apr $64– $76 S; $70–$82 D; from $175 ste. Extra person $6. Children under 20 stay free. Lower rates off-season. Spec packages avail. Pking: Outdoor, free. Maj CC.

≣≣ **Ramada Inn Kennedy Space Center**, 3500 Cheney Hwy, Titusville, FL 32780; tel 407/269-5510 or toll free 800/2 RAMADA; fax 407/269-3796. Exit 79 off I-95. Composed of 1- and 2-story buildings surrounding a sunny deck. **Rooms:** 124 rms and stes. CI noon/CO noon. Nonsmoking rms avail. **Amenities:** 🛎 ⚬ A/C, cable TV w/movies. **Services:** ✗ 🚐 🖼 ⌟ Car-rental desk. **Facilities:** 🛆 ⚑ ⚑ 🔟 ⚿ 1 rst, games rm, lawn games, steam rm, whirlpool, playground, washer/dryer. **Rates:** HS Jan–Apr $66 S or D; from $89 ste. Extra person $6. Children under 18 stay free. Lower rates off-season. Higher rates for spec evnts/hols. Spec packages avail. Pking: Outdoor, free. Maj CC.

Motels

≡≡ **Comfort Inn–Kennedy Space Center**, 3810 S Washington Ave, Titusville, FL 32780; tel 407/267-9111 or toll free 800/525-2765; fax 407/267-0750. 7 mi NW of Kennedy Space Center, exit 79 off I-95. Well-kept 2-story property has guest rooms that open to the pool and courtyard. **Rooms:** 102 rms. CI 3pm/CO 11am. Nonsmoking rms avail. **Amenities:** 🛏 ⚱ A/C, cable TV w/movies. Some units with microwaves and refrigerators. **Services:** ⚐ ⟲ Car-rental desk. **Facilities:** �🔥 ⟦80⟧ 1 rst, 1 bar, lawn games, washer/dryer. **Rates (CP):** HS Jan–Apr $59 S; $54 D. Extra person $5. Children under 18 stay free. Lower rates off-season. Higher rates for spec evnts/hols. Pking: Outdoor, free. Maj CC.

≡≡ **Howard Johnson Lodge**, 1829 Riverside Dr, Titusville, FL 32780; tel 407/267-7900 or toll free 800/654-2000; fax 407/267-7080. Exit 79 off I-95. Offers unobstructed views of space shuttle launches from Kennedy Space Center. **Rooms:** 104 rms. CI 2pm/CO noon. Nonsmoking rms avail. **Amenities:** 🛏 ⚱ ⊠ A/C, cable TV w/movies. All units w/terraces. **Services:** ✕ ⚐ ⟲ ⟲ Car-rental desk, babysitting. **Facilities:** �🔥 🏓 ⟦100⟧ ⚐ 1 rst, 1 bar (w/entertainment), playground, washer/dryer. Boat docks on premises. **Rates:** HS Jan–Apr $59–$99 S or D. Children under 18 stay free. Lower rates off-season. Higher rates for spec evnts/hols. AP and MAP rates avail. Spec packages avail. Pking: Outdoor, free. Maj CC.

Attractions ⚏

US Astronaut Hall of Fame, 6225 Vectorspace Blvd; tel 407/269-6100. Exhibits honoring the first 20 Americans in space include Wally Schirra's *Sigma 7* capsule, Gus Grissom's *Mercury* space suit, rare film footage, and many other artifacts and mementos. A 20-minute film "Shuttle to Tomorrow" is screened aboard a full-scale space shuttle mock-up, and visitors may climb into a re-created *Mercury* capsule for a short tour narrated by John Glenn. Also here is US Space Camp, where children from across the country spend 5 days learning how math and science are applied in astronaut training (advance reservation required). **Open:** Daily 9am–5pm. Closed Dec 25. $$$

Valiant Air Command Museum, 6600 Tico Rd; tel 407/268-1941. Rotating exhibits of usually 10–12 restored and flyable aircraft from the World War II era and afterward. A C-47 transport plane is open for inspection, and kids can jump into a cockpit trainer to get a feel for the controls. Exhibits include rebuilt airplane engines and a large memorabilia room with artifacts from both World Wars. Guided tours are available on request. The VAC also hosts an annual airshow in March or April. **Open:** Daily 10am–6pm. Closed some hols. $$$

TREASURE ISLAND
Map page M-8, A1

Hotel 🛏

≡≡ **Bilmar Beach Resort Hotel**, 10650 Gulf Blvd, Treasure Island, FL 33706; tel 813/360-5531 or toll free 800/826-9724; fax 813/360-2915. 5th Ave N exit off I-275. A delightful beach complex with some commanding views of the gulf. **Rooms:** 172 stes and effic. CI 2pm/CO 11am. Nonsmoking rms avail. **Amenities:** 🛏 ⚱ ⊠ ⚐ A/C, cable TV, refrig, in-rm safe. Some units w/terraces. **Services:** ✕ ⚐ ⟲ Babysitting. **Facilities:** �🔥 ⟦200⟧ ⚐ 1 rst, 2 bars (w/entertainment), 1 beach (ocean), whirlpool. Dixieland jazz offered Wednesday and Sunday evenings. **Rates:** HS Feb 8–Apr 17 from $189 ste; from $110 effic. Extra person $8. Children under 12 stay free. Min stay spec evnts. Lower rates off-season. Spec packages avail. Pking: Outdoor, free. Maj CC.

Motel

≡≡ **Ramada Inn Treasure Island**, 12000 Gulf Blvd, Treasure Island, FL 33706; tel 813/360-7051 or toll free 800/228-2828; fax 813/367-6641. Exit 4 off I-275. Beachfront location in a quiet neighborhood. Some great views and lots of sun. **Rooms:** 121 rms and effic. CI 3pm/CO noon. Nonsmoking rms avail. **Amenities:** 🛏 ⚱ A/C, TV w/movies, VCR, in-rm safe. **Services:** ✕ ⚐ ⟲ **Facilities:** �🔥 1 rst, 2 bars (1 w/entertainment), 1 beach (ocean), games rm, whirlpool, playground, washer/dryer. Poolside bar. **Rates:** HS Feb–Apr $110–$120 S or D; from $120 effic. Extra person $10. Children under 18 stay free. Lower rates off-season. Pking: Outdoor, free. Maj CC.

Resort

≡≡ **Sand Pebble Resort**, 12300 Gulf Blvd, Treasure Island, FL 33706; tel 813/360-1845; fax 813/367-9309. At 123rd Ave. An all-condominium vacation resort. Some marvelous sunset views from the beach below. **Rooms:** 49 effic. CI 4pm/CO 10am. Fully equipped units, many updated in Key West style. **Amenities:** 🛏 ⚱ ⊠ ⚐ A/C, cable TV w/movies, refrig. Some units w/terraces. **Services:** ⟲ Children's program, babysitting. **Facilities:** �🔥 ⚐ 1 beach (ocean), games rm, whirlpool, washer/dryer. **Rates:** HS Feb–mid Apr from $85 effic. Extra person $8. Children under 12 stay free. Min stay. Lower rates off-season. Pking: Outdoor, free. Maj CC.

VENICE
Map page M-8, C2

Hotels 🛏

≡≡ **Best Western Sandbar Beach Resort**, 811 The Esplanade N, Venice, FL 34285; tel 813/488-2251 or toll free 800/822-4853; fax 813/485-2894. Exit 35 off I-75. Boasts a private beach; located near marinas and restaurants. **Rooms:** 44 rms and stes. CI 2pm/CO 11am. Nonsmoking rms avail. **Amenities:** 🛏 📶 A/C, cable TV w/movies. **Services:** 🛎 🍴 **Facilities:** 🏊 1 rst, 1 beach (ocean), washer/dryer. **Rates:** HS Dec–Apr $100–$130 S; $130–$150 D; from $180 ste. Extra person $18. Children under 16 stay free. Min stay spec evnts. Lower rates off-season. Higher rates for spec evnts/hols. Spec packages avail. Pking: Outdoor, free. Maj CC.

≡≡ **Best Western Venice Resort**, 455 US 41 Bypass, Venice, FL 34292; tel 813/485-5411 or toll free 800/237-3712; fax 813/484-6193. 10 mi S of Sarasota, exit 35 off I-75. About 1 mile from the water, this 2-story lodging receives a mix of guests, from golfers to American families and European tourists. **Rooms:** 160 rms and stes. CI 3pm/CO 11am. Nonsmoking rms avail. **Amenities:** 🛏 📶 A/C, cable TV. **Services:** 🛎 🍴 🐕 Babysitting. **Facilities:** 🏊 350 👤 1 rst, 1 bar (w/entertainment), whirlpool, playground, washer/dryer. Dinner theater operates mid-summer and October to March. **Rates:** HS Jan–Apr $86–$99 S or D; from $150 ste. Extra person $6. Children under 18 stay free. Lower rates off-season. Spec packages avail. Pking: Outdoor, free. Maj CC.

≡≡ **Days Inn**, 1710 S Tamiami Trail, Venice, FL 34293; tel 813/493-4558 or toll free 800/325-2525; fax 813/493-1593. 2½ mi S of Venice. Satisfactory for short stays or budget business trips. **Rooms:** 73 rms and stes. CI 2pm/CO 11am. Nonsmoking rms avail. **Amenities:** 🛏 A/C, satel TV. 1 unit w/terrace. **Services:** 🛎 🍴 🐕 **Facilities:** 🏊 100 👤 1 rst, 1 bar, washer/dryer. **Rates:** HS Jan–Apr $74–$84 S; $84–$94 D; from $145 ste. Extra person $6. Children under 12 stay free. Lower rates off-season. Higher rates for spec evnts/hols. Spec packages avail. Pking: Outdoor, free. Maj CC.

Restaurant 🍴

The Crow's Nest Marina Restaurant, 1968 Tarpon Circle Dr, Venice; tel 813/484-9551. **Seafood/Steak.** The menu changes daily according to the availability of fresh seafood. Views of Intracoastal Waterway. **FYI:** Reservations not accepted. Guitar/singer. **Open:** HS Oct–May lunch Mon–Sat 11:30am–4:30pm, Sun noon–10pm; dinner Mon–Sat 5–10pm. Reduced hours off-season. Closed some hols. **Prices:** Main courses $9.95–$16.95. Maj CC. 🏔

VERO BEACH
Map page M-9, A3

Hotels 🛏

≡≡ **Days Inn Vero Beach**, 8800 20th St, Vero Beach, FL 32966; tel 407/562-9991 or toll free 800/325-2525; fax 407/562-0716. Exit 68 off I-95. Popular budget stop with motorists, not far from Dodgertown and 8 miles to the beaches. **Rooms:** 231 rms and stes. CI 4pm/CO 11am. Nonsmoking rms avail. **Amenities:** 🛏 A/C, cable TV. **Services:** 🛎 🍴 🐕 Babysitting. **Facilities:** 🏊 50 👤 1 rst, washer/dryer. **Rates:** HS Dec–Apr $58 S; $63 D; from $75 ste. Extra person $5. Children under 17 stay free. Lower rates off-season. Higher rates for spec evnts/hols. Pking: Outdoor, free. Maj CC.

≡≡≡ **Guest Quarters Suite Resort**, 3500 Ocean Dr, Vero Beach, FL 32963; tel 407/231-5666 or toll free 800/841-5666; fax 407/234-4866. Take Fla 60 to end at Ocean Dr. The area's best facility, offering an all-suites arrangement in a 4-story contemporary building with Mediterranean accents. **Rooms:** 55 stes. CI 3pm/CO noon. Express checkout avail. Nonsmoking rms avail. Spacious rooms proffer handsome furnishings and an efficient layout. **Amenities:** 🛏 📶 📶 A/C, cable TV, refrig, VCR. All units w/terraces. **Services:** ✕ 🛎 🍴 Babysitting. **Facilities:** 🏊 50 👤 2 rsts, 1 bar, 1 beach (ocean), washer/dryer. **Rates:** HS Dec–Apr from $185 ste. Extra person $10. Children under 18 stay free. Lower rates off-season. Higher rates for spec evnts/hols. Spec packages avail. Pking: Indoor/outdoor, free. Maj CC.

≡≡ **Holiday Inn–West Countryside**, 8797 20th St, Vero Beach, FL 32966; or toll free 800/HOLIDAY; fax 407/569-8558. Exit 68 off I-95. Standard lowrise family hotel. **Rooms:** 217 rms. CI 2pm/CO noon. Express checkout avail. Nonsmoking rms avail. **Amenities:** 🛏 📶 A/C, cable TV. **Services:** ✕ 🛎 🍴 🐕 Children under 12 eat free. **Facilities:** 🏊 350 👤 1 rst, 1 bar (w/entertainment), playground, washer/dryer. Volleyball. **Rates:** HS Jan–Apr $58 S; $62 D. Extra person $6. Children under 19 stay free. Lower rates off-season. Spec packages avail. Pking: Outdoor, free. Maj CC.

≡≡ **Riviera Inn**, 1605 S Ocean Dr, Vero Beach, FL 32963; tel 407/234-4112; fax 407/234-4112 ext 118. Attractive accommodations with oversized rooms. **Rooms:** 17 rms and effic. CI 2pm/CO 11am. Nonsmoking rms avail. **Amenities:** 🛏 📶 A/C, cable

TV. Some units w/terraces. **Services:** ✗ 🍴 Babysitting. **Facilities:** 🔲 🔲 ᵴ 1 rst, 1 bar (w/entertainment). Well-regarded, popular restaurant. **Rates:** HS Feb–Apr $69 S or D; from $89 effic. Extra person $10. Children under 12 stay free. Lower rates off-season. Pking: Outdoor, free. Maj CC.

Motels

▤▤ **Islander Motel**, 3101 Ocean Dr, Vero Beach, FL 32963; or toll free 800/952-5886; fax 407/231-4431 ext 31. Well located in downtown Vero Beach, this small, modest, aqua-colored motel is fine for undemanding couples. The beach is nearby. **Rooms:** 16 rms and effic. CI 1pm/CO 11am. Nonsmoking rms avail. Some rooms have refrigerators. **Amenities:** 🔲 ᵹ A/C, cable TV, VCR. Some units w/terraces. **Services:** 🍴 **Facilities:** 🔲 1 beach (ocean), washer/dryer. Small, walk-up cafe. Barbecue area. **Rates:** HS Mid-Jan–mid-Apr $89 S or D; from $99 effic. Extra person $7. Children under 12 stay free. Lower rates off-season. Pking: Outdoor, free. Maj CC.

▤▤ **Vero Beach Inn**, 4700 N Fla A1A, Vero Beach, FL 32963; or toll free 800/227-8615; fax 407/231-9547. This white-columned, 4-story brick structure set on the beach is a short drive from most local shops, restaurants, and attractions. **Rooms:** 108 rms and stes. CI noon/CO noon. Comfortable rooms. **Amenities:** 🔲 A/C, cable TV, in-rm safe. **Services:** ✗ 🚐 🍴 **Facilities:** 🔲 🔲 ᵴ 1 rst, 1 bar (w/entertainment), 1 beach (ocean), washer/dryer. Pool is partly enclosed by the hotel and partly outside. Restaurant has ocean and pool views. A lively tiki bar operates every day in season and on weekends out of season. **Rates:** HS Feb–Apr $100 S or D; from $125 ste. Children under 16 stay free. Lower rates off-season. Spec packages avail. Pking: Outdoor, free. Maj CC.

Restaurants 🍽

The Black Pearl, 1409 Fla A1A, Vero Beach; tel 407/234-4426. 1 mi S of 17th St Causeway. **Regional American/French.** A casually elegant establishment with pink and green decor reminiscent of the famed Polo Lounge in Beverly Hills. The daily menu is centered around seafood dishes—6 to 8 different ones are usually available. The British owners also own the nearby Pearl's Caribbean Bistro, a scaled-down, more festive spot. **FYI:** Reservations recommended. Children's menu. Beer and wine only. **Open:** Daily 6–10pm. Closed some hols. **Prices:** Main courses $16.50. Maj CC. 🔲 ᵴ

★ **Charley Brown's**, 1410 S Fla A1A, Vero Beach; tel 407/231-6310. ¼ mi S of 17th St Bridge. **American.** A comfortable eatery with an animated atmosphere that's fun for the whole family. Great steaks, chicken, and seafood entrees. **FYI:** Reserva-

tions accepted. Children's menu. **Open:** Mon–Thurs 5–9:30pm, Fri–Sat 5–10pm. Closed Thanksgiving. **Prices:** Main courses $9.95–$17.50. Maj CC. 🔲 ᵴ

Ocean Grill, 1050 Sexton Plaza, Vero Beach; tel 407/231-5409. At the end of US 60. **American.** An elegant restaurant with shining hardwood floors, lovely antiques, and superb views of the water. Prime rib, chicken Oscar, and filet mignon are just a few of the house specialties. **FYI:** Reservations not accepted. Children's menu. **Open:** Lunch Mon–Fri 11:30am–2:30pm; dinner daily 5:45–10pm. Closed 2 weeks in Sept. **Prices:** Main courses $11–$20. Maj CC. 🔲 ᵴ

Attractions 💼

McClarty Center Museum, 13180 N Fla A1A; tel 407/589-2147. Dealing primarily with the sinking of a Spanish fleet off the coast here in 1715, this museum is built on the site where survivors came ashore. On view are replicas and some original pieces of the salvaged treasure. Dioramas, talking displays, 28-minute video. **Open:** Daily 10am-4:30pm. $

Center for the Arts in Vero Beach, 3001 Riverside Park Dr; tel 407/231-0707. The Main Gallery features major national and international exhibitions, ranging from American photography to Asian ceramics; the Florida Gallery is devoted to exhibits by Floridians. A sculpture garden is devoted to large-scale works. "Tuesday Cinema at the Center" screens foreign and independent American films every Tuesday at 3pm and 8pm. Guided tours available Wed–Sun 1:30–3:30pm. Gift shop. **Open:** Fri–Wed 10am–4:30pm, Thurs 10am-8pm. Closed Mon (summer only) and some hols. $

Dodgertown, 4101 26th St; tel 407/569-4900. The winter home of the LA Dodgers, this 450-acre sports and recreation complex includes 2 golf courses and a country club where baseball players can sometimes be sighted. Spring training games are played here at Holman Stadium, as are regular home games of the minor-league Vero Beach Dodgers. **Open:** Daily 8am-11pm. $$$

WAKULLA SPRINGS

Map page M4, C-1

Attraction 💼

Edward Ball Wakulla Springs State Park, 1 Spring Dr; tel 904/922-3632. This is one of the world's largest and deepest freshwater springs. The Tarzan movies starring Johnny Weissmuller were filmed in this park. Visitors can take a river cruise to view indigenous wildlife of the area or a glass-bottom boat tour over the spring that includes limestone formations, the opening of the spring, and mastodon bones in the spring bed. Swimming, hiking, nature trails. **Open:** Daily 8am–dusk. $$

WALT DISNEY WORLD

See Lake Buena Vista. *See also* Altamonte Springs, Apopka, Clermont, Kissimmee, Maitland, Orlando, Winter Garden, Winter Park

WESLEY CHAPEL

Map page M-6, D3

Resort ▥

▤▤▤▤ **Saddlebrook**, 5700 Saddlebrook Resort, Wesley Chapel, FL 33543; tel 813/973-1111 or toll free 800/729-8383; fax 813/973-4504. Exit 58 off I-75. 500 acres. This sprawling complex dotting the fairways offers an array of dining and entertainment choices to complement its many sports facilities. **Rooms:** 780 rms and stes. CI 3pm/CO noon. Nonsmoking rms avail. Rooms may be combined to form suites, which include cooking facilities. **Amenities:** ▥ ▥ A/C, cable TV w/movies. All units w/minibars, all w/terraces. **Services:** ▥▥▥▥▥▥▥▥ Car-rental desk, social director, masseur, children's program, babysitting. **Facilities:** ▥▥▥▥36▥▥37▥▥▥▥1K▥▥▥ 3 rsts, 3 bars (1 w/entertainment), lifeguard, games rm, lawn games, spa, sauna, steam rm, whirlpool, beauty salon, washer/dryer. The tennis complex is one of the largest in Florida. **Rates:** HS Jan–Apr $190 S or D; from $220 ste. Extra person $20. Children under 13 stay free. Lower rates off-season. Spec packages avail. Pking: Outdoor, free. Maj CC.

WEST PALM BEACH

Map page M-9, D4

Hotels ▥

▤▤ **Courtyard by Marriott**, 600 Northpointe Pkwy, West Palm Beach, FL 33407; tel 407/640-9000 or toll free 800/321-2211; fax 407/471-0122. Suitable for both business travelers and families on holiday. Convenient to area restaurants. **Rooms:** 149 rms and stes. CI 4pm/CO noon. Nonsmoking rms avail. **Amenities:** ▥ ▥ ▥ A/C, cable TV w/movies. All units w/terraces. **Services:** ▥ ▥ ▥ ▥ Babysitting. **Facilities:** ▥

▥▥ ▥ ▥ 1 rst, 1 bar, whirlpool, washer/dryer. **Rates:** HS Jan–Apr $89 S; $99 D; from $110 ste. Children under 17 stay free. Lower rates off-season. Pking: Outdoor, free. Maj CC.

▤▤ **Hampton Inn–Airport**, 1505 Belvedere Rd, West Palm Beach, FL 33406 (Palm Beach Int'l Airport); tel 407/471-8700 or toll free 800/888-0175; fax 407/689-7385. Well-run middle-grade establishment with a friendly staff. **Rooms:** 136 rms. CI 3pm/CO noon. Nonsmoking rms avail. **Amenities:** ▥ ▥ A/C, cable TV w/movies. **Services:** ▥ ▥ ▥ **Facilities:** ▥ ▥20 ▥ **Rates (CP):** HS Dec–May $79–$89 S; $83–$99 D. Children under 18 stay free. Lower rates off-season. Spec packages avail. Pking: Outdoor, free. Maj CC.

▤▤▤ **Holiday Inn–Airport**, 1301 Belvedere Rd, West Palm Beach, FL 33405 (Palm Beach Int'l Airport); tel 407/659-3880 or toll free 800/HOLIDAY; fax 407/655-8886. Belvedere Rd exit off I-95. This V-shaped highrise of concrete and glass sits on a wider base that contains public areas nestled around an L-shaped pool. Attracts mainly business travelers. **Rooms:** 199 rms and stes. CI 2pm/CO 11am. Nonsmoking rms avail. **Amenities:** ▥ ▥ A/C, cable TV w/movies. Some units w/terraces. **Services:** ▥▥▥▥ **Facilities:** ▥▥270▥ 1 rst, 1 bar, sauna. **Rates (CP):** HS Jan–Apr $89 S; $99 D; from $125 ste. Children under 18 stay free. Lower rates off-season. Higher rates for spec evnts/hols. Spec packages avail. Pking: Outdoor, free. Maj CC.

▤▤▤ **The Omni West Palm Beach Hotel**, 1601 Belvedere Rd, West Palm Beach, FL ; tel 407/689-6400 or toll free 800/THE-OMNI; fax 407/683-7150. Belvedere Rd exit off I-95, near Palm Beach Int'l Airport. Often busy airport hotel. **Rooms:** 220 rms and stes. CI 4pm/CO 1pm. Express checkout avail. Nonsmoking rms avail. **Amenities:** ▥ ▥ A/C, cable TV. Some units w/terraces. **Services:** ▥▥▥▥▥▥ **Facilities:** ▥▥400 ▥ 1 rst, 1 bar (w/entertainment), spa, whirlpool, beauty salon. **Rates:** HS Jan–Apr $129 S; $139 D; from $149 ste. Extra person $10. Children under 18 stay free. Min stay spec evnts. Lower rates off-season. Spec packages avail. Pking: Outdoor, free. Maj CC.

▤▤▤ **Palm Beach Airport Hilton**, 150 Australian Ave, West Palm Beach, FL 33406 (Palm Beach Int'l Airport); tel 407/684-9400 or toll free 800/445-8667; fax 407/689-9421. Southern Blvd exit off I-95. Offers a bit more pizzazz than the nearby competition. Pleasant, small lake in back is an unusual feature for an airport hotel. Smart-looking lobby is sometimes understaffed. **Rooms:** 247 rms and stes. CI 3pm/CO noon. Nonsmoking rms avail. **Amenities:** ▥ ▥ A/C, cable TV. **Services:** ▥▥▥▥▥ **Facilities:** ▥▥500▥ 1 rst, 1 bar (w/entertainment), games rm. **Rates (CP):** HS Dec–Apr $119 S; $129 D; from $450 ste. Extra person $10. Children under 18 stay free. Lower rates off-season. Higher rates for spec evnts/hols. Spec packages avail. Pking: Outdoor, free. Maj CC.

≣≣≣ Radisson Suite Inn–Palm Beach Airport, 1808 Australian Ave, West Palm Beach, FL 33409; tel 407/689-6888 or toll free 800/333-3333; fax 407/683-5183. Exit 51 off I-95. A popular rendezvous for business travelers who drop in for both long and short stays and who appreciate the extra space in their private quarters. **Rooms:** 174 stes. CI 3pm/CO noon. Express checkout avail. Nonsmoking rms avail. **Amenities:** 🛏 ⚸ 🖵 A/C, cable TV w/movies, refrig, VCR, stereo/tape player, in-rm safe. All units w/minibars. **Services:** ✕ 🚐 🖵 ⤸ ⟨♦⟩ Babysitting. **Facilities:** 🔥 🛁 🔳 ⚹ 1 rst, 1 bar, spa, sauna, steam rm, whirlpool, washer/dryer. **Rates:** HS Jan–Mar from $119 ste. Extra person $10. Children under 18 stay free. Lower rates off-season. Spec packages avail. Pking: Outdoor, free. Maj CC.

≣≣≣ Ramada Hotel & Conference Center, 630 Clearwater Park Rd WPB, West Palm Beach, FL 33407 (Palm Beach Int'l Airport); tel 407/833-1234 or toll free 800/228-2828; fax 407/833-1255. Exit 52A off I-95. Go under Australian Ave overpass; make left into parking lot. The colorful 10-story building houses a Key West–style dining room and a dance club. **Rooms:** 350 rms and stes. CI 3pm/CO noon. Express checkout avail. Nonsmoking rms avail. Pleasant, though unstylish, rooms may have city views or views of the lake. **Amenities:** 🛏 ⚸ A/C, cable TV w/movies, shoe polisher. Some units w/terraces. **Services:** 🍽 ✕ ⓋⓅ 🚐 ⤸ **Facilities:** 🔥 🔳 🛁 🔲 ⚹ 2 rsts, 2 bars (1 w/entertainment). **Rates:** HS Jan 15–Apr 15 $135–$175 S or D; from $225 ste. Children under 5 stay free. Lower rates off-season. Spec packages avail. Pking: Outdoor, free. Maj CC.

Motels

≣≣ Comfort Inn, 1901 Palm Beach Lakes Blvd, West Palm Beach, FL 33409; tel 407/689-6100 or toll free 800/228-5150; fax 407/686-6177. Exit 53 off I-95. Just 10 minutes from beaches and easily accessible from I-95, this polished mid-priced offering has some lofty 2-story suites in addition to its standardized guest rooms. **Rooms:** 157 rms and stes. CI 2pm/CO noon. Nonsmoking rms avail. **Amenities:** 🛏 ⚸ 🖵 A/C, cable TV w/movies. Some units w/terraces. **Services:** ✕ 🚐 🖵 ⤸ ⟨♦⟩ **Facilities:** 🔥 🔳 ⚹ 1 bar. **Rates (CP):** $60 S; $80 D; from $80 ste. Extra person $10. Children under 18 stay free. Lower rates off-season. Higher rates for spec evnts/hols. Spec packages avail. Pking: Outdoor, free. Maj CC.

≣≣≣ Wellesley Inn, 1910 Palm Beach Lake Rd, West Palm Beach, FL 33409; tel 407/689-8540 or toll free 800/444-8888; fax 407/687-8090. Exit 53 off I-95. Solid budget accommoda-

tions. Restaurants are nearby. **Rooms:** 106 rms. CI 2pm/CO 11am. Nonsmoking rms avail. **Amenities:** 🛏 ⚸ A/C, cable TV w/movies. **Services:** 🖵 ⤸ ⟨♦⟩ **Facilities:** 🔥 ⚹ Washer/dryer. **Rates (CP):** HS Dec–Apr $69 S; $79–$89 D. Extra person $6. Children under 18 stay free. Lower rates off-season. Spec packages avail. Pking: Outdoor, free. Maj CC.

Resort

≣≣≣ Palm Beach Polo and Country Club, 13198 Forest Hill Blvd, West Palm Beach, FL 33414; tel 407/798-7000; fax 407/798-7330. Forest Hill Blvd off I-95. 2,200 acres. Located in a gated, self-contained enclave, it offers much for the golfer, tennis player, and polo pony. This high-brow establishment is best suited to thoroughbreds and not Mr Eds. **Rooms:** 100 stes and effic; 65 ctges/villas. CI 3pm/CO noon. Varied accommodations range from small units to multi-bedroom villas with individual decor. **Amenities:** 🛏 ⚸ 🖵 A/C, cable TV, refrig, VCR. Some units w/minibars, some w/terraces, some w/fireplaces, some w/Jacuzzis. **Services:** ☛ 🖵 ⤸ Car-rental desk, social director, masseur, children's program, babysitting. **Facilities:** ⛳▶🔪 ♠ 🎿 🎣14 ◯🔟 🔳 🔲 ⚹ 3 rsts, 5 bars (2 w/entertainment), lifeguard, lawn games, racquetball, spa, sauna, steam rm, whirlpool, playground. **Rates:** HS Dec 21–Apr 15 from $290 ste; from $195 effic. Children under 12 stay free. Min stay HS. Lower rates off-season. Spec packages avail. Pking: Outdoor, free. Maj CC.

Restaurants 🍴

Aleyda's, 1890 S Military Trail, West Palm Beach; tel 407/642-2500. At Forest Hill Rd. **Mexican.** Tex-Mex food presented in an authentic Mexican setting. Festive and affordable. **FYI:** Reservations accepted. **Open:** Mon–Thurs 11am–10pm, Fri–Sat 11am–11pm, Sun 5–10pm. **Prices:** Main courses $7–$16. Maj CC. ⚹

Bimini Bay Cafe, 104 Clematis St, West Palm Beach; tel 407/833-9554. Between Datura and Clamitis Sts. **American.** Enjoy a cool breeze and a cool libation as you dine on the outdoor patio of this casual eatery. Inside there's a jungle of hanging plants. Specialties include lobster bisque served with a small chicken caesar salad; buffalo shrimp; and Maryland lump crab cakes. **FYI:** Reservations accepted. Singer. **Open:** Daily 10am–1am. Closed Dec 25. **Prices:** Main courses $5.95–$19.95. Maj CC. 🍺 🍴 💙 ⚹

L & N Seafood Grill, 2031 Palm Beach Lakes Blvd, West Palm Beach; tel 407/697-4602. Between I-95 and Okeechobee Blvd. **Seafood.** A simple, appealing, family-oriented seafood eatery with nautical decor. Dinner specials are offered 4–6pm weekdays and all day on weekends. **FYI:** Reservations accepted. Children's menu. **Open:** Sun–Thurs 11:30am–10pm, Fri–Sat 11:30am–11pm. **Prices:** Main courses $7–$15. Maj CC. ♥ &

Morton's of Chicago, in Phillips Point Building, 777 S Flagler Dr, West Palm Beach; tel 407/835-9664. **Seafood/Steak.** An upscale restaurant with romantic ambience. Extensive wine list. **FYI:** Reservations recommended. Dress code. **Open:** HS Nov–Apr daily 5–10pm. Reduced hours off-season. Closed some hols. **Prices:** Main courses $15.95–$29.95. Maj CC. ♥ VP &

Narcissus, 200 Clematis St, West Palm Beach; tel 407/659-1888. Between Olive and Flagler Aves. **American/Continental.** Dine with Palm Beach's yuppie crowd on chicken fillet, pasta, and salmon entrees. A great value. **FYI:** Reservations recommended. Jazz. Children's menu. **Open:** Lunch Mon–Fri 11am–4:30; dinner daily 5pm–midnight. Closed Dec 25. **Prices:** Main courses $11.50–$20. Maj CC. ♥ VP &

Orchids of Siam, 3027 Forest Hill Blvd, West Palm Beach; tel 407/969-2444. At Congress Rd. **Continental/Thai.** An unassuming dining room serving traditional Thai specialties as well as Thai-inspired twists on such dishes as seafood pasta, Norwegian salmon, and veal marsala. **FYI:** Reservations accepted. **Open:** Lunch Mon–Fri 11:30am–2:30pm; dinner Mon–Thurs 4:30–10pm, Fri–Sat 4:30–11pm, Sun 4:30–10pm. **Prices:** Main courses $8.95–$10.95. Maj CC. ♥ &

Proctor's, 2511 S Dixie Hwy, West Palm Beach; tel 407/832-6686. 1 block N of Belvedere Rd. **American.** The accent is more on food than decor in this family-oriented fish house. The seafood dishes are very popular, as is the roast beef with gravy and the T-bone steaks. A good value at any hour, but the early afternoon specials, featured from 2–5pm, are absolute bargains. **FYI:** Reservations not accepted. Beer and wine only. **Open:** Mon–Sat 11am–8:30pm. Closed some hols. **Prices:** Main courses $6.30–$9.90. No CC. &

Randy's Bageland, in The Village Shopping Center, 911 Village Blvd, West Palm Beach; tel 407/640-0203. **Jewish/Kosher.** A very casual eatery offering fresh bagels, pastries, deli sandwiches, and kosher dishes. **FYI:** Reservations not accepted. Children's menu. No liquor license. **Open:** Mon–Thurs 7am–7:30pm, Fri–Sun 7am–8pm. Closed Dec 25. **Prices:** Main courses $4.99–$8.99. Ltd CC. &

Sagami, in Village Commons Shopping Center, 871 Village Blvd, West Palm Beach; tel 407/683-4600. Between Community Dr and Palm Beach Lakes Blvd. **Japanese.** An intimate, tidy, traditional Japanese cafe and sushi bar serving familiar pan-Asian dishes like spare ribs, shrimp tempura, and ginger pork. **FYI:**

Reservations accepted. Beer and wine only. **Open:** Lunch Mon–Fri noon–2:30; dinner Sun–Thurs 5–10:30pm, Fri–Sat 5–11pm. **Prices:** Main courses $10.75–$19.85. Maj CC. &

Zuccarelli's, in Pine Trail Shopping Center, 1937 N Military Trail, West Palm Beach; tel 407/686-7739. **Italian.** This old-world Italian family restaurant offers a wide variety of pizzas, pastas, and chicken specialties at affordable prices. **FYI:** Reservations accepted. **Open:** Mon–Thurs 11am–10pm, Fri–Sat 11am–11pm–Sun 3:30–10pm. Closed some hols. **Prices:** Main courses $7–$18. Maj CC. &

Attractions 💼

South Florida Science Museum, 4801 Dreher Trail N; tel 407/832-1988. The more than 40 exhibits deal mainly with the physical sciences and include Gravity Well, Fly's Eye, Electric Fleas, Plasma Ball, Echo Tube, Garden of Smells, and Spectroscopy. Fifteen new exhibits dealing with color, sound, light, and motion are expected to be added by early 1995. The Aldrin Planetarium has shows daily and laser shows Friday nights. The Gibson Observatory is open for star-gazing Fridays from sunset to 10pm, weather permitting. **Open:** Sat–Thurs 10am–5pm, Fri 10am–10pm. Closed Dec 25. $$

Norton Gallery of Art, 1451 S Olive Ave; tel 407/832-5194. Collections include 19th- and 20th-century European paintings and drawings by Gauguin, Klee, and Picasso, among others; as well as highly regarded 20th-century American works. Also exhibited is a stunning collection of Chinese art that includes 7th-century sculptured Buddhas. **Open:** Tues–Sat 10am–5pm, Sun 1-5pm. $$

Dreher Park Zoo, 1301 Summit Blvd; tel 407/533-0887. More than 500 animals, representing over 100 different species, inhabit this 22-acre zoo, including the endangered Florida panther. Special features include the ARK (Animals Reaching Kids) Encounter Area, Reptile House, a boardwalk nature trail, and the Baker Lake Boat Tour. Also here is the nation's first outdoor exhibit of Goeldi's monkeys. **Open:** Daily 9am–5pm. $$

Lion Country Safari, Southernmost Blvd W; tel 407/793-1084. A 500-acre, cageless, drive-through wildlife preserve inhabited by 1,300 animals from around the world. The preserve serves as a breeding ground for endangered species. Adjacent amusement park; picnic and camping facilities. **Open:** Daily 9:30am–5:30pm. $$$$

WEWAHITCHKA

Map page M-3, C2

Attraction 🎬

Dead Lakes State Recreation Area; tel 904/639-2702. Located 1 mile north of Wewahitchka off Fla 71, near the Apalachicola River and Apalachicola National Forest. Along the nature trails pine, magnolia, and cypress trees border wetlands where visitors can spot alligators and other critters. Fishing, boating, and overnight camping. For information write to PO Box 989, Wewahitchka, FL 32465. **Open:** Daily 8am–dusk. $$

WILTON MANORS

Map page M-11, A2

Restaurant 🍽

Old Florida Seafood House, 1414 NE 26th St, Wilton Manors; tel 305/566-1044. 4 blocks S of Oakland Park Blvd. **Seafood.** This seafood palace, decorated with sunset murals and nautical embellishments, caters to an older crowd. The fish is fresh and the oyster bar menu offers raw specialties. **FYI:** Reservations not accepted. Children's menu. **Open:** Mon–Sat 5–10pm, Sun 4–9pm. Closed some hols. **Prices:** Main courses $12–$22. Maj CC. ♿

WINDLEY KEY

Map page M-11, D1

Motel 🛏

≡≡ Howard Johnson Lodge, 84001 US 1 MM 84, Windley Key, FL 33036; tel 305/664-2711 or toll free 800/327-7070; fax 305/664-2703. Standardized accommodations offered in a low-rise property, with an L-shaped pool surrounded by lawn. **Rooms:** 56 rms. CI 3:30pm/CO 11am. Nonsmoking rms avail. **Amenities:** 🕿 A/C, cable TV w/movies, in-rm safe. All units w/terraces. **Services:** ⚟ **Facilities:** 🍴 ⛺ 🛥 ⚓ 🎿 🏀 ♿ 5 rsts, 2 bars (w/entertainment), 1 beach (ocean), games rm, snorkeling, playground, washer/dryer. **Rates:** HS Dec–Apr $75–$135 S or D. Extra person $10–$15. Children under 18 stay free. Min stay wknds and spec evnts. Lower rates off-season. Higher rates for spec evnts/hols. Pking: Outdoor, free. Maj CC.

WINTER HAVEN

Map page M-7, E1

Hotels 🛏

≡≡ Best Western Admiral's Inn, 5665 Cypress Gardens Blvd, Winter Haven, FL 33884; tel 813/324-5950 or toll free 800/247-2799; fax 813/324-2376. Popular among visitors to Cypress Gardens for its great location, just a 5-minute walk from the front gate. Many groups and families here. **Rooms:** 160 rms and stes. CI 3pm/CO 11am. Nonsmoking rms avail. **Amenities:** 🕿 A/C, cable TV w/movies. Some units w/terraces. **Services:** ⚟ **Facilities:** 🍴 600 ♿ 1 rst, 1 bar, games rm. Olympic-sized pool. Lounge offers karaoke singing. **Rates:** HS Jan–Apr $59–$69 S or D; from $134 ste. Extra person $5. Children under 9 stay free. Lower rates off-season. Spec packages avail. Pking: Outdoor, free. Maj CC.

≡≡ Holiday Inn Winter Haven/Cypress Gardens, 1150 SW 3rd St, Winter Haven, FL 33880; tel 813/294-4451 or toll free 800/465-4329; fax 813/293-9829. A spring-training hotel for the Cleveland Indians, with nearby access to Cypress Gardens and Bok Tower Gardens. Much of the action arrives with the start of the Grapefruit League season, when the team arrives with loyal fans in tow. **Rooms:** 225 rms and stes. Exec-level rms avail. CI 3pm/CO noon. Nonsmoking rms avail. **Amenities:** 🕿 🍴 A/C, cable TV. **Services:** ✕ 🖨 ⚟ ⚓ Babysitting. **Facilities:** 🍴 200 ♿ 1 rst, 1 bar, washer/dryer. **Rates:** HS Feb–Apr $85–$93 S or D; from $200 ste. Extra person $8. Children under 12 stay free. Lower rates off-season. MAP rates avail. Spec packages avail. Pking: Outdoor, free. Maj CC.

≡≡ Howard Johnson Lodge, 1300 3rd St SW, Winter Haven, FL 33380; tel 813/294-7321 or toll free 800/654-2000; fax 813/299-1673. Casual family atmosphere. Friendly staff. **Rooms:** 98 rms. CI 3pm/CO noon. Nonsmoking rms avail. **Amenities:** 🕿 A/C, cable TV w/movies. **Services:** ✕ 🖨 ⚟ ⚓ Car-rental desk. **Facilities:** 🍴 35 ♿ 1 rst, 2 bars, lawn games, playground, washer/dryer. Miniature golf course. The pizza parlour will please the kids. **Rates:** HS Feb–Apr $66–$92 S; $74–$94 D. Extra person $5. Children under 12 stay free. Lower rates off-season. Pking: Outdoor, free. Maj CC.

Motel

≡≡ Days Inn, 200 Cypress Gardens Blvd, Winter Haven, FL 33880; tel 813/299-1151 or toll free 800/329-7466; fax 813/297-8019. 3 mi W of Cypress Gardens. Stay here and walk to the Chain of Lakes Stadium, the winter home of baseball's Cleveland Indians. Also close to shopping. **Rooms:** 106 rms. CI 2pm/CO noon. Nonsmoking rms avail. **Amenities:** ☎ A/C, cable TV. **Services:** 🛏 ⟐ **Facilities:** 🔲 ◼ 🔳 ⅃ Games rm, playground, washer/dryer. Volleyball courts. **Rates (CP):** HS Jan–Apr $49–$59 S or D. Extra person $4. Children under 18 stay free. Lower rates off-season. Higher rates for spec evnts/hols. Spec packages avail. Pking: Outdoor, free. Maj CC.

Attraction 💼

Cypress Gardens; tel 813/324-2111 or toll free 800/237-4826 or 282-2123. At its founding in 1936, Cypress Gardens occupied 16 acres of land on the shores of Lake Eloise, with cypress-wood-block pathways and thousands of tropical and subtropical plants. Today it has grown to more than 200 acres, with ponds and lagoons, waterfalls, Italian fountains, sculptures, topiary and lush, manicured lawns, all against the backdrop of ancient, moss-shrouded cypress trees and ever-changing floral displays.

Three shows are scheduled several times each day: the Greatest American Ski Team performs waterski acrobatics, Feathered Follies features a variety of performing birds, and Variété International showcases specialty acts from all over the world. Exhibits include Wings of Wonder, a butterfly aviary in a Victorian-style glass conservatory; Kodak's Island in the Sky, an observation platform 153 feet in the air; Carousel Cove, with kiddie rides and arcades; and Cypress Junction, an elaborately landscaped model railroad. Museums, lake cruises; restaurants, shops. **Open:** Daily 9:30am–5:30pm; extended hours during peak seasons. $$$$

WINTER PARK

Map page M-7, C2

Hotels 🛏

≣≣ Best Western Mount Vernon Inn, 110 S Orlando Ave, Winter Park, FL 32789; tel 407/647-1166 or toll free 800/99-BEDS-9; fax 407/647-8011. Adequate offering is convenient to outlying attractions. **Rooms:** 147 rms. CI 3pm/CO 11am. Nonsmoking rms avail. **Amenities:** ☎ ⅄ A/C, cable TV w/movies, refrig. **Services:** ✕ 🚗 🔲 🛏 **Facilities:** 🔲 🔳 ⅃ 1 rst, 1 bar. **Rates:** HS Feb–Mar $79–$85 D. Extra person $7. Children under 18 stay free. Lower rates off-season. Higher rates for spec evnts/hols. Spec packages avail. Pking: Outdoor, free. Maj CC.

≣≣≣ The Langford Resort Hotel, 300 E New England Ave, Winter Park, FL 32789; tel 407/644-3400; fax 407/628-1952. Friendly, family-run establishment was, in pre-Disney days, one of central Florida's most popular resorts, entertaining many celebrity guests. Still attractive, it offers extensive facilities at very reasonable rates. Set on a lovely street lined with oaks draped with Spanish moss, just a block from Park Avenue, Winter Park's ritzy shopping street. **Rooms:** 218 rms and stes. CI 2pm/CO 11am. Nonsmoking rms avail. East Wing rooms feature rattan and bamboo furnishings. Many units have fully equipped kitchenettes. **Amenities:** ☎ ⅄ A/C, cable TV w/movies, refrig. Some units w/terraces. **Services:** ✕ 🚗 🚗 🔲 🛏 ⟐ Car-rental desk, social director, masseur. **Facilities:** 🔲 🔳 ⅃ 1 rst, 3 bars (1 w/entertainment), games rm, spa, sauna, steam rm, beauty salon, washer/dryer. **Rates:** $75 S; $85 D; from $180 ste. AP and MAP rates avail. Spec packages avail. Pking: Outdoor, free. Maj CC.

Motel

≣ Days Inn, 901 N Orlando Ave, Winter Park, FL 33789; tel 407/644-0032 or toll free 800/DAYS INN. Exit 46 off I-4. Not one of this chain's best efforts. Adequate, but needs more work to give it broader appeal. **Rooms:** 105 rms. CI 3pm/CO 11am. Nonsmoking rms avail. **Amenities:** ☎ A/C, cable TV w/movies, refrig. **Services:** 🔲 🛏 ⟐ **Facilities:** 🔲 🔳 ⅃ 1 rst, 1 bar. **Rates:** HS June–Aug $79 S; $89 D. Lower rates off-season. Higher rates for spec evnts/hols. Spec packages avail. Pking: Outdoor, free. Maj CC.

Restaurants 🍽

Boston's Fish House, 7325 Aloma Ave, Winter Park; tel 407/678-2107. Between Forsyth Rd and Palmetto Rd. **Seafood.** This small, nondescript eatery keeps customers coming back by serving acclaimed seafood at great prices. Come early to avoid a wait. Dishes range from fish and chips to a full Boston-style haddock dinner. **FYI:** Reservations not accepted. Children's menu. Beer and wine only. **Open:** Tues–Thurs 11am–8:30pm, Fri–Sat 11am–9:30pm, Sun 11am–8:30pm. **Prices:** Main courses $8–$15. Maj CC. ⅃

Cafe de France, 526 S Park Ave, Winter Park; tel 407/647-1869. Fairbanks Ave exit off I-4, E to Park Ave. **French.** This intimate, elegantly casual cafe is the perfect spot for a romantic dinner. Specialties include chicken stuffed with mushrooms, bell peppers, cheese, and herbs. **FYI:** Reservations accepted. Beer and wine only. **Open:** Lunch Tues–Sat 11:30am–2:30pm; dinner Tues–Sat 6–10pm. **Prices:** Main courses $15–$20. Maj CC. ♥ ⅃

Le Cordon Bleu, 537 W Fairbanks Ave, Winter Park; tel 407/647-7575. At Pennsylvania Ave. **Continental/French.** Originally established as Harper's Tavern in 1927, now an elegant bistro serving French cuisine. Chateaubriand for two, roasted to order, is the specialty. Entertainment is provided in adjoining Harper's Tavern, which is still a part of the main structure. **FYI:** Reservations accepted. Band. **Open:** Lunch Mon–Fri 11:30am–2:30pm; dinner Mon–Sat 5:30–11pm. Closed Dec 25. **Prices:** Main courses $16.95–$40.90. Maj CC. VP &

Maison des Crepes, in Hidden Gardens, 348 N Park Ave, Winter Park; tel 407/647-4469. **Continental/French.** A charming, casual cafe. The crepes are made fresh on the premises. Seafood chowder is a popular starter. Three fresh fish entrees daily. **FYI:** Reservations accepted. Children's menu. Beer and wine only. **Open:** Lunch Mon–Fri 11:30am–3pm, Sat 11:30am–4pm; dinner Tues–Thurs 5:30–10pm, Fri–Sat 5:30–10:30pm. Closed some hols. **Prices:** Main courses $9.25–$25.95; PF dinner $45. Maj CC. ♥ &

Outback Steakhouse, in Winter Park Corners Shopping Center, 1927 Aloma Ave, Winter Park; tel 407/679-1050. **Steak.** A family-oriented steakhouse offering excellent quality beef. Specialties include smoked and grilled baby-back ribs served with Aussie chips. The prime rib can be ordered in 8-, 12-, or 16-ounce cuts. Two-for-one drinks are available during happy hour (4–7pm). Also at: 1301 Florida Mall Ave, Orlando (407/240-6857); Winter Park Corners, 1927 Aloma Ave, Winter Park (407/679-1050); 5891 Red Bug Lake Rd, Winter Springs (407/699-0900); 3109 W Vine St, Kissimmee (407/931-0033). **FYI:** Reservations not accepted. Children's menu. **Open:** Sun–Thurs 4–10:30pm, Fri–Sat 4–11pm. Closed some hols. **Prices:** Main courses $10.95–$17.95. Maj CC. &

Park Plaza Gardens, 319 S Park Ave, Winter Park; tel 407/645-2475. At New England Ave. **Continental.** An enclosed garden with skylights, live plants, and a relaxed atmosphere. Popular dishes include rack of lamb and red snapper baked in a potato crust. Large wine selection. Pastries and ice cream are made on the premises. **FYI:** Reservations accepted. Piano. **Open:** Lunch Mon–Sat 11:30am–3pm; dinner daily 6–10pm. Closed some hols. **Prices:** Main courses $18–$26. Maj CC. &

Seaside Grill, 326 Park Ave, Winter Park; tel 407/740-7575. **American.** A seafood house adorned with exposed brick, pine beams, mirrors, ceiling fans, and hanging plants. Popular dishes include yellowfin tuna, salmon alfredo, and Cajun-style blackened grouper. **FYI:** Reservations accepted. Children's menu. **Open:** Mon–Thurs 11am–10:30pm, Fri–Sat 11am–11:30pm, Sun 10am–10:30pm. Closed some hols. **Prices:** Main courses $3.95–$12.95. Maj CC. &

Attraction ▪

Charles Hosmer Morse Museum of American Art, 133 E Welbourne Ave; tel 407/644-3686. (The museum is scheduled to relocate to 445 Park Avenue North, a few blocks away, in 1995.) This museum's holdings include a variety of American pottery, European and American glass, furniture, and other decorative arts, as well as paintings and graphic arts of the late 1800s to the early 1900s. The unique Tiffany collection contains pieces designed and crafted by Louis Comfort Tiffany himself. The famous All Saints Chapel, created by Tiffany and first presented at Chicago's Columbian Exposition in 1893, is here, as are several massive Tiffany stained-glass windows. **Open:** Tues–Sat 9:30am–4pm, Sun 1–4pm. Closed some hols. $

INDEX

 THE ROAD GUIDE FOR TODAY'S TRAVELER.

 SPLASHTACULAR FUN FOR THE WHOLE FAMILY!
See Reverse Side for Special Discount

 **DO THE WILD THING!**
See Reverse Side for Special Discount

 **$3.00 OFF**
Valid for up to 6 people through 12/31/95.
See back of coupon for details.

Thrill to over 400 acres of incredible rides, shows and attractions! Face the all out attack of JAWS®! Face the fury of King Kong. Rocket Back To The Future® on the greatest ride in history! All of this and more! Universal Studios Florida — the only place on earth where you can Ride The Movies®!

 **$2.50 off**
Admission to Sea World!
Up To Six Guests

This is your chance to see the exciting new attractions, Big Splash Bash,℠ Mermaids, Myths & Monsters,℠* Shamu: World Focus℠ and Shamu: Close Up!℠
*This show is seasonal. Check park for hours.

 **Save Up To $15.00**
on an unforgettable day at
Silver Dollar City!

Present this coupon at any Silver Dollar City ticket booth and SAVE $2.50 on each one day regular admission ($1.50 off during Old Time Country Christmas). (Limit 6)
1-800-831-4FUN
Coupon must be presented at time of purchase and may not be combined with any other offer. Offer expires 12/31/96. Back portion must be filled out to be valid.
1902

 Save 10%
on a Twilight Dinner Cruise aboard
The Showboat Branson Belle!

Present this coupon and SAVE 10% on each twilight (8:00 pm) dinner cruise. Reservations recommended. (Limit 6)
1-800-227-8587
Coupon must be presented at time of purchase and may not be combined with any other offer. Valid May through December. Offer expires 12/31/96. Back portion must be filled out to be valid. 9902

White Water. **Save Up To $12.00**
on a *splash-filled* day at
White Water!

Present this coupon at any Branson White Water ticket booth and SAVE $2.00 on each one day regular admission. (Limit 6)
1-800-831-4FUN
Coupon must be presented at time of purchase and may not be combined with any other offer. Offer expires 9/6/96. Back portion must be filled out to be valid.
6902

 Save Up To $15.00
on a *spectacular* show at
The Grand Palace

Present this coupon at The Grand Palace Box office and SAVE $2.50 on each ticket. For Reservations Call
1-800-5-PALACE
Not valid in conjunction with any other offer or previously purchased tickets. Offer expires 12/31/96. Back portion must be filled out to be valid.(Limit 4)
3902

THE ROAD GUIDE FOR TODAY'S TRAVELER.

SAVE $4 OFF
GENERAL ADMISSION

Present coupon at Front Gate before bill is totalled. Not valid with any other discounts or special offers. Limit 6 guests per coupon. Photocopies not accepted. Operating hours and general admission prices subject to change without notice.

COUPON VALID THRU 12/31/95

PLU# 3175c/23176a

BUSCH GARDENS.
TAMPA BAY, FLORIDA

SAVE $4 OFF
GENERAL ADMISSION

Present coupon at Front Gate before bill is totalled. Not valid with any other discounts or special offers. Limit 6 guests per coupon. Photocopies not accepted. Operating hours and general admission prices subject to change without notice.

COUPON VALID 3/31/95 THRU 10/29/95

PLU# 3175c/23176a

ADVENTURE ISLAND
TAMPA'S WATER PARK

Limit six guests per certificate. Not valid with other discounts or on purchase of multi-park/multi-visit passes or tickets. Present certificate at Front Gate before bill is totalled. Redeemable only at time of ticket purchase. Photocopies not accepted. Certificate has no cash value. Operating hours and general admission price subject to change without notice. Valid through 3/31/95 only.

Sea World.
Orlando, Florida
Anheuser-Busch Theme Parks.

Make Contact With Another World®

©1994 Sea World of Florida, Inc.   PLU# 4556/4555

Discount valid for up to 6 people through 12/31/95.
Coupon has no cash value and is not valid with any other offers.
Offer subject to change without notice. Parking fee not included.
©1994 Universal Studios Florida. All Rights Reserved.

6101944075662

Name _____

Address _____

City _____ State _____ Zip _____

Phone (____) _____

Name _____

Address _____

City _____ State _____ Zip _____

Phone (____) _____

Name _____

Address _____

City _____ State _____ Zip _____

Phone (____) _____

Name _____

Address _____

City _____ State _____ Zip _____

Phone (____) _____

THE ROAD GUIDE FOR TODAY'S TRAVELER.

BUSCH GARDENS.
WILLIAMSBURG, VA.
An Anheuser-Busch Theme Park.

Present this coupon and receive $3.50 OFF the ONE-DAY ticket price. No cash value and cannot be used with any other offers or discounts. Expires 10/29/95.

PLU 382R
383C

INTERNATIONAL DRIVE, ORLANDO

Save $2 off all-day admission

Save up to $16 at these great parks!

Paramount's Carowinds
Charlotte, NC
(800) 888-4386

Paramount's Great America
Santa Clara, CA
(408) 988-1776

Paramount's Kings Dominion
Richmond, VA
(804) 876-5000

Paramount's Kings Island
Cincinnati, OH
(800) 288-0808

Paramount Canada's Wonderland
Toronto, Ontario
(905) 832-7000

Parks are open weekends in spring and fall and daily during the summer. Operating dates and times, admission prices and policies vary. Call the parks directly for more detailed information.

SAVE UP TO $18 AT UNIVERSAL STUDIOS HOLLYWOOD

PRESENT THIS COUPON AND RECEIVE $3 OFF ADMISSION FOR UP TO 6 PERSONS AT THE UNIVERSAL STUDIOS HOLLYWOOD BOX OFFICE. OFFER VALID THROUGH 12/31/95.

Save up to $16 at these great parks!

Paramount's Carowinds
Charlotte, NC
(800) 888-4386

Paramount's Great America
Santa Clara, CA
(408) 988-1776

Paramount's Kings Dominion
Richmond, VA
(804) 876-5000

Paramount's Kings Island
Cincinnati, OH
(800) 288-0808

Paramount Canada's Wonderland
Toronto, Ontario
(905) 832-7000

Parks are open weekends in spring and fall and daily during the summer. Operating dates and times, admission prices and policies vary. Call the parks directly for more detailed information.

WATER COUNTRY USA
WILLIAMSBURG, VA.
An Anheuser-Busch Theme Park.

Present this coupon and receive $3.50 OFF the ONE-DAY ticket price. No cash value and cannot be used with any other offers or discounts. Expires 09/10/95.

PLU 382R
383C

20% Off LAS VEGAS TRAVEL 1(800)449-2892

Bally's • Caesars Palace • Tropicana Hotel • The Plaza
Las Vegas Hilton • Bourbon Street • San Remo Hotel
Sands • Holiday Inn • Flamingo Hilton • Stardust
Maxim • Rio Suites • Sahara • Quality Inn • Super 8

Get 100 Rolls Of KODAK Film & 35mm CAMERA...Just $9.95

Simply fill out the coupon on the back and we'll send you a photo finishing package that gives you FREE, fresh KODAK film returned with your pictures. Most film sizes and film speeds available.

PLUS—GET 40% OFF PROCESSING

© 1995 U.S. Express. Void where prohibited. Film offer valid with purchased processing. This promotional is not an offer of Eastman Kodak Co.

THE ROAD GUIDE FOR TODAY'S TRAVELER.

Save $2 on all-day admission to America's Favorite Waterpark. Good for up to six people. Not to be used in conjunction with any other offer or afternoon pricing. Expires 12/31/95. PLU 6A 7C. For more information, call Wet 'n Wild at 1-800-992-WILD.

BUSCH GARDENS®
WILLIAMSBURG, VA.
An Anheuser-Busch Theme Park™

At Universal Studios Hollywood you'll scream through time on BACK TO THE FUTURE®...THE RIDE. Feel 10,000 degrees of excitement in BACKDRAFT. Rock out with THE FLINTSTONES® SHOW--A Live Rockstravaganza, and much, much more!

Present this certificate at the USH box office. Good for up to 6 people. Offer not valid for separately ticketed events or at Universal Studios Florida. Cannot be combined with other offers or per capita sightseeing tours. Distribution of this certificate on USH property is prohibited. NOT FOR SALE. Offer valid through 12/31/95. ©1994 Universal City Studios, Inc. ALL RIGHTS RESERVED. Closed Thanksgiving and Christmas day. 94-TRA-24

Save up to $16 with this coupon.
Get $4 off each admission (up to four people) at any of the Paramount Parks during the 1995 season.

Coupon valid for $4.00 off purchase price of up to four (4) regular general admission tickets at Paramount's Carowinds, Paramount's Great America, Paramount's Kings Dominion or Paramount's Kings Island, or $4.00 (Canadian funds) off the purchase of each Regular (ages 7-59) Pay-One-Price Passport (up to a total of four) at Paramount Canada's

Wonderland. Offer not valid in conjunction with any other discount offer or special pricing including the purchase of children's or senior citizen's tickets. Offer valid only during regularly scheduled 1995 operating season. Void where prohibited. This original coupon must be presented at any open ticket booth, surrendered at time of purchase and may not be sold/redistributed.

Paramount Parks

For office use:
PCW 151 PC 014 PGA 201 PKD 101 PKI 29   # of tickets

WILLIAMSBURG, VA.
An Anheuser-Busch Theme Park™

Save up to $16 with this coupon.
Get $4 off each admission (up to four people) at any of the Paramount Parks during the 1995 season.

Coupon valid for $4.00 off purchase price of up to four (4) regular general admission tickets at Paramount's Carowinds, Paramount's Great America, Paramount's Kings Dominion or Paramount's Kings Island, or $4.00 (Canadian funds) off the purchase of each Regular (ages 7-59) Pay-One-Price Passport (up to a total of four) at Paramount Canada's

Wonderland. Offer not valid in conjunction with any other discount offer or special pricing including the purchase of children's or senior citizen's tickets. Offer valid only during regularly scheduled 1995 operating season. Void where prohibited. This original coupon must be presented at any open ticket booth, surrendered at time of purchase and may not be sold/redistributed.

Paramount Parks

For office use:
PCW 151 PC 014 PGA 201 PKD 101 PKI 29   # of tickets

Credit card orders call
(615) 584-2626

☐ Enclosed is $9.95, shipping and handling included. Rush my 35mm camera and film offer to:

Name: _____
Address: _____
City: _____
State: _____
Zip: _____ AUTHORIZATION #769

Enclose $9.95 payment (check or money order) and coupon mail to:

U.S. EXPRESS ™

7035 Middlebrook Pike, P.O. Box 51730, Knoxville, Tn 37950

LAS VEGAS TRAVEL
20% Off
Most Major Casino Hotels in Las Vegas.
1 (800) 449-2892

Advance reservations required with Las Vegas Travel.
Valid Sunday-Thursday only. (Holidays/City-Wide Conventions excluded.)
For Show – Wedding – Casino info: 1 (900) RESORT CITY
For Golf Reservations: 1 (800) 627-4465

THE ROAD GUIDE FOR TODAY'S TRAVELER.

Save 10% At Thousands Of Choice Hotels Worldwide!

The next time you're traveling, call **1-800-4-CHOICE** and request the "America On Wheels Travelers' Discount." You'll save **10%** at thousands of **Sleep, Comfort, Quality, Clarion, Econo Lodge, Rodeway** and **Friendship** hotels!

CHOICE HOTELS
INTERNATIONAL

Sleep | Comfort | Quality | Clarion
Friendship | Econo Lodge | RODEWAY

 STAY WITH US & SAVE!

We invite you to stay at any of our over 750 Ramada Limiteds, Inns, Hotels, Resorts and Plaza Hotels throughout the United States. Present this coupon at check-in, and we'll take an additional 10% off your room rate.

This coupon cannot be combined with other promotions, group rates, or packages. Availability may be limited and advance reservations are required, so call now.

For reservations call your travel consultant or 1-800-228-2828 and mention this Ramada 10% discount coupon.

 RAMADA   Expires 12/31/95

10% OFF   10% OFF

 DAYS INN
The Best Value Under The Sun.™

The Best Value Under The Sun Just Got Better

Now you can save even more at any of more than 1,600 Days Inns throughout the United States and internationally. Just present this coupon upon check-in and Days Inn will take 10% off your regular room rate for your entire length of stay! Advance reservations required, so call now! **1-800-DAYS INN**
See details on back

$10 Off   ## A Weekly Rental!

Rent an Intermediate through a Full Size 4-Door car for a week and you can get **$10 off** when you present this coupon at a participating Avis location in the continental U.S. Subject to complete Terms and Conditions on back. Offer expires December 31, 1995. To request this offer, call your travel consultant or an Avis employee-owner at: **1-800-831-8000.**   Coupon # MUFA527

Avis features GM cars.   **AVIS**®

$20 OFF WEEKLY RENTAL
Five or more days Unlimited Mileage

Receive a $20 discount off standard weekly rates when you rent a compact through luxury car. Simply mention promotion code **TCB/MCBC087** at time of reservation and present this certificate at start of rental. For information and reservations, **call Budget at 800-527-0700.**

 **Budget**
The Smart Money is on Budget.

$10 off Weekly Rental
PC#65376

Hertz®

This certificate entitles you to $10 off a weekly rental when you rent any mid-size through Luxury car (class C, D, F, G or I) | at participating Hertz locations in the U.S. For reservations and details, call your travel agent or Hertz at 1-800-654-2210.

Free Class Upgrade

Reserve an economy or compact size car, then present this coupon to any Dollar rental agent when you arrive, and you'll receive a complimentary upgrade to the next car class at no extra charge.

For reservations call, 1-800-800-4000.

 **DOLLAR**® RENT A CAR

Dollar features quality products of the Chrysler Corporation like the Chrysler Neon.

10% OFF TIME & MILEAGE

RENT A ROLLING HOLIDAY!

See the great North American outdoors on an unforgettable RV Adventure Vacation. It's the ultimate for people who like the freedom to go anywhere. The flexibility to set their own pace. We have the right size RV you need...Ready-to-go. Call for reservations and information.

Not combinable with other offers. US & Canadian residents only. Expires 6/30/96.   **1-800-327-7799**

 CRUISE AMERICA
MOTORHOME RENTAL & SALES

THE ROAD GUIDE FOR TODAY'S TRAVELER.

10% STAY WITH US & SAVE! 10%

Ramada Limiteds, Inns, Hotels, Resorts and Plaza Hotels offer you the value and accommodations you expect . . . And so much more!

- Over 750 convenient locations
- Children under 18 always stay free
- Non-smoking and handicap rooms available

For reservations call 1-800-228-2828

10%   10%

1-800-4-CHOICE
(1-800-424-6423)

Advance reservations through 1-800-4-CHOICE required. Based on availability at participating hotels and cannot be used in conjunction with any other discount.

TERMS AND CONDITIONS

Offer valid on an Intermediate (Group C) through a Full Size 4-Door (Group E) car for a 5-day minimum rental. Coupon must be surrendered at time of rental; one per rental. May not be used in conjunction with any other coupon, promotion or offer. Coupon valid at Avis corporate and participating licensee locations in the continental U.S. Offer not available during holiday and other blackout periods. Offer may not be available on all rates at all times. **An advance reservation is required.** Cars subject to availability. Taxes, local government surcharges and optional items, such as LDW, additional driver fee and refueling, are extra. Renter must meet Avis age, driver and credit requirements. Minimum age is 25 but may vary by location. Offer expires December 31, 1995.

Rental Sales Agent Instructions
At Checkout: • In CPN, enter **MUFA527.**   • Complete this information:
    RA#_____   Rental Location_____
• Attach to COUPON tape.

© 1995 Wizard Co., Inc. 1/95 DTPS/

AVIS *We try harder.*

DAYS INN
The Best Value Under The Sun.℠

- Available at participating properties.
- This coupon cannot be combined with any other special discount offer.
- Limit one coupon per room, per stay.
- Expires December 31, 1996.

1-800-DAYS INN

Terms and Conditions

Advance reservations are required and blackout periods may apply. Present this certificate at time of rental or, for Gold rentals, at time of return, and receive $10 off Hertz Leisure Weekly rates at participating locations in the U.S. This certificate has no cash value, must be surrendered and may not be used with any other rate, discount or promotion. Standard rental qualifications, rental period and return restrictions must be met or offer is void. Weekly rentals require a minimum rental period of five days, including a Saturday night. Minimum rental age is 25. Taxes and optional items, such as refueling, are not included and are not subject to discount. All cars are subject to availability at time of rental. Certificate expires 12/31/95.

Hertz rents Fords and other fine cars.

HERE ARE SOME OF THE DETAILS YOU SHOULD KNOW:

Just mention promotion code TCB/MCBC087 when you reserve a compact through luxury size car and receive $20 off your weekly rental. Five-day minimum rental necessary to qualify for discount. This offer is valid at participating budget locations through 3/3/96 and is subject to vehicle availability. Car must be returned to renting location, except in some metro areas where inter-area drop-offs are permitted. Local rental and age requirements apply. Discount applies to time and mileage only and is not available in conjunction with any other discount, promotional offer, CorpRate™, government, or tour/wholesale rate. Refueling services, taxes and optional items are extra. Additional driver, under-age driver and other surcharges are extra. Blackout dates may apply.

Terms and Conditions

- Offer includes 10% discount off all time and mileage charges on Cruise America or Cruise Canada vehicles only.
- Offer not available in conjunction with other discount offers or promotional rates.
- Excludes other rental charges, deposits, sales tax, and fuels.
- Normal rental conditions and customer qualification procedures apply.
- Members must reserve vehicles through Central Reservations only, at least one week in advance of pick up and mention **Frommer's America on Wheels** at time of reservation.

For reservations: 1-800-327-7799 - US and Canada

Rental Rates and Conditions

This offer is subject to availability and may not be used in conjunction with any other certificate or promotion. Offers apply only to economy through intermediate size car. Blackout periods may apply. This coupon has no cash value, and must be surrendered at time of rental. Coupon valid at all participating locations in the U.S. Taxes, fuel, LDW/CDW, under age and additional driver fees are extra. Some additional charges may apply.

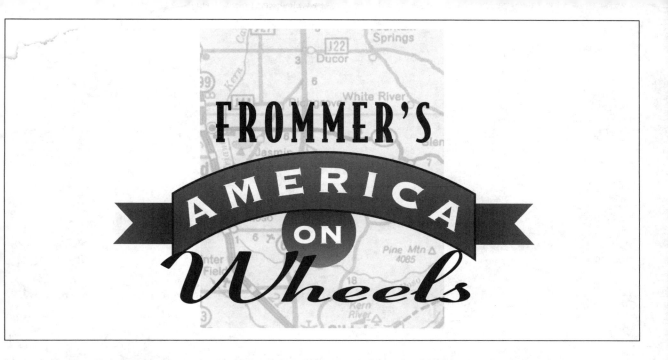

FROMMER'S AMERICA ON Wheels

THE ROAD GUIDE FOR TODAY'S AMERICA FROM THE FIRST NAME IN TRAVEL

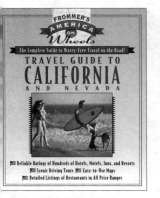

ISBN:0-02-860146-7

ISBN:0-02-860144-0

ISBN:0-02-860145-9

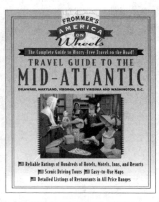

ISBN:0-02-860143-2

New titles coming in 1996

Northeast (includes Maine, Vermont, New Hampshire, Connecticut, Rhode Island, New York, and Massachusetts)

Northwest & North Central (includes Oregon, Washington, Idaho, Montana, Wyoming, North Dakota, South Dakota, Nebraska, Iowa)

Great Lakes (includes Michigan, Wisconsin, Illinois, Indiana, Ohio, Minnesota)

Southeast (includes South Carolina, North Carolina, Kentucky, Tennessee, Mississippi, Georgia, Alabama)

South Central (includes Louisiana, Arkansas, Oklahoma, Texas, Missouri)

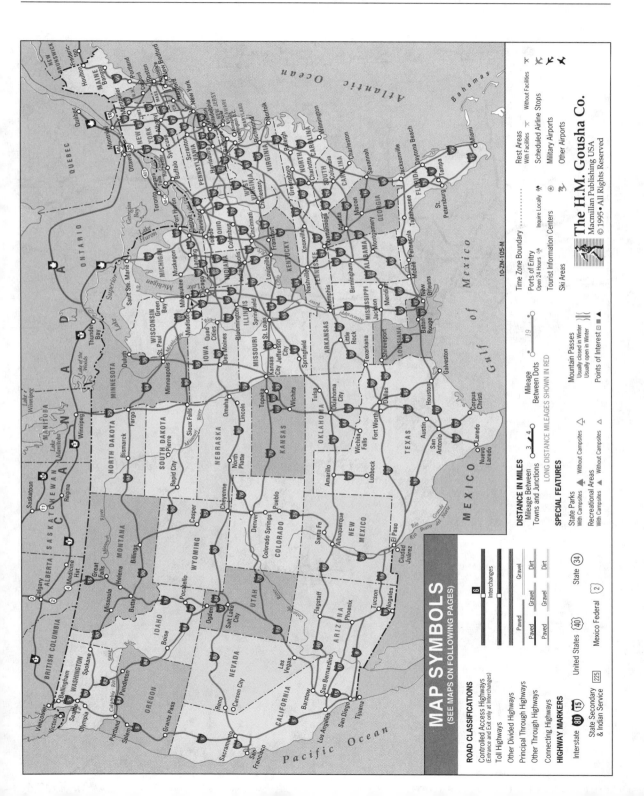

MAP SYMBOLS
(SEE MAPS ON FOLLOWING PAGES)

ROAD CLASSIFICATIONS

Controlled Access Highways
(Entrance and Exit only at Interchanges)

Toll Highways

Other Divided Highways

Principal Through Highways

Paved	Gravel	Dirt

Other Through Highways

Paved	Gravel	Dirt

Connecting Highways

Paved	Gravel	Dirt

6 Interchanges

HIGHWAY MARKERS

Interstate 80 15

State Secondary & Indian Service 225

United States 40

State 34

Mexico Federal 2

DISTANCE IN MILES

Mileage Between Towns and Junctions   3   4

Mileage Between Dots   19

LONG DISTANCE MILEAGES SHOWN IN RED

SPECIAL FEATURES

State Parks With Campsites / Without Campsites

Recreational Areas With Campsites / Without Campsites

Mountain Passes
Usually closed in Winter
Usually open in Winter

Points of Interest

Time Zone Boundary

Ports of Entry Open 24 Hours / Inquire Locally

Tourist Information Centers

Ski Areas

Rest Areas With Facilities / Without Facilities

Scheduled Airline Stops

Military Airports

Other Airports

The H.M. Gousha Co.

Macmillan Publishing USA
© 1995 • All Rights Reserved

10-ZM-105-M

Pacific Ocean

Atlantic Ocean

Gulf of Mexico

MEXICO

CANADA

GULF OF MEXICO

© The H.M. Gousha Co.

FLORIDA

SCALE IN MILES AND KILOMETERS

ONE INCH=19 MI

ONE INCH=30 KM

10-NA-1625-S

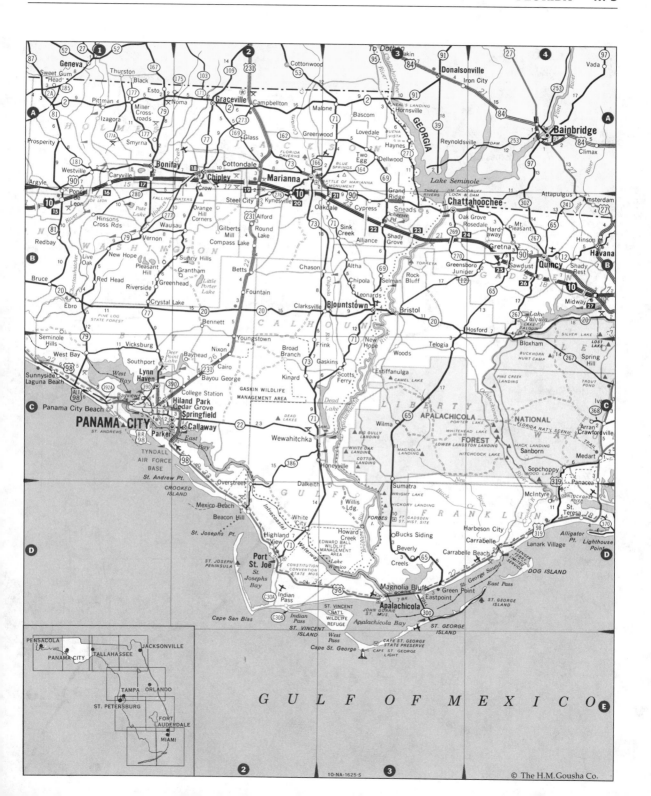

© The H.M. Gousha Co.

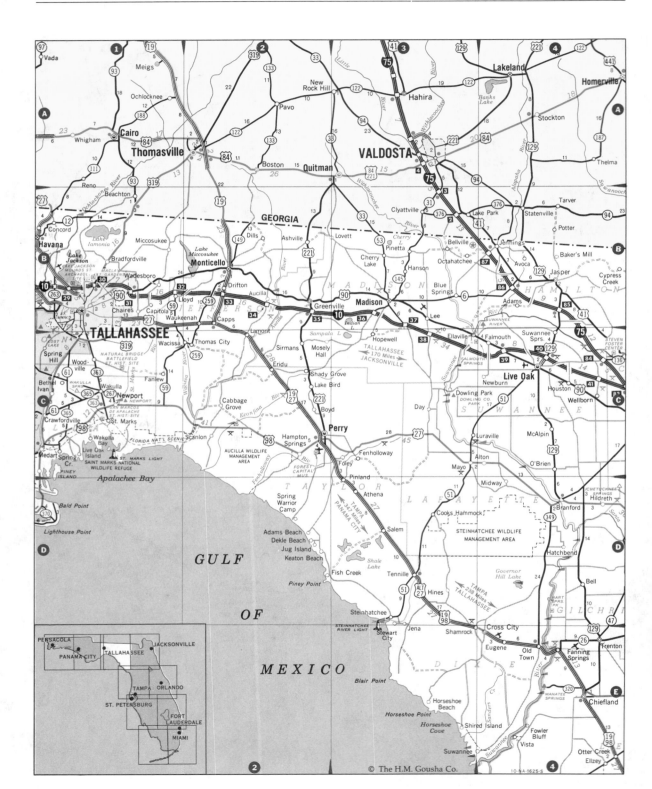

© The H.M. Gousha Co.

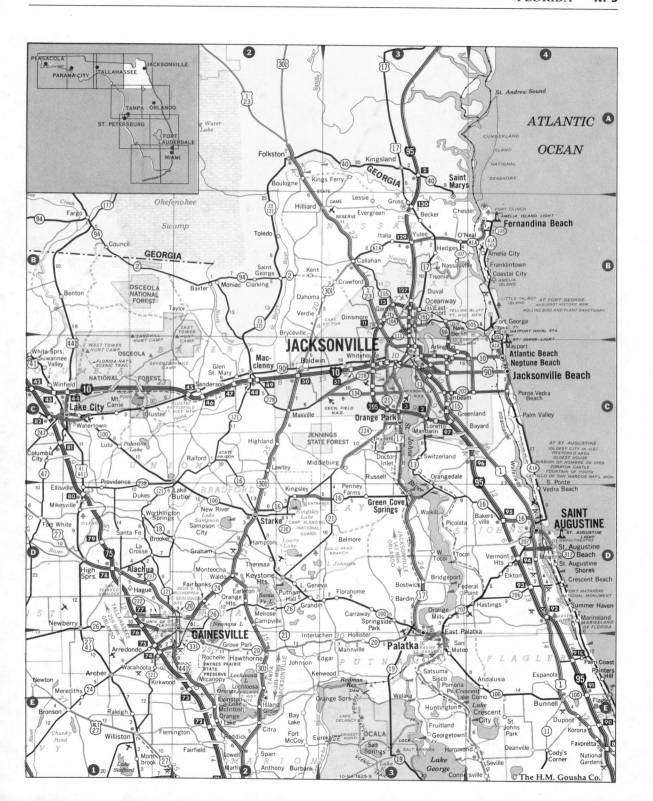

ATLANTIC OCEAN

GEORGIA

© The H.M. Gousha Co.

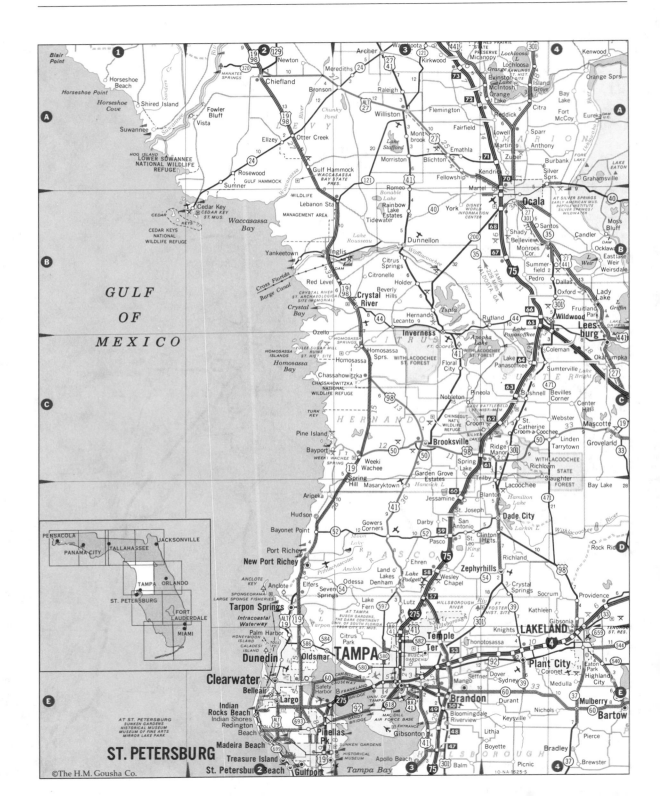

GULF
OF
MEXICO

PENSACOLA
PANAMA CITY
TALLAHASSEE
JACKSONVILLE
TAMPA
ORLANDO
ST. PETERSBURG
FORT LAUDERDALE
MIAMI

ST. PETERSBURG

©The H.M. Gousha Co.

10-NA-1625-5

© The H.M. Gousha Co.

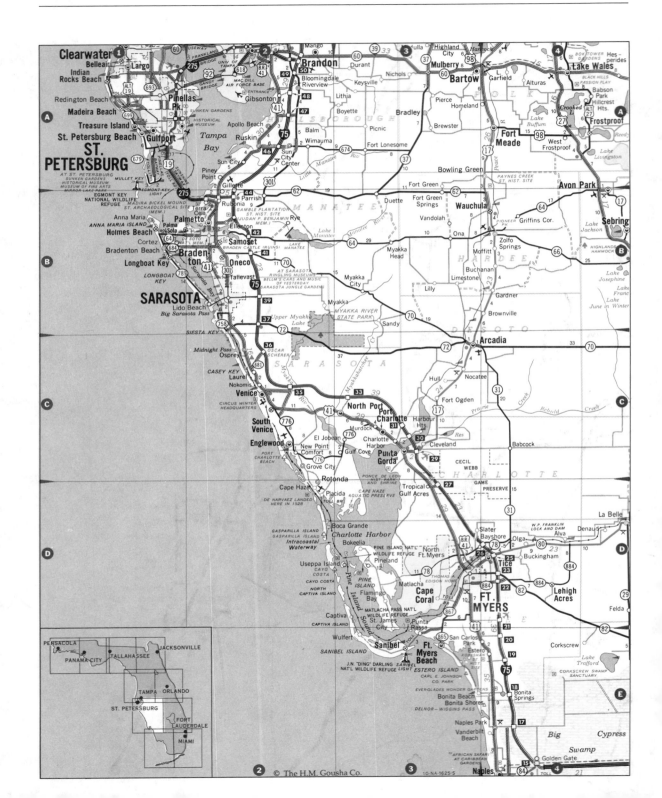

© The H.M. Gousha Co.   10-NA-1625-5